# The Sicilian Sozin

## Mikhail Golubev

First published in the UK by Gambit Publications Ltd 2001

ISBN 1 901983 38 2

DISTRIBUTION:
Worldwide (except USA): Central Books Ltd, 99 Wallis Rd, London E9 5LN.
Tel +44 (0)20 8986 4854 Fax +44 (0)20 8533 5821.
E-mail: orders@Centralbooks.com
USA: BHB International, Inc., 41 Monroe Turnpike, Trumbull, CT 06611, USA.

For all other enquiries (including a full list of all Gambit Chess titles) please contact the publishers, Gambit Publications Ltd, P.O. Box 32640, London W14 0JN.
E-mail Murray@gambitchess.freeserve.co.uk
Or visit the GAMBIT web site at http://www.gambitbooks.com

Edited by Graham Burgess and Helen Milligan
Typeset by John Nunn
Printed in Great Britain by The Cromwell Press, Wiltshire.

10 9 8 7 6 5 4 3 2 1

**Gambit Publications Ltd**
*Managing Director:* GM Murray Chandler
*Chess Director:* GM John Nunn
*Editorial Director:* FM Graham Burgess
*German Editor:* WFM Petra Nunn

# Contents

# Symbols

| | | | |
|---|---|---|---|
| + | check | Z | zonal event |
| ++ | double check | Cht | team championship |
| # | checkmate | Wch | world championship |
| !! | brilliant move | Wcht | world team championship |
| ! | good move | Ech | European championship |
| !? | interesting move | Echt | European team championship |
| ?! | dubious move | ECC | European Clubs Cup |
| ? | bad move | OL | olympiad |
| ?? | blunder | jr | junior event |
| +− | White is winning | wom | women's event |
| ± | White is much better | mem | memorial event |
| ⩲ | White is slightly better | rpd | rapidplay game |
| = | equal position | simul | game from simultaneous display |
| ∞ | unclear position | corr. | correspondence game |
| ⩱ | Black is slightly better | 1-0 | the game ends in a win for White |
| ∓ | Black is much better | ½-½ | the game ends in a draw |
| −+ | Black is winning | 0-1 | the game ends in a win for Black |
| Ch | championship | (n) | nth match game |
| Ct | candidates event | (D) | see next diagram |
| IZ | interzonal event | | |

Transpositions are sometimes displayed by a dash followed by the moves (in *italic*) of the variation to which the transposition occurs. The moves start with the first one that deviates from the line under discussion. All the moves to bring about the transposition are given. Thus, after 1 e4 c5 2 ♘f3 d6 3 d4 cxd4 4 ♘xd4 ♘f6 5 ♘c3 ♘c6 6 ♗c4 ♕b6 7 ♘db5 a6 8 ♗e3 ♕a5 9 ♘d4 e6 10 0-0 the comment "10...♕c7!? 11 ♗b3 – *6...e6 7 ♗b3 a6 8 ♗e3 ♕c7 9 0-0*" signifies that the reader should locate material on 1 e4 c5 2 ♘f3 d6 3 d4 cxd4 4 ♘xd4 ♘f6 5 ♘c3 ♘c6 6 ♗c4 e6 7 ♗b3 a6 8 ♗e3 ♕c7 9 0-0, to which play has transposed.

# Bibliography

## Books

Koblenc, *Sitsilianskaya Zashchita*, Moscow 1955
Boleslawski, *Skandinavisch bis Sizilianisch*, Sportverlag Berlin 1971
Zak, *Puti Sovershenstvovaniya*, Moscow 1981
*Encyclopaedia of Chess Openings* (Volume B, 2nd edition), Šahovski
  Informator 1984
Kasparov and Nikitin, *Sitsilianskaya Zashchita: Scheveningen*, Moscow 1984
Lepeshkin, *Sitsilianskaya Zashchita: Variant Najdorfa*, Moscow 1985
Beliavsky and Mikhalchishin, *B86-87*, Šahovski Informator 1995
Beliavsky and Mikhalchishin, *B88*, Šahovski Informator 1995
Akopian, *B89*, Šahovski Informator 1996
Nunn and Gallagher, *The Complete Najdorf: Modern Lines*, Batsford 1998
Nunn, Burgess, Emms and Gallagher, *Nunn's Chess Openings*,
  Gambit/Everyman 1999
Kosten, *Easy Guide to the Najdorf*, Gambit/Everyman 1999
Yrjölä, *Easy Guide to the Classical Sicilian*, Gambit/Everyman 2000
and various other chess books

## Periodicals

*Informator* (1-81)
*New in Chess Yearbook* (1-60)
and various other chess magazines

## Electronic

*Sicilian in The Nineties* CD-ROM (Interchess BV 1999)
ChessBase Mega Database 2001
ChessBase Magazine 80-83
Chess Assistant HugeBase 2000
TWIC (up to number 361)
and others

# Foreword

It would probably not be an easy task to find a chess-player who had never heard of the Sicilian Sozin – the famous attacking system for White associated with the move ♗c4. It has been many decades since club players as well as top grandmasters started playing it, so you should not be surprised to see this book, wherein your obedient servant has aspired to consolidate the entirety of the vast amount of material accumulated on this issue.

Before you there is a standard openings book which has been written with a view to combining the functions of a textbook and a handbook, presenting the necessary theoretical basis for all interested chess-players. The book's format is more or less typical and the only thing requiring clarification is the author's understanding of the generally accepted chess assessments. Like many others, I use the term 'unclear' to describe something like 'a complicated position with probably approximately equal chances'. In addition, the assessment '±' is intended to mean something closer to '+−' than to '⩲' (and, respectively, '∓' is closer to '−+' than to '⩱').

The author has collected together all the essentials that he has managed to discover and establish on the subject, both during 18 years of practice and in the course of writing this book, and hopes that this work will help players seeking landmarks in the hazardous territory of the Sozin Attack.

The accuracy of the assessments and variations was one of my main priorities, but only one who knows very little about chess could aspire to write a Sozin book free from inaccuracies. I would be grateful for any messages about possible errors (addressed to gmi@europe.com) and hope these errors will not be too numerous.

All in all, it is simpler and more intriguing to play the Sozin than to present this system from a theoretical viewpoint, and I am looking forward to successful Sozin games played by my readers!

Mikhail Golubev
*Odessa, Ukraine*
October, 2001

# Introduction

My serious acquaintance with the Sicilian Sozin began in 1982 when I chanced upon an interesting though still largely unknown article by the master Mochalov, published in the magazine *Shakhmaty, Shashki v BSSR* (1980).

The article contained plenty of interesting games and lines where White attacked desperately and Black defended doggedly, but the following piece of analysis constituted the main topic:

**1 e4 c5 2 ♘f3 d6 3 d4 cxd4 4 ♘xd4 ♘f6 5 ♘c3 ♘c6 6 ♗c4 e6 7 ♗e3 ♗e7 8 ♕e2 a6 9 ♗b3 0-0 10 0-0-0 ♕c7 11 g4 ♘d7!? 12 g5 ♘c5 13 ♖hg1 b5 14 ♕h5 b4!? 15 ♘xc6 ♘xb3+ 16 axb3 ♕xc6 17 ♗d4!** *(D)*

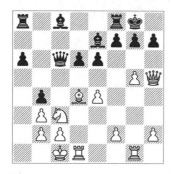

B

**17...♗b7!**

This was Mochalov's main idea (not 17...bxc3? 18 ♕h6! e5 19 ♗xe5! +−). His main line now continued **18 ♖g4 bxc3! 19 ♖h4 cxb2+ 20 ♗xb2 ♕xe4! 21 ♖xe4 ♗xe4**, when Black has an advantage.

It is not easy to improve on White's play. This was confirmed both by the subsidiary lines in the article (the most important being 18 ♗f6 bxc3 19 ♕h6 cxb2+ 20 ♔xb2 ♕xc2+!! and 21...♖fc8+ followed by 22...gxh6, Rudnev-Mochalov, USSR 1976) and by the game Chandler-Yudasin, Minsk 1982, where White could not find anything better than the 21...♗xe4 line. Nevertheless, I managed to find a not-so-complicated solution that had evaded the attention of others: **18 ♘d5! exd5 19 ♖d3!** with a strong attack (instead of 19 ♕h6 ♕xc2+! as indicated by Mochalov). I was very happy with this finding at the time because it was the first time I had managed to find something of importance to theory.

Since that time I have played about eighty serious games with the move ♗c4; as it happens, four of them resulted in the position shown in the diagram, and they brought me 3½ points. I do not mean to say that events always evolved happily on the board but the ratio of wins to defeats (45-8) proves that my choice was correct. Here is one of my pleasant reminiscences:

**Golubev – Mantovani**
*Biel open 1992*

**1 e4 c5 2 ♘f3 d6 3 d4 cxd4 4 ♘xd4 ♘f6 5 ♘c3 a6 6 ♗c4 e6 7 ♗b3 b5 8**

0-0 ♗b7 9 ♖e1 ♘bd7 10 ♗g5 ♕b6 11 a4 b4 *(D)*

12 ♘d5! exd5 13 exd5+ ♔d8 14 ♘c6+ ♔c7 15 a5 ♕b5 16 ♘d4 ♕c5 17 ♗e3 ♗xd5 18 c4! bxc3 19 ♖c1 ♕xa5 20 ♖xc3+ ♘c5 21 ♗xd5 ♘xd5 *(D)*

22 ♕f3! ♘xc3 23 ♕c6+ ♔b8 24 bxc3 ♔a7 25 ♖b1 ♖b8 26 ♕xc5+! ♕b6 27 ♘c6+ ♔a8 28 ♖xb6 1-0

Actually, the Sicilian Sozin and also this book are intended primarily for those chess-players who, like me, enjoy attacking without a backward glance. Nevertheless, I do not wish to discourage the supporters of Black still

more – the defence is not easy but it is certainly not hopeless and I shall try to be objective throughout.

## Theoretical Basis

Conceptually, the Sicilian Sozin is not a single opening but three opening systems. This generic name describes the entire range of opening lines that arise when, after **1 e4 c5 2 ♘f3 d6 3 d4 cxd4 4 ♘xd4 ♘f6 5 ♘c3**, White plays **6 ♗c4** in response to **5...e6**, **5...a6** or **5...♘c6**. Despite the obvious possibilities for these three lines to transpose, each of them has its own reputation and occupies its own place in opening theory.

### 6 ♗c4 against the Scheveningen Variation

**5...e6 6 ♗c4** *(D)*

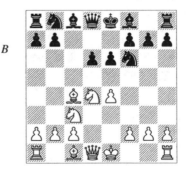

At least half of all games starting this way result in positions from the *Fischer Attack* or the *Sozin/Velimirović Attack* because Black plays ...a6 or ...♘c6. However, a stronger plan for Black is 6...♗e7! with a quick transfer of the knight to c5 if White plays 7 &b3 (e.g., 7...&a6!). Due to this, and also because White has the dangerous Keres Attack (6 g4) in his arsenal, the move 6 &c4 is not in the list of main responses to 5...e6.

## 6 &c4 against the Najdorf Variation (or Fischer Attack)

**5...a6 6 &c4** *(D)*

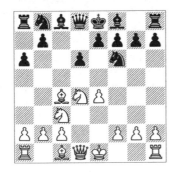

This is the version of 6 &c4 that is most difficult to assess. Black does not often take the opportunity to transpose to the lines with ...&c6 and White has to struggle in double-edged lines such as 6...e6 7 &b3 b5 or 6...e6 7 &b3 &bd7 8 f4 &c5 where Black has less direct control over the centre but more chances to devalue the bishop on b3 and to organize counterplay quickly through ...b5 and ...b4.

If Black does play ...&c6, he often does not do it at once (6...e6 and 7...&c6). In such lines as 6...e6 7 &b3 &e7 and 6...e6 7 0-0 &e7 the idea ...&c6 remains in reserve.

6 &c4 is one of the four main answers to the Najdorf (the others are 6 &g5, 6 &e3 and 6 &e2).

## The Classical Sozin and Velimirović Attack

**5...&c6 6 &c4** *(D)*

Now, after **6...e6**, we get the starting position of the *Sozin/Velimirović complex*. White's most aggressive plan, connected with 7 &e3, 8 ♕e2 and 9 0-0-0 (often with the inclusion of &b3) is traditionally called the *Velimirović Attack*, while the other plans, usually involving 0-0 and f4, are called the *Classical Sozin Attack*.

It is important to know that both *Velimirović Attack* and *Classical Sozin Attack* mean not a single specific position but a multiplicity of similar variations. White may aspire to the arrays of the Velimirović Attack by starting from 7 &e3 or 7 &b3, while to prepare the Classical Sozin Attack at least three moves are suitable: 7 &e3, 7 &b3 and 7 0-0. In all instances the lines with a further ...a6 for Black comprise the majority of the accumulated theoretical material.

Besides 6...e6, Black has a rather popular opportunity to make the game atypical for the Sicilian Sozin by playing **6...♕b6!?** (or, also, **6...&d7!?**).

6 ♗c4 is the second most important answer to 5...♘c6 (after the Richter-Rauzer Attack, 6 ♗g5).

So, the Sicilian Sozin exists in three different versions. Theoretically, the most dangerous of them is 5...♘c6 6 ♗c4, and the least dangerous is 5...e6 6 ♗c4. However, all such assessments are made within the range of '=' to '±' and supported by thousands of games, while the outcome of an individual game is decided by quite different factors.

## Strategic Features

Even just a quick glance at the Sicilian Sozin shows that the sides do not manoeuvre at all, or at least very seldom. The pieces retreat, as a rule, only if the adversary attacks them with pawns and even that happens quite infrequently. The struggle may often become aggravated to such an extent that strategy ceases to exist as an independent category and completely gives way to tactics or, more precisely, fuses with tactics.

Nevertheless, the initial reasons that oblige the sides to struggle in precisely such a manner are found in a purely strategic domain.

Having played 6 ♗c4 and then ♗b3, White has transferred the bishop to a position where it will, from a certain viewpoint, exert pressure on the centre and, from another viewpoint, be aimlessly set against the defended e6-pawn. It is this contradiction that forms the basis for the strategic conflict. White takes on an obligation to create dynamic threats rapidly in the centre and

on the kingside. If he succeeds, the value of the active bishop on the a2-g8 diagonal may be exceedingly high (a simple example: 5...a6 6 ♗c4 e6 7 0-0 ♘bd7 8 ♗xe6!? with an attack). In the opposite case, the potential of the b3-bishop will not be used and this piece may become a useless extra or a target for Black's attack through ...b5, ...a5 and ...a4. Therefore, the result of the opening struggle is reduced to the question of whether White succeeds in using the bishop in his operations.

Given the above, it is not surprising, for instance, that White's plan connected with f3, g4 and g5, which is not bad in other varieties of the Sicilian, is usually too slow and unsuccessful here as it fails to generate a rapid threat to e6 and makes no use of the b3-bishop. If the f-pawn is to be moved, it should go not to f3 but to f4 followed by f5 or e5 – such a scheme corresponds to the classical concept of the Sicilian Sozin.

More advanced schemes envisage the attack without the participation of the f-pawn, by means of a quick g4 and g5 and, in individual cases, e.g., in the line 5...a6 6 ♗c4 e6 7 ♗b3 b5 8 0-0 ♗e7 9 ♕f3, by piece activity only, without the participation of pawns. Still, use of the b3-bishop remains an important component of White's idea (e.g., 9...♗b7 10 ♗xe6! in the line I have just mentioned).

Black's success depends on how he prepares for his opponent's activity. He has a standard set of ideas of which we mention here just three:

a) Ideally, the best way to neutralize the bishop on b3 is to transfer one of the black knights to c5, where it defends the e6-pawn, attacks the e4-pawn and is ready to exchange itself for the bishop when necessary. However, in practice White quickly mobilizes his forces and often Black cannot afford to lose time with the knight manoeuvre.

b) The other typical manoeuvre for the Sozin, ...♘c6, ...♘a5 and ...♘xb3, is generally less dangerous for White, who can count on preserving his advantage in the centre.

c) Black's universal resource and a component of almost all his plans is the advance of the b-pawn to b4 with a threat to the c3-knight and the e4-pawn. Having spent some time on the transfer of the bishop to b3, White (as a rule!) cannot afford a further loss of time to make defensive moves after ...b5 and has to react by creating threats in another area of the board.

The above explains the strategic predetermination of the rapid aggravation of the struggle in the Sicilian Sozin. An example:

**1 e4 c5 2 ♘f3 d6 3 d4 cxd4 4 ♘xd4 ♘f6 5 ♘c3 a6 6 ♗c4 e6 7 ♗b3 ♗e7 8 f4 b5** *(D)*

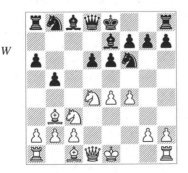

a)  9 a3?! 0-0 10 0-0 ♗b7 11 ♕e2?! (White should try 11 f5!?) 11...♘bd7!

and Black is already better: 12 e5 (too late) 12...dxe5 13 fxe5 ♗c5! 14 ♗e3 ♕b6! ∓. White should not play like that. The long-term factors favour Black and slow play is disastrous for White – at least until the first manifestation of his activity and the appearance of weak points in his opponent's centre.

b) The active 9 f5 does not work properly here due to 9...e5 or maybe 9...b4!?, but in other cases (for example, 8...♕c7 instead of 8...b5) f5 will probably be the strongest move, while a3 almost never is.

c)  9 e5! dxe5 10 fxe5 ♘fd7 11 ♗xe6 ♘xe5 12 ♗xc8 ♕xc8 13 ♘d5 with quite a promising position. An example of strategically correct play by White with the bishop on b3 – not a single 'preventive' move was made!

It appears to me that White's play is in practice reduced to a choice of active continuations and is psychologically easier than the task facing Black, who has to maintain a delicate balance between defensive and counter-attacking actions. Be that as it may, it is high time to start telling you about this practice in more detail.

# Historical Background

## The Story Begins: Veniamin Sozin

A participant in four USSR championships, master Veniamin Sozin (1896-1956) was not the first to develop the bishop on c4 in the Sicilian, but the system is rightfully named after him. Sozin was the first to link the bishop's manoeuvre with an orderly system of attack in the centre and on the kingside.

### Sozin – Ilyin-Zhenevsky
*USSR Ch (Moscow) 1931*

**1 e4 c5 2 ♘f3 ♘c6 3 d4 cxd4 4 ♘xd4 ♘f6 5 ♘c3 d6 6 ♗c4 e6 7 0-0 ♗e7 8 ♗e3 a6** *(D)*

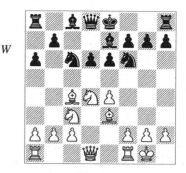

W

**9 f4**

That is the beginning of the story of the Sozin Attack. White prepares further assaults that can be associated with three different ideas: e5, f5 or g4.

**9...♕c7**

9...d5!? is also possible. Modern chess-players prevent this by playing 9 ♗b3! first, and only then 10 f4.

**10 ♗b3 ♘a5 11 ♕f3! ♘xb3 12 axb3 0-0 13 g4! ♖b8**

Not 13...b5? 14 ♘cxb5.

**14 g5 ♘d7** *(D)*

White has a substantial advantage. Sozin continued with 15 ♕h5 g6 16 ♕h6 and his follower, Fischer (in Fischer-Cardoso, New York (2) 1957) preferred 15 f5 ♘e5 16 ♕g3, but probably the most precise line of all is 15 ♕h3 ♖e8 16 ♖f3! ♗f8 17 ♕h4 b5 18 ♖h3 h6 19 gxh6 g6 20 f5 b4 21 ♖f1! (Suetin/Boleslavsky).

Ilyin-Zhenevsky won the game eventually and, possibly because of

W

that, Sozin's plan only came into fashion in the 1950s...

## 1950

This was an important year. White won several spectacular games and the move 6 ♗c4 (primarily as an answer to the plan with ...♘c6) was acclaimed among Soviet masters.

### Geller – Vatnikov
*Kiev 1950*

**1 e4 c5 2 ♘f3 ♘c6 3 d4 cxd4 4 ♘xd4 ♘f6 5 ♘c3 d6 6 ♗c4 e6 7 0-0 ♗e7 8 ♗e3 0-0 9 ♗b3 ♘a5 10 f4 b6** *(D)*

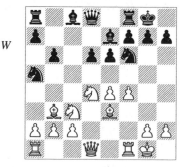

W

**11 e5! ♘e8**

Possibly better is 11...dxe5 12 fxe5 ♘e8 (but not 12...♘d7? 13 ♖xf7!).

**12 f5! dxe5**

Or: 12...exf5 13 e6!; 12...♘xb3 13 ♘c6!.

**13 fxe6! f6? 14 ♘f5 ♘xb3 15 ♘d5! ♘d4 16 ♘dxe7+ ♚h8 17 ♘g6+! 1-0**

In the 1950s heated discussions began on the Sozin Attack. It was at this time that Fischer appeared on the scene...

## Fischer

The eleventh World Champion, Bobby Fischer, used 6 ♗c4 from the very moment he appeared on the international stage in 1957 until he left it in 1972. His contribution to the development of the system cannot be overestimated. He used all the basic varieties of the Sicilian Sozin when playing White, and contested one of them (5...a6 6 ♗c4), which deservedly bears his name, when playing both colours.

Some of his victories:

### Fischer – Bednarski
*Havana OL 1966*

**1 e4 c5 2 ♘f3 d6 3 d4 cxd4 4 ♘xd4 ♘f6 5 ♘c3 a6 6 ♗c4 e6 7 ♗b3 ♘bd7 8 f4 ♘c5 9 f5 ♘fxe4?** *(D)*

**10 fxe6! ♕h4+**

The alternatives are also very bad for Black: 10...♗xe6 11 ♘xe4 ♘xe4 12 ♘xe6 fxe6 13 ♕g4; 10...fxe6 11 ♘xe4 ♘xe4 12 0-0.

**11 g3 ♘xg3 12 ♘f3! ♕h5 13 exf7+ ♚d8 14 ♖g1 ♘f5 15 ♘d5! ♕xf7 16 ♗g5+ ♚e8 17 ♕e2+ ♗e6 18 ♘f4 ♚d7 19 0-0-0 ♕e8 20 ♗xe6+ ♘xe6 21 ♕e4! g6 22 ♘xe6 1-0**

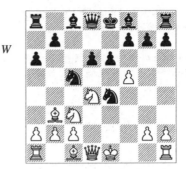

W

### Fischer – Dely
*Skopje 1967*

**1 e4 c5 2 ♘f3 d6 3 d4 cxd4 4 ♘xd4 ♘f6 5 ♘c3 ♘c6 6 ♗c4 e6 7 ♗b3 a6 8 f4 ♕a5 9 0-0 ♘xd4 10 ♕xd4 d5? 11 ♗e3 ♘xe4 12 ♘xe4 dxe4 13 f5 ♕b4 14 fxe6 ♗xe6 15 ♗xe6 fxe6** *(D)*

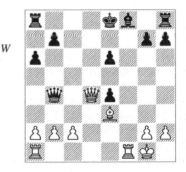

W

**16 ♖xf8+! ♕xf8 17 ♕a4+! b5 18 ♕xe4 ♖d8 19 ♕c6+ ♖d7 20 ♖d1 ♕e7 21 ♖d3 1-0**

### Fischer – Rubinetti
*Palma de Mallorca IZ 1970*

**1 e4 c5 2 ♘f3 d6 3 d4 cxd4 4 ♘xd4 ♘f6 5 ♘c3 e6 6 ♗c4 a6 7 ♗b3 b5 8**

0-0 ♗b7 9 ♖e1 ♘bd7 10 ♗g5 h6 11 ♗h4 ♘c5? *(D)*

12 ♗d5! exd5 13 exd5+ ♔d7 14 b4! ♘a4 15 ♘xa4 bxa4 16 c4! ♔c8 17 ♕xa4 +– ♕d7 18 ♕b3 g5 19 ♗g3 ♘h5 20 c5 dxc5 21 bxc5 ♕xd5 22 ♖e8+ ♔d7 23 ♕a4+ ♗c6 24 ♘xc6 1-0

Wonderful games! The 1960s were the heyday of the Sicilian Sozin, due not only to the American champion...

## The Velimirović Attack

The Yugoslav grandmaster Dragoljub Velimirović was the second outstanding follower of Sozin. Starting in 1965, Velimirović put into practice a most dangerous attacking scheme against the 5...♘c6 system. It featured the development of the queen on e2 and queenside castling, substituting a quick g4 and g5 for Sozin's basic idea (f4), when the forced retreat of the knight from f6 to d7 nourished White's mind with various tactical ideas. The concept was taken on at once by a number of chess-players, including Fischer himself.

**Velimirović – Sofrevski**
*Yugoslavia 1965*

1 e4 c5 2 ♘f3 ♘c6 3 d4 cxd4 4 ♘xd4 ♘f6 5 ♘c3 d6 6 ♗c4 e6 7 ♗e3 ♗e7 8 ♕e2 a6 9 0-0-0 ♕c7 10 ♗b3 *(D)*

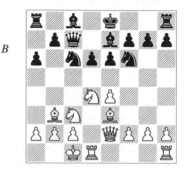

This has been the most important line of the Velimirović Attack. One possibility here is 10...0-0, after which White plays 11 g4 or 11 ♖hg1. Alternatively, Black can start counterplay, while leaving his king in the centre:
**10...♘a5 11 g4 b5 12 g5 ♘xb3+**
Not 12...♘d7? 13 ♗xe6!.
**13 axb3 ♘d7** *(D)*

14 ♘f5!? exf5 15 ♘d5 ♕d8 16 exf5 0-0? 17 f6! gxf6 18 ♗d4 ♘e5 19

gxf6 ♗xf6 20 ♖hg1+ ♗g7 21 ♗xe5
dxe5 22 ♕xe5 f6 23 ♘e7+ ♔f7 24
♕h5+ 1-0

The game attracted the glare of publicity in the chess world and some decades passed before the theoreticians came to a more-or-less definite opinion that 16...♗b7! (instead of 16...0-0?) enables Black to equalize.

## Recoil

Fischer is linked to the sharp tumble of popularity of the Sicilian Sozin in the 1970s, as well as its previous peak. The games Fischer-Larsen and Fischer-Spassky (given below) administered a blow to White's position and raised a lot of questions. Fischer ceased to play chess and the questions remained unanswered. However, the first blow was delivered by Fischer himself in 1967 and it fell upon the system 5...a6 6 ♗c4.

### R. Byrne – Fischer
*Sousse IZ 1967*

1 e4 c5 2 ♘f3 d6 3 d4 cxd4 4 ♘xd4
♘f6 5 ♘c3 a6 6 ♗c4 e6 7 ♗b3 b5 8 f4

A popular plan at the time. The extremely important idea 8 0-0 ♗e7 9 ♕f3!, used by Fischer against Olafsson in 1960, ironically, was not developed at all in the 1960s.

8...♗b7 9 f5 e5 10 ♘de2 ♘bd7 11
♗g5 ♗e7 12 ♘g3 ♖c8 13 0-0 *(D)*

White is ready to use the resource ♘h5 to develop his initiative but he will face a great disappointment.

13...h5! 14 h4 b4 15 ♗xf6 ♗xf6 16
♘d5 ♗xh4 17 ♘xh5 ♕g5

Now it is Black who attacks on the kingside and has an advantage.

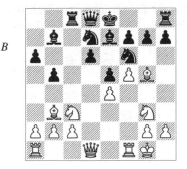

The reputation of the Velimirović Attack suffered seriously from an innovation by Bent Larsen.

### Fischer – Larsen
*Palma de Mallorca IZ 1970*

1 e4 c5 2 ♘f3 d6 3 d4 cxd4 4 ♘xd4
♘f6 5 ♘c3 ♘c6 6 ♗c4 e6 7 ♗b3 ♗e7
8 ♗e3 0-0 9 ♕e2 a6 10 0-0-0 ♕c7 11
g4 *(D)*

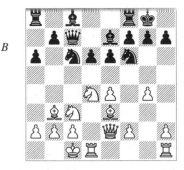

**11...♘d7**

This manoeuvre was carried out for the first time in this game and it still remains an important tool for Black against the Velimirović Attack. The immediate 11...b5 is unsuccessful because of 12 g5 ♘d7? 13 ♘d5! +−, so Black transfers the knight to c5 in advance. After that, ...b5 and ...b4 will become a very serious threat.

**12 h4?**

Even Fischer's brilliance was not enough to reject this enticing but utterly inefficient move.

**12...♘c5 13 g5 b5! 14 f3 ♗d7 15 ♕g2 b4 16 ♘ce2 ♘xb3+ 17 axb3 a5 18 g6 fxg6 19 h5 ♘xd4 20 ♘xd4**

20 ♖xd4 g5! 21 ♗xg5 ♗xg5+ 22 ♕xg5 a4.

**20...g5 21 ♗xg5 ♗xg5+ 22 ♕xg5 h6! 23 ♕g4 ♖f7!**

Later Black energetically made use of his advantage and won.

In the 1971 match against Larsen, Fischer managed to take his revenge by turning back to the Classical Sozin with 0-0 and winning twice. And yet, in the 1972 World Championship match – Fischer's last contest until 1992 – the last word was Black's.

### Fischer – Spassky
*Reykjavik Wch (4) 1972*

**1 e4 c5 2 ♘f3 d6 3 d4 cxd4 4 ♘xd4 ♘f6 5 ♘c3 ♘c6 6 ♗c4 e6 7 ♗b3 ♗e7 8 ♗e3 0-0 9 0-0 a6 10 f4 ♘xd4 11 ♗xd4 b5** *(D)*

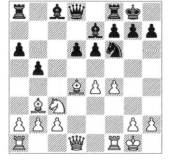

This plan, rare at the time, was specially prepared by Spassky.

**12 a3 ♗b7 13 ♕d3 a5!**

The point.

**14 e5 dxe5 15 fxe5 ♘d7 16 ♘xb5 ♘c5 17 ♗xc5 ♗xc5+ 18 ♔h1 ♕g5!?**

Black's chances are somewhat superior. The game ended in a draw on the 41st move, but on the way Spassky missed a good opportunity to pose serious problems for his opponent.

Certainly, the development of ideas in the 1970s did not stop at that. White's adherents went on with their search. Still, in the absence of Fischer these attempts did not bring the desired results. The Classical Sozin was committed to oblivion. The Velimirović Attack preserved more followers but all attempts in Larsen's variation 11 g4 ♘d7 were stuck because of the line 12 g5 ♘c5 13 ♖hg1 ♗d7!, which was very thoroughly analysed by the Soviet theoretician Nikitin. Finally, in the Fischer Attack, 5...a6 6 ♗c4 e6 7 ♗b3 b5, White persisted with the line 8 0-0 ♗e7 9 f4 although practice proved that Black had no real problems after 9...♗b7!. "Currently Sozin's Attack has been completely ousted by Rauzer's Attack [i.e. the Richter-Rauzer Attack]" wrote Mochalov in his article (1980).

Still, White's resources were far from being exhausted and the proof appeared quite soon.

### Revival

It was the game Sax-Timman, London 1980 that indicated where it was possible to strengthen White's play in the game Fischer-Spassky. Instead of the sluggish continuation 12 a3, White should go in for the following forcing variation:

**12 e5! dxe5 13 fxe5 ♘d7 14 ♘e4 ♗b7 15 ♘d6! ♗xd6 16 exd6** *(D)*

This position is of paramount importance for the entire Classical Sozin. The play is complicated and White possesses resources to fight for an advantage after 16...♕g5 17 ♖f2 (or 17 ♕e2). The final verdict has not yet been declared.

The Velimirović Attack was invigorated by a brilliant win by Andrei Sokolov.

## A. Sokolov – Salov
*Nikolaev 1983*

**1 e4 c5 2 ♘f3 ♘c6 3 d4 cxd4 4 ♘xd4 ♘f6 5 ♘c3 d6 6 ♗c4 e6 7 ♗e3 a6 8 ♕e2 ♕c7 9 0-0-0 ♗e7 10 ♗b3 0-0 11 ♖hg1 ♘d7 12 g4 ♘c5** *(D)*

**13 ♘f5!**

This knight sacrifice had not previously attracted serious theoretical attention. Sokolov and his coach Yurkov did a great job that was fully reflected in this game.

**13...b5 14 ♗d5 ♗b7 15 g5 exf5? 16 g6 hxg6 17 ♖xg6 ♘e5 18 ♖xg7+! +– ♔xg7 19 ♖g1+ ♘g6 20 exf5 ♖h8 21 ♗d4+ ♗f6 22 fxg6 fxg6 23 ♕g4 ♖h6 24 ♗xf6+ ♔h7 25 ♖e1 ♗xd5 26 ♘xd5 ♕c8 27 ♖e7+ ♔g8 28 ♖g7+ ♔f8 29 ♖g8+ ♔xg8 30 ♘e7+ 1-0**

In neither the 1980s nor the 1990s could Black find complete security in the Classical Sozin and Velimirović Attack. It is not by accident that one of the chess world leaders of the 1990s, Vladimir Kramnik, invariably avoids these positions by playing 6...♕b6.

## Development of the Fischer Attack

Of all the subsystems of the Sozin, the greatest change and commotion in the last 15-20 years of the 20th century were seen in the theory of 6 ♗c4 in the Najdorf system.

First of all, by about 1985 it finally became evident that in the main variation **1 e4 c5 2 ♘f3 d6 3 d4 cxd4 4 ♘xd4 ♘f6 5 ♘c3 a6 6 ♗c4 e6 7 ♗b3 b5** White can still fight for the initiative by making use of an old idea of Fischer's:

**8 0-0 ♗e7 9 ♕f3!** *(D)*

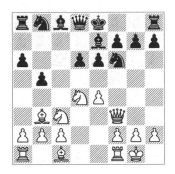

B

Black's early advance on the queen-side has somewhat weakened his position and this allows White to alter his plan completely. In contrast to other lines of the Sicilian Sozin, White is able to create serious threats without any pawn moves.

An example:

**9...♛b6**

This and 9...♛c7 are the main continuations.

**10 ♗e3 ♛b7 11 ♛g3 0-0 12 ♗h6 ♘e8 13 ♖fe1 ♗d7 14 ♖ad1** *(D)*

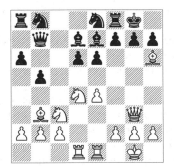

B

**14...♘c6? 15 ♘d5! ♗d8 16 ♘f5! exf5 17 exf5 ♘e5 18 ♖xe5! dxe5 19 f6 g6 20 ♘e7+**

The two lines 20...♖xe7 21 fxe7 and 20...♚h8 21 ♗xf8 are dismal for Black. The earliest game that ended thus was Gurieli-G.Sakhatova, USSR wom Ch (Erevan) 1985.

Although Black can avoid fatal consequences if he defends accurately, and although 7...b5 has many followers (the most important of them being Boris Gelfand), Black's chances after 9 ♛f3 are overall a little worse. In the 1980s the question of whether 7...b5 'stops' the Fischer Attack was answered.

Black also has at his disposal a powerful resource, quite logical and undeservedly rejected after the game Fischer-Bednarski, i.e. 7...♘bd7!. The year 1989 witnessed a real burst of popularity for this forgotten variation, for two reasons. First, 7...♘bd7 was played by Kasparov. In Ehlvest-Kasparov, Skellefteå World Cup 1989, Black had no problems at all after 8 ♗g5 h6 9 ♗h4 ♛a5 10 0-0 ♛h5! =. Second, at the same time Ashot Anastasian demonstrated to the chess community how it is possible to fight against Fischer's recipe 8 f4 ♘c5 9 f5:

**1 e4 c5 2 ♘f3 d6 3 d4 cxd4 4 ♘xd4 ♘f6 5 ♘c3 a6 6 ♗c4 e6 7 ♗b3 ♘bd7 8 f4 ♘c5 9 f5 ♗e7 10 ♛f3 0-0 11 ♗e3**

In his book *My 60 Memorable Games*, Fischer assessed this position as advantageous for White.

**11...e5!? 12 ♘de2 ♘xb3 13 axb3 b5!** *(D)*

Now both 14 ♘xb5? d5 15 exd5 ♘xd5 16 ♘g3 ♗b7, Akopian-Anastasian, Tbilisi jr 1989, and 14 ♗g5?! ♗b7 15 ♗xf6 ♗xf6 16 0-0-0? b4 17 ♘d5 a5 18 ♚b1 a4, Kruppa-Anastasian, USSR Cht (Podolsk) 1989, give Black a big advantage.

The boom for the move 7...♘bd7 was assured and from the beginning of the 1990s this continuation became the main tool against the Fischer Attack. Both White and Black were finding new ideas and the Sicilian Sozin entered a period of active development. The match between Short and Kasparov turned out to be the climax of this period.

### Short – Kasparov

The 1993 world championship match did not promise any news for the Sicilian Sozin. Short did not use this system at all and the spectacular win by Kasparov when playing White against Gelfand at Linares 1993 (in the line 5...a6 6 ♗c4 e6 7 ♗b3 b5 8 0-0 ♗e7 9 ♕f3 ♕c7 10 ♕g3 0-0 11 ♗h6 ♘e8 12 ♖ad1 ♗d7 13 ♘f3!?) was clearly just an episode in his openings research. A great surprise followed: in Short's games with White – from the sixth game to the twentieth – the same position emerged:

**1 e4 c5 2 ♘f3 d6 3 d4 cxd4 4 ♘xd4 ♘f6 5 ♘c3 a6 6 ♗c4 e6 7 ♗b3** *(D)*

Kasparov now tried three different moves.

In the first three games (6, 8 and 10) he played 7...♘bd7 8 f4 ♘c5 and each time Short reacted differently. Three draws followed and the openings were always favourable for Kasparov who, nevertheless, should have lost at least two of these games due to later mistakes.

There followed 7...♘c6 in the next two games. After 8 f4 ♗e7 9 ♗e3 0-0, Kasparov managed to strike a blow against one of the popular lines in the 12th game (10 ♕f3!? ♘xd4! 11 ♗xd4 b5 12 ♗xf6 ♗xf6 13 e5 ♗h4+ 14 g3 ♖b8) but when in game 14 Short chose the classical 10 0-0, Kasparov faced some problems. These two games also ended in draws.

In all three remaining games Kasparov resorted to 7...b5 8 0-0 ♗e7 9 ♕f3 ♕c7 and Short never managed to obtain an appreciable advantage, though he won one of the games.

Generally speaking, the Short-Kasparov match proved that defence is not the strongest side of Kasparov's talent since he clearly underperformed when under attack in these Sozin middlegames. However, from the theoretical viewpoint these games did not yield many answers.

The most significant were the games with **7...♘bd7 8 f4 ♘c5**. The move **9 e5** was successfully neutralized in the 8th game (9...dxe5 10 fxe5 ♘fd7 11 ♗f4 b5!) and Kasparov's deep concept from the 10th game (**9 ♕f3** b5! 10 f5 ♗d7!?) was developed by Short himself later – **9 f5** b5(!) (instead of the very playable 9...♗e7, as in Short-Kasparov, 6th game) 10 0-0 ♗d7, Istratescu-Short, Erevan OL 1996.

Kasparov probably avoided 7...♘bd7 in the course of the match not because of the results of the opening fight but due to the very fact that White has a wide choice. Later he came back to this move and the discussion was resumed in the 1996 Amsterdam tournament: **9 0-0!?** ♘fxe4!? 10 ♘xe4 ♘xe4 11 f5 e5 12 ♕h5 with an extremely sharp game (12...♕e7!?, Topalov-Kasparov; 12...d5!?, Topalov-Short).

To all appearances, by about 1996/7 the leading players of the world had decided that Black is close to equality in the line 7 ♗b3 ♘bd7 and it is not by accident that during their two post-match games, Short selected another (quite rare) sequence of moves when playing against Kasparov – **7 0-0!?** (D).

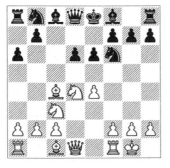

This devalues 7...♘bd7?!, which can be answered by 8 ♗xe6, 8 ♖e1 or 8 ♗g5.

After 7...♗e7 8 ♗b3 0-0 9 f4 (D), the two Short-Kasparov games went:

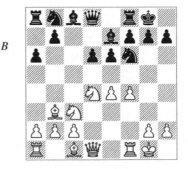

a) 9...♘c6 10 ♗e3 (the game has moved into Classical Sozin territory) 10...♘xd4 11 ♗xd4 b5 12 e5 dxe5 13 fxe5 ♘e8!? 14 ♘e4 ♗b7 15 ♕d3 ± Short-Kasparov, Amsterdam 1996.

b) 9...b5! (on this occasion Kasparov avoids the Classical Sozin; there appears on the board a double-edged variation, well known as a result of the 'wrong' but once popular move-order 7...b5 8 ♗b3 ♗e7 9 f4 {instead of 9 ♕f3!} 9...0-0 – instead of 9...♗b7!) 10 e5 dxe5 11 fxe5 ♘fd7 12 ♗e3! ♘xe5! 13 ♕h5 ♘bc6 14 ♘xc6 ♘xc6 15 ♖f3 b4!? 16 ♖h3 h6 17 ♖d1 ♕a5 18 ♘d5 exd5 19 ♖g3 d4 20 ♗d5 ♗g5 21 ♗xg5 ♕xd5 22 ♗f6 ♕xh5 23 ♖xg7+ ♔h8 24 ♖g6+ ♔h7 25 ♖g7+ ½-½ Short-Kasparov, Novgorod 1997.

Perpetual check is quite a logical outcome of the 9...b5 line. Such a result can hardly suit White in the Fischer Attack, so the ball is in his court! One of the interesting ideas is to play 7 0-0 ♗e7 anyway, and now the rare 8 a4!?, as in Emms-Shipov, Hastings 1998/9: 8...♘c6 9 ♗e3 0-0 10 ♔h1 ♗d7 11 f4 ♖c8 12 ♗a2 ♕c7 13 ♕e2 ♘a5 14 ♖ad1 ♘c4 15 ♗c1 ♖fd8 16 g4 ♕c5 (D)

17 g5 ♘e8 18 f5 e5 19 ♘d5 ♗f8 20 b4 ♕a7 21 ♗xc4 exd4 22 g6 ♔h8 23 gxf7 ♘c7 24 ♘f4 1-0.

## History Never Ends!

With so many games and so much detailed analysis having been performed, it sometimes appears impossible that anything new could be invented. Fortunately, the complexity of chess is vast, as was demonstrated by the lesson that all sceptics received from Dragoljub Velimirović in 1997:

### Velimirović – Popović
*Bar 1997*

**1 e4 c5 2 ♘f3 d6 3 d4 cxd4 4 ♘xd4 ♘f6 5 ♘c3 ♘c6 6 ♗c4 e6 7 ♗e3 a6 8 ♗b3 ♗e7** (D)

This position has occurred hundreds, if not thousands, of times in practice, but nobody chanced to make the following interesting pawn sacrifice: **9**

g4!? ♘xd4 10 ♕xd4 e5 11 ♕d3 'with unclear play'. History never ends!

We are about to enter the main theoretical part of this book. I have to admit that the work on this theoretical coverage turned out to have some pitfalls, and it might be useful to indicate what these pitfalls (i.e. the peculiar features of the Sicilian Sozin) mean for the reader. Briefly, Sozin theory is a limited set of critical trunk variations and a huge number of theoretically secondary but practically very playable lines (particularly in the move range 7-11) which are very difficult for a theoretician to describe and almost impossible for a player to memorize completely. Additionally, the Sozin features an abundance of possible transpositions – practically all the main lines and plenty of the secondary variations may arise by various routes. Therefore, choose several main variations that you are ready to play, and don't limit your attention to the main lines as given in the book. Then you will know ways to punish your opponents if they make an unusual move, and how you can use move-order tricks to lure them into lines that you like!

# 1 5...e6 6 ♗c4 ♗e7

**1 e4 c5 2 ♘f3 d6 3 d4 cxd4 4 ♘xd4 ♘f6 5 ♘c3 e6 6 ♗c4** *(D)*

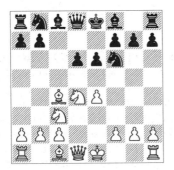

**6...♗e7!**

In this chapter our main focus is on the plan associated with this move and the further rapid transfer of the knight from b8 to c5, if White plays 7 ♗b3. According to everything that is currently known, after 6...♗e7 White has fewer chances for an advantage than after 6...a6 or 6...♘c6.

Two other moves need to be mentioned:

a) 6...♘a6!? is a less successful version of the same idea. Until White has played ♗b3, it is somewhat premature to transfer the knight, and thus White can fight for the initiative:

a1) 7 ♗g5!? ♘c5 8 ♕e2 ♗e7 (8...a6 9 0-0-0 b5 10 ♗d5 exd5? 11 ♘c6!) 9 0-0-0 ♘fxe4 (9...0-0 10 ♘db5!?) 10 ♗b5+.

a2) 7 ♕e2!? is also of some interest.

b) Interestingly, 6...♘bd7!? has almost never occurred. This can be ascribed only to an irrational fear of 7 ♗xe6. In fact, 7 ♗xe6?! is no better here than in the variation 6...a6 7 ♗b3 ♘bd7 8 ♗xe6?!.

**7 ♗b3** *(D)*

If White delays ♗b3, the effectiveness of the plan with ...♘c5 is less, but with the bishop on c4 Black has some extra possibilities in the centre (...d5 or ...♘xe4) and ideas involving a quick ...a6 and ...b5 at a favourable moment:

a) 7 ♕e2 has no real independent value since after 7...0-0 (7...a6) White plays 8 ♗e3 or 8 ♗b3.

b) 7 a3!? is likely to transpose to the variations with ...a6 or ...♘c6 and ♗a2.

c) 7 g4 0-0!? (7...♘c6?! can be met by 8 g5, with the point 8...♘d7 9 ♗xe6) 8 g5 (8 ♗b3 – *7 ♗b3 0-0 8 g4*) 8...♘xe4! 9 ♘xe4 d5 10 ♘f6+ ♗xf6! 11 gxf6 dxc4 12 fxg7 ♖e8 with a good game for Black, Svistunov-Kharitonov, Pinsk 1993.

d) 7 0-0 0-0 8 f4 d5 (or 8...♘xe4 9 ♘xe4 d5) 9 exd5 exd5 10 ♗b3 ♘c6 and Black stands at least no worse; e.g., 11 ♔h1 ♖e8 12 ♗e3 ♗a3!, Saltaev-Lutsko, Minsk 1994.

e) 7 f4 0-0! 8 ♕f3. Now normal variations for White arise following 8...♘c6 9 ♗e3 or 8...a6 9 ♗e3! ♘c6 (9...b5? 10 e5) 10 0-0-0, so Black should choose between 8...♘xe4!? and 8...d5!? – in both cases White will be in great danger if he accepts the pawn sacrifice.

f) 7 &e3!? and now:

f1) 7...a6 and then:

f11) White can play 8 a4!?, with a probable transposition to the positions of Chapter 12 after ...&c6.

f12) Sometimes White is prepared to transpose to a risky side-variation of the Fischer Attack: the position resulting from 8 &e2 b5 9 &b3 will be discussed in Line B of Chapter 5 (*5...a6 6 &c4 e6 7 &b3 b5 8 &e2 &e7! 9 &e3*).

f2) 7...0-0 and then:

f21) 8 &e2 and now:

f211) 8...a6 9 0-0-0 b5 10 &b3 is again the risky line discussed in Line B of Chapter 5 (*5...a6 6 &c4 e6 7 &b3 b5 8 &e2 &e7! 9 &e3 0-0 10 0-0-0*).

f212) There is also 8...d5!? 9 exd5 exd5 10 &b3. It is likely that chances are equal; for example, 10...&b4 11 0-0-0 &xc3 12 bxc3 (Nisipeanu-Suba, Romanian Cht 1997) 12...&e7!? (Nisipeanu/Stoica) or 10...&c6 11 0-0 &e8 12 &b5 &b4 13 &g5 &d7 14 &xb7 &b8 15 &xa7 &a8 with a repetition of moves, Zamora-Yermolinsky, USA Ch (Chandler) 1997.

f22) Another concept for White is 8 &b3 – see 7 &b3 0-0 8 &e3 (White has avoided 7 &b3 &a6 8 f4 &c5 9 &f3 a5!?).

**7...&a6**

Or:

a) 7...&bd7?! looks dubious because of 8 &xe6.

b) After 7...0-0 the play generally transposes to the lines with ...&a6, but there are some independent possibilities:

b1) 8 &e3 &a6 9 f4 – 7...&a6 8 f4 0-0 9 &e3.

*B*

b2) 8 f4 &a6 – 7...&a6 8 f4 0-0.

b3) 8 g4. Now not bad is 8...d5!? (less convincing are the lines 8...&c6 9 g5 &xd4 10 &xd4 &d7 and 8...g6 9 &h6 &e8) 9 exd5 &xd5 10 &xd5 exd5 with sufficient counterplay for Black; for example, 11 &e3 &c6 12 h3 &g5, Shaplyko-Kraschl, Zagan jr Ech 1995.

b4) 8 &e2 a6! (8...&a6 involves some risk in view of 9 g4 &c5 10 g5 and 11 &g1) 9 &c3 (9 g4 &c6! and now 10 &e3?! &xd4! 11 &xd4 e5 or 10 &xc6 bxc6 11 g5 &d7, and Black is at least no worse, Minasian-Sakaev, Frunze 1989) 9...b5 10 0-0-0. If White agrees (or aspires) to play this position, he should start with 7 &e3 (or with 7 &e2) – see above.

**8 f4** *(D)*

After other moves, Black has few problems:

a) 8 0-0?! &c5! deprives White of activity.

b) 8 &e2 &c5 9 g4 g6! (threatening 10...e5!) 10 g5 (alternatively, 10 h3 h5) 10...&h5 gives Black a good game. 11 &g1 can be met by 11...a6!? 12 f4 (12 &e3 is more circumspect) 12...0-0 13 &e3 (Kiefer-Bischoff, Bundesliga 1985/6) 13...e5! or 11...0-0 12

♗e3 a6 13 0-0-0 (Golubev-Suba, Romanian Cht 1996) 13...♗d7!.

c) 8 ♗e3 ♘c5 9 ♕f3 0-0. White's arrangement is somewhat artificial and Black's chances are in no way worse. Several examples:

c1) 10 g4 a5! (10...♗d7 11 g5 ♘e8 12 ♖g1 g6!? 13 0-0-0 ♘g7, Al.Sokolov-V.Neverov, Kstovo 1997) 11 a4 (11 g5 ♘fd7 ∓) 11...d5! with an excellent game for Black, Bokan-Rõtšagov, Tallinn 1989.

c2) 10 0-0-0 ♗d7!? (10...a5?! 11 e5!; however, 10...♕c7 is not bad; e.g., 11 g4 a6 12 g5 ♘fd7 13 ♖hg1 b5 14 ♕h5 g6 15 ♕h6 ♖e8 16 ♖g3 ♗f8 17 ♕h4 ♗g7 with double-edged play, Rublevsky-Sergienko, Podolsk 1992) 11 g4 ♘e8!? (11...a5!?; 11...b5!?) 12 ♖hg1 ♘c7 13 g5?! (13 ♘f5!? is a better try) 13...b5 14 ♕h5 g6 15 ♕h6 ♖e8 16 ♖g3 ♗f8 17 ♕h4 a5 ∓ Golubev-Cools, Belgian Cht 1995/6. Black's attack is faster than White's.

B

Again Black has to choose between two continuations of almost equal value: 8...♘c5 and 8...0-0. The difference between them is about the same as the difference between the lines 8...♘c5 9 e5 and 8...0-0 9 0-0 ♘c5 10 e5.

**8...0-0** *(D)*

Or 8...♘c5, and then:

a) 9 ♕f3. Now 9...0-0 – *8...0-0 9 ♕f3 ♘c5*. Possibly even more precise is 9...a5!? 10 0-0 0-0 with roughly equal play after 11 a4 e5 12 ♘db5 ♘xb3!? 13 cxb3 ♗e6 or 11 ♗e3 a4 12 ♗c4 ♘cxe4, Kreiman-Ehlvest, New York 1993.

b) 9 e5!? dxe5 (9...♘fe4 10 ♘xe4 ♘xe4 11 0-0 0-0 12 c3 ± Skrobek-Pedzich, Warsaw 1989) 10 fxe5 ♘fd7 11 ♗f4 and then:

b1) 11...0-0?! 12 ♕g4 ♘xb3 (or 12...♔h8 13 0-0-0 a6 14 ♖he1 ♕c7 15 ♖e3 ± Golubev-Barsky, Ukrainian open Ch (Yalta) 1996) 13 axb3 f5 14 ♕e2 ♘c5 15 0-0-0 ± Bednarski-Ornstein, 1976.

b2) 11...a6 transposes to a line of the Fischer Attack that is dangerous for Black (see *5...a6 6 ♗c4 e6 7 ♗b3 ♘bd7 8 f4 ♘c5 9 e5 dxe5 10 fxe5 ♘fd7 11 ♗f4 ♗e7?!* in Line B21 of Chapter 7).

b3) 11...♘f8! 12 ♘db5 ♘g6 13 ♕xd8+ ♔xd8 probably leads to equality.

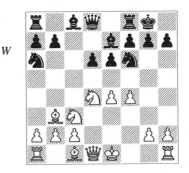

W

**9 ♕f3**
Other possibilities:

a) 9 e5?! ♘d7 ∓.

b) 9 ♗e3 ♘c5 10 ♕f3 – *9 ♕f3 ♘c5 10 ♗e3*.

c) 9 f5 ♘c5 (or 9...e5!? 10 ♘de2 ♘c5 11 ♘g3 b5) 10 ♕f3 e5 (10...♗d7; interesting is 10...d5!? 11 exd5 e5 12 ♘de2 e4, Hendriks-Pliester, Dutch Cht 1994) 11 ♘de2 b5 12 ♗g5 ♘xb3 (12...b4 13 ♘d5!) 13 cxb3 (Hendriks-Timman, Dutch Ch (Amsterdam) 1996) 13...b4 14 ♗xf6 bxc3 15 ♗xe7 cxb2 16 ♖b1 ♕xe7 17 ♖xb2 with equality – Timman.

d) 9 0-0 ♘c5 10 e5 (10 ♕f3 is not dangerous – see *9 ♕f3 ♘c5 10 0-0*) 10...dxe5 (10...♘fe4 11 ♘xe4 ♘xe4 – *8...♘c5 9 e5!? ♘fe4 10 ♘xe4 ♘xe4 11 0-0 0-0 ±*) 11 fxe5 ♘xb3! (11...♘fd7?! 12 ♗f4 a6 – *5...a6 6 ♗c4 e6 7 ♗b3 ♘bd7 8 f4 ♘c5 9 e5 dxe5 10 fxe5 ♘fd7 11 ♗f4 ♗e7 12 0-0-0*) 12 axb3 ♗c5 (12...♘d5 could be considered) 13 ♗e3 and now:

d1) 13...♘d5 14 ♗f2. Compared with the position from the Fischer Attack, Black has made the more useful move ...0-0 instead of ...a6. Still, he has some problems; for example, 14...♘xc3 15 bxc3 ♕c7 16 ♕e2 ♗d7 17 ♖ad1 ♖ad8 (17...a5!?) 18 ♖d3 ♗c6 19 ♖h3, K.Müller-Stohl, Munich 1992.

d2) Therefore, 13...♘d7!? deserves attention.

**9...♘c5 10 ♗e3** *(D)*

10 f5 is considered under *9 f5 ♘c5 10 0-0*.

After 10 0-0 the most precise is 10...a5! – *8...♘c5 9 ♕f3 a5 10 0-0 0-0*. Less convincing is 10...e5!? 11 fxe5 dxe5 12 ♘f5 ♗xf5 13 exf5 e4 14 ♕e2, Liukin-V.Neverov, Ukrainian open Ch (Yalta) 1996.

Now Black faces a major decision.

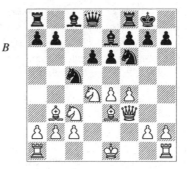

**10...a5**

This move seems to be the most critical. Others:

a) 10...a6 transposes to the positions of the Fischer Attack (see Line A of Chapter 3 for 11 0-0, and Line B42 of Chapter 7 for the other moves).

b) 10...d5 11 exd5 exd5 12 f5! ± (Beliavsky/Mikhalchishin).

c) 10...e5 remains difficult to assess. 11 ♘f5 (11 fxe5 dxe5 12 ♘f5 ♗xf5 13 ♕xf5 ♘xb3! 14 axb3 ♕c8! =) 11...♗xf5 12 exf5 and then:

c1) 12...♘xb3 13 axb3 ♕c8 14 0-0-0! ♕xf5 15 ♕xb7 exf4 16 ♖hf1 gives White the better chances, Moraru-Dumitrescu, Romanian Cht 1994.

c2) 12...e4 and now:

c21) 13 ♕e2 d5 (other ideas are 13...♕a5 14 ♗xc5!? and 13...♘xb3!) 14 0-0-0 (14 ♗xc5! is equal – Quinteros) 14...♘xb3+ 15 axb3 ♕a5 16 g4 ♖ac8 17 g5 ♗b4! brings Black real counterplay, Garcia Toledo-Donoso, Fortaleza Z 1975.

c22) 13 ♕h3 ♘xb3 14 axb3 d5 15 0-0-0, and now 15...♕a5!? is better than 15...h5 16 ♗d4 ♕a5 17 ♔b1 ♖fd8 18 g4! ± Ankerst-Vogt, Baden-Baden 1993.

**11 0-0-0**

11 e5? dxe5 12 fxe5 ♘fd7 13 ♗f4 a4 14 ♗c4 ♘b6 −+.

If 11 a4 then 11...e5! 12 ♘f5 ♗xf5 13 exf5 ♘xb3 (13...e4!?) 14 cxb3 exf4, followed by ...d5, gives Black an excellent position, Poutiainen-Balashov, Teesside students Wch 1974.

11 a3 is no better.

**11...a4** *(D)*

11...♗d7!? 12 ♗c4 (12 e5?! ♘e8) 12...♕c7 (12...a4!?) 13 ♘db5 ♗xb5, Golubev-V.Neverov, Ukrainian open Ch (Yalta) 1996, and now 14 ♘xb5, with the point 14...♕c6 15 ♘xd6 ♗xd6 16 e5 ♘ce4 17 ♗d3!, looks dangerous for Black.

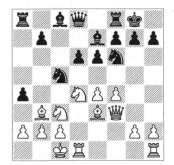

W

**12 ♗c4 a3 13 b3**

Black is better after 13 ♘db5?! axb2+ 14 ♔b1 ♕a5 15 e5 dxe5 16 fxe5 ♘fd7 17 ♕g3 ♔h8 (Istratescu-Stohl, Budapest Z 1993): 18 ♖d4 f6! or 18 ♗g5 f6!.

13 e5 also brings no success to White; e.g., 13...axb2+ 14 ♔b1 dxe5 15 ♘c6 ♕c7 16 ♘xe7+ ♕xe7 17 fxe5 ♘fd7 18 ♕g3 ♔h8 19 ♖d4 ♘a4, Shtyrenkov-Kharitonov, Smolensk 1986.

**13...♘cxe4**

Or:

a) 13...♘fxe4 comes to the same thing.

b) 13...♗d7!? requires investigation.

c) 13...♕a5 and now:

c1) 14 ♘db5 ♗d7 15 e5 dxe5 (not 15...♗c6?! 16 exf6!, Istratescu-Suba, Romanian Cht 1992) 16 fxe5 ♘d5 leads to complications that are satisfactory for Black:

c11) 17 ♗d4 ♘b6! 18 ♗e2 ♗c6! and 19...♘bd7.

c12) 17 ♖xd5 ♗c6! ∞ (17...exd5?! 18 ♘xd5 ♗xb5 19 b4!!; 17...♗xb5 18 ♗xc5 ♗xc4 19 ♗xe7 ♗xd5 20 ♘xd5 exd5 21 ♖f1 ±) and now 18 ♖f1 ♔h8! or 18 ♖hd1 ♔h8!?.

c13) 17 ♗xd5 ♗xb5 18 ♗xc5 ♗xc5 19 ♗xb7 ♖ad8 20 ♘xb5 (½-½ Istratescu-Golubev, Romanian Cht 1996; 20 ♘e4 ♗d4 21 c4 ♗e8!) 20...♕xb5 with compensation.

c2) However, 14 ♗d2!? may present some danger for Black; for example, 14...♕b6 (14...♕c7 15 ♖he1) 15 e5 d5 16 ♗d3 ♘fe4 17 ♗xe4 ♘xe4 18 ♘xe4 ♕xd4 19 ♘f6+! ± Moraru-Parligras, Romanian Cht 2001.

**14 ♘xe4 ♘xe4 15 ♕xe4 d5 16 ♗xd5**

16 ♕f3?! dxc4 17 ♘xe6 ♗xe6 18 ♖xd8 ♖fxd8 gives Black more than enough compensation, D.Gross-Orsag, Czech Cht 1993/4.

**16...exd5 17 ♕f3 ♖e8!?**

It appears that Black should have sufficient counter-chances; for example, 18 ♘b5 ♗f5 19 ♖xd5 ♕c8.

# 2  5...a6 6 ♗c4: Introduction to the Fischer Attack

**1 e4 c5 2 ♘f3 d6 3 d4 cxd4 4 ♘xd4 ♘f6 5 ♘c3 a6 6 ♗c4** *(D)*

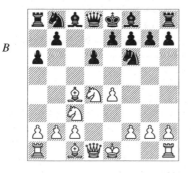

Now 6...e6 is, of course, the main move. 6...e6 7 0-0 will be discussed in the next chapter, and then we shall discuss 6...e6 7 ♗b3. Here we consider rare answers to 6 ♗c4 and the sidelines for White after 6 ♗c4 e6.

**A: 6...b5**      27
**B: 6...♘bd7**    28
**C: 6...e6**       29

In Line C, we only discuss lines without 7 0-0 or 7 ♗b3.

Other moves:

a) 6...g6?! transposes to a dubious variation of the Dragon after 7 f3!, followed by ♗e3 and ♕d2.

b) 6...e5?! is strategically dubious. Now of interest is 7 ♘f5!? ♗xf5 8 exf5 ♕c8 9 ♗b3 ♕xf5 10 0-0 ♘c6 11

f4, Minasian-Trifunov, Novi Sad 1988, but in any case the moves 7 ♘de2 and 7 ♘f3 are sufficient for an untroubled advantage.

c) 6...♘c6. As compared with 6...e6 and 7...♘c6, this does not have any advantages, only disadvantages, because 7 ♘xc6! bxc6 8 e5 ♘d7 9 e6 promises White a sustained initiative.

d) 6...♕c7!? 7 ♗b3 e6 – *6...e6 7 ♗b3 ♕c7*.

## A)

**6...b5 7 ♗b3**

White may attempt to punish his opponent by playing 7 ♗d5!?. Then 7...♘xd5 8 exd5! appears to be in White's favour but 7...♖a7 8 ♗e3 ♖c7 is stronger. As I see no evident benefits for White there, I advise him to remain unprovoked.

**7...♗b7**

Black should play 7...e6 and be satisfied that he has avoided lines like *6...e6 7 a3* and *6...e6 7 a4*. Further avoidance of ...e6 is unjustified.

**8 0-0! ♘bd7 9 ♖e1**

Now:

a) 9...e6 leads to a promising variation for White (Line E1 of Chapter 5).

b) 9...♘c5 can be answered with the unpleasant 10 ♗g5!.

c) 9...g6 10 a4 b4 11 ♘d5 ♗g7 12 ♘xb4! ♕b6 13 c3 also favours White.

d) 9...♖c8 10 a4! bxa4 11 ♗xa4 e6 12 ♘d5! also clearly favours White, Kindermann-Hölzl, Haifa Echt 1989.

**B)**

**6...♘bd7** *(D)*

A rare move. The idea can be linked to 7 ♗b3?! ♘c5! or 7 0-0 ♕c7!? (7...♘c5 8 ♖e1!) 8 ♕e2 b5.

However, a good continuation for White is:

**7 ♗g5**

This transposes to a rare line of the 6 ♗g5 Najdorf, i.e. *5...a6 6 ♗g5 ♘bd7 7 ♗c4!*. In the 1960s this line was often played at high level but later it was discarded by Black in favour of the more reliable *5...a6 6 ♗g5 e6*.

**7...e6**

Black should play extremely cautiously as his adversary's mobilization permanently threatens to become a decisive factor. Otherwise:

a) 7...h6 8 ♗xf6 ♘xf6 9 ♕e2 and 0-0-0! gives White a huge advantage in development.

b) 7...b5 8 ♗d5! is also dangerous for Black.

c) 7...g6 does not give Black equality; e.g., 8 ♕d2 (8 ♕e2 ♗g7 9 0-0-0

0-0 10 f4 is less convincing; then 10...♘b6 11 e5!? ♗g4 12 ♘f3 might favour White, but 10...♕c7!? looks stronger) 8...♗g7 9 f3 h6 10 ♗e3 b5 11 ♗b3 ♗b7 (Howell-Hodgson, British Ch (Plymouth) 1992) 12 0-0-0.

d) 7...♕a5 8 ♕d2 e6 has been the most frequent choice for Black. Here, either 9 0-0 (see *7...e6 8 0-0 ♕a5 9 ♕d2*) or 9 0-0-0 b5 10 ♗b3 is possible (not 10 ♗d5?! in view of 10...b4! 11 ♗xa8 bxc3 12 bxc3 ♘b6, which was discovered by Spassky and Rovner) 10...♗b7 11 ♖he1 0-0-0 12 a3 ±. I think the text-move (7...e6) offers White less choice.

**8 0-0**

The immediate 8 ♗xe6?! is dubious, so White prepares a better version of this blow. Instead, 8 f4!? leads to another rare line of the 6 ♗g5 Najdorf (*5...a6 6 ♗g5 e6 7 f4 ♘bd7 8 ♗c4*) where it is very doubtful that White has any advantage after, for instance, 8...♕b6.

**8...♕a5**

Otherwise:

a) 8...b5? is bad due to 9 ♗xe6 fxe6 10 ♘xe6 ♕b6 11 ♘d5 ♘xd5 12 ♕xd5 +–.

b) 8...♗e7 9 ♗xe6 gives White a powerful attack

c) 8...♕c7 9 ♗xe6! fxe6 10 ♘xe6 ♕c4 11 ♘d5 assures a strong attack for White, Keres-Sajtar, Amsterdam OL 1954.

d) After 8...h6, a good reply is 9 ♗xf6 ♘xf6 10 ♗b3 ± Stean-Browne, Nice OL 1974.

e) Maybe attention should be paid to 8...♘c5!? with the point that 9 b4 can be met by 9...♕b6.

**9 ♕d2 ♗e7** *(D)*

9...b5?! 10 ♗d5! exd5 11 ♘c6 ♕b6 12 exd5 ♘e5 13 ♖ae1 ♗b7 14 ♗e3 ♕c7 15 f4 with an initiative, Mnatsakanian-Zurakhov, USSR 1958. "The fatal deficiency of the entire system is that Black is constantly exposed to danger from one of the typical sacrifices!" – Shamkovich in 1971.

**10 ♖ad1 h6**

10...0-0 11 ♘d5!.

**11 ♗h4**

After 11 ♗e3, 11...♘c5 12 ♘b3! gave White an advantage in Ivanchuk-Ehlvest, Elista 1998, but 11...♘g4!? (Ivanchuk) 12 ♗f4 ♘ge5 is less clear.

**11...♘e5 12 ♗e2 g5 13 ♗g3**

White continues f4, with the better prospects.

**C)**

**6...e6** *(D)*

Out of the secondary moves for White, five deserve to be mentioned, and two are significant enough to deserve their own section:

**C1: 7 a4**      29
**C2: 7 a3**      30

The other three are:

a) After 7 ♕e2, White's priorities are 8 ♗e3 (8 ♗g5) and 9 0-0-0. With

the black knight on b8, this looks rather adventurous. As a rule, play now develops along the lines 7...b5 8 ♗b3, 7...♗e7 8 ♗e3 b5 9 ♗b3 or 7...♗e7 8 ♗b3 0-0 9 ♗e3 b5 (all these will be discussed under *7 ♗b3 b5 8 ♕e2*). One more option for Black is 7...♕b6!?.

b) 7 ♗e3 is another risky move:

b1) 7...♗e7 is quite normal, but if White plays 8 ♗b3, Black should delay 8...b5 no further. Instead, 8...0-0 9 f4 (or 9 g4) and 8...♘bd7 9 f4!? ♘c5 10 ♕f3 are perilous for Black.

b2) The main continuation is 7...b5! 8 ♗b3 – *7 ♗b3 b5 8 ♗e3*.

c) 7 ♗g5 (here this move is harmless as Black is neither weaker nor behind in development) 7...♗e7!. Black wishes to play, primarily, ...♘c6 so as to exert pressure on the centre. He also has the idea of ...b5 and, if possible, the blow ...♘xe4. The g5-bishop is misplaced and Black has no problems. For instance, after 8 ♗b3 ♘c6 9 f4 not bad are 9...♕b6!? and 9...0-0 10 ♘f3 (10 ♕d2 h6 11 ♗h4? ♘xe4) 10...h6 11 ♗h4 d5 12 e5 ♘e4 13 ♗xe7 ♕xe7, Soloviov-Simagin, Gorky 1954.

**C1)**

**7 a4** *(D)*

An atypical idea for the Sicilian Sozin. White nips ...b5 in the bud, but weakens the b4-square and sharply reduces his own capacity for active play.

a) 7...♘c6 8 0-0 (or 8 ♗e3 and 9 0-0) will be discussed in Line B of Chapter 12.

b) 7...♗e7 8 0-0 0-0 often also leads to Line B of Chapter 12 because Black plays ...♘c6 next move. The most common continuation is 9 ♗e3 ♘c6 10 ♔h1 (or 9 ♔h1 ♘c6 10 ♗e3).

c) 7...♕c7 is also linked to ...♘c6 after 8 ♕e2 or 8 ♗a2.

d) 7...♘xe4!? 8 ♘xe4 d5 is another solution for Black. It might be enough to equalize. Now:

d1) 9 ♗d3 dxe4 10 ♗xe4 ♘d7 11 0-0 ♗e7 12 c3 ♘c5 13 ♗c2 e5 = Kavalek-Tarjan, USA Ch (South Bend) 1981.

d2) 9 ♘d2 dxc4 10 ♘xc4 ♕c7 11 ♕e2 = Galdunts-Allwermann, Böblingen 1998.

d3) 9 ♗g5 ♗e7! and now 10 ♗xe7 ♕xe7 11 ♗d3 dxe4 12 ♗xe4 e5 and ...♕b4+, or 10 ♕g4 ♗xg5 11 ♘xg5 ♕a5+!? 12 c3 dxc4.

d4) 9 ♘f3 ♘c6! (better than 9...dxe4 10 ♕xd8+ ♔xd8 11 ♘e5 or 11 ♘g5)

10 ♘ed2 dxc4 11 ♘xc4 ♕xd1+ 12 ♔xd1 ♗c5 13 ♗e3 ♗xc3 14 fxe3 a5 15 c3 f6 16 ♘b6 ♖a6 17 ♘xc8 ♔d7 is equal, V.Gurevich-Dvoirys, Le Touquet 1997.

White can try to avoid the last line by playing 7 0-0, and if 7...♗e7 (or 7...♘c6), then 8 a4. Of course, he needs to be ready for 7...b5 8 ♗b3 in this case.

## C2)

### 7 a3 (D)

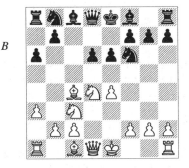

In the usual lines of the Fischer Attack with ♗b3, there is no advantage at all for White in playing a3 at an early stage. Here this move is more appropriate as White desires to compensate for the time loss by shifting the bishop to a less vulnerable position on a2 (the difference is quite important in some variations).

**7...b5**

Other possibilities:

a) 7...♘c6 8 0-0 (or 8 ♗a2 and 9 0-0) will be considered in Chapter 12.

b) 7...♗e7 8 ♗a2 0-0 9 0-0 and then:

b1) 9...♘c6 – 7...♘c6 8 0-0 ♗e7 9 ♗a2 0-0.

b2) The position resulting from 9...b5 will be discussed under *7...b5 8 ♗a2 ♗e7 9 0-0 0-0*.

b3) 9...♕c7 keeps ...b5 and ...♘c6 in reserve. However, after 10 f4!, the variation 10...b5 11 f5 e5 12 ♘de2 ♗b7 13 ♘g3 ♘bd7 14 ♗g5, as in Babula-Dabrowski, Koszalin 1998, appears better for White and it is safer for Black to play 10...♘c6, thereby meaning that this is no improvement for Black over ...♘c6 at an earlier stage.

c) 7...♘xe4 8 ♘xe4 d5 9 ♗g5 ♗e7 and now:

c1) After 10 ♗xe7 ♕xe7 11 ♗d3 dxe4 12 ♗xe4 0-0 (Saltaev-Roshchina, Moscow 1996) White scarcely has any real advantage.

c2) 10 ♕g4!? ♗xg5 11 ♘xg5 dxc4 12 0-0-0 therefore deserves attention. White has the initiative for a pawn; e.g., 12...♕f6 13 h4! 0-0 14 ♕e4!, Petrushin-Zhelnin, Sverdlovsk 1985. 12...♕e7 is a better method of defence: 13 ♖he1 0-0! 14 ♘f5 ♕f6! or 13 ♕h5 g6 14 ♕h6 ♕f8!? 15 ♕h4 ♕e7.

**8 ♗a2** *(D)*

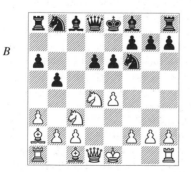

We now discuss:

**C21)**
**8...♗e7 9 0-0 ♗b7**
The alternative is 9...0-0 *(D)*:

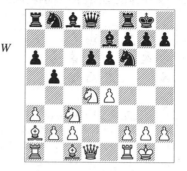

a) 10 ♕e2 ♗b7 – *9...♗b7 10 ♕e2 0-0*.

b) 10 f4 ♗b7 and now:

b1) 11 ♕e2 – *9...♗b7 10 ♕e2 0-0 11 f4*.

b2) White gains nothing by 11 f5, in view of 11...e5 12 ♘de2 ♘bd7! (12...♘xe4?! 13 ♘xe4 ♗xe4 14 ♘g3) 13 ♘g3 ♖c8 14 ♗g5 (14 ♘h5 ♘xh5 15 ♕xh5 ♖xc3! followed by 16...♘f6) 14...♖xc3 (Fischer's 14...♘b6 is not bad) 15 bxc3 ♘xe4 16 ♘xe4 ♗xe4 17 ♗xe7 ♕xe7 18 c4 ♖c8! with great play for Black, Ermenkov-Portisch, Skara Echt 1980.

b3) No better for White is 11 ♕f3 ♘bd7 12 f5 e5 13 ♘de2 a5!, as in Orendy-Szabo, Hungarian Ch (Budapest) 1959, and other games.

c) 10 ♕f3 ♗b7 11 ♕g3 ♘h5!? (11...♘xe4 12 ♘xe4 ♗xe4 is unsuccessful due to 13 ♗xe6! ♗f6 14 ♗f5, but Black can try 11...♘c6 12 ♘xc6 ♗xc6 13 ♗h6 ♘e8, as in Belikov-V.Neverov, Odessa 1990) 12 ♕h3 ♘f6 13 ♖e1 ♘bd7 14 ♗g5 ♖c8 15 ♖ad1 (Korchnoi-Ribli, Reykjavik 1988) and now 15...②e5! (Korchnoi) gives Black good play.

**10 ♕e2**

10 f4 ②bd7 11 f5 e5 12 ②de2 ♖c8! 13 ②g3 h5! is favourable for Black, Westerinen-Lehmann, Palma de Mallorca 1968.

**10...0-0**

Or:

a) 10...②bd7?! is risky in view of 11 ♗xe6!.

b) 10...②c6 is an alternative. After 11 ②xc6 ♗xc6 12 f4 0-0 13 f5, Black can choose between 13...e5!? (with the point that 14 ♗g5? runs into 14...②xe4) and 13...exf5 14 ♖xf5 ♗d7 followed by 15...♗e6, Smailbegović-Bobotsov, Sarajevo 1962.

**11 f4 ②bd7**

11...②c6!? 12 ②xc6 ♗xc6 – 10...②c6 11 ②xc6 ♗xc6 12 f4 0-0.

**12 e5! dxe5 13 fxe5 ♗c5 14 ♗e3 ②xe5**

The variation 14...♕b6? 15 ♖ad1 ②xe5 16 b4! is a good illustration of the benefits of the a2-square for the bishop. If the bishop is on b3, 16 b4 is impossible and the assessment is radically altered.

**15 ②xe6 ♗xe3+ 16 ♕xe3 fxe6 17 ♕xe5 ♕b6+ 18 ♔h1**

White has a slight positional advantage, Kupreichik-Shipov, Aalborg 1997.

**C22)**

**8...♗b7 9 0-0**

9 ♕e2!? ②bd7 10 g4 (Giaccio-Sunye, Villa Gesell 1998) is interesting.

**9...②bd7!** *(D)*

There is no need to hurry with ...♗e7. 9...②c6 is also possible, but 9...②xe4?! 10 ②xe4 ♗xe4 11 ♖e1! is risky for Black.

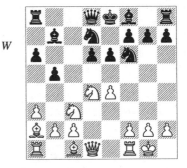

**10 ♕e2**

After 10 f4 it is normal to proceed with 10...♗e7 or 10...♖c8, but probably it is better still to grab the pawn with 10...②xe4!.

Complications with roughly equal chances can be obtained after 10 ♖e1!? ♖c8 11 ♕f3 (after 11 f4, both 11...②b6 and 11...②c5!? are good for Black) 11...②e5 12 ♕g3 ②c4 13 ♔h1 ♕b6 14 ②f3 h5!? (Lepeshkin).

**10...♖c8 11 ♗g5**

11 f3 = Kavalek-Ree, Eersel (9) 1969.

**11...h6 12 ♗h4 ♕b6 13 ♖ad1 ♗e7**

White has no advantage; e.g., 14 ②xe6 fxe6 15 ♗xe6 ♖xc3 16 bxc3 g5 Kupreichik-Åkesson, Mariehamn 1997, or 14 ♔h1 g5 15 ♗g3 (Ćirić-Velimirović, Yugoslavia 1964) 15...♖xc3!? 16 bxc3 ②xe4.

To avoid the line with 8...♗b7 and 9...②bd7, White may try to start with 7 0-0 (7...♗e7 8 a3 or 7...②c6 8 a3).

# 3  5...a6 6 ♗c4 e6 7 0-0

**1 e4 c5 2 ♘f3 d6 3 d4 cxd4 4 ♘xd4 ♘f6 5 ♘c3 a6 6 ♗c4 e6 7 0-0** *(D)*

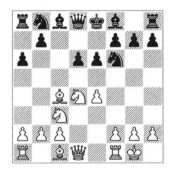

*B*

Bobby Fischer almost exclusively preferred 7 ♗b3 in his games, and the same choice was made by the majority of his followers. It is therefore logical to compare 7 0-0 with the main continuation.

Given that the white bishop is almost certain to move to b3, it is clear that White cuts down his further choices by playing 7 0-0 – this is noticeable in the variations with ...♘c6 and ...♗e7. However, 7 0-0 is advantageous because it renders 7...♘bd7 dubious (see below), so 7 0-0 should be viewed as narrowing the choice for both sides. In Fischer's time ...♘bd7 was not considered a serious idea for Black and White saw no benefits in 7 0-0 at all...

As a follow-up: White can start with 7 0-0 if he desires to play a3 or a4 and avoid variations such as 7 a3 b5 8 ♗a2 ♗b7 or 7 a4 ♘xe4.

**7...♗e7**

This is one of three critical replies to 7 0-0 which are stronger now than after 7 ♗b3. The other good replies (7...♘c6 and 7...♕c7!?) tend to transpose to a Classical Sozin.

a) 7...♘xe4? 8 ♘xe4 d5 9 ♗g5!.

b) 7...♘c6 – *5...♘c6 6 ♗c4 e6 7 0-0 a6*.

c) 7...b5 8 ♗b3 is the same as *7 ♗b3 b5 8 0-0* (there 8 0-0 is not forced but it is still the main move, so for adherents of 7...b5 systems there is little difference between 7 0-0 and 7 ♗b3).

d) 7...♕c7!? 8 ♗b3 and now:

d1) 8...♘c6 – *5...♘c6 6 ♗c4 e6 7 0-0 a6 8 ♗b3 ♕c7*. This move-order makes some sense as it avoids the lines *7...♘c6 8 a3* and *7...♘c6 8 a4*.

d2) 8...♗e7 (see *7...♗e7 8 ♗b3 ♕c7*) is also possible.

d3) 8...♘bd7 is risky in view of 9 ♗xe6 (9 f4 is best answered by 9...b5!, rather than 9...♘c5 – *7 ♗b3 ♘bd7 8 0-0 ♘c5 9 f4 ♕c7* in Chapter 7) 9...fxe6 10 ♘xe6 ♕c4 11 ♘d5 ♘xd5 12 exd5 ♔f7 13 b3 with serious compensation, Milu-Vajda, Bucharest 1999.

e) 7...♘bd7?! is very risky:

e1) 8 ♗g5 – *6...♘bd7 7 ♗g5 e6 8 0-0*.

e2) 8 ♖e1 is good; e.g., 8...♗e7 9 ♗xe6, 8...♕c7 9 ♗xe6! or 8...♘c5 9 b4 ♘cxe4 10 ♘xe4 ♘xe4 11 ♖xe4 d5 12 ♘xe6!.

e3) 8 ♗xe6 fxe6 9 ♘xe6 is also very dangerous: 9...♕b6 (9...♕a5 10

♘d5!? ♘xd5 11 exd5 ♔f7 also does not guarantee safety; e.g., 12 ♗d2!? ♕a4 13 ♖e1) 10 ♘d5 ♘xd5 11 exd5 ♘c5 (11...♘f6? 12 ♗e3 ♕a5 13 b4; 11...♔f7 12 ♗e3!?) 12 ♘xf8! ♔xf8 (12...♖xf8 13 ♕h5+!) 13 ♕f3+ ♔g8 14 ♖e1 ♗d7 (14...♕d8 15 ♗g5 ♕f8 16 ♕xf8+ ♔xf8 17 ♗e7+ ±) 15 ♖e7 ♖f8 (15...♗e8? 16 ♗h6!) 16 ♕g3 ♖f7 17 ♖xf7 ♔xf7 18 ♕f4+ ♔g8 19 ♗e3! with an advantage for White, Istratescu-Badea, Romanian Ch (Bucharest) 1994.

**8 ♗b3**

After 8 a3!?, 8...♘xe4?! 9 ♘xe4 d5 is dubious because of 10 ♕g4 g6 11 ♖d1; e.g., 11...f5 12 ♘xe6 ♗xe6 13 ♕h3 ♗d7 (13...♕b6 14 ♗xd5!) 14 ♘d6+!, and Black would be better to transpose to normal variations with 8...b5 9 ♗a2 (Chapter 2) or 8...♘c6 (Chapter 12).

One more option for White is 8 a4!?.

**8...0-0**

8...♘c6 and 8...b5 9 ♕f3 lead to the other main lines. 8...♘bd7?! fails to 9 ♗xe6!.

After 8...♕c7 9 f4, it is again normal to play 9...♘c6. However, the much less studied 9...b5!? is interesting. Then 10 ♕f3, 10 ♔h1 0-0 11 ♕e2 (Golubev-Alterman, Yaroslavl jr 1983) and 10 f5 b4 (10...e5!?) 11 fxe6 (11 ♘a4 e5! 12 ♘e2 ♗b7) 11...bxc3 12 exf7+ ♔f8, Fischer-Blackstone, USA simul 1964, are all unclear.

**9 f4** *(D)*

Other moves don't make much sense. Here, Black has a 'last chance' to transpose to the Classical Sozin (with 9...♘c6). We shall discuss the other two continuations:

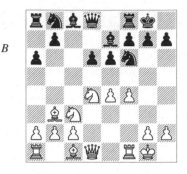

**A: 9...♘bd7**　　34
**B: 9...b5!**　　36

Other alternatives are dubious; e.g., 9...♕c7 10 f5! e5 11 ♘de2 b5 12 ♗g5 ♘bd7 13 ♘g3 ♗b7 14 ♘h5 with better chances for White, Gligorić-Attard, Madrid 1960.

*Note: the plan with f5 and meeting ...e5 with ♘de2 works better for White if the black queen is on c7 and Black has castled as then Black lacks the resources ...♖xc3 and ...h5.*

**A)**

**9...♘bd7 10 ♗e3**

Or:

a) After 10 f5, there is 10...e5!? as well as 10...♘c5.

b) 10 ♔h1!? has been tried, with the idea of meeting 10...♘c5 with 11 e5!; for example, 11...dxe5 12 fxe5 ♘fd7 (12...♘d5 ±) 13 ♗f4 ♗g5 14 ♕h5!, K.Müller-Heinemann, Hamburg 1997. However, 10...♕c7!? is interesting, as in Ciocaltea-Gheorghiu, Bucharest 1961.

c) 10 ♕f3 is a common alternative. Black can choose to delay ...♘c5 by means of 10...♕c7!?, or else settle for 10...♘c5, when 11 f5 and 11 g4 will be discussed in Chapter 7, while 11 ♗e3 is the same as *10 ♗e3 ♘c5 11 ♕f3*.

**10...♘c5**

Here too, Black can delay this move by playing 10...♕c7!?, but it is not clear whether he benefits from this.

**11 ♕f3**

11 e5!? dxe5 12 fxe5 ♘fd7 13 ♕h5 g6 14 ♕h3 ♘xe5 15 ♖ad1 ♕c7 16 ♗f4 doesn't promise much for White, Kaidanov-Wojtkiewicz, New York 1994.

The position after 11 ♕f3 is found at the crossroads of three variations (10...a6 11 0-0 in the main line of Chapter 1, 10...0-0 11 0-0 in Line B42 of Chapter 7, and the present line).

**11...♕c7** *(D)*

Maybe 11...♘fd7!? 12 g4 ♖e8 13 g5 ♗f8 is playable, as in D.Frolov-Dvoirys, Russian Ch (Samara) 2000. Another little-studied move is 11...♗d7.

**12 g4!?**

12 f5 transposes to *7 ♗b3 ♘bd7 8 f4 ♘c5 9 f5 ♗e7 10 ♕f3 0-0 11 0-0 ♕c7 12 ♗e3*.

**12...b5**

After 12...♘xb3 (see note 'b24' to Black's 11th move in Line C221 of Chapter 9) 13 axb3, 13...b5 is impossible.

**13 g5 ♘fxe4**

13...♘fd7!? 14 f5 (14 ♘f5?! exf5 15 ♘d5 ♕d8) 14...♘e5 deserves serious attention:

a) 15 ♕h5 b4 16 ♘ce2 ♘xb3 17 axb3 g6! 18 ♕h4 exf5 19 exf5 ♖e8 ∓ I.Marković-Dobes, Czech Cht 1995/6.

b) 15 ♕h3 b4 16 ♘ce2 ♘xe4 and now 17 fxe6 ♘xg5! or 17 f6 gxf6! 18 gxf6 ♘xf6 ∓.

c) 15 ♕g2!, with the point 15...b4 16 ♘ce2 ♘xb3 17 axb3 exf5 18 ♘xf5 ♗xf5 19 exf5 ♕xc2 20 f6, is probably best.

**14 ♘xe4 ♗b7 15 ♘xe6!**

After 15 ♘xc5, Black may either get an acceptable endgame through 15...dxc5 16 ♘xe6 ♕c8! 17 ♗d5 ♗xd5 18 ♕xd5 ♕xe6 19 ♕xe6 fxe6 (Golubev-Mowsziszian, Berlin 1993) or occupy the b7-square with the queen: 15 ♗xf3 16 ♘cxe6 ♕b7!? 17 ♖xf3 fxe6 (as in Vasiukov-Aronin, Riga 1954).

**15...fxe6**

15...♘xe6 16 ♖ad1 ♖fd8!? 17 ♗d5! ♗xd5 18 ♖xd5 ♕xc2 19 ♖d2 with an initiative for the pawn.

**16 ♘xc5!**

16 ♗xc5?! dxc5 17 ♗xe6+ ♔h8 suits Black.

**16...♗xf3 17 ♘xe6 ♕c8**

Not: 17...♕b7? 18 ♘c5+; 17...♕b8? 18 ♖xf3 ♖c8 19 ♗d5! ± Golubev-Vl.Belov, Alushta 1999.

**18 ♖xf3**

White has more than adequate compensation for the sacrificed material:

a) 18...♖f5 19 ♘d4+!? (19 ♗d4!? d5 20 ♖e1 ♗f8 21 ♖fe3 {Stoica} 21...♕d7 22 ♖e5 ♖xe5 23 ♖xe5 ♔h8

24 f5 ♖e8 25 ♖xd5 ♕c8) 19...d5 20 ♖d1!, Florean-C.Popescu, Romanian Cht 1994.

b) 18...d5 19 ♗xd5 (19 f5!? is possible) 19...♕d7 20 ♗b3 ♖f7 21 g6 (21 f5!?) 21...hxg6 22 ♖af1 ♔h8 23 ♖h3+ ♔g8 = Velker-Vitolinš, corr. 1996.

## B)

**9...b5!** *(D)*

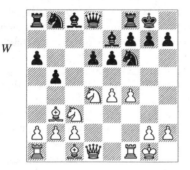

## 10 e5

Risky, but otherwise Black has nothing to worry about:

a) 10 f5? b4! 11 ♘a4 (after 11 ♘ce2 e5 12 ♘f3, Fischer-Smyslov, Bled/Zagreb/Belgrade Ct 1959, Black can play 12...♘xe4! 13 ♗d5 ♗b7 ∓ Mednis) 11...e5 12 ♘e2 ♗b7 13 ♘g3 ♘bd7 14 ♕e1 a5 with better chances, Anand-Ivanchuk, Linares 1991.

b) 10 a3 (no better than 8 a3 and ♗a2) 10...♗b7 (even 10...♘bd7 11 f5 ♘c5!? is not bad) 11 f5 (11 ♕f3 ♘bd7!; 11 ♕e2 ♘bd7! and here, with the bishop on b3, 12 e5 dxe5 13 fxe5 ♗c5 14 ♗e3 ♕b6 ∓ is bad for White) 11...e5 12 ♘de2 ♘bd7 (12...♘xe4?! 13 ♘xe4 ♗xe4 14 ♘g3) 13 ♘g3 ♖c8 (13...♘c5!? 14 ♗d5! ♗xd5 15 exd5 ♖c8! 16 ♗g5 ♘cd7 17 ♗xf6 ♘xf6 18 ♘ce4 ♖c4!, Kotkov-Polugaevsky, Russian Ch 1959) 14 ♗g5, and rough equality is achieved by both 14...♘b6 15 ♗xf6 (15 ♘h5 ♘c4) 15...♗xf6 16 ♖f3 and 14...♖xc3!? 15 bxc3 ♘xe4 16 ♗xe7 ♕xe7 17 ♘xe4 ♗xe4 18 c4, while Gutman's 14...a5 is also playable.

c) 10 ♗e3!? and now:

c1) 10...♗b7?! 11 e5!.

c2) 10...b4 11 ♘a4 ♗b7 (the alternative 11...♘xe4!? 12 f5 d5 13 fxe6 fxe6 14 ♘f5 ♗g5 is interesting, Valvo-Browne, San Mateo rpd 1989) 12 e5 dxe5 13 ♘xe6! (13 fxe5 ♘d5 14 ♗f2 ♘d7 with good prospects for Black, Golubev-Kadyrov, Baku jr 1984) 13...fxe6 14 ♗xe6+ ♔h8, and in this complicated line, White possibly has no advantage: 15 ♕xd8 (15 fxe5 ♘fd7 16 ♖xf8+ ♘xf8 17 ♕xd8 ♗xd8 18 ♗b3 ♘c6 19 ♘c5 ♗b6 20 ♖e1 with compensation, Einarsson-Lautier, Reykjavik 1988) 15...♖xd8 16 fxe5 ♘g8 (16...♘e4!?) 17 ♘b6 ♖a7, Kaidanov-de Firmian, Las Vegas 1994.

c3) 10...♕c7 is more reliable; e.g., 11 a3 (or 11 f5 b4! 12 ♘a4 e5 13 ♘e2 ♘bd7 = Yakovich-Novikov, Uzhgorod 1987) 11...♗b7 (or 11...♘c6!?, when after 12 ♘xc6 ♕xc6 13 f5, there is 13...♘xe4; instead, 12 f5 ♘xd4 13 ♗xd4 = leads to a position of the Classical Sozin) 12 f5 (12 ♕f3 ♘bd7 13 f5 e5 14 ♘de2 ♘c5 – 7 ♗b3 ♘bd7 8 f4 ♘c5 9 f5 ♗e7 10 ♕f3 0-0 11 ♗e3 ♕c7 12 0-0 b5! 13 a3 e5 14 ♘de2 ♗b7, which is approximately equal) 12...e5 13 ♘de2 ♘bd7 (13...♘g4 14 ♗f2; 13...♘xe4?! 14 ♘xe4 and 15 ♘g3) 14 ♘g3 ♘c5 15 ♗d5 ♘a4!, D.Hansson-Fridh, Swedish Ch (Skellefteå) 1972.

**10...dxe5 11 fxe5 ♘fd7!**

11...♗c5?! 12 ♗e3! ♘c6?! 13 ♘xc6! ♗xe3+ 14 ♔h1 ±.

**12 ♗e3!**

Otherwise:

a) Not 12 ♕f3? ♘xe5! 13 ♕xa8 ♕xd4+ 14 ♔h1 ♘bc6.

b) 12 ♗f4 ♘c5! 13 ♘ce2 ♗b7 is good for Black.

c) After 12 ♕h5, it appears that White risks even more than Black:

c1) 12...♘c6 13 ♘xc6 (the alternative 13 ♗e3 gives Black a choice between 13...♘dxe5, transposing to Line B2, and 13...♘xd4! 14 ♗xd4, which is note 'b' to White's 14th move in Line C222 of Chapter 9) 13...♕b6+ 14 ♗e3 ♕xc6 15 ♖f3 ♗b7, and now:

c11) Not 16 ♔h1? b4 17 ♗a4 ♕c7 18 ♖h3 h6 (Levy) 19 ♗xh6 ♕xe5 20 ♗g5 ♗xg2+.

c12) 16 ♖af1 g6!? (16...♗c5 17 ♖1f2 ♗xe3 18 ♖xe3 ∞) 17 ♖g3 b4.

c13) 16 ♖g3 g6 (16...♗c5 17 ♖e1 ♖ad8 {17...g6 18 ♕g5!?} 18 ♕h6 g6 19 ♗d5 exd5 20 ♖h3 ♖fe8 21 ♕xh7+ = Howell-D.Hansson, Reykjavik 1990) 17 ♕h6 ♗c5! 18 ♖e1 ♖fd8 with good chances for Black, Milu-Navrotescu, Bucharest 1999.

c2) After 12...♗c5 13 ♗e3 ♗xd4 14 ♗xd4 ♘c6 15 ♗e3 (15 ♖ad1 ♘xd4 16 ♖xd4 ♕b6! 17 ♖f4 ♕c5 18 ♘d5 ♖a7! 19 ♖h4 h6 20 ♘f6+ ♔h8 is much better for Black, Bareiss-G.Müller, corr. 1986) 15...♘cxe5, White's attacking prospects are unconvincing:

c21) 16 ♘e4 ♕e7 17 ♖ad1 ♗b7 18 ♘d6 ♗c6 19 ♖d4 (or 19 ♗g5 f6 20 ♘f5 ♕e8, Ostojić-Minić, Vrnjačka Banja 1970) 19...♘g6 20 ♗g5 ♘f6, Stisis-Gutman, Biel 1994.

c22) 16 ♖ad1 ♗b7 17 ♖d4 ♘g6 18 ♘e2 ♕e7 (18...♕c7!?) 19 ♘f4 and

now 19...e5? failed to 20 ♘xg6!! in Anand-Kasparov, Moscow rpd 1996. Instead Black should try 19...♘c5!? or Vaïsser's 19...♘f6!?.

**12...♘xe5!**

It is too late for Black to opt for a quiet life, as we can see from the following lines:

a) 12...♗g5? 13 ♗xg5 ♕xg5 14 ♘xe6! is much better for White, Christiansen-Andersson, Hastings 1981/2.

b) 12...♕c7? 13 ♖xf7! ♖xf7 14 ♘xe6 ♕xe5 15 ♗d4 ♕f5 16 ♘xg7 ♕f4 17 ♘e2 ♕g5 (17...♕e4 18 ♕f1 ♗f6 19 ♘f5! +− Rosenberger-Barta, corr. 1983) 18 ♕f1!? ±.

c) 12...♘c5 13 ♕g4!, Golubev-Aliev, Baku jr 1984.

d) 12...♗c5 13 ♘e4 ♗xd4 14 ♕xd4! (14 ♗xd4 ♘c6 15 ♗e3 {15 c3!?} 15...♘cxe5 16 ♕h5 – *12 ♕h5 ♗c5 13 ♗e3 ♗xd4 14 ♗xd4 ♘c6 15 ♗e3 ♘cxe5 16 ♘e4*) 14...♘c6 15 ♕c3 and now:

d1) 15...♘dxe5 16 ♗c5!.

d2) 15...♗b7 16 ♘d6 (16 ♖ad1!? Gallagher) 16...b4 and now White should play 17 ♕e1!, Bouaziz-Psakhis, Las Palmas IZ 1982, but not 17 ♕c4 ♘dxe5!.

d3) 15...♘cxe5 16 ♗d4 b4 17 ♕g3!? (Gallagher) 17...♘g6 18 ♘d6 gives White the initiative.

e) 12...♗b7 13 ♕h5 (not 13 ♖xf7? ♖xf7 14 ♘xe6 ♕c8 15 ♘d5, Bosch-Golod, Hoogeveen 1998, 15...♘xe5! ∓) and here:

e1) Not 13...♘c5? 14 ♖xf7! +−.

e2) 13...♕c7 14 ♖xf7 ♖xf7 15 ♗xe6 ♘xe5 16 ♗f4 and now 16...♘f3+ 17 ♕xf3 ♗xf3 18 ♗xc7 ♗c5 19 ♗xf7+ ♔xf7 20 ♖f1 ± (Nunn) or 16...♗d6 17 ♗xe5 ♗xe5 18 ♗xf7+.

e3)  After 13...♗c5!? White can try 14 ♖ad1 ♘c6 15 ♔h1, as in Zviag-intsev-Mitenkov, Moscow 1989 or 14 ♔h1, but not 14 ♖xf7? ♗xd4!.

e4)  13...g6 14 ♕h3 ♗g5 (14...♘c5 15 ♖xf7! ±; 14...♘xe5 15 ♘xe6!) 15 ♖xf7 ♗xe3+ 16 ♕xe3 ♖xf7 17 ♗xe6 (17 ♘xe6 ♕b6!) 17...♘f8 18 ♗xf7+ ♔xf7 19 e6+ ♔e8 (Shipov) 20 ♖e1!? ♕e7 21 ♖f1, with an attack.

**13 ♕h5** *(D)*

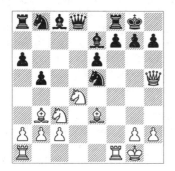

The critical position, in which Black can fight back by two methods.
**B1: 13...♘c4**      38
**B2: 13...♘bc6**     38

Other moves:

a)  13...♘bd7? is unsuccessful in view of 14 ♗xe6!.

b)  13...♗f6 14 ♘e4 ♘g4 15 ♖ad1!! ♘xe3 16 ♘xe6 (Sokrustov-Sozinov, corr. 1988) also favours White.

c)  13...♘g6 is not so easy to refute. After 14 ♖f3 (14 ♖xf7 and 14 ♖ad1 ♕c7 are unclear), 14...♘d7? is weak in view of 15 ♖xf7 ♖xf7 16 ♘xe6 ♕a5 17 ♕d5 ♘b6 18 ♕c6, but there are 14...♕d6, 14...b4 and even 14...e5 (e.g., 15 ♖xf7 ♖xf7 16 ♖f1 ♗f6 17 ♘f3 ♕e8) to consider.

**B1)**

**13...♘c4 14 ♗xc4 bxc4 15 ♖ad1**
Or:

a)  15 ♖f3? g6! 16 ♖g3 (16 ♕h6 e5! 17 ♖d1 exd4 18 ♗xd4 f6 is much better for Black) 16...♗d6 17 ♖g5 ♗f4! −+ Tarjan-Byrne, USA Ch (South Bend) 1981.

b)  15 ♕f3 ♖a7! 16 ♘f5 ♖d7 17 ♘xe7+ ♕xe7 18 ♕f2!? ♖e8 19 ♗c5 with compensation – Gallagher.

**15...♕c7 16 ♖f3 g6 17 ♕h6 f6!**
17...f5 18 ♗f4! ± (suggested by de Firmian).

**18 ♘e4**
18 ♖df1 e5 19 ♖g3 ♗d8 20 ♘f3 ♘c6 21 ♗c5 ♗e7 22 ♖xg6+ hxg6 23 ♕xg6+ ♔h8 ½-½ de Firmian-Ivanchuk, Amsterdam 1996 (here there are more chances to improve Black's play than White's). 18 ♘de2 does not look too convincing either; e.g., 18...♘c6!?.

**18...e5 19 ♖g3 ♗d8 20 ♘f3**
20 ♘e6? ♗xe6 (Bouaziz-de Firmian, Tunis IZ 1985) 21 ♖xd8 ♖xd8 22 ♖xg6+ ♔h8 is much better for Black.

**20...♗f5!**
20...♕g7 21 ♕h4 ♘c6 22 ♗h6 ♕a7+ 23 ♔f1! f5 24 ♖xd8 gives White an attack.

**21 ♘c5**
Now 21...♕g7 22 ♘h4! ♕xh6 23 ♗xh6 is probably better for White, but after 21...♕e7!? 22 ♘h4 ♗xc2 or 21...♗e7 the chances are equal.

**B2)**

**13...♘bc6** *(D)*
**14 ♘xc6**
After 14 ♖ad1 ♕e8 (14...♕c7!?) 15 ♘xc6 (15 ♘e4 ♗b7!) 15...♘xc6 16 ♘e4 ♘a5!? (16...f6!?) 17 ♘f6+ ♗xf6

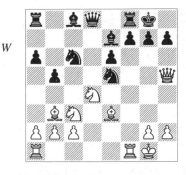

*W*

18 罝xf6 ②xb3 19 axb3 (Golubev-Shu-shkovsky, Donetsk 1984) 19...&b7 (or 19...豐e7!) Black has excellent pros-pects.

**14...②xc6 15 罝f3 豐d6!?**

After this move, White has not yet managed to prove any meaningful ad-vantage. Other moves:

a) 15...b4 16 罝h3 h6 and then:

a1) 17 罝d1 豐a5 18 ②d5 exd5 19 罝g3 d4 20 罝xg7+ (or 20 &d5 &g5 21 &xg5 豐xd5 22 &f6! − Short-Kas-parov, Novgorod 1997) 20...&xg7 21 &xh6+ (21 豐xh6+ =) 21...&h7 22 &g5+ = (not 22 &d5? 豐xd5!).

a2) 17 ②e4 豐a5 18 ②c5 罝b8 19 罝g3 &g5 20 罝e1 ②e7 21 罝xg5 (Nisi-peanu/Stoica) has not been tested.

a3) 17 &xh6!? g6 (17...gxh6 18 罝d1! 豐b6+ 19 &h1 &g5 20 ②e4 +−) 18 豐f3 bxc3 19 豐xc6 cxb2 20 罝f1 &d7 21 豐c3 &f6 22 罝xf6 b1豐+ 23 罝f1 豐b6+ 24 罝e3 豐xf1+ 25 &xf1 f6 is slightly better for White, as in the computer game *MChess8-Nimzo99*, SSDF 1999.

b) 15...g6 16 豐h6 and now:

b1) 16...f5?! 17 罝d1 豐e8 18 ②d5! ②e5 (18...豐f7 19 罝h3) 19 罝h3 豐f7 20 &d4 ②c6 21 &f6 &c5+ 22 &h1 罝a7 23 &c3 exd5 (Golubev-Golod,

Ukrainian jr Ch (Lutsk) 1987) 24 罝xd5! ±.

b2) After 16...f6! Black retains de-fensive resources:

b21) 17 罝d1 豐e8 and now:

b211) 18 罝h3 is best answered by 18...罝f7! (Kengis), rather than 18...豐f7 19 ②d5! ②a5 (19...罝d8!?) 20 罝f1 ②xb3 21 ②xf6+ &xf6 22 罝xf6.

b212) 18 ②e4 ②e5 (18...②a5?! 19 &d4! ②xb3 20 &xf6 ± J.Todorović-D.Lazić, Belgrade 1988) 19 罝h3 (19 罝g3 豐c6 Nickoloff) 19...罝f7.

b22) 17 罝g3!? is also very unclear; e.g., 17...豐e8 18 罝f1 豐f7 19 ②e2 ②a5 20 ②f4 &d6 21 ②h5 (Soderberg-Del-abie, corr. 1990) and now 21...&xg3.

**16 罝h3 h6 17 罝d1**

Or:

a) 17 &xh6 豐c5+ ∓.

b) 17 罝g3 豐e5! 18 豐f3?! (18 豐xe5 ②xe5 19 &xh6 is better) 18...&c5! ∓ Kulaots-Nisipeanu, Medellin jr Wch 1996.

c) 17 豐f3 &b7 and now White can play 18 罝d1 豐c7 or 18 罝g3 &h4! (Nisipeanu/Stoica).

**17...豐e5 18 豐f3 &c5! 19 &xc5 豐xc5+ 20 &h1 &b7!**

20...f5?! 21 ②d5.

**21 ②e4**

Not 21 罝d7? ②e5! −+.

Now, Golubev-Vit.Scherbakov, Nov-aya Kachovka 1988 ended peacefully after 21...豐e7 22 罝d7! 豐xd7 23 ②f6+. 21...豐e5 22 ②d6! ②d4 23 豐xb7 罝ad8! is no real improvement, but 21...豐f5! 22 豐xf5 exf5 23 ②d6 ②a5 ∓ forces White to seek a draw with 24 ②xf5!?.

It is not a good idea to make hasty conclusions, but if there is a deadlock, White will have to recollect, for exam-ple, 8 a3!? or 8 a4!? after 7 0-0 &e7.

# 4  5...a6 6 ♗c4 e6 7 ♗b3: 7...♗e7 and 7...♛c7

**1 e4 c5 2 ♘f3 d6 3 d4 cxd4 4 ♘xd4 ♘f6 5 ♘c3 a6 6 ♗c4 e6 7 ♗b3** *(D)*

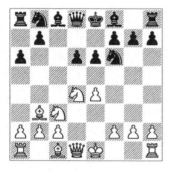

Black enjoys a wide choice here. Current theory has three main continuations: 7...b5, 7...♘bd7 and 7...♘c6 – these were selected by Kasparov in the 1993 World Championship match. We shall discuss these topics in succession in the chapters to follow and here we concentrate on less current but still interesting directions:

**A: 7...♛c7!?**     40
**B: 7...♗e7**       40

We can dispose of other moves:

a) 7...d5? 8 exd5 ♘xd5 9 ♘xd5 exd5 10 0-0 ♗e7 11 ♛f3 ♘c6 12 ♗xd5! +− Golubev-D.Miroshnichenko, Yalta open 1995.

b) 7...g6? 8 ♗e3 ♗g7 9 f3! ± Ziane-Brooks, New York 1993.

c) After 7...♗d7, White may well transpose to the Classical Sozin via 8 f4 ♘c6 9 ♗e3. 8 g4 is also interesting.

**A)**

**7...♛c7!?**

Now:

a) 8 0-0 is the most common but not the most critical move. This position was mentioned in connection with *7 0-0 ♛c7 8 ♗b3*; 8...♘c6 and 8...♗e7!? are the normal replies for Black.

The interesting reply 8...b5 may be used when responding to other moves:

b) 8 ♗e3 b5!?.

c) 8 f4 b5 (8...♘c6 9 f5!) with the idea of meeting 9 f5 with 9...b4 10 ♗a4+ ♔e7!.

d) 8 g4 b5 9 g5 can be met by 9...b4!? 10 gxf6 bxc3 or 9...♘fd7!?.

7...♛c7 still awaits a serious test. By the way, *6...♛c7 7 ♗b3 e6* is one more path via which to achieve this position.

**B)**

**7...♗e7**

Now:

**B1: 8 f4**    41
**B2: 8 g4!?**  42

Instead, 8 ♗e3 b5! promises little for White, while 8 0-0 was studied in the previous chapter.

**B1)**

**8 f4** *(D)*

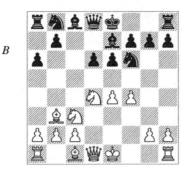

**8...0-0**

Otherwise:

a) 8...♘c6!? transposes to the Classical Sozin.

b) 8...♕c7?! 9 f5! (9 g4!? ♘c6 10 g5 ♘d7? 11 ♗xe6! ± Stein-Chistiakov, Leningrad 1960) and then:

b1) 9...e5 10 ♘de2 h6 (10...♘bd7 11 ♗g5!) 11 ♘g3!, and White wins the fight for the d5-square.

b2) After 9...exf5 White's chances are better, as with the queen on c7 it is hard for Black to arrange ...d5.

c) 8...b5 9 e5! dxe5 10 fxe5 ♘fd7 11 ♗xe6! ♘xe5 (11...0-0?! 12 ♗d5 ♖a7 is insufficient in view of 13 ♘f3!) 12 ♗xc8 (12 ♗f4 fxe6 13 ♗xe5 0-0 14 ♕e2 b4 15 ♘e4 ♕d5 ∓ Nunn) 12...♕xc8 13 ♘d5! (13 ♗f4 ♘bc6 = Sax-Nunn, London 1980) 13...♗c5 (13...♖a7 14 ♕h5!) 14 b4 and now:

c1) 14...♗xb4+? 15 ♘xb4 ♕c3+ 16 ♕d2 ♕xa1 17 0-0.

c2) 14...♕d7 15 ♘f3 ♗d6 16 0-0 ♘bc6 17 ♘b6 ♕a7 18 ♗e3 ♖d8 19 ♘c4 ♕e7 20 ♘xd6+ ♖xd6 21 ♕e1 with an initiative, Yagupov-Moiseev, Podolsk 1992.

c3) 14...♗a7 15 ♗f4 ♕d7 16 ♗xe5 (16 ♘f3 ♘bc6! 17 ♗xe5 0-0-0 Morozevich/Yurkov) 16...♕xd5 17 ♗xg7 (17 ♕e2? 0-0 18 0-0-0 f6!) 17...♕xg2 18 ♕e2+ ♕xe2+ 19 ♔xe2 (Morozevich-Agrest, St Petersburg Z 1993) 19...♖g8 20 ♘f5 ♘c6 21 ♖ad1! ±.

**9 ♗e3!?**

Other moves:

a) 9 0-0 is Chapter 3.

b) 9 g4!? has not been studied at all.

c) 9 ♕f3 allows Black to transpose to satisfactory lines with ...♘c6:

c1) 9...♕c7!? 10 f5 (10 ♗e3?! b5!; 10 g4 ♘c6 11 ♘xc6 bxc6 12 g5 ♘d7 ∞ Ciocaltea-Jansa, Bad Liebenstein 1963) 10...♘c6! (10...e5?! 11 ♘de2 b5 12 g4! b4 13 g5 bxc3 14 ♘xc3!, Soltis-Maeder, Dresden 1969) 11 ♗e3 transposes to note 'c' to White's 11th move in Line C211 of Chapter 9.

c2) 9...♘c6!? 10 ♗e3 transposes to Line C21 of Chapter 9.

d) 9 f5 exf5 10 exf5 (10 ♘xf5 ♗xf5 11 exf5 ♕b6!, Ehlvest-Portisch, Rotterdam 1989) 10...♘c6 11 0-0 d5 and Black is close to equality; e.g.:

d1) 12 ♗e3 ♖e8 13 ♔h1 ♘a5 (13...♘e5 14 ♗g5 ±; 13...♗a3!?) 14 ♕f3 b5! = Balashov-Chistiakov, USSR 1969.

d2) 12 ♔h1 ♗c5 (12...♖e8!?) 13 ♗e3 ♗a7 14 ♗g1 ± Lombardy-Böök, Munich OL 1958.

d3) 12 ♗g5!? Lepeshkin.

**9...b5**

Or:

a) 9...♕c7 10 g4! is probably unsafe for Black.

b) 9...♘c6 is the main line of the Classical Sozin.

**10 e5 dxe5 11 fxe5 ♘fd7**

Now:

a) 12 0-0 transposes to Line B of Chapter 3. White is not doing so well there, and it is worthwhile to look for an alternative.

b) 12 ♕g4?! ♘xe5 13 ♕e4 ♕c7 14 ♕xa8 ♘ec6, Podgaets-Tukmakov, USSR 1975.

c) 12 ♕h5?! ♕c7!?.

d) 12 ♘xe6 fxe6 13 ♗xe6+ ♔h8 14 ♗d5 ♘b6!.

e) Interesting is 12 ♕f3!? ♖a7, and then 13 0-0 is better than 13 ♘f5 ♗c5!? or 13 0-0-0 ♖c7 14 ♕h3 ♖xc3.

## B2)

**8 g4!?** *(D)*

This is a complicated variation, and with only a couple of dozen serious games to work with, it is impossible to do more than outline the theory.

Let us discuss the following:

**B21: 8...♘c6**      42
**B22: 8...0-0**      42
**B23: 8...h6**      43

Other moves:

a) 8...b5? 9 g5 ♘fd7 10 ♗xe6 is bad for Black.

b) 8...d5?! 9 exd5 ♘xd5 (9...exd5 10 g5) 10 ♘xd5 exd5 11 ♘f5! ♗xf5

12 gxf5 favours White; e.g., 12...d4 13 ♖g1 ♗f6 14 ♕h5 ± Istratescu-Arsović, Belgrade 1994.

c) 8...♕a5!? is possible, and if 9 ♕e2, then 9...♕b4!, T.Horvath-Gutman, Schoneck 1988. Instead, White should play 9 f3 or 9 ♕f3.

## B21)

**8...♘c6 9 g5 ♘xd4**

Not 9...♘d7? 10 ♗xe6!.

**10 ♕xd4 ♘h5 11 ♖g1 b5 12 ♗e3 0-0**

12...♗d7!? 13 0-0-0 a5 14 a3 (the alternative 14 e5!? deserves serious attention) 14...♖b8(?!) 15 e5 d5 16 ♘xd5 exd5 17 ♕xd5 ♖f8 18 e6! (18 ♕e4 ♕c8! 19 ♕xh7 ♗f5!) 18...fxe6 (K.Müller-Kempinski, Hamburg 1999) 19 ♕e5! ♖f5 20 ♕e4 e5 21 ♕d5 ♕c7 22 ♕g8+ ♖f8 23 ♕xh7 ♘f4 24 ♗xf4 ♖xf4 25 ♕xg7 with an attack – K.Müller.

**13 0-0-0**

White's chances are probably better. However, if Black does not permit the strike in the centre (13...♖b8 14 e5! d5 15 ♕h4 g6 16 ♘e4 ± Yakovich-Zilbershtein, USSR 1987), but plays 13...♕c7 (as in Zapata-Sunye, Linares {Mexico} 1992), he preserves resources for counterplay.

## B22)

**8...0-0!?** *(D)*

**9 g5**

9 ♗e3 d5!? (9...♘c6 10 g5 ♘d7 11 ♖g1!? is risky for Black) 10 exd5 exd5 11 ♖g1 (11 f3 ♖e8 and now rather than 12 ♕d3 ♗xg4!, White can try 12 0-0!?) 11...♗b4 = Chepurnoi-Pisarev, corr. 1992.

**9...♘fd7**

9...♘e8 looks suspicious.

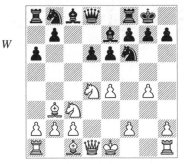 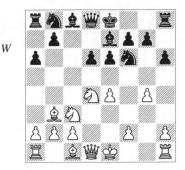

**10 ♖g1**

10 h4!? (as in the game Djurhuus-Van Wely, Gausdal 1994) and especially 10 ♗xe6!? are interesting here.

**10...♘c5 11 ♗e3**

11 ♕h5!? g6 (11...b5 12 ♗e3) 12 ♕h6 ♖e8 13 ♗e3 b5 transposes to the main line.

**11...b5**

Or:

a) 11...g6!? 12 h4 b5 13 h5 ♗d7 14 hxg6 fxg6 15 ♘xe6!?

b) 11...♕a5!? is also interesting, Nikolenko-V.Neverov, USSR Ch (Moscow) 1991.

**12 ♕h5 g6**

12...b4 13 ♘a4 ♘xb3 14 axb3 ♗b7?! 15 ♖g4 ± ♖e8 16 ♖h4 h6 17 0-0-0!, Golubev-Watzke, Chemnitz 1998.

**13 ♕h6 ♖e8 14 0-0-0 ♗f8 15 ♕h4 ♘bd7**

Black has good counterplay, Sofronie-Navrotescu, Romanian Cht 1998.

**B23)**

**8...h6** *(D)*

This is the most frequently chosen continuation for Black.

**9 ♗e3**

9 ♖g1 ♕a5!? (9...♘c6 10 ♗e3) 10 ♗d2 ♕c7 11 h4 (11 ♗e3 b5!?) 11...♘c6

(Chuprov-Zagrebelny, Akmola 1995) 12 ♘xc6!? ♕xc6 13 ♕e2 Zagrebelny.

**9...♘c6**

The line 9...♕c7 10 f4 ♘c6 11 f5 e5 12 ♘xc6 bxc6 13 ♕f3 (de Firmian-D.Thorhallsson, Reykjavik 1994) is in White's favour. Instead, 9...b5 and 9...♕a5!? have hardly been tested.

**10 ♖g1 ♕a5**

10...g5 11 ♕e2 ♕c7 12 0-0-0 ♖g8 favours White after both 13 h3 ♗d7 14 f4, Zapata-Martin del Campo, Linares {Mexico} 1994, and 13 ♘xc6!? bxc6 14 f4 gxf4 15 ♗xf4 e5 16 g5! Gavrikov.

After 10...♘a5, the line 11 ♕e2 b5 12 0-0-0, Stoica-Ghitescu, Timisoara 1987, leaves White's prospects uncertain (e.g., 12...b4!? 13 ♘a4 ♘xe4). Therefore, 11 f4 deserves attention.

**11 ♘xc6**

It appears that both 11 f3 ♘d7, with the idea of ...♗h4+, and 11 ♕d2 g5 12 f3 ♘e5 13 0-0-0 ♗d7 14 h4 ♖g8! 15 ♔b1 ♘h7, Wells-Loginov, Hungarian Cht 1993, are acceptable for Black.

**11...bxc6 12 ♕f3 ♘d7 13 0-0-0 ♖b8 14 h4 g5**

14...♗xh4!? 15 ♖xd6 ♗e7 (Loginov).

**15 hxg5 hxg5 16 ♖h1 ♖g8 17 ♖h5 c5**

The game is complicated, Emelin-Loginov, St Petersburg 1998.

# 5  5...a6 6 ♗c4 e6 7 ♗b3 b5: Sidelines

1 e4 c5 2 ♘f3 d6 3 d4 cxd4 4 ♘xd4
♘f6 5 ♘c3 a6 6 ♗c4 e6 7 ♗b3 b5 *(D)*

*W*

Historically, 7...b5 was Black's dom-
inant reply and the vast supply of material defined the main sequence of
moves: 8 0-0 ♗e7 9 ♕f3. The position
after 9 ♕f3 will be discussed in Chapter 6 and the remaining material is the
subject of this chapter. We consider
the following lines:

**A: 8 f4** 44
**B: 8 ♕e2** 45
**C: 8 ♕f3!?** 47
**D: 8 ♗g5!?** 48
**E: 8 0-0** 51

After 8 ♗e3, the strongest answer is
8...♗b7!. Then: 9 f3 is very unambi-
tious; 9 f4 – *8 f4 ♗b7! 9 ♗e3?!*; 9 0-0
♘bd7! 10 f4 – *8 f4 ♗b7! 9 ♗e3?!
♘bd7 10 0-0*.

## A)
**8 f4**

Fischer played this at the beginning
of his career, but he later cast doubt on
this move when playing Black against
Byrne (1967). Now 8 f4 is obsolete.

**8...♗b7!**

8...♘bd7 is less accurate – see
*7...♘bd7 8 f4 b5*.

After 8...b4!? 9 ♘a4 there are no
clear assessments of these two lines:

a) 9...♗b7!? 10 e5! (10 0-0 ♗xe4!
favours Black – see note 'a3' to White's
10th move in Line E23) 10...dxe5
(10...♘d5 11 0-0 ♕c7?! 12 f5 dxe5 13
fxe6 f6 14 ♘f5 ♕c6 15 ♘xg7+! +–) 11
fxe5 ♘d5 12 0-0 ♘c6!? (12...♕h4).

b) 9...♘xe4!? 10 0-0 and now:

b1) 10...d5?! 11 f5!.

b2) After 10...♗b7 both 11 f5 and
11 ♗e3 are dangerous.

b3) 10...♘f6!? might be worth investigating.

b4) 10...g6 11 f5 gxf5 12 ♘xf5
(Fischer-Tal, Bled/Zagreb/Belgrade Ct
1959) and now 12...♗b7 (or 12...d5
Fischer).

**9 f5**

Or:

a) After 9 0-0, both 9...♗e7 (see *8
0-0 ♗e7 9 f4 ♗b7!*) and 9...♘bd7 (see
*7...♘bd7 8 f4 b5 9 0-0 ♗b7*) are good
replies. Less convincing is 9...b4 10
e5!, Dely-Szabo, Budapest 1962.

b) 9 ♗e3?! is dubious:

b1) 9...b4 10 ♘a4 ♗xe4! is probably good for Black.

b2) 9...♘bd7 10 0-0 ♖c8!? (there are some alternatives: 10...♗e7!? – *8 0-0 ♗e7 9 f4 ♗b7 10 ♗e3 ♘bd7*; 10...b4 is less precise in view of 11 ♘a4 with the point 11...♗xe4 12 f5 e5 13 ♘e6!, Velimirović-Suba, Pinerolo 1987, or 11...♗e7 12 c3!? bxc3 13 f5!, M.Pavlović-Rashkovsky, Vrnjačka Banja 1988) 11 ♕e2 (11 f5 e5 ∓ 12 ♘e6? fxe6 13 fxe6 ♘c5 –+ Velimirović-Portisch, Szirak IZ 1987) 11...b4 12 ♘a4 (12 e5 dxe5 13 fxe5 ♘xe5 14 ♖ad1, Velimirović-Vaulin, Belgrade 1993, 14...bxc3! 15 ♘xe6 fxe6 16 ♖xd8+ ♖xd8 17 ♗f4 ♗c5+! wins for Black) 12...♘xe4 (12...♕a5?! 13 a3 bxa3 14 ♖xa3 ♕h5 15 ♕xh5 ♘xh5 16 f5 e5 17 ♘e6!, Velimirović-Gutman, Metz 1988) 13 f5 e5 14 ♘e6 ♕e7!? seems to be in Black's favour, Feletar-Palac, Pula 1999.

c) 9 e5 dxe5 10 fxe5 ♘e4!? is fine for Black.

**9...e5 10 ♘de2 ♘bd7**

10...♘xe4 is little-studied; e.g., 11 ♗d5 ♘xc3 12 ♘xc3 ♗xd5 and now 13 ♘xd5 ♕h4+ 14 ♔f1 ♕c4+ 15 ♔f2 (Boleslavsky) or 13 ♕xd5 ♘d7 14 ♗g5! ♕c8 15 0-0-0 (Averbakh/Beilin).

**11 ♗g5**

Or 11 ♘g3 ♖c8.

**11...♗e7**

In the 1960s it became clear that Black has at least equal chances here.

**12 ♗xf6**

12 ♘g3 ♖c8 (12...h5!?) 13 ♗xf6 (13 0-0?! h5! ∓ Byrne-Fischer, Sousse IZ 1967; 13 ♘h5 ♘xh5 14 ♕xh5 0-0 ∓) 13...♗xf6 14 ♘h5 (or 14 ♕d3 h5!) 14...♖xc3! (14...♘xe4!? is less strong,

Shmit-Ma.Tseitlin, USSR 1968) and if 15 bxc3, then 15...♘xe4!.

After 12 0-0, good is 12...♘xe4 13 ♘xe4 ♗xe4 with the idea of meeting 14 ♘g3 with 14...♗xc2.

**12...♘xf6 13 ♕d3 ♕b6!**

This is more precise than 13...♖c8 14 0-0 (14 0-0-0!? ♕b6 15 h3 b4 = Platonov-Polugaevsky, USSR Ch (Leningrad) 1971) 14...♖c5 15 ♘d5 ♗xd5 16 ♗xd5 0-0 17 c3 ± Platonov-Tal, USSR Ch (Moscow) 1969.

After the text-move (13...♕b6), 14 h3 0-0 15 0-0-0 a5 16 ♘d5 ♗xd5 17 ♗xd5 ♖ac8 18 ♔b1 ♖c5! 19 g4 ♖fc8 is in Black's favour, Suetin-Platonov, USSR 1971. In the case of other replies he also has nothing to worry about: 14 0-0-0 ♘g4!? 15 ♕g3 ♕e3+ or 14 ♘d5 ♗xd5 15 ♗xd5 ♖c8.

### B)

**8 ♕e2 ♗e7!**

Or:

a) 8...b4 9 ♘a4 ♗b7 10 ♗g5 is the same as *8...♗b7 9 ♗g5 b4 10 ♘a4*.

b) 8...♗b7!? 9 ♗g5 ♘bd7 (9...♗e7? 10 ♗xe6 0-0 11 ♗b3 ±; 9...b4 10 ♘a4 ♘bd7 11 0-0-0 ♕a5 12 ♗xf6 ♘xf6 13 f3 ∞ Radulov-Garcia Martinez, Havana 1969) 10 0-0-0 (10 ♗xe6?! fxe6 11 ♘xe6 ♕a5 *Schach-Archiv*) and now:

b1) Not 10...♘c5? 11 e5.

b2) 10...b4?! 11 ♘d5! exd5 12 exd5+ and now 12...♗e7 13 ♘f5 ♔f8 14 ♖he1 ♘e5 15 ♕d2 or 12...♕e7 13 ♕c4.

b3) 10...♕b6 is best met by 11 f4!.

b4) 10...♖c8 and then:

b41) 11 ♖he1 ♖xc3! (11...h6 12 ♗h4 g5 13 ♗g3 ♖xc3 14 bxc3 ♕a5 15 f3 d5?!, Rossetto-Panno, Buenos

Aires 1968, 16 ♘xe6!) 12 bxc3 ♕a5 with good compensation, Hendriks-Mirumian, Groningen 1997.

b42) 11 ♘d5 exd5 and rather than 12 exd5+ ♕e7!? ∓, White could try 12 ♘f5!?.

**9 ♗e3**

A risky plan. The assessment varies from 'unclear' to 'better for Black'. Instead, 9 g4 b4! is good for Black, while 9 ♗g5 will be examined via the more logical sequence *8 ♗g5 ♗e7 9 ♕e2*.

**9...0-0!**

Or:

a) 9...♗b7 10 ♗xe6 fxe6 11 ♘xe6 gives White compensation for the sacrificed piece.

b) 9...b4 10 ♘a4 ♗d7 (10...♘xe4 11 ♘xe6 ♗xe6 12 ♗b6; 10...♗b7!?) 11 0-0-0 ♕a5 12 ♘b6! is unsafe for Black, Sandrin-Labin, Ermelo blind Wch 1987.

c) 9...♕c7 10 0-0-0 (10 f3 ♘c6!? =) 10...0-0 – *9...0-0! 10 0-0-0 ♕c7*.

**10 0-0-0** *(D)*

The disadvantages of 10 f3 are stressed not by 10...♗b7 11 0-0-0 ♘bd7 12 g4 ♘c5 13 g5 with double-edged play, but 10...♗d7! 11 g4 b4!, Heuer-Mikhalchishin, Riga 1975.

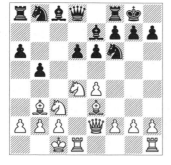

**10...b4**

Black envisages 11 ♘a4 ♕a5, planning 12...♗d7. Other tries with the same idea are 10...♗d7!? and 10...♕a5!?. Otherwise:

a) 10...♗b7?! is doubtful because of 11 e5!.

b) 10...♕c7 11 g4 (11 f3 ♘c6!? is a 'good Velimirović' for Black) 11...b4 (11...♘c6? is the 'bad Velimirović' – see note 'b' to Black's 11th move in Line B21 of Chapter 10), and now:

b1) 12 g5?! bxc3 13 gxf6 ♗xf6 14 ♕f3 (or 14 ♖hg1 g6) 14...♘d7.

b2) 12 ♘a4 ♘xe4 13 ♘b6! ♕xb6 – *10...b4 11 ♘a4 ♕a5 12 g4!? ♘xe4 13 ♘b6! ♕xb6*.

**11 ♘a4 ♕a5**

Black plans 12...♗d7. Other moves:

a) 11...♗d7 12 e5! suits White.

b) 11...♘xe4 and then:

b1) 12 ♘xe6? ♗xe6 13 ♗b6 ♕e8! 14 ♕xe4 ♗xb3 15 axb3 ♗g5+.

b2) 12 f4 d5 (12...♗d7 13 ♘xe6!; 12...♗b7!? Stoica) 13 f5 ∞ Cozianu-Suba, Romania 1998.

b3) 12 ♘b6 ♕xb6 13 ♘xe6 ♘c5 14 ♗xc5 dxc5 15 ♘xf8 ♔xf8 (15...♖a7!? 16 ♘xh7! Veličković) 16 ♗xf7 ♔xf7! 17 ♕f3+ ♗f6 18 ♕xa8 ♕b7 ∞ Stoica.

c) 11...♕c7 12 f4 (12 g4!? is possible) 12...♘xe4 13 ♘b6 (13 f5 e5!) 13...♕xb6 14 ♘xe6 is unclear again, Goossens-Vetemaa, Belgian Ch 1996.

After the text-move, White faces a difficult choice.

**12 g4!?**

Other moves are unpromising for White:

a) 12 ♘f3 ♘bd7!, Ljubojević-Polugaevsky, Amsterdam 1972.

b) 12 c3 bxc3 13 ♘xc3 ♗b7! 14 f3 ♘c6, Bönsch-Adamski, Dečin 1976.

c) 12 ♘b6 ♕xb6 13 ♘xe6 ♕c6, Boiko-Gozman, corr. 1992.

d) 12 f3 ♗d7 13 ♘b6 ♕xb6 14 ♘xe6 ♗b5!? 15 ♕f2 ♕b7, Wirth-M.Löffler, Germany tt 1992.

e) 12 f4 ♗d7 (12...♘xe4 13 ♘b6 ♕xb6 – *11...♕c7 12 f4 ♘xe4 13 ♘b6 ♕xb6*) 13 ♘b6 ♕xb6 14 ♘xe6 ♕b7 15 ♘xf8 ♗xf8 (or 15...♗g4!? first) 16 e5 ♗g4 17 ♕d3 ♗xd1 18 ♖xd1 doesn't give White serious compensation.

**12...♗d7**

12...♘xe4 13 ♘b6! ♕xb6 14 ♘xe6 ♕b5 15 ♕xb5 axb5 16 ♘xf8 ∞.

**13 ♘b6 ♕xb6 14 ♘xe6**

Now 14...♕b7 15 ♘xf8 ♗xf8 16 f3 ♗b5 17 ♕g2 gave chances for both sides in N.Rogers-Byrne, Philadelphia 1992. Possibly 14...♕b5! is stronger.

## C)

**8 ♕f3!?** *(D)*

This is better than 8 ♕e2. Nevertheless, White can hardly hope for an advantage.

*B*

**8...♗b7**

Other moves:

a) 8...♕c7 9 0-0 (9 ♗g5!? gives Black a choice between 9...♗e7 – *8 ♗g5 ♗e7 9 ♕f3 ♕c7* and Lepeshkin's

proposal 9...♘bd7) 9...♘c6?! (9...♗b7 10 ♖e1!; 9...♗e7! is Line B of Chapter 6; 9...b4!?) 10 ♘xc6 ♕xc6 11 ♗g5 ♗e7 12 ♘d5! exd5 13 ♗xf6 dxe4 14 ♕h5 ♗xf6 15 ♕xf7+ ♔d8 16 ♗d5 ± Cheremisin-Makarov, Moscow 1957.

b) 8...♕b6!? 9 ♗e3 ♕b7 supplies plenty of chances for both sides:

b1) 10 0-0 and now:

b11) 10...♗e7 is Line A2 of Chapter 6.

b12) 10...♘bd7!? is little-investigated. After 11 ♖fe1 b4 (11...♘c5!? has the point 12 ♗g5 ♗e7 13 ♘f5 exf5 14 ♗xf6 ♘xb3!) 12 ♘a4 (12 ♘d5?! exd5) 12...♘xe4 13 ♘xe6 fxe6 14 ♗d4 d5 (Kengis-Oll, Pinsk 1986), Kengis gives 15 c4!.

b2) 10 0-0-0 and then:

b21) 10...b4 11 ♘a4 ♘bd7 12 ♖he1 ♗e7 13 ♕g3!, Velimirović-Ilinčić, Yugoslav Cht 2001.

b22) 10...♗e7 11 g4 (11 ♕g3!?) 11...b4 12 ♘a4 ♘bd7 (12...♘xe4? 13 ♘b6!) 13 g5 ♘xe4 14 ♗xe6 fxe6 (not 14...♘xg5? 15 ♗xd7+) 15 ♘xe6 ♘g5 (15...♘ec5!?) 16 ♘xg7+ ♔d8 17 ♕g3 (Lerch-Dydyshko, Czech Cht 1994/5) 17...♘e4 18 ♕f4 ∞.

b23) 10...♘bd7 and now:

b231) 11 ♖he1 ♗e7 12 ♕g3 b4?! (12...♘c5!?) 13 ♘f5!!, Doghri-Ilinčić, Istanbul OL 2000.

b232) 11 ♕h3 ♘c5! (11...♘xe4? 12 ♗xe6; 11...b4 12 ♘a4 ♕xe4 13 ♖he1 ♕g4 14 ♕xg4 ♘xg4 15 ♗g5 Emelin) 12 f3 ♗d7!? with good play for Black: 13 g4 a5 14 g5 ♘g8 (or 14...a4!?) 15 g6 (Emelin-Biriukov, St Petersburg Russia 1998) 15...♘f6! ∞ Emelin.

**9 0-0**

Or:

a) 9 a3 ♘bd7!? =.

b) 9 ♗g5 b4!? (9...♘bd7 =; 9...h6!?
10 ♗xf6 ♛xf6) 10 ♘a4 ♘bd7 with the
idea 11...♛a5, R.Byrne-Evans, USA
Ch (New York) 1966.

**9...♘bd7**

Otherwise:

a) Not 9...♗e7? 10 ♗xe6.

b) 9...b4 (this is risky) 10 ♗a4+ (10
♘d5 exd5 11 ♗a4+! ♘fd7!?) 10...♘bd7
(10...♘fd7!?) 11 ♘d5! exd5 (11...♘xd5
12 exd5 ♗xd5 13 ♛xd5! exd5 14 ♖e1+
♗e7 15 ♘c6 with compensation – Bez-
godov) 12 exd5 ♗e7 (12...♗xd5 13
♖e1+ ♗e7 14 ♛g3! Lepeshkin) 13 ♘c6
♛c7 14 ♖e1 ♗xc6 15 ♗xc6 ± (Bezgo-
dov-Vaulin, Petropavlovsk 1999) and
if 15...♖b8 then 16 ♗h6! – Lepeshkin.

c) 9...♘c6!? 10 ♘xc6 ♗xc6 11 ♖e1
♗e7 12 ♛g3 0-0 13 ♗h6 ♘e8 14 ♖ad1
♛c7 (Tal-Browne, San Francisco 1989)
transposes to note 'd3' to White's 13th
move in Line B21 of Chapter 6, which
is approximately equal.

**10 ♖e1 ♘c5**

It is unsafe to play 10...♖c8 11
♗g5!? or 10...♛b6 11 ♗e3!, Mowszi-
szian-Enders, German Ch (Binz) 1994,
but 10...♗e7!? 11 ♗xe6 fxe6 12 ♘xe6
♘e5! deserves attention, as in Lanc-
Van Oosterom, corr. 1994.

**11 ♗d5**

After 11 ♗g5 ♗e7! Black is OK.

Now (after 11 ♗d5), 11...exd5? is
weak in view of 12 exd5+ ♔d7 13 b4
♘a4 14 ♘xa4 bxa4 15 c4 ± Meister-
Svirin, USSR 1987, but after 11...♛c7!
or 11...♛b6!, Black has good play.

**D)**

**8 ♗g5!?** (D)

This is possibly the most interesting alternative to 8 0-0.

**8...♗e7!**

B

Other moves are less reliable:

a) 8...h6 9 ♗xf6! ♛xf6 10 0-0.

b) 8...b4 9 ♘a4 (9 ♗xf6!? ♛xf6 10
♘a4 ♘d7 11 ♛d2 ♖b8 12 0-0 ♗b7 13
f4!, Meister-Dvoirys, Voronezh 1988)
9...♗e7 10 ♛f3 ♗b7 (10...♛a5!?) 11
♗xe6! is better for White, Meister-
Dydyshko, Hlovonec 1994.

c) 8...♘bd7 and now:

c1) 9 ♛e2 ♗b7! (not 9...b4? 10
♘d5!) – 8 ♛e2 ♗b7 9 ♗g5 ♘bd7.

c2) 9 ♗xe6 fxe6 10 ♘xe6 ♛a5
(10...♛b6?! 11 ♘d5!) 11 0-0 ♔f7 12
♗xf6 ♘xf6 13 ♘g5+ ∞ K.Müller-
Mirumian, Lippstadt 1999.

c3) 9 0-0! (with the idea of 10 ♖e1)
– 8 0-0 ♘bd7 9 ♗g5.

d) 8...♗b7!? and now: 9 ♛e2 – 8
♛e2 ♗b7 9 ♗g5; 9 0-0! – 8 0-0 ♗b7 9
♗g5.

**9 ♛f3!** (D)

9 0-0?! 0-0 10 ♛f3 ♗b7!.

9 ♛e2 is not very dangerous:

a) 9...b4 10 ♘a4 ♗d7 11 f4 ♛a5?!
(11...0-0 12 0-0-0!) 12 e5! dxe5 (or
12...♗xa4 13 exd6!, T.Horvath-Vegh,
Hungary 1986) 13 ♛xe5!, Donchev-
Savon, Varna 1982.

b) 9...♛c7 and now: 10 0-0-0 0-0 –
9...0-0 10 0-0-0 ♛c7; 10 0-0 – 8 0-0
♗e7 9 ♛f3 ♛c7 10 ♗g5.

c) 9...♕a5!? 10 f4 (10 ♗d2 ♕c7 = Donchev-Dorfman, Lvov 1983) and now 10...h6 11 ♗h4 g5 (Dorfman) or 10...♗b7.

d) 9...h6!?.

e) 9...0-0 and then:

e1) 10 f4 can be met by 10...b4 11 ♘a4 ♗b7 = Vasiukov-Gligorić, Belgrade 1961 or 10...h6!? 11 ♗xf6 ♗xf6 12 0-0-0 b4 13 ♘a4 ♕a5 14 ♕d2 ♗b7, Radulov-O.Jakobsen, Forssa/Helsinki Z 1972.

e2) 10 0-0-0 ♘xe4 (10...♕c7 11 f4!; 10...b4 11 ♘a4 ♕a5 12 f4! ♗d7 13 e5, Romanovich-Vaulin, Dečin 1996; 10...♘fd7!? 11 ♗e3 b4 12 ♘a4, Eppinger-Chandler, Bundesliga 1986/7, 12...♗b7) 11 ♕xe4 ♗xg5+ 12 f4 d5 13 ♘xd5 exd5 14 ♗xd5 ♗xf4+ (14...♖a7!?; 14...♖e8!? 15 ♗xf7+) 15 ♔b1 ♖a7 16 ♕xf4 ♕xd5 17 ♕xb8 ♖d7 = Radulov-Padevsky, Sofia 1970.

*B*

Now:
**D1: 9...♕b6!?** 49
**D2: 9...♕c7** 50

Or:

a) 9...♗b7? is met by 10 ♗xe6 ±.

b) If 9...♕d7!?, then White can play 10 0-0 (see *8 0-0 ♗e7 9 ♕f3 ♕d7*

10 ♗g5) or 10 0-0-0 ♗b7 11 ♖he1!? ♘c6 (11...0-0 12 ♕h3) 12 ♕g3.

## D1)
**9...♕b6!? 10 0-0-0!?**

10 0-0-0!? leads to Line A1 of Chapter 6.

**10...♘bd7**

Or:

a) 10...0-0 11 ♗e3 (11 g4!?; 11 ♖he1 ∞) 11...♕b7 (11...♕c7!?) 12 g4!? and then:

a1) 12...♘c6? 13 g5 ♘xd4 14 ♗xd4 ± Emelin-Nepomnishay, St Petersburg 1996.

a2) 12...b4 13 g5 ♘fd7 14 ♘d5.

a3) 12...♘bd7 can be met by 13 ♘f5!? or 13 g5 ♘e5 14 gxf6 ♘xf3 15 fxe7 ♕xe7 16 ♘xf3.

b) 10...♕b7 11 ♖he1 (11 ♕g3 0-0 12 ♗h6 ♘e8 13 a3!?, K.Müller-Kempinski, Hamburg 1998) 11...0-0 (not 11...b4? 12 ♘f5 ± Lazarev-Moiseev, USSR 1985) 12 a3 ♘bd7 ∞ Yakovich/Lazarev.

c) 10...b4 11 ♘f5!? ∞ exf5 12 ♗xf6 ♗xf6 13 ♘d5 ♕d8.

**11 ♖he1**

11 ♗e3 ♕b7 12 ♕g3 b4 (more reliable is 12...0-0!? 13 ♘d5 ♘c5 14 ♘xe7+ ♕xe7, Trapl-Stohl, Czechoslovak Ch (Prague) 1986) 13 ♘d5 exd5 14 ♘f5! gives White a serious initiative for the piece, K.Müller-Lutz, German Ch (Gladenbach) 1997.

**11...0-0**

11...♗b7!?; 11...b4!? 12 ♘a4 ♕c7 13 ♕g3 0-0, Bereziuk-Mirumian, Pardubice 2000, with a possible idea being 14 ♗xe6 fxe6 15 ♘xe6 ♕a5!.

**12 ♕g3**

12 ♕h3!? Olthof/Hendriks.

**12...♘c5 13 ♗h6**

Now:

a) 13...♘e8?! 14 ♘f5! (14 ♗d5!? Bangiev) 14...exf5 15 exf5 ♕d8 16 ♖xe7 ♕xe7 17 ♘d5 ♕d8 18 ♖e1 ♘e6 19 fxe6 fxe6 20 ♗g5 ± Hendriks-Van Wely, Dutch Cht 1999.

b) 13...♘h5!? 14 ♕g4 ♔h8 15 ♕xh5 gxh6 16 ♕xh6 ♖g8 with compensation for Black, Meister-K.Grigorian, Togliatti 1985.

## D2)
**9...♕c7 10 0-0-0**

Or:

a) 10 ♗xf6?! ♗xf6 11 e5 ♗xe5! Lepeshkin.

b) 10 e5!? (a new idea) 10...♗b7 11 exd6 ♗xd6 12 ♕e3 and then:

b1) 12...♘bd7 13 ♘xe6!.

b2) 12...0-0 13 0-0-0! h6 14 ♘dxb5! Wahls.

b3) 12...♗e5!? 13 0-0-0 ♘bd7 and now, rather than 14 ♗xe6?! fxe6 15 ♘xe6 ♕b6! 16 ♕h3 ♔f7 17 ♗xf6 ♘xf6 18 ♘g5+ ♔g6 19 ♕d3+ ♔xg5 20 h4+ ♔h6 21 ♕f5 g6 22 ♕xe5 ♖hd8 ∓ Jose-Gual, Badalona 2001, White should play 14 f4!.

b4) 12...♗c5 13 0-0-0 (13 ♗xf6 gxf6 ∓) 13...♘c6! (13...♘bd7 14 ♗xe6! 0-0 15 ♗b3 ± K.Müller-Wahls, German Ch (Gladenbach) 1997) 14 ♗xf6 gxf6 15 ♘e4? (15 ♘d5 ♕d8 16 c3 ∞ Wahls) 15...♗xd4! (15...♗e7? 16 ♘f5! +−) 16 ♖xd4 ♘xd4 17 ♘xf6+ ♔f8! 18 ♕xd4 ♖d8! ∓ Lobron-Novikov, Bad Wiessee 1999.

**10...♘bd7**

10...0-0?! 11 e5 dxe5 (11...♗b7 12 exf6! ±) 12 ♗xf6! (12 ♘dxb5 ♕c6! = Bakhmatov-Bangiev, Simferopol 1986) 12...exd4 (or 12...♗xf6 13 ♘xe6!; 12...gxf6 13 ♘f5!) 13 ♗xe7 ♕xe7 14

♕xa8 ± Meister-Kuporosov, USSR 1986.

If 10...♘c6, then not 11 e5 ♘xd4! or 11 ♘xc6 ♕xc6 12 ♗xf6 ♗xf6 13 ♘d5 ♗e5!, but 11 ♗xf6! ♗xf6 12 ♘d5! ±.

**11 ♖he1**

Alternatively:

a) 11 ♕g3?! ♘c5! 12 ♗d5 ♖b8! 13 ♗c6+ ♔f8 ∓ Illescas-Gelfand, Linares 1990.

b) 11 ♗xf6! ♘xf6! 12 e5? ♗b7 13 ♕h3 dxe5 14 ♘xe6 fxe6 −+.

c) I think that Bangiev's advice to play 11 e5 ♗b7 12 ♕g3 ♘xe5 (or 12...dxe5 13 ♗xe6) 13 ♗xe6 fxe6 14 f4 is quite doubtful.

**11...0-0**

Or:

a) 11...b4?! 12 ♗xf6! ♗xf6 (or 12...♘xf6 13 ♗a4+ ♘d7 14 ♘d5! ±) 13 e5 ♗b7 14 ♘d5 ♗g5+ 15 ♔b1 ± Bangiev.

b) 11...♘c5?! 12 ♘f5! exf5 13 ♗xf6 gxf6 14 ♘d5.

c) 11...♘e5!?.

**12 ♕h3**

12 ♕g3 ♘c5 13 ♗h6 (13 f4? b4!) 13...♘e8 14 ♗d5 b4 (14...♖b8!?) 15 ♘cb5 axb5 16 ♗xa8 ♗d7 17 e5 dxe5 offers Black good compensation, Garcia Martinez-Pigusov, Havana 1986.

**12...♘c5**

Not very good is 12...b4 13 ♘xe6 (13 ♘a4 ♘c5! Bangiev) 13...fxe6 14 ♕xe6+ ♔h8 15 ♕xe7 bxc3 16 ♕xd6! or 12...♘e5 13 f4.

**13 f4**

Now:

a) 13...b4 14 e5 dxe5 15 fxe5 bxc3 16 exf6 ♘xb3+!? (16...♗xf6 17 ♗xf6 ♕f4+ 18 ♔b1 ♕xf6 19 ♕xc3 ± Timmerman-Wojtkiewicz, Antwerp 1994)

17 ♘xb3! ♗xf6 18 ♗xf6 ♕f4+ 19 ♖e3 ♕xf6 20 ♖xc3 ♗b7 is complicated, Timmerman-Soltau, corr. 1988-91.

b) 13...♗b7 14 e5 dxe5 15 fxe5 ♘fe4!? *Schach-Archiv*.

## E)
### 8 0-0 *(D)*

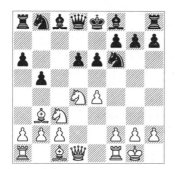

Now:

**E1: 8...♗b7**    51
**E2: 8...b4!?**    53
**E3: 8...♗e7**    58

In Line E3, we only discuss the alternatives to 9 ♕f3.

Or:

a) 8...♕c7 is rare. Then 9 ♕f3!? (– *8 ♕f3 ♕c7 9 0-0*) is probably best.

b) 8...♗d7 is also unusual. Ideas for White then include 9 a3 and 9 f4! b4, when White can play 10 e5!? (or 10 ♘a4 – *8...b4!? 9 ♘a4 ♗d7 10 f4*).

c) 8...♘bd7 should lead to the same positions as 8...♗b7. Flinching will bring no advantage to Black:

c1) 9 ♗g5 ♘c5 (9...♗b7 10 ♖e1 – *8...♗b7 9 ♖e1 ♘bd7 10 ♗g5*) 10 ♖e1 ♘xb3 (10...h6 11 ♗d5!) 11 cxb3! ♗b7 (11...♗d7 12 ♘f5! ♗c6 13 ♘d5! exf5? 14 e5! +–) 12 a4!? bxa4 13 ♘d5 with

an initiative for White, Golubev-Gohil, Schwäbisch Gmünd 1994.

c2) 9 ♖e1, and if 9...♘c5 (better is 9...♗b7 – *8...♗b7 9 ♖e1 ♘bd7*), then there is 10 ♗d5!, besides 10 ♗g5.

## E1)
### 8...♗b7 *(D)*

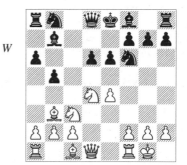

**9 ♖e1!**

Black must now be constantly on the alert to the ideas ♘d5 and ♗d5, as he lacks the time to hide his king away (see the next note for, e.g., the consequences of 9...♗e7?). Other moves:

a) The immediate 9 ♗xe6 fxe6 10 ♘xe6 is too unclear; e.g., 10...♕d7 (10...♕c8 is also possible) 11 ♘d5 ♔f7!? 12 ♘g5+ ♔g8 13 ♘b6 ♕c6 14 ♘xa8 h6!, Volchok-Kopylov, corr. 1984.

b) 9 ♗g5!? and then:

b1) Not 9...h6 10 ♗xf6 ♕xf6 11 f4 g6 12 f5 ♗g7 13 ♘cxb5 ± Ivanchuk-Ljubojević, Moscow blitz 1993.

b2) If 9...b4, then 10 ♘d5!? is interesting.

b3) 9...♘bd7 10 ♖e1! – *9 ♖e1! ♘bd7! 10 ♗g5!*.

b4) 9...♘c6!? is stronger, when Black has chances for equality.

**9...♘bd7!**

Other moves do not promise equality:

a) 9...♕c7? 10 ♗xe6! fxe6 11 ♘xe6 ±.

b) 9...b4? 10 ♘d5 ±.

c) 9...♗e7? 10 ♗xe6!; e.g., 10...fxe6 11 ♘xe6 ♕d7 12 ♘xg7+ ♔d8 13 ♘d5! ♗xd5 14 exd5 ♕g4 15 ♕xg4 ♘xg4 16 ♘f5 ± Golubev-Kottke, Deizisau 1997.

d) 9...♘c6 and now 10 ♘xc6 ♗xc6 11 ♘d5! or 10 a4 b4 11 ♘xc6 ♗xc6 12 ♘d5!.

e) 9...h6 can be met by 10 ♕f3 ± or 10 a4!?.

**10 ♗g5!**

Other moves:

a) 10 ♗xe6 fxe6 11 ♘xe6 ♕c8 12 ♗f4 ♔f7! = Barden-Kottnauer, Helsinki OL 1952.

b) 10 ♘d5 leads to unclear play after 10...♗e7!?, 10...♘c5!? 11 ♗g5 exd5 12 exd5+ ♔d7 and maybe also 10...exd5!?.

c) 10 a4 b4 11 ♘d5 and now 11...♕a5?! 12 ♗g5! gives White the initiative, Cukier-Sunye, Brazilian Ch 1995. 11...♘c5 is better though, with unclear play.

**10...h6**

Other moves:

a) 10...b4? 11 ♘d5 ±.

b) 10...♗e7 11 ♗xe6! fxe6 12 ♘xe6 ♕a5 is dangerous for Black though not completely clear.

c) 10...♖c8 11 a4 bxa4 (11...b4 12 ♘d5) 12 ♗xf6! ♕xf6 13 ♗xa4 ♖c7 14 ♘f3 ♗e7 15 e5 ± del Rio-Shirov, Madrid rpd 2000.

d) 10...♘c5 11 ♘d5! ♕c7 (11...b4 12 ♗xb7 ♘xb7 13 ♘d5 exd5 14 exd5+ ♔d7 15 c3! ± Tal-Mukhin, USSR Ch

(Baku) 1972 or 11...exd5 12 exd5+ ♔d7 13 b4 ♘a4 14 ♘xa4 bxa4 15 c4 ±) 12 ♗xf6 gxf6 13 b4! ♘d7 14 ♗xb7 ♕xb7 15 ♕h5 with an initiative, Palermo-Najdorf, Mar del Plata 1965.

e) 10...♕b6 11 a4! b4 12 ♘d5 (12 a5!?) 12...exd5 13 exd5+ ♔d8 (or 13...♘e5 14 a5 ♕c5 15 ♗e3! ± Adams-Sadler, Dublin Z 1993) 14 a5! (14 ♘c6+!?, Golubev-Mantovani, Biel open 1992, 14...♗xc6! 15 dxc6 ♕xc6 ∞) and now 14...♕c7 15 c3 with an attack (Adams) or 14...♕c5 15 c4!.

f) After 10...♕c7!?, it appears to me that 11 ♗xe6 fxe6 12 ♘xe6 ♕c4 13 ♘xf8 ♖xf8 14 ♕xd6 0-0-0 15 ♘d5 (Nei-Tolush, Riga 1959) 15...♗xd5! 16 exd5 ♘b8 and 11 a4!? b4 12 ♘d5 (Nei) 12...exd5! are not clear.

**11 ♗xf6!**

11 ♗h4 g5! 12 ♗g3 ♘e5 13 ♕e2 (13 ♗xe6?! fxe6 14 ♘xe6 ♕d7 15 ♘d5 ♔f7!; 13 ♘f3 ♕c7) 13...♗e7 14 ♖ad1 ♕b6 15 ♘f3 ♕c7 is satisfactory for Black, Ferrera-Sunye, Mexico 1991.

**11...♘xf6**

11...♕xf6 12 a4 b4 13 ♘a2 ♘c5 (13...a5 14 c3! ± Boleslavsky) 14 ♘xb4 a5 15 ♘bc6 (15 ♘a2!? ♘xe4 16 ♕e2 0-0-0!? 17 ♕c4+ ♘c5) 15...e5 16 ♗d5 exd4 (Golubev-Zagorskis, Karvina 1992/3) 17 ♖a3! with an attack for White.

**12 ♕d3**

Or:

a) 12 ♕f3 ♕b6! 13 ♖ad1 0-0-0 14 a4 b4 15 ♘a2 ♖d7!, as Dvoirys has played as Black three times, is unclear.

b) One dangerous idea is 12 a4!? b4 13 ♘d5 exd5 14 exd5+ ♔d7 15 a5 (15 c3!? bxc3 16 a5) 15...♕c7 (15...♗e7 16 ♗a4+ ♔c7 17 ♗c6 – del Rio) and now 16 c3 (del Rio-Aranda Martin,

Madrid 1995) or 16 ♗a4+ ♔c8 17 ♗c6 (del Rio).

**12...♘d7**

12...♘g4 13 ♕e2 ±.

**13 ♕h3 ♘c5 14 ♗d5 ♕c7 15 ♗xb7 ♕xb7 16 b4**

± de Firmian-Ehlvest, Polanica Zdroj 1995.

## E2)

**8...b4!?**

This move has recently come into fashion.

**9 ♘a4** *(D)*

Other moves are seldom played. Just an example: 9 ♘ce2 ♘xe4 10 ♘f4 ♘c5 11 ♖e1 ♖a7!? 12 ♗xe6 ♗xe6 13 ♘dxe6 ♘xe6 14 ♘xe6 fxe6 15 ♖xe6+ ♔d7! 16 ♕g4 ♔c7 ∓ Brenjo-Ilinčić, Vrnjačka Banja 1998.

This position is very unbalanced. White should try to arrange an attack in the centre before Black completes his development or, at least, to clear the air on the queenside by playing a3 or c3 while preserving possibilities for exerting some pressure. We shall consider:

**E21: 9...♘xe4?** 53
**E22: 9...♗e7** 54
**E23: 9...♗b7** 54
**E24: 9...♗d7** 56

In all these lines (except 9...♘xe4?) no orderly theory exists as many promising continuations around the 10th and 11th moves have not been actually tested as yet.

## E21)

**9...♘xe4? 10 ♖e1! d5**

Or:

a) 10...♘c5? 11 ♘xc5 dxc5 12 ♗a4+ ♗d7 13 ♘xe6 fxe6 14 ♖xe6+ wins for White, Soltis-T.Müller, New York 1965.

b) 10...♗b7 11 f3! ♘f6 (11...♘c5 12 ♘xc5 dxc5 13 ♗a4+ ♘d7 14 ♘xe6 fxe6 15 ♖xe6+ ♔f7 16 ♗xd7) 12 ♗xe6 fxe6? 13 ♘xe6 ♕a5 14 ♘xf8+! ♔f7 15 ♕xd6 +−.

c) 10...♘f6 11 ♗g5 ♗e7 12 ♘f5! ± Jovčić-Slatau, corr. 1957.

**11 ♗f4!**

Another known idea is 11 c4!?, but then 11...bxc3 12 ♘xc3 ♗b4 13 ♗a4+ ♗d7 14 ♘xe4 dxe4 is not so clear.

**11...♗e7**

Or:

a) 11...♘d7? 12 ♗xd5 exd5 13 ♘c6 +−.

b) 11...♕f6? 12 ♘xe6 fxe6 13 ♗xd5 +− d'Amore-Bonatti, corr. 1978.

c) 11...♗b7 12 ♘xe6 (or 12 ♕h5! ± Suetin) 12...fxe6 13 ♕h5+ (13 ♖xe4 dxe4 14 ♕h5+ g6 15 ♕e5 ♕d6!) 13...g6 14 ♕e5 ♕d6 15 f3! ± Pieretti-La Rosa, corr. 1972.

d) 11...♗d6 12 ♖xe4! (12 ♗xd6 ♕xd6 13 ♘f5 {not 13 f3? ♘f6 14 ♘f5 ♕d8!} 13...exf5 14 ♕xd5 ♕xd5 15 ♗xd5 ±) 12...dxe4 13 ♘xe6 ♗xe6 14 ♗xd6 ± Boleslavsky.

e) 11...♗d7 12 c4! and now:

e1) 12...dxc4 13 ♗xc4 ♘f6 (alternatively, 13...♘c5 14 ♘xc5 ♗xc5 15 ♘xe6 +−) 14 ♗xe6 fxe6 15 ♘xe6 ♗xe6 16 ♖xe6+ ♗e7 17 ♕xd8+ ♔xd8 18 ♘b6 +−.

e2) 12...bxc3 13 ♘xc3 ♘xc3 (or 13...♗e7 14 ♘xd5 +−) 14 bxc3 ♗e7 15 ♗xd5! (even 15 ♘f5 0-0 16 ♗xd5 is much better for White, Nei-Chukaev, USSR Cht 1955) 15...exd5 16 ♗d6 ♗e6 17 ♘xe6 fxe6 18 ♖xe6 and White wins, Schindler-Schulz, Germany 1981.

e3) 12...♕f6 13 ♗e3 dxc4 14 ♗c2! ♘c5 15 ♘b6 ♖a7 16 ♘xc4 ♖c7 17 ♘f3 ♕d8 18 ♗g5 ± Guaimare-Simon, corr. 1997.

**12 ♗xb8**

12 ♘f5!? exf5 13 ♕xd5! is also good.

**12...♖xb8 13 ♘c6 ♕c7 14 ♘xb8 ♕xb8 15 c4**

White has a large advantage.

## E22)

**9...♗e7 10 f4**

With the knight on a4, after e5 and the exchange of pawns, Black has no ...♗c5 resource, and White wants to make use of this...

Black experiences no problems after 10 ♖e1 0-0!? and 10 ♗e3 0-0 11 f3 ♗b7, while 10 ♕f3 ♗b7! 11 ♖e1 ♘c6 12 ♗e3 0-0 13 ♖ad1 ♘e5 14 ♕h3 ♗xe4 15 ♘xe6 fxe6 16 ♘c5 ♔h8 left Black better in Magomedov-Kupreichik, Daugavpils 1989.

**10...♕c7!?**

Or:

a) 10...♘xe4? 11 f5 exf5 (11...d5 12 fxe6 fxe6 13 ♘xe6! ♗xe6 14 ♕h5+ +− Delanoy-Touzane, Montpellier

1997) 12 ♘xf5 ♗xf5 13 ♖xf5 ♘f6 14 ♗xf7+! is much better for White, Larsen-Olsen, corr. 1983.

b) 10...♗b7 11 e5! ♘d5 12 ♘f5!?.

c) 10...0-0 11 e5! ♘e4 (11...dxe5? 12 fxe5 ♘e4 13 ♗e3 ♕c7 14 ♕g4 ♕xe5 15 ♘f3 ± Giles-Gratz, USA 1982) 12 ♗e3 ♕c7 (12...♗b7?! 13 ♕g4 ± Ilić), and now 13 ♕h5 ♘d7 14 ♖ae1 g6 15 ♕h6 (Mirumian-Dao, Erevan OL 1996) 15...dxe5! 16 fxe5 ♗b7 is unclear, but 13 ♕g4! ♔h8 (Gallagher-V.Atlas, Wohlen 1993) 14 ♖ad1! (V.Atlas) favours White.

The position occurring after the text-move (10...♕c7) requires serious testing:

a) 11 ♔h1, 11 ♕e2 and 11 c3 have not been investigated at all.

b) 11 ♗e3 0-0!? (11...♘xe4? 12 f5 wins for White; 11...♘bd7 12 c3 bxc3 13 ♘xc3 ♘c5 14 ♗c2 0-0 15 e5! with an advantage, de Firmian-Van Wely, Buenos Aires 1995), and now 12 f5 leads to a good position for Black (*7 0-0 ♗e7 8 ♗b3 0-0 9 f4 b5 10 ♗e3 ♕c7 11 f5 b4! 12 ♘a4*).

c) The main line runs 11 e5 dxe5 (11...♘fd7? 12 ♗xe6!; 11...♘e4?! 12 f5!) 12 fxe5 ♕xe5, when 13 ♘b6 ♗c5 looks quite satisfactory for Black and 13 ♗f4 ♕e4 14 ♕d2 0-0!? (or 14...♘c6 15 c3 Ovseevich) is very unclear.

## E23)

**9...♗b7** *(D)*
**10 ♖e1**

The other possibilities include two moves that offer White little and several interesting but under-explored ideas:

a) 10 f4 has not justified White's hopes:

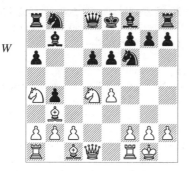

W

a1) 10...♘xe4? 11 f5! (11 ♗e3!? ♘d7 12 f5 e5 13 ♘e6!) 11...e5 12 ♘e6! ±.

a2) 10...♘c6!? could be considered.

a3) 10...♗xe4! and then:

a31) 11 ♗e3 d5!? 12 f5 (12 c3 bxc3 13 ♘xc3 ♗c5 ∓ Couso-Åström, Stockholm 1994) 12...e5 13 ♘f3 ♘bd7 14 ♘g5 ♕c7! (14...♗e7?! 15 ♘xe4 dxe4 16 ♖f2 ♕c7 17 g4! h6 18 h4, Velimirović-Ilinčić, Jagodina 1993) 15 ♘xe4 (15 c3 h6! Ilinčić) 15...dxe4 – *11 f5 e5 12 ♘f3 ♘bd7!? 13 ♘g5 d5 14 ♘xe4 dxe4 15 ♗e3 ♕c7! ∓.*

a32) 11 f5 e5 and now:

a321) 12 ♖e1 ♗e7!?.

a322) 12 ♘f3 ♘bd7!? 13 ♘g5 d5 14 ♘xe4 dxe4 15 ♗e3 ♕c7! 16 ♕e2 (16 g4?! h6 ∓ Todorović-Marjanović, Kavala 1998) 16...h6!? 17 ♖ac1 ♗e7 18 c3 ♕b7 19 c4 0-0 ∓ Sofronie-Marjanović, Bucharest 1998.

a323) 12 ♗g5! ♘bd7 (12...♗e7!? 13 ♗xf6 ♗xf6! {13...gxf6?? 14 ♗xf7+ +– Ilić} 14 ♕e1 d5 15 ♘e2 ♘c6 16 ♖d1 0-0 17 c4 ∞ Browne-Saidy, Atlanta 1967) 13 ♖e1 (13 ♘e6? fxe6 14 fxe6 ♘b6!) 13...♗b7! (13...♗e7? 14 ♗xf6 ♘xf6 15 ♖xe4!; 13...♕c7? 14 ♖xe4! ♘xe4 15 ♘b5! +–) 14 ♘e6 fxe6

15 fxe6 ♘b8 and White's chances are questionable, Kaps-Novak, Ljubljana 1999.

b) 10 ♗e3 ♗xe4 11 ♖e1 is also unconvincing:

b1) 11...♘bd7!?.

b2) 11...♗e7!? and now 12 ♗xe6 fxe6 13 ♘xe6 ♕d7! or 12 ♘b6 ♖a7!? 13 ♗xe6?! ♖b7!.

b3) 11...d5 12 f3 ♗g6 13 f4 (13 ♗f4!?) 13...♗d6 with good chances for Black, Olesen-Åström, Stockholm 1994.

c) 10 c3 bxc3 (10...♗e7 11 ♗xe6!?) 11 ♘xc3 ♘bd7 12 ♗a4 ♗e7!? =.

d) 10 f3 ♘bd7 11 ♕e1!? has hardly been investigated.

e) 10 ♕e1!? (also rare) 10...a5 11 e5 ∞ Gurieli-Smagin, Bad Wiessee 1999.

f) 10 ♗g5!? deserves serious attention: 10...♘bd7 (10...♗e7 11 ♗xe6) 11 ♖e1 ♗e7 12 a3 (12 c3!? bxc3 13 ♗xe6, Borik-Bouaziz, Dortmund 1979) 12...bxa3 13 ♖xa3 0-0 14 ♗xe6! fxe6 15 ♘xe6 ♕e8 16 ♖g3 with an advantage for White, Short-Van Wely, Garmisch rpd 1994.

**10...♘bd7**

It is likely that there is a better move here:

a) 10...♘c6 11 c3 (11 ♘xc6!? ♗xc6 – *9...♗d7 10 ♖e1 ♘c6 11 ♘xc6 ♗xc6*) 11...♗e7!? 12 cxb4 ♘xb4 13 ♘c3 0-0 (13...♘c6!?) 14 ♗a4!? and now 14...♘c8 15 ♕b3 d5 16 ♖d1 ♗c5 17 a3 dxe4 18 ♘xe6 ♗xf2+ 19 ♔f1 ♕a5 20 ♕xb4 ♕f5 21 ♘f4 may favour White, Shtyrenkov-Dvoirys, Kursk 1987.

b) 10...♗e7 11 c3 (11 a3!? is possible) 11...bxc3 (11...0-0 12 cxb4 ♘xe4 13 f3 ♘f6 14 ♖xe6! ± Virostko-Paramonov, Plzen 1998) 12 ♘xc3 0-0 13 f4 ♘bd7 (13...♘c6!?) 14 e5 dxe5 15 fxe5 ♘e8 16 ♘xe6 fxe6 17 ♗xe6+ ♔h8, and, instead of 18 ♕xd7 ♗c5+ 19 ♗e3 ♕b6 with a draw, Yakovich-Dvoirys, Kursk 1987, it is worth studying 18 ♗xd7 ♗c5+ 19 ♗e3 ♕g5 20 ♕d2 ♖f3 21 ♘d1.

**11 c3**

Otherwise:

a) 11 f4?! ♗xe4!.

b) 11 a3 bxa3 (11...♘xe4 12 ♘xe6 fxe6 13 ♗xe6 ♘df6 14 f3 d5 15 fxe4 ± de Firmian-Hort, Baden-Baden 1981) 12 ♗xe6 fxe6 13 ♘xe6 is exceedingly unclear.

c) 11 ♗g5 – *10 ♗g5!? ♘bd7 11 ♖e1*.

d) 11 ♗d2 also deserves attention.

**11...bxc3**

11...♘xe4 12 f3 ♘ec5 13 ♘xc5 ♘xc5 14 ♗a4+!! ± Savon-Simović, Lvov 1961.

**12 ♘xc3 ♘c5**

12...♗e7?! 13 ♗xe6 fxe6 14 ♘xe6 ♕c8 15 ♘xg7+ ♔f7 16 ♘f5 ♘c5 17 ♘xe7 ♔xe7 18 ♗g5 ±.

**13 ♗d5! ♕c7 14 ♗g5 ♗e7 15 b4!**

White is better, Istratescu-Van Wely, Moscow OL 1994.

## E24)

**9...♗d7** *(D)*

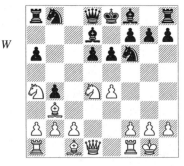

This continuation was introduced by Dvoirys in 1987, and has become very popular recently.

**10 f4**

Or:

a) 10 ♗g5 ♗e7 (10...♕a5!? Ilić), and now 11 ♘f5?! is dubious in view of 11...exf5 12 ♗xf6 ♗xf6 13 ♕d5 0-0 (or 13...♕c7) 14 ♕xa8 ♕e8!.

There are three other, more serious, alternatives:

b) 10 ♗e3 ♘c6 (10...♘xe4?! 11 f4 ♘f6 12 f5 e5 13 ♘e6 fxe6 14 ♘b6 ♗c6 15 fxe6 ♗e7 16 ♖xf6!, Velimirović-Ilinčić, Cetinje 1991; 10...♗e7 11 ♘b6!?) 11 ♖e1 (11 f3 ♗e7 12 ♖c1 ♖b8 13 c4 bxc3 14 ♖xc3 ♘a5 15 ♗c2 e5 = Lautier-Sadler, Tilburg 1998; 11 f4!? – *10 f4 ♘c6 11 ♗e3*) 11...♖b8 (11...♗e7 12 ♘b6 ♕xb6 13 ♘xe6 ♕a5 14 ♘xg7+ ♔f8 15 ♗h6 ♔g8 16 ♗d5 ♘xd5 17 exd5 ♘e5 18 ♘e6 ± Caminade-Boudre, Creon 1998) 12 c3 and here Black should play 12...bxc3 13 ♘xc3 ♗e7 =.

c) 10 ♖e1 and then:

c1) 10...♘c6 11 ♘xc6!? (11 c3 – *10 c3 ♘c6 11 ♖e1*; 11 ♗e3 – *10 ♗e3 ♘c6 11 ♖e1*) 11...♗xc6 12 ♕d4 ♖b8 with a possible continuation 13 ♗g5 ♗e7 14 ♖ad1 ♕a5 15 e5 dxe5 16 ♖xe5 ♖b5 =.

c2) 10...♗e7 and now:

c21) 11 c3 a5 12 ♕f3 ♘c6 13 ♕g3 0-0 14 ♗h6 ♘e8 is slightly better for Black, Juviček-Jaworski, Moravian Cht 1998/9.

c22) 11 f4 ♘c6 12 e5 dxe5 13 fxe5 ♘xd4 14 ♕xd4 ♘d5 and Black is OK, Cetković-Ilinčić, Becici 1993.

c23) 11 a3 a5 12 axb4 axb4 13 ♗d2 ♘a6 = Dekić-Ilinčić, Yugoslav Cht 1992.

c24) 11 ♗d2 ♘c6?! (11...a5 is better) 12 ♘xc6 ♗xc6 13 ♗xb4 ♗xe4 14 ♕d4 with an advantage, Golubev-Balcerak, Bundesliga 1996/7.

d) 10 c3 and then:

d1) 10...♘xe4? 11 ♕f3 d5 12 c4! ♕f6 (or 12...♘c6 13 ♘xe6! +–) 13 cxd5 ♕xd4 14 ♗e3 ♕e5 15 ♗f4 ♕f5 16 ♖fe1 +– Lautier-Sadler, Enghien-les-Bains 1999.

d2) 10...a5 11 ♗e3!? ♗e7 12 ♘b6 ♕xb6 13 ♘xe6 with compensation, Nijboer-Janssen, Dutch Cht 2000/1.

d3) 10...bxc3 is probably a bit premature: 11 ♘xc3 ±.

d4) 10...♘c6 11 ♖e1 (11 ♘xc6 ♗xc6 12 f3 d5 13 exd5 ♘xd5 = Pokorna-Lakos, Ostrava 1999; 11 cxb4!? ♘xb4 12 ♗g5, Schwartz-Gorissen, Dutch jr Ch (Nijmegen) 2001) 11...♖b8 (11...♗e7 12 cxb4 ♘xb4 13 ♗e3 0-0 14 ♖c1! ± Berzinsh-Kulaots, Latvia-Estonia 2000; 11...bxc3!? 12 ♘xc3 ♗e7) and here:

d41) 12 cxb4 ♖xb4 13 ♘xc6 ♗xc6 14 ♘c3 ♗e7 is equal, Sieiro-Gonzalez – Ortega, Holguin 1989.

d42) 12 f3 ♗e7 (12...♘a5!?) 13 ♘xc6 ♗xc6 14 cxb4 ♖xb4 15 ♗e3 0-0 16 ♖c1! ± Rogić-Pavasović, Dresden Z 1998.

d43) 12 f4 bxc3!? (12...♗e7? 13 e5 dxe5 14 fxe5 ♘d5 15 ♕g4 ± Badii-Relange, Villecresnes 1998) 13 ♘xc3 ♘xd4 14 ♕xd4 ♗e7 15 ♗e3 0-0 16 ♔h1 ♗c6 with an acceptable position, Malakhov-Berezin, Ukrainian Ch (Alushta) 1999.

We now return to 10 f4 *(D)*:

**10...♘c6**

10...♕a5 11 c3 is risky for Black.

**11 ♗e3**
Others:

*B*

a) 11 e5?! dxe5 12 fxe5 ♘xe5 13 ♕e2 ♘g6!?.

b) 11 c3!?.

c) 11 f5 is quite dangerous, but it looks like Black holds on: 11...e5! (11...♘xd4?! 12 ♕xd4 e5 13 ♕xb4!) 12 ♘e6 (12 ♘e2 ♗e7 13 ♗e3 ♖b8 14 ♘g3 0-0 15 ♘h5 ♘d4! with a slight advantage for Black, West-Blumenfeld, New York 1989; 12 ♘f3!? h6 13 ♕e1 ♗e7 14 ♕g3 ♔f8 15 ♕e1 ♖b8 is slightly better for Black, Reinderman-Anand, Wijk aan Zee 1999) 12...fxe6 13 fxe6 ♗c8, and here White has tested two possibilities:

c1) 14 ♖xf6?! ♕xf6 15 ♕d5 and then:

c11) After 15...♘d4 16 ♗e3 ♖b8 17 ♗xd4 (Ardeleanu-Marjanović, Predeal 1999) Black can, at least, rely on a draw: 17...exd4!? 18 ♕c6+ ♔d8 19 ♖f1 ♕g5 20 ♗d5 ♗e7 21 ♘b6 ♖f8! (21...♗xe6 22 ♘a8!) 22 ♖xf8+ ♗xf8 23 ♘xc8 ♕e3+ =.

c12) 15...♗b7 16 ♘c5 ♗e7! (not 16...♘d4? 17 ♗a4+ ♔d8 18 ♘xb7+ ♔c7 19 ♗e3 ♕xe6 20 ♕a5+ ♔xb7 21 c3!!; 16...0-0-0? 17 ♘xb7 ♔xb7 18 ♗e3 followed by 19 a3!! – Ardeleanu) 17 ♗e3 0-0 18 ♘xb7 ♘d4 with the following possibilities:

c121) 19 ♗xd4 exd4 20 ♗c4 (20 h3 ♕f2+ 21 ♔h1 ♕g3 22 ♘a5, Echavarria-Borges, Cali 2000, 22...♗g5!! –+ Uribe) 20...d3! ∓ Echavarria.

c122) 19 h3 ♘e2+ and again Black has good chances.

c2) 14 ♗g5 and then:

c21) 14...♗e7 15 ♗xf6 ♗xf6 16 ♖xf6! ♕xf6 17 ♕xd6 ♘d4 18 ♘b6 gives Black problems:

c211) 18...♗xe6 19 ♗xe6! (19 ♘xa8 ♘e2+ 20 ♔h1 ♘g3+ 21 hxg3 ♕h6+ 22 ♔g1 ♕e3+ = {Kalegin-Dvoirys, USSR 1988} 23 ♔f1? ♖f8+ 24 ♕xf8+ ♔xf8 25 ♗xe6 ♕h6!) 19...♕xe6 (19...♖d8 20 ♗d7+ ♔f7 21 ♕d5+! del Rio) 20 ♕xe6+ ♘xe6 21 ♘xa8 ±.

c212) 18...♘e2+ 19 ♔h1 ♘g3+ 20 hxg3 ♕h6+ 21 ♔g1 ♕e3+ 22 ♔f1 ♖f8+ 23 ♕xf8+ ♔xf8 24 e7+ ♔e8 25 ♗a4+ ♗d7 26 ♗xd7+ ♔f7 27 ♘xa8 ♔xe7 28 ♖d1! ♕xe4 29 ♘b6 ♕xc2 30 ♗a4 (Kalegin/Dvoirys).

c22) 14...h5(!) 15 ♗xf6 gxf6 16 ♗d5 ♗b7 17 c3 (Anand is sceptical about White's chances here) 17...♖b8 ½-½ Milu-Marjanović, Bucharest 1999.

**11...♖b8!**

Not: 11...♘xe4? 12 f5; 11...♗e7? 12 f5! e5 (12...♘xd4 13 ♕xd4 e5 14 ♕xb4 d5 15 ♕e1! ± Anand) 13 ♘e6! ± Ciocaltea-Creculescu, Romanian Ch (Bucharest) 1955.

**12 ♕f3**

Or:

a) 12 e5 dxe5 13 fxe5 ♘xe5 14 ♗f4 and now, instead of 14...♕c7 15 c4 bxc3 16 ♖c1 ♗d6 17 ♖xc3 ♕a7 18 ♔h1 0-0 19 ♘xe6! ± (A.Kovačević-Ilinčić, Arandjelovac 1993), Black should play 14...♘g6!.

b) 12 c3 and then:

b1) 12...bxc3 13 ♘xc3 ♗e7 14 ♕e2 (14 ♖c1 0-0 15 ♕e2 ±; 14 ♕f3 0-0 15 e5?! ♘xd4 16 ♗xd4 dxe5 17 fxe5 ♗c6!) 14...♕a5 15 f5 (15 ♖ac1 ±) 15...♘xd4 16 ♗xd4 ♖b4! = Gormally-Rowson, British Ch (Scarborough) 1999.

b2) 12...♗e7 13 e5?! (13 cxb4 ♖xb4 14 ♘c3 0-0 = Anand; 13 ♖c1!? 0-0!?) 13...dxe5! 14 fxe5 ♘xe5 15 ♗f4 ♘g6! with the better chances for Black, Lautier-Anand, Biel 1997.

**12...♕c7**

Otherwise:

a) Not 12...♕a5? 13 e5!.

b) 12...♘xd4 13 ♗xd4 ♗c6 14 ♗xf6! ♕xf6 15 c3 (15 ♕e3 ♗e7; 15 ♖ae1!? Bruzon/Y.Gonzalez) 15...g6 16 ♖ae1 bxc3 17 ♘xc3 is slightly better for White, Y.Gonzalez-Lesiège, Havana 1999.

**13 ♖ae1**

Now, instead of 13...♘xd4 14 ♗xd4 ♗c6 15 c3 ♗e7 16 ♕g3 0-0 17 e5 ± Y.Gonzalez-Borges, Cuban Ch (Santa Clara) 2000, 13...♗e7 deserves attention.

Summing up: currently, 9...♗d7 looks playable while 9...♗b7 is more risky, and 9...♗e7 should be checked very thoroughly.

**E3)**

**8...♗e7** (D)

Now there is currently no serious alternative to 9 ♕f3 (see the next chapter), so in this section we are just tying up a few loose ends.

**9 f4**

White gains nothing by 9 ♗e3 0-0 10 f4 (see note 'c' to White's 10th move in Line B of Chapter 3).

*W*

9 a4!? b4 10 ♘a2 is playable but it
is hardly possible to talk about an advantage for White; e.g., 10...0-0 11
♘xb4 ♗b7 12 c3 ♘xe4 (or 12...a5 13
♘d3 ♗xe4 14 ♖e1 ♘a6 15 ♗g5 ♗xd3
16 ♕xd3 ♘c5 = Kavalek-Andersson,
Tilburg 1980) 13 a5 d5 14 ♗c2 ♗d6
15 ♕h5 ♘d7 16 f3 ♘ef6 17 ♕h4 ♖c8
18 ♖a4 ♖e8 with a good position for
Black, Velimirović-M.Pavlović, Yugoslav Ch (Belgrade) 1999.

**9...♗b7!**

Or:

a) 9...b4 10 ♘a4!? transposes to
Line E22.

b) 9...0-0!? transposes to Line B of
Chapter 3.

**10 e5?!**

10 f5 is harmless in view of 10...e5
11 ♘de2 ♘bd7 12 ♗g5 – *8 f4 ♗b7 9
f5 e5 10 ♘de2 ♘bd7 11 ♗g5 ♗e7 12
0-0*.

10 ♗e3 is the main alternative, but
Black has a variety of good replies:

a) 10...0-0?! is weak in view of 11
e5! (here this move is good).

b) 10...♘c6 is, on the whole, satisfactory for Black.

c) 10...b4!? 11 e5 (11 ♘a4 ♗xe4!)
11...bxc3 12 exf6 ♗xf6 leads to quite

unclear play. In his *Easy Guide to the
Najdorf*, Kosten assesses the lines 13
♗a4+?! ♘d7 14 f5 0-0!, 13 bxc3 0-0
14 ♕d2 ♕c7 15 ♖ad1 d5! and 13 f5 e5
14 ♗a4+ ♔e7! as in Black's favour.

d) 10...♘bd7 appears simpler, with
the idea 11 ♗xe6 fxe6 12 ♘xe6 ♕c8
13 ♘xg7+ ♔f7 14 ♘f5 b4! (14...♗f8
is not bad either) 15 ♘xe7 ♔xe7 16 e5
♕c6!, Galla-Cordara, Turin 1984.

**10...dxe5 11 fxe5 ♗c5! 12 ♗e3
♘c6**

12...♗xd4!? (recommended by Kosten) is good enough; e.g., 13 ♕xd4
♕xd4 14 ♗xd4 ♘c6 15 ♗c5 ♘d7!
(Kosten) or 13 ♗xd4 ♘c6 14 ♖f4 (14
♗c5 ♘xe5!, Sus-Kaluza, corr. 1994)
14...♕c7 15 ♕e2 0-0-0 16 ♗e3 ♕xe5
17 ♕f2 h5 18 ♗b6 ♘g4 19 ♕g3 ♖d7!?.

**13 exf6 ♗xd4! 14 fxg7**

Even if the sacrifice is incorrect, it
is at least dangerous in practice. After
the timid 14 ♕e1 ♗xe3+!? 15 ♕xe3
♕d4 (as in Stein-Bobotsov, Bulgaria-
Ukraine 1965 and other games) Black
has no problems at all.

**14...♗xe3+ 15 ♔h1 ♖g8 16 ♗xe6**

16 ♕f3 ♖xg7 17 ♗xe6 (17 ♕xe3
♕d4!) 17...♕e7 18 ♗d5 ♘d4 19 ♕h3
♗d2!! and Black wins, Inkiov-Ribli,
Plovdiv 1986.

**16...♖xg7**

The position has been assessed in
Black's favour many times, although it
is not so easy to prove it exhaustively.
The variations are:

a) 17 ♕h5 ♘e5! 18 ♗d5 ♖g5 ∓
(Nunn).

b) 17 ♗xf7+ ♖xf7 18 ♕h5 ♕d7
19 ♘e4 ♔f8 20 ♕xh7 (20 ♘d6 ♖f2!
Nunn) 20...♗d4.

c) 17 ♗d5!? ♗d4 18 ♕h5 ♕d7!.

# 6  5...a6 6 ♗c4 e6 7 ♗b3 b5 8 0-0 ♗e7 9 ♕f3!

**1 e4 c5 2 ♘f3 d6 3 d4 cxd4 4 ♘xd4 ♘f6 5 ♘c3 a6 6 ♗c4 e6 7 ♗b3 b5 8 0-0 ♗e7 9 ♕f3!** *(D)*

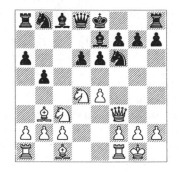

*B*

This is a strong move associated with a plan which involves pieces only. By preventing 9...0-0? (in view of 10 e5!) and 9...♗b7?! (which allows 10 ♗xe6!), White gains time for ♕g3 with the idea of answering ...0-0 with ♗h6! and obtaining an advantage in development after the forced ...♘e8. The threats of various strikes in the centre (♘d5, ♘f5) and the possibility of deploying the rooks (♖ad1, ♖fe1) make Black proceed very cautiously.

Within White's concept, the future of the f2-pawn is an indefinite factor: in the variations with ...♘c6 and an exchange on c6, it is often necessary to play f3, while in other variations White may prepare f4.

## Main Lines

Currently, 9...♕c7 and 9...♕b6 are of about equal importance. 9...♕c7 with the main variations 10 ♕g3 0-0 and 10 ♕g3 ♘c6 is considered more reliable and 9...♕b6 braver, as it leaves Black the chance to continue with ...♘bd7 (with the queen on c7 this is precluded by the threat of ♗xe6!). After 9...♕b6, the main continuation is 10 ♗e3 ♕b7 11 ♕g3, when Black has a choice of several lines, the main one being 11...b4 12 ♘a4 ♘bd7. Lately, 10 ♗g5!? has become popular instead of 10 ♗e3.

## Transpositions

9 ♕f3 is a genuine subsystem that is almost unconnected by transposition to other lines of the Sozin. However, it is inherently somewhat entangled as the sides have many standard moves. The greatest number of transpositions occur in the positions with ...♘c6, ♘xc6 ♕xc6, that arise, as a rule, in various lines after 9...♕c7 but may sometimes be obtained even after 9...♕b6 10 ♗e3 ♕b7 (if Black rejects ...♘bd7 in favour of ...♘c6).

## General Assessment

Black's delay in development precludes him from organizing quick counterplay and his real strategic aim is to neutralize his adversary's activity gradually. If Black defends accurately, he may get an acceptable game. The chances of the sides in the position after 9 ♕f3 may be assessed as in the initial position: somewhere between '=' and '±'.

As usual in the Sozin, in the variations with ...♕b6 and ...♘bd7, White bears relatively greater strategic risk than in the variations with ...♕c7 and ...♘c6, and, at the same time, the ever-increasing lag in Black's mobilization makes his own risk no less.

We shall discuss:

**A: 9...♕b6** 61
**B: 9...♕c7** 73

Sometimes, two other moves by Black occur:

a) 9...♖a7 10 a4!? (the alternative is 10 ♕g3 0-0 11 ♗h6 ♘e8 12 ♗e3 ♖c7 13 a4 b4 14 ♘a2, Mukhutdinov-Agrest, Budapest 1991) 10...b4 11 ♘a2 ♖b7 (in White's favour is 11...d5 12 exd5 ♘xd5 13 ♘f5 Gallagher, or 11...a5 12 c3!) 12 ♗d2 e5 13 ♘f5 ± Sion Castro-Vera, Mondariz 1995.

b) 9...♕d7 and now:

b1) 10 ♕g3 does not reveal the drawbacks of Black's idea since after 10...♘c6!?, 11 ♘xc6 ♕xc6 transposes to Line B22, while 11 ♗e3 is hardly stronger.

b2) 10 ♗g5!? ♗b7 11 ♖ad1 ♘c6 12 ♕g3 enables White to hope for a small advantage, Lerch-Ftačnik, Czechoslovak Cht 1988.

b3) A similar assessment applies to 10 ♖d1!? ♕b7 (10...♗b7 11 ♕h3!?) 11 ♕g3, Zapata-Infante, San Salvador Z 1998.

b4) Possibly the main continuation here is 10 a4 b4 11 a5 0-0 12 ♘a4 ♗d8

(12...♘c6 13 ♘b6! ♘xd4 14 ♕d1 Bangiev), and now 13 ♖d1!?.

**A)**

**9...♕b6** *(D)*

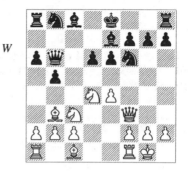

Now:

**A1: 10 ♗g5!?** 61
**A2: 10 ♗e3** 74

**A1)**

**10 ♗g5!?**

This interesting move attracted attention only after the game Ivanchuk-Kamsky, Monaco Amber rpd 1996, but it was first played by Brooks in 1982 (by the way, the position after 10 ♗g5 may also arise via *8 ♗g5 ♗e7 9 ♕f3 ♕b6 10 0-0*).

Let us consider:

**A11: 10...♘bd7** 62
**A12: 10...0-0** 63

Other moves:

a) 10...♕xd4? 11 e5 ±.

b) 10...b4?! 11 e5 ♗b7 12 ♘a4! ♕c7 (12...♕a7 13 ♕d1 dxe5 14 ♘xe6! +−) 13 exd6 ♗xd6 14 ♕h3 with an initiative, Alvim-Valiente, corr. 1989.

c) 10...♗b7 11 ♗e3! ♕a5 (but not 11...♕c7?! 12 ♗xe6!) 12 a3 ♘c6 13

♕g3 0-0 14 f4 ± Ganguly-Farkas, Szeged 1998.

d) 10...h6. Now White can play 11 ♗e3 ♕b7 12 ♕g3 or 11 ♗xf6!? ♗xf6 12 e5 ♗b7 13 ♘d5 exd5 14 exf6 ♕xd4 15 ♖fe1+ (Alvim) 15...♔d8 16 fxg7 ♕xg7 17 ♗xd5 ♗xd5 18 ♕xd5 followed by a4, with compensation.

e) 10...♕b7!? is playable:

e1) 11 a3 0-0 (11...♘bd7) 12 ♕g3 ♘bd7 13 ♖fe1 ♗e5 (13...♔h8!?) 14 ♖ad1 ♗d7 15 f4 ± Ciemniak-Kempinski, Polish jr Ch (Czestochowa) 1992.

e2) 11 ♖fe1 and now:

e21) 11...♘bd7 and then: 12 ♕g3 0-0 13 ♗h6 ♘h5 14 ♕h3 ♘hf6 15 ♗g5 ♘c5 = Alvim-Vujanović, corr. 1999; 12 ♖ad1!? transposes to Line A11.

e22) 11...0-0 12 ♕g3 (12 ♖ad1!? b4 13 ♘a4 – 10...0-0 11 ♖ad1 b4 12 ♘a4 ♕b7 13 ♖fe1) 12...b4 13 e5 (13 ♘a4? ♘xe4) 13...dxe5 14 ♗xf6 ♗xf6 15 ♘e4 ♗e7 (15...exd4!? 16 ♘xf6+ ♔h8 Van der Weide) 16 ♕xe5 ♘c6 17 ♘xc6 ♕xc6 = Mirumian-A.Petrosian, Armenian Ch (Erevan) 1996.

## A11)
**10...♘bd7 11 ♖ad1 ♕b7**
Or:

a) 11...0-0 – *10...0-0 11 ♖ad1 ♘bd7.*

b) 11...♘c5?! 12 ♗xf6! gxf6 13 ♖fe1 (Nunn recommended 13 e5 ♗b7 14 ♘d5! exd5 15 exf6) 13...♖a7 (Ivanchuk-Kamsky, Monaco Amber rpd 1996; 13...♕b7 14 ♘f5 ±) 14 ♕g4! Nunn.

c) 11...♘e5 12 ♕g3 b4 13 ♘a4 ♕b7 and now both 14 ♖fe1 (Nijboer-Timman, Amsterdam 2000) and 14 ♗xf6 are dangerous for Black.

d) 11...♗b7!? is another relatively rare option; e.g., 12 ♖fe1 (both 12 ♗xe6 and 12 ♗e3 should be investigated) 12...♘c5 (12...0-0!? – *10...0-0 11 ♖ad1 ♗b7 12 ♖fe1 ♘bd7*) 13 ♕g3 (13 ♕h3!?), and now:

d1) 13...0-0-0?! 14 ♗e3, Jaracz-Smirin, Groningen 1996.

d2) 13...0-0! – *10...0-0 11 ♖ad1 ♗b7 12 ♖fe1 ♘bd7 13 ♕g3 ♘c5!*.

e) 11...b4 12 ♘a4 ♕b7 13 ♖fe1 – *11...♕b7 12 ♖fe1 b4 13 ♘a4.*

**12 ♖fe1** *(D)*

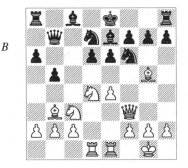

**12...b4**
Or 12...0-0 13 ♕g3 ♔h8:

a) 14 a3 and now:

a1) 14...♘c5 15 ♗xf6 gxf6 16 ♘d5!? ± Lang-Kask, corr. 1994.

a2) 14...h6!? 15 ♕h4 ♘e5 16 f4 ♘g6 17 ♕h3 e5 18 ♘f5 ♘xf4 = Snarheim-Leskiewicz, Gausdal 2000.

b) 14 ♖e3 b4 15 ♘ce2 (15 ♘d5?! exd5 16 ♘f5 ♘h5 17 ♕h4 ♗xg5 18 ♕xg5 ♘df6) 15...♘xe4 16 ♖xe4 ♗xg5, and Black has at least equality; e.g., 17 ♖xe6 (Nunn-Ftačnik, British League (4NCL) 1999/00) 17...♘f6! or 17 ♖g4 ♗e7!? 18 ♖xg7 ♘f6! ∓ Van der Weide.

c) Interesting is 14 ♘d5!? exd5 15 ♘f5 ♘h5 16 ♕h4 ♗xg5 17 ♕xh5.

**13 ♘a4 0-0**

Two other ways to reach this position are *10...♕b7 11 ♖fe1 0-0 12 ♖ad1 b4 13 ♘a4* and *10...0-0 11 ♖ad1 b4 12 ♘a4 ♕b7 13 ♖fe1 ♘bd7*.

**14 ♕g3**

Or:

a) 14 ♕h3 ♖e8 15 f4? ♘xe4 ∓ Peter-Amigues, Bescanon 1999.

b) 14 c3!? ♘e5 (14...bxc3 15 ♘xc3 ♘c5 16 e5!! ±; 14...a5!) 15 ♕e2 bxc3 16 ♘xc3 with an advantage, Srebrnić-Gruskovnjak, Ljubljana 2000.

**14...♖e8**

14...♘xe4? fails to 15 ♖xe4 ♗xg5 16 ♖xe6! ♘f6 17 ♖ee1 – Van der Weide.

14...♔h8 15 c3 (15 ♘f3!? ♕c7 16 ♖d4 a5 17 ♗xf6 gxf6, Prokopchuk-Kempinski, Koszalin 1997, 18 c3!?) 15...a5 (15...♘xe4!?) 16 ♗c2 ♘e5 17 f4 ♘g6 (Nijboer-Van Wely, Dutch Ch (Rotterdam) 2000) 18 e5 (Van Wely) ±.

**15 f3 ♔h8 16 ♔h1**

± Reinderman-Danailov, Wijk aan Zee 2000.

## A12)

**10...0-0 11 ♖ad1** *(D)*

Not 11 e5? dxe5!.

*B*

Here Black faces a crucial choice:

a) 11...♘c6 12 ♘xc6 ♕xc6 13 ♘d5 (13 ♖fe1 ♗b7 14 a3 transposes to note 'c11' to White's 11th move in Line B1) 13...exd5 14 ♗xf6 dxe4 15 ♕e2 ♗xf6 16 ♗d5 ♗g4 17 ♕xg4 ♕c8 18 ♕xe4 ♖a7 (Ryvlin-Ar.Karpov, corr. 1991) 19 c3 with a minimal advantage for White.

b) 11...b4 12 ♘a4 ♕b7 and now:

b1) 13 ♖fe1 ♖e8 (13...♘bd7 transposes to Line A11) 14 c3 a5 15 ♗c2 ♘bd7 16 ♕g3 ♗f8 17 f4 e5 18 fxe5 dxe5 19 ♘f5 ± Reinderman-Bosboom, Hoogeveen 1999.

b2) 13 c3 a5 14 c4 ♘bd7 15 ♘b5 ♕b8 16 ♕e2 ♗b7 17 f3 ♗c6 18 ♘d4 ♖c8 19 ♖d2 h6 20 ♗h4 ♘e5 21 ♘xc6 ♖xc6 (21...♘xc6!?) 22 f4 ♘g6 23 ♗g3 ♕c7 24 f5 ± Emms-Van den Doel, Isle of Man 1997.

Two other moves can be linked to one and the same development pattern:

c) 11...♗b7 and then:

c1) 12 ♕h3!? ♔h8 13 ♖d3 (13 ♖fe1 looks more natural) 13...♘bd7 14 ♖fd1 b4 15 ♘a4 ♕a5 16 f4 ♘c5 17 ♘xc5 ♕xc5 18 ♖e3 ♗d8! with counterplay, del Rio-Gallagher, Lugano 1999.

c2) After 12 ♕g3!?, 12...♘bd7?! is dubious in view of 13 ♗e3!. Gallagher analysed 12...b4 13 ♘a4 ♕a5 (13...♕c7 14 ♗h6 ♘e8 15 ♗xe6!) 14 ♗xf6 ♗xf6 15 ♕xd6 ♖d8 16 ♕c5!, and recommended 12...♘c6.

c3) 12 ♖fe1 ♘bd7 (12...b4 13 ♘a4 ♕a5 14 ♗d2! ♘bd7 15 a3 ♕d8 16 ♗xb4 ♘e5 17 ♕e3 ♘xe4 18 f3 is better for White, Alvim-Ma.Adams, corr. 1999) 13 ♕g3 (13 ♕h3!? is possible) 13...♘c5! (after 13...b4 14 ♘a4 ♕c7, 15 ♗h6 ♘e8 16 ♗xe6 fxe6 17 ♘xe6 is suspicious due to 17...♕xc2! 18 ♘xg7 ♖f6 19 ♘f5+ ♔f7; however,

15 c3 {Alvim} is not bad) 14 ♗h6 ♘e8 15 ♔h1 ♔h8 16 ♗g5 ♗xg5 17 ♕xg5 ♘f6 = M.Sorin-Lefebvre, French Cht 1999.

d) 11...♘bd7 and now:

d1) 12 ♕g3 ♘c5 (12...♔h8) and then:

d11) 13 ♖fe1 ♘h5 (13...♗b7! transposes to line 'c3') 14 ♕h4 ♗xg5 15 ♕xg5 ♘f6 16 ♖e3 h6 17 ♕h4 ♗b7 18 a3 ± del Rio-Gyimesi, Siofok jr Ech 1996.

d12) 13 ♗h6!? ♘e8 14 ♗d5!? exd5 15 ♘xd5 ♕d8 (15...♕b7!? 16 ♘c6 ♔h8 17 ♘cxe7 gxh6 18 ♕f4 Van der Weide) 16 ♘c6 ♗h4! 17 ♘de7+! ♕xe7 18 ♘xe7+ ♗xe7 (Brooks-Browne, USA 1982) 19 ♖fe1 ∞.

d2) 12 ♖fe1 and here:

d21) 12...♘e5 13 ♕g3 (Robović-Danner, Oberwart 1996) and now both 13...♔h8!? and 13...♘g6!? are possible.

d22) 12...♕b7 transposes to the note to Black's 12th move in Line A11.

d23) 12...♗b7!? transposes to line 'c3'.

d24) 12...♘c5 13 ♕h3!? ♗b7 14 a3 (14 ♖e3 b4!) 14...♕c7 15 ♕h4 ♖fe8 16 ♖e3 offers White the better chances, del Rio-R.Fernandez, Leon 1997.

**Summary:** Apart from 10...0-0 11 ♖ad1 ♘c6, Black's possibilities may be subdivided into:

1) Variations with ...♕b7 (here White has had some success).

2) The arrangement ...♗b7, ...♘bd7, ...0-0. In this case there exist three ways to proceed: 10...♘bd7 11 ♖ad1 ♗b7!?, 10...0-0 11 ♖ad1 ♗b7 and 10...0-0 11 ♖ad1 ♘bd7/10...♘bd7 11 ♖ad1 0-0. It is not yet clear which is best.

**A2)**

**10 ♗e3 ♕b7 11 ♕g3** *(D)*

Other moves are quite harmless; e.g., 11 a3 0-0 12 ♖fe1 ♘bd7 and now:

a) 13 ♗g5 ♘c5 14 ♗a2 ♕c7 15 ♖ad1 ♗b7 16 b4 ♘cd7 17 ♕h3 ♘e5 18 f4 ♘c4 with counterplay, Mowszi-szian-Gelfand, Minsk 1986.

b) 13 ♕g3 ♘c5 (13...♔h8 =) 14 ♗h6 ♘e8 15 ♘d5 (15 ♘f5?! can be met by 15...♗f6 16 ♖ad1 {Gobet-Ftačnik, Biel 1984} 16...♗e5! or even 15...exf5!?) 15...♘xb3 = G.Kuzmin-Perun, Ukrainian Ch (Alushta) 1997.

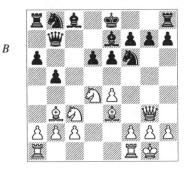

We shall consider:

| A21: 11...♘c6?! | 65 |
|---|---|
| A22: 11...0-0 | 65 |
| A23: 11...♘bd7!? | 67 |
| A24: 11...b4! | 69 |

Other moves:

a) 11...h5? 12 ♘f5! is much better for White.

b) 11...♗d7? 12 ♘f5! exf5 (12...b4 13 ♕xg7 ♖g8 14 ♕xf6!) 13 ♕xg7 ♖f8 14 ♗g5! ± Ivanchuk-Shakhvorostov, USSR jr Ch (Jurmala) 1985.

c) 11...g6 12 f3!? ♘bd7 13 ♖ad1 with a slight advantage for White, Zaid-Anikaev, Lvov 1978.

## A21)

**11...♘c6?!**

This move is inconsequential – if Black wants to play this way, then why not *9...♕c7 10 ♕g3 ♘c6*, when the white bishop is still on c1? Now:

a) 12 ♘f5 exf5 13 ♕xg7 ♖f8 is unclear.

b) 12 ♖ad1 0-0 13 ♘xc6 ♕xc6 14 ♗h6 ♘e8 and now there are various transpositions to Line B2:

b1) 15 ♘d5?! ♗d8 16 ♖fe1 – *9...♕c7 10 ♕g3 ♘c6 11 ♘xc6 ♕xc6 12 ♖e1 0-0 13 ♗h6! ♘e8 14 ♘d5 ♗d8 15 ♖ad1!?*.

b2) 15 ♖fe1 – *9...♕c7 10 ♕g3 ♘c6 11 ♘xc6 ♕xc6 12 ♖e1 0-0 13 ♗h6! ♘e8 14 ♖ad1!?*.

b3) 15 a3 – *9...♕c7 10 ♕g3 0-0 11 ♗h6 ♘e8 12 a3 ♘c6 13 ♘xc6 ♕xc6 14 ♖ad1*.

c) 12 ♖fe1 ♗d7 (12...0-0 13 ♘xc6 ♕xc6 14 ♗h6 – *9...♕c7 10 ♕g3 ♘c6 11 ♘xc6 ♕xc6 12 ♖e1 0-0 13 ♗h6*) 13 ♖ad1 (13 a3 0-0 gives Black satisfactory play, while after 13 f4 b4!, the sacrifice 14 ♘d5 exd5 15 e5 is very inconclusive) 13...b4 (Black can consider 13...♘a5!?, but he should avoid 13...0-0? 14 ♗h6 ♘e8, transposing to note 'b' to Black's 14th move in Line A22) 14 ♘ce2 0-0 15 ♗h6 ♘e8 with a defensible position, Bouaziz-Marin, Szirak IZ 1987.

d) 12 ♖ae1!? ♗d7 (12...0-0 13 ♘xc6 ♕xc6 14 ♗h6 ♘e8 15 ♘d5 ♗d8 deserves attention) 13 f4 b4?! (13...g6!? Beliavsky/Mikhalchishin) 14 ♘d5! exd5 15 e5!, and, with the rooks on e1 and f1, White's initiative is very dangerous, A.Sokolov-Armas, Wijk aan Zee 1993.

e) 12 ♘xc6!? ♕xc6 and now:

e1) 13 ♖fe1 is inaccurate in view of 13...♗b7! (13...0-0 14 ♗h6 – *9...♕c7 10 ♕g3 ♘c6 11 ♘xc6 ♕xc6 12 ♖e1 0-0 13 ♗h6!*) 14 ♖ad1 (14 f3!?) 14...♘xe4! 15 ♘xe4 ♕xe4 16 ♗f4 (16 ♕xg7 ♕g6!) 16...♗h4!? (16...♕g6 17 ♕h3!?) 17 ♕g4 h5 18 ♖xe4 hxg4 19 ♖ee1 = (Armas).

e2) White should prefer 13 f3! 0-0 14 ♘e2 with some advantage, Hübner-Armas, Bundesliga 1989/90.

f) 12 f4!? 0-0 (12...♘xd4 13 ♗xd4 b4 14 e5!, Anand-Badea, Manchester 1990, and 12...♘a5 13 e5 ♘h5 14 ♕h3 ♘xb3 15 ♘xb3 g6 16 ♖ad1!? are both dangerous for Black) 13 a3 (13 e5! is critical) 13...♘a5 14 e5 ♘e4 15 ♘xe4 ♕xe4 16 f5 (Mirumian-Movsesian, Tbilisi 1993) 16...♕xe5! with good play (Mirumian/Nadanian).

## A22)

**11...0-0**

Here, the knight also usually goes to c6, but only after ♗h6 and ...♘e8 (by which White 'returns' the tempo gained by 10 ♗e3).

**12 ♗h6**

After 12 f3, 12...♘c6 13 ♘xc6 ♕xc6 transposes to *11...♘c6?! 12 ♘xc6!? ♕xc6 13 f3! 0-0* ±, but 12...♔h8!? and 12...♗d7!? are both possible.

**12...♘e8** *(D)*

The same position, but with Black's queen on c7, results from the important variation *9...♕c7 10 ♕g3 0-0 11 ♗h6 ♘e8*. With the queen on b7, White has to defend the e4-pawn more carefully, but Black needs to supervise his d6-pawn. My general appraisal is that Black has slightly fewer resources with the queen on b7.

**13 ♖ad1!**

W

Other moves:

a) 13 ♘d5 ♗d8!, with the possibility of 14 ♘f4 ♔h8 15 ♗xe6 fxe6 16 ♘dxe6 ♗xe6 and 17...gxh6, is good for Black.

b) 13 ♖fe1 ♗f6! (an important idea; 13...♔h8 is weaker owing to 14 ♗g5) 14 ♘f3 (14 ♗e3 b4!; 14 ♖ad1? ♗e5!) 14...♘d7 15 ♖ad1 a5 and Black has strong counterplay, Gdanski-Kempinski, Polish Ch playoff (Warsaw) 1997.

c) If 13 ♖ae1, then 13...♗f6! is again possible.

d) After 13 a3 ♗f6, there is 14 ♗e3 but, on the whole, 13 a3 does not make much sense as 13 ♖ad1 also prevents 13...b4 (albeit indirectly).

**13...♗d7**

Or:

a) 13...b4 14 ♘d5! ♗d8 15 ♖fe1 with an unpleasant initiative, Ardeleanu-Florean, Romanian Cht 1999.

b) 13...♔h8 14 ♗g5! (more logical than 14 ♗c1 = or 14 ♗e3 ♘d7!? 15 f3 ♘c5 16 a3 ♘xb3! = A.Ivanov-Kamsky, USA Ch (Los Angeles) 1991) 14...♗xg5 (14...♘f6 is answered by 15 ♗xf6!) 15 ♕xg5 ♘f6 (Gallagher proposed 15...h6) 16 ♖fe1 (16 f4!? ♘xe4 17 ♘xe4 ♕xe4 18 f5, Palac-Beran, Toulouse 1990) 16...b4 17 ♘a4

♘bd7, and instead of 18 f3 ♘e5! 19 ♘e2?! ♕a7+! 20 ♔h1? ♘eg4!! −+ Kudrin-Hellers, New York 1993, 18 ♘f3!? ♘xe4 19 ♕e7! is enticing (±).

**14 ♖fe1**

Or:

a) 14 a3 ♘c6 15 ♗g5 ♗xg5 16 ♕xg5 ♘xd4 17 ♖xd4 ♗c6 = Tisdall-Browne, Lone Pine 1976.

b) 14 f4!? is a double-edged alternative:

b1) 14...♔h8 15 ♗g5 (15 f5?! gxh6) 15...♗xg5 (15...f6!? is more demanding) 16 fxg5! with better chances for White, Reefat-Malishauskas, Dhaka 1997.

b2) 14...b4 15 f5 bxc3 16 fxe6 fxe6 17 ♘xe6 ♗xe6 (17...♕xb3? 18 ♘xg7 +−) 18 ♗xe6+ ♔h8 with unclear play; e.g., 19 ♖xf8+ (19 ♕xc3!?) 19...♗xf8 20 ♗d5!? (20 ♖f1? ♘d7! ∓).

b3) 14...♘c6 15 f5!? (15 ♘xc6 ♗xc6 16 f5 ♔h8 17 f6 {17 ♗g5 b4!} 17...♗xf6 18 ♖xf6 ♖g8 19 ♖f4 gxh6 20 ♕f3 ♖a7 21 ♖f1, Najer-Biriukov, St Petersburg 1998, 21...a5!? with counterplay) 15...♘xd4 16 ♖xd4 ♗f6 (16...♔h8?! 17 f6!) 17 ♖d3 (17 ♖dd1!?) 17...b4 (17...♔h8!?) 18 fxe6 fxe6 19 ♘d5 ♗b5! 20 e5 (20 ♗e3! is better), and now 20...dxe5? 21 ♘xf6+ +− Golubev-Lambert, Bundesliga 1997/8 is wrong, but 20...♗xd3! ∓ is very strong, with the point that 21 exf6 can be met by 21...♗b5!!.

**14...♔h8**

Not:

a) 14...b4?! 15 ♘f5!.

b) 14...♘c6? 15 ♘d5! ♗d8 16 ♘f5! exf5 17 exf5 ♘e5 18 ♖xe5! dxe5 19 f6! +− Gurieli-G.Sakhatova, USSR wom Ch (Erevan) 1985.

**15 ♗g5! ♘c6!?**

15...♗xg5 16 ♕xg5 ♘c6 17 ♖e3! is also slightly better for White, Snape-Twitchell, corr. 1995.

**16 ♘xc6**

16 ♖e3?! f6!.

**16...♗xc6 17 ♗xe7 ♕xe7**

White has a slight advantage, Auer-V.Neverov, Porz 1993.

## A23)

**11...♘bd7!?** (D)

The most critical move and a risky one at the same time. Attempts to refute it lead to utterly mad positions.

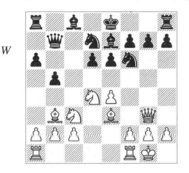

**12 ♖fe1**

Frankly speaking, I find it hard to state the strongest move for White, and I have defined the main line in accordance with the amount of accumulated material – at least it is convenient to read it this way...

a) 12 ♘f5 exf5 13 ♕xg7 ♖f8 14 ♘d5 is recommended by Gallagher in view of 14...♘xd5 15 ♗xd5 ♕b8 16 ♖fe1!? ♗b7 17 ♗h6! f4 18 ♕xh7 ♘f6 (alternatively, 18...♘e5 19 ♗xf4!?) 19 ♕f5 ♖g8 20 ♗g5 ♖g6 21 h4 ± Firnhaber-Eliseev, corr. 1994. I would regard 14...fxe4 15 ♘xe7 ♔xe7 16 ♖ad1 ♕c6 17 ♗g5 ♗b7 18 ♖fe1 ♕c5

−+ Boudy-Novikov, Villa Clara 1987 as more of a problem.

b) 12 f4!? and then:

b1) 12...♘xe4 13 ♘xe4 ♕xe4 14 ♖ae1! ♗b7 15 f5 ♗h4 16 ♕h3 ♗xe1 17 fxe6 0-0, Golubev-Kruppa, Kiev 1995. After several weeks of analysis of the game I came to the conclusion that it is only 18 ♖f4! that gives a chance for an advantage.

b2) 12...b4 13 ♘d5!? (as far as I can determine, other moves promise White nothing: after 13 f5, 13...bxc3 14 fxe6 fxe6 15 ♘xe6 ♘e5 is possibly satisfactory for Black, but 13...♘c5! is even stronger; 13 ♘a4 allows Black an excellent game – *11...b4! 12 ♘a4 ♘bd7 13 f4?!*) 13...exd5 14 e5 dxe5 15 fxe5 ♘xe5 16 ♗a4+ (it was not worth starting all that just to settle for 16 ♕xe5 0-0 ∓) 16...♗d7 (16...♘ed7 17 ♖ae1!) 17 ♕xe5 ♗xa4 (17...0-0 18 ♕xe7 ♖fe8 19 ♕d6 ♗xa4 20 ♖xf6!) 18 ♘f5 with the point 18...♔d8 19 ♗d4. This line awaits testing.

c) 12 f3!? and then:

c1) 12...b4 13 ♘ce2! 0-0 14 ♗h6 ♘e8 15 ♗a4 ± Semeniuk-Moiseev, USSR 1987.

c2) 12...0-0 13 ♘d5 (with the pawn on f3, 13 ♗h6? is bad in view of 13...♘h5!, though 13 a4!? b4 14 ♘d5 is possible) 13...♘xd5 (no better is 13...♗d8 14 ♘xf6+ ♗xf6 15 ♖ad1 or 13...♘e5) 14 exd5 ♘c5 15 ♘c6 ± Repkova-Novikov, Cairo 1997.

c3) 12...♘c5!? 13 ♖fd1 (13 ♕xg7 ♖g8 14 ♕h6 is important; then 14...♖g6 15 ♕h3 ♗d7 {Seirawan} seems to be stronger than the alternative 14...e5 15 ♘f5 ♗xf5 16 exf5 ♘xb3 17 axb3 ♖xg2+ 18 ♔xg2 ♘g4 19 ♕xh7 ♘e3+ 20 ♔h1) 13...♗d7 14 ♔h1 (14 ♕xg7

♖g8 15 ♕h6 b4 16 ♘ce2 ♘xb3!)
14...b4 15 ♘ce2 0-0 with roughly equal
chances, Milos-J.Polgar, Bali 2000.

d) 12 ♖ae1 is hardly a critical
move:

d1) 12...♘xe4? is bad for the same
reason as after *12 ♖fe1*.

d2) After 12...♘c5 13 ♘f5, the
rook is no longer on a1 and there is no
chance for 13...♘xb3. However, White
is deprived of the ♖ad1 resource, and
after 13...exf5 Black has some chances
to hold on.

d3) 12...0-0 13 ♘d5 ♗d8 seems
satisfactory as the white rooks are not
best placed.

d4) 12...b4!?. Now the sacrifice 13
♘d5 exd5 14 ♘f5 ♘e5 (Yurtaev-Nov-
ikov, Tashkent 1986) 15 ♘xg7+!? ♔d8
16 exd5 (Novikov) has not found followers. 13 ♘a4 – *11...b4 12 ♘a4
♘bd7 13 ♖ae1* (I should mention that
after *11...b4 12 ♘a4 ♘bd7* White, as a
rule, plays neither *13 ♖ae1* nor *13
♖fe1*).

We now return to the position after
12 ♖fe1 *(D)*:

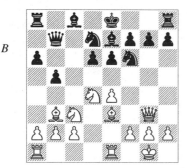

**12...♘c5**
If my further analysis is correct,
this move leads to problems for Black.

Therefore, it is very important to ex-
amine the alternatives:

a) 12...♘xe4? 13 ♘xe4 ♕xe4 14
♘xe6 fxe6 15 ♗g5 ♕g6 16 ♖xe6 ♘f6
17 ♖xe7+!.

b) 12...0-0 13 ♘d5 ± (13 ♗h6 – *10
♗g5 ♕b7 11 ♖fe1 ♘bd7 12 ♕g3 0-0
13 ♗h6*).

c) 12...g6 13 ♗h6!? ±.

d) 12...b4!? is possibly critical:

d1) The unpretentious 13 ♘a4
transposes to *11...b4 12 ♘a4 ♘bd7 13
♖fe1*.

d2) After 13 ♘f5(?) bxc3, Grilc-
Gruskovnjak, Ljubljana 2000, I see
nothing good for White.

d3) Only 13 ♘d5 exd5 remains. As
of now, I assess 14 ♘f5 ♘e5 15 ♘xg7+
♔d8! more likely to be in Black's favour, and the same assessment applies
to 14 ♗g5 dxe4!?, Roese-Neurohr,
Bundesliga 1988/9. 14 ♗a4 appears to
be more dangerous, however.

**13 ♘f5 ♘xb3**
13...exf5 14 ♗xc5 dxc5 15 ♕xg7
♖f8 16 ♗d5! (16 exf5 ♗e6!) 16...♘xd5
17 exd5 ±.

**14 ♘xg7+!**
14 ♘xe7 ♘xa1! 15 ♕xg7 ♖f8 (or
15...♘xc2!? 16 ♗g5 ♘xe1 17 ♕xf6
♔d7 18 ♕xh8 b4) 16 e5 ♘xc2 (not
16...dxe5? 17 ♗c5 ♘d7, Ki.Georgiev-
Zaichik, Palma de Mallorca 1989, 18
♘f5!! ±; 16...♘h5!? 17 ♕xh7 ♕xe7 18
♘e4 ♘xc2 19 ♘xd6+ ♕xd6 20 exd6
♘xe1 21 ♕e4! followed by ♕h4 –
Ki.Georgiev) 17 ♗h6 ♘xe1 18 ♕xf8+
♔d7 19 ♘ed5! = Ki.Georgiev.

**14...♔f8**
14...♔d7 15 ♖ad1!! (di Luca; after
this move White is much better)
15...♖g8 (15...♘xe4 16 ♘xe4 ♕xe4
17 ♗f4; 15...♘a5 16 e5 ♘d5 17 exd6

♗xd6 18 ♗f4!) 16 axb3 ♘e8!? 17
♘xe6! ♖xg3 18 ♘c5+ ♔c7 19 ♘xb7
♖xe3 20 ♘d5+.

**15 ♗h6!**

15 axb3? h6!.

**15...♘xa1! 16 e5! ♘xc2**

Or:

a) 16...♘g8 17 ♘xe6++ ♔e8 18
♘g7+ ♔d8 19 exd6 ♗f6 20 ♖e8+
♔d7 21 ♕h3+ ♔c6 22 ♕f3+ ♔d7 23
♕f5+ ♔c6 24 ♕e4+ ♔d7 25 ♖d8+!
+−.

b) 16...dxe5 17 ♖d1! ♗d7 (17...♘d7
18 ♘f5+! ♔e8 19 ♕g7 ♖f8 20 ♘xe7
♘xc2 21 ♘g8! ♘d4 22 ♘f6+ ♔e7 23
♘ce4) 18 ♘h5+! ♔e8 19 ♕g7 ♖g8! 20
♘xf6+ ♗xf6 21 ♕xg8+ ♔e7 22 ♕g4
and White is better!

**17 ♖d1 ♘d7 18 ♘xe6+ ♔e8 19
♘g7+ ♔d8**

19...♔f8 20 ♘f5+ ♔e8 21 exd6 ±.

**20 exd6 ♗f6 21 ♗g5 ♖g8**

Or: 21...♗xg5? 22 ♕xg5+ winning
for White; 21...h6 22 ♗xf6+ ♘xf6 23
♕h4 ♗d7 24 ♕xf6+ ♔c8 25 ♖c1;
21...♕c6!? 22 ♘d5!.

**22 ♗h4!! ±**

22 ♕f4 ♕xg2+!! ∞ di Luca-Kin-
nunen, corr. 1991.

## A24)

**11...b4!** *(D)*

Nowadays this is the main move.

**12 ♘a4**

Otherwise:

a) 12 ♘ce2 is suspicious in view of
12...♕xe4.

b) Zapolskis has tried 12 ♘f5 here:
12...bxc3 13 ♘xg7+ ♔d7 14 e5 ♘d5
15 bxc3 and now 15...♘xc3 16 ♖fe1
d5 17 ♗d2 ♘b5 (Zapolskis-Ki.Geor-
giev, Batumi Echt 1999) can hardly be
considered as a refutation, but possibly

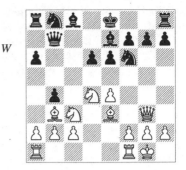

W

stronger is 15...♖g8 (as in Zapolskis-
Vökler, Cuxhaven 2000).

**12...♘bd7**

Or:

a) 12...♘xe4 13 ♕xg7 gives White
a development advantage.

b) 12...♗d7 13 ♘b6 (after 13 f3,
Black should try 13...0-0!? rather than
13...♘c6 14 ♘xc6 ♗xc6 15 ♘b6 ♖b8
16 ♘c4 ±) 13...♕xb6 14 ♘xe6 with a
dangerous attack for White, Krueger-
Penna, corr. 2000.

c) 12...0-0!? is seldom played: 13
♗h6 (after 13 f3, 13...♘bd7 transposes
to the main line, while 13...♘c6!? is
possible) 13...♘e8 14 ♖ad1 (14 ♖fe1
and now there is 14...♔h8?! 15 ♗g5 ±,
14...♗f6! or 14...♘d7 – *12...♘bd7 13
♖fe1 0-0 14 ♗h6 ♘e8*) 14...♘d7 (or
14...♔h8 15 ♗g5 with a slight advantage for White) 15 ♖fe1 – *12...♘bd7
13 ♖fe1 0-0 14 ♗h6 ♘e8 15 ♖ad1*.

**13 f3**

Other moves are rare:

a) 13 f4?! 0-0! ∓ Giaccio-Quin-
teros, Trelew 1995.

b) 13 ♕xg7!? deserves attention.

c) 13 ♖ae1 (this and, to a greater
extent, 13 ♖fe1 are interesting in
view of the move-order *11...♘bd7 12
♖fe1/12 ♖ae1 b4 13 ♘a4*) 13...0-0

(13...♕xe4 14 f4, Kudrin-Yedidia, Maryland 1993, and 13...♘xe4 14 ♕xg7 ♗f6 15 ♕g4, Kudrin-Freeman, Philadelphia 1991, are dangerous for Black) 14 ♗h6 ♘e8 with good play (15 f4? ♕a7).

d) 13 ♖fe1 and then:

d1) 13...♘xe4?! is met by 14 ♕xg7.

d2) 13...♕xe4!?. Now, instead of 14 ♘xe6?! fxe6 15 ♗f4 ♕g6 16 ♕f3 ♖b8 17 ♗xe6 ♘e5 18 ♗xe5 dxe5 19 ♖xe5 ∓ Tabatadze-Gelfand, Leningrad 1985, I suggest 14 ♖ad1!? with the point 14...♕g4 15 ♕xg4 ♘xg4 16 ♗d2 ±.

d3) 13...0-0 14 ♗h6 ♘e8 (another idea is 14...♘h5!?) 15 ♖ad1 (15 ♘xe6!? ∞ Byrne/Mednis). Now 15...♘c5? is weak due to 16 ♘xc5 dxc5 17 ♗a4. 15...♔h8 16 ♗g5 ♗xg5 17 ♕xg5 ♘ef6 transposes to note 'b' to Black's 13th move in Line A22. 15...♘e5!? is critical and unclear; e.g., 16 f4 ♘g6 17 ♗g5 ♗xg5 18 fxg5, Borge-Djurhuus, Gausdal 1995.

d4) Strangely, nobody has yet tried 13...♘e5!?.

**13...0-0** *(D)*

13...♘e5?! is dubious; e.g., 14 ♕xg7 ♖g8 15 ♕h6 ♘xe4 16 ♘b6 (Emms) 16...♕xb6 17 ♘xe6.

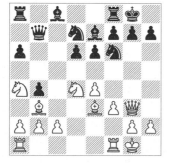

This is one of the key positions for 9...♕b6 and the entire 9 ♕f3 system.

The struggle is above all strategic. Black's plan consists not of 14...♘c5 (following which 15 ♘xc5 dxc5 16 ♘e2 gives White a structural advantage), but of 14...♘e5! and 15...♗d7. After ...♘e5 Black will be ready to counter White's ♘b6 not only with ...♖ab8 but also with ...♘h5!. The development of White's play should be linked to c3, or c4 in the advantageous version, sooner or later.

**14 ♖fd1**

White enjoys a very wide choice:

a) 14 ♗h6? ♘h5! 15 ♕h3 gxh6 16 ♕xh5 ♕a7 ∓ J.Polgar-Gelfand, Dos Hermanas 1994.

b) 14 c3 (this is a bit premature) 14...bxc3 15 bxc3!? (15 ♘xc3 ♘c5! =; 15 ♖ab1 ♘e5! =) 15...♘e5 (15...♘c5 16 ♘xc5 dxc5 17 ♘c2 ± Morozevich-Nevostruev, Orel 1992; not wholly clear is 15...♕c7 16 ♗xe6 ♘h5) 16 ♖ab1 ♕c7 17 ♘b6 (17 f4?! ♘xe4 18 ♕h3, Chapman-Freeman, Melbourne 1996, 18...♘g6!) 17...♖b8 18 ♘xc8 ♕xc8!, and Black is no worse.

c) 14 ♔h1 (I do not see any real advantage in such a preventive step) 14...♔h8 (14...a5?! 15 c4; 14...♘e5 15 ♘b6 ♖b8 leads to unclear play, for instance, 16 a3 ♕xb6!?) 15 ♖ac1 (no advantage is gained by 15 c4 bxc3 16 bxc3, when Black can choose between 16...♘e5 or 16...♕c7!?) 15...♘e5 16 c3 bxc3 (16...♘d3 17 ♖cd1 ♘h5 18 ♕g4 ♘hf4? 19 ♗xf4 e5 20 ♗d5! does not work for Black) 17 ♖xc3 ♗d7. Now after 18 ♘b6 there is the reply 18...♕xb6!? 19 ♘xe6 (by the way, with the kings on g1 and g8, ♘f5! is winning) 19...♘h5!.

d) 14 ♖ac1!? (straightforward and interesting) 14...♘e5! (14...♘c5 15 ♘xc5 dxc5 16 ♘e2, 14...a5 15 c4 and 14...♖h8 15 c3 bxc3 16 ♖xc3 are somewhat better for White) and then:

d1) 15 ♘b6 ♖b8 (15...♘h5!? 16 ♕h3 ♘f4 17 ♗xf4 ♕xb6 18 ♗e3 ♗f6 19 ♖fd1 ♘c6! Gallagher) 16 ♘xc8 ♖bxc8 17 ♘xe6 fxe6 18 ♗xe6+ ♔h8 19 ♗xc8 ♕xc8 gives Black good play, Ayapbergenov-Ki.Georgiev, Komotini 1993.

d2) 15 ♖fd1 is not dangerous for Black; see *14 ♖fd1 ♘e5 15 ♖ac1.*

d3) 15 c3!? and now:

d31) 15...♘d3 16 ♖cd1 ♘h5 17 ♕g4 (with the point 17...♘hf4 18 ♗xf4 e5 19 ♘f5 ♗xf5 20 exf5 ♘xf4 21 f6 ♗xf6 22 ♖xd6) somewhat favours White.

d32) 15...bxc3 16 ♖xc3 ♗d7 17 ♘b6 ♘h5 (17...♕xb6? 18 ♘f5) 18 ♕h3 ♘f4 19 ♗xf4 ♕xb6 20 ♗e3 ♕b7 21 f4 is also quite good for White, Gi.Hernandez-Morović, Havana 1997.

d33) 15...♗d7! probably equalizes; e.g., 16 ♘b6 ♘h5 17 ♕h3 ♕xb6! (17...♘f4 18 ♗xf4 ♕xb6 19 ♗e3 ♘d3 20 ♘f5 exf5 21 ♗xb6 ♘f4 22 cxb4) 18 ♕xh5 ♘d3 19 ♘f5 exf5 20 ♗xb6 ♘f4 21 ♗a4 ♘xh5 22 ♗xd7 bxc3, or 16 cxb4 ♕xb4 17 ♘c2 ♕b7, German-Spangenberg, Villa Martelli 1997.

d4) 15 c4!? ♘d3 (15...bxc3 – *15 c3 bxc3*) 16 ♖cd1 ♘h5 17 ♕g4 ♘hf4 18 ♗xf4 e5 19 ♘f5 ♗xf5 20 exf5 ♘xf4 21 f6! ♗xf6 22 ♖xd6 deserves to be investigated.

e) 14 ♘e2!? (so as to ensure ...♘e5 can be met by ♘b6):

e1) 14...♖b8 15 c4 bxc3 16 ♘exc3 ± ; e.g., 16...♕a8 17 ♖fd1 a5 18 ♔h1 ♗a6 19 ♗h6!, Istratescu-Röder, Groningen open 1997.

e2) 14...♘e5 15 ♘b6!? (15 ♖ad1 – *14 ♖ad1 ♘e5 15 ♘e2*).

e3) 14...a5!? 15 c4 bxc3 (15...♖a6!? Gallagher) 16 ♘exc3 (16 ♘axc3!?), and now 16...♕b8 (Gallagher) seems quite playable for Black.

e4) The immediate 14...♕b8!? is interesting (generally, this is a typical answer to an early ♘e2); for example, 15 c4 bxc3 16 ♘exc3 ♗b7!? with equality, Macieja-Vasilchenko, Zlin 1995.

f) 14 ♖ad1!? *(D)* (White refuses to attack solely along the c-file but instead amasses his forces across the entire board). Now:

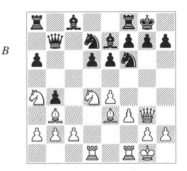

*B*

f1) 14...a5?! 15 c4!.

f2) 14...♘e5 and then:

f21) Black experiences no problems after 15 ♖fe1 ♗d7 16 ♘b6 ♘h5 17 ♕h3 ♘f4 18 ♗xf4 ♕xb6 19 ♗e3 ♕c7 20 f4 ♘c4, Petelin-Galkin, St Petersburg 1993.

f22) 15 ♖d2 is also answered by 15...♗d7!, with the same ideas.

f23) 15 ♘b6 ♘h5 16 ♕h3 ♘f4 (16...♕xb6!?) 17 ♗xf4 ♕xb6 with good chances for equality: 18 ♕g3 ♕c7 19 ♗g5 (19 ♗e3 can be met by 19...♗f6 or 19...♘c4) 19...♗xg5 20

♕xg5 ♘c4!? 21 ♗xc4 ♕xc4 22 ♕e7 ♕xa2.

f24) 15 ♘e2!? ♗d7 (15...a5 16 c4 bxc3 17 ♘exc3 is slightly better for White) 16 ♘b6 ♗b5 17 ♖fe1 (17 ♖d2!? Zapolskis; 17 ♘xa8 ♗xe2 18 ♘b6 ♖b8! is good for Black, Pokorna-Bojković, Batumi wom Echt 1999) 17...♖ab8 18 c4 ♗e8 (18...bxc3!?), and instead of 19 ♖d2 with sharp play, Zapolskis-Lalić, Olomouc ECC 1996, also interesting is 19 ♘f4!? with the point 19...♕c6 (19...♕c7 20 c5!) 20 c5 dxc5 21 ♘c4 ♘xc4 22 ♗xc4 ♗d6 23 ♕h4.

f3) 14...♔h8 is the most frequent answer:

f31) 15 ♕f2 ♘e5!? with a normal game.

f32) 15 ♖fe1 ♖b8 (15...♘e5!?) 16 ♔h1 (16 c3 bxc3 17 ♘xc3 ♘c5!?) 16...♘e5 17 ♘e2 ♕c7 18 c3 ♗d7 and Black stands at least no worse, Short-Kasparov, London rpd (2) 1993.

f33) 15 ♔h1 ♘e5 (15...♖b8!? 16 ♕e1 ♕a8 17 c4 bxc3 18 ♕xc3 ♗b7 gave Black a good game in Hamdouchi-Topalov, Cap d'Agde 1994) 16 ♘b6 ♘h5 17 ♕h3 ♘f4 18 ♗xf4 ♕xb6 19 ♗e3 ♕c7 followed by ...♘c4 =.

f34) 15 ♘e2 and then:

f341) After 15...a5 16 c4 (16 ♖d2!? is also interesting) 16...bxc3 White has 17 ♘axc3 (17 ♘exc3 ♕b8 transposes to line 'f342') 17...♖b8 18 ♘d4!?.

f342) 15...♕b8! 16 c3 bxc3 17 ♘exc3 a5 18 ♖f2 ♗a6 19 ♕h3 ♘e5 20 ♗d4 ♘c6 21 ♗e3 ♘e5 = Mitkov-Gelfand, Moscow OL 1994.

f35) 15 ♖d2 ♘e5 16 ♘e2 (16 ♘b6 ♖b8 17 ♘e2 ♕c6 =) 16...a5 17 ♖fd1 ♗d7 is possibly also satisfactory for Black, Pinus-D.Popović, corr. 1999.

We now return to 14 ♖fd1 *(D)*:

**14...♘e5!**

Other moves:

a) 14...♖e8 15 ♖ac1 ♗f8 16 c4 ± Mikhalchishin-A.Petrosian, Lviv 1994.

b) 14...a5 15 c4 bxc3 16 bxc3 ♕a6 17 c4 ± Bouaziz-Ady, Erevan OL 1996.

c) 14...♖b8 15 ♖ac1 ♘e5 16 c4! (16 c3 ♗d7! = Firnhaber-Schmidt, corr. 1996) 16...bxc3 17 ♘xc3 (17 ♖xc3 ♗d7 18 ♘b6 ♕xb6!? 19 ♘xe6 ♕xe3+ 20 ♖xe3 ♗xe6 is a less convincing line) 17...♗d7 18 f4 with an initiative, Veröci-Farkas, Hungarian Cht 1997.

d) 14...♔h8 15 ♖ac1 (15 ♘e2 ♕b8! 16 ♖ac1 a5 17 c4 bxc3 18 ♕xc3 ♗b7 ½-½ Istratescu-A.Petrosian, Berlin 1996; 15 ♖d2!?) 15...♘e5 (15...♘c5 16 ♘xc5 dxc5 17 ♘e2 ±) and now:

d1) 16 ♘e2 a5 (16...♖b8!? *Fritz6*-Van Wely, Eindhoven rpd 2000) 17 c4 bxc3 18 ♖xc3 (18 ♘exc3!? ♖a6 19 f4 ♘g6 20 ♗c4 ♖c6 21 ♗d3 ♕b8 22 ♕f3 with a complicated game and possibly some advantage for White, Zapata-Morović, Yopal 1997) 18...♗d7 (Gallagher suggests 18...♗a6!?, with the point 19 ♖dc1 ♗d7 20 ♖c7 ♕b4) 19 ♘b6 ♖a6 20 ♘xd7 ♘exd7 21 ♖dc1 a4

22 ♗c2 ± Zapata-Morović, Havana 1997.

d2) 16 c4!?.

d3) 16 c3 ♗d7 17 ♘b6 ♘h5 18 ♕h3 ♕xb6 19 ♕xh5 ♕b7 20 ♗g5 is slightly better for White, Neelakantan-King, Calcutta 1993.

**15 c4**

Or:

a) 15 ♖ac1 ♗d7! gives Black good play: 16 c4 bxc3 17 ♖xc3 ♗xa4 (17...♖fc8!?) 18 ♗xa4 ♕xb2 19 ♕e1 ♕b4 or 16 ♘b6 ♘h5 17 ♕h3 (Emms-Gallagher, Bundesliga 1996/7) and now Gallagher gives 17...♕xb6 18 ♕xh5 ♕b7!.

b) 15 a3 bxa3 16 ♖xa3 ♗d7 17 ♘e2 (17 ♘b6 ♘h5) 17...♗b5 18 ♘ec3 ♘ed7 and Black is OK, K.Müller-Wahls, Hamburg 1995.

c) 15 ♘e2 ♖b8 (Gallagher's idea 15...a5!? is better; e.g., 16 a3 ♖a6 ∞) 16 ♘b6 ♕c7 17 ♘xc8 ♖fxc8 18 c4 (18 c3 ♘c4!) 18...bxc3 (18...♘xc4 19 ♖ac1! ±) 19 ♖ac1 ± Zapata-Herrera, Santa Clara 1996.

d) 15 ♘b6 ♘h5 (15...♖b8!?) 16 ♕h3 ♘f4 (16...♕xb6!?) 17 ♗xf4 ♕xb6 18 ♗e3 ♕c7 with roughly equal chances: 19 c3 ♘c4!? (19...bxc3 20 ♖ac1 ♕b7 21 ♖xc3 ♗d7 22 f4) 20 ♗xc4 ♕xc4 21 cxb4 ♗f6!, Vujadinović-Schoonhoven, corr. 2000.

e) 15 c3 bxc3 transposes to the main line.

**15...bxc3**

15...♗d7 16 c5!?.

**16 ♘xc3**

16 bxc3 (Hakki-Gallagher, Istanbul OL 2000) 16...♕c7!?.

**16...♘g6!**

16...♗d7 17 f4 ±.

**17 ♖ac1**

17 f4? ♘xe4 18 ♘xe4 ♕xe4 19 ♖ac1 ♗h4 ∓.

**17...♗d7 18 ♗c2 ♖fc8 19 ♕f2 ♕c7 20 ♖dc1 ♖ac8**

The chances are equal, Kobaliya-Gallagher, Biel 1997.

Therefore, after 9...♕b6 10 ♗e3 ♕b7 11 ♕g3, both the extremely risky 11...♘bd7!? and the reliable 11...b4! appear to be viable. As regards 10 ♗g5!?, Black has to work out the most precise move-order.

**B)**

**9...♕c7** *(D)*

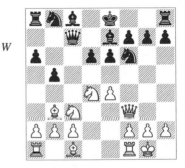

Now, after 10 ♕g3, Black has two main possibilities. The first is 10...0-0 11 ♗h6 ♘e8, and then 12 ♖ad1 ♗d7. The second is 10...♘c6 11 ♘xc6 ♕xc6 12 ♖e1 ♗b7!.

The tricky move 10 ♖e1!? slightly devalues the early ...♘c6 but provides Black with other good possibilities, such as 10...0-0 11 ♕g3 ♔h8 (or 11...b4).

Thus, we shall discuss:

**B1: 10 ♖e1!?**  74
**B2: 10 ♕g3**  76

White's alternatives are less interesting:

a) 10 e5?! ♗b7! (10...dxe5? is met by 11 ♘dxb5!) 11 exd6 ♗xd6 12 ♕h3 0-0.

b) 10 a3 allows Black to play 10...♘bd7! 11 ♕g3 ♘c5 = in addition to the standard 10...♘c6 and 10...0-0.

c) 10 ♗g5 ♘bd7! = Lutikov-Polugaevsky, USSR Ch (Leningrad) 1960. Now 11 ♖fe1 0-0 – *10 ♖e1 0-0 11 ♗g5 ♘bd7.*

## B1)
**10 ♖e1!? 0-0**

Other moves:

a) 10...♗b7? 11 ♗xe6 fxe6 12 ♘xe6 ♕d7 13 ♘xg7+ ♔f7 14 ♘f5 ±.

b) 10...♘bd7 11 ♕g3 ♘c5? (Black should try 11...b4!?) 12 ♘f5! ± Emms-Rashkovsky, Hastings 1995/6.

c) 10...♘c6 11 ♘xc6 (11 e5?! ♘xd4 12 ♕xa8 dxe5 13 ♗g5 0-0, Vink-Najer, Groningen 1999) 11...♕xc6 and then:

c1) 12 ♕g3 transposes to Line B22.

c2) 12 a3 ♗b7! (12...0-0 transposes to note 'c1' to White's 11th move) 13 ♕g3 again transposes to Line B22.

c3) 12 ♗g5! and now:

c31) 12...0-0? 13 ♘d5! exd5 14 ♗xd5! ±.

c32) 12...♗b7 13 ♗xf6! gxf6 14 ♖e3!? ♕c5 looks dubious though there is no straightforward win. 15 ♗d5 and 15 ♘d5 are both answered by 15...exd5 16 exd5 ♔d8, while 15 a4 ♖g8 (or 15...f5!?, but not 15...b4? 16 ♘d5 exd5 17 exd5 ♔d8 18 ♖ae1 ♖e8 19 ♖xe7 ♖xe7 20 ♕xf6 ♕c7 21 a5 +–) isn't clear-cut either.

c33) 12...♖b8 13 ♖ad1 is slightly better for White.

c34) 12...♖a7!? 13 a4 b4 14 a5 0-0 15 ♘a2, followed by 16 ♗d2, gives White slightly the better chances.

d) 10...b4 11 ♘a4 0-0 12 c3 (12 ♕g3/12 ♗g5 transposes to *10...0-0 11 ♕g3/11 ♗g5 b4 12 ♘a4* but 12 e5!? appears interesting) 12...bxc3 13 ♘xc3 ♘bd7 14 ♕g3 ♘e5 15 ♗g5 ♗d7 = K.Müller-Lutz, Berlin 1989.

e) 10...♗d7 is interesting; e.g., 11 ♘d5? exd5 12 exd5 ♗g4; 11 a3 ♘c6 12 ♘xc6 ♗xc6 =; 11 e5!? dxe5 12 ♗f4; or 11 ♕g3 ♘c6!?.

**11 ♕g3**

Otherwise:

a) 11 a4 b4 12 ♘a2 ♗b7 13 ♗d2 ♕b6 14 c3 with roughly equal chances, Bronstein-Slutsky, Moscow 1979.

b) 11 ♗g5 is not strong here:

b1) 11...b4 12 ♘a4 ♘c6 (Black can investigate 12...♗d7!? and 12...♘bd7!? with the point 13 e5 dxe5 14 ♘xe6 fxe6 15 ♕xa8 ♗b7 16 ♕a7 ♗c5!) 13 ♘xc6 ♕xc6 14 c3 ± del Rio-Van Zyl, Medellin jr Wch 1996.

b2) 11...♘bd7 is enough for equality: 12 e5? dxe5 13 ♘xe6 fxe6 14 ♕xa8 ♗b7 –+; 12 ♖ad1 ♘e5 (12...♘c5!?); 12 ♕g3 ♘e5 13 ♖ad1 b4!?, Ma.Ankerst-Shneider, Pula 1994.

c) 11 a3 gives Black a satisfactory choice:

c1) 11...♘c6 12 ♘xc6 ♕xc6 and then:

c11) 13 ♗g5 ♗b7 14 ♖ad1 ♖fd8 15 ♕g3 a5 16 ♗h6 ♗f8 17 ♗g5 ♗e7 = Vasiukov-Polugaevsky, USSR Ch (Moscow) 1969.

c12) 13 ♕g3 ♔h8 (13...♘h5?! 14 ♕h3 ♘f6 15 ♗g5 ♗b7 16 ♖e3!, Short-Ehlvest, Moscow rpd 1994) – *11 ♕g3 ♔h8 12 a3 ♘c6 13 ♘xc6 ♕xc6.*

c2) 11...♗d7!? 12 ♕g3 ♘c6 13 ♘xc6 ♗xc6 14 ♗h6 ♘e8 – *10 ♕g3 0-0 11 ♗h6 ♘e8 12 a3 ♗d7 13 ♖fe1 ♘c6 14 ♘xc6 ♗xc6 =.*

c3) 11...♗b7!? 12 ♕h3 ♘c6 =.

c4) 11...♘bd7!? 12 ♕g3 ♘e5 with good play after 13 f4 (or 13 ♗h6 ♘h5 14 ♕h3 ♘f6 15 ♕g3 ♘g6!?, Emms-Lutz, Hamburg 1995) 13...♘c4 14 ♗xc4 ♕xc4 15 ♗e3 ♗b7, Ardian-syah-Ljubojević, Manila 1973.

We now return to the position after 11 ♕g3 *(D)*:

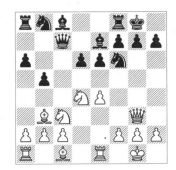

**11...♔h8**

Or:

a) 11...♘c6 12 ♘xc6 ♕xc6 transposes to *10 ♕g3 ♘c6 11 ♘xc6 ♕xc6 12 ♖e1 0-0* (White avoids *12...♗b7!*).

b) 11...♗d7 12 ♗h6 ♘e8 transposes to *10 ♕g3 0-0 11 ♗h6 ♘e8 12 ♖fe1 ♗d7* (White avoids *12...♗f6!*).

c) 11...♖d8 12 ♗h6 ♘e8 13 ♖ad1 (13 ♘f5?! exf5 14 ♘d5 f4!) 13...♘c6? 14 ♘d5 +− Emms-Glenne, Gausdal 1995.

d) 11...♖e8 12 a3! ♘c6 13 ♘xc6 ♕xc6 14 ♗h6 ♗f8 15 ♖ad1 ♗b7 16 ♖d3 ♔h8 17 ♕h4 ♘d7 18 ♗c1 with an advantage for White, Ehlvest-H.Olafsson, St John 1988.

e) 11...♘h5 12 ♕h3 ♘f6 13 a3 ♖e8 14 f4 (14 ♗g5!) 14...♘c6 15 ♘xc6 ♕xc6 16 ♔h1 ♗d8 ∞ Õim-Hertel, corr. 1988.

f) 11...b4!? is probably a good option: 12 ♘a4 (12 ♘d1 ♘c6 13 ♘xc6 ♕xc6 14 ♗h6 ♘e8 15 c3 ♔h8 = Repkova-Vasilchenko, Zlin 1995) 12...♗d7 (12...♘c6 13 ♘xc6 ♕xc6 14 ♗h6 ♘e8 15 c3 ± Riegler-Grosar, Maribor 1993; 12...e5 13 ♘f5 ±) 13 c3 (13 ♗h6 ♘h5!; 13 a3!?) 13...♕a5 14 cxb4 ♕xb4 and Black is no worse, Van Riemsdijk-Mecking, São Paulo Z 1993.

**12 ♗g5**

12 f4?! is weaker in view of 12...b4 13 ♘a4 ♘c6!.

12 a3 is not bad, however:

a) 12...♘c6 13 ♘xc6 ♕xc6 14 ♗g5 ♘h5 (14...♗b7!? 15 ♖ad1 ♖ad8 is roughly equal) 15 ♕h4 ♗xg5 16 ♕xg5 ♘f6 17 ♖ad1 ♗b7 transposes to note 'd' to Black's 15th move in Line B221.

b) 12...♗d7 13 ♗g5 ♘c6 14 ♘xc6 (14 ♖ad1!? – *12 ♗g5 ♗d7 13 ♖ad1 ♘c6 14 a3*) 14...♗xc6 15 ♖ad1 and there followed 15...♖fd8!? 16 ♖d3 a5 17 ♕h4 ♘g8 with sharp play in Dabrowska-Mukhutdinov, Cappelle la Grande 1995.

**12...b4**

Alternatively:

a) 12...♘c6? 13 ♘xc6 ♕xc6 14 ♘d5 ±.

b) 12...h6 13 ♕h4 b4 14 ♘a4 ♕a5 (14...♗d7!?; 14...♗g8!? 15 ♗xh6 gxh6 16 ♕xh6 ♘g4 17 ♕h5 ♘f6) 15 f4 e5 (15...♗g8 16 ♗xh6 gxh6 17 e5!) 16 ♘f5 with an initiative, Gi.Hernandez-Pigusov, Santa Clara 1991.

c) 12...♗d7 13 ♕h4!? (13 ♖ad1 ♘c6 14 a3 brought White success in one game: 14...♘a5 15 ♖e3 ♘h5 16 ♕h4 ♗xg5 17 ♕xg5 ♘f6 18 ♖g3 ♖g8 19 ♖h3 ♕c5?! 20 ♘f3 ♘xb3 21 e5! ± Motylev-Leitão, Guarapuava jr Wch

1995) 13...♘c6 14 ♘ce2 (14 ♘xc6 ♗xc6 15 ♖e3 ♘g8 16 ♗xe7 ♘xe7 17 ♖d1 a5 is unclear, Liepold-Kuczynski, Erlangen 1990) 14...h6 (14...♘e5!? Mikhalchishin) 15 ♖ad1 ♘e5 16 f4! ♘g6 17 ♕h3 gives White the initiative, Minasian-Zagorskis, Frunze 1989.

**13 ♘a4 ♗d7**

13...♘c6 14 ♘xc6 ♕xc6 15 c3 (or 15 ♕h4!?) is insufficient for equality, but 13...♗b7!? is interesting.

**14 c3 ♘c6!**

Black has good play, Drozdov-Shneider, Voroshilovgrad 1987.

**B2)**

**10 ♕g3** *(D)*

Now:

**B21: 10...0-0** 77
**B22: 10...♘c6** 85

Other moves seldom occur:

a) After 10...♗d7, it is necessary to take into account not only 11 ♕xg7 but also 11 ♘f5!? exf5 12 ♕xg7 ♖f8 13 ♗g5 ♕d8 14 exf5.

b) 10...g6 11 ♖e1 (11 ♗h6!? is possible) 11...♗d7 12 ♕f3!? gives White the better chances, Mortensen-Frick, Manila OL 1992.

c) 10...♗b7 11 ♗xe6! (11 ♖e1 ♘c6! =; 11 f3 ♘c6 12 ♘xc6 ♕xc6 13 ♕xg7 ♖g8 14 ♕h6 0-0-0 ∞ A.Sokolov-Renet, Clichy 1993) 11...fxe6 12 ♘xe6, and Black has problems:

c1) 12...♕c4 13 ♘xg7+ ♔d8 14 ♗g5 ♘bd7 15 ♖ad1 ♖g8 (15...♔c7? 16 ♗xf6 ♘xf6 17 e5) 16 ♘f5 ±.

c2) 12...♕d7 13 ♘xg7+ ♔d8 (or 13...♔f8 14 ♘f5 ♖g8 15 ♗g5!? b4 16 ♘xe7 ♕xe7 17 ♘d5) 14 ♗g5! (but not 14 e5?! ♖g8!).

d) 10...b4!? and now:

d1) 11 ♘ce2 and then:

d11) 11...♘xe4 12 ♕xg7 ♗f6 13 ♕h6!? is good for White.

d12) 11...♕b7 12 f3 g6 13 ♗g5! is also better for White, Mitkov-Sorena, Olot 1993.

d13) 11...0-0 12 ♗h6 ♘e8 13 c3 bxc3 14 ♘xc3 ♗f6 (14...♘d7? 15 ♗xe6! fxe6 16 ♘xe6 ♕c4 17 ♘xg7 +−) 15 ♗e3 ±.

d14) 11...g6 12 ♗h6! (Fischer; 12 c3? ♘xe4 13 ♕e3 ♘f6!? 14 cxb4 0-0 ∓ Fischer-F.Olafsson, Buenos Aires 1960; 12 f3? e5 ∓; not wholly clear is 12 ♕e3 0-0 13 c3 a5 14 cxb4 axb4 15 ♗d2 ♕b7 16 ♘g3, Pikula-Kuczynski, Katowice 1991) 12...♘xe4 (or 12...e5 13 ♗g7 ♖g8 14 ♗xf6 ♗xf6 15 ♘f5 Mikhalchishin) 13 ♕e3 ♘c5 (13...d5 14 c4!) 14 ♗g7 ♖g8 15 ♕h6 ♗f8 16 ♗xf8 ♖xf8 17 ♘f4 with an initiative, Dementiev-Mukhin, USSR 1974.

d15) 11...♘c6!? appears quite playable.

d2) 11 ♘a4 and now:

d21) 11...♘xe4 12 ♕xg7 ♗f6 13 ♕g4 d5 (13...♕b7 14 ♘xe6! fxe6 15 ♖e1) 14 ♗e3 h5 (14...♗d7 15 c4! bxc3 16 ♘xc3 ♘xc3 17 ♖ac1 ± M.Hoffmann-Rechel, Bochum jr 1989) 15 ♕e2 with an advantage, Jaracz-Van der Stricht, Arnhem jr Ech 1990.

d22) 11...g6 12 f3 ♘c6 13 ♘xc6 ♕xc6 14 &e3 is clearly better for White, Kapić-Klaić, corr. 1996.

d23) 11...0-0 12 &h6 ♘e8 13 c3 (13 &e3 &d7!? 14 ♘b6 ♕xb6 15 ♘xe6 ∞) 13...&f6 (13...bxc3 14 ♘xc3 – *11 ♘ce2 0-0 12 &h6 ♘e8 13 c3 bxc3 14 ♘xc3* ±; 13...♘c6 14 ♘xc6!? ♕xc6 15 ♖fe1 ±) 14 &e3 &b7 15 f3 ±.

d24) 11...♘c6 12 ♘xc6 (12 c3 should be met not by 12...&d7 13 ♖e1 bxc3 14 ♘xc6! ±, but 12...&b7! with good play; e.g., 13 ♖e1 ♘xd4 14 cxd4 &xe4 15 ♘c5 &f5 16 &a4+ ♔f8, Bosboom-Vanheste, Dutch Ch (Hilversum) 1988) 12...♕xc6 13 f3 (13 ♖e1 Ehlvest) 13...0-0 14 &h6 (14 &e3!?) 14...♘h5 (14...♘e8 15 &e3 ♖b8 16 ♕f2 &d8, Ehlvest-Timman, Reykjavik 1988, 17 ♖ad1 f5 18 e5!? ±) 15 ♕g4 g6 16 &xf8 ♔xf8 17 e5! dxe5 18 ♖fe1 ± (Nikitin).

## B21)
**10...0-0 11 &h6**
Or:

a) 11 ♖e1 – *10 ♖e1 0-0 11 ♕g3*.

b) 11 a3 is seldom played. Then:

b1) 11...♘c6 12 ♘xc6 ♕xc6 13 &h6 ♘e8 – *11 &h6 ♘e8 12 a3 ♘c6 13 ♘xc6 ♕xc6*.

b2) 11...&d7 12 &h6 ♘e8 – *11 &h6 ♘e8 12 a3 &d7*.

b3) 11...♔h8!? is one more option; e.g., 12 &e3 (12 ♖e1 – *10 ♖e1 0-0 11 ♕g3 ♔h8 12 a3*) 12...♘c6 13 ♘xc6 (13 f4 transposes to note 'b2' to White's 10th move in Line B3 of Chapter 14) 13...♕xc6 14 &d4 with double-edged play, Waitzkin-Fedorowicz, New York 1992.

**11...♘e8** (D)

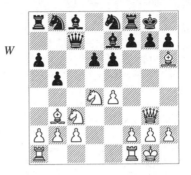

Many grandmasters, headed by Gelfand, prefer this line where Black has a very compact position and plans, above all, to complete his mobilization (e.g., 12...&d7 and 13...♘c6).

**12 ♖ad1**
White has made plenty of other attempts to maintain the initiative:

a) 12 &e3 retreats the bishop prematurely; e.g., 12...&b7 (12...♘d7!?) 13 f3 ♘c6 14 ♖ad1 ♘a5 with good play for Black.

b) 12 &g5 = is also premature.

c) 12 a4 &f6!? (12...b4) 13 ♖fd1 b4 14 ♘ce2 ♔h8 15 &e3 ♘d7 16 c3 bxc3 17 ♘xc3 (Donges-Davis, corr. 1995) 17...♖b8 with counterplay.

d) 12 ♔h1 is Morozevich's move; the idea is f4. Then:

d1) After 12...&f6, 13 ♖ad1 is a logical reply, with the point 13...&e5 14 f4.

d2) 12...♘c6 and now neither 13 ♘xc6 ♕xc6 14 a4 b4 15 ♘d5 &d8 16 a5 ♕b7 nor 13 ♘d5 exd5 14 ♘xc6 dxe4 15 ♘xe7+ ♕xe7 16 a4 is wholly clear.

d3) 12...b4!? is an interesting possibility.

d4) 12...♗b7!? has the point 13 ♗xe6?! ♗f6! 14 ♘d5 ♕d8.

d5) 12...♗d7 13 f4 ♘c6 and now:

d51) 14 ♘xc6 ♗xc6 15 f5!? ♔h8 16 fxe6 gxh6 17 ♖xf7 ♖xf7 18 exf7 ∞ Morozevich.

d52) 14 ♖ad1 ♘xd4!? (14...b4) 15 ♖xd4 and now Black should continue 15...a5! 16 f5 ♗f6. Weaker is 15...♗f6 16 ♖d3!; e.g., 16...♔h8 (16...b4 17 e5!; 16...a5 17 e5!) 17 ♗g5 b4 (or 17...♗xg5 18 fxg5! b4 19 ♖df3!?) 18 ♗xf6 ♘xf6 19 e5!.

d53) 14 ♘f3 b4 (or 14...♘a5!? 15 e5 ♗c6 16 f5 dxe5 17 ♘xe5 ♘xb3 18 cxb3 exf5 19 ♖xf5 ♗b7 with good play, Kobaliya-Vaulin, Krasnodar 1997) 15 ♘e2 ♘a5 (15...a5!?) 16 ♘ed4 (16 e5 ♘xb3 17 cxb3 ♕c2 18 ♘ed4 ♕g6 Morozevich) 16...♕b7 (16...♘xb3 17 cxb3 ♔h8 18 ♗g5 f6 19 ♗h4 e5 ∞ Morozevich) 17 e5 ± Morozevich-Gelfand, Madrid 1996.

d4) 14 ♘ce2 ♔h8 15 ♗g5 ♘f6 16 ♕h4 ♖ae8 17 f5 ♘xd4 18 ♘xd4 exf5 19 ♖ae1 ♗d8 20 ♘xf5 ♗xf5 21 ♖xf5 ♖e5 = Morozevich-Vaulin, Krasnodar 1997.

e) 12 a3 (D) (this has no advantages over 12 ♖ad1 ♗d7 13 a3), and now:

e1) Inexact is 12...♔h8 13 ♗e3 (13 ♗g5!?) 13...♘c6 (13...♘f6 14 f4 and now 14...♘c6 15 f5 ± or 14...♕b7 15 f5!) 14 ♘xc6 (14 ♘d5?? ♘xd4!; 14 f4 ♘a5!?) 14...♕xc6 15 f4! with better chances for White.

e2) 12...♘c6 13 ♘xc6 ♕xc6 14 ♖ad1 (14 ♘d5 ♗d8! suits Black; instead, 14 ♖fe1 ♗b7 transposes to Line B221) 14...a5 (14...♗b7 is better; then 15 ♖fe1 again transposes to Line B221) 15 ♖fe1 a4 16 ♗a2 ♖b8 17 ♖d4 ± ♗f6?! 18 e5!, Mowsziszian-Bangiev, Simferopol 1985.

e3) 12...♗f6!? 13 ♗e3 ♘c6 is playable, since Black need not worry about 14 ♘xc6 ♕xc6 15 ♘d5 ♗d8 16 ♗b6 ♕d7.

e4) 12...♗d7 13 ♖fe1 (13 f4? ♕c5 −+; the main move 13 ♖ad1 transposes to Line B211) 13...♘c6 (also good here is 13...♗f6) 14 ♘xc6 (14 ♖ad1 – 12 ♖ad1 ♗d7 13 a3 ♘c6 14 ♖fe1 =) 14...♗xc6 15 ♖e3?! (Arizmendi-Pelletier, Bermuda 1999; 15 ♖ad1 transposes to note 'c' to White's 15th move in Line B211; 15 ♗g5 =) 15...♔h8! 16 ♗g5 f6 Ftačnik.

It remains only to discuss the moves of the rooks:

f) 12 ♖ae1 ♔h8 (12...♗f6!?) 13 ♗e3 ♗d7 (13...b4!?) 14 f4 (14 a3!?) 14...b4 15 ♘ce2 ♘c6 16 f5 e5 17 ♘xc6 ♗xc6 18 ♕f3 ♘f6 19 ♘g3 (Baciu-Vasiesiu, Bucharest 1998) 19...♕b7 with unclear play.

g) 12 ♖fd1 ♗d7 and then:

g1) 13 ♘f3 ♘c6 (13...b4!? is playable) 14 ♘e2 ♘e5!? (14...♖d8 15 ♘f4 ♔h8 16 ♗g5 ± Waitzkin-Lesiège, Bermuda 1995) 15 ♘fd4 ♔h8 16 ♗c1 ♘f6 17 f3 ♘c4 with good play, Ashley-Wojtkiewicz, New York 1994.

g2) 13 ♘ce2 ♕b7 14 f3 a5 15 a3 ♘c6 16 ♘xc6 ♗xc6 17 c3 (Zapata-Paramos Dominguez, Varadero 2000) and I see no advantage for White after 17...b4!?.

h) 12 ♖fe1 (Kasparov played this in the first of his games against Gelfand but in the next two he chose the more useful 12 ♖ad1). Now:

h1) 12...♘c6?! can be countered by 13 ♘d5!.

h2) 12...♗b7 appears risky but no direct refutation can be found; e.g., 13 ♗xe6 ♗f6 14 ♘d5 ♕d8 15 e5 ♗h4!.

h3) 12...b4 has not yet been played.

h4) 12...♔h8 13 ♗g5 (13 ♗e3 ♘f6 =) 13...♘f6 (13...♗xg5 14 ♕xg5 and now, rather than 14...h6 15 ♕h4 ♘c6 16 ♘xc6 ♕xc6 17 a4 b4 18 ♘d5! ± T.Thorhallsson-Arnason, Hafnarfirdi 1992, 14...♕c5!? gives Black chances of equalizing, Coleman-Arnason, Philadelphia 1993) 14 ♖ad1 ± (14 f4? ♕a7) transposes to *12 ♖ad1 ♔h8 13 ♗g5 ♘f6 14 ♖fe1*.

h5) 12...♗d7 (we were interested in this position in connection with *10 ♖e1 0-0 11 ♕g3 ♗d7*) and now:

h51) 13 a3 – *12 a3 ♗d7 13 ♖fe1*.

h52) 13 ♖ad1 – *12 ♖ad1 ♗d7 13 ♖fe1*.

h53) 13 ♘f5 is at best unclear: 13...exf5 14 ♘d5 ♕d8 15 exf5, and now Black can play 15...♗f6!?.

h54) No advantage is achieved after 13 ♗g5 ♗xg5 14 ♕xg5 ♘c6 15 ♘xc6 ♗xc6 16 a3 ♘f6 17 ♖ad1 ♖ad8 =, as in Kutuzović-Wojtkiewicz, Nova Gorica 1997.

h55) 13 ♘ce2 ♘c6 14 ♘xc6 ♕xc6 15 ♘f4 ♔h8 16 ♗g5 ♗xg5 17 ♕xg5 ♘f6 = Minasian-Am.Rodriguez, Lucerne Wcht 1993.

h56) 13 a4!? b4 (13...♗f6!? is another idea) 14 ♘ce2 ♘c6 (14...♕b7 15 ♖ad1!; 14...♔h8 15 ♗g5 ♗xg5 16 ♕xg5 ♘f6 17 ♘g3 ♘c6 18 ♘xc6 ♗xc6 19 ♖ad1 ± Kasparov-Gelfand, Paris rpd 1991) 15 ♘xc6 ♗xc6 16 ♘d4 ♗b7 17 ♖ad1 and now, instead of 17...♗f6?! 18 ♗c1! with an advantage, Magomedov-Vaulin, Cheliabinsk 1990, better is 17...♔h8 18 ♗g5 ♗xg5 19 ♕xg5 ♘f6 (Magomedov).

h6) 12...♗f6(!) and now:

h61) 13 ♖ad1? ♗e5! is most likely winning for Black; e.g., 14 ♕g4 ♗xd4 (14...♔h8!?) 15 ♖xd4 e5 16 ♕g5 exd4 17 ♘d5 ♕c5 18 e5 (18 ♘f6+ ♔h8 19 ♗xg7+ ♘xg7 20 ♕h6 ♗f5 wins for Black) 18...♔h8! 19 ♖e4 (Gdanski-Kempinski, Polish Ch (Gdansk) 1994) and now 19...gxh6!? 20 ♕xh6 ♖g8 21 ♘f6 ♗f5! or 19...♗e6!.

h62) 13 ♗e3 leads to approximately equal play.

h63) If 13 ♘f3, then Black should avoid 13...♗xc3 14 bxc3 ♕xc3 15 ♖ad1 ♗b7 16 ♖d3 ♕c7 17 ♘g5! ± Vavra-Lesiège, Parana jr Wch 1991. Instead, 13...♘d7 or 13...b4!? gives Black good chances.

We now return to the position after 12 ♖ad1 *(D)*:

*B*

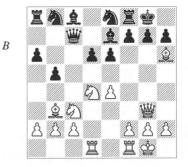

**12...♗d7**

Other moves have occurred much less frequently:

a) 12...♗b7?! 13 ♗xe6! ±.

b) 12...♘c6 13 ♘d5! ♘xd4 (alternatively, 13...exd5 14 ♘xc6 dxe4 15 ♘xe7+ ♕xe7 16 ♗g5 ♕d7 17 ♕h4!) 14 ♘xe7+ ♕xe7 15 ♖xd4 is slightly better for White, Velička-Hybl, Pardubice 1995.

c) 12...♗f6 13 ♗g5 (13 f4? ♗xd4+! 14 ♖xd4 ♕a7; 13 ♘ce2!? ♘c6 14 c3 ♔h8 15 ♗g5 ♗b7 16 ♖fe1 ♗xg5 17 ♕xg5 ♘f6 is satisfactory for Black, Macieja-Kempinski, Warsaw 1995; 13 ♗e3!? could be tried) 13...♗xg5 14 ♕xg5 ♕c5 15 ♕d2 (15 ♕e3!? Ehlvest) 15...♗d7 16 ♖fe1 with a slight advantage for White, Ehlvest-Gavrikov, USSR Ch (Moscow) 1988.

d) 12...♔h8 13 ♗g5 (13 ♗e3!? is an idea) 13...♘f6 (13...♗xg5 14 ♕xg5 ±; 13...b4 14 ♗xe7 ♕xe7 15 ♘a4, and now 15...♖a7 16 ♖fe1 ± or 15...♗b7 16 ♘b6 ♖a7 17 ♕e3 ♘f6 18 ♘d5 ±) and now:

d1) 14 ♕h4 is unclear; for example, 14...♖e8 (14...b4!?) 15 ♖d3 ♘bd7, and now 16 f4 b4! was good for Black in Rudensky-Cabarkapa, blind 1980.

d2) Calmer is 14 ♖fe1 b4 (14...♖e8 15 a3!?) 15 ♘a4 with some advantage.

d3) Or 14 a3 ±; e.g., 14...♘bd7?! 15 ♗xe6; 14...♘c6?! 15 ♘xc6 ♕xc6 16 ♗xf6!, K.Grosar-Stiri, Wuppertal wom ECC 1998.

e) 12...b4!? has not been sufficiently studied:

e1) 13 ♘ce2 ♘c6 (13...♗f6!?; 13...a5 is weaker in view of 14 ♘f4!, Bennedik-Cijs, corr. 1999) 14 ♘f3 (14 ♖fe1 ♘e5!? and 14 ♘xc6 ♕xc6 15 ♘d4 ♕xe4 are both unclear) 14...♗f6

15 c3 bxc3 16 ♘xc3 (Macieja-Warszawski, Brzeg Dolny 1995) 16...♘a5!? is unclear.

e2) 13 ♘a4 and now:

e21) 13...♘c6 14 ♗e3 (14 ♘xc6!? ♕xc6 15 ♖fe1) 14...♖b8 (14...♘f6 is well answered by 15 ♘b6!; 14...♗d7 – *13...♗d7 14 ♗e3 ♘c6*) 15 ♘xc6 ♕xc6 16 f3 ± Tokmachev-Ottenburg, corr. 1999.

e22) 13...♗d7 14 ♗e3 ♘c6 and now nothing is gained by 15 ♘f3 ♖b8! (15...♘f6 16 ♘b6! ±). Instead, 15 c4!? deserves attention.

We now return to the position after 12...♗d7 *(D)*:

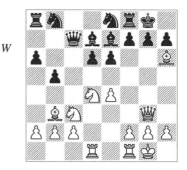

We have reached another important crossroads. We shall discuss these three moves separately:

**B211: 13 a3**     81
**B212: 13 f4**     82
**B213: 13 ♘f3**     84

There remain:

a) 13 h4 (Lepeshkin) does not appear very logical.

b) 13 ♗e3 ♘c6! (13...b4 14 ♘a4 – *12...b4 13 ♘a4 ♗d7 14 ♗e3*), and after 14 f4 b4! Black takes over the initiative.

c) 13 ♔h1 ♘c6 14 f4 – *12 ♔h1 ♗d7 13 f4 ♘c6 14 ♖ad1*.

d) 13 ♖fe1 ♘c6 (13...♔h8 14 ♗g5!; 13...b4!?), and now:

d1) 14 ♔h1?! ♘a5 15 f4 ♘xb3 16 axb3?! b4 ∓ Ruisinger-de Firmian, Ticino 1993.

d2) 14 a3 – *13 a3 ♘c6 14 ♖fe1*.

d3) 14 ♘xc6 ♗xc6 15 ♗g5 (15 a3 – *13 a3 ♘c6 14 ♘xc6 ♗xc6 15 ♖fe1*) 15...♗xg5! (less convincing is 15...b4 16 ♘d5) 16 ♕xg5 b4!? = Veröci-Ruck, Hungary 1993.

d4) 14 ♗g5 ♗xg5 15 ♕xg5 b4 (15...h6 has also occurred) 16 ♘a4 (16 ♘ce2 ♘xd4 and 17...a5) 16...♖b8 17 c3 ♘xd4 18 ♖xd4 ♖xa4 19 ♗xa4 bxc3 20 b3 with approximately equal play, Oll-Gelfand, Sverdlovsk 1987.

d5) 14 ♘ce2!? ♘e5 (14...♔h8 15 ♗g5 gives White some advantage; 14...♘a5 15 ♘f4; 14...♘xd4 15 ♘xd4 a5 16 a3; 14...b4!?) 15 c3 ∞ Collas-Das, Calcutta 2000.

e) 13 ♘ce2!? (this is little studied, like line 'd5') 13...♘c6 (13...♔h8 14 ♗g5 ♗xg5 15 ♕xg5 ♘f6 16 ♘g3 ♘c6 17 c3 was the actual move-order of Lautier-Gelfand) 14 c3 (14 ♘f3 – *13 ♘f3 ♘c6 14 ♘e2*; 14 ♖fe1 – *13 ♖fe1 ♘c6 14 ♘e2*) 14...♔h8 (14...♘e5!?) 15 ♗g5 ♗xg5 16 ♕xg5 ♘f6 17 ♘g3 ♘a5 (17...♖ad8 18 f4 ±; 17...♘e5 18 ♖fe1! ♖ad8 19 ♘h5 Lautier) 18 ♖fe1 (18 f4 ♕c5! leads to equality – Lautier) 18...♕b6?! (18...♖ad8 Lautier) 19 ♘f3! ± Lautier-Gelfand, Las Vegas FIDE 1999.

**B211)**
    **13 a3** *(D)*
    **13...♘c6 14 ♘xc6**
Otherwise:

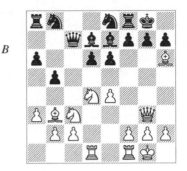

*B*

a) Not 14 f4? ♕b6 −+.

b) 14 ♗g5 is best met by 14...♘f6 = (rather than 14...♗xg5 15 ♕xg5, and now 15...♘e5 16 f4 ♘c4 17 ♗xc4 followed by 18 ♖f3, or 15...♘a5 16 ♖d3 ♘c4 17 ♖h3 ♘xb2? 18 ♘f5 +− Lepeshkin).

c) 14 ♖fe1 promises White little after 14...♗f6!?, 14...♘a5 15 f4!? or 14...♘xd4!? 15 ♖xd4 ♗f6 16 ♖d3 a5 17 ♗g5 b4.

d) 14 ♗e3 ♗f6 (14...♘a5?! 15 ♘f5!; 14...♘xd4 15 ♗xd4 a5 16 e5 ♗c6 17 ♖fe1 ± Emms-Coleman, Gausdal 1996; 14...♘f6!?) 15 ♘xc6 ♗xc6 16 ♗d4 ♖d8 17 ♕e3 ♗xd4 18 ♖xd4 ♘f6 19 ♖fd1 gives White a small advantage, Emms-Lutz, Bundesliga 1995/6.

**14...♗xc6 15 ♗f4**
First used by Short against Kasparov. Other possibilities:

a) 15 ♗g5 ♗xg5 16 ♕xg5 ♘f6 =.

b) 15 f4 ♔h8 (15...♗f6!? 16 f5 {16 ♗g5 is answered by 16...♕a7+! and 17...♗xc3} 16...♕e7 17 ♕g4 ♔h8 18 ♗d2, Shtyrenkov-Vaulin, Budapest 1991, 18...♗d4+!? 19 ♔h1 ♘f6 ∞) 16 ♗g5 and then:

b1) 16...♗xg5?! 17 fxg5.

b2) After 16...♘f6 White can try 17 ♕h4!?, rather than 17 f5 ♘xe4 =

Cabello-Roiz, Asturia 1995 or 17 e5 dxe5 18 fxe5 ♗c5+ =.

b3) 16...a5 17 f5 b4 18 axb4 axb4 19 ♘e2 (19 fxe6? bxc3 20 exf7 ♗xg5! 21 ♕xg5 cxb2 ∓ Istratescu-Kuczynski, Budapest Z 1993). Now 19...♗xg5 20 ♕xg5 ♘f6 21 fxe6, Skrobek-Engel, corr. 1990-1, is slightly better for White, and 19...♗xe4 is not wholly clear. Instead, 19...♘f6! gives Black good play.

c) An important position arises after 15 ♖fe1 a5:

c1) 16 f3 ♗f6 17 ♗g5 ♗xg5 18 ♕xg5 ♘f6 = Martin del Campo-Sunye, Merida 1993.

c2) 16 ♖e3 b4 17 axb4 axb4 18 ♘e2 ♖a5 = Macieja-Vaulin, Warsaw 1992.

c3) 16 ♖d3 b4 (16...♗f6!?) 17 axb4 axb4 18 ♘a2 ± J.Polgar-Csonkics, Hungarian Ch 1988.

c4) 16 ♗f4 b4! is probably good for Black.

c5) 16 ♗g5 ♗xg5 17 ♕xg5 and now 17...♖b8 is roughly equal, Gobet-Pinter, Thessaloniki OL 1984, whereas 17...b4 18 axb4 axb4 19 ♘a2 ♗a4 20 ♕g3!, Alvim-Weber, corr. 1999, and 17...♕b7 18 ♖d4 ♘f6 19 ♖xd6!? are less convincing.

**15...♖d8**

This is the latest attempt to improve Black's play. The previous main line ran: 15...♕b7 (15...a5 16 e5!) 16 ♖fe1! (16 e5 dxe5 17 ♗xe5 ♖d8 transposes to the main line) 16...a5 (not 16...♖d8?! 17 ♘d5!) 17 e5 (17 ♘d5? ♗d8) 17...dxe5 (17...d5 ±) 18 ♗xe5 ♗f6 (18...b4 19 axb4 axb4 20 ♘e2 ±; 18...♘f6 19 ♖d4; 18...a4 19 ♗a2 b4 20 axb4 and 21 ♖d4!; 18...♖d8!?) 19 ♖d4! ♖d8 (19...b4 20 axb4 axb4 21 ♘a2 ♗xe5 22 ♕xe5 ♗xg2 23 ♖xb4

♕c6 24 ♕c3 ± Short) 20 ♖xd8 ♗xd8 21 ♘e2! a4 (21...♗f6!?) 22 ♗a2 b4 23 axb4 (23 ♘d4!? ♗d5? 24 ♗xd5 ♕xd5 25 axb4 f6 26 ♕h3) 23...♕xb4 24 ♗c3 ± Short-Kasparov, London PCA Wch (20) 1993.

**16 e5 dxe5 17 ♗xe5 ♕b7 18 ♖xd8 ♗xd8 19 ♖d1 ♗e7**

19...♗f6 is also possible.

**20 ♘e2 ♘f6 21 ♘f4 ♖d8**

= Mirumian-Vaulin, Minsk 1997.

It might be concluded that Black can reach equality after 13 a3, if he proceeds accurately.

## B212)

**13 f4** *(D)*

Most likely, this interesting continuation is not stronger than 13 a3.

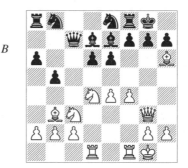

**13...♘c6**

Or:

a) 13...b4 14 ♘ce2 (14 f5? bxc3 15 fxe6 fxe6 16 ♘xe6 ♗xe6 17 ♗xe6+ ♔h8 18 ♖xf8+ ♗xf8 19 ♕f1 ♘d7! 20 ♗xd7 ♘f6 21 ♗e6 cxb2! −+ Olivier-Dunis, Monaco 2000) 14...♔h8 15 ♗g5 ♘c6 16 f5!? (16 ♖d3 ♗f6 =; 16 ♗xe7 ♘xe7 is unclear) 16...♘xd4 (16...e5!?) 17 ♘xd4 ♗xg5 (17...♘f6 18 ♕h4!, Almasi-Vaulin, Kecskemet

1993, with the point 18...e5? 19 ♖f3) 18 fxe6 ♗f6 19 exd7 ♕xd7 20 ♔h1 ± Voitsekhovsky-Vaulin, Kstovo 1994.

b) 13...♔h8!? 14 ♗g5 ♘c6 (the inferior 14...♗xg5?! should be met by 15 fxg5! rather than 15 ♕xg5?! ♘c6 16 ♘xc6 ♗xc6 17 f5 transposing to note 'c' to White's 16th move) 15 ♗xe7 ♘xe7 16 f5 (16 a3 a5) 16...e5 17 ♘e6 fxe6 18 fxe6 ♖xf1+ 19 ♖xf1 ♘f6! = Tischbierek-H.Grünberg, East German Ch (Zittau) 1989.

**14 ♘xc6**

Or:

a) 14 ♔h1 – *12 ♔h1 ♗d7 13 f4 ♘c6 14 ♖ad1*.

b) 14 ♗g5 ♗xg5 15 fxg5 ♘xd4 16 ♖xd4 ♕c5 (Morozevich-Gelfand, Istanbul OL 2000) is good for Black.

c) 14 f5!? ♘xd4 15 ♖xd4 and now:

c1) 15...b4 should be met by Kasparov's 16 e5! (instead of 16 fxe6 fxe6 17 ♖xf8+? ♔xf8! or 16 ♘e2 exf5!? 17 exf5 ♗f6 ∞ Hage-Alvebring, corr 1999).

c2) 15...♗f6 16 ♖d3 and then:

c21) 16...♔h8 17 fxe6 (17 ♗f4!? Shipov) 17...fxe6 18 ♗e3 (18 e5?! dxe5 19 ♗g5 b4!) 18...b4 19 ♘e2 (Macieja-Wojtkiewicz, Warsaw 1995) 19...♕c6! ∞ Nisipeanu/Stoica.

c22) 16...e5 17 ♕g4 (17 ♕g5?! b4! 18 f6 ♕c5+ 19 ♔h1 ♗xf6 ∓; 17 ♗f4 ♘f6! ∞; very interesting is 17 fxe6!? ♗xg3 and now 18 exf7+ or possibly even 18 e7 – Morozevich) 17...b4 18 f6! g6! 19 ♘e2 (19 ♘d1!? Shipov) 19...a5! 20 ♗xf8 (20 ♕h4 a4 21 ♗g5 h5! 22 g4 {∞ Kasparov} 22...hxg4!! 23 ♕xg4 ♗b5! Morozevich) 20...♗xf8 21 ♕h4 (21 c3!? Shipov) 21...a4 22 ♕xh7 ♕a7+ (the alternative is 22...♘xf6!? 23 ♕h8+ ♔h7 24 ♖df3? f5 Kasparov) 23 ♔h1 ♘xf6 24 ♕h6+ ♔e7 gave Black good compensation in Morozevich-Kasparov, Astana 2001.

c23) 16...b4!? 17 fxe6 fxe6 18 e5 (18 ♘e2!?) 18...♗xe5 (18...♕c5+!? 19 ♖e3 ♗xe5 20 ♖xf8+ ♔xf8 and now 21 ♕f2+ ♔g8! or 21 ♕f3+ ♔e7! – Morozevich) 19 ♖xf8+ ♔xf8 20 ♕f3+ (20 ♖f3+ ♔e7!) 20...♗f6 21 ♘e4 (21 ♘d5?! exd5 22 ♕xd5 ♗c6! 23 ♕g8+ ♔e7 24 ♗f4!? Morozevich) 21...♗c6 ∞ Kasparov.

**14...♗xc6**

14...♕xc6? 15 f5 ±.

**15 f5**

15 a3 – *13 a3 ♘c6 14 ♘xc6 ♗xc6 15 f4*.

**15...♔h8 16 ♗e3**

Or:

a) 16 f6 ♗xf6 (16...gxh6!?) 17 ♖xf6 b4!? ∞ Manker-Golmon, theme corr. 1994.

b) 16 fxe6!? gxh6 17 ♖xf7 (17 exf7 ♘f6!?) 17...♖xf7 18 exf7 ♘g7 is probably satisfactory for Black, Kelleher-de Firmian, Woburn 1994.

c) 16 ♗g5 ♗xg5 (16...b4!?) 17 ♕xg5 ♘f6 18 fxe6 fxe6 19 ♗xe6 ♕a7+ 20 ♔h1 ♘xe4 21 ♘xe4 ♗xe4 = Sieiro-Gonzalez – Vera, Cuban Ch (Sagua la Grande) 1981/2.

**16...b4 17 ♘a4**

17 ♘e2?! e5!.

**17...♘f6!**

The simplest. 17...♖b8?! 18 fxe6 fxe6 19 ♖xf8+ ♗xf8 20 ♖f1 ♕e7 (not 20...♘f6 21 ♘c5!) 21 e5 with an advantage, A.Sokolov-Gelfand, USSR Ch (Odessa) 1989. Not quite clear are 17...e5 18 ♘b6 ♘f6!? and 17...♗xe4.

**18 fxe6 ♘xe4 19 ♕h3 fxe6 20 ♕xe6 ♗f6**

20...罝f6 21 罝xf6 奧xf6 is possibly satisfactory, since 22 ♘b6 罝e8 23 ♘d5 seems suspicious.

**21 ♘b6**

Or 21 ♕c4 ♕b7 22 ♘b6 罝ae8 23 ♕xb4 奧xb2 = Damaso-Arnason, Novi Sad OL 1990.

**21...罝ae8 22 ♘d5 ♕d8 23 ♕g4 奧d7 24 ♕e2**

= Olivier-Polak, Baden 1999.

## B213)

**13 ♘f3!? (D)**

This was introduced by Kasparov against Gelfand (1993) where White achieved a spectacular win. After a small boom, the fashion for playing 13 ♘f3 shrank by the end of the 1990s.

**13...♘c6**

Or:

a) 13...奧c6 has not yet been tested.

b) 13...b4 14 ♘e2 a5?! (14...♘c6 15 ♘f4!? ♚h8 16 奧g5 gives White an advantage, Abashev-Kostin, Russia 1996; 14...奧b5 15 ♘fd4!; 14...♚h8!?) 15 ♘f4! ♚h8 (not 15...a4? 16 奧xg7 +−) 16 奧g5 ♘f6 (16...f6? 17 奧xe6 +−; 16...奧xg5 17 ♘xg5 ± a4 18 ♕h4 {alternatively, 18 ♕h3} 18...♘f6 19 奧xe6!) 17 ♕h4! (17 e5? ♘e4), and

instead of 17...奧b5? 18 ♘d4! +− Kasparov-Gelfand, Linares 1993 or 17...a4?! 18 ♘h5! ±, Black should try 17...♘c6 with the idea 18 ♘h5 ♘xh5 19 奧xe7 ♘xe7 20 ♕xe7 罝ae8! 21 ♕xd6 ♕xd6 22 罝xd6 奧b5 (Bönsch) or 17...奧d8!? (Nikitin).

c) 13...a5 is a major alternative:

c1) 14 e5?! gives White a draw at the most: 14...a4 15 罝d4 axb3 (Black may try to improve via 15...g6!? 16 奧d5 罝a5 or 15...♚h8!?, but not 15...dxe5 16 罝g4 奧f6 17 ♘e4 g6 18 奧xf8!) 16 奧xg7 ♘xg7 17 罝g4 bxa2 18 罝xg7+ ♚h8 19 ♘e4!? (19 罝xh7+ =), and now 19...♕xc2! = is simpler than 19...a1♕ 20 罝xh7+ ♚xh7 21 ♘eg5+ 奧xg5 22 ♘xg5+ ♚g6 23 ♘xe6+!? ♚f5 24 ♘xc7.

c2) 14 a3 b4 (14...奧f6 15 e5!?) 15 axb4 axb4 16 ♘e2 奧f6 (or 16...♘c6 17 ♘f4 罝a5! Makarychev) 17 奧g5 奧b5! is good for Black, Zapata-Renteria, Bogota 1995.

c3) 14 a4 b4 15 ♘e2 (15 ♘b1 ♘a6!? 16 e5 ♘c5 with counterplay, Gelashvili-Banikas, Zagan jr Ech 1995) 15...♘c6 (Black has several risky but interesting alternatives: 15...♘a6!?, 15...奧c6!? or 15...奧f6!? with the point 16 奧g5 奧xb2 17 奧e7 奧b5 18 奧xf8 奧xe2 19 奧xd6 ♘xd6 20 ♕xd6 ♘a6) 16 ♘f4 (16 ♘ed4 ♘xd4 17 ♘xd4 =; 16 奧g5 奧xg5 17 ♘xg5 h6 18 ♘f3 罝d8 = Berndt-Jacoby, Hamburg 1997) 16...奧f6 (16...♚h8 17 奧g5 gives White the initiative) 17 ♘d3! (17 ♘h5? 奧xb2 18 e5? ♘xe5!; 17 ♘g5? ♘e7!? ∓; 17 c3?! ♚h8 18 奧g5 bxc3) 17...e5! 18 奧e3, Short-Kasparov, London PCA Wch (18) 1993. The knight on d3 looks strange, but White still might have a slight plus.

**14 ♗f4**

Or:

a) 14 ♖fe1 b4!? (14...♗f6) 15 ♘e2 ♗f6 with counterplay, Hamdouchi-A.Luft, Sitges 1995.

b) 14 ♗g5 ♗xg5 (14...♘c8 15 ♗f4!? Gallagher) 15 ♘xg5 ♖d8 (15...h6 16 ♘h3!? Bangiev) 16 f4?! (16 ♖d2!? Shipov) 16...h6 17 ♘f3 b4 18 ♘e2 ♘f6 19 e5 ♘e4 ∓ Sax-Wojtkiewicz, Budapest Z 1993.

c) 14 ♘e2, and now Black can play 14...a5 15 c3 (15 a4!?) 15...a4 16 ♗c2 e5 17 ♘d2 ♗e6 = Ashley-Arnason, St Martin 1993, or 14...♘e5 15 ♘ed4 ♘xf3+ 16 ♘xf3 ♗c6 17 ♖fe1 ♕b7 = Rublevsky-Vaulin, Kurgan 1993.

**14...♖d8**

Otherwise:

a) 14...b4 15 e5! ± dxe5 16 ♘xe5 (Nijboer-Pelletier, Istanbul OL 2000) 16...♗d6 17 ♖xd6 ♕xd6 18 ♖d1! ♘d4 19 ♕e3 bxc3 20 bxc3 ♗b5 21 cxd4 with compensation – Nijboer.

b) 14...♕b7!? 15 ♖fe1 (15 ♗g5!? Beliavsky/Mikhalchishin; 15 e5 dxe5 16 ♘xe5 ♘xe5 17 ♗xe5 ♗c6 =) 15...b4 (15...♘a5 16 e5!) 16 ♘e2 (16 ♘a4 ♘a5! Shipov) 16...e5 (16...♗f6!? 17 ♗xd6 ♘xd6 18 ♕xd6 ♖fd8 19 e5! ♘xe5 20 ♘xe5 ♗e8! 21 ♕c5 ♖xd1 22 ♖xd1 ♕e4 or 16...♘a5 17 e5 dxe5 18 ♘xe5 ♗b5 19 ♘d4 ♘xb3 20 axb3 f6! ∞ Nikitin) 17 ♗g5 ♗e6 (17...♗xg5 18 ♕xg5 ♗e6 19 ♘g3 ± Shipov) 18 ♘h4! ± Kasparov-Gelfand, Moscow OL 1994.

**15 e5!**

15 ♖fe1 ♗c8 16 e5 dxe5 17 ♘xe5 ♖xd1 (17...♗d6 = Lamoureux-Wojtkiewicz, Cannes 1998) 18 ♖xd1 ♘xe5 19 ♗xe5 ♕c6 = Winants-Wojtkiewicz, Wijk aan Zee 1994.

After the text-move (15 e5), Black has some problems:

a) 15...dxe5 16 ♘xe5 is risky for Black:

a1) 16...♗d6 17 ♖xd6! ♘xd6 and now rather than 18 ♘g4 e5 19 ♘d5 ♕b7 20 ♘gf6+ ♔h8 21 ♕h4 ♗f5 22 ♘xh7 ♗xh7 23 ♘f6 = or 18 ♘xc6 ♗xc6 19 ♖d1 b4! ∞ Istratescu-Wojtkiewicz, Odorheiu Secuiesc Z 1995, Istratescu recommends 18 ♖d1! b4 19 ♘xf7! ♖xf7 20 ♗xd6 ♕a7 21 ♘e4 ±.

a2) 16...♘xe5 17 ♗xe5 ♕b7 18 ♖d4 ♗c6 (or 18...♘f6 19 ♘c4 ♘h5 20 ♕h3 ♗c6 21 ♘d6) 19 ♖g4 ♔h8 (or 19...g6 20 ♗xe6 fxe6 21 ♖xg6+ ♔f7 22 ♖h6 ♖g8 23 ♕f4+ ♘f6 24 ♖xf6+ ♔e8 25 f3) 20 ♖xg7 f6 21 ♖xh7+ ♔xh7 22 ♕h3+ ♔g7 23 ♕g4+ ♔h7 24 ♕h5+ ♔g7 25 ♗f4! with a strong attack for White.

b) 15...♗c8 16 exd6 (16 ♘e4 dxe5 17 ♘xe5 ♘d4!?) 16...♗xd6 17 ♗xd6 (17 ♖xd6 ♘xd6 18 ♖d1 b4! is much better for Black) 17...♖xd6 18 ♘e4 gives White some advantage.

On the whole, the line 10 ♕g3 0-0 11 ♗h6 ♘e8 remains interesting for both sides.

**B22)**

**10...♘c6** *(D)*

Another major option. Black wishes to simplify the position.

**11 ♘xc6**

Otherwise:

a) 11 ♘de2 (nothing is gained by retreating the knight) 11...0-0 12 ♗h6 ♘e8 13 ♖ad1 ♘a5 (Kosten).

b) 11 ♘f3 0-0 12 ♗h6 ♘e8 13 ♖ad1 ♗b7, Vavra-Neumann, Bundesliga 1998/9.

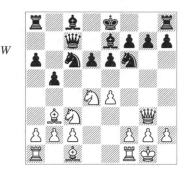

c) 11 ♘f5 (this sacrifice is not considered to work here) 11...exf5 12 ♕xg7 ♖f8 and then:

c1) 13 ♗g5 b4!? (13...♕d8!? is an alternative; 13...♘xe4 14 ♘d5 is unclear) 14 ♘d5 ♘xd5 15 ♗xd5 (or 15 exd5 ♘e5 16 ♗xe7 ♕xe7 17 f4 f6! Kosten) 15...♗xg5 16 ♕xg5 f4 ∓ Guseinov-Magerramov, Baku 1986.

c2) 13 exf5 ♗xf5 (13...♘e5 14 ♘d5!; 13...b4!?) 14 ♗g5 b4 15 ♗xf6 bxc3 16 ♖ae1 0-0-0!? 17 ♗xe7 ♘xe7 18 ♖e3 cxb2 19 ♕f6 (19 ♕xb2!?) 19...♗e6 ∓ Mukhutdinov-Shneider, St Petersburg 1993.

d) 11 ♗e3 gives Black a choice:

d1) 11...♘a5 12 ♕xg7 (12 ♘f5?!) 12...♖g8 13 ♕h6 ♘xb3 14 axb3 ♗b7 15 f3 b4 16 ♘a4 ♖g6 17 ♕h3 d5 18 f4!, Alvim-Kiese, corr. 1999.

d2) 11...♘xd4 12 ♗xd4 0-0 (alternatively, 12...♗b7 13 ♖ad1!? b4 14 ♗a4+, and instead of 14...♔f8 15 e5 ♘h5 16 ♕e3! with a dangerous initiative, Ivanović-Marjanović, Yugoslav Ch (Subotica) 1984, Black should play 14...♗c6 – Marjanović) 13 a3 (13 e5 dxe5 14 ♗xe5 ♕c6 15 ♖fe1 ♗b7 16 ♘e4 ♔h8 with a defensible position, Gara-Khukhashvili, Oropesa del Mar jr Wch 1999) 13...e5 (13...♗b7 is

better) 14 ♗e3 ♗e6 15 ♗g5 with an advantage for White, Raud-Ilić, Bela Crkva 1990.

d3) 11...♗b7!?.

d4) 11...0-0 (now ♗h6 will lose a tempo) 12 ♘xc6 (12 a3 =) 12...♕xc6 13 ♗h6 (13 ♗d4 ♗b7 = 14 ♖ad1?! b4!, V.Ivanov-Zhidkov, USSR 1977) 13...♘e8 14 a4 (14 ♖fe1 ♗b7 15 ♖ad1 – *11 ♘xc6 ♕xc6 12 ♗g5 ♗b7 13 ♖ad1 0-0 14 ♗h6 ♘e8 15 ♖fe1*; 14 ♖ad1 ♗b7 – *11 ♘xc6 ♕xc6 12 ♗g5 ♗b7 13 ♖ad1 0-0 14 ♗h6 ♘e8*; White achieves nothing by 14 ♘d5 ♗d8!) and now:

d41) 14...b4 15 ♘d5 ♗d8 16 a5 (16 ♖fe1!?) 16...♕b7 17 ♗d2 exd5 (17...♗d7 18 ♘xb4 ±) 18 ♗xd5 ♕a7 19 ♗xa8 ♕xa8 20 e5!, J.Polgar-H.Olafsson, Egilsstadir 1988.

d42) 14...♗d7!?.

d43) 14...♗b7 is probably best: 15 axb5 axb5 16 ♖xa8 ♗xa8 followed by 17...♗f6 = Nikolenko-Yuferov, Moscow 1990.

**11...♕xc6** (D)

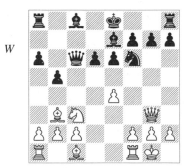

**12 ♖e1**

Other moves:

a) 12 ♕xg7? ♖g8 13 ♕h6 ♘xe4 14 ♘xe4 ♕xe4 ∓.

b) 12 a3 ♘xe4!?.

c) 12 ♗g5 (as in the case of 11 ♗e3, ♗h6 will now lose a tempo) 12...♗b7 (12...0-0? 13 ♘d5!) and then:

c1) 13 ♖fe1 0-0 (13...0-0-0?! 14 a4) and now:

c11) 14 a3 gives Black a choice of transpositions: 14...♖ad8 – *12 ♖e1 ♗b7 13 a3 ♖d8 14 ♗g5 0-0*; 14...♖fd8!? 15 ♖ad1 transposes to note 'c11' to White's 11th move in Line B1, which is equal.

c12) 14 ♖ad1 – *13 ♖ad1 0-0 14 ♖fe1*.

c13) 14 ♗h6 ♘e8 = gives Black an extra tempo compared to Line D221.

c2) 13 ♖ad1 0-0! (13...♖d8 14 ♖fe1 0-0, transposing to line 'c241', has its disadvantages) and then:

c21) 14 a3 =.

c22) 14 ♗xf6 ♗xf6 15 ♖xd6 ♕c5! gives Black compensation.

c23) After 14 ♗h6 ♘e8 15 ♖fe1, a good reply is 15...♔h8! (less convincing is 15...♗f6 16 ♗g5 ♗xg5 – *12 ♖e1 0-0 13 ♗h6 ♘e8 14 ♖ad1 ♗b7 15 ♗g5 ♗xg5*) 16 ♗g5 ♗xg5 17 ♕xg5 ♘f6 = 18 ♖d3? b4!, Moutousis-Cvetković, Vrnjačka Banja 1990.

c24) 14 ♖fe1 and here:

c241) 14...♖ad8 is well met by 15 ♖d3! (nothing is gained by 15 ♗d5 ♕c7 =). Then Black must avoid 15...♔h8? 16 ♕h4 +–, 15...♘h5? 16 ♕h4 ♗xg5 17 ♕xg5 ♘f6 18 ♖g3 +–, 15...b4? 16 ♘d5 exd5 17 exd5 ♕c7 18 ♖xe7! and 15...a5 16 a4!? b4 17 ♘d5. There remains only 15...♕c5, when 16 ♕h4 (Pawlak-Ferens, corr. 1996) is not convincing in view of 16...h6!, so 16 ♗e3!? deserves attention.

c242) 14...♖fd8!. Now 15 ♖d3?! does not work because of 15...b4! 16

♘d5 exd5 17 exd5 ♕d7! 18 ♖xe7 (18 ♖de3 ♖e8) 18...♕xe7 19 ♖e3 ♕f8! (the difference!) 20 ♗xf6 ♖e8. Also dubious is 15 f4?! (G.Kuzmin-Polugaevsky, USSR Ch (Leningrad) 1977), when Black can play, e.g., 15...b4!? (Kosten). Better is 15 f3 or 15 a3, transposing to note 'c11' to White's 11th move in Line B1 (=).

d) 12 f3!? (this occurs much more seldom than 12 ♖e1 ♗b7 13 f3), and now:

d1) 12...♕c5+!? 13 ♔h1 0-0.

d2) 12...0-0 13 ♗h6 (13 ♔h1!?; 13 ♗e3!? ♗b7 – *12...♗b7 13 ♗e3 0-0*) 13...♘c8 (13...♘h5! =) 14 ♗o3 (14 ♘e2 ♕c5+ 15 ♔h1 ♔h8 = Labuckas-Zagorskis, Lithuanian Ch (Vilnius) 1994; 14 ♔h1!?) 14...♘f6 15 ♔h1 ♗b7 16 a4 ♖fd8 17 ♘e2 e5 18 ♗g5 b4 19 ♕e1! with an advantage for White, Gdanski-Brustman, Aegina 1993.

d3) 12...♗b7 13 ♗e3 0-0 (13...♖g8 14 a4 b4 15 a5 ±) with a complicated game after both 14 ♖fd1 ♖fd8 15 ♖d2 ♘d7 16 ♘e2 (Bereziuk-Kalod, Czech Cht 1998) and 14 a4 ♖fd8 (14...b4!?) 15 ♘e2 e5 16 ♘c3 b4 17 ♘d5 ♘xd5 18 exd5 ♕d7 19 a5!, Morozevich-Hohn, Moscow 1991.

We now return to 12 ♖e1 *(D)*:

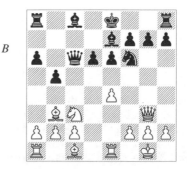

*B*

## 12...♗b7!

There is at least one important alternative, but the majority of the rare continuations look dubious:

a) 12...a5? 13 a4 b4 14 ♘d5 exd5 15 ♕xg7 ♖f8 16 exd5 ♘xd5 17 ♗g5 ±.

b) 12...g6?! 13 ♗g5!?.

c) 12...♕c5?! 13 ♗e3 ♕h5 14 ♗f4 e5 15 ♘d5 ±.

d) After 12...♗d7?! White is able to choose between 13 ♗g5 ♕c5 ±, 13 ♕xg7 ♖g8 14 ♕h6 b4? 15 ♘d5 and 13 ♘d5!? exd5 14 ♕xg7 0-0-0 15 exd5 ♘xd5 16 ♕xf7 ♘f6 17 ♖e3 ♖hg8 18 g3.

e) 12...♕c7!? is interesting; e.g., 13 a4 b4 14 ♘a2 ♕b7 ∞ Mirumian-Mozny, Czech Cht 1996/7.

f) 12...0-0 13 ♗h6! ♘e8 has occurred rather frequently. Now:

f1) 14 a3 ♗b7 transposes to Line B221.

f2) 14 ♖ad1!? and then:

f21) 14...♕c7 15 a3 ♗f6 16 ♖d3 ♗b7 transposes to note 'a' to Black's 15th move in Line B221 (±).

f22) 14...♕b7 15 a3 ±.

f23) 14...♔h8 15 ♗g5 (or 15 ♗e3!?) 15...♘f6? 16 ♗xf6 is much better for White, H.Olafsson-Teitsson, Icelandic Cht 1995.

f24) 14...♗b7 and then:

f241) 15 a3 again transposes to Line B221.

f242) 15 ♖d3 ♔h8!? (15...♖d8 16 ♗g5 ♕c7 17 ♗xe7 ♕xe7 18 f3 ± Canda-Vera, Bayamo 1989) 16 ♗g5 ♗xg5 17 ♕xg5 b4 and 18...♘f6 ∞, Yurtaev-Rashkovsky, USSR 1985.

f243) 15 ♗g5!? ♗xg5 16 ♕xg5 ♘f6 (16...b4 17 ♘a4 ♘f6 18 ♖d4 ±) gives White some chances on the

kingside; e.g., 17 ♖e3 h6 18 ♕f4 ♖ad8 19 ♖dd3 b4? 20 ♖g3 +− or 17 ♖d3 h6 18 ♕h4 ♖fd8 19 ♖g3 ♔f8 (Mariano-Browne, Las Vegas blitz 1995) 20 ♖ee3!.

f3) 14 a4!? ensures a slight advantage: 14...♗b7 (or 14...♔h8 15 axb5!? axb5 16 ♖xa8 ♕xa8 17 ♗g5 ±) 15 axb5 axb5 16 ♖xa8 ♗xa8 (J.Polgar-Schandorff, Åbenrå rpd 1989) 17 ♘a2!?.

Practice has shown that White is often tempted to advance the knight:

f4) 14 ♘d5 ♗d8! and, so far, Black has managed to defend very successfully in this position:

f41) 15 ♗g5?! ♗xg5 16 ♕xg5 exd5 17 ♗xd5 ♕c5! 18 b4 ♕a7.

f42) 15 c3 ♗d7! (15...♗b7!? 16 ♘f4 ♔h8 17 ♗g5 ♗xg5 18 ♕xg5 ♘f6) 16 a4 ♕b7 = Zso.Polgar-Browne, New York 1989.

f43) 15 ♗e3 ♗d7 16 ♗d4 ♕b7! = Bach-Szuhanek, Timisoara 1993.

f44) 15 a3 ♗b7 16 ♖ad1 ♔h8 17 ♘b4 ♕c7 18 ♗f4 a5 19 ♘d3 e5! was good for Black in Brooks-Kraai, Los Angeles 1991.

f45) 15 ♖ad1 and then:

f451) 15...♗b7 and now: 16 a3 – *15 a3 ♗b7 16 ♖ad1*; 16 ♘f4 ♔h8 17 ♗g5 – *15...♔h8 16 ♗g5 ♗b7 17 ♘f4*.

f452) 15...♔h8 16 ♗g5 (16 ♗c1 is equal) 16...♗b7 17 ♘f4 (17 ♗xd8 ♖xd8 18 ♕h4 ♖d7 = Browne-Ghitescu, Rovinj/Zagreb 1970) 17...♗xg5 18 ♕xg5 ♘f6, and there is nothing special for White.

f453) 15...a5!? is possibly even stronger; e.g., 16 ♘f4? ♔h8! ∓ Raud-Zagrebelny, Tallinn 1988, with the point 17 ♗d5 exd5 18 exd5 ♕xc2! −+.

f46) 15 a4 ♔h8 (15...♗b7 16 axb5 axb5 17 ♖xa8 ♗xa8 18 ♘b4! ±

Mikhalchishin; 15...♕b7 16 axb5!?; 15...♕d7!? is playable) 16 ♗f4 (16 axb5? axb5 ∓; 16 ♘b4!?; 16 ♗g5!?) 16...♕d7 17 ♘c3 b4 18 ♘a2 ± Tomescu-Minasian, Dečin 1996.

f47) 15 ♘f4 ♗f6 (not 15...♔h8? 16 ♗d5!; 15...♖a7 16 ♘h5!? f6 ±; 15...♕c5 16 ♘d3 ♕h5 ±) 16 ♘d3 (16 ♘d5 ♗d8 is a repetition; after 16 c3, instead of 16...♔h8 17 ♗g5 ±, 16...♗e5! is strong, Macieja-Kempinski, Poland 1991) 16...a5!? (16...♗b7 17 a4! ± Firnhaber-Schwierzy, corr. 1992).

f48) 15 ♖e3 is popular though very unclear:

f481) 15...♗b7? is bad in view of 16 ♖c3! ♕d7 17 ♖c7!.

f482) 15...♕b7 16 ♘f4 ♔h8 17 ♗g5 ♗b6?! (17...♗xg5 18 ♕xg5 h6 19 ♖h3?! ♕xe4 = Hislop-Hughson, corr. 1995) 18 ♖f3 ♕xe4 19 ♔f1! ± de Firmian-Browne, USA Ch (Long Beach) 1989.

f483) 15...♕d7 16 ♘f4 ♕e7 (not 16...♗f6? 17 ♘h5! ±) 17 ♘h5 f6 ± Gdanski-Jasnikowski, Polish Ch (Cetniewo) 1991.

f484) 15...♔h8 16 ♗g5 f6!? (other ideas are 16...♗xg5 17 ♕xg5 ± and 16...♕d7 17 ♘f4 ♖a7!?, Love-Kask, corr. 1995), and instead of 17 ♖f3?! ♗d7 (17...a5!?) 18 ♘f4 (or 18 ♕h4 exd5 19 g4?! ♗e6! 20 ♖h3 ♗g8) 18...♘c7! (Szuhanek), the correct move is 17 ♕f3 ∞.

f485) 15...♖a7!? 16 ♘f4 ♗f6 17 ♘h5? (17 ♘d3) 17...♗xb2 18 c3 f6 ∓ Voitsekhovsky-Minasian, Kstovo 1994.

f486) 15...♕c5!? is important; for example, 16 ♘f4? ♔h8 or 16 ♖ae1 ♔h8 17 ♖c3 ♕d4, and there seems nothing concrete for White, Korneev-Karpman, Smolensk 1991.

We now return to 12...♗b7! *(D)*:

### 13 a3

13 a4? b4 14 a5 0-0 is bad for White and 13 ♗g5 has already been discussed under *12 ♗g5 ♗b7 13 ♖fe1*.

There are two more options for White:

a) 13 f3 (not very dangerous for Black) 13...0-0 (both 13...♖g8!? and 13...h5!? are interesting) 14 ♗h6 (14 ♗e3 −) 14...♘e8 and here:

a1) In the case of 15 ♔h1, instead of 15...♔h8 16 ♗g5 ♗xg5 17 ♕xg5 ♘f6 18 a4 b4 19 ♘e2 with a slight advantage to White, Movsesian-Jirovsky, Mlada Boleslav 1993, 15...♗f6 is interesting; e.g., 16 ♖ad1 a5! ∓ Sluka-Jirovsky, Plzen 1996 or 16 ♗g5 ♗xc3 17 bxc3 ♕c7!?.

a2) 15 ♗g5 ♗xg5 16 ♕xg5 is adequately met by 16...♕c5+!? 17 ♕e3 ♘c7, Bielczyk-Kuczynski, Bydgoszcz 1990.

a3) 15 ♖ad1 and then:

a31) 15...b4 16 ♘e2 (16 ♘a4! ± Magerramov) 16...♕c5+ 17 ♔h1 ♗f6 = Rublevsky-Magerramov, USSR Ch (Moscow) 1991.

a32) 15...♔h8 16 ♗f4 (16 ♗g5!?) 16...♖d8 17 a3 ♘f6 18 ♗e3 ♘d7 (not obligatory) 19 ♗d4! ♗f6 20 ♗xf6 ♘xf6 ± Gormally-Kosten, British Ch (Scarborough) 1999.

a33) Interesting is 15...♗f6!? 16 ♗g5 (16 ♖d3 b4 17 ♘a4 a5 with strong counterplay, Boll-Van Oosterom, corr. 1991) 16...♗xc3 17 bxc3 a5 with unclear consequences, Y.Hernandez-Martin del Campo, Havana 1993.

a34) 15...♖d8 16 ♔h1 (16 ♖d3 ♔h8 =) and then:

a341) 16...♔h8 17 ♗g5 ♗xg5 18 ♕xg5 ♘f6 and now:

a3411) 19 e5?! is met by 19...dxe5 with the point 20 ♖xd8 ♖xd8 21 ♘e4 h6 22 ♕h4 ♕c7! 23 ♘xf6 ♕e7.

a3412) 19 a3 transposes to note 'b' to White's 16th move in Line B222 (=).

a3413) 19 a4!? h6 20 ♕d2 b4 (Magomedov-Magerramov, USSR 1991) 21 ♘e2.

a3414) 19 ♕d2!? Magerramov.

a3415) 19 ♖d4! ♖d7 20 a4 ± Magomedov-Isaev, Dushanbe 1999.

a342) 16...♗f6 17 ♗g5 ♖d7 (or 17...♗xg5 18 ♕xg5 ♘f6 19 e5! ±) 18 ♗d5!?. Now both 18...♕c8 19 ♗xb7 ♕xb7 20 ♗xf6 ♘xf6 21 ♖xd6 ♘h5 22 ♕e5 ♕c7 23 ♖ed1 b4, Magomedov-Magerramov, USSR Cht 1991, and 18...exd5(!) are probably satisfactory for Black.

b) 13 ♕xg7!? ♖g8 14 ♕h6 0-0-0. Black has acquired a sustainable initiative on the kingside for the pawn. Some variations:

b1) 15 a3? d5!.

b2) 15 f3 ♖g6 (15...b4!?) 16 ♕d2 (16 ♕h4?! ♘g4! 17 ♕xe7 ♕c5+ 18 ♗e3 ♘xe3 19 ♔h1 ♖d7 20 ♕e8+ ♔c7 ∓ A.Pachmann-Cermak, corr. 1995; 16 ♕h3 ♔b8 – 15 ♕h3 ♔b8 16 f3

♖g6) 16...♖dg8 (16...b4!?) 17 ♖e2 ♗d8 (17...♕c5+!? 18 ♕c3 ♕h5) 18 ♕d3 h5 19 ♗f4 ♗c7 ∞ Vavra-Kalod, Prague 1995.

b3) 15 ♕h3 ♔b8 (15...♘g4?! 16 ♗d5! Sutovsky) and then:

b31) 16 a3 and now 16...♖g6 17 ♖e2 ♖dg8 18 f3 transposes to line 'b32', while 16...h5!? is also possible.

b32) If 16 ♕d3 ♖g6 17 f3 ♖dg8 18 ♖e2, then Black can play 18...♘d7!? or 18...h5 19 ♗f4 h4 20 ♖d1 ♘h5!, Lupkowski-Warszawski, Brzeg Dolny 1995.

b33) 16 f3 ♖g6 and now:

b331) 17 a3 ♖dg8 18 ♖e2 h5 and then:

b3311) 19 ♗e3 – 17 ♗e3 ♖dg8 18 ♖e2 h5 19 a3.

b3312) 19 ♗d2 can be met by 19...♘d7!?, intending ...♘e5, Wanke-Hodges, corr. 1992. If instead 19...h4, 20 ♕xh4!? is interesting.

b3313) 19 ♔h1 ♕c7 and now, instead of 20 ♘d1? h4 21 ♘e3 ♘h5 22 ♘g4 ♕d8 23 ♗d2 ♗g5 24 g3 f5 ∓ Ki.Georgiev-Ivanchuk, Tilburg 1993, Bönsch recommends 20 ♗f4 or 20 ♗e3.

b332) 17 ♗e3 ♖dg8 (17...h5 allows 18 a4!? b4 19 ♘e2 ♖dg8 20 ♘f4, Klauner-Koeneke, corr. 1991) 18 ♖e2 h5 (18...♘d7? 19 ♘d5! ± Ivanchuk-Polugaevsky, Monaco blindfold 1993; 18...b4!?; 18...♗d8!? 19 a4 b4 20 ♘d1 gives Black a choice between 20...d5 21 ♗f4+ ♔a8 22 e5 ♘d7 ∞ Krueger-Kissinger, corr. 1999, and 20...♔a8!?) 19 ♖d1 (19 a4!? b4 20 ♘a2 Psakhis; after 19 a3 Black can play either 19...♕c7 or 19...♗d8 20 ♔h1 h4 21 ♖g1 ♕e8!?, Kalod-Jirovsky, Czech U-16 Ch (Svetla) 1994) and now:

b3321) 19...♘d7? fails to 20 ♘d5!, Nijboer-Shneider, Ohrid Ech 2001.

b3322) 19...♕c7 can be met by 20 a4 b4 21 ♘a2 d5 22 e5 ♘h7!? 23 ♕xh5 ♘g5 with compensation or 20 ♔h1 h4 21 ♖ed2 ♘h5 (Olivier-V.Gurevich, Cappelle la Grande 1999) 22 g4 ♘f6 23 a3 with chances for both sides.

b3323) 19...♕e8!? 20 a4 b4 21 ♘a2 e5! 22 ♘xb4 (22 ♗c1 a5! Sutovsky; 22 ♖ed2 ♗c8 23 ♕h4 ∞ Psakhis) 22...a5 23 ♘d5! (23 ♘d3 ♗c8 24 ♕h4 ♘g4 ∓ Nijboer-Sutovsky, Essen 2001) 23...♗c8 (23...♘xd5!? 24 ♗xd5 ♗c8 25 ♕xh5 ♖h8! 26 ♗xf7 ♕xf7 27 ♕xh8 ♗f6 28 ♕h6 ∞ Ftačnik) 24 ♘xf6 ♗xf6 25 ♕xh5 ♖h8 26 ♕xg6 fxg6 27 ♖xd6 ♗d8 28 ♖ed2 ∞ Psakhis.

We now return to 13 a3 *(D)*:

The last big crossroad:
**B221: 13...0-0**      91
**B222: 13...♖d8!?**    93

Other moves:

a) 13...♕c5 14 ♗e3 ♕h5 15 f3 (15 ♗f4 ♕c5) 15...0-0 16 ♖ad1 (or 16 ♘e2) 16...♖ad8 17 ♘e2 ♕e5 18 ♕xe5 dxe5 19 ♘c1 ± Vrenegoor-Van der Stricht, Dutch Cht 1996.

b) 13...♕c7!? has not been tested.

## B221)
**13...0-0 14 ♗h6 ♘e8**
14...♘h5?! 15 g4 ♕c5 16 ♖ad1!?.
**15 ♖ad1**
15 ♗g5 ♗xg5 16 ♕xg5 ♘f6 (or 16...h6!? 17 ♕e3 ♘f6 18 ♖ad1 ♖fd8 = Matsuura-Mecking, Americana 1994) 17 ♖ad1 ♖fd8 and ...♕c5 = (17...♖ad8 transposes to note 'd2' to White's 14th move in Line B222, which is equal).
**15...♖d8**
Other moves:

a) 15...♕c7 16 ♖d3 ♗f6 17 ♗g5 ♖d8 (17...♕e7 18 ♗xf6 ♕xf6 19 f4!) 18 ♖ed1 ♗xg5 19 ♕xg5 h6 20 ♕d2 ± Shtyrenkov-A.Petrosian, Sevastopol 1986.

b) 15...♗f6 16 ♖d3 (16 ♗f4 ♗xc3 17 bxc3 ±) 16...♗e5 17 f4 (17 ♗f4) 17...♕c5+ 18 ♔h1 ♗d4 19 ♘d1 is slightly better for White, Macieja-Mikulcik, Zlin 1995.

c) 15...a5 16 a4 b4 17 ♘b5 ± de la Riva-Lesiège, Parana jr Wch 1991.

d) 15...♔h8 (slightly less reliable than 15...♖d8) 16 ♗g5 (16 ♗f4 ♖d8 and now 17 ♖d3 ♘f6 18 ♗g5 ♘h5!? 19 ♕h4 ♗xg5 20 ♕xg5 ♘f6 transposes to *15...♖d8 16 ♖d3 ♔h8 17 ♗g5 ♗xg5 18 ♕xg5 ♘f6*, while 17 ♕e3 can be met by 17...♖d7 = or 17...♕c7) 16...♗xg5 (16...♕c7 17 ♗xe7 ♕xe7 18 ♖d3 ♖c8 19 ♖ed1 ± Macieja-Stypka, Polish Cht 1995) 17 ♕xg5 ♘f6 (17...♖c8 can be met by 18 a4 b4 19 ♘a2 {19 ♘e2!?} 19...♘f6 or 18 ♕f4!? ±) and now:

d1) 18 ♖d3 is the most popular move:

d11) 18...♕c5 19 ♕d2! ±.

d12) 18...♖ac8 19 ♕d2 ♖fd8 20 f3 h6 (20...♖d7 transposes to the note to White's 20th move) 21 ♔h1 ♕b6?

22 ♖d1 with an advantage for White, Sulskis-Nordahl, Gausdal 1995.

d13) 18...h6 19 ♕d2 (19 ♕f4 ♖ad8 20 f3 ♖d7) 19...♖fd8 20 f3 ♖d7 21 ♖d1 ♖ad8 22 ♔h1 (22 ♕f2!? ♕c5 23 ♘e2 with a minimal advantage for White, Emms-H.Olafsson, Hillerød 1995) 22...♕c7 (22...♔g8 23 ♘e2 ♕c7 24 ♕e3 ± Dembo-Carstensen, Budapest 1999) and now, instead of playing 23 ♘e2?! d5!, as in Shtyrenkov-Titlianov, USSR 1987, 23 ♕f4 ♗c6 24 ♕g3 a5 25 ♖d4 (∞ Dembo) or 23 ♕e1!? is interesting.

d14) 18...♖ad8 transposes to the main line.

d2) 18 ♖e3!? has the point that 18...♖ad8? is bad in view of 19 ♖g3! ♖g8 20 e5 ♘e4 (20...h6? 21 exf6 +−) 21 ♘xe4 ♕xe4 22 ♖e3.

d3) 18 ♖d4!? ±.

**16 ♖d3**

Or: 16 ♘e2!? ♔h8 17 ♘d4 ♕c8 18 ♗g5 ♗xg5 19 ♕xg5 ♘f6 with an acceptable game, Garber-Freeman, Philadelphia 1991; 16 f3 transposes to Line B222.

**16...♔h8**

16...♗f6!? 17 ♗g5 ♖d7 (17...♗xg5 18 ♕xg5 ♘f6? 19 ♖g3 +−) 18 ♗xf6 ♘xf6 19 f3 (19 ♖f3!?; 19 ♕h4!?) 19...♖fd8 20 ♖ed1 ♕c5+ = Ciemniak-Skalik, Polish Ch (Bielsko-Biala) 1991.

**17 ♗g5 ♗xg5 18 ♕xg5 ♘f6** (D)
**19 ♕d2**

Other attempts:

a) 19 ♖f3 ♕c5 20 ♘d5?! exd5 21 ♖xf6 dxe4! ∓ Velimirović-Tukmakov, Amsterdam 1974.

b) 19 f3 and now 19...♕c5+ 20 ♕e3 ♖d7 21 ♖ed1 ♖fd8 transposes to Line B222. The alternative is 19...♘d7!?.

c) 19 ♕e3 a5 (19...♘d7 is A.Sokolov's suggestion; Black should avoid 19...♕c5 20 ♖ed1! and 19...♖d7 20 ♘d5!) 20 f3 ♘d7 21 ♖ed1 ♘c5 22 ♖d4 and White's chances are possibly better, Vavra-Anapolsky, 1991.

d) 19 ♕h4 ♕c5 20 ♖ed1 (20 ♖ee3!?) 20...a5 21 ♕f4 b4 22 ♘a4 ♕c7 23 f3 ♗c6 = Halwick-Reichardt, corr. 1999.

e) 19 ♖ee3!? ♕c5 20 ♕h4 (20 e5 h6!).

f) 19 ♖g3 ♖g8 and now:

f1) 20 ♖f3 ♕c5 21 ♘d5?! ♘xe4! 22 ♖xe4 ♗xd5 is much better for Black.

f2) 20 ♖h3 ♕c5 and now 21 ♕h4 a5!? (21...g5!?) or 21 ♕f4 ♕e5!? with a good game for Black.

f3) 20 ♕h4 a5 (20...♕c5 21 ♖g5 ♕b6 22 ♖e3!?) 21 ♖g5 (21 ♖ee3 b4 22 ♘e2 bxa3 23 bxa3 a4 ∓ Mowsziszian-Shneider, Tallinn 1988) 21...b4 (21...a4!? 22 ♗a2 b4; 21...♗a6!?) 22 axb4 axb4 23 ♘a2 ♕b6 (Hamdouchi-James, Moscow OL 1994) 24 e5!.

g) 19 ♖d4!?.

**19...♖d7**

19...♕b6?! 20 ♖d1, Ki.Georgiev-Ftačnik, Budapest Z 1993.

**20 ♖d1**

20 f3 ♖c8!? (20...♖fd8! 21 ♖d1 –
*20 ♖d1 ♖fd8 21 f3*) 21 ♖d1 ♘e8 22
♕f2 ± Dolmatov-Polugaevsky, Moscow TV 1987.

**20...♖fd8**

20...♘xe4 21 ♘xe4 ♕xe4 22 f3 ±.

**21 f3**

White has some advantage:

a) 21...♕c7 (with the idea of 22...d5)
22 ♕e1 (22 ♕e3 ♕c5 transposes to
Line B222) 22...♔g8 23 ♔h1 ♕c5 24
a4 (Golubev-Jirovsky, Hamburg 1999;
24 ♘e2!?) 24...b4 25 ♘e2 a5 26 ♘d4
♕e5 27 ♖e3.

b) 21...♕c5+ 22 ♕f2 (22 ♔h1!?
with the idea of ♖d4) 22...♔g8 23 ♘e2
♕xf2+ (23...♕e5 24 ♕d4 ± A.Sok-
olov-Portisch, Rotterdam 1989) 24
♔xf2 ± Golubev-Zagorskis, Senden
1994.

c) 21...♔g8 yields equality after 22
♘e2 ♕c5+ = or 22 ♕f2 ♕c7 =, but
White can try 22 ♖d4!? or 22 ♔h1!?.

**B222)**

**13...♖d8!?** *(D)*

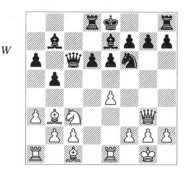

This move of Magerramov's is aimed
at transposing to positions similar to
but slightly safer than the previous
line.

**14 f3**

Other possibilities:

a) 14 ♕xg7? ♖g8 15 ♕h6 d5! 16
f3 dxe4 ∓.

b) After 14 ♘d5 exd5 15 exd5
♘xd5 16 ♕xg7 ♔d7 17 ♕g4+ (17
♕xf7? ♖de8) 17...♔c7 (17...♔e8?! 18
♗h6) 18 ♗xd5 ♕xd5 19 ♖xe7+ ♔b8
20 ♕f3, White gets no more than a
draw.

c) 14 a4!? b4 15 ♘d5 exd5 16
♕xg7 ♔d7! *(D)* doesn't promise White
any advantage either:

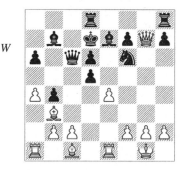

c1) 17 ♕xf7?! ♘xe4!.

c2) 17 exd5 ♘xd5 18 ♕g4+ (18
♕xf7? ♖de8! 19 a5 ♘c7) 18...♔c7 19
♗xd5 ♕xd5 20 ♖xe7+ ♔b8 21 ♕f3?!
♕xf3 22 gxf3 ♖hg8+ 23 ♔f1 a5!.

c3) 17 a5 ♕c5 18 exd5 and then:

c31) 18...♘xd5 19 ♕g4+ ♔c7! 20
♗xd5 ♕xd5 21 ♖xe7+ ♔b8 22 ♖xb7+
(not 22 ♕f3? ♕xf3 23 gxf3 ♖hg8+ 24
♔f1 ♗c6!; 22 c4 bxc3 23 bxc3 ♖hg8
24 c4 ♕c6!?) 22...♕xb7 23 ♕d4! with
compensation.

c32) 18...♖hg8!? 19 ♕xf7 ♖de8 20
♕e6+ (20 ♗e3? ♕xd5!; 20 ♗a4+?
♔c8!) 20...♔c7 21 ♗e3 ♕b5 22 ♗b6+
♔b8 23 ♗a4 ♕xd5 (23...♕c4!?) 24
♕xd5 ♗xd5 25 ♗xe8 ♗xg2! =.

d) 14 ♗g5 0-0 and then:

d1) 15 ♗h6 ♘e8 16 ♖ad1 (this is Line B221 but with White a tempo down) 16...♔h8 17 ♗g5 (17 ♗c1 ♘f6 18 ♖d3 a5!) 17...♗xg5 18 ♕xg5 ♘f6, etc.

d2) 15 ♖ad1 ♘h5 (15...a5!? 16 ♗h6 ♘e8 17 ♖d3 ♔h8 18 ♗g5 ♗xg5 19 ♕xg5 ♘f6 has also been played) 16 ♕h4 ♗xg5 17 ♕xg5 ♘f6 18 ♖d3 h6 (18...♔h8 transposes to Line B221; 18...♕c5!?) 19 ♕h4 (19 ♕d2!? is another idea) 19...♕c5 20 ♕f4 (20 ♖g3 ♔h7!) 20...♖d7 = Kudrin-Browne, USA Ch (Modesto) 1995.

**14...0-0** *(D)*

**15 ♗h6**

15 ♗e3 ♘d7 16 ♗d4 ♗f6 17 ♗xf6 ♘xf6 18 ♖ad1 ♖d7 19 ♖d2 ♖fd8 20 ♖ed1 ♕c5+ 21 ♕f2 ♔f8 = Lamoureux-Renet, French Ch (Nantes) 1993.

**15...♘e8 16 ♖ad1**

Or:

a) 16 ♘e2 ♕c5+ 17 ♔h1 ♗f6 (17...♔h8!?) 18 c3 ♗e5 19 f4 ♗f6 20

♘d4 ∞ Shtyrenkov-Magerramov, Smolensk 1991.

b) 16 ♔h1 ♔h8 (Short's 16...♗f6 is simpler) 17 ♗g5 ♗xg5 18 ♕xg5 ♘f6 19 ♖ad1 (19 a4!? b4 20 ♘d1) 19...♖d7 (19...♕c5!?) 20 ♖d3 ♖fd8 21 ♖ed1 (21 a4!?) 21...♕c5 22 ♕e3 (22 ♕d2!?) 22...♗g8! with an equal position, Short-Kasparov, London PCA Wch (16) 1993.

**16...♔h8**

16...♗f6 17 ♗g5 (more interesting is 17 ♖d3! a5 18 ♗g5, Kissinger-Krueger, corr. 1999) 17...♗xg5 18 ♕xg5 ♘f6 19 ♖d3 ♕c5+ 20 ♕e3 (Zapata-Mecking, San Jose do Rio Preto 1995) 20...♖d7 =.

**17 ♗g5 ♗xg5**

17...♘f6 18 ♔h1 ♘h5 19 ♕h4 ♗xg5 20 ♕xg5 ♘f6 21 ♖d4 h6 (Van Blitterswijk-Rowson, Wijk aan Zee 2000) 22 ♕d2 is slightly better for White.

**18 ♕xg5 ♘f6**

Now Mirumian-Kaufman, Olomouc 1999 continued 19 ♕e3 ♖d7 (alternatively, 19...♕c5 20 ♖d3) 20 ♖d3 ♖fd8 21 ♖ed1 ♕c5 22 ♘e2! ♕xe3+ 23 ♖xe3 ♔g8 24 a4, and Black still had some problems.

Generally speaking, White definitely appears to be more comfortable after 10 ♕g3 ♘c6 11 ♘xc6 ♕xc6 12 ♖e1 ♗b7! 13 a3 but Black's position has a reasonable safety margin. Alternatively, 13 ♕xg7!? still seems to be risky for White.

# 7  5...a6 6 ♗c4 e6 7 ♗b3 ♘bd7!

**1 e4 c5 2 ♘f3 d6 3 d4 cxd4 4 ♘xd4 ♘f6 5 ♘c3 a6 6 ♗c4 e6 7 ♗b3 ♘bd7!** *(D)*

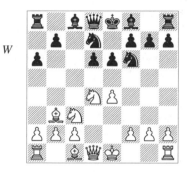

W

Having played 7 ♗b3, White not only ensures a wide choice of further plans but, at the same time, introduces a certain delay, so that after 7...♘bd7 his most aggressive ideas do not work very effectively. Surely, 7...♘bd7 is the most important move.

We shall discuss the following separately:

**A: 8 ♕e2**     96
**B: 8 f4**     97

Other moves:

a) 8 ♗xe6?! fxe6 9 ♘xe6 is dubious; e.g., 9...♕b6 10 ♗e3 ♘c5 11 ♘xf8 ♖xf8.

b) 8 g4 ♘c5 9 ♕f3? b5 10 g5? ♘fxe4! 11 ♘xe4 ♗b7 12 ♘c6 ♕d7! −+.

c) 8 ♗e3 ♘c5 9 f3. I do not like this interpretation of the Sozin at all.

Here, I do not see any difficulties for Black after, for instance, 9...b5.

d) 8 0-0!? ♘c5 and then:

d1) 9 ♖e1?! ♗e7! (it is extremely important for Black to hide the king) 10 ♕f3 (after 10 f4 0-0 11 ♕f3, one of the good ideas is 11...♕c7 12 ♗e3 b5 – Gallagher) 10...0-0 11 ♕g3 ♔h8 (or 11...♘d7!? 12 ♗h6 ♘e8 13 ♖ad1? ♘xb3 14 axb3 ♗h4 −+ Gallagher) 12 ♗g5 (12 f3?! ♘d5!!, Re.Gonzalez-Herrera, Cuban Ch (Matanzas) 1997) 12...h6 (de Firmian-Ivanchuk, Lucerne Wcht 1989) 13 ♕h3 ♔g8 14 ♗h4 ♕c7 (Ivanchuk) with a good game.

d2) 9 ♕f3?! ♗e7 10 ♕g3 0-0 11 ♗h6 ♘e8, and bad is 12 ♖ad1? ♘xb3 13 axb3 ♗h4 14 ♕g4 f5, Magomedov-Dvoirys, Cheliabinsk 1991.

d3) 9 f4(!) will be discussed under *8 f4 ♘c5 9 0-0* (note that the move-order here, *8 0-0 ♘c5 9 f4*, makes it possible to avoid the line *8 f4 b5!?*).

e) 8 ♗g5 and then:

e1) 8...h6!? 9 ♗h4 (9 ♗xf6!?) 9...♕a5 10 0-0 (10 ♕d2 ♗e7! or 10 f3 ♗e7 11 ♕e2 ♘c5 12 0-0 ♗d7 13 ♖ad1 b5 14 e5 dxe5 15 ♕xe5 b4 = Ehlvest-Tal, Skellefteå World Cup 1989) 10...♕h5! = Ehlvest-Kasparov, Skellefteå World Cup 1989.

e2) 8...♘c5 and now:

e21) 9 ♕e2 – *8 ♕e2 ♘c5 9 ♗g5*.

e22) After 9 ♕f3 ♗e7, Black gets a good game; e.g., 10 0-0-0 ♗d7 and now 11 h4 ♖c8 12 ♔b1 b5, Gdanski-Adorjan, Polanica Zdroj 1991, or 11

♖he1 ♕c7 12 ♔b1 0-0 13 g4 b5, Ivan-ović-Rashkovsky, Skopje 1991.

e23) 9 f4 ♗e7 (9...b5!? 10 e5 dxe5 11 fxe5 ♕c7, L.Steiner-Najdorf, Warsaw 1937). Now 10 ♕e2 transposes to Line A, and the idea 10 ♕f3 ♕c7 11 0-0-0 b5 12 ♗xf6 ♗xf6 13 ♘f5 ♘xb3+ 14 axb3 exf5 15 ♘d5 ♕b7 16 exf5 0-0 (Istratescu-Akopian, Mamaia jr Wch 1991) 17 ♘xf6+ gxf6 18 ♕g4+ ♔h8 19 ♕h4 ♕e7 20 ♖he1 ♕d8 21 g4 (Stoica/Istratescu) has not found followers.

## A)

**8 ♕e2 ♘c5** *(D)*

8...b5 9 ♗g5 ♘c5 – *8...♘c5 9 ♗g5 b5*.

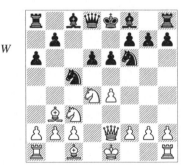

W

**9 ♗g5**

9 g4 is worth mentioning:

a) It is probably premature to play 9...d5 in view of 10 ♗g5!, Borkowski-Kr.Georgiev, St John 1988.

b) 9...g6!? (Marin/Stoica) is quite good.

c) Also good is 9...b5 10 g5 ♘fd7 (10...b4!?); e.g., 11 ♗d5 (11 ♘d5?! ♗b7!?; 11 f4 ♗b7!; 11 f3 ♗b7 12 h4 b4 13 ♘d1 ♕c7 14 ♘e3 ♘xb3 15 axb3 d5 16 exd5 ♗c5 17 dxe6 ♘e5 with

compensation, Rigo-Balinov, Austrian Cht 1995/6) 11...exd5! (less convincing is 11...♗b7 12 ♗xb7 ♘xb7 13 a4) 12 ♘c6 ♕b6 13 exd5+ ♘e5 14 f4 ♗g4 15 ♕e3 (Fierro-Bruzon, Havana 1997) and now 15...♘cd3+!? is at least sufficient.

**9...♗e7**

9...h6!?; 9...b5 10 ♗d5!?, Velimirović-Bertok, Yugoslavia 1974.

**10 f4**

10 0-0-0 ♘fxe4! 11 ♗xe7 ♘xc3 12 ♗xd8 ♘xe2+ 13 ♘xe2 ♔xd8 14 ♖xd6+ is slightly better for Black.

**10...h6**

This is still the main move but it is not necessary to create weaknesses in the kingside. After 10...0-0 11 0-0-0 ♕c7 Black is OK in the following examples:

a) 12 ♔b1 b5 (12...h6 13 h4) 13 e5 dxe5 14 fxe5 ♘e8 15 ♗d5 ♗b7, Dobos-Baburin, Györ 1990.

b) 12 g4 b5 13 ♗xf6 ♗xf6 14 g5 ♗e7, Veröci-Wang Pin, Subotica wom IZ 1991.

c) 12 h4 ♖e8 (12...b5!? 13 e5 ♘e8) 13 g4 b5 14 e5 (14 ♗xf6 ♗xf6 15 g5 ♗d8!?, Boros-Purtov, Zalakaros 1992) 14...dxe5 15 fxe5 ♘fd7 16 ♗xe7 ♖xe7, Sax-Dao, Balatonbereny 1996.

**11 ♗xf6**

Not 11 ♗h4? ♘fxe4!.

**11...♗xf6 12 0-0-0 ♕c7**

Or:

a) 12...♘xb3+ 13 axb3 ♕a5 14 ♔b1 ♗d7 15 g4 (15 ♖he1!? 0-0-0 16 e5 dxe5! 17 fxe5 ♗e7) 15...0-0-0 16 h4 ♔b8 with chances for both sides, S.Farago-Mas, Budapest 1997.

b) 12...♗d7 and now:

b1) 13 ♔b1 ♕c7 – *12...♕c7 13 ♔b1 ♗d7*.

b2) Interesting is 13 e5 dxe5 14 fxe5 ♗g5+ 15 ♔b1 ♕c7 16 ♘e4!? (16 h4 ♗f4!; 16 ♖hf1!?) 16...♕xe5!? 17 ♘xc5 ♕xc5 18 ♗xe6! ♗xe6 19 ♘xe6 fxe6 20 ♕xe6+ ♕e7 21 ♕f5 ♕f7 22 ♕c5 ♗e7 23 ♖he1 ♔f8 24 ♕c7 ∞ Krogh-Hutters, Denmark 1992.

**13 ♖he1**
Other moves:

a) 13 ♔b1 ♗d7 (not 13...b5?! 14 ♘dxb5! axb5 15 ♘xb5 ♕a5 16 ♘xd6+ ♔e7 17 ♘c4!, Balinov-Nagel, Austria 1993) and then:

a1) 14 ♖he1 0-0-0! (unsafe for Black is 14...0-0 15 g4!, as in Pilnik-Rubinetti, Argentine Ch (Buenos Aires) 1972) 15 e5 ♗e7 = Palac-Badea, Khania 1989.

a2) 14 g4. Now 14...b5?! is inaccurate due to 15 a3 ♘xb3 (15...0-0-0 16 ♗a2) 16 cxb3 ♖c8 17 h4 ± Istratescu-Votava, Rishon-le-Zion 1991. Black should play 14...g5!? or 14...0-0-0, when White can choose between 15 f5!? and 15 h4 (Marin/Stoica).

b) 13 g4!? ♗d7 14 h4 0-0-0 15 ♕f2 (15 ♔b1!? Marin/Stoica; 15 ♕f3 ♔b8 16 g5 ♗xd4 17 ♖xd4 ♗c6 gives Black a satisfactory game, S.Farago-Roehrich, Budapest 1995) 15...b5 16 g5 ♗e7 17 a3 ♕b6 18 ♗a2 a5 with a good game for Black, A.Kovačević-Tringov, Arandjelovac 1993.

**13...0-0**
13...♗d7 is more cautious. For example, 14 ♔b1 transposes to *13 ♔b1 ♗d7 14 ♖he1*.

**14 g4**
After 14 e5 dxe5 15 fxe5, 15...♗e7! gives Black a good game, Medvegy-Zhu Chen, Erevan wom OL 1996. Less convincing is 15...♗g5+ 16 ♔b1 b5 17 h4!? ♗xh4 18 ♖h1 with

compensation, Golubev-Serebrjanik, Novy Bečej 1991.

**14...b5 15 g5!? hxg5 16 e5 dxe5 17 fxe5 ♗e7 18 ♕h5 ♖d8**
Possibly Black can maintain the balance after 19 ♘e4 (or 19 ♖e3!? g6 20 ♕h6 ♗f8! 21 ♕xg5 ♗b7 Serebrjanik) 19...♘xe4 20 ♖xe4 g6 21 ♕h6 a5 22 ♖d3 ♗f8, Mitkov-Serebrjanik, Vrnjačka Banja 1991.

**B)**
**8 f4**
This is White's main choice.
**8...♘c5** *(D)*
Black usually plays this. Alternatively:

a) 8...♕c7!? is possible:

a1) 9 f5 ♘c5 – *8...♘c5 9 f5 ♕c7*.

a2) 9 0-0 and then: 9...b5 – *8...b5 9 0-0 ♕c7*; 9...♘c5 – *8...♘c5 9 0-0 ♕c7*.

b) 8...b5!? is possibly no worse than the main continuation:

b1) 9 f5 ♘c5! transposes to Line B32 (9...e5 is weaker in view of 10 ♘c6! – Fischer).

b2) After 9 ♗e3, it is a good idea to play 9...♗b7! (see *7...b5 8 f4 ♗b7! 9 ♗e3 ♘bd7!*).

b3) 9 0-0 and then:

b31) 9...♘c5 – *8...♘c5 9 0-0 b5*.

b32) 9...b4 10 ♘a4 (10 ♘d5?! exd5 11 exd5 ♗e7 12 ♖e1 ♘b8) 10...♗b7 (10...♘xe4 11 f5!), and now:

b321) 11 f5 e5 12 ♘e6 fxe6 13 fxe6 ♘b8 is hard to assess.

b322) 11 ♗e3!? – *7...b5 8 f4 ♗b7 9 ♗e3 ♘bd7 10 0-0 b4 11 ♘a4*.

b33) 9...♕c7 is less logical than 9...♗b7. White may proceed with 10 ♖e1 ♘c5 11 e5 or 10 f5 e5 11 ♘de2.

b34) 9...♗b7! 10 ♖e1!? (10 f5 e5! and 10 ♗e3 ♖c8! result in lines that are advantageous for Black) 10...♘c5 11 ♗d5 and here 11...♕c8, or even 11...exd5 12 exd5+ ♔d7 13 b4 ♔c8!, as in the game Hoogendoorn-Bosch, Dutch Cht 2000/1, appears satisfactory for Black.

*W*

At this point there are four interesting moves:

**B1: 9 0-0**          98
**B2: 9 e5**           101
**B3: 9 f5**           105
**B4: 9 ♕f3**          114

9 ♗e3 has also occurred:

a) 9...b5 10 e5 dxe5 11 fxe5 ♘fd7 (11...♘xb3 transposes to the Classical Sozin – Line C2 of Chapter 8) 12 0-0 (12 ♕f3 ♗b7 13 ♕g3 ∞ Jaracz-Jasnikowski, Polish Ch (Cetniewo) 1991; after 12 ♕e2, 12...♗b7 13 0-0-0 ♕c7 is good for Black) 12...♗b7 13 ♕h5 (13 ♖xf7 ♔xf7 14 ♕f1+ ♔e8 looks dubious for White) 13...g6 14 ♕h3 ♕e7! *Schach-Archiv*.

b) 9...♗e7 10 e5 dxe5 11 fxe5 ♘fd7 12 ♕h5 0-0 (12...g6?! 13 ♕e2 ♘xe5 14 0-0-0 ♕c7 15 ♗h6!, Velimirović-Wojtkiewicz, Palma de Mallorca 1989) 13 0-0-0 ♕a5 14 ♗f4 ∞ Lejlić-Grilc, Bled 1993.

c) The likelihood is that the simple 9...♘fxe4! 10 ♘xe4 ♘xe4 favours Black; e.g., 11 0-0 ♘f6!? or 11 ♕f3 ♘c5!?. The optimistic recommendation of Mikhalchishin (1991), 11 f5!?, with the ideas 11...e5 12 ♕h5 ♕f6 (?!) 13 ♕g4 and 11...♕h4+ 12 ♔f1 ♘g3+ 13 ♔g1, has not yet found followers.

**B1)**
**9 0-0**
Now:
**B11: 9...♗e7**       99
**B12: 9...♘fxe4**     100

There are two other possibilities:

a) 9...b5 10 e5! (10 f5?! – *9 f5 b5 10 0-0*) 10...dxe5 11 fxe5 ♘xb3 (this position may also arise from the Classical Sozin) 12 axb3 ♗c5 13 ♗e3 ♘d5 14 ♕f3! 0-0 15 ♘xd5 ♕xd5 (not 15...exd5? 16 ♘c6 ± Gheorghiu-Basman, Hastings 1967) 16 ♕xd5 exd5 17 b4 ± Mikhalchishin-Ubilava, Kuibyshev 1986. I am not sure that White has serious winning chances.

b) 9...♕c7!? and now:

b1) 10 f5?! e5.

b2) 10 ♗e3?! can be answered by 10...♘cxe4!? or 10...b5!?.

b3) 10 e5?! dxe5 11 fxe5 ♕xe5 12 ♖e1 ♕c7 (12...♕d6!?) 13 ♗g5 ♘xb3! (and not 13...♗e7? 14 ♘f5!, as in Vavra-Votava, Czech Ch (Luhačovice) 1993).

b4) 10 ♕f3 – *9 ♕f3 ♕c7 10 0-0*.

b5) 10 ♕e2!? ♗e7 (10...b5? 11 e5) 11 e5 (11 ♔h1 0-0 12 e5 ♘fd7!; 11 g4!?), and then 11...♘xb3 12 axb3 dxe5 13 fxe5 ♗c5 14 exf6 ♗xd4+ 15 ♔h1 with compensation, Caruso-Penttinen, Tallinn 1991, or 11...dxe5 12 fxe5 ♘fd7 13 ♗f4 0-0, when White may play 14 ♔h1 or 14 ♖f3 (14 ♖ad1 b5 15 ♘d5 exd5 16 ♗xd5 ♘e6! is very unclear, Tkaczyk-Rogaliewicz, corr. 1994).

## B11)

**9...♗e7** *(D)*

W

**10 e5**

Or:

a) 10 ♕f3!? – *9 ♕f3 ♗e7 10 0-0*.

b) 10 f5 – *9 f5 ♗e7 10 0-0*.

c) 10 ♗e3 ♕c7 (10...♘fxe4!?) 11 e5 (11 ♕f3 – *9 ♕f3 ♗e7 10 ♗e3 ♕c7!? 11 0-0?!*) 11...dxe5 12 fxe5 ♕xe5 13 ♘f5 (a beautiful but dubious idea) 13...♘g4! 14 ♘d6+ ♕xd6 (14...♗xd6!? 15 ♗f4 ♘d3!) 15 ♕xg4 0-0 16 ♗h6 (better is 16 ♖ad1!? – Peng Zhaoqin) 16...♕e5 17 ♖ae1 f5! ∓ Velimirović-Peng Zhaoqin, Pozarevac 1995.

**10...dxe5**

10...♘fe4 11 ♘xe4 ♘xe4 12 c3! ±.

**11 fxe5 ♘xb3**

11...♘fd7 and then:

a) 12 ♖xf7? ♔xf7 13 ♘xe6 ♘xe6 14 ♗xe6+ ♔e8 –+ Sandler.

b) 12 ♕h5 ♘f6! (12...g6 13 ♕e2 ± Gi.Hernandez-Browne, Linares (Mexico) 1994; 12...0-0 13 ♖f3!? Minasian) and now 13 ♕d1 ♘fd7 repeats, Sandler-Danailov, Adelaide 1990. Instead, both 13 exf6 ♕xd4+ 14 ♔h1 gxf6! (Sandler) and 13 ♖xf6 ♕xd4+!? 14 ♖f2 0-0 15 ♗f4 ♘xb3 16 ♖d1 ♕b4! are unconvincing for White.

c) 12 ♕e2!?.

d) 12 ♗f4!? transposes to note 'a1' to Black's 11th move in Line B21.

**12 axb3 ♗c5 13 ♗e3 ♘d5 14 ♗f2!**

14 ♕f3 0-0 15 ♘xd5 ♕xd5 16 ♕xd5 exd5 = Kunze-Stohl, Munich 1992.

After the text-move (14 ♗f2), White enjoys some advantage:

a) 14...0-0 15 ♘e4 ♗e7 16 c4 (16 ♕f3 f6 = Rogers-Dao, Erevan OL 1996; 16 ♕g4 f5 Shipov) 16...♘f4 17 ♕g4 ♘g6 (17...♘d3 18 ♘f3!? Shipov), and now:

a1) 18 ♖ad1 ♘xe5 19 ♕g3 (19 ♕h5 ♕a5 20 ♗e1 ♕c7 21 ♗g3 f6 22 ♔h1 b5! Shipov) 19...♕c7 (19...♘d7!?) 20 ♗e3 f6 21 ♗h6 ♖f7 22 ♗f4 ♗d7 = Velimirović-Shipov, Belgrade-Moscow 1998.

a2) An attempt to improve is 18 ♘f3!? ♕c7 (18...f5!?) 19 ♖ad1 ♘xe5 20 ♘xe5 ♕xe5 21 ♗d4 h5 (or 21...f5 22 ♗xe5 fxg4 23 ♖xf8+) 22 ♕e2 ♕a5 23 ♗c3 ♕b6+ 24 ♔h1 e5 25 ♕xh5 f6 (Shipov) 26 ♗xe5!.

b) 14...♘xc3 15 bxc3 and then:

b1) 15...♕c7 and here:

b11) 16 ♕h5 0-0 (or 16...♗d7 17 ♗h4!) 17 ♖ae1 (17 ♗h4!?) 17...♗d7 18 ♖e4 f5! with a good game, Arakhamia-Ftačnik, Sydney 1991.

b12) 16 ♕g4 0-0 17 ♗h4 (17 ♖ae1!? is better) 17...♕xe5 18 ♖ae1 ♗xd4+ 19 cxd4 f5!, and Black holds on, Velimirović-Aleksić, Yugoslav Cht 1992.

b2) 15...0-0 16 ♕h5 (other possibilities are 16 b4!? {Ftačnik} and 16

♕g4) 16...♗e7 17 ♖ad1 ♕c7 18 ♖d3 g6 19 ♕e2 with a slight advantage for White, Gdanski-Rõtšagov, Manila OL 1992.

## B12)
**9...♘fxe4**
Or 9...♘cxe4.
**10 ♘xe4 ♘xe4 11 f5 e5! 12 ♕h5!**
*(D)*

Other moves are dubious for White: 12 ♕e2 ♘f6; 12 ♘f3 ♘f6!?; 12 ♘e6 ♕b6+! 13 ♔h1 fxe6! 14 ♕h5+ ♔d8 15 ♗g5+ ♔c7! 16 fxe6 ♘f2+ (or 16...♗xe6! 17 ♗xe6 ♘f2+ 18 ♖xf2 ♕xf2 Marin/Stoica) 17 ♖xf2 ♕xf2 18 ♕e8 (18 e7 ♗d7), and White cannot get real compensation after, for example, 18...♕f5!?.

This is an amazingly rich and very unclear position.

**12...♕e7**
The most uncompromising continuation, but nobody knows whether it is the best. 12...♕b6?! 13 ♕xf7+ ♔d8 14 c3! exd4 15 ♖e1 (Stoica) and 12...♕c7? 13 ♘e6 have been unsuccessful.

The alternative is 12...d5!? 13 ♖e1! (13 ♘f3?! ♘f6!?; 13 ♘e6?! ♗xe6 14 fxe6 ♕b6+!; 13 ♗f4?! exf4! 14 ♖ae1

♕f6 15 c3 ♗c5 and Black wins, Astrahantsev-Stoica, Romanian Cht 1970) 13...♗c5! 14 ♖xe4, and then:

a) 14...0-0 15 ♖g4! (15 ♖h4? ♗xf5! ∓; 15 ♗g5 ♕b6!) 15...♗xd4+ 16 ♔h1 offers substantial compensation for White:

a1) 16...♔h8 17 ♗xd5! ♕xd5 18 ♖h4 ♗xf5 19 ♕xf5 g6 20 ♕f6+ ♔g8 21 ♖xd4 +−.

a2) 16...g6 and now, rather than 17 fxg6 fxg6 18 ♖xg6+ hxg6 =, maybe 17 c3 is stronger.

a3) 16...e4 17 ♗g5 is dangerous for Black according to Stoica's analysis; e.g., 17...♕d7 (17...♗f6 18 ♕h6! ±) 18 ♖f1 ♕b5 (18...g6 19 ♖g3! ♕b5 20 ♕d1) 19 ♖gf4 g6 (19...f6 20 a4! ♕c5 21 ♖h4!; 19...♗xb2 20 a4 ♕c6 21 f6) 20 fxg6 hxg6 21 ♕d1 ♗e5 22 ♗xd5!.

b) 14...♗xd4+ and then:

b1) 15 ♔h1 ♕f6! (15...0-0 16 ♖h4! ♗xf5 17 ♖xd4!? g6 18 ♖g4) 16 ♖e1 (not 16 ♗xd5?! ♗xf5 17 ♗g5 ♕g6!) 16...♕xf5 (16...♗xf5 17 c3 is unclear) 17 ♕xf5 ♗xf5 18 c3 =.

b2) 15 ♗e3 0-0 (15...♗xb2 is hazardous for Black) 16 ♖xd4 (16 ♗xd4? dxe4 17 ♗xe5 ♕b6+ 18 ♔h1 ♕h6) 16...exd4 17 ♗xd4. Black is no worse: 17...f6 (17...♖e8!? {Short} 18 f6 ♖e4 19 c3 ♖xd4!?) 18 ♗c5 (18 ♖d1 ♔h8 I.Rogers; 18 ♕f3 ♔h8 19 ♗xd5 ♕c7! Kavalek) 18...♖e8! 19 ♖d1 ♔h8, Topalov-Short, Amsterdam 1996.

b3) 15 ♖xd4!? ♕b6! (15...exd4? 16 ♗g5) 16 c3! (16 ♕g5? 0-0 17 f6 ♕xd4+ 18 ♗e3 ♕g4; 16 ♗a4+? ♔f8 17 f6 ♕xd4+ 18 ♔h1 h6) 16...exd4 (16...0-0 17 ♗e3 exd4 18 ♗xd4 ♕h6 19 ♕xh6! gxh6 20 ♖f1 Stoica) 17 ♕e2+. White has compensation:

b31) 17...♔d8 18 ♕e5 dxc3+ (alternatively, 18...♗d7 19 ♕xg7 dxc3+ 20 ♔h1 ♖e8 21 ♗g5+ ♔c8 22 ♕xc3+ ♕c7 23 ♕d2 ♗c6 24 ♖c1) 19 ♗e3 ♕c6!? 20 ♗xd5 ♖e8 (20...♕f6 21 ♗g5!!) 21 ♕d4 is analysis by Stoica.

b32) 17...♔f8 18 ♕e5!! (Stoica and Stanciu) 18...♕f6 (another possibility is 18...♗d7 19 cxd4! ♖d8 20 ♗f4 with compensation) 19 ♕xd5 (or maybe 19 ♕xf6!?) 19...h6! 20 ♗f4 ♗xf5 with very unclear play (Stoica).

**13 ♕f3!**

13 ♗e3 ♘f6 14 ♕f3 ♕c7 ∓.

**13...♘c5**

If 13...♘f6, then 14 ♗g5! (rather than 14 ♗a4+?! ♔d8 15 ♗d2 ♕c7). Stoica and Marin suggested 13...♕h4!? 14 ♗a4+ ♔d8 15 ♘c6+ ♔c7 16 ♘b4 ♘f6.

**14 ♘c6**

14 f6? gxf6 15 ♘c6 ♕c7 16 ♕xf6 ♘xb3 17 ♕xh8 ♘xc1!.

**14...♕c7 15 ♗d5**

15 ♘b4 ♘xb3 16 ♕xb3 b5 17 ♘d5 ♕c6 18 f6 ♗b7! ∓ is given by Topalov.

After the text-move (15 ♗d5) the situation is rather complex:

a) 15...♗d7 16 ♘b4 ♗e7 (16...a5? 17 ♗xf7+! ♔xf7 18 ♘d5 +− Kasparov), and now attention should be paid to 17 ♗xf7+!? ♔xf7 18 ♘d5 ♕d8 19 b4 ♘a4 (19...♗b5 20 ♕h5+ and 21 f6) 20 ♕h5+ ♔g8 21 f6 ♗xf6 (21...gxf6 22 ♗g5!) 22 ♗g5 ♗e8 23 ♕h3! – Stoica/Marin.

b) 15...♗e7!? and now 16 ♗xf7+?! ♔xf7 17 ♕h5+ ♔g8! 18 ♕e8+ (18 f6 gxf6 19 ♕e8+ ♔g7!) 18...♗f8 19 f6 ♗e6! favours Black, but 16 ♘xe7 ♕xe7 17 ♗e3!? is better.

c) 15...a5 16 ♗g5 (16 ♗e3 ♖a6 17 ♘d4 is dubious, TV viewers-Kasparov,

Spain 1991 – although the game later turned in the viewers' favour) 16...♗d7 (16...♖a6? 17 ♘d8! ± Topalov-Kasparov, Amsterdam 1996) 17 ♘e7 (17 f6!? g6 18 ♘e7 demands attention, Areshchenko-Averianov, Ukrainian jr Ch (Kiev) 1999), and Stoica gives 17...♗xe7! (17...f6?! 18 ♕h5+! ♔d8! 19 ♘g6 ♗e8 20 ♗e3! with an initiative) 18 ♗xe7 (18 f6 ♗xf6! 19 ♗xf6 ♗e6! 20 ♗xg7 ♖g8) 18...f6! 19 ♕g4 ♗e6!, with unclear play.

**B2)**

**9 e5** *(D)*

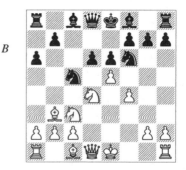

This thrust can give Black practical worries but, generally speaking, it appears to be poorly prepared.

**B21: 9...dxe5**   101
**B22: 9...♘fd7!?**   104

The only other possibility is 9...♘fe4 10 ♘xe4 ♘xe4 11 0-0 ±.

**B21)**

**9...dxe5 10 fxe5 ♘fd7!**

A weaker line is 10...♘xb3 11 axb3: 11...♘d5 12 0-0 (12 ♕g4!? Pugachov) 12...♘xc3 (12...♗e7 13 ♕g4 g6 14 ♗h6 ± Rublevsky – Har-Zvi, Oakham

1992) 13 bxc3 ♕d5 14 ♕e1 ± or
11...♗c5 12 ♗e3 ♘d5 13 ♘xe6! ±
Pugachov-Boger, USSR 1991.

**11 ♗f4**

11 ♕e2? ♕h4+.

**11...b5!**

Other moves:

a) 11...♗e7?! is risky for Black:

a1) 12 0-0 with chances for both
sides:

a11) 12...0-0?! 13 ♕g4 ♘f6 14 exf6
♕xd4+ 15 ♔h1 ♗xf6 16 ♖ad1 is
much better for White, Mowsziszian-
Anastasian, Erevan 1987.

a12) 12...b5!? is an interesting idea,
Gdanski-Pieniazek, Slupsk 1992. The
point is 13 ♘c6 ♕b6 14 ♘xe7 ♘xb3+.

a13) 12...♘f8 13 ♕f3 ♘g6 (but
not 13...♕xd4+?! 14 ♗e3 ♕xe5 15
♕xf7+ ♔d8 16 ♖ad1+ ♘fd7 17 ♗d4)
14 ♖ad1 ♕c7 15 ♘e4 ∞ Borulia-Yez-
ersky, Karvina 1992/3.

a2) 12 ♕h5 should probably be met
by 12...g6!?, since 12...♘f8!? (Velim-
irović-Ninov, Ulcinj 1998) 13 ♘f5!
(Burgess) is good for White.

a3) 12 ♕e2 ♗g5 13 ♗xg5 ♕xg5 14
♘f3 ♕f4 15 ♖d1 b5 16 ♖d4 ± Gi.Her-
nandez-Nedobora, Benasque 1993.

a4) 12 ♕g4!? g5 (12...g6 looks
good for White) 13 ♘xe6! (13 ♗g3 h5
14 ♕e2 h4 is unclear) 13...♘xe6 (or
13...fxe6 14 ♕h5+ ♔f8 15 0-0 ♔g7 16
♗xg5 ♗xg5 17 ♖f7+ ♔g8 18 ♖f5!)
14 ♗xe6, with an advantage after both
14...gxf4 15 ♗xf7+! (Vavra-Golod,
Ostrava 1993) and 14...fxe6 15 ♕h5+
♔f8 16 0-0 ♔g7 17 ♗xg5 ♗xg5 18
♖f7+ ♔g8 19 ♖af1 ♘xe5 20 ♘e4 h6
21 ♘f6+ ♗xf6 22 ♖1xf6.

b) 11...g5 and now:

b1) 12 ♘xe6 ♘xe6 13 ♗xe6 gxf4 14
♗xf7+ (14 ♕h5 ♘xe5 15 ♕xe5 ♗xe6

16 ♕xh8 f3! Sokolov) 14...♔xf7 15
♕h5+ ♔g7 ensures Black a draw,
A.Sokolov – Har-Zvi, Biel open 1992.

b2) Therefore, 12 ♗g3! h5 13 h4
♗g7 14 ♕e2 gxh4 15 ♗f4 is stronger,
Zontakh-Taborov, Kiev rpd 1994.

c) 11...♘xb3 12 axb3 ♗c5 13 ♘e4
± Mikhalchishin-Stangl, Dortmund
1991.

d) 11...g6 12 ♕e2 ♗g7 13 0-0-0!?
♗xe5 (13...♕c7 14 ♖he1 0-0 15 h4!
has also occurred) 14 ♗h6! gives
White a serious initiative for the pawn;
e.g., 14...b5 15 ♘c6 ♕h4 16 ♕e3 ♗xc3
17 bxc3 ♗b7 18 ♖d4 ♕h5 19 ♗d5!,
Vavra-Wojtkiewicz, Pardubice 1995.

**12 ♕e2**

12 ♕g4 h5! (12...♗b7 13 0-0-0 is
unclear) 13 ♕g3 h4 14 ♕g4, and now:

a) 14...g5!? 15 0-0-0!, and now both
15...♕e7 16 ♘c6! ♘xb3+ 17 axb3
♕c5 18 ♘e4! ♕xc6 19 ♗xg5 ♗b7 20
♖d6!, Short-Kasparov, London PCA
Wch (8) 1993, and 15...gxf4 16 ♘xe6
(for example, 16...♘xe6 17 ♗xe6 ♕e7
18 ♗xd7+ ♗xd7 19 ♕f3 ♖a7 20
♖he1) are dangerous for Black. After
15...♗h6 (Kasparov) 16 ♗e3! White
also preserves his attacking chances:
16...♘xe5 17 ♘c6 or 16...♗b7 17 ♘f3
(P.H.Nielsen).

b) 14...h3!? (Short) has not been
tested.

c) 14...♘f6 15 exf6 ♕xd4 16 fxg7
♕xg7 17 ♕e2 (± Hübner) 17...♗e7 18
♗e5 f6 19 ♗d4 ♘xb3 20 axb3 e5 21
♕f3 ♖b8 22 ♗e3 ♗b7 23 ♘d5 ♔f7
gave Black a slight plus in P.H.Niel-
sen-The World, Internet 2000.

**12...♗b7**

Possibly 12...♕h4+ 13 g3 ♕h3 (as
in Figlio-Frost, corr. 2000) deserves
some attention.

**13 0-0-0** *(D)*

13 0-0!? b4 14 ♘a4 ♘xb3 15 axb3 ♘c5 16 ♖ad1 ♘xa4 17 bxa4 ♗c5 (Zapolskis-Slekys, Mariampole 1992) 18 ♔h1 (Zapolskis).

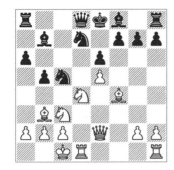

This position is hard to play for both sides. The white pieces are concentrated in the centre and Black should be very careful. However, if Black manages to squirm out of his adversary's threats, then in five to ten moves the e5-pawn might develop into a real weakness.

**13...♕b6**

Or:

a) 13...♗e7?! 14 ♕g4 g6 15 ♗h6!.

b) 13...♕a5 is a risky but interesting move:

b1) 14 a3 ♘xb3+ 15 ♘xb3 ♕c7 16 ♖hf1 is equal, Reefat-Wojtkiewicz, Dhaka 1999.

b2) 14 ♖he1 leads to unclear play after 14...♖c8 or even 14...b4!?.

b3) *Schach-Archiv* suggests 14 ♗g5!? b4 (or 14...h6 15 ♘xe6 hxg5 16 ♘xg5) 15 ♘a4 with the variations 15...♘xa4 16 ♘xe6 fxe6 17 ♗xe6 ♘ac5 18 ♕g4! +− and 15...♘xb3+ 16 axb3 ♕xe5 17 ♕d2 followed by ♖he1.

b4) 14 ♖hf1 and here:

b41) 14...♗e7?! 15 ♕g4 g6 (15...g5 16 ♗xg5 and now either 16...♘xe5 17 ♕f4 ♗xg5 18 ♕xg5 b4 19 ♘d5! or 16...♖g8 17 ♘xe6!) 16 ♗h6! (16 ♗g3 ♕b6 is unclear) 16...♘xe5 (16...b4 is risky due to 17 ♖xf7!?; e.g., 17...♔xf7 18 ♗xe6+ ♔e8 19 ♗xd7+! ♘xd7 20 ♘e6 or 17...bxc3 18 ♖xe7+ ♔xe7 19 ♗xe6 with the point 19...♕b6 20 ♗g5+ ♔e8 21 ♗xd7+ ♘xd7 22 ♘b5 ♘xe5 23 ♕b4 +−) 17 ♕f4 b4 (Vavra-Ftáčnik, Czech Cht 1994/5) and now Ftáčnik gives 18 ♘cb5! ♘ed3+ 19 cxd3 ♘xb3+ 20 ♘xb3 ♕xb5 21 ♕xf7+ ♔d7 22 d4 with an attack.

b42) 14...♘xb3+!? 15 ♘xb3 (15 cxb3 – Gallagher; 15 axb3!?) 15...♕c7 16 ♘d4 (16 ♘e4) 16...♘c5 = Motwani-Pigott, British Ch (Plymouth) 1989.

b43) 14...b4!? is interesting; e.g., 15 ♘d5 ♗xd5 16 ♗xd5 exd5 17 e6 ♘f6 18 e7 ♘ce4!, Vavra-V.Popov, Pardubice 2000.

c) 13...♕c7 14 ♖hf1 b4 and now 15 ♘a4 ♘xb3+ 16 axb3 transposes to line 'd', while 15 ♘d5 ♘xb3+ 16 ♘xb3 ♗xd5 17 ♖xd5 exd5 18 e6 ♗d6 19 exd7+ ♔f8 20 ♕g4 is not clear.

d) 13...b4!? 14 ♘a4 ♘xb3+ 15 axb3 ♕c7 16 ♖hf1 (16 ♖he1!?) and now:

d1) 16...♗e7?! 17 ♘f5.

d2) 16...g6? 17 ♗g5!, Kobaliya-Verner, Moscow 1995.

d3) 16...♖c8!? and then: 17 ♘f5 exf5 18 e6 ♕xc2+!; 17 ♖d2 ♘c5 18 ♘xc5 ♗xc5 19 ♘f5? exf5 20 e6 ♕e7 21 ♖d7 ♕xe6; 17 ♔b1 ♘c5 – *16...♘c5 17 ♔b1 ♖c8!?*.

d4) 16...♘c5 and here:

d41) 17 ♘f5?! exf5 18 e6 ♘xb3+ 19 ♔b1 ♕c6 20 ♘b6?! (Emms-A.Petrosian, London 1991) 20...fxe6!? ∓ A.Petrosian.

d42) 17 ♗g5 ♘e4!?.

d43) 17 ♔b1 ♖c8!? (17...♘xa4 18 bxa4 ♗c5 19 ♕g4 0-0-0 and now 20 ♗g3 was unclear in Riegler-Osterman, Slovenian Ch 1992, but maybe 20 ♘b3!? is stronger still) 18 ♘f5 exf5 (18...♘xa4!?) 19 e6 ♕e7!? (19...♕c6 20 exf7+ ♔xf7 21 ♘xc5 ♗xc5 22 ♕c4+) 20 ♘xc5 ♖xc5 21 ♖d7 ♕xe6 22 ♕xe6+ fxe6 23 ♖xb7 g5.

**14 ♖hf1**

Other options are:

a)  14 ♔b1 ♗e7 15 h4 and now:

a1)  15...0-0-0 16 a3 (according to Ftačnik, the line 16 ♖hf1 b4 17 ♘a4 ♘xa4 18 ♗xa4 ♘c5 19 ♗b3 ♖xd4 20 ♖xd4 ♘xb3 21 ♖c4+ ♘c5 is unclear) 16...♘b8 17 ♗e3 ♘c6 18 ♗a2 ♘xd4 19 ♗xd4 ♕c6 was roughly equal in Topalov-Anand, Wijk aan Zee 1996.

a2)  15...0-0! and now Topalov assesses both 16 ♗g5 ♖ae8 and 16 ♕g4 ♔h8 as '∓'.

b)  14 ♖he1!? ♗e7 15 ♕g4 g5 (or 15...g6 16 ♗h6) 16 ♗g3 h5 17 ♕e2 with very unclear play, Macieja-Kaminski, Polish Cht (Lubniewice) 1994.

**14...♗e7 15 ♕g4 g6**

The alternative 15...g5 16 ♗xg5 ♖g8 17 h4 ♘xe5 18 ♕f4 gives White an advantage, Oral-Tkebuchava, Mlada Boleslav 1994.

**16 ♗h6!?**

Topalov gave this as unclear. For example, 16...♘xe5 17 ♕f4 f6 18 ♗g7 0-0-0 (Yu Ting-Wang Pin, Hei Bei wom Z 2001) 19 ♗xf6.

## B22)

**9...♘fd7!? (D)**

This move differs in principle from 9...dxe5. Black endeavours to obtain a position with a greater safety margin.

**10 exd6**

Scarcely justified is 10 ♗e3 dxe5 11 fxe5 ♘xe5 12 ♕h5 ♗d6!? or 10 f5 ♘xe5 11 0-0 (11 fxe6 ♕h4+!) 11...♗e7 (11...exf5!?) 12 fxe6 fxe6.

**10...♘f6! 11 ♗e3**

11 ♕e2 ♗xd6 12 ♘f5 0-0 13 ♘xd6 ♕xd6 is good for Black, Velimirović-Popović, Belgrade 1998.

**11...♗xd6! 12 ♕f3 0-0**

12...♕c7 13 0-0-0 ♗d7 (or 12...♗d7 13 0-0-0 ♕c7), and then:

a)  An approximately equal game can be obtained after 14 ♖he1 0-0-0 (14...♘xb3+ 15 axb3 0-0-0 16 ♔b1 e5!? Moiseev) 15 h3 ♔b8 16 ♔b1 h5!, Vavra-Timoshenko, Topolcianky 1994.

b)  14 ♔b1 0-0!? (14...0-0-0 15 g4 ♘xb3 16 cxb3 ♗c6 17 ♘xc6 ♕xc6 18 ♕e2 {Gallagher} 18...♔b8!?) 15 g4 ♘xb3 (Saulin-Shipov, Moscow 1995) 16 axb3 ♖fe8! = 17 g5 ♘d5 (Shipov).

c)  14 g4!? 0-0-0 15 g5 ♘xb3+ 16 axb3 ♘d5 17 ♘xd5 exd5, and now 18 ♖d3, as in Florean-Bekker Jensen, Hallsberg 1997, preserves a slight advantage for White.

**13 0-0-0 ♕c7**

Otherwise:

a)  13...e5? 14 fxe5 ♗g4 15 ♕g3 +−.

b) 13...♘xb3+ 14 axb3 (14 ♘xb3 ♕c7 15 ♖xd6 ♕xd6 16 ♗c5 ♕c7 17 ♗xf8 ♔xf8 18 ♖d1 ♗d7 = Moroze-vich-Mukhutdinov, Moscow 1992) 14...♕c7 (14...♕a5!? 15 ♔b1 ♗b4 T.Thorhallsson-Van Wely, Akureyri 1994) and now:

b1) Nothing is achieved by continuing 15 f5 exf5 16 ♘xf5 ♗e5 17 ♗d4 ♗xd4! 18 ♖xd4 ♕e5, Lopez-Gongora, Cuba 1996.

b2) 15 ♔b1 is better.

b3) 15 g4!? is interesting: 15...b5!? 16 ♕xa8 ♗b7 17 ♕a7 ♗c5 (17...♖a8? 18 ♘xe6) 18 ♘xe6 ♗xa7 19 ♘xc7 ♗xe3+ 20 ♔b1 ♗xh1 21 ♖xh1 ♗xf4 22 ♘xa6 ♘xg4 23 h3 (Kobalia-Sad-vakasov, Gala Galdana jr Wch 1996) 23...♘f2 24 ♖f1 ♘xh3 25 ♖f3 ♖a8 26 ♘c5 ♗d6 27 ♘5e4 ♘g1 28 ♖f1 ♗h2 (Gallagher) 29 ♘xb5.

**14 g4?**

Probably 14 ♔b1 is better as it prevents 14 b5? in view of 15 ♕xa8 ♗b7 16 ♕a7 ♖a8 17 ♘dxb5 +–. Instead, 14...♗d7 transposes to note 'b' to Black's 12th move.

**14...b5!**

14...♗d7 15 g5 ±.

**15 ♖hf1**

15 ♕xa8 ♗b7 16 ♕a7 ♖a8 ∓.

**15...♗b7 16 ♕h3 ♖fc8**

After 17 g5 ♘fe4 18 f5 (Bezgodov-Solodovnichenko, Ukrainian open Ch (Alushta) 1999), Black's position must be close to winning; for example, 18...♘xb3+!? 19 axb3 exf5 20 ♘xf5 ♘xc3 21 ♖xd6 ♗e4.

**B3)**

**9 f5** *(D)*

For a long time it was believed that 9 f5 discredited the entire plan of

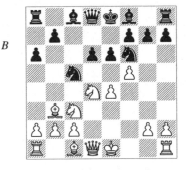

B

7...♘bd7 owing to the game Fischer-Bednarski (9...♘fxe4?) and the variation suggested by Fischer (9...♗e7 10 ♕f3 0-0 11 ♗e3 d5 12 exd5 ♘xb3 13 ♘xb3 exd5 14 0-0-0 +–). Nowadays it is clear that Black has a great number of sufficiently reliable alternatives.

**B31: 9...♗e7**   106
**B32: 9...b5!?**   112

The other continuations are:

a) 9...♘fxe4? 10 fxe6! ± Fischer-Bednarski, Havana OL 1966.

b) 9...exf5?! has not been played.

c) 9...e5 (this is probably premature) 10 ♘de2! and then:

c1) 10...h6 11 ♘g3! ♗d7 12 ♘h5 ± Ciríc-Bogdanović, Kraljevo 1967.

c2) 10...b5 11 ♗g5!.

c3) After 10...♗e7!?, 11 0-0 transposes to 9...♗e7 10 0-0 e5 11 ♘de2, while 11 ♘g3 h5 and 11 ♗e3 ♘xb3, followed by 12...b5, are unclear.

c4) 10...♘xb3 11 axb3 and then:

c41) 11...♗e7 12 ♗g5!.

c42) 11...h6 12 ♘g3! ♗d7 13 ♘h5 ♘xh5 14 ♕xh5 ♗c6 15 ♗e3 ± Zap-ata-Fedorowicz, Philadelphia 1993.

c43) 11...b5 12 ♗g5 ♗b7 ±. Now 13 0-0?! is inaccurate due to 13...♕b6+!. 13 ♘g3 and 13 ♗xf6!? are better.

c44) 11...d5 12 ♗g5 (12 ♘xd5!?)
12...d4 13 ♗xf6 gxf6 14 ♘d5 ♗d7
(Sieiro-Gonzalez – Vilela, Santa Clara
1983) 15 ♘g3! ♗c6 16 c4 ± Polugaevsky.

d) 9...♕c7!? occurs very rarely, although 10 0-0 (– *9 0-0!? ♕c7!? 10 f5*)
and 10 ♕f3 (– *9 ♕f3 ♕c7 10 f5*) both
appear quite good for Black. 10 fxe6
fxe6 doesn't seem bad for Black either; e.g., 11 0-0 ♗e7 or 11 ♕f3 ♗e7.

e) 9...♗d7!? is another interesting
move. 10 fxe6 fxe6 11 0-0 ♗e7 is
good for Black. After 10 ♕f3, 10...b5
transposes to Line B41 and 10...e5 11
♘de2 ♗c6 deserves attention. After
10 0-0, besides 10...b5 and 10...♗e7,
there is also 10...e5!? followed by
11...♗c6.

**B31)**
**9...♗e7 10 ♕f3**
Instead:

a) 10 fxe6 proves premature. After
10...fxe6 11 0-0, Black has a pleasant
choice between 11...♘xb3! 12 axb3
0-0, Akopian-Ivanchuk, Erevan 1989,
and 11...♗d7!? with good play for
Black, Grünfeld-Wojtkiewicz, Palma
de Mallorca 1989.

b) 10 0-0 is quite popular (and
harmless!):

b1) 10...♘xb3?! 11 axb3 0-0 (11...e5
12 ♘de2 b5 13 ♗g5! – *10...e5 11
♘de2 b5 12 ♗g5 ♘xb3 13 axb3*) 12
♕f3! (not wholly clear is 12 ♕e2 ♗d7
13 g4 e5 14 ♘f3 ♘xg4 15 ♘d5, Shtyrenkov-Dvoirys, Budapest 1991) – *10
♕f3 0-0 11 0-0 ♘xb3 12 axb3*.

b2) 10...♗d7!? is an good option:

b21) 11 fxe6 fxe6 12 ♗g5 b5
transposes to note 'b3' to White's 11th
move in Line B32 (=).

b22) 11 ♗g5 b5!? (11...0-0 is also
satisfactory) 12 ♕f3 transposes to note
'b' to White's 12th move in Line B41.

b23) 11 ♕e2 0-0 – *10...0-0 11 ♕e2
♗d7*.

b24) 11 ♕f3 and now: 11...b5 –
*9...b5 10 f5 ♗d7 11 0-0 ♗e7*; 11...0-0
– *10 ♕f3 0-0 11 0-0 ♗d7!?*; 11...e5!?
12 ♘de2 ♗c6 13 ♗d5 is unclear.

b3) 10...e5 11 ♘de2 and then:

b31) 11...h6 12 ♗e3!? ♘xb3 13
axb3 0-0 14 ♘g3 b5 15 ♘h5 with an
advantage for White, Anand-King,
Calcutta 1992.

b32) 11...♗d7!? 12 ♘g3? (White
should try 12 ♗e3!?) 12...h5! 13 ♗g5
h4 14 ♗xf6 (Sluka-Shtyrenkov, Pardubice 1997) 14...hxg3! ∓ (e.g., 15 ♗xe7
♕b6 16 ♘d5 ♘xe4+! and mate in
two).

b33) 11...b5 12 ♗g5 b4!? (12...♘xb3
13 axb3 ♗b7 14 ♗xf6 ♗xf6 15 ♘d5
0-0 16 b4!, Istratescu-Vasiesiu, Romanian Ch (Bucharest) 1994, and 12...0-0
13 ♗xf6, Istratescu-Genov, Mangalia
1992, both favour White) 13 ♗xf6
♗xf6 14 ♗xf7+ (14 ♗d5 ♖b8 15 ♗c6+
♔f8 16 ♘d5 ♘xe4 ∓ Ninov/Kostak-
iev; 14 ♘d5!? ♘xe4 15 ♘d4 is interesting; for example, 15...♗d7 16 ♘e6)
14...♔xf7 15 ♕d5+ ♔e8 16 ♕xa8
bxc3 (Telbis-Ninov, corr. 1994) 17 b4!
♘a4 18 ♘xc3 with unclear play (Gallagher).

b4) 10...0-0 11 fxe6 (11 ♕f3!? –
*10 ♕f3 0-0 11 0-0*; 11 ♕e2 is inaccurate; e.g., 11...e5!? 12 ♘f3 ♘xb3! 13
axb3 h6, Ciric-Bogdanović, Titograd
1965, or 11...♗d7 12 fxe6 fxe6 13 ♘f5
b5 14 a3 ♘xb3, etc., J.Polgar-Wojt-
kiewicz, Budapest Z 1993) 11...fxe6
12 ♘f5 (otherwise Black has not a
shadow of a problem), and then:

**b41)** 12...♘fxe4?! 13 ♕g4 ♖xf5 14 ♕xf5 ♘xc3? 15 ♕f7+ ♔h8 16 ♗g5 +–.

**b42)** 12...♘xb3 13 ♘xe7+ ♕xe7 14 axb3 and then:

**b421)** 14...♗d7 15 ♗f4! (15 ♗g5 ♗c6 =) 15...e5 (15...d5!?) 16 ♗g5 ± Istratescu-Gutkin, Biel open 1993, with the point 16...♗e6 17 ♘d5! ♗xd5 18 ♗xf6.

**b422)** 14...h6 15 ♕d3 ♗d7 (another idea is 15...e5!?) 16 ♗f4 e5 17 ♗g3 ♗c6 18 ♖ad1 ♖ad8 19 ♗h4! with better chances for White, Vlad-Ceteras, Bucharest 1992.

**b423)** 14...b5 15 ♗f4 (15 ♗g5 may come to the same thing after 15...♗b7 16 ♕d4 e5!? 17 ♕d3) 15...e5 16 ♗g5 ♗b7 17 ♕d3 ♕e6 18 ♗xf6 ♖xf6 19 ♖xf6 ♕xf6 20 ♘d5 ♕h4 with good chances for a draw, German-Kasparov, Buenos Aires simul 1997.

**b43)** 12...b5 and then:

**b431)** 13 ♗f4?! ♘fxe4! 14 ♘xe4 (14 ♕g4 is met by 14...♖xf5! 15 ♕xf5 ♘xc3) 14...♖xf5! – Gallagher.

**b432)** 13 ♗g5 b4!? (13...♘xb3 is liable to transpose to line 'b423') 14 ♘xe7+ ♕xe7 15 ♘d5 (15 ♗xf6 ♖xf6 16 ♖xf6 ♕xf6 17 ♘d5 ♕d8! ∞ Topalov) 15...exd5 16 ♗xf6 gxf6 17 ♗xd5+ ♗e6 18 ♗xa8 ♖xa8 19 ♕d4 ♖e8! with chances for both sides, S.Nikolov-Topalov, Sumen 1991.

**b5)** 10...b5!? is an interesting possibility.

We now return to 10 ♕f3 *(D)*:

**10...0-0**

This is logical, but nevertheless Black has several alternatives:

a) 10...♕a5 is interesting.

b) 10...♗d7!? 11 ♗e3! (11 0-0 – *10 0-0 ♗d7 11 ♕f3*), with interesting play:

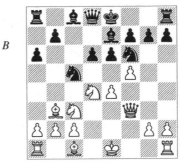

**B**

b1) 11...b5?! 12 fxe6 fxe6 transposes to note 'e1' after Black's 11th move in Line B32.

b2) 11...♖c8 12 g4!?.

b3) 11...0-0 – *10...0-0 11 ♗e3 ♗d7*.

b4) 11...♕c7 12 g4!? e5 (Black can also continue 12...♘xb3!?) 13 ♘de2 ♘xb3 14 axb3 (14 cxb3!?) 14...♗c6! 15 0-0 (Vombek-Balinov, Austrian Cht 1995/6) 15...h6! – Gallagher.

b5) 11...e5 12 ♘de2 ♘xb3 (12...♗c6 13 ♗xc5!) 13 axb3 ♗c6 14 0-0-0 (14 0-0 h5!?) 14...h6!? 15 g4 b5 with great complications, Anka-Purtov, Budapest 1993.

c) 10...♕c7 and then:

c1) 11 g4 d5!?.

c2) 11 ♗g5 Gallagher.

c3) 11 0-0 e5!? 12 ♘de2 ♘xb3 13 axb3 b5 14 ♗g5 ♗b7!?.

c4) 11 ♗e3 e5?! (11...b5? 12 fxe6 fxe6 13 e5! ♗b7 14 ♕h3 ± Goloschapov-Zso.Polgar, Pardubice 1995; better is 11...♗d7 – *10...♗d7!? 11 ♗e3! ♕c7*, or 11...0-0 – *10...0-0 11 ♗e3 ♕c7*) 12 ♘de2 ♘xb3 13 axb3 (13 cxb3 b5 14 ♖c1 ♕b7 15 ♗g5 ♗d7 16 ♗xf6 ♗xf6 17 0-0 ± Martens-Boriss, Santiago jr Wch 1990) 13...♗d7 (or 13...h6 14 g4!?) 14 ♗g5 with an advantage, Magomedov-Mahmud, Doha 1992.

d) 10...e5 11 ♘de2 and then:

d1) 11...♕a5 12 ♗d2 (12 ♗d5 ♘xd5 13 exd5 b5 ∞) 12...♘xb3 13 cxb3 b5 14 ♘d5 (14 g4 b4 15 g5 ∞) 14...♕d8 15 ♘xe7 ♕xe7 16 ♗g5 ♗b7 17 ♘g3 h6 18 ♗xf6?! (18 ♗h4! is stronger) 18...♕xf6 is fine for Black, Votava-Serebrjanik, Rishon-le-Zion 1992.

d2) 11...♗d7 and now 12 ♗g5!? (Veličković) or 12 ♗e3 – *10...♗d7 11 ♗e3 e5 12 ♘de2.*

d3) 11...♘xb3 12 axb3 b5 13 ♗g5 ♗b7 14 ♗xf6 ♗xf6 15 0-0-0!? (15 0-0 0-0 transposes to note 'b21' to White's 11th move) 15...0-0 16 ♘d5 a5 17 ♘ec3 a4 18 b4 a3 19 b3 turned out to be better for White in Mortensen-Browne, Reykjavik 1990.

**11 ♗e3**

11 g4 is quite well met by 11...♘fd7 followed by ...♘e5, while 11...d5 12 exd5 e5! might be even stronger.

The better-known alternative is 11 0-0, and then:

a) After 11...♔h8, 12 g4 ♘fd7 13 ♗e3 ♘e5 afforded Black good counterplay in Honfi-Vogt, Trnava 1982, but 12 ♗e3 and 12 ♗g5 are probably stronger.

b) 11...e5 12 ♘de2 and then:

b1) 12...b5!? and then: 13 ♗g5 ♘xb3 14 axb3 – *12...♘xb3 13 axb3 b5 14 ♗g5*; 13 g4 ♗b7!; 13 ♗d5!?.

b2) 12...♘xb3 13 axb3 (13 cxb3!?) 13...b5 and here:

b21) 14 ♗g5 ♗b7 is OK for Black; e.g., 15 ♗xf6 ♗xf6 16 ♘g3 ♖c8!.

b22) 14 ♗e3 – *11 ♗e3 e5 12 ♘de2 ♘xb3 13 axb3 b5! 14 0-0 ∞.*

b23) 14 g4!? b4 (14...h6! Vera) 15 g5 bxc3 (15...♘e8 16 ♘d5 ♗xg5 17 ♗xg5 ♕xg5+ 18 ♔h1 with compensation, Istratescu-Olimid, Romanian

Cht 1993) 16 gxf6 ♗xf6 (16...cxb2 17 fxe7 bxa1♕ 18 exd8♕ ♖xd8 19 ♗h6 or 19 ♕g3 ±) 17 ♘xc3 ♗b7 18 ♗e3 ♖c8 19 ♖ad1 with an advantage, Zapata-Vera, Matanzas 1993.

c) 11...♘xb3 12 axb3 e5 (12...♗d7?! 13 g4! – *11...♗d7 12 g4 ♘xb3? 13 axb3 ±*; 12...♕c7 13 ♗e3 transposes to note 'b12' to Black's 11th move in Line C221 of Chapter 9, where White is a little better) 13 ♘de2 – *11...e5 12 ♘de2 ♘xb3 13 axb3.*

d) 11...♕c7 and now:

d1) 12 ♗e3 – *11 ♗e3 ♕c7 12 0-0.*

d2) 12 ♗g5 b5 13 a3 ♘xb3 14 cxb3 h6 15 ♗e3 (15 ♗h4!? may also be tried) 15...e5 (15...♗d7! 16 ♖ac1 ♕b7 Beliavsky/Mikhalchishin) 16 ♘de2 b4 (16...a5!?) 17 axb4 ♕b7 18 ♘g3 ± Mortensen-Hölzl, Novi Sad OL 1990, with the point 18...♕xb4 19 ♘h5!.

d3) Critical is 12 g4!? ♘xb3 (12...d5 13 exd5 e5 14 ♘de2 ♘xb3 15 axb3 ♗c5+ 16 ♔h1; 12...h6 13 g5 hxg5 14 ♗xg5 ± Honfi-Cirić, Čačak 1969) 13 axb3 d5 14 exd5 ♗c5 15 ♗e3, when 15...e5 16 ♘db5 (16 ♘de2?! e4!) 16...♕b6 17 ♗xc5 ♕xc5+ 18 ♔h1 probably favours White, Christoffel-Herschel, corr. 1991. After 15...♕e5, White has, for example, 16 ♔h1!?.

e) 11...♗d7!? seems to be the most reliable:

e1) 12 ♗g5 ♘xb3 (or 12...b5) 13 axb3 b5 creates no problems for Black.

e2) 12 ♗e3 – *11 ♗e3 ♗d7 12 0-0.*

e3) 12 g4?! e5! (12...♘xb3? 13 axb3 ± h6 14 g5!, Istratescu-Ghitescu, Romanian Cht 1992) 13 ♘de2 ♗c6! gives Black excellent play; e.g., 14 ♗d5 ♘cxe4! 15 ♗xe4 d5, R.Pert-Bates, London 1997.

We now return to 11 ♗e3 *(D)*:

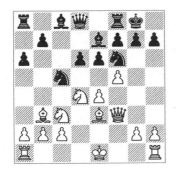

B

**11...e5**

Other possibilities:

a) 11...d5 12 exd5 e5 13 ♘de2 e4 14 ♕h3 (14 ♕g3 is unclear) 14...♘xb3 (14...g6 15 0-0!, Matulović-Bogdanović, Yugoslavia 1969) 15 axb3 ♘xd5 (15...b5 16 ♖d1 ± Yakovich-Vaulin, Kursk 1987). Now, instead of 16 0-0-0?! ♗xf5!, Romanishin-Dorfman, USSR Ch (Moscow) 1976, Black experiences some problems after 16 0-0! (Dorfman) or 16 ♘xd5!? ♕xd5 17 0-0, Badii-Dorfman, French Cht 1995.

b) 11...♘xb3 12 axb3 and now:

b1) 12...♘d7 is somewhat better for White after 13 0-0 ♘e5 14 ♕h3 or 13 0-0-0 ♘e5 14 ♕h3.

b2) 12...♗d7 13 g4! e5 14 ♘de2 – *11...♗d7 12 g4 e5 13 ♘de2 ♘xb3 14 axb3*.

b3) 12...e5! 13 ♘de2 – *11...e5 12 ♘de2 ♘xb3 13 axb3*.

c) 11...♗d7 12 g4! (12 0-0 b5! gives Black a good game, as 13 a3 is forced; 12 0-0-0!?). Now:

c1) 12...♕a5 13 0-0-0 e5 14 ♘de2 ♘xb3+ 15 cxb3 ♗c6 16 ♘g3 is much better for White, Winants-Christiansen, Wijk aan Zee 1993.

c2) 12...b5 13 g5 ♘e8 14 ♖g1 b4 (Kuksov-Yudasin, USSR 1989) 15

♘ce2! ♘xb3 16 axb3 e5 17 f6 exd4 18 ♗xd4 gives White an advantage.

c3) 12...e5 13 ♘de2 ♘xb3 14 axb3 d5 (14...♗c6 15 g5! {15 0-0-0 ♕a5} 15...♘xe4 16 ♘xe4 d5 17 f6 ♗b4+ 18 c3 dxe4 19 ♕f2 ± Tomescu-Ungureanu, Wattens 1997) 15 exd5 e4 16 ♕g2 ± Fischer-Bielicki, Mar del Plata 1960.

c4) 12...♘e8!? 13 0-0-0 (13 g5!? ♗xg5 14 0-0-0 Yudasin) 13...b5 gives Black counterplay.

c5) 12...d5!? is possibly playable: 13 exd5 ♘xb3 14 axb3 ♘xd5 15 ♘xd5 ♗h4+ ∞ Infante-H.Leyva, San Salvador 1997.

d) 11...♕c7 is a very important alternative, especially due to transpositions from other lines:

d1) 12 g4 b5! 13 g5 ♘fxe4 14 ♘xe4 ♗b7 15 fxe6 (both 15 f6!? ♗xe4 16 fxe7 ♕xe7 17 ♕f1 and 15 ♘xe6!? fxe6 16 ♗xc5 dxc5 17 ♗xe6+ ♔h8 18 0-0! ♗xg5 19 ♖ae1 are unclear – Shipov) 15...♗xe4 16 exf7+ ♔h8. Now, instead of 17 ♕h3? ♗xg5! ∓ Bezgodov-Shipov, Russian Ch (Elista) 1994, 17 ♕h5 is better. However, Black is no worse in any case.

d2) Of possible interest is 12 0-0-0!? b5 13 fxe6 fxe6 14 ♕h3 ♘xb3+ 15 axb3 e5 16 ♘e6, as in Hendriks-Van Blitterswijk, Netherlands 1994.

d3) 12 0-0 and now:

d31) 12...♗d7 13 g4!.

d32) 12...♔h8 13 g4 b5 14 g5 ♘fxe4 (I.Rogers-Baburin, Erevan OL 1996) 15 fxe6! ♗b7 (15...♘xc3 16 ♕xa8 ♗b7 17 ♕xf8+!) 16 ♘d5 ♗xd5 17 ♗xd5 fxe6 18 ♘xe6 – Baburin.

d33) 12...e5 13 ♘de2 ♘xb3 transposes to note 'b13' to Black's 11th move in Line C221 of Chapter 9.

d34) 12...♘xb3 transposes to note 'b12' to Black's 11th move in Line C221 of Chapter 9.

d35) 12...b5! is the most precise move:

d351) 13 fxe6 fxe6 and now one possibility is 14 ♘f5 ♘xb3 15 ♘xe7+ ♕xe7 16 axb3 ♗b7 = Istratescu-Ceteras, Bucharest 1992. There has also occurred 14 ♕h3 ♘xb3 15 axb3 (or 15 cxb3) 15...e5! 16 ♘f5 b4, when Black stands at least no worse.

d352) 13 a3 is playable, given the position of the black queen. Then:

d3521) 13...e5!? 14 ♘de2 (also possible is 14 ♘d5!?) 14...♗b7 15 ♘g3 ♘xb3 (Black can deviate with 15...♗c6 16 ♗d5 ♘a4, Veröci-Kotronias, Greece 1985) 16 cxb3 – *13...♘xb3 14 cxb3 e5 15 ♘de2 ♗b7 16 ♘g3*.

d3522) 13...♘xb3 14 cxb3 e5 15 ♘de2 ♗b7 16 ♘g3 (16 ♖ac1 ♕d7 17 ♘g3 ♖ac8 18 ♗g5? ♘xe4! Moutousis-Stangl, Tunja jr Wch 1989) with chances for both sides; e.g., 16...♖ac8 (16...♗c6; 16...d5!?) 17 ♖ad1 and now 17...♖fd8 18 ♘h5 ♗c6 19 ♖d3 ± Velimirović-Aleksić, Svetozarevo 1990 or 17...♕d7 (Mirallès-Khuzman, Luxembourg ECC 1998) 18 ♘h5!?.

**12 ♘de2 (D)**

**12...♘xb3**

It is well-known that in his 1993 match Kasparov played 12...b5!? here only after long thought. Other players have also hesitated to play it, as there is almost no fresh material on this topic at all:

a) Nothing is gained by 13 ♘d5 ♘xb3 14 ♘xf6+ ♗xf6 and 15...d5!, Bogdanović-Matulović, Sarajevo 1960.

b) 13 g4 ♗b7 (13...b4!? 14 ♘d5 ♘fxe4; 13...♘xb3) 14 ♗xc5 dxc5 15 g5 c4! 16 gxf6 ♗xf6 (unclear, Kasparov).

c) 13 0-0-0 ♘xb3+! 14 cxb3. Now, instead of 14...♗b7 15 ♔b1 (Mikhalchishin), 14...a5! is stronger.

d) 13 ♗d5 ♖b8 and then:

d1) 14 ♗xc5 dxc5 15 0-0-0 and now 15...♕b6 gives Black counterplay – Kasparov. Instead, 15...♕a5 16 g4 b4 17 g5 is unclear.

d2) 14 b4 ♘cd7 (14...♘a4!?) 15 0-0 ♘xd5 (15...♘b6! ∓ Kasparov) 16 ♘xd5 ♗b7 17 ♘ec3 with complications and roughly equal chances, Short-Kasparov, London PCA Wch (6) 1993.

d3) 14 a3 a5 15 b4 (15 ♗xc5?! dxc5 16 ♗c6 b4!) 15...♘a4 16 0-0 (Munteanu-Tugui, Romania 1995) 16...♘b6 (Stoica) with unclear play.

**13 axb3 b5!**

Or 13...d5, and now:

a) 14 ♘xd5 is possible.

b) 14 0-0-0!? (Dorfman/Perelshtein).

c) 14 exd5 e4 and now 15 ♕h3 transposes to note 'a' to Black's 11th move, while 15 ♕g3!? and 15 ♘xe4!? are also possible.

**14 g4**

This sharp idea of Mikhalchishin's (linked with 14...b4 15 ♘a4) might possibly allow Black to obtain a better endgame by force. Let us see what else there is:

a) 14 ♘xb5?! d5!, Akopian-Anastasian, Tbilisi 1989.

b) 14 ♗g5?! ♗b7! (14...b4!?) 15 ♗xf6 ♗xf6 16 0-0-0? b4 17 ♘d5 a5 ∓ Kruppa-Anastasian, Podolsk 1989.

c) 14 0-0-0?! b4! 15 ♘d5 (15 ♘a4 ♗b7!) 15...♘xd5 16 exd5 a5!.

d) 14 ♘d5!? ♘xd5 15 exd5 e4!? 16 ♕f2 ♗f6 17 c3 ♗b7 18 ♘f4? (18 ♖d1!) 18...♕c8 ∓ Lastin-Loskutov, Moscow 1995.

e) 14 ♖d1 ♗b7 (14...b4!? 15 ♘d5 ♘xd5 16 ♖xd5 ♗b7 17 ♖d2 ♗h4+!? 18 g3 ♗e7; 14...♕a5!?) and now:

e1) 15 0-0 – *14 0-0 ♗b7 15 ♖ad1*.

e2) 15 ♘g3 b4!? with good counterplay, Kuczynski-Stempin, Polish Cht 1989.

f) 14 0-0 ♗b7 15 ♖ad1 ♖c8 (or 15...b4!? 16 ♘d5 ♗xd5 17 exd5 ♖b8, Bakhmatov-Kabatiansky, USSR 1991) 16 ♖d2 ♕a5 (16...b4 17 ♘d5 and now, rather than 17...♘xd5 18 exd5 ± Golubev-G.Ginsburg, Ukrainian Ch (Simferopol) 1992, Black could try instead 17...♗xd5!?) 17 g4 (17 ♘g3 b4 ∞ Somborski-Timm, corr. 1998-2000) 17...♕b4! (17...b4 18 g5 bxc3 19 gxf6 cxd2 20 fxe7 ♖fe8 21 f6 ± Gudmunsson; 17...d5!?) 18 ♘g3 d5 19 ♘xd5 ♗xd5 20 exd5 ♗c5 ∞ Gudmunsson-Gislason, corr. 1990-2.

**14...b4** *(D)*

**15 ♘a4**

Neither 15 ♘d5 ♘xd5 16 exd5 ♗h4+ nor 15 g5 bxc3 is much good for White.

**15...♗b7**

Or 15...d5!? 16 ♘g3 (16 0-0-0!?) 16...♘xe4 (16...dxe4?! 17 ♕e2) 17

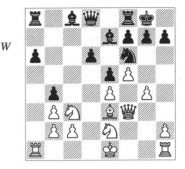

0-0-0 ♘d6 (17...♘xg3 18 hxg3!?) 18 f6!, with an utterly unclear position:

a) 18...♗xf6 19 ♕xd5 ♗xg4 20 ♕xd6 ♗xd1 (Zapata-Van Wely, Wijk aan Zee 1995) 21 ♕xd1!? (Zapata).

b) 18...gxf6 19 ♘f5!? (there are five or six other ideas as well) 19...♗b7 20 ♖hg1 d4 (20...♔h8? 21 ♗b6!) 21 ♕h3 ♔h8 (21...dxe3?? 22 ♖xd6 +− Ankerst-Wojtkiewicz, Amsterdam 1994) and now 22 ♖g3 is met by 22...♗e4!, but 22 ♘c5!? is interesting.

**16 ♘g3 ♕c7!**

A better-known continuation for Black is 16...d5 17 0-0-0 (17 g5 dxe4 18 ♕e2 ♘d5 19 f6 gxf6 20 gxf6 ♗xf6 21 0-0-0 ♗g5 22 ♘f5 ♘xe3 23 ♖xd8 ♘xf5+ 24 ♔b1 ♖axd8 25 ♕g4 f6! 26 ♕xf5 e3 27 ♖e1 is unclear according to Veličković), and then:

a) 17...♘xe4? 18 ♘xe4 dxe4 19 ♖xd8 exf3 20 ♖d7 +−.

b) 17...dxe4? 18 ♕e2 ♕a5 19 g5 ±.

c) 17...d4?! 18 ♗d2 (18 g5? ♘xe4 19 ♘xe4 ♕d5 −+ Winants) 18...♖c8 19 ♔b1 ♘d7 (19...♕c7 20 ♖c1) 20 h4, Yedidia-Akopian, Las Vegas 1994, favours White according to Akopian.

d) 17...♕c7!? 18 g5 (18 ♘b6 d4!? 19 ♘xa8 ♖xa8, Sluka-Vasilchenko, Zlin 1995). Now 18...♖ac8 19 ♖d2 transposes to note 'a' after White's 18th move. Alternatively, Nedobora recommended the immediate 18...♘xe4 19 ♘xe4 dxe4.

e) 17...♖c8!? 18 g5 (Veličković gave the line 18 ♘b6 ♕c7! 19 ♘xc8 ♖xc8, with the point 20 ♖d2 d4 21 ♗f2 ♘xe4!! 22 ♘xe4 ♗g5 –+; following 20 ♕e2 Black has 20...♘xg4 or 20...d4) 18...♕c7 and now:

e1) 19 ♕e2 ♘xe4 20 ♘xe4 is bad in view of 20...d4!! 21 ♗f2 ♕xc2+!! – Veličković.

e2) 19 ♖d2 transposes to note 'a' after White's 18th move.

**17 0-0-0**

17 g5? ♘xe4 18 ♘xe4 ♕c6 19 f6 ♗d8.

**17...♖ac8!**

Better than 17...♘xe4 18 ♘xe4 ♕c6?! 19 f6.

**18 ♖d2**

Black now has two options:

a) 18...d5 19 g5, and now not 19...d4? 20 gxf6 dxe3 21 ♕xe3 ♗xf6 22 ♘h5 ♕e7 23 ♖g1 ± Vega-Lopez Gomez, corr. 1995-7, but 19...♘xe4! 20 ♘xe4 dxe4 with a little-studied position, Barr-Russell, corr. 2000. If the next variation is correct, however, it will not be necessary to study it!

b) 18...♘xe4 19 ♘xe4 ♕c6 20 ♘b6 (20 f6 gxf6 seems dubious for White) 20...♕xe4 21 ♕xe4 ♗xe4 22 ♘xc8 ♖xc8 23 ♖e1 d5 with a better ending for Black, Kobaliya-Sotnikov, Moscow 1995.

**B32)**

**9...b5!?** *(D)*

Short played this move against Is-tratescu at the Erevan Olympiad in 1996, probably based on analysis of a

similar variation, 9 ♕f3 b5 10 f5 (Line B41), that occurred in his 1993 match versus Kasparov.

**10 fxe6**

Otherwise:

a) The main alternative is 10 ♕f3 – *9 ♕f3 b5 10 f5*; see Line B41.

b) 10 ♗g5 is not a very good idea; for example, 10...b4!? 11 ♘a4 (11 fxe6?! ♘xb3!) 11...♘xb3 12 axb3 e5!, Tomescu-Vajda, Bucharest 1995.

c) 10 0-0 is rather harmless:

c1) 10...♘xb3!? – *5...♘c6 6 ♗c4 e6 7 ♗b3 a6 8 0-0 ♘a5 9 f4 b5 10 f5 ♘xb3*.

c2) 10...♗d7!? and then:

c21) 11 fxe6 fxe6 – *10 fxe6 fxe6 11 0-0 ♗d7*.

c22) 11 ♕f3 – *10 ♕f3 ♗d7 11 0-0*.

c3) 10...♗e7!?.

c4) 10...e5(!) 11 ♘f3 (11 ♘de2 ♗b7!) 11...♘xb3 12 axb3 ♗b7 with a good game for Black, Vink-Lautier, Antwerp 1998.

**10...fxe6 11 ♕f3**

Or:

a) 11 ♗g5 can be well answered by 11...b4!?.

b) 11 0-0 and now:

b1) 11...♕d7?! 12 ♕f3 – *11 ♕f3 ♕d7?! 12 0-0*.

b2) 11...♗d7 is possible: 12 ♗g5 (12 ♕f3 – *11 ♕f3 ♗d7 12 0-0*) 12...♗e7 – *11...♗e7 12 ♗g5 ♗d7.*

b3) After 11...♗e7!? 12 ♗g5 ♗d7 Black suffers no problems:

b31) 13 ♔h1 b4 14 ♘a4 ♘xb3, Hendriks-Hoeksema, Enschede 1993.

b32) 13 ♕f3 ♘xb3! 14 axb3 0-0, Hamdouchi-Hellers, Biel IZ 1993.

**11...♗d7!** *(D)*

Or: 11...♕c7?! 12 ♗g5 (12 ♘xe6!? is interesting) 12...♗e7 13 e5! ♗b7 14 ♕h3; 11...♕d7?! 12 0-0 ♗b7 (12...b4 13 ♘a4!; 12...♗e7 13 ♘xe6!?) 13 ♕h3 e5 14 ♘e6 ± Balashov-Zlotnik, Moscow 1969; 11...e5, 11...♘xb3 and 11...b4 have not been tested.

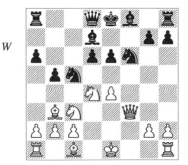

*W*

This is the critical position. Should Black manage to complete his development without trouble (12...♗e7, 13...0-0), his chances may improve. White should look for active possibilities connected, first of all, with the advance e5.

It is difficult to single out a main line as yet:

a) 12 ♕h3? e5 13 ♘f5 ♘xb3 14 axb3 b4 −+.

b) 12 ♗g5 ♗e7! (12...b4? 13 e5! dxe5 14 ♗xf6 gxf6 15 ♖d1!) 13 0-0-0 (13 e5 dxe5 14 ♘c6 ♗xc6 15 ♕xc6+ ♔f7! ∓; 13 0-0 transposes to note 'b3' to White's 11th move) 13...0-0! (the alternative 13...♕c8 is unclear) 14 e5 ♘d5! (14...♘fe4? 15 ♗xe7 ♕xe7 16 ♘xe4!! ♖xf3 17 exd6, Short-Kasparov, London PCA Wch (10) 1993) 15 ♗xe7 ♘xe7! and 16...d5! with an advantage for Black, Doghri-Dao, Budapest 1996.

c) After 12 ♖f1, good enough is 12...b4! (12...♗e7?! 13 e5!) 13 ♘a4?! ♘xa4 14 ♗g5 ♘c5 15 e5 dxe5 16 ♗xf6 gxf6 17 ♖d1 ♗g7! 18 ♘f5 0-0 19 ♕g4 ♖f7 ∓.

d) 12 0-0!? and then:

d1) 12...b4!? 13 ♘ce2 and now 13...♘xb3 14 axb3 e5 15 ♘f5 ♗xf5 16 ♕xf5 ♕d7 17 ♕f3 seems promising for White, Repkova-Chilingrova, Chrudim 1994, but Black may try to improve via, for example, 13...e5 or 13...♗e7.

d2) 12...♗e7 and now:

d21) 13 ♕g3 b4 (13...♘xb3 is OK) 14 ♘ce2 ♘cxe4!? 15 ♕xg7 ♖g8 16 ♕h6 d5 ∞ Waitzkin-Jaracz, Matinhos jr Wch 1994.

d22) 13 e5 dxe5 14 ♘c6 ♗xc6 15 ♕xc6+ ♔f7 16 ♘e4! (16 ♗e3 ♕c8 ∓ Istratescu-Short, Erevan OL 1996; after 16 ♗g5 possibilities include 16...♕d4+! 17 ♔h1 ♕g4 ∓ Istratescu) 16...♕d4+ 17 ♔h1 ♕xe4 18 ♗xe6+ ♔g6 19 ♗f5+ ♕xf5 20 ♖xf5 ♔xf5 21 g4+ ♔g6 22 g5. All this was forced. After 22...♖ac8 (or 22...♖hc8) 23 ♕g2 and 24 b4! White might have good chances.

d3) 12...♕c8 13 g4 is unstudied.

d4) 12...♖c8 is also worth investigating.

e) 12 ♗e3 and then:

e1) 12...≗e7?! 13 e5! ⟁xb3 (after 13...dxe5 White continues 14 ⟁c6) 14 exf6!? ⟁xd4 15 ≗xd4 is much better for White, Ardeleanu-Badea, Romanian Ch (Bucharest) 1994.

e2) 12...b4 and here:

e21) 13 e5? dxe5 14 ⟁c6 ♕c8 and Black wins.

e22) 13 ⟁ce2 opens up good possibilities for Black; for example, 13...⟁xb3; 13...e5; 13...≗e7 14 0-0 0-0 (14...⟁xb3!?) 15 ⟁f4 (Kotsur-Neverovsky, Smolensk 1997) 15...d5!?; or 13...♕c8 14 ⟁g3 ≗e7 15 0-0 ⟁xb3 16 axb3 0-0 ∓ Macieja-Spisak, Brzeg Dolny 1995.

e23) 13 ⟁a4!? ⟁xa4 (13...≗xa4? 14 ≗xa4+ ⟁xa4 15 e5!; playable is 13...⟁xb3!? 14 axb3 ≗e7) 14 ⟁xe6! ≗xe6 (14...♕c8?! 15 e5 ±) 15 ≗xe6, and Black must defend with 15...♖c8.

e3) 12...♖c8!? 13 0-0 b4!? 14 ⟁ce2 ⟁xb3 followed by 15...e5 with a double-edged game, Meister-Golod, Hlovenec 1994.

e4) 12...♕c8! 13 g4 (13 a3 ⟁xb3! {13...≗e7? 14 ≗a2!, Macieja-Dao, Budapest 1996} 14 cxb3 ≗e7 15 ♖c1 ♕b7 ∓ Macieja) 13...h5!? (another unclear possibility here is 13...h6 14 h4 b4 15 ⟁ce2 ♕b7 16 ⟁g3 e5 17 ⟁df5 ⟁xb3, Garcia Martinez-Zhang Zhong, Linares open 2001) 14 h3 (14 gxh5 ♖xh5 ∓; 14 g5 ⟁g4 ∞ Vera) 14...hxg4 15 hxg4 ♖xh1+ 16 ♕xh1 b4 with a complicated game, Re.Gonzalez-Vera, Cuban Ch (Matanzas) 1997.

## B4)

**9 ♕f3** *(D)*

Quite often the game transposes to variations with f5, but if Black develops straightforwardly via 9...≗e7 and

10...0-0, White can transpose to the interesting Line A of Chapter 3.

We shall discuss the following separately:

**B41: 9...b5**     115
**B42: 9...≗e7**    117

The first move is critical, beyond all doubt, while the second is the most reliable.

Black has two other possibilities:

a) 9...♕d7. Generally speaking, it seems almost impossible that such a move could be the strongest, but the verdict has not yet been returned:

a1) 10 ≗e3 b5 11 e5 ≗b7 is good for Black.

a2) 10 0-0 b5! 11 f5! (11 e5 ≗b7, Cirić-Bogdanović, Novi Sad 1965) 11...e5! (11...b4? 12 fxe6 fxe6 13 ⟁a4) 12 ⟁de2 has not yet been studied.

a3) 10 f5!? e5 11 ⟁de2 ⟁xb3 12 axb3 d5, and 13 ⟁xd5 ⟁xd5 14 exd5 ♕xf5 turned out to be good for Black in Jansa-Cirić, Sochi 1965. White would do better to choose 13 ♕g3 or 13 0-0 d4 14 ⟁d5 ⟁xd5 15 exd5, Reefat-Alzate, Erevan OL 1996.

b) 9...♕c7 is quite a playable alternative:

b1) 10 ≗e3?! b5.

b2) 10 f5 e5!? (10...b5?! – *9...b5 10 f5 ♕c7?!*; 10...♗d7?! 11 g4!; 10...♗e7 – *9...♗e7 10 ♕f3 ♕c7*; 10...♘xb3!?) 11 ♘de2 ♘xb3 (11...b5?! 12 ♘d5!), and now:

b21) 12 axb3 b5! 13 ♘xb5!? (13 ♗g5?! b4!) 13...♕xc2 14 ♘ec3. Now the continuation 14...axb5!? (which is not necessary at all) 15 ♖xa8 ♕xc1+ 16 ♔f2 ♕xh1! (16...♕xb2+?! 17 ♘e2, H.Olafsson-Gislason, Icelandic Cht 1995; 16...♕c2+ 17 ♕e2) 17 ♖xc8+ ♔d7 18 ♘xb5 ♕b1 19 ♖c7+ ♔d8 20 ♖c8+ looks like a draw.

b22) Better is 12 cxb3!? b5 13 ♗g5 b4 ∞ (Beliavsky/Mikhalchishin).

b3) 10 0-0 b5 (10...♗e7 – *9...♗e7 10 0-0!? ♕c7!?*) 11 f5! e5!? (11...b4?! 12 fxe6 fxe6 13 e5!; 11...♘xb3 12 axb3 b4 13 ♘cb5!?) 12 ♘d5 ♘xd5 13 ♗xd5 ♗b7 14 ♘e2 ♗xd5 15 exd5 with good prospects for White, Kimelfeld-Chistiakov, Moscow 1966.

## B41)
**9...b5 10 f5** *(D)*

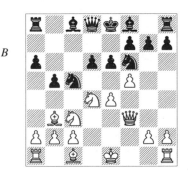

Forced! This position also arises after *9 f5 b5 10 ♕f3*, but there White may choose another 10th move.

**10...♗d7**

This is similar to Line B32. However, with the pawns on f5 and f7, Black enjoys a much more interesting choice. First, two unsuccessful lines:

a) 10...♕c7?! 11 fxe6 fxe6 – *9 f5 b5 10 fxe6 fxe6 11 ♕f3 ♕c7?!*.

b) 10...♕d7?! 11 fxe6 (11 ♗g5 and now 11...b4 12 fxe6 fxe6 13 ♘a4! Stoica, or 11...♗e7!?, P.Andersen-Psakhis, Copenhagen 2000) 11...fxe6 – *9 f5 b5 10 fxe6 fxe6 11 ♕f3 ♕d7?!*.

Three other moves are very interesting and barely investigated:

c) 10...b4!? and now:

c1) 11 ♘a4 and then:

c11) 11...e5 12 ♘c6 (12 ♘xc5!? dxc5 13 ♘e2) 12...♕c7 13 ♘xb4 ♕a5!? (13...♘cxe4!? 14 ♘d5!; 13...♗b7 14 ♘xc5 ♕xc5 15 ♘d5) 14 ♗d2 ♘cxe4 15 0-0-0 ♕b5!? (15...♗b7?! 16 ♘d5) is difficult to assess.

c12) 11...♘xb3 and then:

c121) 12 axb3 e5! 13 ♘c6 ♕c7 14 ♘xb4 a5 doesn't seem bad for Black: 15 ♕c3 ♕b7 or 15 ♘c3 axb4 16 ♖xa8 bxc3 17 ♕xc3 ♔d7.

c122) 12 cxb3 ♗b7?! (12...e5?! 13 ♘c6; 12...♗d7! is playable) 13 fxe6 fxe6 14 ♗g5 h6 15 ♕h3 ± Golubev-Shevchenko, Ukrainian Ch (Alushta) 1997.

c2) 11 fxe6!? ♘xb3! (11...fxe6 12 ♘a4) 12 axb3 bxc3 13 e5 dxe5 14 ♕c6+ ♗d7 15 exd7+ ♘xd7 16 ♘f5 ♖c8 17 ♕xa6 cxb2 18 ♗xb2 ♖xc2 19 ♗a3!? is very unclear.

d) 10...♘xb3!? 11 axb3 (11 cxb3 e5!) 11...b4. Now 12 ♘a4 transposes to line 'c121' while 12 fxe6 transposes to line 'c2'.

e) 10...e5!? 11 ♘c6 (better than 11 ♘de2?! ♗b7) 11...♕d7! (11...♕c7?! 12 ♘d5!?) 12 ♘b4 and then:

e1) 12...♘xb3 13 axb3 ♗b7 14 ♗e3!? (not 14 ♗g5? ♘xe4!, Bebchuk-Kalinsky, USSR 1966; 14 ♘bd5 is possible, however) 14...a5?! 15 ♘bd5 ♗xd5 16 ♘xd5 ♘xd5 17 exd5 ♗e7 18 0-0 0-0 19 ♕h5!? favours White, Golubev-Bliumberg, Odessa 1995.

e2) 12...♗b7! and now:

e21) 13 ♗d5 is bad in view of 13...♘cxe4! 14 ♗xb7 ♕xb7 15 ♗g5 ♖b8 16 ♗xf6 ♘xc3!.

e22) After 13 ♘cd5 ♘cxe4/♘fxe4 14 ♘b6 ♕d8 15 ♘xa8 ♕xa8! Black has menacing compensation.

e23) Instead, 13 ♘bd5 ♘cxe4!? 14 ♘xe4 (14 ♘b6 ♘xc3!) 14...♘xd5 15 ♗g5!? (15 ♘g5 ♘f4! 16 ♗xf7+ ♔e7!?; 15 f6?! ♘xf6 16 ♘xf6+ gxf6 17 ♕xf6 ♗xg2!) 15...♘b6 16 0-0-0 is critical. Possibly White has compensation. If not, and if 12...♗b7 favours Black, then both 9 ♕f3 and 9 f5 b5 10 ♕f3 may not be playable!

**11 ♗g5!?**

Or:

a) 11 fxe6 fxe6 transposes to Line B32.

b) 11 a3?! e5 (or 11...♘xb3!) 12 ♘de2 ♘xb3!.

c) 11 ♗e3 can be met by 11...e5!? or 11...♕c8!? 12 a3 (12 fxe6 fxe6 transposes to Line B32) 12...♘xb3 13 cxb3 ♕b7 ∓ Reefat-Short, Dhaka 1999.

d) 11 0-0 and then:

d1) After 11...♗e7, 12 ♗g5 transposes to *11 ♗g5 ♗e7 12 0-0*. More interesting is 12 fxe6(!) fxe6, transposing to note 'd2' to White's 10th move in Line B32.

d2) 11...b4!? 12 fxe6 fxe6 transposes to note 'd1' to White's 10th move in Line B32.

d3) 11...e5 12 ♘de2 can be met by 12...b4!?, winning the pawn (rather than 12...♘xb3 13 axb3 b4 14 ♘d5 ± D.Frolov-V.Popov, St Petersburg 1995).

**11...♗e7**

11...b4? 12 fxe6 fxe6 13 e5!.

**12 e5!?**

I found this idea over the board in 1995 but later discovered that Crouch had recommended it as early as 1993. The alternatives are:

a) 12 fxe6?! fxe6 transposes to note 'b' to White's 10th move in Line B32.

b) 12 0-0 ♘xb3 (12...0-0!?) 13 axb3. Here both 13...0-0 (Istratescu-Jaracz, Duisburg jr Wch 1992) and 13...b4 14 ♘a4 e5 (Istratescu-Timoshenko, Calimanesti 1992) are not bad for Black.

**12...dxe5 13 ♘c6! ♗xc6!**

13...e4!? 14 ♘xe4 ♕c7 (14...♕b6 15 ♘xf6+!? ♗xf6 16 ♘e5 ♗c6 17 ♘xc6 ♗xg5 18 fxe6 ±) 15 ♘xe7! ♘fxe4! (15...♘e5? 16 ♗xf6 gxf6 17 fxe6 fxe6 18 0-0 ♘xe4 19 ♖ae1 f5 20 ♗xe6 +−; 15...♘cxe4? 16 ♗xf6 ±) 16 0-0-0! (16 fxe6? ♘xg5 17 ♕xa8+ ♔xe7 18 ♕xh8 ♕e5+ −+), and Black is in danger.

**14 ♕xc6+**

Here, Black does not have the usual f7-square for the king...

**14...♔f8**

14...♘fd7? 15 ♗xe7 ♔xe7 16 fxe6 fxe6 17 ♗xe6! ♘xe6 18 0-0-0 ± Golubev-Borić, Kiev 1995.

**15 fxe6 b4!**

...instead, there is time to drive back the white knight (15...♕c8?! 16 ♕f3! e4 17 ♕e2, Istratescu-Badea, Bucharest 1997).

**16 ♘e2**

Not 16 ♘d5? ♖c8! −+.

The text-move (16 ♘e2), gives White an opportunity to fight (for example,

16...♕c8 17 ♕f3 e4 18 ♕e3 or 16...♖c8 17 ♕f3 ♘xe6 18 ♗xf6) but we can hardly talk about an advantage.

**B42)**

**9...♗e7** *(D)*

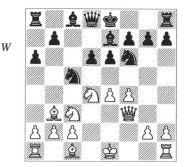

**10 ♗e3**

Otherwise:

a) 10 g4 d5!? 11 e5 (11 exd5 exd5 12 f5 ♘fe4! Akopian) 11...♘fe4 12 0-0 ♕c7! is satisfactory for Black, Filipenko-Akopian, Rostov 1993.

b) 10 0-0-0!? 0-0 11 ♗e3 transposes to Line A of Chapter 3. An alternative for Black is 10...♕c7!? (10...b5? 11 ♘c6! and 10...e5 11 fxe5 dxe5 12 ♘f5 are weaker) and now 11 f5 transposes to note 'c3' to Black's 10th move in Line B31 (where 11...e5 is possibly more precise than 11...0-0 12 g4!?). 11 ♗e3?! is dubious because of 11...b5 and 11 g4 should be verified; e.g., 11...b5 12 g5 ♘fxe4 13 ♘xe4 ♗b7 14 ♖e1 or 11...♘fd7!?.

**10...♕c7!?**

10...0-0 and then:

a) 11 f5 transposes to Line B31.

b) 11 g4 d5 (11...b5!? 12 ♘c6 ♕c7 13 ♘xe7+ ♕xe7 is an interesting idea,

Grilc-A.Pachmann, Stockerau jr 1991) 12 exd5 (12 e5 ♘fe4 13 ♘xe4 dxe4 14 ♕h3 ♕a5+!, Bednarski-Malich, Skopje OL 1972) 12...♘xb3 13 ♘xb3 exd5 14 f5 (14 g5 ♘e4 =) 14...♗b4 with chances for both sides, Kakabadze-Nasybullin, Moscow 1991.

c) 11 0-0-0 ♕c7 12 ♔b1 (12 g4?! b5!; 12 f5!? transposes to note 'd2' to Black's 11th move in Line B31) 12...b5 13 e5 ♗b7! (13...dxe5?! 14 ♘c6! ± Golubev-Zagrebelny, Pavlikeni 1990) 14 exf6 ♗xf3 15 fxe7 ♗xd1 16 exf8♕+ ♖xf8 17 ♖xd1 ♕b7, with good prospects for Black, Panchenko-Suba, Sochi 1977.

d) 11 0-0 transposes to Line A of Chapter 3 (11...♕c7 12 g4!?, etc.).

**11 0-0?!**

11 g4?! b5 12 g5 ♘fxe4 13 ♘xe4 ♗b7 favours Black, Wagner-H.Schuh, Walldorf 1986. Better is 11 f5(!), transposing to note 'c4' to Black's 10th move in Line B31.

**11...b5! 12 e5**

12 f5 e5 (12...♘xb3 13 axb3 e5? 14 ♘dxb5) 13 ♘de2 (difficult to assess is 13 ♘d5 ♘xd5 14 ♗xd5 exd4 15 ♗xd4 Shipov) 13...♘xb3 14 cxb3 ♗b7 ∓ Shipov; e.g., 15 a3 ♖c8!?.

**12...♗b7 13 ♕g3 dxe5!**

Better than 13...♘xb3?! or 13...♘h5 14 ♕g4! (14 ♕f2 0-0 15 exd6 {15 g4? ♘xf4!} 15...♕xd6 16 ♖ad1 ♕c7 =) 14...g6 15 f5 – Shipov.

**14 fxe5 ♘h5 15 ♕f2 0-0 16 g4 b4!**

This recommendation of Shipov's gives Black a very good game. Instead, 16...♘xb3!? (Emms-Shipov, Thessaloniki 1996) transposes to the Classical Sozin (note 'b342' to Black's 10th move in Line C12 of Chapter 9).

# 8  5...♞c6 6 ♝c4 e6 7 ♝b3 a6

**1 e4 c5 2 ♞f3 d6 3 d4 cxd4 4 ♞xd4 ♞f6 5 ♞c3 ♞c6 6 ♝c4 e6 7 ♝b3 a6** *(D)*

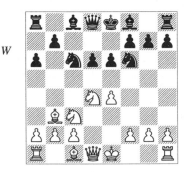

Now we start discussing the lines of the Classical Sozin and the Velimirović Attack, continuing the theme of the Fischer Attack. It is obvious that the position in the diagram can also be achieved after 5...a6 6 ♝c4 e6 7 ♝b3 ♞c6. The most important lines of the Sozin and Velimirović can originate from that position, and we shall start their discussion in this chapter (including the plan 8...♛c7 and 9...♞a5 for Black, and other lines). We will continue our discussion of these systems in two separate chapters to follow:

Chapter 9: **8 ♝e3 ♝e7** (including 9 0-0 and the main lines of the Classical Sozin);

Chapter 10: **8 ♝e3 ♝e7 9 ♛e2** (including the main lines of the Velimirović Attack).

Note that with the Classical Sicilian move-order, 5...♞c6 6 ♝c4 e6, the continuation 7 ♝b3 a6 is no more than one of the possible set-ups. We shall have a chance to discuss all the associated nuances in the introductions to Chapters 11, 12 and 13.

So:

**A: 8 f4!?** 118
**B: 8 0-0** 119
**C: 8 ♝e3** 121

## A)

**8 f4!?**

This works successfully against the plan with 8...♛c7. However, we shall see that Black gets an additional possibility...

a) 8...♝e7. Here it is normal to play 9 ♝e3 or 9 0-0 with the usual variations. The only line of note is 9 f5. After 9...♞xd4 (9...♛b6!? 10 ♝e3? e5) 10 ♛xd4 exf5 11 exf5 ♝xf5 12 0-0 ♝e6 White has a certain amount of compensation for the pawn; e.g., 13 ♝g5 ♛a5 14 ♝xe6 fxe6 15 ♝xf6 ♝xf6 16 ♛xd6 ♛e5 ∞ Korzubov-Kovaliov, Byelorussia 1987.

b) 8...♛a5 9 0-0, and instead of 9...♞xd4 10 ♛xd4 d5 11 ♝e3! ± Fischer-Dely, Skopje 1967, Fischer recommended 9...d5 10 ♞xc6 (I propose 10 ♝a4!?) 10...bxc6 11 f5 ♝c5+ 12 ♚h1 0-0.

c) 8...♞a5 9 f5!? (9 ♝e3 – *8 ♝e3 ♞a5 9 f4*; 9 0-0 – *8 0-0 ♞a5 9 f4*) 9...♞xb3, and we transpose to the variations that have been described earlier in Line B3 of Chapter 7; e.g., 10 axb3 ♗e7 11 ♕f3 0-0 and now 12 ♗e3 e5 13 ♘de2 b5 or 12 0-0.

d) 8...♗d7 and now:

d1) 9 f5 ♘xe4! 10 fxe6 fxe6 11 ♘xe6 ♗xe6 12 ♘xe4 ♗xb3 and then 13...♕h4+! = (Donaldson/Tangborn).

d2) 9 ♗e3! transposes to Line C1.

e) 8...♕c7 9 f5! (Fischer's idea, and the main point of the move-order 8 f4) 9...♘xd4 (here 9...♕b6 is clearly worse than in line 'a') 10 ♕xd4 and now:

e1) 10...♗d7 11 fxe6 fxe6 12 ♗g5 ♗e7 13 0-0-0 ± Golubev-Gutkin, Biel 1994.

e2) After 10...exf5, White is able to choose between 11 exf5 ♗xf5 12 0-0 with an attack (Fischer), and 11 0-0!? (*Schach-Archiv*), when 11...d5 12 ♘xd5 ♘xd5 13 ♕xd5 ± does not solve all Black's problems.

e3) 10...♗e7 and now:

e31) 11 g4 ♘xg4!? 12 ♕xg7 ♗f6 appears inconclusive.

e32) 11 ♗e3 exf5!? leads to nothing obvious for White either.

e33) 11 fxe6 fxe6 (11...♗xe6 12 ♗g5) 12 ♗g5 (12 0-0!? ♕c5 13 ♕xc5 dxc5 14 a4), and Black must defend by 12...h6! (12...b5?! 13 a4!, Dvoirys-Lesiège, Koszalin 1999; 12...♕c5 13 ♕d2 ♘g4?! 14 ♗xe7 ♔xe7 15 0-0-0! ± Golubev-Istratescu, Romanian Cht 1996) 13 ♗h4 ♕c5!, as 14 ♕d2?! can be answered either with 14...♘g4 or with 14...♘xe4!?.

e34) 11 0-0 0-0 (11...♕c5!? and maybe also 11...d5!? deserve attention) 12 ♕d3 (12 ♔h1 – *8 0-0 ♕c7 9 ♔h1 ♗e7 10 f4 0-0 11 f5 ♘xd4 12 ♕xd4*) 12...b5 13 fxe6 ♗xe6 14 ♗f4 favours White, Stoica-Redlich, Warsaw 1970.

e35) 11 ♕d3!?.

f) 8...d5!?. It is possible that this unusual move exploits the drawbacks of 8 f4. After 9 exd5 exd5 10 ♗e3 ♗b4! Black stands well. After 9 e5, Black may play 9...♘d7 10 ♗e3 ♗c5 11 ♕d2 ♘xd4 12 ♗xd4 b5 = Mikhalchishin-Lerner, Leningrad 1983. Instead, a tense game may result after 9...♘xd4 10 ♕xd4 ♘d7 11 f5!; e.g., 11...♕c7 12 ♗f4 ♗c5 13 ♕d2 ♗b4 14 0-0-0 ♗xc3 15 bxc3 ♘c5 16 ♕d4 ♕a5 17 f6, Mortensen-Van der Wiel, Århus 1983.

## B)

**8 0-0** *(D)*

Having played this, White will have less choice (as compared to 8 ♗e3) after both 8...♕c7 and 8...♗e7. Still, this does not have any fatal consequences, and besides, the position is important for the line 5...a6 6 ♗c4 e6 7 0-0 ♘c6 (or 7...♕c7!? 8 ♗b3 ♘c6) 8 ♗b3.

*B*

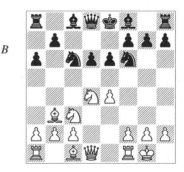

Now:

**B1: 8...♘a5**          120
**B2: 8...♕c7**          120
**B3: 8...♗e7**          121

Other moves:

a) 8...♘xd4 9 ♕xd4 ♗e7 10 ♗g5!? ± (10 f4 – 8...♗e7 9 f4 ♘xd4 10 ♕xd4).

b) After 8...♗d7!?, White may play 9 ♗e3 b5 10 f4, which transposes to note 'a' to White's 10th move in Line C1, or 9 f4. Probably the latter is more precise; e.g., 9...b5 10 f5! ± (10 ♘xc6 ♗xc6 11 f5, Fischer-Gadia, Mar del Plata 1960, 11...b4!?).

## B1)
**8...♘a5 9 f4**
Now:

a) 9...b5 and then:

a1) 10 ♗e3 transposes to note 'b' to White's 10th move in Line C2.

a2) 10 f5 e5 11 ♘de2 ♘xb3 12 axb3 ♗b7 (12...b4 13 ♘d5 ♘xe4 14 ♗e3 ♖b8 15 ♕d3 with an initiative, Daum-Morlo, Bundesliga 1995/6; 12...♕b6+ 13 ♔h1 ♗b7 14 ♘d5 ♗xd5 {14...♘xd5 15 exd5 ± Vasiukov-Kotov, Erevan 1955} 15 exd5 ♕c5 {15...♗e7!?} 16 c4 bxc4 17 ♘c3 ♗e7 18 ♗g5 with compensation, Suetin-Ilivitsky, Erevan 1955) and here:

a21) 13 ♘g3?! can be answered by 13...h5! (Boleslavsky) or 13...b4!?.

a22) 13 ♕d3 ♕b6+ 14 ♔h1 ♕c6! 15 ♘g3 h5! (Boleslavsky).

a23) 13 ♗g5 ♕b6+ 14 ♔h1 ♘xe4!.

a24) 13 ♘d5 ♘xe4 (for the continuations 13...♗/♘xd5 14 exd5 ♕b6+ see *12...♕b6+*), and now 14 ♘ef4! (Nunn) gives White more hope than 14 ♗e3 ♖c8 (Kasparov/Nikitin).

a3) 10 e5 dxe5 11 fxe5 ♗c5 12 ♗e3 ♘xb3 (12...♘c6 is well met by 13 ♕f3 or 13 ♘xc6!) 13 axb3 transposes to note 'a' to Black's 9th move in Line B1 of Chapter 7 (±).

b) 9...♕c7 is more precise. Then 10 ♗e3 transposes to Line C32, while

10 f5!? e5 11 ♘de2 ♘xb3 12 axb3 b5 has not been studied.

## B2)
**8...♕c7 9 ♔h1!?**
This particular idea of 8 0-0 hardly promises anything. Otherwise:

a) The main move 9 ♗e3 will be examined under *8 ♗e3 ♕c7 9 0-0* (Line C3).

b) White seldom plays 9 f4 because of the hazard of 9...d5!?; e.g., 10 ♘xc6 bxc6 11 f5 (11 e5?! ♘d7, Suetin-Tal, USSR Cht 1953) 11...♗d6 12 fxe6 fxe6 13 ♔h1 0-0 14 ♗g5 ♔h8 15 exd5 exd5 16 ♕d4 ♗e5 17 ♕h4 (Parma-F.Olafsson, Bled 1961) 17...♗e6 =. There are many other little-studied variations (9...♘a5 transposes to Line B1; 9...b5!?; 9...♘xd4 10 ♕xd4 d5 11 ♗e3! dxe4 12 ♘xe4 ♗e7; 9...♗d7!?).

**9...♗e7**
Or:

a) 9...b5!? is a good possibility for Black.

b) 9...♘a5!? is more critical:

b1) 10 f4 b5 and now:

b11) 11 e5 dxe5 12 fxe5 ♕xe5 13 ♗f4 and now 13...♕h5 14 ♘d5!? exd5 15 ♖e1+ ♗e6 16 g4 led to unclear play in Tal-Gurgenidze, Poti 1970. It is also not obvious how Tal would have attacked after 13...♕c5.

b12) It appears dubious to follow 11 f5 ♘xb3 (11...e5 12 ♘d5!) 12 axb3 b4 13 ♘cb5?! ♕b7.

b2) White may try 10 ♗a4+!?.

**10 f4 0-0**
10...♘a5 is not very logical here; e.g., 11 f5 ♘xb3 (11...e5 12 ♘de2 ♘xb3 13 axb3 ±) 12 cxb3!? b5 13 ♗e3 e5 (13...b4 14 ♘a4 ♕b7 15 ♖c1 ♗d7 16 fxe6 fxe6 17 ♘b6! ♕xb6 18 ♘f5,

Langner-Dončević, Prague 1986) 14 ♘c2 ♕b7 (14...♗b7 15 ♘b4!) 15 ♗g5!, Langner-Bartak, corr. 1987.

**11 f5 ♘xd4 12 ♕xd4 b5!**

12...♗d7 13 ♗g5 ± Sidorov-Bannik, USSR Cht 1952.

Now (after 12...b5):

a) 13 a4?! b4! ∓ Ivanchuk-Salov, Linares 1991.

b) 13 ♗e3 exf5 14 ♘d5 (or 14 exf5 ♗b7! = Minasian-Akopian, Erevan 1996) 14...♘xd5 15 ♗xd5 ♗f6 16 ♕b6 ♕xb6 17 ♗xb6 ♗b7! – Ivanchuk.

c) Ivanchuk recommended the line 13 ♗g5!? h6 14 ♗h4 exf5 15 ♕d3! (15 ♖ad1 ♖b8! =) as the only attempt to fight for the advantage.

**B3)**

**8...♗e7** *(D)*

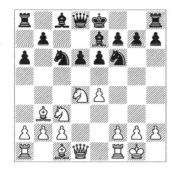

**9 f4**

Or:

a) 9 ♗e3, followed by 10 f4, is the most popular move-order – see Line B of Chapter 9.

b) Quite harmless here is 9 ♔h1 0-0 10 f4 ♘xd4 (10...♗d7 11 f5; 10...♕c7 – *8...♕c7 9 ♔h1!? ♗e7 10 f4 0-0*) 11 ♕xd4 b5!; for example, 12 f5 (12 a4 ♗b7!?; 12 a3 ♘d7!) 12...exf5!?

(12...♕c7 transposes to Line B2, while 12...♘g4, 12...b4 and 12...♖b8 are all playable) 13 exf5 ♗b7 = Honfi-Spassov, Vrnjačka Banja 1976.

**9...0-0**

Or:

a) 9...♕c7 10 ♗e3 transposes to Line C12 of Chapter 9 (10 f5? ♕b6!; 10 ♔h1 transposes to Line B2).

b) 9...♘xd4 10 ♕xd4 0-0 11 f5 ♔h8 (11...♕c7 – *8 f4 ♕c7 9 f5 ♘xd4 10 ♕xd4 ♗e7 11 0-0 0-0*; 11...b5!?) 12 ♔h1 ♗d7 13 ♗g5 ± Illescas-Andersson, Ubeda 1997.

c) 9...♗d7 10 f5!? (10 ♗e3 transposes to note 'c2' to Black's 9th move in Line C of Chapter 9) 10...♘xd4 (10...♕b6?! 11 fxe6) 11 ♕xd4 exf5 12 exf5 0-0 13 ♗g5 ♗c6 ± Medina Garcia-Gligorić, Hastings 1969/70.

d) 9...♘a5. Now, apart from 10 ♗e3, White has 10 f5!? ♘xb3 11 axb3, transposing to note 'b1' to White's 10th move in Line B31 of Chapter 7, and 10 e5!? ♘xb3 11 axb3 dxe5 12 fxe5, transposing to Line B11 of Chapter 7.

e) 9...d5 10 exd5 (10 e5!? is a serious alternative) 10...exd5 11 f5 0-0 transposes to note 'd' to White's 9th move in Line B1 of Chapter 4.

**10 ♗e3**

Play has transposed to a main line of the Classical Sozin (Line C22 of Chapter 9).

Otherwise: 10 f5? ♕b6 –+; 10 ♔h1 – *9 ♔h1 0-0 10 f4* =.

**C)**

**8 ♗e3** *(D)*

The most flexible continuation.

White has in mind both Sozin's plan with 9 f4 and Velimirović's 9 ♕e2, followed by 10 0-0-0.

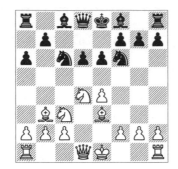

B

To my mind, 9 ♕e2 is sound after 8...♗e7 (and, additionally, after the untried 8...♘xd4 9 ♗xd4 b5, when 10 ♕e2!? transposes to note 'a' to White's 8th move in Chapter 11), but not in other lines.

We consider:

**C1: 8...♗d7**    122
**C2: 8...♘a5**    122
**C3: 8...♕c7**    124

The main continuation, 8...♗e7, will be discussed in Chapters 9 and 10.

**C1)**

**8...♗d7 9 f4!**

9 ♕e2 and here:

a) 9...♖c8!? and then:

a1) 10 0-0-0 ♘a5! 11 ♗g5 ♗e7 12 f4 0-0, Timmermann-S.Larsen, Copenhagen 1995.

a2) 10 f4 b5! 11 0-0-0 ♘a5 12 e5 ♖xc3, Istratescu-Porper, Rishon-le-Zion 1990.

a3) 10 0-0! b5 11 ♘xc6!?.

b) 9...b5! 10 0-0-0 and now with 10...♘a5! Black quickly organizes counterplay, Ricardi-I.Rogers, Spanish Cht 1999. 10...b4 is less accurate because of 11 ♘a4 ♘xe4 12 ♘xc6 ♗xc6 13 ♘b6.

**9...b5**

9...♕c7 – 8...♕c7 9 f4 ♗d7 ±; the alternative 9...♗e7 transposes to note 'c' to Black's 9th move in Line C of Chapter 9.

**10 f5!**

Otherwise:

a) 10 0-0 and then:

a1) 10...h5!? 11 f5 ♕c8 12 fxe6 fxe6 ±; then 13 ♖xf6 gxf6 14 ♕f3 ♗e7 is hardly dangerous for Black, Brenjo-Ilinčić, Yugoslav Cht 2000.

a2) 10...b4 11 ♘a4 ♖b8! transposes to a variation of the Fischer Attack (Chapter 5, Line E24) that is difficult to assess.

b) 10 ♕f3 ♘xd4 (10...♕c8!? 11 0-0 ♗e7 12 ♖ae1 0-0 13 a3 ♖b8, Hendriks-Kupreichik, Groningen 1995; 10...♖c8!?) 11 ♗xd4 ♗c6 (11...b4!? has been played) 12 0-0-0 b4 (Mikhalchishin) is unclear.

**10...♘xd4**

10...b4 11 fxe6 fxe6 12 ♘xc6!? ♗xc6 13 ♘e2.

10...♕c8!? 11 fxe6 fxe6 12 0-0, and now 12...♗e7 – 8...♗e7 9 f4 ♗d7 10 0-0 b5 11 f5 ♕c8 12 fxe6 fxe6 ±; 12...h5 – 10 0-0 h5!? 11 f5 ♕c8 12 fxe6 fxe6 ±.

**11 ♕xd4 ♗e7 12 fxe6**

12 g4!? Mikhalchishin.

**12...♗xe6**

12...fxe6 13 e5!?.

**13 0-0-0 0-0 14 ♗xe6 fxe6 15 e5**

± Mikhalchishin-Saltaev, Groningen 1992.

**C2)**

**8...♘a5 9 f4!**

9 0-0 b5 10 f4 – 9 f4 b5 10 0-0.

Not clear is 9 g4; e.g., 9...h5 10 g5 ♘g4 11 g6 fxg6 12 ♗xe6.

**9...b5** (D)

More reliable is 9...♕c7! (Line C32).

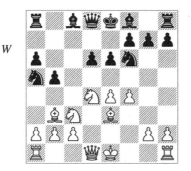

W

**10 e5**

Or:

a) 10 f5 e5 11 ♘de2 ♘xb3 12 axb3 (12 cxb3 d5!) and then:

a1) 12...♗b7 can be met by 13 ♗g5 ± (*Schach-Archiv*) or 13 ♘d5!?.

a2) 12...♕c7!? transposes to note 'c32' to White's 10th move in Line C32.

a3) 12...b4 13 ♘d5 ♘xd5 14 ♕xd5 ♖b8 15 0-0 ♗e7 (Parma-Tukmakov, Moscow 1971) and now Kasparov and Nikitin's suggestion 16 c4! is unclear.

b) 10 0-0 is important:

b1) 10...b4 11 e5! is another line from Kasparov and Nikitin.

b2) 10...♕c7! transposes to Line C32.

b3) 10...♘xb3 (or 10...♗b7 11 e5, and then 11...♘xb3) is sharp and dangerous for Black:

b31) 11 cxb3!? (less studied than White's alternative recapture 11 axb3) 11...♗b7 12 e5 dxe5 (the continuation 12...♘d5 13 ♘xd5 ♗xd5 14 f5!, Fershter-Osnos, Leningrad 1972, has the point 14...dxe5 15 ♘xe6 fxe6 16 ♕h5+) 13 fxe5 and then:

b311) 13...♘d7 14 ♕h5 g6 15 ♕h3 ♕e7 16 ♖ad1 (16 ♖ae1!? is similar to line 'b3214') 16...♗g7 17 ♗g5 ♕xg5 18 ♖xf7? (18 ♘xe6! fxe6 19 ♖xd7 ♔xd7 20 ♖f7+ ♔d8 21 ♕d3+ ♗d5 22 ♘xd5 ♔e8 23 ♘f6+ =) 18...♔xf7 19 ♕xe6+ ♔f8 ∓ Damjanović-Krogius, Sochi 1967.

b312) 13...♘d5 14 ♕f3 ♕d7 15 ♘e4?! (15 ♘xd5) 15...♘xe3 16 ♕xe3 ♕d5 (possibly better is the alternative 16...♖d8!?) 17 ♕f2 0-0-0 18 ♖ac1+ ♔b8 19 ♖fd1 (Voigt-Wahls, Hamburg 1993) 19...♖d7! with unclear play.

b32) 11 axb3 ♗b7 (11...b4?! 12 ♘c6!) 12 e5! (12 f5 can be met by Nunn's 12...b4! or 12...e5) 12...dxe5 (12...♘d5 13 ♘xd5 ♗xd5 14 c4!) 13 fxe5 and then:

b321) 13...♘d7 14 ♕h5 (14 ♖xf7? ♔xf7 15 ♘xe6 ♕e7!?) 14...g6 15 ♕h3 ♕e7 (15...♘xe5 16 ♖ad1 ♕c7 looks risky, but should be checked) and now:

b3211) 16 ♘dxb5? axb5 17 ♘xb5 does not work because of 17...♘xe5! 18 ♖ad1 ♗g7 19 ♘d6+ ♔f8 20 ♗c5 ♔g8.

b3212) 16 ♖ad1 ♗g7 17 ♗g5 ♕xg5 18 ♘xe6 fxe6 19 ♖xd7 ♔xd7 20 ♖f7+ ♔d8 21 ♕d3+ ♗d5 22 ♘xd5 leads to a draw.

b3213) 16 ♘f3 ♗g7 and then:

b32131) 17 ♘g5 ♘xe5 18 ♘ce4 (18 ♘ge4 0-0!) and now Black should avoid 18...h6? 19 ♘xe6! (Kotov), and play 18...♖c8!?.

b32132) 17 ♗h6 0-0!? 18 ♘g5? (18 ♖ae1) 18...♗xh6 19 ♕xh6 f6 is slightly better for Black, Kakabadze-Dzhandzhgava, Tbilisi 1992.

b3214) The last word is 16 ♖ae1! ♗g7 17 ♗h6 ♗xe5 (17...0-0 18 ♗xg7 ♔xg7 19 ♘e4!) 18 ♖xe5 ♘xe5 19

♗g7 ♕c5 20 ♕e3! (20 ♗xh8 ♕xd4+
= Jovcić-Hybl, corr. 1971) 20...♘g4
21 ♕f4 ± Kasparov/Nikitin.

b322) 13...♘d5!? 14 ♕f3 is an interesting transposition to the main line.
**10...dxe5 11 fxe5 ♘xb3**
11...♘d7? 12 ♗xe6! ±.
**12 axb3 ♘d5**
12...♘d7 13 ♕f3!? is better for White.
**13 ♕f3 ♗b7**
13...♘xe3!? 14 ♕xa8 is very complicated but should end, in the long run, in White's favour:

a) 14...♘xg2+ 15 ♔f1 ♘e3+ 16 ♔e2 +−.

b) 14...♕d7 15 ♘cxb5 ♗b4+ (the alternatives are 15...axb5 16 ♖a7 ± and 15...♘xg2+?! 16 ♔xg2 ♗b7 17 ♕f1 axb5 18 0-0-0 +− Ehlvest-Smirin, USSR Ch (Leningrad) 1990) 16 c3 with an advantage; e.g., 16...0-0 17 ♕c6 (17 ♕e4!?) 17...♘c2+ 18 ♔e2 ♘xa1 19 ♖xa1!?.

c) 14...♗b4!? 15 ♔e2 ♗xc3 16 ♕c6+!? (16 bxc3 ♘d5) 16...♗d7 17 ♕xc3 ♘xg2 18 ♕g3.

**14 0-0 ♕c7**
14...♕d7 15 ♘xd5 ♗xd5 16 ♕g3 h5 (16...g6 17 ♖ad1 ± Kasparov/Nikitin) 17 ♖f4 ♕c7 18 c4 ± Mezsaros-Titz, Eger 1990.

**15 ♘xd5**
15 ♘cxb5 axb5 16 ♘xb5 ♕d7 17 ♖xa8+ ♗xa8 18 c4 ♗c6! (and not 18...♘b6? 19 ♕f2 ♘c8 20 ♗b6! ± Kozlov-Petrushin, Penza 1972, but 18...♗b4!? is interesting) with the point 19 cxd5 ♗xb5 20 ♖a1 ♕xd5 21 ♖a8+ ♔d7 22 ♕xf7+ ♗e7 23 ♖a7+ ♔c8.

**15...♗xd5**
Now White has two lines that give Black problems:

a) 16 ♘xb5? is bad due to 16...♕d7.

b) 16 ♕f2 ♕b7? (16...b4 Sokolov; 16...♗e4!?) 17 ♘xb5 +− A.Sokolov-Timoshenko, Moscow 1990.

b) 16 ♕g3 h5 (16...g6 17 c4!, Bednarski-Gromek, Poland 1970; 16...♕b7 17 ♕f2!, Bednarski-Mititelu, Varna 1972) 17 c4 bxc4 18 bxc4 ♕xc4 19 ♖ac1 ♕d3 20 ♖c7 h4 21 ♕f2 f5 22 exf6 gxf6 (de Firmian-D.Gurevich, San Francisco 1987), and it is likely that 23 ♗g5! wins; e.g., 23...♖g8 24 ♘xe6! (but not 24 ♕xf6? ♕e3+! =), or 23...♗d6 24 ♕xf6! ♗xh2+ 25 ♔h1, etc.

**C3)**
**8...♕c7** *(D)*

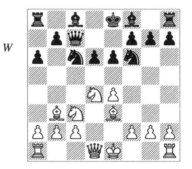

This is the most popular alternative to 8...♗e7. It has independent value, since Black is not obliged to follow up with 9...♗e7. Now:

Or:

a) 9 0-0 is possible, but it has no advantages compared to 9 f4, and only narrows the choice for White on move 10:

a1) 9...♘e5 10 ♕e2 ♘eg4 11 f4 and rather than 11...♘xe3 12 ♕xe3 ♕c5 13 ♖ad1 ♗e7 14 e5! ± Liberzon-Portisch, Erevan 1965, Black could try 11...b5!?.

a2) 9...b5!? 10 f4 – *9 f4 b5 10 0-0*.

a3) 9...♘a5 10 f4 (10 ♗a4+!? ♗d7! 11 ♗xd7+ ♕xd7! 12 ♕e2, Adams-Wolff, Biel IZ 1993, 12...♗e7 = Wolff) 10...b5 transposes to Line C32.

b) Maybe 9 g4 ♘xd4 10 ♗xd4 e5 11 ♗e3 ♗xg4 12 ♘d5!? deserves attention.

## C31)
### 9 ♕e2 ♘a5!

One of the variations that might be called 'Anti-Velimirović'. Other moves:

a) 9...♗e7 transposes to Line B of Chapter 10.

b) 9...♘d7 is unsafe in view of 10 ♗xe6!? fxe6 11 ♘xe6 ♕a5 12 0-0-0.

c) 9...b5 is suspect; e.g., 10 ♘xc6 ♕xc6 11 ♗d1 (11 ♗g5 ♗b7 12 ♘d5 {12 ♗xf6!?} 12...♘d7 13 0-0-0 h6!?, A.Frolov-Ryskin, Budapest rpd 1992) 11...♗e7 (11...♗b7 can be met by 12 ♗xf6!?, 12 ♘d5!? or 12 0-0-0!? ♘xe4 13 ♖he1!), and White has two promising possibilities: 12 ♘d5 (when Black must play 12...♗b7, since 12...exd5? fails to 13 ♗xf6 dxe4 14 0-0-0!), and 12 0-0-0 – *8...♗e7 9 ♕e2 ♕c7 10 0-0-0 b5?! 11 ♘xc6! ♕xc6 12 ♗d4*.

d) 9...♗d7!? 10 0-0-0 (I am not sure whether the pawn sacrifice 10 g4 ♘xd4 11 ♗xd4 e5 12 ♗e3 ♗xg4 13 f3 ♗e6 14 ♖g1 is correct), is interesting:

d1) 10...♘a5 11 g4! b5 12 g5 and here:

d11) 12...b4 and now: 13 gxf6 is liable to transpose to 'd12'; 13 ♘d5 ♘xd5 14 exd5 e5 15 f4 exd4 16

♗xd4+ ∞ Ilinčić-Madl, Balatonbereny 1988.

d12) 12...♘xb3+ 13 axb3 b4 14 gxf6 bxc3 15 fxg7 ♗xg7 16 ♖hg1 ♗f6 (16...cxb2+ 17 ♔xb2 ♗f6 18 ♗g5!) 17 bxc3 (17 ♗g5? ♕a5 –+; 17 ♕d3!?) 17...♕xc3 18 ♔b1 a5 19 ♖g3 (19 ♗c1 ♗xd4!?) 19...♕b4 20 ♗c1 a4 21 ♗b2 (Velimirović-Ivanović, Vrbas 1980) 21...♗e5! ∞ Krnić.

d2) 10...b5 and now:

d21) Black need not fear 11 ♖he1 ♗e7!.

d22) 11 ♗g5 ♗e7 12 f4 (12 ♗xf6 gxf6!) 12...0-0 13 f5 ♘a5 is also fine for Black, Ulybin-Sher, Smolensk 1987.

d23) Probably White should go down the road of unclear sacrifices; e.g., 11 ♘xc6 ♗xc6 12 ♘d5 exd5 13 exd5 ♗b7 14 ♗d4+.

d24) 11 g4!? is another such idea, with variations like 11...b4 12 ♘a4 (12 ♘d5?! exd5 13 g5) 12...♖b8!? or 11...♘xd4 12 ♗xd4 (12 ♖xd4?! e5 13 g5 exd4 14 ♗xd4) 12...e5 13 ♗e3 (13 ♘d5 ♘xd5 14 ♗xd5?! ♖c8 15 ♗c3 b4!; 13 g5?! exd4) 13...♗xg4 14 ♘d5 ♘xd5 15 ♕xg4.

### 10 g4!

Or:

a) 10 0-0-0?! transposes to the note to White's 10th move in Line B of Chapter 11, which is good for Black.

b) 10 ♗a4+ ♗d7 11 ♗xd7+ ♘xd7! 12 0-0 ♘c4 = Rogić-Sax, Bled 1994.

c) 10 a4 ♗e7 11 0-0 0-0 = Liukin-Morozevich, Ukrainian Cht (Alushta) 1994.

### 10...b5

Or:

a) 10...h6 is inaccurate: 11 0-0-0 b5 12 f3 ± Velimirović-Stein, Kapfenberg Echt 1970.

b) 10...♘xb3?! 11 axb3 ♗e7 (11...h5 12 g5 ♘g4 13 ♗d2 ♕c5 14 h3!, Vavra-Borik, Czech Cht 1994/5) 12 g5 ♘d7 13 h4!, Planinc-Ungureanu, Bucharest 1970.

c) After 10...h5!? 11 g5 ♘g4, 12 g6 ♘xe3 is OK for Black, while White may consider 12 0-0-0 or 12 ♗d2!?.

d) 10...g6!? 11 g5 ♘h5 12 f4 ♗g7 13 f5 ♘xb3 14 axb3 ♗e5 is unclear, Mikhalchishin-Kapengut, USSR 1982.

**11 g5 ♘d7** *(D)*

11...♘xb3?! 12 axb3 b4 (otherwise 13 ♘cxb5) 13 gxf6 bxc3 14 ♘b5!.

11...b4?! and now:

a) 12 ♘cb5?! axb5 13 gxf6 ♘xb3 14 cxb3 ♗d7.

b) 12 ♘d5 ♘xd5 leads to unclear play:

b1) 13 ♗a4+ ♗d7 14 ♗xd7+ ♕xd7 15 exd5 and now 15...e5 (Kupreichik-Anikaev, Kiev 1970) or 15...♕b7.

b2) 13 exd5 and then 13...♘xb3 14 cxb3!? ♗b7 15 ♘c6 (Tatai-Belotti, Reggio Emilia 1996/7) or 13...e5 14 ♘c6!? ♘xc6 15 dxc6 ♕xc6 16 0-0-0, Moraru-Burnoi, Bucharest 1998.

c) 12 gxf6! bxc3 (12...♘xb3 13 ♘d5! exd5 14 axb3 dxe4 15 0-0-0 Ribli) 13 ♗a4+ ♗d7 14 ♗xd7+ ♕xd7 15 fxg7 (15 b3!? gxf6 16 0-0-0 Ribli) 15...♗xg7 16 b3 ± Korchnoi-Ribli, Skellefteå World Cup 1989.

The text-move (11...♘d7) brings us to the critical position.

**12 ♘xe6!?**

This is very unclear, but in the other lines White has not achieved much:

a) 12 a3 ♘b6 13 0-0-0, and instead of 13...♖b8 14 f4 ♘bc4 15 f5 ♘xa3 16 fxe6 ♘xb3+ 17 cxb3, Velimirović-Ivanović, Yugoslav Ch (Vrbas) 1982, stronger is 13...♘bc4! (Nunn).

b) 12 h4 ♗b7 (unclear is 12...♘c5 13 f3 b4 14 ♘d1; 12...b4!? 13 ♘a4 ♗b7 14 f3 ♘xb3 15 cxb3 d5) 13 f3 ♘c4 14 ♗xc4 ♕xc4 15 ♕xc4 bxc4 with an acceptable position for Black, Ljubojević-Ivanchuk, Monaco Amber blindfold 1994.

c) 12 ♗xe6 fxe6 13 ♘xe6 ♕c4! 14 ♕xc4 ♘xc4 15 ♘c7+ ♔d8 16 ♘xa8 ♘xe3 17 fxe3 ♗b7 with a good ending.

d) 12 f4 and now:

d1) 12...♘xb3!?.

d2) 12...♘c5 13 f5 b4 (13...♗d7!?) 14 ♘a4 ♘axb3 15 cxb3 ♕b7 16 fxe6 fxe6 17 ♘xc5 dxc5 18 ♘f3, and now 18...♕xe4 19 0-0-0 is unclear, while 18...♗e7 is sufficient for equality, Ljubojević-Salov, Belgrade 1987.

d3) 12...b4 13 ♘a4 (13 ♘d5?! exd5 14 exd5 ♘c5 15 ♘c6 ♘xc6 16 ♗xc5+ ♗e7 17 ♗a4 ♗d7! 18 dxc6 ♗xc6 19 ♕f3 ♗xa4! 20 ♕xa8+ ♔d7 Kasparov/Nikitin) and here:

d31) 13...♘c5?! 14 ♘xc5 dxc5 15 ♗a4+ ±.

d32) 13...♘xb3 14 cxb3 and then:

d321) 14...♗b7 15 f5 e5 16 ♖c1 is good for White after 16...♕a5?! 17 ♘e6!, Vlad-Istratescu, Bucharest 1992, or 16...♘c5 17 ♘f3.

d322) 14...♕b7 15 ♕c2 ♘c5 16 ♘xc5 dxc5 17 ♘f3 ± Baimuratov-Serper, Bishkek Z 1993.

d33) 13...♗b7! and now:

d331) 14 ♗d2 e5 15 ♘f5 g6 16 ♘g3 and rather than 16...exf4 17 ♗xf4 ♘xb3 18 axb3 ♗e7 19 0-0-0 0-0 20 h4 ♘c5 ∞ Gdanski-Istratescu, Manila OL 1992, probably stronger is 16...♘xb3 17 axb3 ♕xc2 18 f5 gxf5 19 0-0 ♗xe4!?.

d332) 14 f5 e5 15 ♘e6 (15 ♗xf7+ ♔xf7 16 ♕h5+ ♔g8 17 f6 ♕c4!? {or 17...g6} 18 ♖f1 ♕f7 ∓ Ardeleanu-Istratescu, Romanian Ch (Herculane) 1996) 15...fxe6 16 fxe6 ♘c5 17 ♘xc5 dxc5 18 ♗d5 0-0-0 19 0-0-0 (Kasparov) – I am not sure that White has real compensation here.

e) 12 0-0-0 and then:

e1) 12...♘xb3+ 13 axb3 ♗e7 transposes to Line B of Chapter 10 (an alternative is 13...♗b7!? 14 f3 g6).

e2) 12...♗b7 13 ♗xe6 fxe6 14 ♘xe6 ♕c4 15 ♕g4 gives White compensation, Smagacz-Sher, Koszalin 1999.

e3) 12...b4!? 13 ♘a4 ♘xb3+ 14 axb3 ♘c5 15 ♘xc5 (15 ♕c4 ♗d7!? 16 ♕xb4 ♖b8 17 ♕c3 ♗xa4 18 bxa4 ♕b7) 15...dxc5 16 ♘f3 (16 ♘f5 exf5 17 exf5 ♗xf5 18 ♕f3 ♕c8 19 ♖he1 ♗e6 –+ Marić) 16...♗e7 17 ♘d2 (17 ♕d2 a5!? 18 ♗f4 ♕b7; 17 h4 a5!, Juarez-Polugaevsky, Mar del Plata 1971, 18 ♘e5 0-0! 19 ♗f4 ♗d6) 17...a5 18 ♘c4 a4 19 ♔b1 ♗a6 20 f3 0-0 21 h4 ♖a7 with strong counterplay, Zapata-Am.Rodriguez, Cienfuegos 1997.

e4) 12...♘c5 and here:

e41) Not 13 f3? b4 –+.

e42) 13 a3 ♗b7 (13...♖b8!? – Lerner; 13...♘axb3+!?) 14 ♗a2 ♘xe4 (Arakhamia-Lerner, Helsinki 1992) 15 ♘xe4 ♗xe4 16 ♖he1 d5 17 f3 ♗g6 18 ♗xd5 ♖c8 with counterplay.

e43) 13 ♖he1 b4 14 ♘d5 exd5 (14...♘cxb3+!?) 15 exd5 (15 ♗xd5!?) 15...♗e7 (A.Frolov-Lerner, Simferopol/Alushta 1992) 16 ♗f4! ♖a7 17 ♕xe7+ ♖xe7 18 ♗xd6 ∞.

e44) 13 ♗d5 exd5 (13...♖b8!? 14 b4 and now Black should play 14...♘d7!, but not 14...♘a4? 15 ♘xa4 bxa4 16 bxa5 exd5 17 exd5 ♗e7 18 ♘c6 0-0 19 f4!, Rechel-Lerner, Metz 1998) 14 ♘xd5 ♕b7 15 b4 (15 ♘f5 ♘c6 16 h4 ♗e6 ∓ Minasian-Lerner, USSR Cht 1991) 15...♘xe4 (15...♘c4 16 bxc5 dxc5 17 ♘f5 ♗e6 ∞ Maksimenko) 16 ♘xb5 axb5 17 ♗b6 ♘c4 (I don't see why Black should avoid 17...♗e6!? 18 ♕xe4 ♘c6) 18 ♕xe4+ ∞ Kozakov-Maksimenko, Lviv 1991.

**12...fxe6 13 ♗xe6**

The position remains difficult to assess. For instance:

a) 13...♘b6 14 ♗xb6 ♕xb6 15 ♘d5 (15 ♕g4! Milos) 15...♕c6 16 ♘f6+ (16 ♕g4 ♔d8! ∓ Lima) 16...gxf6 17 ♗d5 ♕c5 18 ♕h5+ ♔d8 19 ♕f7 ♕d4! ∓ Milos-Lima, Brazilian Ch 1995.

b) 13...♘e5 14 ♘d5 ♕c6 (14...♕b7 15 ♕h5+ g6 16 ♕h3, Kozakov-Nevednichy, France 1999) 15 ♗xc8 ♖xc8 16 ♕h5+! with compensation (Kozakov; 16 0-0-0 ♕c4!).

## C32)
**9 f4** *(D)*

Now, after 9...♗e7, the 'Velimirović' can no longer be obtained, but White may play, besides 10 0-0 (the 'normal' Classical Sozin), also 10 ♕f3!? and 11 0-0-0 – both of which will be discussed in Chapter 9.

**9...♘a5**

Or:

a) 9...♗d7 is inaccurate, as White can reply with 10 f5! ± (or 10 0-0 b5?! 11 f5).

b) 9...b5 is the favourite move of GM Serper:

b1) 10 ♘xc6!? ♕xc6 11 f5! is not bad, and 11...♘xe4 (after 11...♗e7, 12 0-0 transposes to Line C12 of Chapter 9, while White could try 12 fxe6!?) 12 fxe6 ♘xc3 13 exf7+ ♔d8 14 bxc3 ♕xc3+ 15 ♔f2 favours White.

b2) 10 f5 b4!? (10...♘xd4 11 ♕xd4 allows White to struggle for an advantage) 11 ♘a4?! (11 fxe6 bxc3 12 exf7+ ♔d8 ∞ Tkachev-Babula, Calicut jr Wch 1993; *NCO* suggests 11 ♘ce2!? e5 12 ♘xc6 ♕xc6 13 ♗g5 ±) 11...e5 12 ♘f3 (12 ♘xc6 ♕xc6 13 ♕d3 ♖b8 ∓ Willemze-Cvek, Cala Galdana jr Wch 1996, and 12 ♘e2 ♖b8!, Mitkov-Granda, Moscow OL 1994, are no better) 12...♖b8 13 ♕d3 ♗e7 14 0-0-0!? ♘a5 15 ♗g5 ♘g4! 16 ♕d2 ♘xb3+ 17 axb3 h6! with good play for Black, Gi.Hernandez-Serper, Los Angeles 1996.

b3) 10 0-0 b4!? (10...♗b7 11 f5 ♘xd4 12 ♕xd4 e5 13 ♕d3 ♗e7 14 ♗g5 ± Lukin-Serper, St Petersburg

1995; instead, 10...♘a5 is normal – see *9...♘a5 10 0-0 b5!*) 11 ♘a4 (11 ♘ce2 ♗e7!? 12 ♘g3 0-0 13 f5 ♘xd4 14 ♗xd4 e5 15 ♗e3 ♗b7 16 ♗g5 ♘xe4 is good for Black, Nenashev-Dautov, Frunze 1988) 11...♖b8 12 c3 ♘a5 (12...♘xe4 13 cxb4! Serper) 13 cxb4 ♘xb3 14 ♕xb3 ♕b7! 15 e5 dxe5 16 fxe5 ♘g4 17 a3 (possibly better is 17 h3!? – de Firmian) 17...♕e4 18 ♖ae1 ♗b7 19 ♘f3 ♘xe5 20 ♘c5 ♗xc5 21 ♗xc5 ♘xf3+ 22 gxf3 ♕d5 and Black holds the position, de Firmian-Serper, New York 1996.

**10 0-0**

It is a big question whether White should really play this. He has a number of alternatives:

a) 10 ♕f3 b5! has been studied little. It seems that Black has good chances.

b) 10 g4!? ♘c4 (also of interest are 10...d5 and 10...b5 11 g5 b4 12 gxf6 bxc3 13 ♗a4+ ♗d7 14 fxg7 ♗xg7 15 ♘xe6? fxe6 16 ♕h5+ ♔e7 and Black wins, Müller-Mantovani, Montecatini Terme 1993) 11 ♗xc4 ♕xc4 12 g5 (12 ♕f3!? ♗e7 – 8...♗e7 9 f4 ♕c7 10 ♕f3 ♘a5 11 g4 ♘c4 12 ♗xc4 ♕xc4) 12...♘d7 13 ♕d3 ♕c7 14 0-0-0 b5 15 ♖he1 with double-edged play, Canda-Am.Rodriguez, Bayamo 1989.

c) 10 f5 is rather important:

c1) 10...♘c4!? and here:

c11) 11 ♗xc4 ♕xc4 12 ♕f3 ♗e7 (or 12...e5!?) 13 0-0-0 e5 14 ♘de2 b5 15 b3 ♕c6 16 ♗g5 ♗b7 17 ♗xf6 ♗xf6 18 ♘d5 ♖c8! ∞ Reinderman-Van der Weide, Hoogeveen 1999.

c12) 11 fxe6 ♘xe3 12 ♕e2 ♘eg4 13 exf7+ ♔d8 14 h3 (Shtyrenkov-Petrushin, Russia 1984) 14...♘e5 deserves attention.

c2) 10...e5 11 ♞de2. Now, instead of 11...♞c4 12 ♗xc4 ♕xc4 13 b3 ♕c6 14 ♕d3, 11...b5 12 ♞d5 ♞xd5 13 ♗xd5 ♗b7 14 b3 b4 15 c3 ♞c6 16 a3 (*Schach-Archiv*) or 11...♗d7?! 12 ♗g5, it is better to play 11...♞xb3: 12 axb3 – *10...♞xb3 11 axb3 e5 12 ♞de2*; 12 cxb3 – *10...♞xb3 11 cxb3 e5 12 ♞de2*.

c3) 10...♞xb3 and now:

c31) 11 cxb3 and then:

c311) 11...♗e7 12 ♖c1 ♕a5 13 0-0 ±.

c312) 11...b5 12 ♖c1! (12 0-0 – *10 0-0 b5 11 f5 ♞xb3 12 cxb3*).

c313) 11...e5 12 ♞de2 (12 ♞c2 d5!?) 12...b5! (12...♗d7 13 ♗g5 ♗e7 14 ♗xf6 ♗xf6 15 ♞d5 ± Morović-Am.Rodriguez, Cienfuegos 1997; 12...♕a5 13 0-0 h5 14 ♞d5 ± Mikhal-chishin-Chechelian, Moscow 1979) 13 ♖c1 (13 0-0!? – *10 0-0 b5! 11 f5 e5 12 ♞de2 ♞xb3 13 cxb3*) 13...♕a5 14 0-0 (very unclear is 14 b4!? ♕xb4 15 a3 ♕a5 16 b4 ♕d8 17 ♗g5, as I analysed with Istratescu) 14...♗b7 – *10 0-0 b5 11 f5 e5 12 ♞de2 ♞xb3 13 cxb3 ♗b7 14 ♖c1 ♕a5!* ∞.

c32) 11 axb3 e5! (11...exf5 12 0-0! ± Ehlvest-Rashkovsky, USSR 1986; 11...♗e7?! 12 ♕f3!) 12 ♞de2 b5! and now:

c321) 13 ♞xb5? fails to 13...♕c6.

c322) 13 ♗g5? b4 is bad for White.

c323) 13 ♞d5 ♞xd5 14 ♕xd5 ♗b7 15 ♕d3 and now 15...b4 and 15...♖c8 are both quite reasonable for Black.

c324) 13 0-0!? – *10 0-0 b5 11 f5 e5 12 ♞de2 ♞xb3 13 axb3*.

c325) Another try is 13 ♕d3 ♗b7 (½-½ Golubev-Istratescu, Bucharest 1996), with a complicated game.

**10...b5!**

Or:

a) 10...♗e7 transposes to note 'b' to Black's 10th move in Line C12 of Chapter 9 (±).

b) 10...♞c4 11 ♗xc4 ♕xc4 12 ♕f3! with an advantage for White, Kiroski-Abramović, Skopje 1994.

c) 10...♞xb3 11 cxb3 b5 12 ♖c1 ♕b7 13 e5 ♞d5 14 ♞xd5 ♕xd5 15 exd6 ♗b7 (15...♗xd6 16 ♞f5) 16 d7+ ♕xd7 17 f5 e5 (17...♕d5 18 ♕e2 e5 19 ♖fd1) 18 ♞e6 ± Pelikan-Marini, Argentina 1985.

**11 f5** *(D)*

11 ♕f3?! ♗b7!.

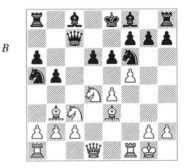

One more important position for the plan with ...♕c7 and ...♞a5.

**11...♞xb3!?**

Obliging White to take with the c-pawn. Otherwise:

a) 11...b4 is risky due to 12 ♗a4+.

b) 11...♞c4?! 12 ♗xc4 ♕xc4 13 fxe6 fxe6 14 ♖xf6 gxf6 15 ♕h5+ (Cio-caltea-Soos, Romania 1954) 15...♚d8 16 ♕f3!? ♗e7 17 e5 d5 18 exf6 is also treacherous for Black.

c) Black's alternative is 11...e5 12 ♞de2, and now:

c1) 12...♞c4!? 13 ♗g5 ♗b7 (Black should avoid 13...♞g4?! 14 ♗xc4 ♕xc4

15 ♕d5!, A.Kuzmin-K.Orlov, Pančevo 1989; 13...b4!? Lalić) 14 ♗xf6 gxf6 15 ♗xc4 ♕xc4 16 ♘d5 (Palac-Kožul, Slovenian Cht 2000) 16...♗xd5 17 exd5 ♖c8 = Lalić.

c2) 12...♘xb3, and again it is not clear how to recapture:

c21) 13 cxb3 ♗b7 14 ♖c1 ♕a5! (14...♕d8 15 ♗g5!?) with an important and unclear position; e.g., 15 a3 (15 ♘g3 h5!?) 15...♗e7 16 ♘g3 (16 ♗g5!?) 16...h5 17 b4 ♕d8 18 ♕f3, T.Horvath-Zeller, Bundesliga 1992/3.

c22) 13 axb3 ♗b7 14 ♘d5 (14 ♘g3 h5! 15 ♘d5 ♗xd5 16 exd5 h4 17 ♘h1 ♗e7 18 ♘f2 ♕b7 19 c4 ♗d8 is good for Black, Ghizdavu-Honfi, Timisoara 1972) 14...♗xd5 15 exd5 ♗e7 16 ♘c3!? 0-0 17 ♗g5 ♕c5+ (17...b4! 18 ♗xf6 bxc3 19 ♗xe7 cxb2 20 ♖b1 ♕xe7 21 f6!? is probably critical) 18 ♔h1 ♘xd5 19 ♗xe7 ♘xe7 20 f6 with an advantage for White, Lalić-S.Pedersen, London 1997.

c3) 12...♗b7 13 ♘d5 (13 ♘g3 ♘c4! ∓ Bena-Mir.Pavlov, Bucharest 1969; 13 ♗g5?! ♘xb3) 13...♘xd5 (13...♗xd5 14 ♗xd5 ♖c8 15 b3! ± Palac-Kožul, Croatian Cht 2000, with the point 15...♕xc2?! 16 ♖c1! ±) 14 ♗xd5 ♘c4 and here:

c31) 15 ♕c1 ♗xd5 16 exd5 ♖c8! 17 ♗f2 ♗e7! (17...h5?! 18 b3 ♘b6 19 ♖d1 ± Honfi-Tarjan, Majdanpek 1976) 18 b3 ♘b6 ∞ Pelletier.

c32) 15 ♗c1 ♕c5+ 16 ♔h1 ♗xd5 17 exd5 ♘b6 18 ♘c3 (18 f6!? ♕xd5 19 ♗e3 with compensation, Palac-Kožul, Croatian Ch (Pula) 2001) 18...♗e7 and now:

c321) 19 ♘e4? is weak: 19...♕xd5 20 ♕f3 ♖c8 21 ♗e3 ♘d7! ∓ de Firmian-Salov, New York 1996.

c322) 19 ♕d3!? ♕c4 20 ♗e3 is also possible.

c323) 19 f6 gxf6 20 ♕f3 ♘d7 21 ♘e4 ♕c7 22 ♗e3 ♖g8 23 ♖ac1 ♖c8 24 c4 bxc4 25 b3 ♕a5 26 bxc4 ♕xa2 27 ♖a1 with a draw, A.Kovačević-Popović, Yugoslav Ch (Nikšić) 1997.

c324) Instead, 19 ♕f3! (Salov) appears to be very strong.

We now return to 11...♘xb3 (D):

**12 cxb3**

12 axb3?! b4! 13 ♘a4 (13 ♘cb5 ♕b7! ∓ Boleslavsky) 13...e5 14 ♘e2 ♖b8 15 ♘g3 h5! ∓ Onoprienko-Van Laatum, Groningen open 1993.

**12...b4!?**

Or:

a) 12...e5 and then:

a1) 13 ♘de2 – *11...e5 12 ♘de2 ♘xb3 13 cxb3* ∞.

a2) White can try 13 ♘c2!? (making use of the fact that he had to play 12 cxb3) 13...♗b7 (13...♕b7 14 ♘b4 ♘xe4 15 ♘cd5) 14 ♘b4 ♘xe4 15 ♘cd5.

b) 12...♗e7?! has a long history:

b1) 13 ♕f3 b4 (Black should try 13...e5!? or 13...♕b7!?) 14 ♘a4 ♕b7 15 ♖ac1! ±.

b2) 13 ♖c1! (±) (D) and now:

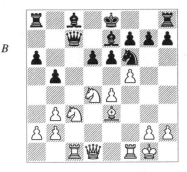

*B*

b21) 13...♕b7 14 fxe6 (14 ♕f3 ♗d7 15 g4 b4!, Khenkin-Fridshtein, USSR Cht 1954) 14...fxe6 15 b4 0-0 16 ♕b3 d5 (Tolush-Taimanov, USSR Ch (Moscow) 1952; 16...♕d7!? is better) 17 ♘c6! ± Koblenc.

b22) 13...♕d7 and then:

b221) 14 fxe6 fxe6 15 ♘c6 (15 b4 0-0 16 ♕b3 ♔h8 17 h3 e5! = Keres-Taimanov, Zurich Ct 1953) 15...♕xc6! 16 ♘d5 ♘xd5 (maybe 16...♕b7 is possible) 17 ♖xc6 ♘xe3 18 ♕c1 ♗d7 ∞ Ekström-Roos, corr. 1964.

b222) 14 ♕f3! and then:

b2221) 14...e5 15 ♘c6! ♗b7 16 ♘a5 ± Boleslavsky.

b2222) 14...♗b7!? 15 fxe6 fxe6 16 ♕h3 ♗c8 17 ♖cd1!? (17 ♘f3 0-0 18 e5 dxe5 19 ♘xe5 ♕d6 20 ♕g3 = Onishchuk) 17...0-0 18 b4 ± F.Olafsson-Johansson, Reykjavik (2) 1959.

b2223) 14...0-0 15 g4 (or 15 e5! ♗b7 16 exf6 ♗xf3 17 fxe7 ♕xe7 18 ♖xf3 Suetin) 15...e5 (15...♘e8 16 g5

♗b7 17 ♕h5 ± Vasiukov-Veiland, Lyons 1955; 15...b4 16 ♘a4 ♕b7 17 ♘c6 ± Onishchuk) and now Khenkin recommends 16 ♘de2! (instead of 16 ♘c6?! ♕xc6 17 g5, Geller-Taimanov, USSR Ch (Kiev) 1954).

**13 ♘a4 e5!** *(D)*

13...♘xe4 can be met by 14 ♖c1 ± (Koblenc) or 14 fxe6 fxe6 15 ♕h5+ g6 16 ♕f3 ± (Nunn).

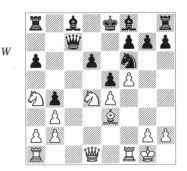

*W*

Now:

a) 14 ♖c1 ♕b7 15 ♘f3 (15 ♘c6? ♗d7 ∓) 15...♘xe4!? (15...♘xe4 16 ♘b6 ♘f6! 17 ♘xa8 ♕xa8 ± Serper; 15...♗e7 16 ♘b6 ♖b8 17 ♖c4! ± de Firmian-Serper, Los Angeles 1997) 16 ♕d2 and now 16...♘d5? 17 ♖fe1 ♗b7 18 ♘c5!! dxc5 19 ♗xc5 and 16...♕b7 17 ♘b6 ♖b8 18 ♕xb4 (Serper) both favour White, but I hesitate to recommend this for White due to 16...♗xf5!?.

b) 14 ♘f3!?, with a tense game, is worthy of attention.

# 9 5...♘c6 6 ♗c4 e6 7 ♗b3 a6 8 ♗e3 ♗e7 without 9 ♕e2

**1 e4 c5 2 ♘f3 d6 3 d4 cxd4 4 ♘xd4 ♘f6 5 ♘c3 ♘c6 6 ♗c4 e6 7 ♗b3 a6 8 ♗e3 ♗e7** *(D)*

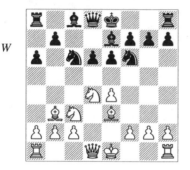

9 ♕e2 is considered in Chapter 10, so we are left with these three moves:

**A: 9 g4!?**      132
**B: 9 0-0**       132
**C: 9 f4**        133

## A)

**9 g4!?**

A curious and fresh idea. There are not many examples of it as yet:

a) 9...♘xd4 10 ♕xd4 and then:

a1) 10...e5 (certainly, this is the most critical) 11 ♕d3 (11 ♕c4 ♗e6 should be good for Black) 11...♗xg4 (11...♘xg4!?) 12 ♖g1 0-0 13 ♗g5 (13 ♘d5!? Popović) 13...♗h5 14 ♕h3 ♗g6 15 ♗xf6 (15 ♕h4!?) 15...♗xf6 16 0-0-0 ♖c8 (Velimirović-Popović,

Bar 1997) 17 ♕g4! with compensation – Popović.

a2) 10...0-0!? 11 ♖g1 (not 11 g5? ♘g4) 11...b5 12 g5 ♘d7 13 0-0-0 ♖b8 (13...♘c5?! 14 e5!) 14 f4 a5 15 a4 (15 a3 ♘c5! 16 e5 b4 Sokolov) 15...bxa4 16 ♕xa4 ♖b4 17 ♕a2 a4! 18 ♗xa4 ♕c7 19 f5 ♘c5 20 f6 ♗d8 offers compensation for Black, Velimirović-A.Sokolov, Yugoslavia 1998.

b) 9...♕a5!? 10 f3 ♘d7 (similar positions may arise in the variation *5...a6 6 ♗c4 e6 7 ♗b3 ♗e7 8 g4*), and now:

b1) 11 ♕d2 ♘c5 12 0-0-0 0-0 13 ♔b1 ♘xd4 14 ♗xd4 ♕c7 (14...b5 15 ♘d5!) 15 g5 b5 16 h4, Velimirović-Popović, Yugoslav Ch (play-off) 1997 (± *Informator*).

b2) 11 h4 0-0 (11...♘c5 12 ♕d2 0-0 13 0-0-0 ♘xd4 14 ♗xd4 b5 15 ♔b1 b4 16 ♘e2 ♘xb3 ∞ Ivanović-Popović, Bar 1997) 12 ♕e2 ♘c5 13 0-0-0 ♘xd4 14 ♗xd4 b5 15 e5 ♕c7 16 f4 ½-½ Velimirović-Popović, Yugoslav Cht 1999.

We see that 9 g4 has not as yet acquired any followers outside Yugoslavia, as the new variations are very unclear while the old continuations are still attractive for White. Nevertheless, it is one more worry for Black.

## B)

**9 0-0**

White has to continue 10 f4 after all Black's main answers, so the immediate 9 f4, preserving the possibility of 10 ♕f3!?, is more flexible. Still I have no great objections to 9 0-0; for example, Black can gain no benefit from 9...♘a5 10 f4 ♘xb3 (10...b5? 11 e5; 10...♕c7 transposes to note 'b' to Black's 10th move in Line C12) 11 axb3 0-0 12 ♕f3! and White achieves the optimal arrangement of pieces.

The difference between 9 f4 and 9 0-0 may, however, be of importance after:

**9...♘xd4!? 10 ♗xd4 b5**

Usually this follows one move later (after 9...0-0 10 f4). One possible idea in playing the move here is that after 11 f4 (– *9 f4 ♘xd4!? 10 ♗xd4 b5 11 0-0*), Black can play 11...♗b7!?. With the pawn on f2, 11 a4!? is possible, when 11...b4 12 a5 0-0! (not 12...bxc3? 13 ♗b6! +–) seems satisfactory for Black

## C)

**9 f4** (*D*)

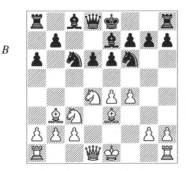

*B*

The two main moves here are:
**C1: 9...♕c7!?**      134
**C2: 9...0-0**           137

Other moves:

a) 9...d5?! 10 e5 ♘d7 11 0-0!? ♗c5 12 ♔h1 gives White the better prospects, Minić-Klemens, Oberhausen Echt 1961.

b) 9...♘a5. Now 10 e5 is unconvincing in view of 10...dxe5 11 fxe5 ♘d7 12 ♗xe6 ♘xe5 13 ♕h5 ♘ac4! (Therrell-Melvin, Alabama 1995) but 10 0-0 is normal, or maybe 10 ♕f3!? b5 11 e5 ♗b7 12 exf6, as in Estrin-Kletsel, Moscow 1962.

c) 9...♗d7 contains few noteworthy ideas:

c1) 10 ♕f3 and now:

c11) 10...b5? is weak due to 11 e5.

c12) After 10...♘xd4 11 ♗xd4 ♗c6, both 12 g4 and 12 f5 e5 13 ♗f2 seem good.

c13) 10...0-0 transposes to note 'c' to Black's 10th move in Line C21.

c2) 10 0-0 b5!? (10...♕c7 – *9...♕c7 10 0-0 ♗d7*; 10...0-0 – *9...0-0 10 0-0 ♗d7*; 10...♖c8?! 11 f5!) 11 f5 (11 a3 has fewer pretensions) 11...♕c8 12 fxe6 (12 ♕f3 ♘xd4 13 ♗xd4 0-0 14 a3 ½-½ de Firmian-Ftačnik, Polanica Zdroj 1995) 12...fxe6 13 ♘xc6 ♕xc6. Now, instead of 14 ♕d4 0-0! = Kaidanov-Ehlvest, New York 1994, White should try something else; for example, 14 ♕d3!? (14 ♔h1!? or even 14 ♖f4) 14...b4 15 ♘a4 ♘xe4 16 ♔h1.

c3) 10 f5!?.

d) 9...♘xd4!? (continuing the theme of 9 0-0 ♘xd4!?), and then:

d1) 10 ♗xd4 b5 and now:

d11) 11 0-0 can be met by 11...0-0, transposing to Line C222, or 11...♗b7!? 12 e5 dxe5 13 fxe5 ♘d7!? – *11 e5 dxe5 12 fxe5 ♘d7 13 0-0 ♗b7!?*.

d12) 11 e5 dxe5 12 fxe5 ♘d7 13 0-0 (13 ♕f3!? ♖b8; 13 ♕g4 0-0), and instead of 13...0-0 (which transposes to Line C222), 13...♗b7!? (preventing 14 ♘e4) is interesting. Surprisingly, I do not see anything for White:

d121) After 14 ♕h5, possible is 14...♘f6 15 exf6 ♕xd4+ 16 ♔h1 ♗xf6 17 ♗xe6 0-0 or 14...0-0 with the point 15 ♖xf7 (15 ♖ad1 ♘c5) 15...♖xf7 16 ♗xe6 ♘xe5 17 ♕xe5 ♗f6 18 ♗xf7+ ♔h8! ∓.

d122) Or 14 ♕g4 0-0! (14...♘c5 15 ♗e3!), and after 15 ♖xf7 ♔xf7 16 ♗xe6+ ♔e8, the known continuation is 17 ♕h5+(?) g6 18 ♕xh7 ♘xe5 −+. Better but still not convincing is 17 ♘e4!? ♗xe4 18 ♕xe4 g6 (possibly even stronger is 18...♖c8; e.g., 19 ♕xh7 ♘xe5!) 19 ♗xd7+ ♔xd7 20 e6+ ♔c7 21 ♖d1 ♖f5 22 ♗e5+ ♖xe5 23 ♕xe5+ ♗d6 =.

d2) After 10 ♕xd4! 0-0 11 0-0-0 Black has suffered difficulties: 11...♕c7 (11...b5 12 e5 dxe5 13 ♕xe5 ± Varavin-Zagrebelny, Alma-Ata 1995) 12 ♖hf1 (or 12 ♕b6!? ♕b8 13 ♖hf1 ♘d7 14 ♕d4 ♘c5 15 f5 with an advantage, Varga-Meissner, Altensteig 1993) 12...b5 13 f5 ± Kindermann-H.Schuh, Bundesliga 1993/4.

## C1)
**9...♕c7!?** (D)

By playing this, Black rejects the popular plan of 9...0-0 10 0-0 ♘xd4 but keeps the possibility of 10 0-0 0-0 (− 9...0-0 10 0-0 ♕c7). Here it is important which of the moves (9...♕c7 or 9...0-0) works better against 10 ♕f3 − the question still remains unanswered!

In addition, the position is important due to the move-order 8...♕c7 9 f4 ♗e7.

As in the main variation 9...0-0, here White has two main moves:

**C11: 10 ♕f3**     134
**C12: 10 0-0**     135

Other ideas:

a) 10 ♕e2 (a rare hybrid of Sozin and Velimirović) 10...b5!? (10...0-0 − 9...0-0 10 ♕e2 ♕c7; 10...♘a5!?) 11 f5 (11 0-0 − 10 0-0 b5 11 ♕e2; 11 0-0-0!? is unclear) 11...♘xd4 12 ♗xd4 b4 13 e5 with complications where White has no apparent advantage, Nijboer-Garcia Ilundain, Groningen 1991.

b) 10 f5!? has not been played at a serious level.

## C11)
**10 ♕f3 ♘xd4!?**
Other moves:

a) 10...0-0 11 0-0-0, transposing to Line C211, might represent a microconcession by Black.

b) 10...b5 11 e5 ♗b7 (11...♘xd4?! 12 ♕xa8) 12 ♘xe6 fxe6 13 exf6 ♗xf6 14 ♕h3 is better for White, Khasidovsky-Siddikov, Uzbekistan 1969.

c) 10...♗d7 11 0-0-0 (11 f5 is also good; e.g., 11...♘xd4 12 ♗xd4 e5 13 ♗e3 ♗c6 14 g4 b5 15 g5 ♘xe4 16 ♘xe4 ♕b7 17 f6! +− Plaskett-Krush,

Hampstead 2001) 11...♖c8 (11...0-0 – *10...0-0 11 0-0-0 ♗d7*) 12 g4! with an advantage, Howell-Bologan, Biel open 1993.

d) 10...♘a5 11 g4!? (11 0-0 – *10 0-0 ♘a5 11 ♕f3*; 11 0-0-0 b5!? 12 e5 ♗b7 13 ♕g3 dxe5 14 fxe5 ♘h5; 11 ♗a4+!?; 11 f5!?) with somewhat superior chances for White:

d1) 11...h6 12 0-0-0 b5 13 g5 ♘xb3+ 14 axb3 hxg5 15 fxg5 ♘d7 16 g6 ± Istratescu-Nevednichy, Bucharest 1994.

d2) 11...d5 12 exd5 ♘xb3 13 ♘xb3 ♘xd5 14 ♘xd5 exd5 15 0-0-0 ± Ostojić-Parma, Yugoslav Ch (Umag) 1972.

d3) 11...♘c4 12 ♗xc4 ♕xc4, and now 13 0-0-0!? b5 14 e5 is possibly more accurate than 13 g5 ♘d7.

d4) 11...0-0 12 g5 (12 0-0-0 – *9...0-0 10 ♕f3 ♕c7 11 0-0-0 ♘a5 12 g4*) 12...♘d7 13 0-0-0 (13 ♗xe6 ♘e5! Kasparov/Nikitin) 13...♘xb3+ (alternatively, 13...b5 – *9...0-0 10 ♕f3 ♕c7 11 0-0-0 ♘a5 12 g4 b5 13 g5 ♘d7*) 14 axb3 b5 – *9...0-0 10 ♕f3 ♕c7 11 0-0-0 ♘a5 12 g4 b5 13 g5 ♘xb3+ 14 axb3 ♘d7* ±.

**11 ♗xd4 b5 12 a3**

Other moves are:

a) 12 0-0-0 ♗b7 with strong counterplay.

b) 12 e5 dxe5 13 fxe5 ♗b7 14 ♕g3 ♘e4! 15 ♕xg7? 0-0-0 16 ♖f1 (16 0-0-0 ♖dg8 –+; 16 ♘xe4 ♗xe4 17 ♖f1 ♗g6) 16...♖hg8 17 ♕xf7 ♖xg2 18 ♕xe6+ ♔b8 19 0-0-0 ♗g5+ 20 ♔b1 ♘d2+ 21 ♖xd2 ♖xd2 22 ♗b6 ♕xc3!! 23 ♗xd8 ♕f3!! –+ Madl-Chiburdanidze, Batumi wom Echt 2000.

c) 12 f5!?, and now 12...0-0 transposes to note 'c' to White's 11th move

in Line C211. Black has two unclear alternatives: 12...b4 and 12...e5 13 ♗f2 (13 ♗e3!?) 13...♗b7 14 0-0-0 b4 15 ♘d5 ♘xd5 16 ♗xd5 (16 ♖xd5!?; 16 ♗a4+!?) 16...0-0, Blees-Lanka, Ljubljana 1994.

**12...0-0**

12...♗b7 13 0-0 (13 0-0-0!?) 13...0-0 transposes to note 'c' to White's 13th move in Line C221.

**13 0-0-0**

13 0-0 – *9...0-0 10 0-0 ♕c7 11 ♕f3 ♘xd4 12 ♗xd4 b5 13 a3!? =*.

**13...♗d7!?**

According to Stoica and Istratescu, both 13...♗b7 14 f5! and 13...♖b8 14 e5! favour White.

After the text-move (13...♗d7!?), 14 ♕d3?! is dubious in view of 14...♗c6 (14...♖fd8!? Kupreichik) 15 f5 e5 16 ♗e3 and now either 16...♖fc8 = Schandorff-Kupreichik, Copenhagen 1993 or 16...a5!? (Kupreichik). White should choose among 14 f5, 14 e5!? dxe5 15 fxe5 ♗c6 16 exf6 and 14 g4!? e5 15 g5.

**C12)**
**10 0-0** *(D)*

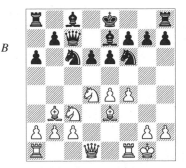

Now 10...0-0 is the main move; see *9...0-0 10 0-0 ♕c7* (Line C221).

**10...b5**

Played by Larsen, Tal and Anand. The other options are:

a) 10...♗d7 does not contain any meaningful ideas (besides 11...0-0):

a1) 11 ♕f3 ♘xd4?! 12 ♗xd4 ♗c6 13 f5 e5 14 ♗e3 b5 15 ♗g5 ♘xe4 16 ♘xe4 ♗xg5 17 ♗xf7+!, Benderac-Gnjatović, Yugoslavia 1996.

a2) 11 f5 ♘xd4 (11...e5? 12 ♘e6! fxe6 13 fxe6 ♗c8 14 ♖xf6 +–) 12 ♗xd4 (12 ♕xd4!?) 12...b5 (12...0-0 – *9...0-0 10 0-0 ♕c7 11 f5 ♘xd4 12 ♗xd4 ♗d7 ±*) 13 a3 (13 fxe6!?). Now, 13...0-0!? transposes to note 'b12 to White's 11th move in Line C221. Instead, 13...e5 14 ♗e3 ♗c6 15 ♗g5! (after 15 ♘d5, rather than 15...♗xd5 16 ♗xd5 ± Fischer-Cardoso, New York (4) 1957, Black should play 15...♕b7!, as in Golubev-Liubarsky, Ukrainian jr Cht (Evpatoria) 1984) 15...♘xe4 16 ♗xe7! favours White.

b) 10...♘a5 contains ideas, but they work rather poorly:

b1) 11 ♗a4+ ♗d7 12 ♗xd7+ ♕xd7! 13 e5?! dxe5 14 fxe5 ♘c4! ∓.

b2) 11 ♕e2 b5 (11...0-0!? =) 12 f5 ♘xb3 (12...e5) 13 cxb3 (13 axb3 b4! ∓ Lipnitsky-Taimanov, USSR Ch (Moscow) 1951) 13...e5 14 ♘c2 ± Ivanović-Cebalo, Pula 1991.

b3) 11 ♕f3 b5! on the whole suits Black:

b31) 12 a3 can be met by 12...♘xb3 or 12...♗b7 =.

b32) Unclear is 12 g4 b4!? (12...h5 13 g5 ♘g4 14 g6! Khenkin) 13 ♘ce2 ♘xb3 14 axb3 ♗b7 15 ♘g3 ♘d7 Boleslavsky.

b33) 12 f5!? e5 (12...♘xb3!? 13 axb3 b4 14 e5? ♗b7) 13 ♘d5 ♘xd5 14 ♗xd5 exd4 15 ♗xd4 ♗f6 (15...♗b7 is

critical) 16 ♗xf6 gxf6 17 ♗xa8 ♕a7+ 18 ♖f2 ♕xa8 19 ♕c3 ± Adorjan-Ribli, Hungary 1969.

b34) 12 e5 ♗b7 13 ♕g3 dxe5! (13...♘xb3 14 cxb3; 13...♘h5 14 ♕h3 ♘xb3 15 cxb3 g6 16 ♖ac1! Boleslavsky) 14 fxe5 ♘h5 (14...♘xb3!?) and now:

b341) 15 ♕h3 ♘xb3 (15...♕xe5? 16 ♗xe6!, Averbakh-Taimanov, Zurich Ct 1953) 16 ♘xb3 ♕xe5 17 ♘a5 b4! is good for Black, Bannik-Taimanov, USSR Ch (Kiev) 1954.

b342) Double-edged play results after 15 ♕f2 0-0 16 g4 ♘xb3; e.g., 17 axb3 f6!? (17...♕xe5 18 gxh5 ♕xh5 19 ♘ce2!) 18 gxh5 fxe5 19 ♕g3 ♗c5 20 h6 g6 21 ♖xf8+ ♖xf8 = Emms-Shipov, Thessaloniki 1996.

b343) 15 ♗xe6 ♘xg3 (15...fxe6? 16 ♕h3 ±) 16 ♗xf7+ ♔d7 17 ♗e6+ ♔e8 (17...♔d8? 18 ♖ad1!) is a draw.

b4) 11 g4!?.

b5) 11 f5! and then:

b51) 11...e5 12 ♘de2 ♘c4 (12...b5 13 ♗g5!; 12...♗d7 13 ♔h1!?) 13 ♘d5!? (13 ♗xc4 ♕xc4 and now 14 b3!? *Schach-Archiv* or 14 ♗g5!?) 13...♘xd5 14 ♕xd5 ♘xe3 15 ♕xf7+ ♔d8 16 ♕xg7 ♖e8 17 ♖f3 ♕b6 18 ♔h1 d5 (Akhmadeev-Ragozin, Russian Ch (Elista) 1994) 19 ♗xd5 with an advantage – Cu.Hansen.

b52) 11...♘c4 12 ♗xc4 ♕xc4 13 ♕f3 0-0 (13...e5 can be answered by Kaidanov's 14 ♘b3! b5 15 ♘d2 or 14 ♘de2 b5 15 b3! ♕c6 16 ♘d5!, Ciocaltea-Halić, Romanian Ch (Bucharest) 1954) 14 ♖ad1 b5?! (14...♖b8 15 g4!; 14...e5 ±; 14...♘d7!? – Kaidanov) 15 fxe6 fxe6 16 e5 ± Kaidanov-Smirin, Groningen PCA qual 1993.

We now return to 10...b5 *(D)*:

W

**11 ♘xc6**

Otherwise:

a) 11 ♕e2 can be answered by 11...♘xd4!? = (Akopian) or 11...♘a5 – *10...♘a5 11 ♕e2 b5*.

b) 11 ♕f3 gives Black a choice between 11...♗b7!? and 11...♘a5 – *10...♘a5 11 ♕f3 b5!*.

c) After 11 a3, 11...0-0 (11...♗b7 12 f5 e5 13 ♘xc6 ♗xc6 – *10...♗d7 11 f5 ♘xd4 12 ♗xd4 b5 13 a3 e5 14 ♗e3 ♗c6 ±; 11...♘a5!?*) is OK; e.g., 12 f5 ♘xd4 13 ♗xd4 – *9...0-0 10 0-0 ♕c7 11 f5 ♘xd4 12 ♗xd4 b5 13 a3*.

d) 11 f5 is popular: 11...♘xd4! (11...b4? 12 ♗a4 ♗b7 13 fxe6 bxc3 14 exf7+), and now:

d1) 12 ♕xd4!? 0-0 and now, rather than 13 fxe6? ♗xe6! (13...fxe6? 14 ♘d5 ♘xd5 15 exd5! ±) 14 ♖ad1 ♖ac8 = Ab.Khasin-Tal, USSR Ch (Leningrad) 1956, Tal recommended 13 ♖ad1!.

d2) 12 ♗xd4 e5!? (12...b4!? 13 ♘a4 ♖b8 ∞ Bitansky-Lerner, Tel-Aviv 2001; 12...0-0 – *9...0-0 10 0-0 ♕c7 11 f5 ♘xd4 12 ♗xd4 b5*) 13 ♗f2 (13 ♗e3 ♗b7 14 ♗g5 {14 ♘d5!?} 14...♘xe4 15 ♘xe4 ♗xe4 16 ♕g4 d5 with a double-edged game, Veröci-Liu Shilan, Thessaloniki wom OL 1984) 13...♗b7 14 a3 (14 ♗h4 ♘xe4 15 ♘xe4 ♗xe4

16 ♕g4 d5 17 ♕xg7 0-0-0 with counterplay – Anand) 14...0-0 15 ♕f3 transposes to note 'c31' to White's 13th move in Line C221 (=).

**11...♕xc6 12 f5! 0-0**

12...♗d7 13 fxe6 fxe6 transposes to note 'c2' to Black's 9th move in Line C.

**13 fxe6 ♗xe6**

13...fxe6 14 ♘d5!.

**14 ♘d5 ♗xd5 15 exd5 ♕d7 16 ♖f4** ± Golubev-Belotti, Grächen 1999.

**C2)**

**9...0-0** *(D)*

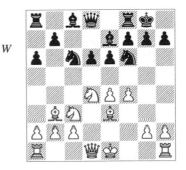

W

Now:

10 ♕e2!? continues the topic of hybrids:

a) 10...♘xd4 11 ♗xd4 b5 12 0-0-0 b4 (12...♗b7 can be met by 13 e5 or 13 f5!? ± Nikitin) 13 ♘a4 ♗b7 (13...e5 14 ♗xe5 ♗g4 15 ♕e3!? ♗xd1 16 ♗xf6 ♗xf6 17 ♖xd1 ♕e7 18 ♘b6 ♖ae8 19 e5! with an advantage, Klimov-Eriksson, Stockholm 1998; 13...♘d7!?) 14 ♗xf6!? ♗xf6 15 ♘c5 ♗c6 (15...♗c8!? Lepeshkin) 16 e5 ♗xe5! 17 ♘xe6! =

Sigurjonsson-Ligterink, Wijk aan Zee 1980.

b) 10...♞a5 11 g4!? gives White attacking chances.

c) 10...♝d7 11 f5 (11 0-0-0 transposes to note 'b' to White's 11th move in Line A1 of Chapter 10; 11 0-0) 11...♞xd4 12 ♝xd4 exf5 13 0-0 fxe4 14 ♞xe4 ♞e5 15 ♞xd6 = Kovaliov-Filipenko, USSR 1986.

d) 10...♛c7 11 f5!? (11 0-0-0 transposes to note 'b' to White's 11th move in Line B2 of Chapter 10) 11...♞xd4 (11...exf5 12 ♞xf5 ♝xf5 13 exf5 d5 14 0-0-0 ± A.Ivanov-Kovaliov, USSR 1986) 12 ♝xd4 b5 (12...exf5 13 0-0! is slightly better for White, Mikhalchishin-Tukmakov, Rostov 1980) 13 fxe6 fxe6 (13...♝xe6!?) 14 0-0 ♚h8 (14...b4?! 15 ♞a4 ♜b8 16 e5 Belikov) 15 a3 ♝d7 (15...e5 16 ♝e3 ±) 16 e5 with a slight advantage for White, Belikov-Mäki, Dresden 2000.

## C21)
**10 ♛f3** *(D)*

This concept, connected with 0-0-0, partially lost its appeal after the 1993 Kasparov-Short match.

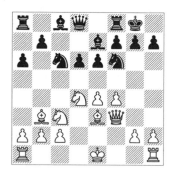

B

Now:

Other moves:

a) 10...♛a5 11 0-0-0 ♞xd4 12 ♜xd4 ♝d7?! (12...♞d7!?) 13 g4! e5 14 ♞d5 (14 ♜d5 ♛d8! Yakovich) 14...exd4 15 ♞xe7+ ♚h8 16 ♝xd4 ± Mitkov-Kožul, Skopje open 1991.

b) 10...♞d7 11 0-0-0 (11 0-0!?) 11...♞c5 12 g4 ♝d7 13 g5 b5 14 ♚b1 ♞xb3 15 axb3 ♞xd4 16 ♝xd4 b4 17 ♞a4 ± Kupreichik-Mukhin, USSR 1973.

c) 10...♝d7 11 0-0-0! (11 0-0 – *10 0-0 ♝d7 11 ♛f3*), and Black faces problems: 11...♛c7 – *10...♛c7 11 0-0-0 ♝d7*; 11...♞xd4 12 ♝xd4 ♝c6 13 g4 or 13 f5! with an advantage; 11...♛b8 12 g4 ♞xd4 13 ♝xd4 e5 14 g5 ♝g4 15 ♛g3 ±; 11...♞a5 12 g4! with an initiative; 11...♜c8 12 g4! (12 f5?! ♞xd4! 13 ♝xd4 e5 ∞ J.Polgar-I.Ivanov, New York 1989).

d) 10...♞a5 11 0-0-0 (11 g4 b5 12 g5 ♞d7 is unclear; e.g., 13 ♜g1 b4 14 ♞ce2 ♞xb3 15 axb3 ♝b7 16 f5, Atanasov-Suba, 1978, 16...e5) 11...b5!? (11...♛c7 – *10...♛c7 11 0-0-0 ♞a5*; 11...♞xb3+ 12 axb3 ♛a5 13 ♚b1 ♛h5 14 ♛f2 ± Enders-Vogt, East German Ch (Nordhausen) 1986) 12 e5 ♝b7 13 exf6 ♝xf3 14 fxe7 ♛xe7 with a complicated game, Filipowicz-Gromek, Polish Ch (Rzeszow) 1966.

## C211)
**10...♛c7 11 0-0-0**
Otherwise:

a) 11 g4? ♞xd4 12 ♝xd4 e5.

b) 11 0-0 – *10 0-0 ♛c7 11 ♛f3*.

c) 11 f5!? ♞xd4! (11...d5? 12 fxe6 fxe6 13 exd5 ±; 11...♚h8?! 12 0-0-0;

11...e5 12 ♘de2 {possibly 12 ♘xc6!?} 12...b5 13 g4 b4 14 ♘a4 ♘d7 15 g5 with an attack, Cheremisin-Bakulin, Moscow 1957; 11...♘e5 12 ♕e2 exf5 13 ♘xf5 and now 13...♗xf5 14 exf5 ± Zuckerman-Schön, New York 1987, or 13...d5 14 ♘xe7+ ♕xe7 15 ♗g5 ± Stefansson-Shirov, Reykjavik 1992) 12 ♗xd4 b5 (12...e5 13 ♗e3 b5 14 a3!?), and now:

c1) 13 a3 and then:

c11) 13...exf5?! 14 exf5 ♗b7 ±.

c12) 13...♗d7 is well met by 14 g4!.

c13) 13...e5 and then:

c131) 14 ♗f2 ♗b7 15 0-0 transposes to note 'c31' to White's 13th move in Line C221.

c132) 14 ♗e3 ♗b7 and now 15 0-0 transposes to note 'c32' to White's 13th move in Line C221, but 15 0-0-0!? is interesting, Zeller-Haist, Württemberg Ch 1995.

c14) 13...♖b8! and now:

c141) 14 0-0-0 b4 15 axb4 ♖xb4 16 g4 – *14 g4 b4 15 axb4 ♖xb4 16 0-0-0*.

c142) Black has good play after 14 0-0 b4! 15 axb4 ♖xb4 16 ♗e3 exf5 17 exf5 ♗b7, del Rio-Lerner, Metz 1998.

c143) 14 fxe6 ♗xe6 15 ♘d5 ♗xd5 16 exd5 ♘d7 is also fine for Black, Apicella-Avrukh, Albufeira ECC 1999.

c144) 14 g4 b4 15 g5 (or 15 axb4 ♖xb4 16 0-0-0 e5 17 ♗f2 ♗b7 18 ♖he1 ♖b8!, Bednarski-Lombard, Skopje OL 1972, with the point 19 g5 ♘xe4 −+) 15...♘e8! 16 axb4 ♗xg5 17 0-0 ♗f6 favours Black, Vera-Lechtinsky, Bratislava 1983.

c2) 13 g4!? b4 (13...♗b7?! 14 g5 ±; 13...e5!? 14 ♗f2 b4 15 ♘d5 ♘xd5 16 ♗xd5 ♗b7) 14 g5 ♘e8. Here, Black

may be happy with 15 f6 bxc3 16 fxe7 ♕xe7, as in Minić-Jansa, Budva 1963, and other games, but 15 ♘d5!? exd5 16 ♕h5 (Baljon) deserves serious attention.

c3) 13 0-0-0!? b4 14 ♘a4. Now 14...exf5 15 exf5 ♗b7 16 ♕g3, Soffer-Loginov, Budapest 1994, and 14...♖b8 15 g4 e5 16 ♗f2 ♗b7 17 ♖he1 ♗c6 18 g5, A.Ivanov-Wessman, Reykjavik tt 1990, do not yield equality. Also dubious seems 14...♗b7 15 fxe6 fxe6 (Yakovich-Aseev, USSR Ch (Moscow) 1991; hardly sufficient is 15...♗xe4 16 exf7+), and now 16 ♕g3!. There remains 14...e5!? with unclear play; e.g., 15 ♗f2 ♗b7 16 ♖he1 ♗c6 17 ♘b6 ♖ab8 18 ♘d5 ♘xd5 19 ♗xd5 a5.

We now return to 11 0-0-0 *(D)*:

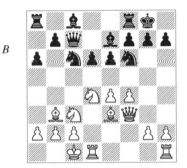

**11...b5(!)**

Others:

a) 11...♘xd4?! is hardly successful:

a1) 12 ♖xd4 b5 and then:

a11) 13 f5 ♗d7!? (13...exf5 14 exf5 ♗b7 15 ♕f2 probably favours White, J.Polgar-Maxwell, Weimar 1989, as does 13...b4 14 ♖xb4 d5 15 ♖d4 dxe4 16 ♘xe4 exf5 17 ♘g5!?) 14 g4 a5 15 g5 a4 16 gxf6 ♗xf6 17 ♗d5 ♖ac8

Medvegy-Somogyi, Hungarian Cht 1992/3, and it appears that Black is ready for complications; e.g., 18 ♕g2 a3 19 ♔b1 axb2 20 fxe6 fxe6 21 ♘xb5 ♕c5.

a12) 13 g4 e5 (13...b4 14 ♖xb4 d5 15 ♖d4 dxe4 16 ♕e2 ± Anand-Piket, Amsterdam 1990) 14 ♘d5 (14 g5!? exd4 15 ♗xd4 ♘d7 16 ♘d5 ♕d8 17 ♖g1 Kasparov) 14...♘xd5 15 ♖xd5 b4! (15...♗e6? 16 f5! ±; 15...exf4 16 ♗xf4 ♗e6 17 ♖d2 ± Anand) 16 f5! (16 fxe5 ♗e6!? {or 16...dxe5 17 ♕g3 ♗b7} 17 exd6 ♗xd6 18 ♖d2 ♗xb3 19 axb3 a5 with an initiative – Kasparov) 16...a5 17 ♗a4! ♗b7 18 g5 (18 ♕g2!? Kasparov) 18...♖fc8! 19 ♕g2 ♗xd5 20 exd5 ♕c4 21 ♔b1 ♕h4! with approximately equal chances, Reinderman-Kasparov, Wijk aan Zee 1999.

a2) 12 ♗xd4! b5 (12...e5 13 fxe5 dxe5 14 ♕g3 ♗d6 15 ♗e3 ± Khenkin-Zlotnik, Moscow 1965; 12...♘d7 13 ♕g3 ♗f6 14 ♖he1 ±) 13 ♗xf6! ♗xf6 (13...gxf6 14 ♖d3 ± Rublevsky-Ionov, Russian Ch (Elista) 1994) 14 e5 ♗b7 15 ♗d5! ± Votava-Bagaturov, Brno 1991.

b) 11...♘a5 12 g4! (12 f5!?) 12...b5 (12...♘xb3+ 13 axb3 b5 will come to the same thing; 12...♘c4 13 g5 ♘d7 14 ♘f5! ± Tringov-Letelier, Havana 1971) 13 g5 ♘xb3+ (13...♘d7 14 ♗xe6!? ♘e5 15 fxe5 fxe6 16 ♕h3) 14 axb3 ♘d7 15 f5 b4 (15...♘e5 16 ♕g3!? is given by Kasparov and Nikitin) 16 ♘a4! (16 ♘ce2 e5 is unclear) 16...♘e5 17 ♕g2 ± Yakovich-Ionov, USSR Ch (Moscow) 1991.

c) 11...♗d7 12 g4! ♘xd4 and then:
c1) 13 ♗xd4 e5 (13...♗c6?! 14 f5!; 13...b5!? 14 f5 b4 15 g5 ♘e8 16 f6 ♗d8) 14 fxe5 dxe5 15 ♕g3! ♘xg4

(15...♗d6 16 ♗e3 ♗c6 17 ♕f3 ±) 16 ♘d5 with a strong initiative, Trepp-Kaenel, Biel 1989.

c2) 13 ♖xd4!? e5 14 ♖d2! with an advantage, Ničevski-Lombard, Polanica Zdroj 1974.

d) 11...♘d7!? (e.g. 12 f5 ♘c5 13 ♕g3 ♔h8) is worthy of attention.

**12 e5**
12 f5 b4 13 ♘ce2 ♘xd4 14 ♖xd4 exf5!? (unclear is 14...e5 15 ♖c4 ♕b8 16 g4 Sokolov) 15 exf5 ♗b7 16 ♕h3? (16 ♕g3!, Sokolov, is unclear again) 16...a5 ∓ Istratescu-A.Sokolov, Groningen FIDE 1997.

12 g4 ♘xd4 (possibly 12...b4! is even stronger) 13 ♗xd4 (13 ♖xd4 – *11...♘xd4 12 ♖xd4 b5 13 g4*) 13...b4! with counterplay, Perez-Smyslov, Havana 1962.

**12...♘xd4**
12...♗b7? 13 ♘xe6.

**13 ♗xd4**
13 ♖xd4? dxe5 14 fxe5 ♕xe5 15 ♕xa8 ♕xe3+ 16 ♖d2 ♘g4 ∓ A.Sokolov.

13 ♕xa8 dxe5 (13...♘c6!?, as suggested by Kasparov/Nikitin, is unclear) 14 fxe5 ♘xb3+ (14...♗b7 15 ♕a7 ♘c6 16 ♕b6 ±) 15 axb3 ♗b7! (15...♕xe5?! 16 ♕a7 ± Yakovich-Ionov, St Petersburg 1995) 16 ♕a7 ♘g4 (or 16...♘d7) with compensation – Ionov.

**13...dxe5!**
13...♘d7 14 ♕xa8!? ♗b7 15 ♘xb5 axb5 16 ♕a3 ±.

**14 ♗xe5**
After 14 fxe5, the reply 14...♘d7 is sufficient.

**14...♗b7 15 ♕g3 b4 16 ♘e2**
16 ♘a4 ♕c6 17 ♖d4 ♗b7 18 ♖c4 ♕b5 19 ♖c7 ♗d8 is OK for Black, A.Kovačević-Arsović, Ulcinj 1988.

**16...a5 17 ♗a4**

White keeps some initiative, Voit-sekhovsky-Loginov, Novgorod 1999.

## C212)

**10...♘xd4 11 ♗xd4 b5** *(D)*

This move is better than 11...e5 ± or 11...♕a5 12 f5 exf5 13 0-0!, Velim-irović-Popović, Yugoslav Ch (Budva) 1986.

W

The line with 10...♘xd4 and 11...b5 was recognized as the strongest after Short-Kasparov (1993). It is easy to understand why in 1999 Kasparov did not play like this against Reinderman: in the main line White has a simple draw and various other tries.

**12 ♗xf6**

Or:

a) 12 e5?! dxe5 13 ♗xe5 (13 fxe5 ♕xd4 14 exf6 ♗c5!, Hermlin-Sham-kovich, Viljandi 1972) 13...♖a7! (but not 13...♕b6? 14 ♕xa8 ♗b7 15 ♗d4 ♕c6 16 ♕a7 ♘d7 17 ♗e3! ♘c5 18 0-0-0 ♖a8 19 ♗d5 +−).

b) 12 0-0-0!? ♗b7 13 ♖he1 is un-clear; e.g., 13...b4!? 14 ♘a4 ♗c6, Honfi-Wells, Budapest 1995.

c) 12 a3 ♗b7 (12...♖b8!? 13 0-0-0 b4 14 axb4 ♖xb4 15 e5 dxe5 16 ♗c5

♕c7 17 ♗xb4 ♗xb4 with compensa-tion, Istratescu-Milu, Romanian Ch (Bucharest) 1992) 13 0-0-0 (13 0-0 transposes to note 'c2' to White's 12th move in Line C222) has frequently oc-curred:

c1) 13...♖c8 14 ♖he1 (14 f5 ♖xc3!) 14...♕a5 15 ♔b1 b4 16 axb4 ♕xb4 17 g4 ♘d7 18 f5 ♔h8 (18...♗h4 19 fxe6 fxe6 20 ♗xe6+ ♔h8 21 ♕h3 ♗xe1 22 ♗xd7 ♗xc3 23 ♗xc3 ♖xc3 24 ♕xc3 ♕xc3 25 bxc3 ♖d8 ± Istratescu-Pan-chenko, Bucharest 1994) 19 g5! e5 20 ♗e3 ♖xc3 21 bxc3 ♕xc3 (21...♕xe4 22 ♕xe4 ♗xe4 23 f6! Istratescu) 22 ♕g4 ♖b8 23 ♗a7 ♗xe4 24 ♕xe4 ♖xb3+ 25 cxb3 ♕xb3+ 26 ♔c1 ♗xg5+ 27 ♖e3! ± Istratescu-Murugan, Lin-ares open 1998.

c2) 13...a5! 14 ♗xf6 ♗xf6 15 ♘xb5 a4 16 ♗c4! (16 ♖xd6 ♕c8! 17 ♗a2 ♕c5! 18 ♕d3, Istratescu-Buturin, Bu-charest 1992, 18...♗c6! with the point 19 ♘c7 ♗xe4 20 ♕xe4 ♗xb2+ −+ Stoica/Istratescu) 16...d5! (possibly best) 17 e5 (17 exd5 ♕b6! 18 ♕e2 exd5 19 ♗xd5 ♖ae8 Stoica/Istratescu) 17...♗e7 18 ♗d3 ♕b6 with serious compensation; e.g., 19 ♖d2 ♖ab8 20 ♘c3 d4 21 ♕h3 ♕xb2+! ∓.

**12...♗xf6 13 e5 ♗h4+ 14 g3 ♖b8! 15 gxh4**

Or:

a) 15 exd6 ♗b7 16 ♘e4 f5 17 ♗xe6+ ♔h8 18 ♗xf5 ♖xf5 19 0-0-0 ♕a5!?.

b) 15 ♖f1 ♗e7 16 0-0-0 a5!? (also possible is 16...♕c7) 17 exd6 ♗xd6 18 f5? (18 ♕d3 ♗e7 19 ♕xb5 ♕c7 20 ♕e5 ♕b6 21 ♘a4 ♕a7 with compen-sation, San Segundo) 18...a4 ∓ Moro-zevich-San Segundo, Madrid 1996.

c) 15 0-0-0!? and then:

c1) 15...♗b7 16 ♘e4 and now:

c11) 16...♗xe4 17 ♕xe4 d5 18 ♕d3 (18 ♕f3 ♗e7 19 f5 a5! 20 c3 a4 21 ♗c2 b4 22 f6 gxf6 23 ♗xh7+ = Ehlvest-Mednis, Las Vegas 1998) 18...♗e7 19 h4 ♕a5 (19...a5 20 c3 b4 21 ♗c2 g6 22 h5 bxc3 23 hxg6 hxg6 24 ♖h6 +− *Russian Chess Review*) 20 f5 ± Morozevich-Mitenkov, Moscow 1991.

c12) 16...♗e7 17 exd6 (17 f5! ± Borkowski-J.Adamski, Polish Ch 1983) 17...♗xd6 18 ♖he1 a5 with a good game for Black, Hmadi-de Firmian, Tunis IZ 1985.

c2) 15...♗e7! 16 ♖he1? (16 exd6 ♗xd6 17 ♘e4 ♗b7 transposes to line 'c12') 16...d5 ∓ Morozevich-de Firmian, Amsterdam 1996.

**15...♗b7 16 ♘e4**

16 ♕g3?! ♗xh1 17 0-0-0 b4!?.

**16...dxe5**

16...♕xh4+ 17 ♕g3 (17 ♔f1 dxe5 ∞) 17...♕xg3+ 18 ♘xg3 ♗xh1 19 ♘xh1 ± Kasparov.

**17 ♖g1 g6!**

Other moves are poor; for example: 17...♗xe4? 18 ♕xe4 ♕xh4+ 19 ♔f1 exf4 20 ♖g2 ± Kasparov; 17...♕xh4+? 18 ♕g3 ♕xg3+ 19 ♘xg3 exf4 20 ♘h5 +− Shamkovich; 17...♕d4? 18 ♘f6+ ♔h8 19 ♕g3 +−.

After the text-move (17...g6!), the critical position arises:

a) 18 ♖d1 ♗xe4 19 ♕xe4 ♕xh4+ and Black stands no worse, Short-Kasparov, London PCA Wch (12) 1993.

b) 18 ♖g5 ♕d4 19 ♖xe5 (or 19 ♘f6+ ♔g7 20 c3 ♗xf3 21 cxd4 ♔xf6) 19...♕g1+ with perpetual check – Kasparov.

What else?

c) 18 ♔f1 f5!? does not seem convincing.

d) Probably 18 ♖f1!? is more interesting; e.g., 18...f5 19 ♗xe6+ ♔g7!? (19...♔h8 20 ♕c3) 20 ♖d1 (20 ♕c3 ♗xe4 21 ♕xe5+ ♔h6!) 20...fxe4 21 ♕g3 ♕f6 22 ♖d7+ ♔h8 23 f5 e3 24 h5.

## C22)

**10 0-0** (D)

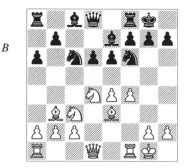

Via a long winding road, we have reached the Classical Sozin main line. The principal continuations are:

**C221: 10...♕c7**              143
**C222: 10...♘xd4**            147

Other moves:

a) 10...d5?! 11 e5 ♘d7 is hardly sufficient (here it is worth mentioning 12 ♕h5 ♖e8? 13 ♘xd5!! exd5 14 ♕xf7+!! +− Troinov-L.Popov, Bulgaria 1962).

b) 10...♘a5, and then:

b1) 11 ♕f3 b5?! (better is 11...♕c7 – *10...♕c7 11 ♕f3 ♘a5*) 12 e5 ♗b7 13 exf6! ♗xf3 14 fxe7 ♕xe7 15 ♖xf3 (Suetin) is dangerous for Black.

b2) 11 f5 ♘xb3 12 axb3 ♗d7 13 ♕f3 (13 g4!? e5 14 g5 exd4 15 ♗xd4!) 13...b5! = Ki.Georgiev-Xu Jun, Moscow OL 1994.

b3) 11 e5! ♘e8 (11...dxe5 12 fxe5 ± ♘d7? 13 ♖xf7!), and both 12 ♕h5 and 12 ♕g4 preserve the initiative.

c) 10...♗d7 requires a precise reaction:

c1) 11 ♕e2 b5! = 12 e5 dxe5 13 ♘xc6 ♗xc6 14 fxe5 ♘e4! 15 ♕f3? ♕c7! −+ Padevsky-Larsen, Moscow OL 1956.

c2) 11 ♕f3 b5! = (Pritchett-Larsen, Dundee 1967) 12 e5 ♘xd4 13 ♗xd4 dxe5 14 fxe5 ♗c6!.

c3) 11 f5! ♘xd4 (11...♕c8? 12 fxe6 ± ♗xe6? 13 ♘xe6 fxe6 14 ♘a4 +− Fischer-Larsen, Denver Ct (3) 1971; 11...e5 12 ♘de2 ±) 12 ♗xd4 (12 ♕xd4 ♘g4 =) 12...exf5 (12...♕c7 transposes to note 'b' to White's 11th move in Line C221; 12...e5 13 ♗e3 ♗c6 14 ♕f3 b5 15 ♗g5 ±; 12...b5 13 ♗xf6!, K.Müller-Heinemann, German Ch (Altenkirchen) 1999) 13 exf5 ♕a5 (or 13...♗c6 14 ♕e1 b5 15 ♕g3 ♖c8 16 ♖ae1 b4 17 ♘a4 ♗b5, Motousis-Greenfeld, Novi Sad OL 1990, 18 ♘b6! ±) 14 ♕d3 (14 ♕e1!) 14...♗c6 15 ♖ae1 ♖ae8 with the idea of ...♗d8 gives Black a defensible position, Lendwai-Brunner, Graz 1991.

## C221)
**10...♕c7** *(D)*

This occurs two or three times less frequently than 10...♘xd4, but a comparable amount of material has been accumulated as a consequence of transpositions from an early ...♕c7.

**11 ♕f3**

Otherwise:

a) 11 ♔h1 ♘xd4 (11...♘a5!?) 12 ♕xd4 b5 (12...♗d7?! 13 ♖ad1 ♘c5 14 f5! ± de Firmian-Stefansson, Moscow OL 1996; 12...♘g4 13 ♕b6 ±

Psakhis) 13 f5 transposes to note 'b' after Black's 12th move in Line B2 of Chapter 8.

b) A worthy alternative is 11 f5 ♘xd4 (11...e5 12 ♘de2! ±) 12 ♗xd4 (12 ♕xd4 b5 transposes to note 'd1' to White's 11th move in Line C12) 12...b5 (12...e5?! 13 ♗e3 b5 14 ♗g5 b4 15 ♗xf6 bxc3 16 ♗xe7 cxb2 17 ♗xf8 bxa1♕ 18 ♕xa1 ♔xf8 19 ♕d1 ± Sax-Muhtarov, Bled 1994; 12...♗d7 ± gives White a good choice among 13 ♕f3 – *11 ♕f3 ♗d7 12 f5 ♘xd4 13 ♗xd4*, 13 g4!?, 13 ♕d3 exf5 14 exf5 ♗c6 15 ♖ae1, Aseev-Ionov, St Petersburg 1996, and 13 fxe6 fxe6 14 ♕d3), when White has two tries:

b1) 13 a3 and then:

b11) 13...exf5?! is answered by 14 ♘d5!.

b12) 13...♗d7 14 g4 (14 ♕d3 ♖ac8 15 ♔h1 ♕b7 = Gorelov-Serper, Russian Cht 1994; 14 ♕e2!?; 14 ♕f3!? – *11 ♕f3 ♗d7 12 f5 ♘xd4 13 ♗xd4 b5 14 a3!?*) 14...h6 (14...e5!? 15 ♗e3 ♗c6 16 ♕f3 ♕b7 17 ♗d5 ∞) 15 h4 ♘h7 (Hartston-Suetin, Hastings 1967/8) 16 g5! with a dangerous attack.

b13) 13...e5!? and now White faces a typical decision:

b131) 14 ♗e3 ♗b7 and now:

b1311) 15 ♕f3 – *11 ♕f3 ♘xd4 12 ♗xd4 b5 13 a3 ♗b7 14 f5 e5 15 ♗e3*.

b1312) 15 ♕d3 h6!? = Cochrane-Mateus, Dubai OL 1996.

b1313) 15 ♗g5 ♘xe4 is satisfactory for Black, Kaminski-Kempinski, Polish Ch (Brzeg Dolny) 1996.

b1314) A curious and risky possibility is 15 g4!? ♘xe4 16 ♘d5 ♕d8 17 ♕f3 ♘c5 18 f6, Roiz-Ahmed, Asturia 1996.

b132) 14 ♗f2 ♗b7 and then: 15 ♕f3 – *11 ♕f3 ♘xd4 12 ♗xd4 b5 13 a3 ♗b7 14 f5 e5 15 ♗f2*. However, 15 ♕e2!? de Firmian-Wharton, Ashville 1990 (15 ♖e1!? is proposed by Beliavsky and Mikhalchishin) leaves more hope for an advantage.

b14) 13...♖b8!?. Now both 14 ♔h1 a5 15 a4 bxa4 16 ♖xa4 ♖b4!, Brenjo-Arsović, Yugoslav Cht 1994, and 14 ♕d3 b4 15 axb4 ♖xb4 16 fxe6 fxe6 17 ♔h1 ♔h8, Lukin-Aseev, St Petersburg 1996 appear good for Black, though 14 g4!? is not wholly clear.

b2) 13 fxe6 seems most important:

b21) 13...♗xe6 and now:

b211) After 14 ♘d5 ♗xd5 15 exd5 ♘d7 16 ♕g4 ♘e5 17 ♕g3 ♖ae8, 18 c3 (Bezgodov-Lutsko, Kstovo 1994) is superior to 18 a4 b4 19 a5 ♗d8! (Illescas-Salov, Linares 1990), but hardly gives any real advantage.

b212) Therefore, 14 ♕d3! is better: 14...♗c4?! 15 ♕g3!; 14...♖ae8 15 ♔h1 (15 ♘d5!?) 15...♘d7 16 a4 ± Mortensen-Radulov, Copenhagen 1991; 14...b4 15 ♘d5 ♗xd5 16 exd5 ♘d7 17 a3 is slightly better for White, Berzinsh-Veingold, Tallinn Z 1998.

b22) 13...fxe6 has not been used by grandmasters but still deserves attention:

b221) 14 ♘d5?! exd5 15 ♗xf6 gxf6! is unsuccessful for White.

b222) 14 ♗xf6 ♗xf6 15 ♘d5 ♕a7+! also looks unconvincing for White.

b223) 14 a4!? b4 15 ♘e2 ♔h8 16 a5 and now rather than 16...♗b7 17 ♗b6 ♕c6 18 ♘d4 ♕xe4 19 ♕d2 ♘d5 20 ♖xf8+ ♖xf8 21 ♖e1 ♕g4?! 22 ♘xe6 ♗h4 23 ♖e2 ± Golubev-Haist, Biel open 1994, Black may be able to improve with 16...♗d7!?.

b224) 14 ♕e2!? transposes to note 'd' to White's 10th move in Line C2.

We now return to 11 ♕f3 *(D)*:

**11...♘xd4**

Let us assume, provisionally, that this is the main line. The same positions can be achieved through 11...b5!? after 12 e5 ♘xd4 (12...♗b7? 13 ♘xe6) 13 ♗xd4, as well as after 12 a3 ♘xd4 (or 12...♗b7 13 f5 ♘xd4 14 ♗xd4) 13 ♗xd4.

The other lines are:

a) 11...♘d7 12 f5 ♘c5 13 ♕g3 gives White a small advantage.

b) 11...♘a5. Now, White has two tries (and both allow possible transpositions into the ...♘bd7, ...♘c5 and ...♘xb3 lines of the Fischer Attack):

b1) 12 f5 and then:

b11) 12...♘c4 13 ♗xc4 (13 fxe6!?) 13...♕xc4 transposes to note 'b52' to Black's 10th move in Line C12.

b12) 12...♘xb3 13 axb3 ♗d7 (or 13...exf5 14 ♘xf5 ± Yurtaev-Lerner, Frunze 1989) 14 g4! with an initiative, Morozevich-Dragomaretsky, Alushta 1993.

b13) 12...e5 13 ♘de2 ♘xb3 14 axb3 (14 cxb3 b5 15 ♖ac1 and now either 15...♕d7 = Shipov or 15...♕a5!?) 14...b5 15 g4 b4 (15...h6!?) 16 g5 bxc3 17 gxf6 ♗xf6 18 bxc3! ± Fischer-Hamann, Netanya 1968.

b2) 12 g4 and then:

b21) 12...d5 13 e5 and then either 13...♘d7 14 ♗xd5! exd5 15 ♘xd5 ♕d8 16 ♘f5 ± (Kimelfeld) or 13...♘e4 14 ♘xd5 ±.

b22) 12...♘c4 13 g5 ♘d7 (13...♘e8 14 f5!?) 14 ♘f5! ± Golubev-Zahn, Bad Wiessee 1999.

b23) 12...b5 13 g5 ♘d7? (13...♘e8 14 f5) 14 ♘xe6! fxe6 15 ♗xe6+ ♔h8 16 ♘d5 ♕d8 17 ♕h5 +− Boleslavsky-Aronin, USSR Ch (Moscow) 1949.

b24) 12...♘xb3 (the main continuation) 13 axb3 (13 cxb3!? e5 14 ♘f5 ♗xf5 15 exf5 ♕c6 16 g5 ♕xf3 17 ♖xf3 ♘d7 18 ♘d5 ♗d8 19 ♖c1 f6 and Black may hold on, Filipowicz-Savon, Moscow 1964) and now:

b241) 13...♖b8 is too slow: 14 g5 ± Sozin – Ilyin-Zhenevsky, USSR Ch (Moscow) 1931.

b242) 13...♘d7 14 g5 ♖e8 15 f5 ♘e5 16 ♕h3 g6 17 ♖f2 ♗d7 18 ♖af1 ♗f8 19 ♖f4 ± Yurtaev-Prasad, Calcutta 1998.

b243) 13...e5 is not the most effective way to land a blow in the centre: 14 ♘f5 (14 fxe5!? ♘xg4 15 ♘d5 ♕d8 16 e6) 14...♗xf5 15 exf5 (15 gxf5!?

b5 16 ♖f2 b4 17 ♘d5 ♘xd5 18 exd5 ♗f6, Golubev-Kudriavtsev, Izhevsk 1997, 19 ♔h1!?) 15...♕c6 16 g5 ♕xf3 17 ♖xf3 is slightly better for White, Honfi-Szily, Budapest 1956.

b244) 13...d5!? 14 e5 (alternatively, 14 exd5 ♘xd5 15 ♘xd5 exd5 16 f5 ♖e8) 14...♘e4! (14...♘d7 15 g5 ♘c5 16 ♕h5 ± Vasiukov-Gurgenidze, USSR Ch (Kharkov) 1967) 15 ♘xe4 dxe4 16 ♕xe4 ♗c5 (Suetin) is not wholly clear.

c) 11...♗d7 is rather a popular plan. Black's relative inactivity makes it possible for White to consider a wide variety of aggressive continuations, but few of them are at all convincing:

c1) 12 g4?! ♘xd4! 13 ♗xd4 e5 is unsuccessful for White; e.g., 14 fxe5 dxe5 15 g5?! (15 ♕g3 ♗c6!? Khenkin) 15...exd4 16 gxf6 dxc3 17 fxe7 ♕c5+ ∓.

c2) 12 ♖ad1 b5! 13 a3 ♘xd4 14 ♗xd4 ♗c6 = Boleslavsky.

c3) 12 ♖ae1 is well met by 12...b5!.

c4) 12 ♔h1 b5 13 a3 ♘a5 (another line is 13...♘xd4!? 14 ♗xd4 ♗c6) 14 ♗a2 ♘c4 15 ♗xc4 ♕xc4 (15...bxc4!?) 16 e5 ♘d5 17 ♘f5 ± Dembo-Hu Yi, Budapest 1999.

c5) 12 ♘de2!? ♘a5 13 g4 is interesting.

c6) The main move is 12 f5:

c61) 12...♔h8!? (consistent!). Now, instead of 13 ♖ad1 b5 14 a3 ♘e5 = Slobodjan-Reddmann, Hamburg 1998, or 13 ♘xc6 ♗xc6!? 14 ♖ae1 b5! = Golubev-Reddmann, Hamburg 1999, it is worth investigating 13 ♕h3!? ♘xd4 14 ♗xd4 e5 15 ♗f2 ♗c6 16 ♖ae1 b5 17 ♗h4.

c62) 12...♘xd4 13 ♗xd4 b5 (better than 13...e5?! 14 ♗e3 and now 14...b5 15 ♗g5 or 14...♗c6 15 g4) and then:

c621) 14 fxe6!? fxe6 (14...♗xe6!? 15 ♘d5 ♗xd5 16 exd5 ♘d7 17 ♕g3 ♘e5) 15 ♕f5!? (15 ♕h3 ♕c8 16 ♖ae1 is also not bad) 15...♕c8 16 e5 ♖f7 17 ♕f4 dxe5 18 ♕xe5 ♕c6 19 ♖ae1 ± Hartley-Bartsch, corr. 1994-6.

c622) 14 g4, and now not 14...h6 15 h4!? ♘h7 16 g5 with a dangerous attack, Bauza Mercere-Moulain, New York 1995, but 14...b4! 15 g5 bxc3 16 gxf6 ♗xf6 17 ♗xf6 gxf6 with good play.

c623) 14 a3!? (a rare case where I find this move interesting – for the explanation see Khenkin's line below) 14...a5 (14...e5 15 ♗e3/15 ♗f2 ♗c6 – *11...♘xd4 12 ♗xd4 b5 13 a3 ♗b7 14 f5 e5 15 ♗e3/15 ♗f2 ♗c6?!*) 15 g4! h6 (15...b4 16 axb4 axb4 17 ♖xa8 ♖xa8 18 g5 bxc3 19 gxf6 ♗xf6 20 ♗xf6 gxf6 21 fxe6 ♗xe6 22 bxc3 ± Khenkin) 16 h4 (both 16 ♖ae1 e5!? and 16 ♖ad1 b4 17 axb4 axb4 18 fxe6 are unclear) 16...♘h7, and now 17 ♕g3 ♕d8 18 fxe6 fxe6 19 g5 hxg5 20 ♕g4 is not clear, V.Nikitin-Smekalin, corr. 1996, but again 17 g5!? looks promising.

**12 ♗xd4 b5** *(D)*

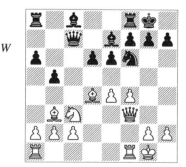

**13 e5**

13 f5?! b4 14 fxe6 bxc3 15 exf7+ ♔h8, followed by ...♗g4, Swan-Muir, St Andrews 1989.

13 a3!? and then:

a) 13...♕b7. There is only one example here: 14 f5 ♔h8 15 fxe6 fxe6 16 ♕g3 ♗d7 17 e5 dxe5 18 ♗xe5 (Rublevsky-Aseev, St Petersburg 1995) 18...♖f7!? = Aseev.

b) 13...♖b8!? (also rarely played) 14 ♖ae1 (14 f5 transposes to note 'c142' to White's 11th move in Line C211) 14...b4 15 e5 bxc3 16 exf6 ♗xf6 17 ♗xf6 gxf6 18 ♖e3 ♕c5 19 ♔h1 ♗b7 (Richardson-Neishtadt, corr. 1990-2) 20 ♕h3!? is all rather unclear.

c) 13...♗b7 is the predominant choice:

c1) 14 ♖ae1 ♖ac8 (14...♗c6 Anand) 15 ♕g3 ♔h8?! 16 ♔h1 ♕c6 17 ♖f3! gives White the initiative, Ljubojević-Anand, Buenos Aires (Sicilian theme) 1994.

c2) 14 g4 d5 15 e5 ♗c5 with counterplay, Bosch-Rõtšagov, Dieren 1997.

c3) 14 f5 e5 is especially important due to transpositions to the following lines:

c31) 15 ♗f2 ♖ac8! (15...♗c6?! appears hazardous for Black after either 16 ♗h4 or 16 g4) 16 ♖fe1 (16 ♖ad1 ♕b8!? 17 ♖fe1 ♕a8; 16 g4 ♕b8!?; 16 ♗h4? ♘xe4) 16...h6 17 h3 (17 ♗h4? ♘xe4) 17...♗c6 18 ♕d3 (½-½ Ivanchuk-Anand, Linares (3) 1992) 18...♕b7 19 ♗h4 ♘h7! 20 ♗f2 ♘f6 with a repetition – Anand.

c32) 15 ♗e3 ♗c6 (15...♖ac8! appears better, and similar to line 'c31'; 15...h6!? *Schach-Archiv*) and now:

c321) 16 g4 – *11 f5 ♘xd4 12 ♗xd4 b5 13 a3 ♗d7 14 g4 e5 15 ♗e3 ♗c6 16 ♕f3.*

c322) 16 ♖ad1?! gives Black an agreeable choice between 16...a5 17 g4 b4, Minić-Janošević, Yugoslav Ch (Ljubljana) 1960, and 16...♖ab8 17 g4 b4!.

c323) 16 ♗g5! ♘e8 (16...♘xe4? 17 ♗xe7 ♘f6 18 ♘d5! ± Honfi-Blubaum, Baden-Baden 1979; 16...a5 17 ♗xf6 ♗xf6 18 ♗d5 b4 19 ♗xc6 ♕xc6 20 ♘d5! ± Honfi) 17 ♗xe7 ♕xe7 18 ♗d5 gives White the initiative.

**13...dxe5**

Or: 13...♗b7 14 exf6! ±; 13...♘d7 should, rather than 14 f5 ♗b7 15 ♕g3 dxe5 16 fxe6 fxe6 17 ♗xe6+ ♔h8 ∞, be met by 14 exd6 ±.

**14 fxe5 ♘d7!**

Not: 14...♗b7?! 15 exf6!; 14...♗c5? 15 ♗xc5 ♕xc5+ 16 ♖f2 ± Onishchuk-Lerner, Bad Zwesten 1997.

**15 ♗xe6!**

Not: 15 ♘e4? ♗b7 ∓ Veröci-Ioseliani, Donji Milanovac wom Ct (5) 1980; 15 ♕xa8? ♗b7 is also slightly better for Black.

**15...fxe6 16 ♕xa8 ♗b7 17 ♖xf8+ ♘xf8**

17...♗xf8 is well met by 18 ♕e8! ♕c6 19 ♔f2 ♕xg2+ 20 ♔e1!. Then there is 20...b4 21 ♕xe6+ ♔h8 22 ♘e2 ♗f3 23 ♘g3 (23 ♕xa6!?) 23...♕xh2 24 ♗f2 ♗c5 25 ♗xc5! ♕xg3+ 26 ♗f2 ♕xe5+ 27 ♕xe5 ♘xe5 28 a3 ±, while 20...♕c6 21 ♖d1 ♘xe5 and 20...♕h1+ 21 ♔d2 ♕xh2+ 22 ♘e2 ♘xe5 23 ♕xe6+ ♘f7 are also insufficient for Black.

**18 ♕e8 ♗c5! 19 ♘e2!**

This is better than 19 ♖d1?! ♗xd4+ 20 ♖xd4 ♕xe5 21 ♖d1 ♕g5 or 19 ♗xc5 ♕xc5+ 20 ♔h1 (20 ♔f1?! ♕xe5) 20...♕f2 =.

**19...♗xd4+**

Or 19...♕xe5 20 ♖f1! ♗xd4+ 21 ♘xd4 ♕xd4+ 22 ♔h1, etc.

**20 ♘xd4 ♕xe5 21 ♖f1!**

21 c3 ♕e4 =; 21 ♘f3 ♕e3+ = Onishchuk-Bologan, Biel 1999.

**21...♕xd4+ 22 ♔h1 ♗xg2+ 23 ♔xg2 ♕d2+**

Now:

a) The stem game, Golubev-Brodsky, Simferopol 1989, continued 24 ♔g3 ♕g5+ 25 ♔h3 ♕e3+ =.

b) 24 ♔f3! ± Mowsziszian-Lerner, Bad Wörishofen 1997. Black is obliged to fight for a draw, since 24...♕xh2? 25 ♔e3! +– and 24...♕xc2? 25 ♔g3! +– are bad for him.

**C222)**

**10...♘xd4 11 ♗xd4 b5** *(D)*

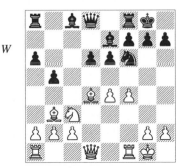

**12 e5**

With other continuations White can scarcely gain an advantage:

a) 12 ♕e1 ♗b7 13 ♖d1 ♕c7 (or 13...b4 14 e5 dxe5 15 fxe5 ♘d7 16 ♘e4 ♗xe4 17 ♕xe4 ♘c5 18 ♗xc5!?) 14 a3 e5 15 fxe5 dxe5 16 ♕g3 ♗c5 with equality, G.Kuzmin-Kaplun, Yalta open 1995.

b) 12 ♕d3 ♗b7 13 ♖ae1 b4 14 e5 bxc3 15 exf6 ♗xf6 16 ♕xc3 a5 =

Kr.Georgiev-Donchev, Bulgarian Ch (Pernik) 1975.

c) 12 a3 ♗b7 and then:

c1) 13 ♕e1 a5!? (or 13...♕c7 =) 14 ♖d1 b4 = Klovsky-Tavadian, Erevan 1981.

c2) 13 ♕f3 a5!? 14 ♖ae1 b4 15 axb4 axb4 16 ♘d1 ♕c7 = Gironella-Pogorelov, St Cugat 1993.

c3) 13 ♕d3 a5! (13...♕c7 can be met by 14 ♖ae1!? or 14 f5 e5 15 ♗e3 h6!? =) and here:

c31) 14 ♕xb5!? ♗a6 15 ♕g5 (15 ♕a4!?) 15...♗xf1 16 ♖xf1 ♕c7 17 ♕g3 ♖fc8 18 ♔h1?! a4! is much better for Black, J.Adams-Thompson, corr. 1985.

c32) 14 ♖ae1 b4 15 ♘b5 a4 16 ♗a2 bxa3 17 ♘xa3 d5 18 e5 ♘e4 with counterplay, K.Müller-D.Gurevich, Bermuda 1998.

c33) 14 e5 dxe5 15 fxe5 ♘d7 16 ♘xb5 (16 ♖xf7? ♖xf7 17 ♗xe6 ♘xe5! –+; 16 ♕e3!? b4 17 ♘b5 is unclear, Voitsekhovsky-Ulybin, Kstovo 1997) 16...♘c5 17 ♕e3 (17 ♗xc5 ♗xc5+ ∓ Fischer-Spassky, Reykjavik Wch (4) 1972) 17...♘xb3 18 ♕xb3 a4! with compensation, Moutousis-Tukmakov, Haifa Echt 1989.

**12...dxe5**

12...♘e8!?.

**13 fxe5 ♘d7**

13...♘e8 14 ♘e4 ♗b7 15 ♕d3 ♗xe4 (15...♕c7 16 c3 ♖d8 17 ♗c2 ♗xe4 18 ♕xe4 g6 19 b4 ± Short-Kasparov, Amsterdam 1996) 16 ♕xe4 ♖c8 (16...g6!?, Ehlvest-Dlugy, Mazatlan rpd 1988) 17 c3 ♗c5 ± Short.

**14 ♘e4!**

An attack on the kingside does not work here:

a) 14 ♕g4 and then:

a1) 14...♗b7!? transposes to note 'd122' to Black's 9th move in Line C.

a2) 14...♗c5!? also seems satisfactory.

a3) 14...♘c5 and here:

a31) 15 ♘e2 ♘xb3 (after 15...♗b7, 16 ♘g3 is well met by 16...♗e4!, but White can try 16 ♖ad1!?) 16 axb3 ♕d5 17 ♘c3 ♕d7 18 ♗e3 ♕c7 19 ♕g3 ♗c5 = Yuneev-Aseev, Daugavpils 1989.

a32) 15 ♗e3 ♘xb3 16 axb3 ♕c7 – *15 ♘e2 ♘xb3 16 axb3 ♕d5 17 ♘c3 ♕d7 18 ♗e3 ♕c7.*

a33) 15 ♖ad1 ♗b7 16 ♔h1 ♘xb3 (possibly 16...♕c7! is simpler) 17 axb3 ♕c7 18 ♖d3 and now 18...♖fd8!? (Hort) is good.

b) Nothing is gained by 14 ♕h5 either:

b1) 14...♗b7!? – *9...♘xd4 10 ♗xd4 b5 11 e5 dxe5 12 fxe5 ♘d7 13 0-0 ♗b7!? 14 ♕h5 0-0.*

b2) 14...♘c5 15 ♖ad1 ♗b7 16 ♗xc5 (16 ♖f4 ∓) 16...♗xc5+ 17 ♔h1 ♕c7 18 ♖d3 ♖fd8 19 ♖h3 h6 20 ♖g3 ♖d2! 21 ♘e2 ♖ad8 22 ♘f4 ♖f2 ∓ G.Kuzmin-Ermenkov, Varna 1976.

**14...♗b7 15 ♘d6**

15 ♕g4 ♗xe4! is good for Black.

**15...♗xd6 16 exd6 ♕g5** *(D)*

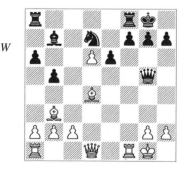

The key position. The white pawn on d6 is as difficult for White to advance as it is for Black to take scot-free – I would call such a situation 'strategically tense'. After the Fischer-Spassky match, the position was considered advantageous for Black. Recently, White has achieved serious progress but nobody can say that the sides have exhausted their resources...

**17 ♖f2**

This move became the main one primarily as a result of Bangiev's efforts. Nevertheless, 17 ♕e2 still represents a serious alternative:

a) 17...♗d5 18 ♖ad1 ♗xb3 19 axb3, followed by c4, is assessed in White's favour.

b) 17...a5?! is not enough:

b1) 18 ♖f2 – *17 ♖f2 a5!? 18 ♕e2*.

b2) 18 a4 b4 19 ♗c4 (19 c4 bxc3 20 bxc3 ♖a6 21 ♖f2 ♖xd6 22 ♕b5 with compensation, Riemersma-Van der Wiel, Dutch Ch (Amsterdam) 1995; 19 ♖f2 – *17 ♖f2 a5!? 18 a4 b4 19 ♕e2*) 19...e5 20 ♗e3 ♕g6 21 ♗b5 ♖ac8 22 ♖f2 ♗c6 23 ♖d1 f5?! 24 ♕c4+ ± Bezemer-Van der Heijden, Dutch Cht 1996/7.

b3) 18 c3 ♖a6 and now:

b31) 19 ♖fd1!? and now Black must avoid 19...♖d8? 20 ♖d3 e5 21 ♖g3 ♕h6 22 ♖f1 +− Hübner-Tischbierek, Bundesliga 1996/7. 19...♖xd6 is met by 20 ♗e3!, while Byrne and Mednis suggest 19...e5.

b32) 19 ♖ad1 ♖xd6 (19...a4 20 ♗c2 ♖xd6 21 ♗e3 ♕e5 22 ♖xd6 ♕xd6 23 ♕xb5 ♗a6 24 ♕h5 g6 25 ♖d1 ± Sax-Jasnikowski, Næstved 1988) 20 ♗xg7 ♖xd1 21 ♖xd1 ♔xg7 22 ♖xd7 ♗c6 23 ♖d4 ± de Firmian-Fishbein, Philadelphia 1997.

c) 17...♔h8!? 18 ♖ad1 (18 ♖f2 e5 19 ♗e3 ♕g6 20 a4 f5!, Stratil-Lanc, Prague 1985; 18 c4 bxc4 19 ♗xc4 e5 20 ♗c3 f5 with counterplay, del Rio-Villavicencio, Spanish Ch (Linares) 1993; 18 a4!? e5 19 ♗c3 ♕g6 20 axb5 axb5 21 ♖xa8 ♗xa8 22 ♖f2 ± Vrenegoor-Cifuentes, Antwerp 1993) 18...♕g6 (18...f5 19 h4! ♕g6 20 h5 ♕g5 21 h6 J.Polgar) 19 c4 (19 ♖d3!? e5 20 ♖g3 ♕xd6 21 ♗c3 f5 ∞ J.Polgar; 19 a4!?) 19...bxc4 20 ♗xc4 f5 21 ♗c3 f4! with strong counterplay, Illescas-J.Polgar, Dos Hermanas 1997.

d) 17...e5 and then:

d1) 18 ♗e3 ♕g6 19 ♖ad1 ♔h8! 20 h4 (20 c3 ♗e4!, Hamann-Gligorić, Skopje OL 1972) 20...f5 (20...♘f6? 21 d7! ♕g3 22 ♖xf6! ± Zapata-Am.Rodriguez, Bucaramanga 1992) 21 h5 ♕f6 22 a4 (Browne-Donner, Wijk aan Zee 1974) 22...♗c6!? ∞.

d2) 18 ♗c3 ♕g6 (18...♘c5?! 19 ♖ad1 ♘xb3 20 axb3 ∓; 18 a5 19 ♖ad1 b4 20 ♗d2 ♕g6 21 ♖f2 ♘f6 22 ♕xe5 ♘e4, Bezemer-Van der Heijden, Dutch Cht 1995/6, 23 ♖f3!? gives White an advantage) 19 ♖ad1 ♔h8 20 ♗d5 (20 a4 bxa4 21 ♗xa4 ♘c5 22 b3 ♖ad8 23 d7 ♘xa4 24 bxa4 ♗c6!) 20...♗xd5 21 ♖xd5 ♕e6 (21...♖ac8!? with the point 22 a4 b4!, Hendriks-Wells, Antwerp 1994) 22 ♖fd1 ♖fc8 (22...f5 23 a4 bxa4 24 ♖a5! Kasparov) and then:

d21) 23 a4 bxa4 24 ♕e4 (24 ♖a5 ♖c4!) 24...♖ab8 with counterplay – Kasparov.

d22) 23 ♗a5 ♖c6 (Short-Kasparov, London PCA Wch (14) 1993) 24 a4 bxa4 25 ♕e4 ♕g6 26 ♖xe5 ♘xe5 27 ♕xe5 ♖xc2 (27...♕g4 28 ♖d2!) 28 ♕d5 ♖g8 29 d7 h6 30 d8♕ ♖xd8 31

♛xd8+ ♔h7 32 ♖d2 ♖c1+ 33 ♖d1
♖c2 (Kasparov) and Black probably
survives.

We now return to the position after
17 ♖f2 (D):

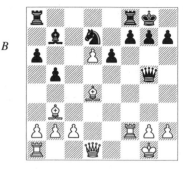

### 17...a5!?

This active attempt occurs most frequently. The other continuations are:

a) 17...e5?! (here 17 ♖f2 works especially well) 18 ♗c3 ♘f6 (or 18...e4
19 ♕f1! ♕g6 20 ♖e1 ± Bangiev-
Shmirin, Volgograd 1973) 19 ♕f1 b4
20 ♗xb4 ♕h4 21 ♗a5 ♘g4 22 h3
♘xf2 23 ♕xf2 ± Kudrin-Dahlberg,
Lone Pine 1981.

b) 17...♗d5 (this move is natural
but probably unsuccessful) 18 ♖d2 (18
♗c3!? ♘b6 19 ♗a5 ♘c4 20 ♗xc4 bxc4
21 ♗c7 ± Beliavsky/Mikhalchishin)
18...♗xb3 (18...♗c4!? – '64') 19 axb3
e5 20 ♗f2 ♖fc8 (Bangiev's 20...♖fe8
21 ♕e2!? e4 22 ♗e3 ♕g6 23 c4 ♘e5
is insufficient because of 24 ♖d5 ♕e6
25 ♗d4 ♘d3 26 ♖f1) 21 ♕e2 ♖c6?!
(21...b4!?) 22 ♗e3!? (22 c4, Bangiev-
Chernikov, Cheliabinsk 1975) 22...♕g6
23 ♕xb5! Bangiev.

c) 17...♖ae8 18 ♕d2 ±.

d) 17...♔h8 18 ♕d2 is also slightly
better for White.

e) 17...♘e5!? (Leluashvili-Rogo-
zenko, corr. 1988-92), with the point
18 ♕c1 ♘f3+! 19 ♖xf3 ♕g4, deserves
at least some attention.

f) 17...♖ac8 and then:

f1) 18 a4 ♗d5 19 ♗xd5 ♕xd5 20
axb5 e5!? 21 ♗c3 ♕xb5 ∞ Kreiman-
I.Ivanov, USA Ch (Key West) 1994.

f2) 18 ♕e2 ♘c5 (18...♗d5!? 19
♖d1 ♗xb3 20 axb3 e5 21 ♗e3 ♕g6 22
c4 ♕e4!) 19 h4 (19 ♖d1 ♖fd8 20 h4!?
♕g6! ∞ Bangiev-Shakarov, Grozny
1974; 19 ♖af1!?) 19...♕g3!? with a
complicated game (19...♕xh4 20 ♗xc5
♖xc5 21 ♗xe6 ♗e4 22 ♖af1!).

f3) 18 ♕d2! ♕xd2 19 ♖xd2 ♘c5 20
♗xc5! ♖xc5 21 a4 with an advantage.

g) 17...♖ad8 and then:

g1) 18 ♕d2 ♕xd2 19 ♖xd2 ♘f6 20
♗xf6 gxf6 21 a4 (also after 21 c4!?
bxc4 22 ♗xc4 ♖d7, it is not easy for
White to make progress) 21...♗d5 22
♗xd5 (or 22 axb5 axb5 23 ♖a5 ♗xb3
24 cxb3 ♖b8) 22...♖xd6 = Kaminski-
Kacheishvili, Guarapuava jr Wch 1995.

g2) 18 ♕e2 ♗d5 (18...♘f6 19 ♗xf6
gxf6 20 ♖d1 ±) 19 ♖d1 ♗xb3 20 axb3
e5 21 ♗c3! (Galdunts-Lauber, Pardubice 1996), and White is probably
better.

### 18 ♕e2

This is the latest height of fashion.
Otherwise:

a) 18 c4?! is unsuccessful:

a1) 18...♖a6 19 c5 a4 (19...e5?!
can be met by 20 ♕f1 or 20 ♕e2!?)
20 ♗c2 ♘xc5 21 h4 (21 ♕e2 ♘d7!)
21...♕d5 22 ♕g4 g6 23 ♖d1 ♖xd6!
with a good game, Vujadinović-Stoica,
Bela Crkva 1986.

a2) 18...a4 19 ♗c2 bxc4 20 ♗xa4
♖fd8! (20...♘c5?! 21 ♗c2 ♘e4 22
♗xe4 ♗xe4 23 d7!, Sax-Timman,

London 1980, with the point 23...♕d5 24 ♗b6 ♖xa2 25 ♖d2 +–) 21 ♗xd7 (21 ♗c2 ♖a6) 21...♖xd7 22 ♗b6 ♖c8 ∓ Kasparov/Nikitin.

b) Earlier, 18 a4 was commonly played:

b1) 18...e5?! 19 ♕e2! (19 ♗c3? b4 is good for Black: 20 ♗e1 ♘f6! 21 ♕d3 ♘e4 ∓ Bangiev-Kaplun, Ukrainian Ch 1974 or 20 ♗d2 ♕g6 21 c3 ♘c5 22 ♗c2 ♗e4!, Yilmaz-Panchenko, Cheliabinsk 1991) 19...exd4 20 ♕e7 ± Yrjölä.

b2) 18...♖a6 19 axb5 (19 ♕e2 – *18 ♕e2 ♖a6 19 a4*) 19...♖xd6 20 ♕d2 ♕xb5 (20...♕g4 21 ♖a4!, Cirić-Suradiradja, Belgrade 1977; 20...♕h5 21 ♕e3! ± Mortensen-Tischbierek, Leningrad 1984) 21 ♖xa5 ♕c6 22 ♕f4 f6! with an acceptable position.

b3) 18...b4 and then:

b31) 19 ♕f1 ♖a6 20 ♖e1 ♖xd6 21 ♗e3 ♕h5 22 ♗c4 ♗d5 is good for Black, J Polgar-Lutz, Frankfurt rpd 1999.

b32) 19 ♕d3 ♗c6 20 ♕e2 ♗d5 21 ♕b5 ♖fb8 22 ♕f1 ♗xb3 23 cxb3 ♕g6 24 ♖c1 e5 25 ♗e3 with a double-edged game, Kindermann-Reeh, Bad Wörishofen 1990.

b33) 19 ♕e2 ♖a6 (19...♗d5!? – *19 ♕d3 ♗c6 20 ♕e2 ♗d5*) 20 ♗e3!? (20 ♗xe6 ♖xd6 21 ♗e3 ♗e5 22 ♗c4 ♕xb2 23 ♖e1 ♕e5 ∓ Morović-Milos, Yopal 1997; 20 ♕b5 ♕xb5 21 axb5 ♖xd6 22 ♗e3 ♖a8 23 ♗f4 = Winants-Tukmakov, Wijk aan Zee 1993) 20...♕e5, with double-edged play after 21 ♕b5 or 21 ♗f4 ♕xb2 22 ♖d1 – Bangiev.

b34) 19 ♕d2 ♖xd2 20 ♖xd2 ♖ac8 (20...♖fd8!? ½-½ de Firmian-Tringov, Niš 1981; 20...♖a6 21 c3 ♖xd6 22

cxb4 axb4 23 ♖ad1 with compensation) 21 ♖e1 ♗a6 22 c3 ♗c4 23 ♗xc4 (23 ♗d1!?, Bosch-Reeh, Amstelveen 1994) 23...♖xc4 24 cxb4 ♖xb4 25 ♖c1 ♖xa4 26 ♖c7 ♖d8 = Oll-Loginov, Sverdlovsk 1987.

b35) 19 ♕e1 ♖a6!?.

**18...♖a6**

18...a4? 19 ♗xe6! ± Sulskis-Piesina, Riga Z 1995.

18...♗c6 19 c3 a4 20 ♗c2 e5 21 ♗e3 with an initiative, Renet-Garcia Paolochi, Linares Z 1995.

**19 ♗c3**

Or: 19 ♗xe6 ♖xd6 20 ♗xd7 ♖xd7 21 c3 =; 19 a4 bxa4 (19...b4 – *18 a4 b4 19 ♕e2 ♖a6*) 20 ♖xa4 ♖xd6 21 ♗xg7 ♗a6! (Bangiev) is good for Black.

The position after the text-move (19 ♗c3) remains difficult to assess:

a) 19...♖xd6?! 20 ♗xa5, and White is better.

b) 19...♕c5!? 20 a3 (20 ♗xe6? fxe6 21 ♕xe6+ ♔h8; 20 ♔h1?! b4; 20 ♕g4 ♘e5 21 ♕g3 ♘g6) 20...e5?! (20...b4! is critical) 21 ♖d1 h6 22 ♗d2 ♖xd6 23 ♗xa5 with an advantage for White, *Fritz5-Junior5*, Riga 1999.

c) 19...b4 20 ♗d2 ♕c5 21 ♗f4 and then:

c1) 21...♖aa8 22 ♖d1 (22 ♗c4!?; 22 c3? bxc3 23 ♖c1 a4! 24 ♖xc3 axb3!) 22...♗a6, and White has an advantage: 23 ♕e1 ♗b5 24 c3 bxc3 (Van der Wiel-Leitão, Wijk aan Zee 1999) 25 ♗e3!, or 23 ♕f3! a4! 24 ♗xa4 ♗e2 25 ♕xe2 ♖xa4 – Leitão.

c2) 21...♘f6 and now 22 ♖d1 ♘e4 23 d7 ♖d8 24 ♗e3 ♕c6! 25 ♖f4 ♖aa8! is probably better for Black, Kudrin-Vigorito, Harvard 2000. White could try 22 ♗c4!?, followed by ♗d3.

# 10  5...♘c6 6 ♗c4 e6 7 ♗b3 a6 8 ♗e3 ♗e7 9 ♕e2

**1 e4 c5 2 ♘f3 d6 3 d4 cxd4 4 ♘xd4 ♘f6 5 ♘c3 ♘c6 6 ♗c4 e6 7 ♗b3 a6 8 ♗e3 ♗e7 9 ♕e2** *(D)*

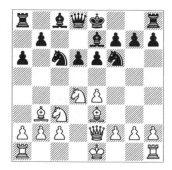

B

This is the basic starting position for the Velimirović Attack. Its peculiar features were aptly described by GM Genna Sosonko: "The price for each and every move in attack and counterattack is so high that one small inaccuracy can change the verdict of any position from +− to −+" *(New in Chess Yearbook)*. So, how should we study such uncertain material? It is worthwhile to recollect an observation made by André Gide – one should believe only those who seek truth and doubt those who claim to have found it.

White's basic plan is 0-0-0, g4, g5, ♖hg1, ♕h5, ♖g3, ♖h3 followed by ♕xh7#, and a critical decision for Black is whether he should castle quickly:

**A: 9...0-0**        152
**B: 9...♕c7**        159

Here we shall consider 9...♕c7 to be 'the main line', where after 10 0-0-0 Black will have to make a critical choice between 10...♘a5 and 10...0-0. At the same time, the line 9...0-0 10 0-0-0 ♕c7 is equivalent to 9...♕c7 10 0-0-0 0-0, so there is no single main move here.

Continuations such as 9...♘xd4 10 ♗xd4 b5 11 0-0-0! and 9...♗d7 10 0-0-0 (or 10 ♖g1!?) are somewhat second-rate. 9...♘a5 is of some interest, though White can simply reply 10 0-0-0 (rather than 10 g4 ♘xb3 11 axb3 h5).

## A)
### 9...0-0 10 0-0-0 *(D)*

It doesn't look promising to play 10 ♖g1 here. For instance: 10...♘xd4 (10...♕c7 – 9...♕c7 10 ♖g1 0-0; 10...♘d7!?; 10...d5!?) 11 ♗xd4 b5 12 0-0-0 (12 g4 b4! = Krnić-Spassov, Athens 1981) 12...b4 (12...♗b7!? 13 e5 dxe5 14 ♗xe5 ♕b6, Rantanen-Unzicker, Nice OL 1974) 13 ♘a4 ♗d7 (13...♘d7!? Ryskin) 14 e5 (14 ♘b6 ♗b5 with counterplay, J.Diaz-Spassov, Vrnjačka Banja 1976) 14...♗b5! (Vaulin-Panchenko, USSR 1987) 15 ♕e3!? =.

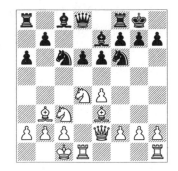

*B*

Certainly, the main continuation here is 10...♕c7 (Line B2). Two of Black's remaining ideas may be singled out:

**A1: 10...♘d7!?** 153
**A2: 10...♕e8** 154

Other continuations are hard to recommend:

a) 10...♘a5 11 g4 (or 11 f4).

b) 10...♗d7 11 f4! (11 ♖hg1?! b5!; 11 g4!?) 11...♕c7 (11...b5 12 e5) 12 g4 ♘xd4 13 ♖xd4, Planinc-Musil, Ljubljana 1969.

c) 10...♕a5?! almost never fits together well with ...a6.

d) 10...♘xd4 11 ♗xd4 b5 is also a concession of sorts. For instance:

d1) 12 g4 b4! (12...e5? 13 ♗xe5 ♗xg4 14 f3 ♗e6 15 ♗xd6 ±) 13 ♘a4 ♗b7 = Rivera-Cifuentes, Villa Gesell 1985.

d2) 12 f4!? transposes to note 'a' to White's 10th move in Line C2 of Chapter 9.

d3) 12 e5 dxe5 13 ♗xe5 ♕b6 14 ♘e4 (14 g4 ♘d7!?). Now, instead of 14...♘d7 15 ♗d4 (15 ♗d6 is slightly better for White) 15...♕c7 16 ♖he1 (16 ♔b1!? Panchenko) 16...♖b8 17 ♕g4 e5 18 ♕g3 ♗b7 19 ♗c3 ♗xe4 20 ♖xe4

♗f6 (Rublevsky-Panchenko, Cheliabinsk 1991) 21 f4 ♘c5 22 ♖xe5 ±, it would be interesting to investigate the risky 14...♘xe4 15 ♕xe4 ♗g5+ 16 f4 (16 ♔b1 ♗b7 17 ♕g4 ♗h6) 16...♗b7 17 ♕e2 ♗h6, Panbukchian-Ermenkov, Bulgarian Ch 1988, with the point 18 ♖d6 ♕c5 19 ♖hd1 a5.

**A1)**
**10...♘d7!?**

The drawbacks of this move may be emphasized only by rejecting the plan with g4, as we shall see in the next note.

**11 ♔b1!?**

Preventing 11...♘c5??, since this would fail to 12 ♘xc6 +–.

Otherwise:

a) 11 g4 ♘c5 12 ♖hg1 and now:

a1) 12...♕c7 transposes to Line B23. Black has alternatives though:

a2) 12...♘xb3+!? 13 axb3 ♘b4 14 ♖g3!? ♕a5 15 ♔b1 (Korneev-Shipov, Moscow 1985) 15...♖e8! Nikitin.

a3) 12...♗d7 13 g5?! (13 ♔b1!? ♘xb3 14 cxb3 b5 15 ♘f5, Ardeleanu-Navrotescu, Romanian Cht 1997; 13 ♘f5!?, Sion Castro-Ragozin, Oviedo rpd 1993) 13...b5! 14 ♕h5 b4 is much better for Black, Ginsburg-Ryskin, Nikolaev Z 1993.

b) 11 f4 ♘c5 and then:

b1) 12 ♔b1 is not entirely logical here.

b2) 12 ♘xc6 ♘xb3+ 13 cxb3 bxc6 14 e5 is of interest; e.g., 14...d5 15 ♘a4 or 14...♕c7 15 exd6 ♗xd6 16 ♕f2, Bosch-Lauber, Schoneck 1996.

b3) 12 ♖hf1 is a serious option. 12...♗d7 13 f5 ♘e5 (13...♘xb3+ 14 axb3 ♘e5 15 fxe6?! fxe6 16 ♘f3 ♕a5! = Emms-Kovaliov, Eupen ECC 1994;

then 17 ♔b1? fails to 17...♗b5!) 14 ♘f3 (14 ♔b1 b5!? Yakovich) 14...♘xb3+ 15 axb3 ♘g4! 16 fxe6 fxe6 17 ♗d4 ± Yakovich-Filipenko, Belgorod 1989.

**11...♕c7**

Otherwise:

a) 11...♕e8 12 f4 ♘c5 does not solve Black's problems in view of 13 ♖hf1 ♗d7 14 f5, Kupreichik-Savon, Odessa 1974.

b) 11...♕a5 12 f4 ♘c5 is likewise not ideal for Black.

c) 11...♘xd4 12 ♗xd4 b5 13 f4 (13 e5 dxe5 14 ♗xe5 ♕b6 =) 13...b4 14 ♘a4 ♗b7 (14...♕a5 15 ♖d3 ♗b7 16 ♖g3 ♗f6 17 e5! dxe5 18 fxe5 ♗xe5 19 ♖g5 ± Chuprov-Mochalov, Kurgan 1994) 15 ♕g4 ♗f6, and instead of 16 e5 dxe5 17 fxe5 ♗xe5! = M.Pavlović-R.Scherbakov, Linares open 1996, 16 ♖he1! is stronger.

**12 f4!**

Or: 12 ♕h5 ♘f6!? =; 12 ♖hg1 – *9...♕c7 10 0-0-0 0-0 11 ♖hg1 ♘d7 12 ♔b1*.

**12...♘c5 13 f5**

Instead, White gains nothing by 13 ♖hf1 ♘xb3 = Cvetković, but 13 ♘xc6!? is worth considering.

After the text-move (13 f5), White is a little better:

a) After 13...♘xb3 14 axb3 ♗d7, besides 15 ♖hf1 ♘e5 (15...♗f6!?) 16 ♘f3 (16 g4!?) 16...♗c6 (16...♗b5!?) 17 ♘xe5 dxe5 18 fxe6 fxe6 19 ♕g4 with an advantage, de Firmian-Ivanchuk, Biel 1989, it is worthwhile to note 15 ♘xc6, as in Reeh-Borik, Bundesliga 1984/5.

b) 13...♘e5 is unsuccessful: 14 ♘f3 ♗d7 15 ♘xe5 dxe5 16 f6! and White is much better, Zapolskis-R.Scherbakov, Warsaw 1991.

c) 13...♘a5!? 14 ♖hf1 ♗f6 15 g4 also seems promising for White.

**A2)**

**10...♕e8** *(D)*

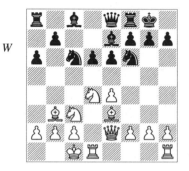

This move was successfully introduced by Beliavsky in 1971/2. Like 10...♘d7, it appears somewhat artificial. The idea is that after 11 g4 ♘xd4! Black wins a pawn.

**11 ♖hg1**

This is the main line, which has been well developed. White also has the plans 11 f4!? ♘xd4 12 ♖xd4 and 11 ♘xc6!?, which have so far rarely been played.

**11...♘d7**

Here, dubious is 11...♘xd4 12 ♗xd4 ♘d7 13 g4 ♘c5 14 g5 b5 (14...♗d7 is scarcely better) 15 ♕h5 ♘xb3+ 16 axb3 e5 (16...b4? 17 ♗f6 +−) 17 ♘d5 ♔h8 (M.Lazić-Kosić, Yugoslav Ch (Kladovo) 1990) 18 ♗c3!? ±. However, of some interest is 11...b5 12 g4 b4, similar to Line B222.

**12 g4**

Not much is promised by 12 ♕h5 ♘c5 13 g4 ♘xb3+ 14 axb3 f6, Wahls-Hausner, Bundesliga 1990/1, nor by 12 ♘xc6 bxc6 13 g4 d5 14 g5 ♘c5,

G.Todorović-Kosić, Yugoslav Ch (Kladovo) 1990.

**12...♘c5 13 g5 b5** *(D)*

13...♗d7 is rare. Then:

a) 14 ♖g3!?.

b) 14 f4 b5 15 f5 b4 16 f6 bxc3 17 ♕h5 cxb2+ (17...♘xd4 18 ♗xd4 ♘xb3+ 19 axb3 cxb2+ 20 ♗xb2 e5 21 ♗a3! ♖c8 22 ♖d3 Bruzon/Gongora) 18 ♔xb2 ♘xb3 (18...♘xe4? 19 ♖df1! ± Velimirović-Vucković, Belgrade 2000) is interesting though unclear.

c) 14 ♕h5 is also interesting; e.g.:

c1) 14...b5!? – *13...b5 14 ♕h5 ♗d7*.

c2) 14...♘xb3+ 15 axb3 and now 15...♘xd4 16 ♗xd4 f5 17 g6 or 15...f5 16 g6 hxg6 17 ♖xg6 ♘e5 18 ♖xg7+ ♔xg7 19 ♕h6+ ♔g8 20 ♖g1+ ♘g4 21 ♘d5!.

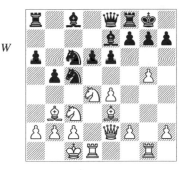

W

The same position though with the queen on c7 arises after *9...♕c7 10 0-0-0 0-0 11 ♖hg1 ♘d7 12 g4 ♘c5 13 g5 b5* in Line B2311. Both there and here White has two possible lines:

**A21: 14 ♘xc6**     155
**A22: 14 ♕h5**     156

Naturally, after 14 ♘xc6 ♕xc6, and after 14 ♕h5 b4 15 ♘xc6 ♕xc6, these variations come to the same thing.

Moreover, in playing 14 ♘xc6, White is guided by the position that may also arise after 14 ♕h5 b4 15 ♘xc6 ♘xb3+ 16 axb3 ♕xc6 17 ♗d4!.

## A21)

**14 ♘xc6 ♘xb3+**

14...♕xc6!? occurs seldom, so the variations without ...♘xb3+ are given here to a limited extent:

a) 15 ♗d5 exd5 16 ♘xd5 looks dubious to me.

b) 15 ♕h5. Now Black can choose between:

b1) 15...♘xe4? 16 ♘d5 ♕b7 (or 16...♗d8 17 ♕f3) and now:

b11) 17 ♗d4? exd5 18 ♗xg7 ∞ (or 18 g6 hxg6 19 ♗xd5 ♗g5+ ∓).

b12) 17 f3! +– (Burgess).

b2) 15...b4 transposes to note 'b' to Black's 15th move in Line A22.

b3) 15...♘xb3+!? 16 axb3 – *14...♘xb3+ 15 axb3 ♕xc6 16 ♕h5.*

c) 15 ♗d4(!) h4 (15 ♘xb3+ 16 axb3 – *14...♘xb3+ 15 axb3 ♕xc6 16 ♗d4*; 15...♗d7 16 ♗d5 exd5 17 ♘xd5 ♖fe8 18 ♕h5 ♖ac8 19 c3 ♘e6 20 ♗xg7 +– Anand-Wegner, London Lloyds Bank 1987; 15...g6!?) 16 ♗d5!? (16 ♕h5!? – *14 ♕h5 b4 15 ♘xc6! ♕xc6!? 16 ♗d4!?*) and then:

c1) 16...♕c7 can be met by 17 ♗xa8!? or 17 ♕h5 – *14 ♕h5 b4 15 ♘xc6! ♕xc6!? 16 ♗d5 ♕c7 17 ♗d4.*

c2) 16...exd5 17 ♘xd5 gives White compensation.

**15 axb3 ♕xc6 16 ♗d4!**

Or 16 ♕h5, and then:

a) 16...b4?! – *14 ♕h5 b4 15 ♘xc6! ♘xb3+ 16 axb3 ♕xc6.*

b) 16...g6!? 17 ♕h6 ♖e8 18 ♗d4 – *16 ♗d4 ♖e8!? 17 ♕h5 g6 18 ♕h6.*

c) 16...♗d7!? is interesting; e.g.:

c1) 17 ♗d4 ♖fc8! 18 ♖d2 (18 ♗xg7? ♔xg7 19 ♕h6+ ♔h8 ∓; 18 ♖d3 e5!; 18 ♗f6 b4!; 18 ♖g4 e5 19 ♖h4 h6 ∓; 18 ♖g3 e5 19 ♖d2 and now 19...exd4 looks best) 18...b4! 19 ♘a4 e5 ∓ Vaerynen-Portilho, corr. 1990.

c2) 17 ♖g4 ♖ac8 (17...b4?! 18 ♗d4 transposes to note 'e' to Black's 17th move in Line A22) 18 ♖h4 h6 19 ♖g1 ♗e8 20 ♔b1 (20 gxh6 f5!; 20 ♗d4 e5!) 20...b4 21 ♗d4 f5! ∓ Guyot-Kožul, Graz 1987.

c3) 17 ♖g3!? ♖ac8!?.

**16...♖e8!?**

Or:

a) 16...♗d7 17 ♗f6 ♖fe8 18 ♖d3!? b4 19 ♖h3 with an attack.

b) 16...b4 17 ♗f6?! (White should of course play 17 ♕h5!) 17...♖e8 18 ♘a4 (18 ♖d3 bxc3 19 ♖h3 ♗f8!, Bonin-Shamkovich, USA 1976) 18...e5 19 ♗xe7 ♖xe7 with good play, Voitsech-Mochalov, Minsk 1976.

**17 ♕h5**

Both 17 ♗f6 ♗f8 (Kasparov/Nikitin) and 17 ♖d3 e5 18 ♗e3 a5 (18...♗e6) 19 ♘d5 ♗e6 20 ♖c3 ♗xd5 21 ♖xc6 ♗xc6, Skrobek-Weglarz, Polish Cht (Mikolajki) 1991, are unclear.

**17...g6**

Not: 17...b4? transposes to note 'b' to Black's 17th move in Line A22; 17...e5? 18 ♘d5 exd4 19 ♘f6+ +−.

**18 ♕h6 ♗f8 19 ♕h4 b4!**

This is far better than: 19...♗e7? 20 ♗f6 +− Balashov; 19...e5? 20 ♘d5 ♗e7 21 ♘f6+ (21 ♕h6! is even better) 21...♗xf6 22 gxf6 ♔h8 23 ♖xg6 (23 ♖d3!? exd4 24 ♖gg3! ♕d7 25 f4) 23...fxg6 24 f7 ± Cornu-Heine, corr. 1992.

**20 ♖d3 h5 21 gxh6 e5! 22 ♘d5 exd4 23 ♖dg3**

23 h7+ ♔h8 24 ♕f6+ ♗g7 25 ♕xf7 ♗e6 26 ♕xg6 ♖a7 ∓; 23 ♖f3 ♗e6? (23...♖a7 ∓ Liberzon) 24 ♖xg6+! +− Sharif-Radashkovich, Netanya 1977.

**23...d3!**

Not: 23...♕b5 24 ♖g5!? +− A.Pereira; 23...♗e6 24 ♖xg6+ fxg6 25 ♖xg6+ ♔h7 26 ♕g5! +−; 23...♖a7 24 ♘f6+ ♔h8 25 ♖xg6 fxg6 26 ♖xg6 ♗e6 27 ♕g5 ♗e7 28 h7! 1-0 A.Pereira-Varabiescu, corr. 1981.

After the text-move (23...d3!), White can force a draw by 24 ♖xg6+ fxg6 25 ♖xg6+ ♔h7 26 ♖g7+, etc. Instead, 24 ♖xd3 is unlikely to prove stronger.

## A22)
**14 ♕h5** (D)

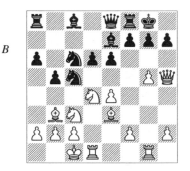

As in the position with the queen on c7, this is the most popular move.

**14...b4**

14...♗d7!?, with the point 15 ♖g3 ♘xd4 16 ♗xd4 f5 (S.Soloviov-Loginov, St Petersburg 2001), deserves serious study.

**15 ♘xc6! ♘xb3+**

Instead:

a) It is hardly any better to play 15...bxc3 16 ♘xe7+ (16 ♗d4 ♘xb3+ 17 axb3 – *15...♘xb3+ 16 axb3 bxc3!?*

*17 ♗d4)* 16...♕xe7 17 ♗xc5 dxc5 18 ♖g4! Baljon.

b) However, 15...♕xc6!? is interesting:

b1) 16 ♖g4? bxc3 17 ♖h4 cxb2+ 18 ♔b1 h6 Nikitin.

b2) 16 ♗d5 ♕c7 (16...exd5 17 ♘xd5 ♗d8 18 ♘f6+ ♗xf6 19 gxf6 g6 20 ♗xc5 dxc5 21 e5 ♔h8 22 ♕h6 ♖g8 23 ♖d8 +− Tisdall) 17 ♗d4 (17 ♖g4? bxc3 18 ♖h4 h6 19 gxh6 g6 −+ Plaskett; 17 ♗xa8 bxc3 18 ♖g4 g6 19 ♕h6 f5 ∞ Nikitin) and then:

b21) It is not easy to prove White's advantage after 17...g6!? 18 ♕h6 e5 19 ♗xa8 bxc3 20 ♗xc3 ♘a4 21 ♖g3 ♘xc3 (or the immediate 21...♕a7) 22 ♖xc3 ♕a7, Berndt-Hausner, Bundesliga 1993/4.

b22) 17...bxc3 18 ♕h6 f6 (18...e5? 19 g6! +− Kobaliya-L.Guliev, Moscow 1996) and here:

b221) 19 gxf6 ♗xf6 20 ♗xa8 (20 ♗xf6? ♖xf6 21 ♕xf6 cxb2+! ∓ Hector-Plaskett, London 1991) and now: 20...cxb2+ 21 ♔b1 ♗xd4 22 ♖xd4 ♖xf2 23 ♕e3 ♖f7 24 ♕g3 ± Ioffe-Liubin, USSR 1969; 20...♔h8 – *19 ♗xa8! ♔h8! 20 gxf6!? ♗xf6.*

b222) 19 ♗xa8! ♔h8! (19...cxb2+ 20 ♔b1 gxh6 21 gxf6+ ♔f7 22 ♖g7+ ♔e8 23 ♖xe7+ ♕xe7 24 fxe7 ♔xe7 25 e5 ± Plaskett; 19...♕b6 20 ♗xc3 gxh6 21 gxf6+ +−). Now 20 ♕xg7+ ♔xg7 21 gxf6++ ♔h6 22 ♗e3+ ♔h5 23 ♖g5+ ♔h4 will bring White a draw after 24 ♖dg1, but hardly more than that. Instead, 20 gxf6!? ♗xf6 21 ♗xf6 ♖xf6 22 ♕e3 cxb2+ 23 ♔b1 ♘a4 is not entirely clear, Baermann-Montalta, corr. 1998.

b23) 17...♗b7!? is possibly stronger.

b3) 16 ♗d4!? ♘xe4 (Nikitin; instead 16...♘xb3+!? 17 axb3 transposes to the main line) 17 ♘d5! (17 ♗d5? exd5 18 ♘xe4 ♗f5! −+; 17 ♗a4?! ♕b7 18 ♘xe4 ♕xe4 19 ♖g4 ♕f3!? 20 ♖d3 ♕f5) 17...exd5 18 g6! (18 ♗xg7!?) 18...♗g5+ 19 ♖xg5 hxg6 20 ♖xg6 fxg6 21 ♗xd5+ ♖f7 22 ♗xc6 gxh5 23 ♗xa8 with an advantage for White.

**16 axb3 ♕xc6**

16...bxc3!? 17 ♗d4 cxb2+ (White wins after 17...♕xc6 18 ♕h6) 18 ♗xb2 e5 19 ♘xe7+ ♕xe7 (again, there is a transposition to the system involving ...♕c7), and the following continuations are known: 20 ♗a3 ♖d8 21 ♖d3 a5 (21...♗b7 22 ♖h3! ♗xe4 23 g6) 22 ♕d1 ♖a6 23 ♕d2 (± according to Baljon, but I am not sure), and also 20 f4 a5 (20...♗b7!?) 21 f5 f6 (21...a4!?) 22 ♖d3 with the initiative, Voss-Kindsvogel, corr. 1986.

**17 ♗d4!** *(D)*

Not: 17 ♖g4? bxc3 18 ♖h4 h6 −+ 19 ♖g1 ♕e8! 20 ♖hg4 f5, Ioffe-Puksansky, USSR 1980; 17 ♖d4? bxc3 18 e5 ♗b7! (18...♗d7!?) 19 ♖h4 h6 20 exd6 cxb2+!! −+ Donchev-Yudasin, Lvov 1983; 17 ♘d5? exd5 18 ♗d4 ♗d7!? ∓ (18...♕d7!? 19 g6! hxg6 20 ♕xd5 ♔h7 21 ♕xa8 ♗b7 gives Black the initiative, Panchenko-Beliavsky, Sukhumi 1971; 18...♖e8 19 ♗xg7 ♕d7! Ciocaltea).

White's successes in the important position after the text-move (17 ♗d4) have led to the loss of popularity of 10...♕e8 and ...♕c7/13...b5.

**17...♗b7**

This is Mochalov's move. There is only one serious alternative:

a) 17...bxc3? 18 ♕h6! e5 19 ♗xe5! +− Baljon-Boersma, Dutch Cht 1974.

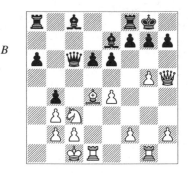

*B*

b) 17...罝e8? 18 奧xg7! 含xg7 (or
18...bxc3 19 g6! +− Ermenkov-Triana,
Cienfuegos 1975) 19 豐h6+ 含h8 (alternatively, 19...含g8 20 g6 fxg6 21
罝xg6+ hxg6 22 豐xg6+ 含f8 23 豐h6+
含f7 24 豐h7+ 含f6 25 罝g1 +− Mochalov) 20 g6 fxg6 21 罝xg6 罝g8 (or
21...含f8 22 罝g8+! +− Balashov) 22
罝dg1 奧b7 23 罝g7 +−.

c) 17...罝d8? 18 罝d3 bxc3 19 罝f3
e5 20 豐xf7+ 含h8 21 豐xe7 罝g8 22
g6 豐xe4 (Grigorov-Spassov, Pernik
1975) 23 豐xg7+! +−.

d) 17...f5 18 gxf6 奧xf6 19 奧xf6
罝xf6 20 e5 ± Nikitin.

e) 17...奧d7!? 18 罝g4 (18 奧xg7
含xg7 19 罝d3 bxc3 20 豐h6+ 含h8 21
罝h3 豐xe4 22 g6 奧g5+! −+) and then:

e1) 18...罝fc8? 19 罝h4 and here:
19...奧xg5+ 20 豐xg5 e5 21 罝g1 g6 22
豐f6 +− Golubev-Kožul, Skopje open
1991; 19...h6 20 gxh6 奧xh4 21 豐g4
+−; 19...含f8 20 豐xh7 奧xg5+ 21 f4
with a decisive advantage; e.g., 21...e5
22 fxg5! exd4 23 豐h8+ 含e7 24 豐xg7
奧e6 25 罝f1!.

e2) 18...bxc3 19 罝h4 奧xg5+ 20
豐xg5 and then:

e21) 20...f6 21 豐h5 cxb2+ (21...e5
22 奧xc3 ±) 22 奧xb2 h6 (22...罝fc8 23
c4 ± Plaskett) 23 罝g1 罝f7 24 豐xh6

含f8 25 罝xg7 1-0 Plaskett-Wahls, Hastings 1989/90.

e22) After 20...cxb2+! 21 奧xb2 e5
White has not yet demonstrated an advantage: 22 罝g1 g6 23 豐h6 罝fc8 24
c4 奧e6 25 豐xh7+ 含f8 with counterplay, Roth-Stanec, Austria 1994, or 22
豐h5!? 罝fc8 23 c4 豐c5! with the point
24 罝d5 豐xf2! 25 豐xh7+ 含f8 = 26
罝xd6? 奧a4!.

**18 ♘d5!**

Not:

a) 18 奧f6? bxc3 (18...罝fc8! Mochalov) 19 豐h6 cxb2+ 20 含xb2 豐xc2+!
∓ Rudnev-Mochalov, USSR 1976.

b) 18 奧xg7? 含xg7 19 豐h6+ 含h8
20 g6 fxg6 21 罝xg6 罝g8 −+ Mochalov.

c) 18 罝g4?! bxc3 19 罝h4 cxb2+
20 奧xb2 豐xe4! ∓ Chandler-Yudasin,
Minsk 1982.

**18...exd5 19 罝d3!**

This is the only move again. Otherwise: 19 豐h6? 豐xc2+! (a typical
counter-sacrifice!) 20 含xc2 罝fc8+ ∓
Mochalov; 19 c3?! bxc3! 20 bxc3 (20
豐h6? cxb2++ 21 含xb2 豐c2+! 22
含a3 豐c5+ −+ Baljon) 20...f6!?.

**19...罝fc8 20 c3 bxc3**

Or:

a) 20...含f8?! 21 罝f3 含e8 22 罝xf7!.

b) 20...dxe4?! 21 罝h3 含f8 22 g6 h6
(Pote-Penquite, corr. 1996-7; 22...fxg6?!
23 豐xh7 含e8 24 罝xg6 +− Howell-
Wahls, Gausdal jr Wch 1986) 23 gxf7!
奧f6, and now 24 奧xf6 gxf6 25 豐g6
含e7 26 罝xh6 d5 27 f8豐+! +− (Pen-
quite) or 24 罝xg7 奧xg7 (24...奧xd4 25
罝h7 +−) 25 奧xg7+ 含e7 26 豐f5! ±.

**21 罝f3!?**

Alternatively:

a) 21 bxc3 dxe4 (21...豐b5 22 罝f3
+− Baljon) 22 罝h3 含f8 23 g6 h6!

(23...fxg6? 24 ♕xh7 ♔e8 25 ♖xg6 ♕d5 26 ♖xg7 1-0 Hadraba-Necesany, corr. 1984), and Black has a chance to protect himself; e.g., 24 gxf7 ♗f6 25 ♖xg7? ♗xd4 26 ♖h7 ♗xc3 –+.

b) 21 ♖h3 cxb2++ 22 ♔xb2 ♔f8 (22...♕c2+ 23 ♔a3 ♕xe4? 24 g6) and now 23 ♖f3?! ♔e8 24 ♕xf7+ ♔d8 is satisfactory for Black, Golubev-Shapiro, Odessa rpd 1983, but 23 g6!? is interesting.

**21...cxb2++ 22 ♔xb2 ♕c2+**

22...♗f8?! 23 ♖h3 (or 23 ♕xf7+ ♔h8 24 g6! ♕c2+ 25 ♔a3 ♕c7 26 gxh7! ±) 23...♕c2+ 24 ♔a3 ♕xe4 (or 24...h6 25 gxh6 +–) 25 g6 fxg6 26 ♕xh7+ ♔f7 27 ♖e3! ♕f5 28 ♖xg6 +–.

**23 ♔a3 ♖f8 24 ♖h3! ♕xe4 25 g6 fxg6 26 ♕xh7+ ♔f7 27 ♗xg7!**

This is better than 27 ♖e3? ♕xd4 –+ or 27 ♕xg7+ ♔e8 28 ♖e3 ♖f7 =.

After the text-move (27 ♗xg7!) Black can reach an endgame a pawn down but with some drawing chances: 27...g5 28 ♗xf8+ ♕xh7 (28...♔xf8 29 ♕h6+ +–) 29 ♖xh7+ ♔xf8 30 ♖c1 (30 h4!?) 30...d4 31 ♖c7 d3 32 ♖cxe7 d2 33 ♖xb7 ♔g8 34 ♖bg7+ ♔f8 35 ♖d7 ♔g8.

## B)

**9...♕c7 10 0-0-0**

10 f4 transposes to note 'a' to White's 10th move in Line C1 of Chapter 9.

10 ♖g1!? does not promise an advantage here either, though it carries some poison:

a) 10...♘a5 11 g4 ♘xb3 12 axb3 ♘d7 13 g5 ±.

b) 10...0-0 11 g4! is unsafe for Black, even though the line 11...♘d7

12 g5 (12 0-0-0; 12 ♘f5) 12...♘c5 13 ♖g3 (13 ♕h5!?) 13...♘xb3!? (13...g6 14 h4!?, Camacho-N.Gonzalez, Cuban Ch 1987) 14 axb3 f5 (Hector-Shirov, Val Maubuée 1989) 15 ♕c4 ♔h8 16 ♘xe6 ♗xe6 17 ♕xe6 ♘d8! turns out well for him.

c) 10...b5 11 g4 (11 0-0-0 ♘a5!; 11 ♘xc6 ♕xc6 12 0-0-0 ♘xe4!?) 11...b4 with almost unstudied complications arising after 12 ♘xc6!? bxc3 13 ♘xe7 or 12 ♘a4, Lamoureux-Lanka, Paris 1990.

d) 10...e5!? makes sense, Qi Jingxuan-G.Kuzmin, Bled/Portorož 1979.

e) 10...♘xd4!? = Akopian.

We now return to 10 0-0-0 (D):

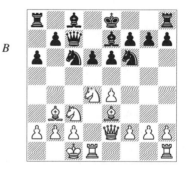

Black must now make a fundamental decision:

**B1: 10...♘a5**     160
**B2: 10...0-0**     167

10...b5?! is unsuccessful because of 11 ♘xc6! (11 g4 ♘a5 transposes to Line B1) 11...♕xc6 12 ♗d4; for instance, 12...♗b7 (12...0-0 13 ♘d5! ±) 13 ♖he1 ♖c8 14 f4 0-0 15 ♘d5 ± Hübner-Hort, Bamberg 1972.

Also better for White is 10...♗d7 11 g4! ♘xd4 12 ♖xd4.

## B1)
**10...♘a5**

From now on Black is obliged to play with his king in the centre in almost all variations, and not many 'Classical Sicilian' players like it. Nevertheless, the line remains very playable.

**11 g4 b5**

Or 11...♘xb3+ 12 axb3, and now:

a) 12...b5 13 g5 – *11...b5 12 g5 ♘xb3+ 13 axb3*.

b) A rare deviation is 12...g6 13 g5 ♘h5 14 f4 (14 ♘f5 exf5 15 ♘d5 ♕c6! 16 ♗d4 ♗xg5+ 17 ♔b1 ♖g8! Kasparov/Nikitin; 14 ♕d2 b5 15 ♘de2 ♗b7 16 ♘g3 0-0! 17 ♘xh5 gxh5 18 f3, Van Riemsdijk-Carlier, Dieren 1989, 18...b4! Akopian) 14...b5 (14...♗d7 15 f5 0-0-0 16 ♕f2 ± Quinteros-Gligorić, Manila 1974; there has also occurred 14...0-0 15 f5 ♖e8 16 ♕f3 ♗f8 17 ♘de2 b5 18 ♘g3 b4 which appears dangerous for Black, because of, for example, 19 ♘xh5 gxh5 20 g6) 15 f5 b4 16 ♘a4 0-0. Now 17 ♕c4 is one interesting idea.

**12 g5 ♘xb3+**

12...♘d7?! 13 ♗xe6 fxe6 14 ♘xe6 ♕c4 15 ♘xg7+ ±.

**13 axb3 ♘d7** *(D)*

This is the key position for 10...♘a5, and White has two well-known moves at his disposal:

**B11:　14 ♘f5**　　160
**B12:　14 h4**　　163

Rare tries for White:

a) 14 b4? a5! 15 ♘dxb5 ♕b8 16 bxa5 ♖xa5 ∓ (Velimirović).

b) 14 ♖hg1 b4 (14...0-0?! transposes to Line B221; 14...♗b7!?) 15 ♘a4 and now both 15...♘c5 and 15...♗b7 are satisfactory, Pukulev-Lysenko, Cheliabinsk 1974.

c) 14 ♔b1 b4 (14...♘c5?! 15 ♘f5!; unclear is 14...♗b7 15 ♕h5 g6 16 ♕h6 ♗f8 17 ♕h3 – Velimirović) 15 ♘a4 ♘c5 16 ♕c4 (16 h4 – *14 h4 b4! 15 ♘a4 ♘c5! 16 ♔h1*) 16...♗d7 17 ♕xb4 ♘xa4!? 18 bxa4 ♖b8 with good play for Black, Noetzel-Eber, Elb 1987.

d) 14 f4!? b4! 15 ♘a4 ♗b7 (after 15...♘c5!? 16 f5 e5 17 ♘xc5 exd4 18 ♗xd4 dxc5 19 ♗xg7 White has compensation, Freise-Rossmann, Rostock 1983) 16 ♗d2 a5 17 ♖he1 0-0 18 ♔b1 ♖fc8 19 ♗c1 ♘c5 20 ♕g2 (Hamdouchi-A.Sokolov, French Cht 1999) 20...g6!? with adequate counterplay.

e) 14 ♕h5 g6! (14...0-0? 15 ♖hg1 ± is unsuccessful and 14...♘c5 15 b4 ♘a4 16 ♖d3 ∞ Honfi-Donner, The Hague Z 1966, deserves particular attention) 15 ♕h6 ♗f8 16 ♕h4 b4 17 ♘a4, and now, for example, 17...♗g7, Mason-Howell, British Ch (Swansea) 1995, and 17...♗b7!? seem very good.

## B11)
**14 ♘f5**

The positional sacrifice developed by Velimirović.

**14...exf5**

14...b4 appears dubious but has not yet been refuted:

a) 15 ♘xg7+ ♔f8 16 ♕h5 (16 ♗d4 ♖g8!?) 16...♔xg7 17 ♗d4+ ♔g8! (17...♘e5 18 f4 ±) 18 ♘d5 (18 ♗xh8 ♔xh8 19 ♕xf7 ♘f8 −+; 18 ♖hg1 ♘e5 19 f4 ♘g6 20 ♗xh8 ♔xh8 21 ♘e2 ♗b7 ∓ Wahls-Rechlis, Berne 1990) 18...exd5 19 g6 fxg6 20 ♕xd5+ ♔f8 ∓ Furhoff-Sanden, Salogernas 1994.

b) 15 ♗d4!? ♗xg5+?! (15...bxc3 16 ♔b1 ♗f6? 17 ♗xf6 ♘xf6 18 ♘xd6+ +− Prié-Muir, Novi Sad OL 1990.

c) 15 ♘xe7 bxc3 (15...♔xe7!? is recommended by Rechlis) 16 ♘xc8 cxb2+ 17 ♔xb2 ♖xc8 18 ♖d4 (or 18 ♖d2 Boleslavsky) with a slight advantage for White.

**15 ♘d5 ♕d8**

Possibly attention should be paid to 15...♕a5; e.g., 16 exf5 (16 ♘xe7!?) 16...♗b7 17 ♘xe7 (17 ♗b6 ♕a1+!). Now bad is 17...♗xh1? 18 ♗b6! ♕a1+ (18...♗f3 19 ♕xf3 ♘xb6 20 ♕c6+ ♔xe7 21 ♕xd6+ ♔e8 22 ♔b1! +−) 19 ♔d2 ♕xb2 20 ♘c6+ ±, but 17...♕a1+ 18 ♔d2 ♕a5+! and 17...♘e5!? are sufficient.

**16 exf5 ♗b7!**

16...0-0? 17 f6! ± Velimirović-Sofrevski, Titograd 1965.

**17 f6**

After 17 ♖he1 ♗xd5 18 ♖xd5 0-0! 19 f6 ♘xf6 20 gxf6 ♗xf6 Black stands at least no worse.

**17...gxf6!**

If 17...♗xd5, it is bad to play 18 fxe7? because of 18...♕a5!. Interesting is 18 ♖xd5 gxf6 19 ♗d4 (19 ♖e1 – *17...gxf6! 18 ♖he1 ♗xd5! 19 ♖xd5*) 19...♔f8 20 ♕h5, as in Gusev-Zotkin, Leningrad 1968, but the most accurate continuation is 18 fxg7 ♖g8 19 ♖xd5

♖xg7 20 f4 ♔f8, when both 21 ♖e1 and 21 h4 give White very strong pressure.

**18 ♖he1**

18 gxf6 ♗xd5 (18...♘xf6?! 19 ♗b6 ♗xd5 20 ♗xd8 ♖xd8 21 ♖he1 seems to be better for White) 19 ♖xd5 (19 fxe7? ♕a5!) 19...♘xf6 20 ♖f5 ♖g8 (20...♕d7!? 21 ♕f3 ♖c8 22 ♗d4 ♕c6 = Reinaldo-Campos, Mondariz 1996) 21 ♗d4 (21 ♖e1 – *18 ♖he1 ♗xd5! 19 ♖xd5 ♖g8 20 gxf6 ♘xf6 21 ♖f5*) 21...♔f8 22 ♕f3 ♖g6 23 h4 h5 and Black defends successfully.

**18...♗xd5!**

18...0-0? 19 gxf6 ♗xf6 20 ♕g4+ ♔h8 21 ♘xf6 ♘xf6 22 ♗d4 ♖g8 23 ♖e8!! ♖xe8 24 ♕g5 ♖e6 25 ♖g1 +− Velimirović.

**19 ♖xd5 ♖g8** *(D)*

Black's alternatives are inferior: 19...♔f8?! 20 gxf6 ♘xf6 21 ♗h6+ ♔e8 22 ♖d3 ♔d7 23 ♕f3; 19...♘e5?! 20 gxf6 ♗xf6 21 f4; 19...0-0? 20 gxf6 ♗xf6 21 ♖g1+ ♔h8 22 ♖h5 ♗g7 23 ♖xg7 ♔xg7 24 ♕g4+ +−.

By making a series of accurate moves, Black has achieved a position where his extra knight is worth no less than White's activity.

**20 gxf6**

Or:

a) 20 ♖f5 fxg5!? 21 ♗xg5 ♘e5 – *20 gxf6 ♘xf6 21 ♖f5 ♘g4!? 22 ♗g5 ♘e5*.

b) 20 ♗d2 ♔f8! 21 ♖a5 (21 ♕h5 ♖g7!) 21...♕xa5 22 ♕xe7+ ♔g7 is much better for Black, Goliak-Petrushin, USSR 1971.

c) 20 h4 ♖c8 (20...fxg5!? 21 ♗xg5 ♘e5) 21 ♗f4 (21 f4?! ♔f8, Ehlvest-Tischbierek, Leningrad 1984) 21...♔f8 22 ♗xd6 ♗xd6 23 ♖xd6 fxg5 (Yrjölä suggests 23...♕c7) 24 ♕d2 ♖c7 25 ♕b4 ♗g7 26 ♕d4+ ♔f8 = Dashko-Tseshkovsky, Novorossiysk 1995.

d) 20 ♗f4 ♔f8 (20...♘e5? 21 gxf6 ♗xf6 22 ♗xe5 ♗xe5 23 f4 ± Golubev-Konarev, Ukrainian jr Ch (Alexandria) 1984) and then:

d1) 21 ♕d2 ♖xg5! (21...fxg5? 22 ♗xd6 ♗xd6 23 ♖xd6 – *21 ♗xd6 ♗xd6 22 ♖xd6 fxg5? 23 ♕d2 ±*) 22 ♗xg5 fxg5 23 h4 a5!, Hector-Fishbein, Stavanger 1991, with the point 24 ♖xb5 ♘c5! ∓.

d2) 21 ♕h5 ♕a5!.

d3) 21 ♗xd6 ♗xd6 22 ♖xd6 ♖xg5 (22...fxg5? 23 ♕d2 ♖a7 24 ♕b4! a5 25 ♖xd7+ axb4 26 ♖xd8+ ♔g7 27 ♖xg8+ ♔xg8 28 ♗e5 ± A.Koroliov; 22...♖a7?! 23 gxf6 ♖g6 24 ♕e3 ♖c7 25 ♕h3; 22...♖c8!? – Kasparov/Nikitin) 23 f4 (23 ♕d2 ♖a7 24 f4 ♖g6 – *23 f4 ♖g6 24 ♕d2 ♖a7*) 23...♖g6 and here:

d31) 24 f5 ♖g5 25 ♕d2 (25 h4?! ♖xf5 26 ♕d2 ♖e5!) 25...♖a7 – *24 ♕d2 ♖a7 25 f5 ♖g5*.

d32) 24 ♕d2 ♖a7 25 f5 (25 ♖d1 f5 ∓) 25...♖g5 26 h4 ♖g4 (26...♖g7!?) 27 ♖d4 (27 ♕h6+ ♔g8 28 ♖d4 ♖g7!? 29 ♕d2 ♕c8 ∓ Moraru-Ardeleanu, Romanian Cht 1998) 27...h5!? 28 ♕h6+ ♔g8 29 ♖xg4+ hxg4 30 ♖e4 ♘e5 31 ♖xe5! = Nisipeanu/Stoica.

**20...♘xf6 21 ♖f5 ♘g4!?**

This is sufficient, but is not the only move:

a) 21...♖g6? 22 ♗b6 ♕d7 23 ♕f3 ♖b8 24 ♖xf6 ♖xb6 25 ♕a8+ ♕d8 26 ♖xe7+ ± Kupreichik-Beliavsky, USSR 1974.

b) 21...♖b8 22 h4 (A.Frolov-Bagaturov, Biel IZ 1993; 22 ♗a7?! ♖b7 23 ♗d4 ♘g4 24 ♕f3 ♕c8 ∓ Taborov-Korsunsky, Tallinn 1976; 22 ♗d4!?) 22...♘g4 23 ♗g5 ♘e5 24 f4 with unclear play.

c) 21...♘d7!? 22 g5 (it is unknown whether White gets compensation after 22 ♕h5; e.g., 22...♖g6 23 ♕xh7 and now 23...♘e5 {*Schach-Archiv*} or 23...♘f6), and now, apart from 22...♘e5 (see *21...♘g4 22 ♗g5 ♘e5*), Black should consider the idea 22...♖xg5!? 23 ♖xg5 ♔f8.

**22 ♗g5**

Black achieves the advantage after other moves:

a) 22 ♕f3 ♖c8 23 ♗d4 ♘e5!, Zapata-Van der Wiel, Wijk aan Zee 1995.

b) 22 ♖g5 ♖xg5 23 ♗xg5 ♘e5 24 ♗xe7 ♕xe7, Howell-Lysenko, Cappelle la Grande 1995.

c) 22 ♖g1 ♘h6! (22...h5? 23 ♖xh5 ♘f6 24 ♖xg8+ ♘xg8 25 ♕g4 ♘f6 26 ♖h8+ ♗f8 27 ♕f3) 23 ♖fg5? ♗xg5! –+.

d) 22 ♗d4 ♖g6!? 23 ♕f3 ♘e5 24 ♗xe5 dxe5 25 ♖xf7 ♖a7!.

**22...♘e5 23 ♗xe7 ♕xe7 24 f4**

A probable draw can be achieved either through 24...♖g2, as in the game Soloviov-Lysenko, Sverdlovsk 1978, or 24...♘d3+ and 24...♕e6 25 ♕e4 ♘d3+, which were played later.

**B12)**
**14 h4** *(D)*

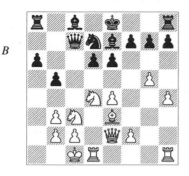

The most popular plan for White – he intends 15 h5 and 16 g6.

**14...b4!**

The other possibilities are:

a) Unsuccessful is 14...0-0?! 15 g6! ♘c5 (15...hxg6 16 h5 ±), when White has two promising roads: 16 b4 ♘a4 17 ♘xa4 (17 ♖d3!? Velimirović) 17...bxa4 (Romanishin-Vaiser, USSR 1972) 18 h5!, or 16 gxh7+ ♔h8 17 ♖hg1 ♗f6 18 ♗g5 with an advantage.

b) 14...♘c5!? and now:

b1) 15 ♘f5?! exf5 16 ♘d5 ♘xb3+ 17 ♔b1 ♕b7.

b2) After 15 b4 ♘a4 16 ♖d3, we have:

b21) 16...♕c4 17 ♘b1! ♕xb4 18 c3 ♕a5 19 ♘c6 ♕c7 20 ♘xe7 ♕xe7 21 ♖hd1 favours White, Radulov-Hamann, Lugano OL 1968.

b22) 16...♗d7 can be met by 17 ♘f5!? exf5 18 ♘d5 ♕d8 19 ♗d4 – Velimirović.

b23) 16...♗b7!? is more reliable for Black.

b24) 16...♘xc3 17 ♖xc3 ♕d7, as given by Kasparov and Nikitin, also looks safer for Black.

b3) 15 h5 b4 16 ♘a4 – *14...b4! 15 ♘a4 ♘c5! 16 h5.*

c) 14...♗b7 is a natural but somewhat inaccurate continuation:

c1) 15 h5 b4 and then:

c11) 16 ♘a4 ♗xe4 17 f3 and here:

c111) 17...♗b7?! 18 g6 hxg6 19 hxg6 ♖xh1 20 ♖xh1 and now, rather than 20...♗f6? 21 ♘xe6! +– M.Gurevich-Ehlvest, USSR 1978 or 20...♘c5?! 21 ♘xc5 dxc5 22 gxf7+ ♔xf7 23 ♘xe6! +– Podgaets-Butnorius, Odessa 1975, Black should try 20...♘f8!?.

c112) 17...♗d5! 18 ♔b1 ♘e5 (the alternatives for Black are 18...♖c8!? 19 ♘f5 ♕c6 and 18...♕b7!?) 19 ♖h3 0-0! (Livshits/Lukin) gives Black good chances.

c12) 16 ♘a2! and then:

c121) 16...♘c5 17 ♘xb4 ♗xe4 18 f3 ♗b7 19 g6 ±.

c122) 16...♗xe4!? 17 f3 ♗b7 18 ♘xb4 (18 g6 ∞ Akopian) 18...a5!?.

c123) 16...♕a5 17 ♔b1 ♗xe4 (after 17...♗xg5 18 ♗xg5 ♕xg5 19 ♘xb4 White has the initiative, de Firmian-Busquesto, New York 1989) 18 f3 ♗f5 (18...♗d5 19 ♗d2! ± Ulybin/Volovik), and now White has an interesting choice:

c1231) 19 ♖h4 h6 20 ♘xb4 (20 ♘c6!?) 20...♗xg5 21 ♘bc6 ♕d5 22 ♗xg5 hxg5 23 ♖hh1 ∞ Ljubojević-Beliavsky, Las Palmas 1974.

c1232) 19 ♘c6!? Šahović.

c1233) 19 ♘xb4 ♕xb4 20 ♘xf5 exf5 21 ♗d4 ♘c5 (21...♕b5!? Minić; 21...♕d8 22 h6 ±) 22 h6 ♘e6 23 hxg7 ♖g8 24 ♗f6 with compensation, Ljubojević-Hamann, Amsterdam 1975.

c2) 15 f3 and now:

c21) 15...♕a5 16 ♔b1 b4 17 ♘a2!? d5 18 h5 dxe4 19 g6, Lerner-Petrushin,

Minsk 1971, has been evaluated in White's favour.

c22) 15...♖c8 16 h5 b4 17 ♘a4 d5 18 g6 hxg6 19 hxg6 ♖xh1 20 ♖xh1 dxe4 21 f4 with the initiative, Radulov-Shamkovich, Varna 1970.

c23) 15...g6 should probably transpose to line 'c254' as after 16 h5 b4, 17 hxg6 bxc3 18 ♖xh7 ♖xh7 19 gxh7 0-0-0 20 g6 ♗f6 seems satisfactory for Black.

c24) 15...♘c5!? 16 ♔b1 0-0-0 was suggested by Nisipeanu and Stoica.

c25) 15...b4 16 ♘a4 and then:

c251) 16...d5?! 17 exd5 ♗xd5 18 ♘f5 ±.

c252) 16...♕a5 17 ♔b1 ♘c5 – *16...♘c5 17 ♔b1 ♕a5*.

c253) 16...♘c5 and here:

c2531) 17 h5 ♘xa4 (17...♕a5 18 ♔b1 – *17 ♔b1 ♕a5 18 h5*) 18 bxa4 ♖c8 and now, rather than 19 g6 ♗f6!, as in Wedberg-Shamkovich, Reykjavik 1982, Nunn recommends 19 ♔b1! ±.

c2532) 17 ♔b1 and now:

c25321) 17...♘xa4 18 bxa4 ♖c8 19 ♗c1! ± Nunn.

c25322) 17...♖c8 18 h5 ♘xa4 (18...0-0 19 g6 ♗f6 20 ♕h2 ♖fe8 21 ♖dg1!? with an attack; 18...♕a5!? – *17...♕a5 18 h5 ♖c8!?*) 19 bxa4 d5 20 g6 ♗f6 21 gxf7+ ♔xf7 (Razuvaev-Shamkovich, USSR Ch (Baku) 1972) 22 f4 dxe4 23 f5 ±.

c25323) 17...♕a5 18 h5 (18 e5?! ♘xa4!?) 18...♘xa4 (18...♖c8!? 19 g6 ♗f6) 19 bxa4 ♕xa4 (19...♗xg5 20 ♘b3 and 19...♖c8 20 g6 favour White) 20 g6 ♖c8 (20...♗f6 21 ♕c4 ±) 21 h6! hxg6 22 hxg7 ♖g8 23 ♖h8 ♔d7 24 ♘b3 ± Nunn-Van der Wiel, Wijk aan Zee 1982.

c254) 16...g6!? and then:

c2541) 17 ♕f2!?.

c2542) 17 ♕d2!? ♕a5 (17...d5!?) 18 h5 0-0-0 19 ♔b1, and now not 19...♔b8? 20 hxg6 hxg6 21 ♖xh8 ♖xh8 22 ♘c6+!! ♗xc6 23 ♕d4 +– Nunn-Nokes, Ramsgate 1981, but 19...d5 20 e5!? ♘xe5, with complications.

c2543) 17 h5! enables White to fight for the initiative; e.g., 17...e5 18 hxg6 fxg6 19 ♘e6; 17...0-0-0 18 ♕f2 ♕a5 19 ♔b1 ♗xg5 (19...d5 20 e5!) 20 ♘f5!, Parligras-Ardeleanu, Romanian Cht 2000; 17...♖f8 18 ♕d2 d5 19 e5!?, P.Petursson-Nykopp, Reykjavik 1984; 17...♖g8 18 ♕f2 ♖c8 19 hxg6 hxg6 20 ♖d2 ± Lukin-Liavdansky, Leningrad 1969.

We now return to 14...b4 *(D)*:

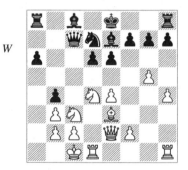

**15 ♘a4**

15 ♘a2 a5! (15...♗b7 16 h5! – *14...♗b7 15 h5 b4 16 ♘a2!*; 15...♘c5 16 ♘xb4 ♘xe4 Kasparov/Nikitin) 16 ♘b5?! (a game with chances for both sides can be obtained through 16 ♔b1 or 16 h5 ♗a6, followed by ...♖c8, Wedberg-Yrjölä, Finland-Sweden 1988) 16...♕b8 (or 16...♕c6 17 ♕c4 ♘c5 18 ♖xd6 ♗xd6 19 ♘xd6+ ♕xd6 20 ♗xc5 ♕c7! Kasparov/Nikitin) 17 ♕d3 ♖a6

(17...0-0 18 ♘xd6 ♘e5!? 19 ♕d4 a4)
18 ♕c4 ♘c5 19 ♔b1 (de Firmian-
Hellers, Reykjavik 1990) 19...♗b7!.

**15...♘c5!**

15...♗b7 and then: 16 f3 – *14...♗b7
15 f3 b4 16 ♘a4*; 16 h5 – *14...♗b7 15
h5 b4 16 ♘a4*.

**16 h5**

The remaining continuations are:

a) 16 ♘xc5?! dxc5 17 ♘f3 – *8...♕c7
9 ♕e2 ♘a5 10 g4 b5 11 g5 ♘d7 12
0-0-0 b4 13 ♘a4 ♘xb3+ 14 axb3 ♘c5
15 ♘xc5 dxc5 16 ♘f3 ♗e7 17 h4.*

b) 16 ♕c4 ♗d7 (16...♕b7 17 e5
♘xa4 18 bxa4 dxe5 19 ♘c6 ♕c7 20
♘xe5 ♕xc4 21 ♘xc4 ♗b7 = Matano-
vić-Hamann, Vrnjačka Banja 1966)
17 ♕xb4 ♗xa4! 18 bxa4 0-0 with an
excellent position.

c) 16 ♔b1 ♘xe4 (16...♗d7 can be
met by 17 f4!? or 17 h5 – *16 h5 ♗d7
17 ♔b1)* 17 ♗f4 and now *Schach-
Archiv* gives 17...e5! ∓ (rather than
17 ♘c5 18 ♘f5 + Raičević)

d) 16 f3 ♗d7! 17 ♔b1 (17 h5?! can
be met by 17...e5!? or 17...♘xb3+ 18
♘xb3 ♗xa4 ∓) 17...♘xa4! (17...♗xa4
18 bxa4 ♘xa4 19 h5 ♘c5 ∞ Yudasin-
Sion Castro, Leon 1993) 18 bxa4 ♗xa4
19 h5 ♗d7 20 g6 and it is not clear
whether White has real compensation.
Black can choose between 20...♗f6
and 20...fxg6!? 21 hxg6 h6, Dervishi-
I.Nikolaidis, Erevan Z 2000.

**16...♗d7**

Otherwise:

a) 16...♗b7?! is well met by 17
g6!, as in Gufeld-Tukmakov, Moscow
1975, or 17 f3!? – *14...♗b7 15 f3 b4
16 ♘a4 ♘c5 17 h5.*

b) 16...♘xa4?! 17 bxa4 ♕a5 18 g6
± Hartston-Mestel, British Ch (East-
bourne) 1973.

c) 16...e5?! 17 ♘f5 ± Nunn-Mur-
shed, Commonwealth Ch (London)
1985.

d) Serious attention should be paid
to 16...♘xe4!? 17 g6 ♗f6 (17...f5 18
h6! ± I.Zaitsev-Utemov, USSR 1983;
17...♘f6?! 18 h6 hxg6 19 hxg7 ♖g8
20 ♖h8 ♗b7 21 ♗g5 ♔d7 22 ♘b5
axb5 23 ♕xb5+ ♗c6 24 ♘c5+! +–;
17...♗d8!?) 18 gxf7+ (18 ♕g4 d5 19
gxf7+ ♔xf7 20 f3 ♕g3! with an advantage, Chuprov-Kalugin, St Petersburg 1999; 18 ♗f4?! e5 19 ♕xe4 ♗b7;
18 h6 hxg6 19 hxg7 ♗xg7 20 ♖xh8+
♗xh8 also looks dubious; e.g., 21 ♖h1
♗f6 22 ♖h7 ♘g5 or 21 ♕g4 ♗b7!)
18...♗xf7 19 ♖hg1 ∞ Emms-Henni-
gan, British Ch (Dundee) 1993.

**17 ♔b1**

17 ♘xc5?! dxc5 18 ♘f3 ♗b5 with
strong counterplay.

17 g6 ♘xb3+! (17...♗f6? 18 e5!! ±
Benjamin-Taborov, Schilde 1976) and
then:

a) 18 ♔b1 ♘xd4! (18...♘c5 19 h6!
gives White sufficient compensation,
Renet-Am.Rodriguez, Pančevo 1985)
19 ♗xd4 ♗xa4 20 ♗xg7 and now
20...♖c8 ∓ Hector-Am.Rodriguez, Se-
ville 1986, or 20...♔d7.

b) 18 ♘xb3 ♗xa4 19 h6!? (this
does not give an advantage but nobody
knows whether there is compensation
after 19 gxf7+ ♔xf7 or 19 ♘d4 ♗f6
20 gxf7+ ♔xf7; e.g., 21 h6 g6 22 b3
♗d7! 23 f4) 19...fxg6 20 hxg7 (20
♘d4 e5!? may well come to the same
thing) 20...♖g8 21 ♘d4 e5 (21...♖c8!?;
e.g., 22 ♖xh7? ♗xc2! 23 ♘xc2 b3 ∓
K.Berg-Trepp, Zug 1985, or 22 b3 ♗b5
23 ♕d2 ♗d7 24 ♖xh7 ♗f6, Lange-
veld-De Koning, corr. 1991) 22 ♘e6
♕c6 (22...♕c8!? 23 ♘f8 ♖xg7 24

♘xh7 ♕e6 25 ♘g5 ♕a2! Akopian)
23 ♖xh7 ♗b3! (23...♖c8? 24 ♗c5! ±
dxc5? 25 ♕c4 +−) 24 ♖d5! (24 ♘c5
♗f7 25 ♘d3 ♕xe4 ∓ Brunner-Van der
Wiel, Lucerne Wcht 1989) 24...♖c8
25 ♖h8 ♕xc2+ (25...♔f7 26 ♘c5!
dxc5! 27 cxb3 c4! 28 bxc4 ♕xc4+ =
Rechlis-Piket, Gausdal jr Wch 1986) 26
♕xc2 ♖xc2+ 27 ♔b1 ♔f7 28 ♖d3(!)
with a roughly equal endgame according to Akopian.

**17...♗xa4**

The prevailing practical choice, although there are some other interesting moves:

a) 17...♘xe4? 18 g6 f5 19 h6! hxg6
20 f3! ♘c5 21 ♘xc5 dxc5 22 ♗f4! ±
Wolff-D.Gurevich, Los Angeles 1991.

b) 17...♖c8?! 18 g6 ♗f6 19 gxf7+
♔xf7 20 e5 ♗xe5 21 ♘xc5 dxc5 22
♘f3 ♗f6 23 ♗f4 ± Wolff-Masculo,
Philadelphia 1990.

c) 17...♕b7 and now:

c1) 18 g6 ♗xa4 (18...♗f6?! 19
gxf7+ ♔xf7 20 h6!, Pugachov-Feher,
Budapest 1992; 18...hxg6?! 19 hxg6
♖xh1 20 ♖xh1 is much better for
White − Wedberg; 18...♘xa4!?) 19
bxa4 − _17...♗xa4 18 bxa4 ♕b7 19 g6_.

c2) 18 e5 ♘xa4 19 exd6 ♗xd6 20
bxa4 ♗xa4!? ∞ (20...0-0-0 21 ♘b3
♗xa4 22 ♘a5 ♕b5 23 ♘c4).

d) 17...♘xa4!? 18 bxa4 ♗xa4 (or
18...g6!? Kasparov/Nikitin), and instead of 19 g6 ♗f6, 19 f4!? deserves
attention (e.g. 19...e5 20 fxe5 dxe5 21
♘f5 b3 22 cxb3 ♗xb3 23 ♖d3).

e) 17...g6!?.

**18 bxa4** (D)

Here, Black has several possibilities:

a) 18...♘xa4 19 g6 (19 f4! Kuczynski) 19...♗f6 (19...♘c5 20 e5!? with

the initiative) 20 gxf7+ (20 f4?! 0-0!
21 gxf7+ ♖xf7 22 ♘xe6? ♕b7 −+)
20...♕xf7 (20...♔xf7?! 21 h6! g6 22
♕f3 ± Planinc-Beliavsky, Hastings
1974/5) 21 ♕c4 (21 h6!? g6 22 ♕c4
0-0 =; 21 f4?! 0-0 22 h6 g6 23 f5 exf5
24 exf5 ♖ae8) 21...0-0 22 ♕xe6 ♕xe6
23 ♘xe6 ♖f7 (Wang Pin-Chiburdan-
idze, Shanghai wom Ct 1992; 23...♘xb2
=) 24 ♗c1 ♘c5 =.

b) 18...♖c8 and then:

b1) 19 ♘b3?! ♘xa4 20 ♖d4 and
now 20...♕c3! is even better than
20...♘c5 ∓ Hector-Cebalo, Montpellier 1985.

b2) 19 g6 ♗f6 20 gxf7+ is best met
by 20...♕xf7!. 20...♔xf7 is weaker in
view of 21 f4!? or 21 ♕c4 b3 22 ♘xb3
♘xa4 23 ♕xc7+ ♖xc7 24 ♖xd6 ±.

b3) 19 f4!? is worth considering.

b4) 19 f3 ♘xa4 20 ♕xa6 (20 g6
♗f6 21 ♕xa6 ♘xb2! Cu.Hansen)
20...♘c5 21 ♕b5+ ♘d7! (21...♕d7 is
best met by 22 b3! ± Rõtšagov-Vein-
gold, Finnish Cht 1996, rather than 22
h6 g6 23 ♕xb4 0-0 ∞) and then:

b41) 22 ♖d2 0-0 23 g6 (23 f4 ♘c5
24 f5 ♘xe4 25 ♖g2 ♖a8 26 ♘c6 ♖fc8
∓) 23...♘c5 (23...♘e5 24 gxf7+ ♖xf7
25 ♘xe6 ♕c4 = Akopian) 24 h6 (24
♕xb4!? Van der Wiel) 24...fxg6 25

hxg7 ♖f7 ∓ Onishchuk-Van der Wiel, Wijk aan Zee 1996.

b42) 22 g6 e5! (22...fxg6? 23 ♖h2 ± Hector-Rõtšagov, Gothenburg 1997), and here Black has a guaranteed draw: 23 h6 (or 23 gxf7+ ♔xf7 24 ♕d5+ ♔e8 25 ♘e6 ♕xc2+, Nunn-Estremera Panos, Leon 1997) 23...exd4 24 gxf7+ ♔xf7 (24...♔d8 25 ♖h2 g6 26 ♗xd4 ♖f8 27 e5 ∞) 25 ♕d5+ ♔e8 26 hxg7 ♕xc2+ = Cu.Hansen.

c) 18...♕b7 and here:

c1) 19 e5 dxe5 20 ♘b3 ♘xb3 21 cxb3 0-0 22 ♔a2 ♖ad8 23 ♖dg1 e4 24 g6 ♗f6! ∓ Nieuwenhuis-Am.Rodriguez, Dieren 1987.

c2) 19 f3!? ♘xa4 20 g6 ♗f6 and now:

c21) 21 gxf7+ and now: 21...♕xf7 22 ♕c4 0-0 – *21 ♕c4 0-0 22 gxf7+ ♕xf7*; 21...♔xf7!? transposes to line 'c323'.

c22) 21 ♕c4 0-0 22 gxf7+ ♕xf7 23 ♕xe6 (23 ♕c6!?) 23...♕xe6 24 ♘xe6 ♘xb2 25 ♘xf8 ♘xd1 26 ♖xd1 ♖xf8 27 ♖xd6 = de Firmian-D.Gurevich, Philadelphia 1995.

c3) 19 g6 ♗f6 (19...hxg6 20 hxg6 ♖xh1 21 ♖xh1!) and then:

c31) 20 f3 and here:

c311) 20...♖c8 21 b3! hxg6 22 hxg6 ♖xh1 23 gxf7+ ♔xf7 24 ♖xh1 (Wolff-D.Gurevich, New York 1994) 24...d5! (Wolff) gives White good possibilities such as 25 ♖h5!?.

c312) Stronger is 20...♘xa4! – *19 f3!? ♘xa4 20 g6 ♗f6*.

c32) 20 gxf7+ ♔xf7 (20...♕xf7?! 21 e5! and now 21...♗xe5 22 ♘c6 or 21...dxe5 22 ♘b5 – Kuczynski) 21 f3 (21 h6 g6; 21 e5 dxe5 22 ♘f5 ♘e4! 23 ♕c4 ♖hd8 ∓ Kolomiets-Tsvetkov, corr. 1991; 21 ♘f5?! ♘xe4!? 22 ♕c4

♖hd8; 21 ♖hg1!? is interesting) and then:

c321) 21...b3 22 cxb3 ♘xb3 gives White a choice between 23 ♘f5!? exf5 24 ♕c4+ (*Schach-Archiv*) and 23 h6! g6 24 ♘xb3 ♕xb3 25 ♗d4 ± (Kuczynski).

c322) 21...♖ac8 22 b3 is slightly better for White, Kuczynski-Am.Rodriguez, Camaguey 1987.

c323) 21...♘xa4! 22 ♕c4 (22 ♘f5? ♘c3+ 23 ♔a1 ♕c6 wins for Black) 22...♕d7 (22...d5 23 ♕a2! Kuczynski) gives Black an extra pawn and good counterplay, Wolff-Piket, Baguio jr Wch 1987.

I dare to conclude that after 14 ♘f5 White is in deadlock and the line 14 h4 remains difficult to assess since White is yet to prove his case not only in our main line, but also after deviations such as 16...♘xe4 or 17...♘xa4.

**B2)**
**10...0-0** *(D)*

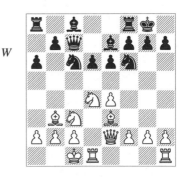

Another very important crossroad. We shall consider:

The last line is a common direction for 11 ♖hg1 and 11 g4.

Other moves are not considered as dangerous for Black and are played surprisingly seldom:

a) 11 ♔b1 b5 (11...♗d7 12 g4! ♘xd4 13 ♖xd4; 11...♘d7 transposes to Line A1, which is a little better for White; 11...♘a5!? 12 g4 ♘xb3 13 axb3 b5 =; e.g., 14 g5 ♘d7 15 h4 b4 16 ♘a2 ♗b7, Kengis-Lukin, Sverdlovsk 1984) 12 ♘xc6 ♕xc6 13 ♗d4 ♗b7 (13...♖b8!? 14 ♖he1 a5) 14 ♖he1. Now, instead of 14...b4? 15 ♘d5, 14...♖fe8?! 15 f4 ♗d8 16 ♖d3!? (16 e5!? dxe5 17 ♕xe5!) 16...e5 17 fxe5 dxe5 18 ♗e3 ♘xe4 19 ♘xe4 ♕xe4 20 ♕f1 ± or 14...♗d8 15 e5!? dxe5 16 ♕xe5, Nunn's 14...♕c7! 15 a3 ♘d7!? appears good.

b) 11 f4 is another hybrid of the Velimirović Attack and the Classical Sozin. Now:

b1) 11...♘a5 (not the best) 12 g4! b5 13 g5 ♘xb3+ (13...♘e8 should be in White's favour) 14 axb3 ♘d7 and now:

b11) 15 h4 is well met by 15...b4!.

b12) 15 f5 is best answered by 15...♘e5!, Timman-Langeweg, Amsterdam 1973, rather than 15...b4?! 16 ♘a4 ♘c5 17 f6! ♗d8 18 e5!?, Pablo Marin-Cuadras, Roses 1992, though 15...♘c5!? is interesting.

b13) White should play 15 ♖hg1!, transposing to Line B221.

b2) 11...♘xd4 12 ♖xd4 leads to play with chances for both sides:

b21) 12...♘d7 13 ♖f1 (13 ♖dd1 b5 14 f5 ♘c5 15 ♗d4 ♘xb3+ 16 axb3 b4!? 17 ♘a4 ♖b8, Kaminski-Av.Bykhovsky, Katowice 1992; 13 g4 – *11 g4*

♘xd4 12 ♖xd4 ♘d7 13 f4) 13...b5 (13...♘c5! is slightly better for Black – Akopian) 14 f5 ♘e5 (14...♘c5? 15 f6!) 15 g4 with the initiative, Korneev-Tourneur, Paris 1991.

b22) 12...b5 13 f5! (13 ♖f1 ♖b8! 14 f5 b4 15 ♘a4 e5 16 ♖c4 ♕a5 17 ♖c6? ♗b7 18 ♗b6 ♕b5 is given by Kasparov and Nikitin; 13 g4!? – *11 g4 ♘xd4 12 ♖xd4 b5 13 f4*) leads to a tough and very unclear struggle:

b221) 13...exf5 14 exf5 ♗xf5 15 g4 ♗e6 16 g5 ♘d7 17 ♕h5 (17 ♘d5!?) 17...♗f5? (17...♘e5!? Lukin) 18 ♖f1 ♗g6 19 ♕d1 ♘c5 20 ♗d5 ♖ab8 21 h4 b4 22 h5!! ± Lukin-Shirov, Daugavpils 1989.

b222) 13...♕b7 14 fxe6!?.

b223) 13...♖b8 14 g4 b4 15 ♘a4, and instead of 15...♕b7 16 g5!? ♘xe4 17 f6 ♘xf6 18 gxf6 ♕xh1+ 19 ♖d1 ♕b7 (Lukin), I like 15...d5, as in Silva-Paoli, Odessa 1976.

b3) 11...b5 appears to be at least an equal alternative:

b31) 12 g4 b4 13 ♘xc6 bxc3!? with strong counterplay, Radev-Spassov, Albena 1970.

b32) 12 f5 ♘a5 (12...♘xd4 13 ♖xd4 – *11...♘xd4 12 ♖xd4 b5 13 f5*; 12...b4 13 ♕c4!) 13 fxe6 ♘xb3+ 14 axb3 fxe6 15 ♗g5 b4 16 ♘a4 ♗d7 and Black has no problems, Suetin-T.Petrosian, USSR 1971.

b33) 12 ♘xc6 ♕xc6 13 e5 (13 g4 b4 14 ♘d5 exd5 15 g5 ♗g4 ∓ Akopian) 13...dxe5 14 fxe5 ♘d7 15 ♘d5, and, quite apart from 15...♗c5 16 ♖he1, Black also has the promising option 15...♗d8!? (Nunn).

**B21)**
**11 g4** *(D)*

The choice between this move and 11 ♖hg1 is mostly a matter of taste.

**11...♘xd4!**

This is the most important move – White must now recapture on d4 with the rook. Otherwise:

a) 11...♘a5?! 12 g5 ♘xb3+ 13 axb3 ♘d7 14 h4 (14 f4 b5 – *11 f4 ♘a5 12 g4! b5 13 g5 ♘xb3+ 14 axb3 ♘d7*; 14 ♖hg1 b5 transposes to Line B221) 14 h5 15 g6!

b) 11...b5?! 12 ♘xc6 (or 12 g5!) 12...♕xc6 13 ♘d5 (Nunn).

c) 11...♘d7 is the popular alternative:

c1) 12 ♘xe6?! fxe6 13 ♗xe6+ ♔h8 14 ♘d5 ♕d8.

c2) 12 ♖hg1 is Line B23.

c3) After 12 g5 ♘c5, 13 ♖hg1 transposes to Line B231. White hardly has anything better: 13 h4 b5! 14 h5 (14 f3 ♗d7 is slightly better for Black, Fischer-Larsen, Palma de Mallorca IZ 1970) 14...b4! (14...♘xd4!?) 15 ♘a4 ♘xd4 16 ♖xd4 ♗d7 Kasparov/Nikitin; 13 f4 b5! 14 f5 b4 ∓; 13 ♔b1 ♗d7 = (or 13...♘xb3); 13 ♕h5 ♗d7!, and White is obliged to play 14 ♖hg1 all the same, which transposes to Line B2312.

c4) 12 f4!? ♘c5 13 f5 (13 ♔b1 b5!) 13...b5 14 ♔b1 leads to a double-edged game; e.g., 14...♗d7 (14...♘xb3 15 axb3 b4 16 ♘a4 ♘xd4 17 ♗xd4 ♖b8 18 f6!? Ghizdavu) 15 ♘xc6 (15 fxe6 fxe6 16 ♘f5 =) 15...♕xc6 16 g5 (16 ♗d5? exd5 17 exd5 ♕c8 18 ♗xc5 dxc5 19 ♕xe7 b4) 16...♘xb3 17 axb3 (17 f6!?) 17...b4 18 f6 bxc3! = White-Butze, corr. 1986.

c5) 12 ♘f5!? is very interesting (and probably strong):

c51) 12...♘c5 13 ♘xe7+ (the alternatives are 13 ♘xg7!? ♔xg7 14 g5 Nikitin and 13 ♖hg1!?, transposing to Line B232) and now:

c511) 13...♘xe7 14 ♕d2 results in a better game for White after 14...♖d8 15 ♗f4! (15 e5!? ♘xb3+ 16 axb3 ♘d5 ±) 15...♘g6 (15...♘xb3+ 16 axb3 e5 17 ♗xe5 ♗xg4 18 ♗xg7! +−) 16 ♗xd6 ♕c6 17 f4 ± Anand-Salov, Dos Hermanas 1997 or 14...♘xb3+ 15 axb3 e5 (Anand recommends 15...d5!, which restricts White to a small advantage) 16 ♖hg1 ± Nunn-Spassov, Buenos Aires OL 1978.

c512) 13...♕xe7 and then:

c5121) 14 ♕d2 ♖d8 15 ♗g5 (15 f4!? b5 16 ♕f2 ♗b7 17 ♖he1, Sahno-Novogrudsky, corr. 1991) 15...f6 16 ♗h4 (16 ♗e3 b5 17 g5 b4!) 16...♕e8 17 g5 ♕h5 is unclear.

c5122) 14 ♖d2!? b5 15 ♖hd1 ♖d8 16 ♗f4 ♘xb3+ 17 axb3 e5 (Lind-Degerman, Swedish Ch (Borlange) 1992) 18 ♘d5!? ♕h4 19 ♗e3 is another try for White.

c5123) 14 f4 ± Anand.

c52) 12...exf5 13 ♘d5 ♕d8 14 gxf5 is critical. Now:

c521) 14...♗g5 15 ♖hg1 ♗xe3+ 16 ♕xe3 ♔h8 (16...♕h4 17 ♖g3) 17 ♕g3

♖g8 18 ♘f4 ♘de5 19 ♘h3 ± Wedberg-Schutz, Enköping 1991.

c522) 14...♘a5 15 ♖hg1! (15 ♘xe7+ ♕xe7 16 ♗d5 ♔h8 17 ♖hg1 ♘f6 18 ♕f3 ♘xd5 19 ♖xd5, Velimirović-Bukal, Yugoslav Ch (Portorož) 1971, and now Nunn gives 19...♘c6!, which looks unclear) 15...♘xb3+ 16 axb3 (Velimirović) seems extremely dangerous for Black, although he can try 16...g6!?.

c523) Possibly critical is 14...♘f6 15 ♖hg1 (15 ♗b6 ♕d7 16 ♖hg1 ♘xd5 17 exd5 ♗f6! was equal in Nunn-Liberzon, Hastings 1979/80) 15...♘xd5 (after 15...♔h8!?, Nikitin's suggestion 16 ♗b6 ♕d7 17 ♘c7 ♖b8 18 f4 is unsuccessful in view of 18...♗d8) 16 ♗xd5 ♗f6 17 ♕h5 (Yakovich-Yudasin, Leipzig 1986), and now 17...♕e7!? 18 ♖g3 ♘b4 or 17...♘b4!? 18 ♗b3 ♕e7.

It is clear that there is not enough information to draw a definite conclusion on the important line 11...♘d7 12 ♘f5.

**12 ♖xd4** *(D)*

12 ♗xd4 e5 is '∓' according to Akopian.

**12...♘d7**

Or:

a) 12...b5 13 g5 (13 f4!? ♘d7 {the alternative 13...♖b8!? is interesting} 14 f5!? ♘c5 15 g5 – *12...♘d7 13 g5 b5 14 f4!? ♘c5 15 f5!*) 13...♘d7 – *12...♘d7 13 g5 b5*.

b) 12...e5?! 13 ♖c4! (13 ♘d5? can be met by 13...♘xd5 14 ♖xd5 ♗e6 ∓ or 13...♗xg4!?) 13...♕d8 14 g5 favours White:

b1) 14...♘g4? 15 ♖xc8!.

b2) 14...♘e8 15 ♖g1 (15 ♖xc8!?; 15 ♘d5!? ♗xg5 16 ♖g1 ♗xe3+ 17 ♕xe3 ♗e6 18 ♖c3; 15 h4!? ♗e6) 15...♗d7 (15...♗e6 16 ♘d5) 16 ♘d5 ♗b5 17 ♕g4!, Fiala-Badura, corr. 1988.

b3) 14...♘d7 and now:

b31) 15 ♖g1 b5 16 ♖xc8 ♖xc8 17 ♕h5 – *15 ♕h5 b5 16 ♖xc8 ♖xc8 17 ♖g1*.

b32) 15 ♕h5 b5 (15...♘c5 16 ♖xc5! dxc5 17 ♖d1 ± Boleslavsky) 16 ♖xc8 ♖xc8 17 ♖g1 (17 g6 hxg6 18 ♕xg6 ♘c5 19 ♗d5 ♗h4!) 17...♘c5 18 ♗d5 ♘e6 19 g6 hxg6 20 ♖xg6 ♘f4! = Kuczynski-Staniszewski, Polish Cht 1995.

b33) 15 ♖xc8!? ♕xc8 16 ♘d5 ♗d8 17 h4 (Nikitin) appears good, as do the next two possibilities.

b34) 15 ♘d5!? ♗xg5 16 ♖g1.

b35) 15 h4!? b5 16 ♖xc8.

**13 g5**

13 f4 ♘c5 14 f5?! ♗f6 15 g5 ♗xd4 16 ♗xd4 b5 17 ♖g1 ♗b7 ∓ de Firmian-Shirov, Tilburg 1993.

**13...b5**

13...♘c5!? is a serious alternative here:

a) 14 h4 b5 – *13...b5 14 h4 ♘c5*.

b) 14 f4 f5! (this is a typical idea in all variations with 11 g4 ♘xd4) and then:

b1) 15 gxf6 ♗xf6 16 e5 dxe5 17 ♖c4 ♘xb3+ 18 axb3 ♕f7! and now 19 ♗c5 b5! ∓ Wedberg-Mednis, Copenhagen 1991, or 19 ♘e4 b5!.

b2) 15 exf5 ♖xf5 is satisfactory for Black.

b3) 15 ♕h5!? fxe4 16 ♘xe4 ♘xe4 17 ♖xe4 d5 18 ♖d4 ♗c5 19 ♖f1 ∞ Sergeev-Veingold, Estonian Cht 1998.

c) 14 e5 (a typical idea for White) 14...dxe5 (14...d5!? Nikitin) 15 ♖h4 g6 (15...f5? 16 ♕h5 h6 17 ♖g1), and then:

c1) 16 ♖g1 f5 (16...b5? – *13...b5 14 ♖g1 ♘c5 15 e5!? dxe5? 16 ♖h4 g6*; 16...♖d8!? Nikitin) 17 gxf6 ♗xf6 (17...♘xb3+!?) 18 ♖hg4 (Aseev-Arakhamia, London Lloyds Bank 1994; 18 ♗xc5!?) 18...♘xb3+ 19 axb3 ♗g7 ∞ Aseev.

c2) 16 ♖h6 and here:

c21) 16...f5 17 h4 ♘xb3+ 18 axb3 f4 (Bronstein-Lein, USSR Ch (Leningrad) 1971) 19 ♗d2! is unsafe for Black.

c22) 16...♘xb3+ 17 axb3 ♖d8 18 ♕g4 ♗f8 19 ♘c4 ♗xh6 20 ♘f6+! is also perilous for Black, Quadri-Leiros, corr. 1999.

c23) 16...b5! 17 ♗xc5 (or 17 h4 ♗b7 18 f3 e4!) 17...♕xc5 18 ♘e4 ♕c6! 19 h4 ♗b7 20 f3 ♕d7 – Nikitin.

d) 14 ♕h5 g6!? and then:

d1) 15 ♕h6 f5 (the reliability of 15...♖d8 and 15...♖e8 16 e5!? ♗f8 17 ♕h3, Nikitin, is unknown) 16 gxf6 (16 f4 ♕c6!? 17 h4? ♖e8 wins for Black) 16...♗xf6 17 ♖dd1 ♘xb3+ 18 axb3 ♗d7 and Black is OK, Simić-Lanka, Budapest 1991.

d2) 15 ♕e2 f5 (15...b5!? – *13...b5 14 ♕h5 g6!? 15 ♕e2!? ♘c5*) 16 exf5 ♖xf5 17 h4 b5 18 h5 ♘xb3+ 19 axb3

♗b7 20 ♖h3 ♗f8 gives Black quite a solid position, Timoshchenko-L.Grigorian, Kiev 1970.

e) 14 ♖g1 and then:

e1) 14...b5 – *13...b5 14 ♖g1 ♘c5.*

e2) 14...f5 15 exf5 ♖xf5 16 ♖h4 (16 ♔b1 d5 17 ♖h4 g6 18 ♗d4 ♘xb3 19 axb3 ∞ Doghri-Mednis, Cannes 1998) 16...♘xb3+ 17 axb3 g6 18 ♖g3 ♗d7?! (18...♖f7!? Ugrinović) 19 ♖gh3 ♖f7 20 ♕d3! ± Szmetan-Liberzon, Buenos Aires 1979.

e3) 14...♗d7!? and now:

e31) 15 f4 f5 appears satisfactory for Black.

e32) 15 ♖g3 g6 16 h4 (16 e5 ∞ Nikitin) 16...f5! is again OK for Black, Koyias-Atalik, Katerini 1993.

e33) 15 ♕h5 ♖fc8 (15...g6) 16 e5!? g6 17 ♕h3 dxe5 18 ♖h4 ♘xb3+ 19 axb3 h5 20 ♖xh5 gxh5 21 ♕xh5 ♗e8 22 g6 = Delgado-Estremera, Lalin 1994.

e34) 15 e5 is interesting: 15...dxe5 (15...d5!?) 16 ♖h4 ♘xb3+ 17 axb3 g6 18 ♘e4 f5 19 gxf6 ♗xf6 20 ♖xh7!! ± Agopov-Veingold, Finnish Cht 1999.

We now return to 13...b5 *(D)*:

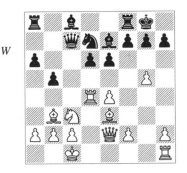

From here, it is difficult to single out the main line.

**14 ♖g1**

Others:

a) 14 e5?! dxe5 (14...d5?! 15 ♖h4; 14...♘xe5!? 15 ♕h5 ♘g6 Nikitin) 15 ♖h4 ♖d8! 16 ♖g1 (16 ♘d5 exd5 17 ♗xd5 ♘f8! 18 ♗xa8 ♘g6 ∓ was first found by Cvetković/Krnić; 16 ♕h5 – *14 ♕h5 ♖d8 15 e5? dxe5! 16 ♖h4 ∓*) 16...♗b7 (16...g6 is simpler) 17 ♖xh7 g6! (Vagner; 17...♔xh7? 18 g6+ fxg6 19 ♖xg6 +−).

b) 14 h4 ♘c5 15 h5 (15 f4 f5! ∓; after 15 ♔b1 or 15 f3, 15...♖b8 is strong, with the idea of 16...a5! ∓) 15...f5! (this is probably most precise; 15...♖b8 16 g6!?) 16 exf5 ♖xf5 is equal, Dely-Paoli, Szombathely 1966.

c) 14 ♕h5 and then:

c1) 14...♘c5?! 15 e5! ±.

c2) 14...♘e5?! 15 f4! ±.

c3) 14...♗b7 is also unreliable in view of 15 ♖g1 g6 (15...♖fc8? 16 g6!) 16 ♕h3! ♖fc8 17 f4, Rogić-Taggatz, Passau 1999.

c4) 14...♖d8 is good enough:

c41) 15 ♖g1 – *14 ♖g1 ♖d8 15 ♕h5*.

c42) 15 e5? dxe5! (15...♘xe5!? Zak) 16 ♖h4 ♘f8 17 ♘e4 ♗b7 18 ♘f6+ ♗xf6! (18...gxf6? 19 ♖g1 f5 20 g6 +−) 19 gxf6 ♗xh1 20 fxg7 ♔xg7 21 ♕g5+ (21 ♗h6+ ♔g8 22 ♕g5+ ♘g6 23 ♕f6 ♖d1+ 24 ♔xd1 ♕d8+ −+ Velimirović) 21...♘g6! 22 ♕h6+ ♔g8 23 ♕xh7+ ♔f8 24 ♗xe6 ♖d1+! ∓.

c43) 15 ♘d5? exd5 16 ♗xd5 ♘e5 17 f4 (Dvoirys-Vainshtein {Kasparov}, USSR jr Ch (Vilnius) 1975) 17...♗g4! 18 ♕h4 (18 ♗xf7+!? Zak) 18...♖ac8 19 c3 h5!? 20 fxe5 dxe5 21 ♖f1 ♖xd5 22 ♖xd5 b4 ∓.

c44) 15 f4!? and now:

c441) After 15...♘c5 16 f5 ♘xb3+ 17 axb3, both 17...exf5?! 18 ♘d5 and 17...♗f8 18 ♖f1 g6 19 ♕h3 d5 20 exd5 exf5 21 ♗f4, de Firmian-D.Gurevich, USA Ch (Estes Park) 1987, favour White.

c442) 15...g6 leads to unclear play:

c4421) 16 ♕h6 ♖b8 17 ♖d3!? ♗f8 18 ♕h4 ♘c5 19 ♖hd1?! ♘xd3+ 20 ♖xd3 (Valenti-A.Schneider, Reggio Emilia 1975) 20...h5! ∞.

c4422) 16 ♕e2 ♘c5 17 h4 ♗b7 18 h5 ♗f8 ∞ Minasian-Akopian, Erevan 1990.

c4423) 16 ♕h3 ♘c5 17 f5 ♖b8 18 e5 ∞ Hawelko-Mäki, Thessaloniki OL 1988.

c5) 14...g6!? and then:

c51) 15 ♕e2!? ♘c5 16 h4 leads to unclear play after 16...h5!?, Ulybin-R.Scherbakov, Borzhomi 1988, or 16...♖b8, Yakovich-Panchenko, Sochi 1989.

c52) 15 ♕h6 ♖e8 (possibly stronger than 15...♖d8 16 ♖g1 – *14 ♖g1 ♖d8 15 ♕h5 g6! 16 ♕h6*) 16 f4 (other attempts: 16 e5 ♗f8 17 ♕h3 and 16 ♖g1 ♗f8 17 ♕h4 ♖b8 18 ♖g3 ♗g7, Vetemaa-Panchenko, USSR Cht 1979, 19 f4!?) 16...♗f8 17 ♕h4 ♘c5 (the other possibilities are 17...♗g7 18 f5!? and 17...♖b8!? R.Scherbakov) 18 ♖g1 ♖b8 19 ♖g3 b4 and now Scherbakov assesses both 20 ♘a4 ♘xb3+ and 20 ♘e2 e5 (Fedulov-R.Scherbakov, Russian Cht 2000) in Black's favour.

d) 14 f4!? looks critical: 14...♘c5 (14...♖b8!? is interesting) 15 f5! (15 ♖f1 b4! 16 ♖xb4 a5 ∞ Yuneev-Lukin, USSR 1984; 15 ♕f2 f5! ∞ Planinc-Langeweg, Wijk aan Zee 1974; 15 ♖g1 ♖b8 16 ♔b1 a5! ∞ de Firmian-Lein, New York 1990, with the typical point 17 ♘xb5? ♖xb5 18 ♕xb5 ♗a6 −+) and then:

d1) 15...b4?! 16 ♖xb4 d5 17 ♗xd5! +– Gik-Krichevsky, USSR 1968.

d2) 15...♖d8 16 ♖g1!?.

d3) 15...♘xb3+ 16 axb3 exf5 17 ♘d5 ♕d8 (17...♕b7? fails to 18 ♖g1: 18...♗e6 19 ♘f6+ ♔h8 20 ♘xh7! +– or 18...fxe4 19 ♘f6+ ♔h8 20 ♕h5! wins for White) 18 ♖g1 (18 ♕h5!?) 18...♖e8 (18...g6 does not equalize in view of 19 h4!, Klundt-Weindl, Bodensee 1995) 19 ♕f2 (19 h4 fxe4!? Nikitin) and here:

d31) After 19...fxe4, 20 ♖xe4 ♗b7 21 ♗b6 ♗xd5 22 ♗xd8 ♗xe4 23 ♗xe7 ♖xe7 looks like a draw, but interesting is 20 ♕f4 g6 21 ♖f1 ♗f5 22 ♖xe4 ♖c8 23 c3 with the initiative, Mallee-Dunhaupt, corr. 1992.

d32) 19...g6 20 exf5 ♗xf5 21 ♖h4 (21 ♖f4!?) 21...♖c8 22 ♕xf5 gxf5 23 ♘f6+ ♔g7 24 ♖xh7+ ♔g6 25 ♖h6+ ♔g7 (Wedberg-L.Schneider, Eksjö 1980). Now White has the draw in his pocket, but 26 ♘xe8+!? is interesting.

d4) 15...exf5 16 ♗d5 (no stronger are 16 ♘d5 ♕d8 17 e5?! dxe5! and 16 exf5 ♗xf5) 16...♖b8 17 exf5 b4 (following 17...♗xf5 18 ♖f1!, as in Wedberg-Trincardi, Eksjö 1979, Black has not yet found any acceptable recipe) 18 g6 (18 ♘e4? ♗xf5 19 ♘g3 ♗e6 ∓ Hübner) 18...hxg6 (18...bxc3? 19 ♕h5 +–) 19 fxg6 ♗e6 and then:

d41) 20 ♘e4 ♗xd5!? (20...b3!?) 21 ♕h5 fxg6 22 ♕xd5+ ♔h7.

d42) 20 ♖c4!? ♕d7 21 gxf7+ ♖xf7 22 ♗xc5.

d43) 20 ♗xe6 ♘xe6 21 ♘d5 ♘xd4 22 ♗xd4 ♗g5+ 23 ♔b1 ♕b7 24 ♕h5 ♗h6 25 ♘f6+ gxf6 26 ♖g1 fxg6 27 ♕xh6 ♖f7 and Black has achieved approximate equality, Wahls-Hübner, Bundesliga 1989/90.

We now return to 14 ♖g1 *(D)*:

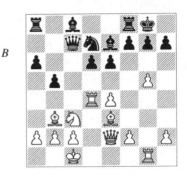

*B*

**14...♘c5**

Again, this is just one of the possible options. The rare cases include 14...♖e8 (it is then worthwhile to investigate 15 g6 hxg6 16 ♖xg6) and 14...b4?!. Others are:

a) 14...♗b7 15 f4 (15 ♕h5!? – *14 ♕h5 ♗b7 15 ♖g1*) 15...♘c5 (15...♖fe8 16 f5 ♗f8, Cebalo, seems to be too passive) 16 f5 ♖fc8 17 f6 (17 g6!?; 17 ♔b1 ♘xb3 18 axb3 ♗f8 19 ♖g3 g6 20 f6 ♗c6 21 e5!? b4! 22 ♖xb4 ♕a5 23 ♖h4 ♕xe5 24 ♖gh3 h6, and it appears that Black has successfully defended, de Firmian-Gomez Esteban, New York 1989) 17...♗f8 18 e5 d5 (a possible improvement here is 18...dxe5 19 ♖h4 g6!? 20 ♖g3 ♕c6) 19 ♖h4 ♕xe5 20 ♖g3 g6 21 ♕f2 b4 22 ♗d4 ♕d6 23 ♖gh3 h5 24 ♖xh5 +– Har-Even – Markland, corr. 1987-92.

b) 14...♖b8!? 15 ♕h5 (15 ♖g3 g6!, Zuev-Panchenko, Rostov 1985; 15 f4 ♘c5!? – *14 f4 ♘c5 15 ♖g1 ♖b8*), and then:

b1) 15...♖d8? 16 g6! is much better for White – Parma.

b2) 15...b4 16 e5 (16 ♘e2 g6 17 ♕h6 ♖d8 18 ♖g3 ♗f8 19 ♕h4 ♗g7

20 f4 ♖b5!? ∞ Shulga-Serov, corr. 1993-4) and then:

b21) 16...bxc3 17 ♖h4 h6 18 gxh6 g6 19 ♖xg6+ ♔h8 20 exd6 ♕xd6! (20...♖xd6? 21 ♖g1! +–) 21 ♗d4+ ♕xd4 22 ♖xd4 fxg6 23 ♕xg6 ♖g8 24 ♕f7! gives White compensation.

b22) 16...♘xe5 17 ♖h4 h6 18 ♘e4 ♖b5 (18...♘g6 19 ♘f6+ ♗xf6 20 gxf6 ♖b5 – 18...♖b5 19 ♘f6+ ♗xf6 20 gxf6 ♘g6) 19 ♘f6+ (19 ♕e2!? ♘g6!) 19...♗xf6 (19...♔h8 20 f4 ±) 20 gxf6 ♘g6 21 ♕e2 (Wang Zili's 21 fxg7!? is probably stronger) 21...♘xh4 22 ♖xg7+ ♔h8 23 ♕g4 ♘g6! 24 ♗xh6 ♕b7 25 ♕h3 ♕h1+ 26 ♔d2 ♖d5+ =.

b3) 15...g6!? 16 ♕h6 ♖d8 deserves attention; e.g., 17 e5 d5 18 ♖xd5 and now 18...b4 19 ♖xd7 ♗xd7 20 ♘e4 ♕xe5 21 ♗c5 ♕xc5!?, while 18...♗f8! is maybe even stronger.

c) 14...g6!? 15 h4 (15 f4 ♘c5 16 f5 exf5 17 ♘d5 ♕d8 18 e5?! dxe5! Gufeld) 15...♘c5 16 h5 (16 f4? ♖b8 17 h5 b4) 16...♖e8 17 e5 (17 ♖h1!? ♗b7 18 ♕g4 ♗f8 19 f3 and here, rather than 19...♖ad8 20 ♖d2 ± Dueball-G.Kuzmin, Nice OL 1974, Black should continue 19...♗c6! – Baljon) 17...dxe5 18 ♖h4 ♗b7 19 f3 ♘xb3+ 20 axb3 ♗d6 21 ♖gh1 ♖e7 22 ♕d3 (22 ♘d1!? Baljon) 22...♖f8! 23 ♗d2 ♖d7 24 ♕f1 ♗a3! = Engel-Sanakoev, corr. 1976-9.

d) 14...♖d8 with the following possibilities:

d1) 15 g6 hxg6 16 ♖xg6 fxg6 17 ♗xe6+ ♔f8 18 ♘d5 ♕b8 possibly favours Black but is still interesting.

d2) 15 h4!? ♖b8 16 h5 ♘c5 17 g6 fxg6 18 hxg6 h6 ∞ Dominguez-Camilleri, Dubai OL 1986.

d3) 15 f4!? deserves attention.

d4) 15 ♖g3!? with little-studied complications; for example, 15...♘c5 (15...g6!? 16 h4 ♖b8 17 h5 a5 Polugaevsky) 16 ♖h3 (16 e5 d5 17 ♖h4 ♘xb3+ 18 axb3 ♕xe5 19 ♕d3 ♕f5! Nikitin) 16...♘xb3+ (16...g6!? with a possible idea being 17 e5 ♗b7 18 ♖dh4 ♘xb3+ 19 axb3 ♗g2) 17 axb3 e5!? 18 ♘d5 ♕d7 (18...♕b7!?) 19 ♖h4 exd4 20 ♕h5 h6 21 gxh6 ♗xh4 22 hxg7 f6 23 ♕h8+ ♔f7 (Bielak-Abramowicz, corr. 1992-4) 24 ♕xh4!?.

d5) 15 ♕h5 is not too promising:

d51) 15...♘c5 16 e5 (16 f4 ♗b7!?; 16 ♖g3 g6 17 ♕h6 ♗f8 18 ♕h4 – 15...g6! 16 ♕h6 ♗f8 17 ♕h4 ♘c5 18 ♖g3) 16...g6, and then:

d511) 17 ♕h6 ♗f8 18 ♕h3 ♗g7 (18...d5 19 ♖h4 ♕xe5!? 20 ♗d4 ♕f5 21 ♕g3 gives White compensation: 21...♗d6 22 f4 ♗b7 23 ♔b1 h5 24 gxh6 ♔h7 25 ♕e3, Kang-Grishchuk, Oropesa del Mar jr Wch 1998) 19 ♖h4! (19 ♖xd6?! ♗b7! ∓ de Firmian-Shirov, Biel 1995) 19...d5! (19...h5?! 20 gxh6 ♗xe5 21 ♗g5!) 20 ♖gg4!? ∞ Shirov.

d512) 17 ♕h3 d5 (17...♗b7? 18 ♖h4 ♘xb3+ 19 axb3 h5 20 ♖xh5! gxh5 21 ♕xh5 ±) 18 ♖h4 ♕xe5 19 ♗d4 ♘xb3+?! (19...♕f5 is similar to 17 ♕h6 ♗f8 18 ♕h3 d5 19 ♖h4 ♕xe5!? 20 ♗d4 ♕f5) 20 axb3 ♕f5 21 ♕g3!? ♗b7 22 ♔b1! (22 ♖h6? ♗d6 23 ♖xh7 ♕f4+!) 22...♗d6 23 f4 (23 ♖xh7!?) 23...h5 24 gxh6 ♔h7 25 ♘d1 with an attack, V.Pavlov-Kharitonov, corr. 1986.

d52) 15...g6! 16 ♕h6 (16 ♕h4?! ♘c5 17 f4 ♖b8 18 f5 a5 ∓ Radulov-Ribli, Kecskemet 1972) and here:

d521) 16...♖b8!? – 14...♖b8 15 ♕h5 g6!? 16 ♕h6 ♖d8.

d522) 16...♘c5 and now: 17 ♖g3 ♗f8 18 ♕h4 – *16...♗f8 17 ♕h4 ♘c5 18 ♖g3*; 17 e5 – *15...♘c5 16 e5 g6 17 ♕h3*.

d523) 16...♗f8 leads to unclear play: 17 ♕h4 (17 ♕h3!? ♗g7 18 e5 ∞ V.Pavlov-Poletukhin, corr. 1998) 17...♘c5 (17...♗e7!?; 17...♗g7!?) 18 ♖g3 (18 f4!? Lysenko) and now 18...♖b8 19 ♖h3 h5! 20 gxh6 ♔h7 (Nikitin), or 18...♗e7 19 f4 ♖b8 20 f5 a5!? (20...h5) 21 f6 ♗f8 22 ♕xh7+ ♔xh7 23 ♖h3+ ♗h6! 24 ♖xh6+ ♔g8 25 e5 ♘xb3+ 26 axb3 ♕c5.

We now return to 14...♘c5 *(D)*:

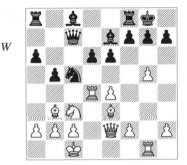

Now:

a) 15 f4 – *14 f4 ♘c5 15 ♖g1*.

b) After 15 ♕h5 g6 16 ♕h6, both 16...f5 17 ♔b1 (17 gxf6 ♗xf6 ∓ Nunn-Langeweg, Malta OL 1980) 17...♖b8!? and 16...♖d8 (see *14...♖d8 15 ♕h5 g6 16 ♕h6 ♘c5*) are satisfactory.

c) 15 ♖g3 g6 (15...f5 16 ♖h3 f4!? 17 ♕h5 ∞) 16 e5 (16 h4!?; 16 f4!? – Lanka) 16...dxe5 (16...d5 Nikitin) 17 ♖h4 f5 18 gxf6 ♘xb3+ 19 axb3 ♗xf6 20 ♖hg4 ♗b7!? 21 h4 ♔h8 22 ♗h6 ♖f7 23 ♘e4 = Boleslavsky.

d) 15 e5!? leads to a very tough struggle:

d1) 15...dxe5? 16 ♖h4 ♘xb3+ (or 16...g6 17 ♖xc5! ♕xc5 18 ♘e4 ♕c7 19 ♘f6+ +– Aseev) 17 axb3 g6 18 ♘e4 (18 ♕f3 e4! is just slightly better for White) 18...f5 19 gxf6 ♗xf6 20 ♖hg4 ♗g7 21 h4 ♖f5 22 h5 ♖xh5 23 ♘f6+! +– Grechikhyn-Glek, Kuibyshev 1981.

d2) 15...♘xb3+ 16 axb3 d5 17 ♖h4 g6 (17...♕xe5 18 ♕d3 g6 can be met by 19 ♗d4 ♕xg5+ 20 ♖xg5 ♗xg5+ 21 ♗e3 ♗xh4 22 ♕d4 ♗e7 23 ♗h6 or 19 f4!?) 18 f4 (18 ♖g3!? ♕xe5 19 f4) 18...♗b7 (18...b4!?) 19 ♖g3 ♗g7 20 f5!? exf5 21 e6 with an attack, Carr-Markland, corr. 1978.

d3) 15...g6 16 exd6!? (16 ♖h4 ♗b7 17 ♖g3 ♘xb3+!? 18 axb3 dxe5 19 ♖gh3 ♗g2) 16...♗xd6 17 ♖xd6 ♕xd6 18 ♖d1 with compensation, Böröcz-Szilardfy, Budapest 1993.

d4) 15...d5!? 16 ♖h4 (I do not think White achieves anything better by 16 f4, 16 ♕h5 ♕xe5!?, 16 ♗xd5 exd5 17 ♘xd5 ♕xe5! 18 f4 ♕e6 19 f5 ♕e5 20 f6 ♗d8!? or 16 ♗d2 ♗b7 17 ♖h4 g6 18 ♖g3 ♖fc8!) 16...♕xe5 17 ♖g3, and besides 17...♕f5 18 ♖gh3 with the point 18...♘xb3+ 19 axb3 ♗xg5 20 ♖xh7 ♗xe3+ 21 ♕xe3 ♕xh7 22 ♖xh7 ♔xh7 23 ♘e4, it is worth studying 17...b4!?.

**Conclusion:** as of now, 13...b5 14 f4 is interesting for White. Therefore, 13...♘c5!? (with possibly 14 f4 f5! or 14 ♖g1 b5) deserves attention.

## B22)

**11 ♖hg1** *(D)*

Now, White can always take on d4 with the bishop. However, 11 ♖hg1 certainly has definite drawbacks as well...

**B221: 11...⑤a5** 176
**B222: 11...b5!?** 177
**B223: 11...⑤d7** 179

11...⑤xd4 12 ⑤xd4 b5 (or 12...⑤d7 13 g4 – *11...⑤d7 12 g4 ⑤xd4 13 ⑤xd4*) 13 g4 followed by 14 g5 will transpose to the variations with *11...⑤d7 12 g4 ⑤xd4 13 ⑤xd4 b5*, which are very risky for Black.

## B221)
**11...⑤a5 12 g4 b5 13 g5 ⑤xb3+**
13...⑤d7 is worth trying; for example, 14 ⑥d5 ⑥b7!? 15 ⑤xe6 (15 g6 exd5!) 15...fxe6 16 ⑥xe6+ ⑥h8.
**14 axb3 ⑤d7 15 f4!**
Other moves seem unclear:

a) 15 h4 b4 16 ⑤a4 ⑥b7!? (or 16...⑤c5 17 h5 ⑥d7 18 ⑥b1 ⑥ac8 19 g6 ⑥f6!?, Ehlvest-Yudasin, Kuibyshev 1986) 17 f3 (17 g6?! hxg6 18 h5 e5!) 17...⑤c5!?.

b) 15 ⑨h5 g6 (15...b4!? 16 ⑤f5 ⑤e5, Velimirović-Cebalo, Titograd 1984; 15...⑥b7!?) 16 ⑨h6 ⑥e8 (after 16...⑥b7 17 ⑥g3 ⑥fc8 18 ⑥h3 ⑤f8 19 ⑤f5 exf5 20 ⑥d4 f6 21 exf5 ⑥d8 22 gxf6! White is winning, Berlin-Sokolov, Jurmala 1977) 17 ⑥g3 ⑥f8 18 ⑨h4 b4!.

c) 15 ⑤f5 exf5 16 ⑤d5 ⑨d8 17 exf5 ⑥e8 (17...⑥b7 18 f6 ⑥xd5 19 fxe7 ⑨xe7 20 ⑥xd5 ±) 18 ⑨f3 (18 g6!?; 18 f6 ⑥f8 19 fxg7 ⑥xg7 20 ⑨h5 ⑥b7 −+) 18...⑥b8 (18...⑥f8 19 ⑤f6+ ⑤xf6 20 gxf6 with compensation – Shakarov) 19 f6 ⑥f8 20 fxg7 (20 g6 hxg6 21 ⑥xg6 ⑤e5 22 ⑥xg7+ ⑥xg7 23 ⑨g3 ⑤g6 −+) 20...⑥xg7 21 ⑤f6+, Trabattoni-Grimaldi, Tripoli 1976.

d) 15 ⑥g3 and then:

d1) 15...⑥b7 16 f4 b4 17 ⑤d5! exd5 18 ⑤f5 ⑤c5!? 19 ⑥d4 ⑤e6 20 exd5 ⑥xd5 21 ⑥b6 ⑨b7 22 ⑤xe7+ ⑨xe7 23 ⑥xd5 ±.

d2) 15...b4!? 16 ⑤f5 (16 ⑤a4!?) 16...exf5 17 ⑤d5 ⑨d8 18 exf5 ⑥e8 19 ⑨f3 (19 f6 ⑥f8 20 fxg7 ⑥xg7 21 ⑨h5 ⑥xe3!?; 19 g6!?) 19...⑥f8 20 ⑤f6+ ⑤xf6 21 gxf6 ⑥b8! 22 fxg7 (22 ⑥d4 g6 23 fxg6 ⑥h6+! ∓ Stean) 22...⑥e7 23 ⑨f4 ⑨a5!? 24 f6 ⑥f5! ∓.

d3) 15...⑥e8 16 f4 (16 h4!?; 16 ⑨h5 g6 17 ⑨h6 – *15 ⑨h5 g6 16 ⑨h6 ⑥e8 17 ⑥g3*) 16...b4 is unclear.
**15...b4**
Or:

a) 15...⑤c5 16 ⑤f5!? ⑤xb3+ 17 ⑥b1! exf5 18 ⑤d5 ⑨b7 19 e5! dxe5 20 ⑤f6+! +− Hoffer-Johnson, corr. 1989.

b) 15...⑥b7 16 f5 (16 ⑥g3!? – *15 ⑥g3 ⑥b7 16 f4*) 16...b4 17 ⑤a4 – *15...b4 16 ⑤a4 ⑥b7 17 f5*.

c) 15...⑥e8 16 f5 (16 ⑥g3 – *15 ⑥g3 ⑥e8 16 f4*) 16...⑤e5 17 h4!? gives White the initiative.

d) 15...⑤b6!? 16 f5 b4 Nikitin.
**16 ⑤f5!**
This is better than:

a) 16 ⑤a2 ⑥b7 17 f5 e5 is slightly better for Black, Van der Wiel-Ligterink, Wijk aan Zee 1985.

b) 16 ♘a4 ♗b7 (16...♘c5!? 17 f5 with complications; 16...♖e8 17 f5 e5?! 18 g6!; e.g., 18...fxg6 19 fxg6 exd4 20 gxh7+ ♔h8 21 ♖xg7 ♘f6?! 22 ♗xd4! ♔xg7 23 ♕h5 +−) 17 f5 e5 18 f6 exd4 19 fxe7 ♖fe8 20 ♖xd4 ♖xe7 = Velimirović-Ivanović, Yugoslav Ch (Belgrade) 1978.

**16...exf5?**

The knight cannot be captured here but it seems Black faces problems either way:

a) 16...♗d8 17 ♘d5! (17 ♘h6+ ♔h8! 18 ♕h5 g6!; 17 ♕h5 bxc3!; 17 ♘xg7 bxc3! 18 ♕h5 ♔xg7!?) 17...exd5 18 ♕h5 ♘c5 19 ♘xg7 d4 20 ♖xd4 ♔xg7 21 ♕h6+ ♔g8 22 f5 ♘xb3+ 23 ♔d1!, with a probable win.

b) 16...bxc3 17 ♘xe7+ ♔h8 18 f5!.

c) 16...♖e8 17 ♘h6+ with the initiative.

d) 16...♘c5 17 ♘xe7+ (17 ♘h6+?! ♔h8!) 17...♕xe7 18 e5! (18 ♗xc5?! dxc5 19 ♘a4 ♗d7 is slightly better for Dlack) 18...bxc3 (18...dxc5? 19 ♗xc5 ♕xc5 20 ♘e4; 18...d5 19 ♕f2, Nunn-Arakhamia, British League (4NCL) 1996/7, 19...♘xb3+!?) 19 exd6 cxb2+ 20 ♔xb2 (20 ♔b1?? ♕d8 21 ♗xc5 ♕a5) 20...♘a4+ (20...♕a7 21 ♗d4! ±) 21 ♔a3! (21 bxa4?! ♕b7+ 22 ♔c1 ♖b8 Nunn) 21...♕e8 (21...♕d7 22 ♕c4) 22 ♗d4 ♕b5 23 ♕e5 – da Costa Junior.

**17 ♘d5 ♕d8 18 exf5 ♖e8 19 ♗d4!!**

Otherwise, the problems are all White's.

**19...♗f8**

Or:

a) 19...g6 20 ♖ge1!? +−.

b) 19...♗f6 20 ♕xe8+ ♕xe8 21 gxf6 g6 (Nijboer-Winants, Wijk aan Zee 1988) 22 ♖de1 ±.

c) 19...♗b7 loses to 20 g6: 20...hxg6 (20...fxg6 21 ♕e6+ ♔h8 22 ♗xg7+!; 20...f6 21 gxh7+ ♔h8 22 ♖xg7 ♗xd5 23 ♖dg1!; 20...♗f6 21 gxf7+ ♔xf7 22 ♕h5+) 21 fxg6 ♘f6 22 ♘xf6+ (22 ♕g2!?) 22...♗xf6 23 gxf7+ ♔xf7 24 ♕h5+ ♔g8 25 ♖xg7+ ♗xg7 26 ♗xg7 ♗f3 27 ♕g6!.

**20 ♕h5 ♖e4 21 ♗f6**

This position arose in the game Wolff-I.Sokolov, Baguio jr Wch 1987. Now 21...♕a5 22 g6 fxg6 23 fxg6 h6 24 ♗xg7 (Nikitin) is much better for White.

**B222)**

**11...b5!?** *(D)*

This is the critical and biting reply to 11 ♖hg1. Virtually no clear-cut assessments have been made here.

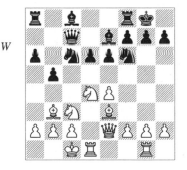

We shall proceed with our discussion along the historical main line, bearing in mind that both sides have significant alternatives at almost every move.

**12 g4**

12 ♘xc6!? ♕xc6 13 g4 ♘xe4 14 ♘d5.

**12...b4(!)**

12...♘a5 and 12...♘xd4 are less important.

**13 ♘xc6**

Other possibilities:

a) 13 ♘a4?! ♘xe4 14 ♘xe6 ♗xe6! ∓.

b) 13 g5!? bxc3 14 gxf6 is very unclear:

b1) 14...cxb2+ 15 ♔b1 ♗xf6 16 ♘xc6 (16 ♕f3 ♗e5 17 ♗h6 – *14...♗xf6! 15 ♕f3 ♗e5 16 ♗h6 cxb2+ 17 ♔b1*) 16...♕xc6 17 ♗h6 and now 17...g6 18 f4!? or 17...♔h8 18 e5 gxh6 19 exf6 ♗b7 20 ♕h5.

b2) 14...♗xf6! is more accurate: 15 ♕f3 (15 ♘xc6 ♕xc6 16 ♗h6 can be met by 16...g6 or 16...♕b5!?) 15...♗e5 16 ♗h6 cxb2+ 17 ♔b1 g6 18 ♕c3 (Matulović-Nikitin, Kislovodsk 1966; 18 ♘xc6!? ♕xc6 19 ♗xf8 ♔xf8 20 ♕e3) 18...♗b7!? 19 f4 ♗f6 20 ♗xf8 ♖xf8 21 ♗a4 ♕a5! – Kasparov/Nikitin.

c) 13 ♘d5 ♘xd5 (13...exd5 14 ♘xc6 ♕xc6 – *13 ♘xc6 ♕xc6 14 ♘d5 exd5*) 14 ♘xc6 (scarcely any better for White is 14 exd5 ♘xd4 15 ♖xd4 a5 16 ♖c4 ♕b8 17 dxe6 ♗xe6 18 ♖c6 d5, Ljubojević-Korchnoi, Tilburg 1985) 14...♘xe3!? 15 ♘xe7+ ♕xe7 16 ♕xe3 a5 with good play for Black, Stean-Velimirović, Nice OL 1974.

**13...♕xc6** *(D)*

Or 13...bxc3!? 14 ♘xe7+ ♕xe7 15 ♗d4 ♗b7! 16 f3 cxb2+ 17 ♗xb2 ♖fd8, Hamdouchi-Dorfman, French Cht 1996.

**14 ♘d5 exd5**

Or:

a) 14...♗d8?! 15 g5!, Matulović-Simagin, Kislovodsk 1966.

b) 14...♘xd5!? 15 exd5 ♕b7 is interesting and quite reliable. For instance, 16 f4 (16 g5!?; 16 dxe6!? fxe6 17 ♗d4 d5 18 g5 ♗d6, Lyly-Karpati, corr. 1987), and now:

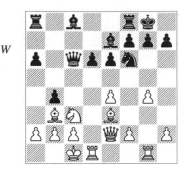

b1) After 16...a5, 17 dxe6 fxe6 18 f5?! a4! favours Black, but 17 ♗d4 a4 18 ♗c4 is stronger, Jovičić-Pesl, corr. 1985.

b2) 16...♖e8 17 ♕d3 ♗f8 18 dxe6 ♗xe6 19 ♗xe6 ♖xe6 seems satisfactory for Black, Kobaliya-Panchenko, Moscow 1996.

**15 g5 ♘xe4**

15...dxe4? 16 gxf6 ♗xf6 17 ♗d5 ♕a4 18 ♕h5! ♗e6 19 ♖xg7+! ♗xg7 20 ♖g1 ♖fc8 21 ♖xg7+ ♔xg7 22 ♕h6+ ♔g8 23 ♗xe4 +− Ostapenko-Yartsev, corr. 1969.

**16 ♗xd5 ♕a4**

16...♘c3?! 17 bxc3 ♕a4 18 ♗b3! ± with the point 18...♕a3+ 19 ♔b1 bxc3 20 ♗c1 – Nikitin.

**17 ♗xe4!?**

Otherwise:

a) 17 ♗d4 is not much good in view of 17...♗f5! 18 ♗xe4 ♗xe4 19 ♕xe4 ♕xa2!? 20 ♕xe7 ♖ae8! 21 ♕c7! ♖e4! 22 ♗e3 ♖c4 23 ♕xd6 b3, Arwedson-Wikström, corr. 1979.

b) 17 ♗xa8 gives White no advantage: 17...♘c3 18 bxc3 ♗e6 (18...bxc3? 19 ♖d4 ♕xa2 20 ♔d1 +−; 18...♕a3+?! 19 ♔b1 ♗e6! 20 ♗d5 ♗xd5 21 c4!) 19 ♗d4 (19 ♗d5 ♗xd5! 20 ♖xd5?! ♕xa2 21 ♗d4 ♖e8! ∓; 19 ♗e4 ♕a3+

=) 19...bxc3 (19...♖xa8? 20 g6! +−) 20 ♗xc3 ♖xa8 21 g6 hxg6 22 ♖xg6 ♕f4+ 23 ♗d2 (23 ♖d2 fxg6 24 ♕xe6+ ♕f7 =) 23...♕d4 (23...♕f5 24 ♖g3 ♖b8!? Nikitin) 24 c3 ♕c5 (24...♕e5?!) 25 ♖dg1 ♕a3+ 26 ♔d1 ♗b3+! 27 ♔e1 fxg6 28 axb3 ♕xb3 29 ♕xe7 ♕b1+ 30 ♔e2 ♕xg1 31 ♕e6+ = Nadenić-Sarenac, corr. 1989.

**17...♗e6 18 ♗d4**

After 18 ♗xh7+?! ♔xh7 19 ♕h5+ ♔g8 20 g6 fxg6 21 ♕xg6 ♗f6 22 ♗d4 b3!! (Nikitin) 23 axb3 ♕a1+ 24 ♔d2 ♕a5+ 25 ♔c1 Black can choose between 25...♕a1+ = and 25...♗xd4!?.

**18...g6!**

The critical position. Now:

a) 19 f4 gives both sides chances.

b) 19 h4 likewise.

c) 19 ♗xa8 ♖xa8 20 b3 ♕xa2 (Stean-Dueball, Nice OL 1974) is unclear; e.g., 21 ♗b2 ♖c8 22 ♖d2 ♕xb3 23 ♕xa6 ♕f3.

d) 19 b3!? is interesting. After 19...♕xa2 20 ♔d2 ♕a5 21 ♖a1 ♕d8 22 ♗xa8 ♕xa8 (Tabatadze-Akopian, USSR 1985) and now, e.g., 23 ♖xa6, the onus is on Black to prove his compensation.

## B223)

**11...♘d7**

This is the main line.

**12 g4**

The same position also arises from *11 g4 ♘d7 12 ♖hg1* and deserves special attention – see Line B23. White has nothing better than this move, as we can see from examining the alternatives:

a) After 12 ♔b1 ♘c5 13 ♕h5, I propose 13...♘xb3 14 cxb3 ♕a5 (instead of the line recommended by

Nikitin: 14...♗d7 15 g4 ♘xd4 16 ♖xd4 f6, which seems somewhat passive), 13...♘xd4!? 14 ♗xd4 ♕a5, Kengis-Lerner, Jurmala 1983, or 13...♕a5!? 14 ♘xc6 bxc6 15 ♗xc5 g6! 16 ♗xd6! ♕xh5 17 ♗xe7 ♖e8 18 ♗f6 ∞ Taborov-Salov, Nikolaev 1983.

b) 12 ♕h5 also intends g4, ♖g3, ♖h3, but Black has two good replies:

b1) Not 12...♘xd4 13 ♗xd4 b5 14 ♖d3! (Larsen).

b2) 12...♕a5! = Jokšić-Langeweg, Plovdiv 1975.

b3) 12...♘f6!? 13 ♕f3 ♘d7 14 g4 ♘de5 15 ♕h3 ♘xd4 with complications, Velimirović-Kelečević, Yugoslav Ch (Herceg Novi) 1983.

## B23)

**11 ♖hg1 ♘d7 12 g4** *(D)*

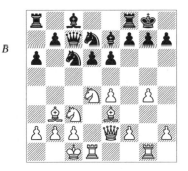

**12...♘c5**

The only alternative worth mentioning is the risky 12...♘xd4 13 ♗xd4 b5 (13...♘c5 14 g5! – *12...♘c5 13 g5 ♘xd4 14 ♗xd4*) 14 g5!, and then:

a) 14...♘c5 – *12...♘c5 13 g5 ♘xd4 14 ♗xd4 b5*.

b) 14...♖d8 15 ♕h5!? g6 16 ♕h6 ♗f8 17 ♕h4 ± Nunn-Podzielny, Groningen jr Ech 1974/5.

c) After 14...♖e8, 15 ♘d5?! exd5 16 g6 hxg6 17 ♗xd5 ♗b7 18 ♖xg6 ♗f6! (Vaulin-Poluliakhov, Sochi 1988) is probably in Black's favour, but White could play 15 ♖d3 or 15 ♕h5.

d) 14...b4 15 ♕h5! (15 ♘d5? exd5 16 ♗xd5 ♗b7 17 g6 ♗f6! 18 ♕h5 ♖fc8! 19 ♕xh7+ ♔f8 20 ♗b3 ♘c5 21 ♗c4 ♘d3+! ∓ de Zeeuw; 15 g6!? hxg6 16 ♘d5 ♕d8! Zak) 15...♘e5 (15...bxc3 16 ♖d3! with an attack which is difficult to refute, Bosch-D.Gross, Schoneck 1996) and now 16 ♗xe5!? dxe5 17 ♖d3 or Bosch's 16 f4!? is more promising than 16 ♘a4 ♗b7!?.

e) 14...♗b7 15 ♕h5 (15 ♖d3!? Zak) 15...♘c5! transposes to note 'd3' to Black's 14th move in Line B2311 (Black must avoid 15...b4? 16 g6 +− and 15...g6? 16 ♕h6 e5 17 ♖d3 +−).

f) 14...g6!? 15 h4 ♘c5 – *12...♘c5 13 g5 ♘xd4 14 ♗xd4! g6!? 15 h4 b5*.

Now (after 12...♘c5):

**B231: 13 g5**     180
**B232: 13 ♘f5!**   186

There are almost no examples of 13 f4. One of them is: 13...b5 14 f5 b4 15 ♘a4 ♗d7!? 16 ♘xc6 ♘xb3+ 17 axb3 ♗xc6, and Black stands no worse, Lukin-N.Popov, Daugavpils 1974.

13 ♔b1!? is not a very strong move but it carries a lot of poison:

a) 13...♗d7 14 ♘f5 exf5 15 gxf5 ♕d8?! 16 ♗h6 leads to an attack for White.

b) 13...b5 14 ♘xc6! (better than 14 ♘f5 ♘xb3!? 15 cxb3 b4 Gagarin; 14 g5 – *13 g5 b5 14 ♔b1*) 14...♕xc6 15 ♘d5 and then:

b1) 15...♗d8?! 16 g5 ♘h8 (alternatively, 16...♘xb3 17 ♘f6+ gxf6 18 gxf6+ ♔h8 19 ♕g4 ♗xf6 20 ♗h6 +−

Akopian or 16...♘xe4 17 ♕f3 ±) 17 ♕h5 ♘xe4 18 ♖d4 ±.

b2) 15...♖a7 16 g5 exd5 17 ♗xd5 ♕e8 18 g6 ♗f6 19 f4 ♘xe4 20 ♕h5 hxg6 21 ♖xg6 ♗e6!? 22 ♗xe4 ♗xa2+ 23 ♔xa2 ♕xe4 24 ♖xf6 ♕xe3 (M.Pavlović-Krakops, Ubeda 1997) 25 ♕g4 with compensation.

c) 13...♖e8 14 g5 ♗d7 15 f4 b5 16 f5 ♘xb3 (16...b4 17 g6 fxg6 18 ♘d5!) 17 axb3 b4 (17...♘xd4 18 ♗xd4 b4 19 g6 fxg6 20 fxg6 h6 21 ♘a4 ±; 17...♘e5!? 18 ♘f3 g6! – Brunner) 18 g6! fxg6 19 fxg6 ± (Brunner-Hübner, Bundesliga 1989/90) 19...h6 20 ♕h5 ♗f6 21 ♗xh6 gxh6 22 ♕xh6 ♖e7 23 ♘f5 ♗e8 24 ♘xe7+ ♕xe7 (Brunner) 25 ♖df1! +− Burgess.

d) 13...♘xd4 14 ♗xd4 b5 15 g5 gives White chances but no real advantage:

d1) 15...♖e8 16 ♕h5 g6 17 ♕h6 ♗f8 18 ♕h4 with a slight advantage for White, M.Pavlović-Arakhamia, Greek Cht 1996.

d2) 15...b4 16 ♕h5 bxc3? (Black should try 16...♘xb3!?) 17 ♕h6! +− M.Pavlović-Atalik, Ilioupolis 1995 (17...e5 18 g6!).

d3) 15...♘xb3 16 axb3 b4 17 ♗f6 bxc3 (17...♗b7!) 18 ♕h5 with an attack, Ochoa-Pablo Marin, Almeria 1989.

d4) 15...♗b7!? 16 ♕h5 ♘xb3 17 axb3 b4 seems adequate, Strauts-Shabalov, Latvian Ch (Riga) 1987.

## B231)
**13 g5** *(D)*
A standard scheme of attack.
Now:

**B2311: 13...b5**     181
**B2312: 13...♗d7!**   183

*B*

Few other moves have been played here. Exchanges are rather premature:

a) 13...♘xd4 14 ♗xd4! and now:

a1) 14...b5 15 ♕h5 (15 ♗d5 – *13...b5 14 ♗d5 ♘xd4 15 ♗xd4*; 15 ♗f6 ♗b7; 15 f4!?) – *13...b5 14 ♕h5 ♘xd4 15 ♗xd4!*.

a2) 14...♖e8 15 ♖g3 (15 ♕h5!) 15...♘xb3+ 16 axb3 ♕a5 (16...g6!) 17 ♔b1 e5 18 b4! ± Hellers-Cebalo, Herning 1991.

a3) 14...g6!? 15 h4 (15 e5!? b5) 15...b5 16 h5 ♘xb3+ 17 axb3 b4 18 ♘a4 e5 with counter-chances, Tobyas-Orsag, Czech Ch (Prague) 1992.

b) 13...♘xb3+ 14 axb3 (14 cxb3!?) and now:

b1) 14...b5 and now 15 ♘xc6 and 15 ♕h5 are both stronger than 15 ♖g3 b4 16 ♕c4!? (Parma), which is unclear.

b2) 14...g6!? is possible.

b3) 14...♗d7! is again the most reliable continuation.

## B2311)
**13...b5**

This move is difficult to assess. Many of the most important lines from here lead to positions that have already been considered via *9...0-0 10 0-0-0 ♕e8* in Line A2.

**14 ♕h5!?**

This is the most popular. Instead:

a) 14 ♖g3?! b4! (Nunn) favours Black.

b) 14 ♔b1 is harmless; for example, 14...♘xb3 (14...♗d7 – *13...♗d7 14 ♔b1 b5*) 15 axb3 ♗d7 (15...b4 16 ♘a4 ♗d7 = Danner/Polajzer) 16 f4 b4 17 ♘a4 ♘xd4 18 ♗xd4 ♗xa4 19 bxa4 e5 = Ljubojević-Korchnoi, Lucerne Wcht 1989.

c) 14 ♗d5 is unconvincing:

c1) 14...exd5(?) 15 ♘xd5 ♘xd4 16 ♗xd4 ♕b7, and now 17 ♘f6+ ♔h8!? (17...♗xf6 18 gxf6 ♕xe4 19 ♖xg7+ ♔h8 20 ♕xe4 ♘xe4 21 f3 ±) 18 ♕h5 ♗xf6 19 gxf6 g6 20 ♕h6 ♖g8! 21 ♗xc5 ♗e6 is not so clear. However, 17 ♕h5(!) and 17 ♗f6 are possible.

c2) 14...♘xd4!? 15 ♗xd4 is possible, and now Black may not venture upon 15...exd5(?) 16 ♘xd5. Instead, 15...b4 transposes to note 'c1' to Black's 14th move in Line A21.

c3) 14...♗b7 and now: 15 ♘f5!? – *13 ♘f5 b5 14 ♗d5 ♗b7 15 g5*; 15 ♘xc6 ♗xc6 – *14...♗d7 15 ♘xc6!? ♗xc6*.

c4) 14...♗d7 15 ♘f5 (15 ♘xc6!? ♗xc6 16 ♗xc5 dxc5 17 ♗xc6 ♕xc6 18 e5 Gufeld) 15...exf5 16 g6 ♗e6 17 exf5 ♗xf5 18 gxf7+ ♖xf7 19 ♗xf7+ ♔xf7 and Black is OK, Gdanski-H.Grünberg, Stara Zagora Z 1990.

d) 14 ♘xc6!? ♕xc6 transposes to the note to Black's 14th move in Line A21.

We now return to 14 ♕h5 *(D)*:

**14...b4**

This is the 'main' move, but is also extremely risky. Other ideas:

a) 14...♗d7?! 15 ♖g3 – *13...♗d7 14 ♖g3 b5?! 15 ♕h5*.

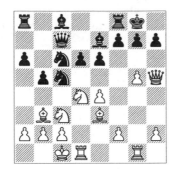

b)  14...罝d8?! 15 ②xc6 彎xc6?! 16
奧d5!, Djurhuus-Kaspersen, Copenhagen 1988.

c)  14...罝e8 15 ②xc6 (other ideas
are 15 奧d5!? g6 16 彎h6 奧d7 17 罝g3
奧f8 18 彎h4, Renet-Piket, Groningen
1984 and 15 ②f5!?) 15...②xb3+ 16
axb3 彎xc6 17 奧d4 transposes to Line
A21.

d)  14...②xd4 (also risky) 15 奧xd4!
and then:

d1)  15...b4? allows both 16 彎h6!?
± and 16 奧f6! 罝e8 17 罝g3 bxc3 18
罝h3 h6 19 彎xh6!! +−.

d2)  15...②xb3+?! 16 axb3 is difficult for Black: 16...b4 17 彎h6 e5 18
②d5 +−; 16...奧b7 17 罝d3; or 16...g6
17 彎h6 f6 18 f4 ± C.Hansson-Tim-
merman, corr. 1982.

d3)  15...奧b7! and now:

d31)  16 奧f6 罝fc8! 17 罝g4 (17 罝d4
②xb3+ 18 axb3 e5 19 罝d2 b4 20 ②d5
奧xd5 21 exd5 a5!) 17...b4! 18 罝h4
奧xe4 19 罝xe4 bxc3 20 罝h4 ②xb3+
21 當b1 ②d2+ 22 罝xd2 h6 23 罝d1
(Bordonada-Mir.Pavlov, Nice OL 1974)
23...cxb2 24 c4 彎a5! is much better
for Black − Akopian.

d32)  16 f3 ②xb3+ 17 axb3 e5 18
奧e3 罝fc8 ∞ Hodges-Malevich, corr.
1995.

d33)  16 罝g4 ②xb3+ (16...罝fc8?
17 罝h4! h6 18 罝g1 +−) 17 axb3 e5 18
奧e3 (scarcely better is 18 罝h4 h6 19
罝g1 exd4, Nedev-Relange, Pula Echt
1997) 18...罝ac8 19 罝d2 g6 20 彎h6 f5
21 gxf6 奧xf6 = J.R.Koch-Relange,
French Ch (Chambéry) 1994.

d34)  16 罝g3 and now:

d341)  16...②xe4?! 17 g6! hxg6 18
罝xg6 fxg6 19 奧xe6+ 罝f7 20 彎xg6
奧g5+ 21 當b1 當f8! 22 ②xe4 奧xe4 23
彎xe4 罝e8 24 彎g6 罝fe7 25 彎h7 罝xe6
26 彎h8+ 當e7 27 彎xg7+ 當d8 28
彎xg5+ ±.

d342)  16...罝fc8 17 f3 ②xb3+ 18
axb3 e5 19 罝h3 favours White, Val-
enti-Toth, Reggio Emilia 1975.

d343)  16...罝ac8! (Paoli) deserves
attention.

*In conclusion:* although things are
far from clear, 14...②xd4 can hardly
be recommended.

e)  14...g6!? (this still seems playable) 15 彎h6 and then:

e1)  15...②xb3+ 16 axb3 f6 17 f4
fxg5 18 f5! ± Gheorghescu-Tratato-
vici, Romania 1977.

e2)  15...罝d8 16 罝g3 (16 奧d5?! 奧f8
17 彎h4 b4!, Stukaturkin-Goichman,
Krasnoiarsk 1974) 16...奧f8 17 彎h4
b4?! (Black should try 17...奧e7!?) 18
②xc6 彎xc6 19 奧d4 ± J.Hartston-
Alexandria, Menorca wom IZ 1973.

e3)  15...罝e8! 16 罝g3 (16 奧d5!? −
*14...罝e8 15 奧d5!? g6 16 彎h6*)
16...奧f8 17 彎h4 b4 (17...奧e7!? is
possible; then 18 ②f5 ②xb3+ 19 axb3
exf5 20 ②d5 彎a5 is unconvincing for
White) and now:

e31)  18 ②a4!? is unclear.

e32)  18 ②xc6!? ②xb3+ 19 axb3
彎xc6 (19...bxc3 20 奧d4 e5 21 ②b4 ±)
20 奧d4 (20 罝h3!? h5 21 gxh6 e5!

A.Pereira) 20...h5! (20...e5 21 ♘d5 ±) 21 gxh6 e5 22 ♘d5 exd4 23 ♖dg1 transposes to Line A21.

e33) 18 ♖h3!? h5 (18...♗g7?! 19 ♕xh7+ ♔f8 20 ♘f5!?) 19 gxh6 bxc3 20 ♘xc6 (better than 20 ♕f6?! ♔h7, Magerramov-Tal, Moscow simul 1974) 20...♘xb3+ 21 axb3 e5! (21...♗b7 22 ♕f6 ♔h7 23 ♗b6! +−) 22 ♖f3 (22 ♘b4 ♕a5!) 22...♗e6 23 ♘d4!? cxb2+ 24 ♔xb2 ♔h7! = V.Khenkin.

Now (after 14...b4):

a) 15 ♖g4? bxc3 16 ♖h4 ♘xb3+ 17 axb3 h6 18 ♘xc6 (18 ♖g1 ♕a5!) 18...♕xc6 −+.

b) 15 ♖g3? bxc3 16 ♖h3 h6 (or 16...♘xb3+ first) 17 ♖g1 ♘xb3+ 18 cxb3 ♘xd4 (or 18...♔h8) 19 ♗xd4 cxb2++ 20 ♔xb2 e5 ∓ Sideif-Zade – Mochalov, USSR 1974.

c) 15 ♘a4?! ♗d7 (15...♘xd4 16 ♗xd4 ♘xb3+ 17 axb3 e5 ∓ Gufeld; 15...♘xb3+ 16 axb3 ♗d7!? 17 ♖g3 ♖fc8 18 ♖h3 h6 Mochalov) 16 ♘xc5 ♘xd4 (16...dxc5? 17 ♘f5!) 17 ♗xd4 (17 ♘xd7 ♘xb3+ 18 axb3 ♖fc8 ∓) 17...dxc5 18 ♗f6 (18 ♗xg7 ♔xg7 19 ♖g4 ♖g8 ∓ Sanz-Gheorghiu, Torremolinos 1974) 18...♗b5 19 e5 ♖fd8 20 ♖xd8+ ♖xd8 21 g6 fxg6! 22 ♖xg6 ♗xf6 23 exf6 ♕f4+! 24 ♔b1 ♕f5.

d) 15 ♘ce2 ♘xb3+ 16 axb3 ♘xd4 (V.Pavlov) gives Black counterplay.

e) White should play 15 ♘xc6!:

e1) 15...♕xc6 transposes to note 'b' to Black's 15th move in Line A22.

e2) 15...♘xb3+ 16 axb3 ♕xc6 transposes to Line A22.

## B2312)

**13...♗d7!** *(D)*
This is the most reliable move.
**14 ♕h5**

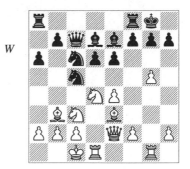

Or:

a) 14 ♖g3 and then:

a1) 14...b5?! 15 ♕h5 b4 16 ♘f5! exf5 17 ♘d5 +− Cappello-Hulak, Rovigo 1972.

a2) 14...♖fd8?! 15 ♔b1!? b5 16 ♘f5!, Z.Nagy-Apro, Hungary 1994.

a3) 14...♘xb3+ 15 axb3 ♖ac8 (other moves are 15...b5?! 16 ♕h5 b4 17 ♘f5! and 15...♖fc8!) 16 ♕h5 g6 17 ♕h6 f6 18 f4 ♖f7 (Soltis-Trincardi, Reggio Emilia 1971) 19 f5! Soltis.

a4) 14...g6!? is interesting.

a5) 14...♖fc8 and then:

a51) 15 f4?! b5! (15...♘xd4 16 ♗xd4 ♘xb3+ 17 axb3 ♗c6 18 f5!?) 16 f5 ♘xb3+ (16...b4!? ∞) 17 axb3 ♘e5 = Seeliger-Kauranen, corr. 1978.

a52) 15 ♔b1 b5! – *14 ♔b1 b5 15 ♖g3 ♖fc8*.

a53) 15 ♕h5 – *14 ♕h5 ♖fc8! 15 ♖g3*.

b) 14 f4?! does not work out well here. 14...b5! (14...♖fc8? 15 f5 ±) and then:

b1) 15 f5?! b4! 16 g6 (16 ♘xc6 ♗xc6 ∓; 16 ♗xe6 ♗xe6 17 g6 bxc3 18 gxh7+ ♔h8 19 ♖xg7 cxb2+ −+ A.Frolov-Krakops, Berlin 1994; 16 f6 bxc3 ∓ Ermenkov-Mednis, Palma de Mallorca 1989; 16 fxe6 can be answered by 16...fxe6 or 16...bxc3!?; 16 ♕h5 is also inadequate) and then:

b11) 16...hxg6!? and then:

b111) 17 fxg6 should be met not by 17...bxc3 18 ♕h5 fxg6 19 ♖xg6 = Golubev-Grasis, USSR jr Cht 1988, but 17...♘e5! ∓.

b112) After 17 ♗xe6!?, rather than 17...bxc3 18 ♖xg6 or 17...♗xe6 18 ♘xe6, Salov-Slesarev, USSR 1974, Black should prefer 17...♘xd4! 18 ♗xf7+ ♔xf7 19 ♗xd4 bxc3, when White's prospects are doubtful.

b12) 16...fxg6!?.

b13) 16...♘xb3+ 17 axb3 fxg6 18 fxg6 bxc3 19 ♕h5 (19 gxh7+ ♔h8 20 ♖xg7 ♕a5! −+) and now, instead of 19...hxg6 20 ♖xg6 ♖f7 (20...♗f6 21 ♖h6 is equal) 21 ♖h6 (21 ♖dg1 ♕a5!) 21...gxh6 (Benjamin-Liberzon, Lone Pine 1980) 22 ♗xh6! =, 19...h6 probably wins.

b2) 15 ♕h5 ♖fc8 and here:

b21) 16 f5 g6! (16...♘xd4 17 ♖xd4 ♘xb3+ 18 axb3 exf5 19 e5) 17 ♕h6 ♗f8 18 ♕h4 b4 19 fxe6 ♘xb3+ is much better for Black, Salgado-Fowell, corr. 1979.

b22) 16 ♔b1 ♘xb3 17 cxb3 b4 ∓.

b23) 16 ♖g3 g6!? 17 ♕h6 – *14 ♕h5 ♖fc8! 15 ♖g3 g6 16 ♕h6 ♗f8 17 ♕h4 ♗e7 18 f4 b5 19 ♕h6.*

c) 14 ♔b1!? probably does not constitute a real threat for Black:

c1) 14...♖fe8(?!) – *13 ♔b1 ♖e8 14 g5 ♗d7.*

c2) 14...♖fc8 and then:

c21) 15 ♖g3 can be answered by 15...♘xb3!? or 15...b5 – *14...b5 15 ♖g3 ♖fc8.*

c22) 15 f4 ♘xd4 (15...b5!?) 16 ♗xd4 b5 17 f5 ♘xb3 18 axb3 b4?! 19 g6 fxg6 20 fxg6 h6 21 ♗xg7! gives

White a dangerous attack, Panchenko-Shestoperov, Cheliabinsk 1977.

c23) 15 ♘f5!? leads to unclear play.

c3) 14...g6!? 15 f4 b5 is satisfactory for Black, Vasiukov-Lukin, Uzhgorod 1972.

c4) 14...♘xb3 15 cxb3 b5 16 ♕h5 b4 17 ♘ce2 ∞ Shamkovich.

c5) 14...b5 and here:

c51) 15 ♖g3 ♖fc8 (15...g6!?) 16 ♘f5 and now:

c511) 16...exf5 17 ♗xf7+ (White can also consider 17 ♘d5!?) 17...♔xf7 18 ♕h5+ ♔g8 19 g6 hxg6 20 ♖xg6 ♘e6!.

c512) 16...♘xb3 17 ♘xe7+ ♘xe7 18 axb3 b4 ∓ Tobyas-Slezka, Czech Cht 1994/5.

c52) 15 ♕h5 and then:

c521) 15...♖fc8 16 ♘f5 g6 (but not 16...♘xb3? 17 ♘h6+ gxh6 18 g6 ♔h8 19 gxf7 ±) and now, rather than 17 ♘xe7+? ♘xe7 18 ♕h6 ♘xb3 ∓ Liepold-Oberst, Bundesliga 1990/1, White should play 17 ♘h6+!?.

c522) 15...g6 16 ♕h6 ♖fc8 17 ♖g3 ♗f8 18 ♕h4 ♘xb3 19 axb3 ♗e7 (= Danner/Polajzer) 20 ♘de2!?.

We now return to the position after 14 ♕h5 *(D)*:

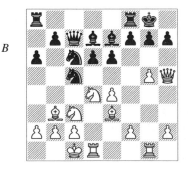

**14...♖fc8!**

14...g6 15 ♕h6 ♖fc8 is also possible.

**15 ♖g3 g6 16 ♕h6 ♗f8 17 ♕h4**

In this critical position 17...♘xd4!? leads to unclear play, and it brings no benefits for White to decline a draw after 17...♗e7.

**17...♗e7**

Or:

a) 17...b5?! 18 ♘xc6 (or 18 ♖h3!) 18...♘xb3+ 19 axb3 ♗xc6 20 ♖h3 ♗g7 21 e5! (Glenn) ±.

b) 17...♘xb3+!? 18 axb3 (18 ♘xb3 ♗e7!?) and now:

b1) 18...b5?! 19 ♖h3 ♗g7 20 ♕xh7+ ♔f8 21 f4 ± Donchev-Semkov, Varna 1978.

b2) 18...♘xd4!? transposes to other lines: 19 ♖xd4 – *17...♘xd4 18 ♖xd4 ♘xb3+ 19 axb3*; 19 ♗xd4 – *17...♘xd4 18 ♗xd4 ♘xb3+ 19 axb3*.

b3) Following 18...♗e7, White has scarcely any more chances than after 17...♗e7.

c) 17...♘xd4!? *(D)* and then:

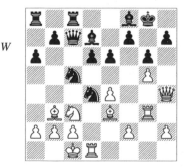

c1) 18 ♖xd4!? makes sense here:

c11) 18...♘xb3+ 19 axb3 e5 (or 19...♗e7!? 20 f4 h5 21 f5 b5 22 ♖d2 a5 Mir.Marković) 20 ♖d2 ♗e6 (20...♕a5!?

21 ♔b1 ♖xc3 Nikitin) 21 ♔b1 (21 ♖h3! h5 22 gxh6 ♔h7 23 ♖f3 Mir.Marković) 21...b5 22 f4 ♗g7 (Velimirović-Mir.Marković, Vrnjačka Banja 1992) 23 fxe5! ± Mir.Marković.

c12) 18...b5 19 f4!? (19 ♖h3 h5! ∓ Veröci-Alexandria, Menorca wom IZ 1973) 19...♗g7 (19...a5!? 20 ♖d2 ∞ Rogaliewicz-Capuano, corr. 1995) 20 ♖h3 ♘xb3+ 21 axb3 e5 22 ♕xh7+ ♔f8 23 ♖h4 exd4 24 ♕xg7+ =.

c2) 18 ♗xd4 ♘xb3+! 19 axb3 e5 20 ♗e3 (20 ♗b6 ♕c6 21 ♖d2 ♗e6 22 ♗e3 a5! ∓ Noetzel-Lanka, Bundesliga 1991/2) 20...b5 21 ♖d2 ♗e6 22 ♖h3 (or 22 ♘d5 ♗xd5 23 exd5 a5 24 ♖h3 ♗g7!, Cheah-Garcia Paolochi, Novi Sad OL 1990). Now, instead of playing 22...♗g7, it is simpler to proceed with 22...h5! 23 gxh6 ♔h7 (Schumi-Wittmann, Austrian Ch (Gamlitz) 1993), with acceptable play.

Now we return to the position after 17...♗e7 *(D)*:

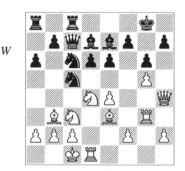

**18 ♕h6**

It appears wisest to take the draw by repetition with the text-move. Otherwise:

a) 18 ♖h3 h5 19 f4 ♘xd4 20 ♗xd4 ♘xb3+ 21 axb3 e5 ∓ Nikitin.

b) 18 ♘f5? ♘xb3+ 19 axb3 exf5 20 ♘d5 ♕d8! (20...♕a5 21 ♘xe7+ ♘xe7 22 ♗d4 ♕a1+! = Panchenko-Kochiev, Riga 1972) 21 ♘f6+ ♗xf6 22 gxf6 ♘e5 23 ♗d4 fxe4 24 ♗xe5 dxe5 25 ♖xd7 ♖xc2+! −+ Zak.

c) 18 ♗c4 h5 (18...b5?! 19 ♘f5!) 19 ♘f5 b5! (19...exf5 20 ♗xc5 dxc5 21 ♘d5) 20 ♘h6+ ♔g7 is probably in Black's favour, Guseinov-Uusi, USSR Cht 1979.

d) 18 f4 b5 (18...♘xb3+!? 19 axb3 b5; 18...♘b4!? 19 f5 ♘xb3+ 20 axb3 e5 Nikitin) and then:

d1) 19 ♘de2? ♘xb3+ 20 axb3 b4 21 ♖h3 h5 22 ♘g3 bxc3 23 ♘xh5 ♘b4 −+.

d2) 19 f5? ♘xb3+ 20 axb3 b4! −+ Zak.

d3) 19 ♕h6 ♗f8 20 ♕h4 b4!? (or 20...♗e7) 21 ♘f5 (21 ♖h3 h5 22 gxh6 ♗e7! −+ Ftačnik) 21...♘xb3+ 22 axb3 bxc3 ∓ Pinski-Pedzich, Koszalin 1999.

d4) 19 ♘xc6 ♕xc6 (19...♘xb3+!?; 19...♗xc6!?) 20 ♗d4 (20 ♗xc5!?) 20...h5 (20...♘xb3+ 21 axb3 e5!?) 21 ♖d2? (21 f5 ♘xb3+!? 22 axb3 b4 ∓; 21 ♗xc5!) 21...b4 22 ♗d5 bxc3! −+ Zhiltsova-Lysenko – Ioseliani, USSR 1976.

d5) 19 ♘f5 ♘xb3+ 20 axb3, and now 20...h5 21 ♘h6+ ♔h7 22 f5 b4!? is interesting. Moreover, it is likely that the continuation 20...exf5 21 ♘d5 (NCO) 21...♕d8! 22 e5 also does not promise White anything after 22...♗e6 or 22...dxe5.

e) 18 ♘de2 and then:

e1) 18...h5 19 f4 (or 19 ♘f4!?) 19...b5 20 f5 ♘xb3+ 21 axb3 b4 22 ♘f4 bxc3 23 bxc3 ♕a5 24 fxg6 fxg6 25 ♘xg6 ♔g7 (Ostapenko/Nikitin) is, to my mind, not quite convincing.

e2) However, 18...♘xb3+ 19 axb3 ♘b4! (19...h5 20 ♘f4!? ♘b4 21 ♗d4 e5 22 ♘xh5 exd4 23 ♖xd4) appears good for Black though the play is rather crazy; e.g., 20 ♔b1 a5!? 21 ♘f4 a4 (21...e5) 22 ♖h3 h5 23 ♘xh5 axb3 24 cxb3 ♖a1+! −+; 20 f4 ♕a5 (or 20...a5) 21 ♔d2?! e5 22 f5 ♗b5!? 23 ♖h3 h5 24 ♘g3 (Ilinčić-Zelić, Yugoslav Cht 1989) 24...♘a2!.

## B232)
**13 ♘f5!** *(D)*

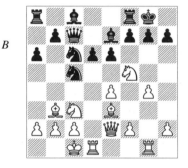

Following A.Sokolov's win over Salov in 1983, this move became more topical than 13 g5.

**13...b5**

Others:

a) 13...exf5?! 14 gxf5 ♘e5 (or 14...♗d7 15 ♘d5 ♕d8 16 ♕h5 ♔h8 17 ♖xg7! +− S.Sokolov-K.Grigorian, USSR 1978) 15 ♘d5 ♕d8 16 ♗xc5!? dxc5 17 f4 ±.

b) 13...♘xb3+ 14 axb3 and then:

b1) 14...exf5?! 15 ♘d5 (the immediate 15 gxf5! is more precise since then 15...♘b4? fails to 16 ♖xg7+! +−) 15...♕d8 (15...♕a5!? Nikitin) 16 gxf5 f6 (16...♔h8 17 ♕h5 f6 18 ♘f4 +−) 17 ♖g3!? ♖f7 18 ♕h5 ♗f8 19 ♖dg1 wins

for White, Coleman-Bologan, Biel
rpd 1993.

b2) 14...b5 15 ♘xe7+ ♘xe7 (after
15...♕xe7 16 g5!? White is slightly
better). Now White has a small advantage after 16 ♕d2 d5 (16...♖d8 17 ♗f4
b4 18 ♘a4 e5 19 ♗xe5 ± Johansson-
Eriksson, Uppsala 1986) 17 exd5 (17
♗f4!? offers White a slight advantage)
17...♘xd5 (17...b4 Ulybin/Volovik)
18 ♘xd5 exd5 19 ♗d4 (Shirov), or after 16 ♕d3 b4 (16...d5 17 exd5 ♘xd5
18 ♘xd5 exd5 ±) 17 ♘a4 d5 (17...♗b7
18 ♕xd6 ±) 18 ♗c5 ±; e.g., 18...dxe4?
19 ♕g3 +− Ulybin-Ermolinsky, Simferopol 1988.

c) 13...♖d8!? (a recent idea) 14
♘xe7+ (14 g5 ♘xb3+!? 15 axb3 exf5
16 ♘d5 ♕a5 17 ♗b6 ♕a1+ 18 ♔d2
♕xb2 19 ♘xe7+ ♘xe7 20 ♗xd8 ♘c6
Yudasin) 14...♕xe7 (14...♘xe7! Yudasin) 15 g5 b5 16 ♕h5 (16 h4!? Yudasin) 16...♗b7? (16...♖b8! 17 ♖g3 g6
18 ♕h6 ♕f8 19 ♕h4 a5 Notkin) 17
♖g3 g6 18 ♕h6 ♕f8 19 ♕h4 ± Yuda-
sin-Sher, St Petersburg 1996.

**14 ♗d5!?** *(D)*

14 ♘xe7+ is less ambitious but also
less risky:

a) 14...♘xe7 and now:

a1) 15 ♗f4 ♘xb3+ (15...e5!?) 16
axb3 e5 17 ♗g5 f6 (17...♗e6 18 ♔b1
♖ad8 19 ♗xe7 ♕xe7 20 ♘d5 gives
White a slight advantage) 18 ♗e3 b4
(18...♗e6!?) 19 ♘a4 ♗e6 20 ♔b1
(Peelen-Jasnikowski, Bielsko Biala
1986) 20...d5! with unclear play –
variations given by Shirov.

a2) 15 ♕d2! ♖d8 (15...b4 16 ♘a4
♘xe4 17 ♕xb4 d5 18 f3 ♘d6 19 ♗f4
♖d8 20 ♔b1 – G.Todorović) 16 e5 (16
♗f4!? ♕c6 17 ♗xd6 ♘g6 18 ♕d4 ♘b7
19 e5, Brunner-Hübner, Haifa Echt

1989) 16...♘xb3+ (16...d5!? 17 f4;
16...b4 17 ♗xc5! ♕xc5 18 ♘e4 ♕xe5
19 ♘xd6 – G.Todorović) 17 axb3 b4
18 ♘a4 ♘d5 19 exd6, G.Todorović-
Kožul, Brezovica 1988 – in all instances White has some advantage.

b) 14...♕xe7 and then:

b1) 15 ♗f4 ♖d8 16 ♕e3 ♗b7 17
♗g5 f6 ∞ Shirov.

b2) 15 g5 ♗b7 (15...b4 16 ♘a4
♗b7?! 17 ♘xc5 dxc5 18 ♕c4) 16 f3
(16 ♕h5!? b4 17 ♘a4 ♘xe4 18 f3)
16...♖ac8 (16...♖fc8!? 17 ♔b1 ♖ab8 –
Shirov) 17 ♔b1 ♖c7 18 ♖d2 ♘e5!
with an acceptable position for Black,
Rõtšagov-Shirov, USSR 1990.

b3) 15 ♕d2 ♖d8 16 ♗g5 f6 17 ♗f4
♘e5 (17...b4 18 ♘d5!) 18 g5 (unclear
is 18 ♕e3 ♗b7 19 g5 ♔h8 – Shirov)
18...♘f3 19 gxf6 ♕xf6 20 ♗g5 (20
♕e3 ♘xg1 21 ♗g5 ♕f3! ∓ Hector-
Shirov, Torcy 1990) and, instead of
20...♘xd2 21 ♗xf6 ♘dxb3+ 22 axb3
♖d7 23 h4! ± (Shirov), 20...♕f7!? 21
♕e3 ♖f8 deserves attention.

*B*

**14...♗b7**

Otherwise:

a) 14...♖e8? 15 ♘xe7+ ♖xe7 16 e5
± Nijboer-Hon, London Lloyds Bank
1992.

b) The rare 14...exd5!? 15 ♘xd5 ♕b7 16 e5 ♘e6 deserves attention:

b1) 17 g5?! dxe5 18 ♕h5 ♘f4!? (or 18...♔h8!? 19 ♘f6 ♗xf6 20 gxf6 g6) 19 ♘fxe7+ ♘xe7 20 ♘f6+ gxf6 21 gxf6+ ♘eg6! 22 ♕h6 ♘e6 23 ♖g3 ♕e4! 24 ♖h3 ♘gf4 25 ♖g3+ ♕g6! (25...♘g6 =).

b2) 17 exd6 ♗d8 and then:

b21) 18 f4 f6 19 ♕f2 ♖f7!? and now 20 ♖ge1 (∓ Shirov) should be preferred to 20 ♗b6 ♘xf4 21 ♘fe7+ ♘xe7 22 dxe7 ♖xe7 23 ♗xd8 ♘xd5 ∓ Hellers-Mednis, Copenhagen 1991.

b22) 18 g5 ♔h8! (18...♗d7 19 ♕h5 ♔h8 20 ♖g4 offers compensation, Hjorth-Andersen, corr. 1984) 19 ♕d3 (19 ♖g3?! ♘f4! ∓) 19...♘e5 with good prospects for Black; e.g., 20 ♕e4 ♘c4 21 ♖g4 ♘xe3 22 ♕xe3 ♕a7 23 ♕g3 ♘c5!?.

b3) 17 ♘dxe7+!? ♘xe7 18 ♘xd6, followed by 19 f4, gives White compensation.

c) Another little-studied option for Black is 14...♖a7 with the point 15 g5 (15 ♗xc6 ♕xc6 16 ♘xe7+ ♖xe7 17 ♖d4 e5!?) 15...exf5 16 g6 ♘e5.

**15 g5 ♖fc8 (D)**
Or:

a) 15...exf5 16 g6! hxg6 (16...♘e5 17 exf5 hxg6 18 fxg6 ♘cd3+ 19 ♖xd3! ± Kobaliya/Cherny) 17 ♖xg6 (17 exf5!? ♘e5 – *16...♘e5 17 exf5 hxg6* ±) 17...♘e5 18 ♖xg7+ leads to a terrific attack for White, A.Sokolov-Salov, Nikolaev 1983.

b) 15...b4 16 ♕h5 ♘e5 (16...g6 17 ♕h6 gxf5 18 ♖g3!? +–; 16...bxc3 17 ♖g3 ♕b6 18 bxc3 exf5 19 ♖h3 +– A.Sokolov; 16...♔h8 17 ♖g3 exf5 18 g6 fxg6 19 ♕xh7+ +–; 16...♖fc8 – *15...♖fc8 16 ♕h5 b4*) 17 ♖g3 exf5 18

exf5 g6 (18...bxc3 19 g6 +– Sion Castro-Rivera, Cordoba 1991; 18...♖fc8!?, Walsh-Raffaele, corr. 1999) 19 fxg6 hxg6 20 ♕h6 +– Shirov.

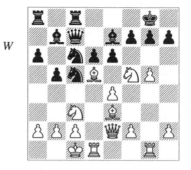

The games that have been played indicate that Black faces serious danger here.

**16 ♖g3**
We cannot rule out the possibility that 16 ♕h5 is stronger:

a) 16...b4 17 ♗xe6 ♘xe6 (17...fxe6? 18 g6) 18 ♘d5 with an attack.

b) 16...♘e5 17 f4 ♘g6 18 ♖g3! (18 ♘xg7?! can be countered by Lanka's 18...b4!? or 18...♔xg7 19 f5 exd5 20 ♖g3!?) 18...b4 19 ♖h3 ♘f8 (19...♔f8 20 ♕xh7 ♔e8 21 ♗xc5 dxc5 22 ♗xe6 +– Ginsburg) 20 ♗d4! exd5 (20...♗d8 21 ♕h6 f6 22 gxf6! +–) 21 ♗xg7 +– Ginsburg-Lanka, Cappelle la Grande 1997.

c) 16...g6 17 ♘h6+ also looks hazardous for Black; e.g., 17...♔g7 18 ♕f3!? ♘e5 19 ♗d4 exd5 20 ♕xf7+ ♔h8 21 f4.

**16...♗f8!?**
First suggested by Romero. Other attempts:

a) 16...g6 17 ♘h6+!? with the initiative.

b) 16...♘e5 and then:

b1) 17 f4 ♘g6 (both the following favour White: 17...b4 18 ♗xc5! and 17...exf5 18 ♗xc5 ♘g6 19 ♗e3! – Shirov) 18 ♘xg7 b4!? (18...♔xg7 19 f5 exd5!?) 19 ♗xc5 ♘xf4 20 ♕f2 dxc5 21 ♗xb7 ♕xb7 22 ♘d5 exd5 (Mezhebitsky-Kirilko, corr. 1996-7) 23 ♕xf4!? =.

b2) 17 ♗xb7 and here:

b21) 17...♕xb7 18 ♘xe7+ ♕xe7 19 f4 ♘ed7! (19...♘c4?! 20 ♗d4 ♘d7 21 ♖h3 b4 22 ♕h5 ♘f8 23 ♗xg7! ♔xg7 24 f5! Shirov) 20 a3! ± Bönsch.

b22) 17...♘xb7 18 ♘xe7+ (18 ♗b6! ♕d7 19 ♗d4 Shirov) 18...♕xe7 with roughly equal play, Sion Castro-Shirov, Leon 1995.

b3) 17 ♖h3 ♘g6? 18 ♕h5 ♘f8 19 ♘xg7!! +– ♗xd5 (19...♔xg7 20 ♗d4+ ♔g8 21 ♕h6) 20 ♕h6 e5 21 ♘h5 +– A.Fedorov-Lanka, Pula Echt 1998.

c) 16...b4 and then:

c1) 17 ♖h3(?) g6 (17...bxc3 18 ♕h5 ♔f8 19 ♘xg7! I.Efimov) 18 ♗xc6 (alternatively, 18 ♘h6+ ♔g7 19 ♗xc6 ♗xc6!) 18...♗xc6 19 ♘h6+ ♔g7 20 ♕f3 ♗e8 21 ♘g4 bxc3 22 ♘f6 ♗xf6 23 gxf6+ ♔g8 –+ Kobaliya-Prokopchuk, Kolontaevo 1997.

c2) 17 ♘xg7!? ♔xg7 (17...bxc3 18 ♕h5 +– A.Fedorov) 18 ♕h5 ♖g8! (18...♖h8? can be met by A.Fedorov's 19 ♗xc5, or 19 ♕h6+ ♔g8 20 ♗xe6! ♗f8 21 g6!! +– Lukacs) 19 ♗xe6! ♘xe6 (19...bxc3? 20 ♗xf7 +– A.Fedorov-Kobaliya, Russian Cht 1998) 20 ♘d5 ♕d8 leads to an insufficiently

explored position: 21 f4 A.Fedorov; 21 ♘f6 ♘f8 22 f4 Kodinets; 21 ♗b6 Notkin.

d) 16...exf5 17 g6 has not yet been verified either.

Now we return to 16...♗f8 (D):

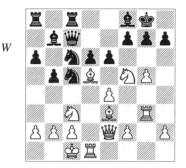

17 ♕h5 g6 18 ♘h6+

18 ♕h4 is a possible attempt to improve.

18...♔h8 19 ♕h4 b4 20 ♖h3

Not 20 ♗xc6? bxc3! ∓ Onishchuk-Shirov, Bundesliga 1996/7. Instead, 20 ♘g4 bxc3 21 ♖h3 (not 21 ♘f6? h6 22 ♘g4 h5 23 ♘f6 cxb2+ 24 ♔b1 ♗g7 25 ♖h3 ♘a4 –+ Shirov) transposes to the main line.

20...bxc3 21 ♘g4 f5!

21...h5? 22 ♘f6.

22 ♘f6 h6 23 ♕xh6+

with perpetual check, I.Rogers-Lanka, Linz 1997.

White can try to improve on this incredible line, but Black still has in reserve, at least, 11 g4 ♘xd4! and 11 ♖hg1 b5!?.

# 11 5...♘c6 6 ♗c4 e6 7 ♗e3 a6 without ♗b3

**1 e4 c5 2 ♘f3 d6 3 d4 cxd4 4 ♘xd4 ♘f6 5 ♘c3 ♘c6 6 ♗c4 e6 7 ♗e3 a6** *(D)*

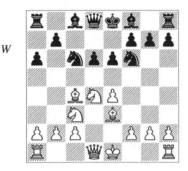

W

With the move-order of the Sozin, 5...♘c6 6 ♗c4, the set-up 6...e6 7 ♗e3 a6, is, undoubtedly, one of the most important. In this chapter we must leave aside the lines with ♗b3 because 8 ♗b3 was completely covered in Chapters 8-10. Nevertheless, this circumstance does not preclude a discussion of the nuances of the position in the diagram (and we should note, first of all, that normally this position should not arise out of the Fischer Attack, since *5...a6 6 ♗c4 e6 7 ♗e3?! ♘c6?!* is quite a hypothetical move-order).

Usually, White wishes to play the Velimirović Attack and to this he has two possible introductions: 8 ♗b3 and

8 ♕e2. Other moves are rare, although **8 0-0** (see *7 0-0 a6 8 ♗e3* in Chapter 12) is quite normal and usually leads to Classical Sozin positions.

Sometimes, White plays **8 a4** and **8 a3**, after which the play usually transposes to the positions of Chapter 12 (one of the few additional ideas for Black is 8 a3 ♕c7 9 ♗a2 ♘e5!?, Minić-Timman, Sombor 1974, and this is interesting).

So, 8 ♗b3 or 8 ♕e2: this is the heart of the matter. If 8...♗e7 is played, it makes no particular difference, but a difference does occur in the 'Anti-Velimirović' lines. After **8 ♗b3**, it is 8...♕c7!?, with the point 9 ♕e2 (9 f4 transposes to the Classical Sozin) 9...♘a5!. After **8 ♕e2** there are both 8...♘a5 and 8...♕c7 9 0-0-0 ♘a5!?, which makes it almost imperative for White to reply ♗d3. Personally, I would prefer 8 ♗b3 (all the more because the Fischer Attack move-order *5...a6 6 ♗c4 e6 7 ♗b3 ♘c6 8 ♗e3* does not leave White any such choice). Objectively, in any case I advise White to arrange ♕e2 and ♗b3 only in the case where the black bishop has *already* been placed on e7. Therefore, choose between 8 ♗b3 ♕c7 9 f4 and 8 ♕e2 ♕c7 (8...♘a5 9 ♗d3) 9 0-0-0 ♘a5 10 ♗d3.

We pass on to the theoretical part of this chapter, consisting of the lines that could not have been discussed earlier. These include, apart from the lines with an early ...♘a5, White's attempts to save on ♗b3 (with an early ♖hg1) in the main lines with ...♗e7.

**8 ♕e2**

Now:

A: **8...♘a5**　　　　　　　　　　191
B: **8...♕c7 (9 0-0-0 ♘a5!?)**　192
C: **8...♕c7 9 0-0-0 ♗e7**　　196
D: **8...♗e7 9 0-0-0 0-0**　　197

We should not forget to mention first two other rare continuations for Black:

a) 8...♘xd4 9 ♗xd4 b5 does not work well here. 10 ♗b3 ♗e7 11 0-0-0 0-0 – *7 ♗b3 a6 8 ♗e3 ♗e7 9 ♕e2 0-0 10 0-0-0 ♘xd4 11 ♗xd4 b5* ±.

b) 8...♗d7!? is not played at grandmaster level for some reason. Then:

b1) The position after 9 ♗b3 (– *7 ♗b3 a6 8 ♗e3 ♗d7 9 ♕e2*) was assessed in Chapter 8 (the note to White's 9th move of Line C1) as not very promising for White (9...b5 10 0-0-0 ♘a5! or 9...♖c8!? 10 0-0-0 ♘a5!).

b2) However, even after 9 0-0-0! it is not easy to avoid such positions: after 9...b5 10 ♘xc6!? ♗xc6 White must sacrifice something; 9...♖c8 10 ♘xc6!?; 9...♘a5 10 ♗d3!? ♖c8 11 ♖hg1 b5 (11...♖xc3?! 12 bxc3, Ljubojević-Spassky, Turin 1982) 12 g4. All this is not wholly clear and deserves further study.

**A)**

**8...♘a5** *(D)*
**9 ♗d3!**

Or:

a) 9 0-0-0 ♘xc4 10 ♕xc4 ♗d7! = Karasev-Yudasin, USSR 1984.

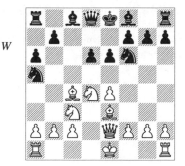

b) 9 ♗b3 and now:

b1) 9...♕c7 (followed by 10...b5) transposes to Line C31 of Chapter 8, which suits Black.

b2) 9...b5!? is at least no weaker.

**9...b5**

Consistent but risky. Others:

a) 9...♕c7 and now:

a1) 10 0-0-0 simply transposes to Line B, so it is unclear what Black hopes to gain by giving White some additional possibilities.

a2) 10 g4 b5 11 g5 ♘d7 12 f4 b4 ∞ Hartston-Liberzon, Reykjavik Z 1975.

a3) 10 0-0 ♗e7 11 f4 should be compared with *10 f4*.

a4) 10 f4 b5 11 0-0 (11 a4!? b4 12 ♘b1) 11...♗b7 12 ♖ae1!? ♗e7 13 ♔h1 enables White to fight for the advantage, Link-Kovaliov, Schwäbisch Gmünd 1994.

b) The rare 9...♗e7 makes a fair amount of sense. For instance:

b1) 10 0-0-0 0-0 (10...b5 11 g4 b4 12 ♘b1 Yudasin) 11 g4 (or 11 ♘b3!?, de Firmian-I.Ivanov, USA Ch (Long Beach) 1989) 11...b5 12 g5 ♘d7 13 f4 ♘c5 14 h4 b4 15 ♘b1 ♕c7 16 ♘d2 ♘xd3+ 17 ♕xd3 ♗d7 18 ♔b1 ♖fc8 19 ♖c1 ♗f8 with mutual chances, Yudasin-Garcia Ilundain, Pamplona 1992/3.

b2) The other line is 10 f4 ♕c7 11 0-0, which is similar to line 'a4', and looks like a promising version of the Scheveningen for White.

**10 a4!?**

As of now, no recognized main move has been defined.

a) Black's idea is not questioned by 10 0-0 ♗b7 11 a3 ♗e7, Minasian-Epishin, Minsk 1990.

b) 10 g4 does not appear logical to me.

c) 10 f4 can be met by 10...b4!? or 10...♕c7 – *9...♕c7 10 f4 b5*.

d) 10 0-0-0 b4!? (10...♕c7 transposes to Line B) 11 ♘b1 (11 ♘a4?! ♗d7!) is quite interesting and playable for both sides; for example, 11...♕c7 (11...♗b7!?) 12 ♘d2 ♗e7 13 g4 ♘d7 14 f4 ♘c5 15 ♔b1 ♗d7 16 g5 0-0 17 f5 ♖fc8 (Brunner-Epishin, Maringa 1991) and now 18 ♖c1!? or 18 ♘2f3!? – Epishin.

e) 10 b4!? ♘c4! (10...♘b7 11 0-0 ± Meštrović-Polugaevsky, Varna 1972) 11 ♗xc4 bxc4 12 ♕xc4 (a slight advantage might be obtained by continuing 12 a3!? ♗b7 13 f3 ♕c7 14 0-0 ♗e7 15 ♗f2, A.Fedorov-Kovaliov, Minsk 1997) 12...♗b7 13 0-0 (13 a3 should be met not by 13...♘xe4 14 ♘xe4 d5 15 ♕b3 dxe4 16 ♖d1 ±, but 13...♖c8!) 13...♖c8 14 ♕b3 (14 ♕d3!? d5 15 e5 ♘d7 16 ♗f4 ♗xb4 17 ♘ce2 is interesting, de Firmian-Zaltsman, Lone Pine 1979) 14...♕c7 15 ♕a4+ ♕d7 16 ♕xd7+ ♘xd7 17 ♘de2 ♖c4 18 f3 ♗e7! with compensation, Solozhenkin-Ionov, St Petersburg Ch 2000.

**10...b4 11 ♘a2**

This move was recommended by Aseev. 11 ♘b1 ♗e7 12 ♘d2 0-0 13 0-0 ♘d7!? 14 f4 ♗f6 is satisfactory

for Black, A.Sokolov-Aseev, USSR Ch (Odessa) 1989.

**11...e5**

After 11...d5 12 e5, Black must avoid 12...♘d7? 13 ♘xe6! +–, while after 12...♘e4, White can continue 13 f3 ♕h4+ 14 ♔d1 ♘g3 15 ♕e1 ±.

**12 ♘f5**

The game Lutovinov-Stepanov, corr. 1994, appeared to favour White after 12...d5 13 ♗g5 ♗b7 (13...♗xf5 14 exf5 ♗d6 15 ♗xa6; 13...h6 14 ♗xf6 ♕xf6 15 ♘e3) 14 ♖d1 d4 15 c3. Certainly, Black has other ideas (e.g. 12...b3) which await investigation.

**B)**

**8...♕c7**

This is the most popular continuation as Black keeps both 9...♗e7 and 9...♘a5 in reserve.

**9 0-0-0**

Other moves are less important:

a) 9 ♖g1?! runs up against 9...b5! 10 ♘xc6 bxc4 11 ♕xc4 ♗b7 12 ♘e5 ♕xc4 13 ♘xc4 ♘xe4, Vujadinović-Lerner, Bela Crkva 1988.

b) 9 ♗b3 transposes to Line C31 of Chapter 8.

c) 9 a3 and 9 f4 are possible here though this version is clearly far from being optimal.

d) 9 a4!? has been played by Kuzmin and a number of other famous players. The usual continuation is 9...♗e7 10 0-0, transposing to note 'b2' to Black's 9th move of Line B in Chapter 12.

**9...♘a5!?** *(D)*

Otherwise:

a) Fortunately for White, 9...b5? does not work because of 10 ♘xc6! ♕xc6 (or 10...bxc4 11 ♕xc4 ♗b7 12

♘e5 ♕xc4 13 ♘xc4, attacking the d6-pawn) 11 ♘xb5 ♘xe4 12 ♘a7 ±.

b) 9...♗d7!? 10 ♗b3 transposes to note 'd' to Black's 9th move in Line C31 of Chapter 8.

c) The main continuation here is still 9...♗e7 – see Line C.

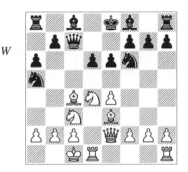

W

**10 ♗d3!**

White should always try to avoid the position after 10 ♗b3?! b5!, where Black has gained the initiative:

a) 11 f3. Now Black often plays 11...♗e7 12 g4 0-0 with a double-edged position, but at least no weaker is 11...♘d7!? 12 ♗xe6 (12 g4 ♖b8 13 g5 ♘c5 favours Black, Golubev-V.Neverov, Kharkov 1984) 12...fxe6 13 ♘xe6 ♕c4 14 ♕xc4 ♘xc4, as in the game Gormally-S.Pedersen, Hampstead 1998.

b) 11 g4 b4!? (11...♗e7 transposes to Line B1 of Chapter 10; 11...♘xb3+ leads, as a rule, to various transpositions; 11...♗b7!? 12 f3 ♖c8 13 g5 ♘d7 14 h4 is double-edged, Golubev-Borodach, Odessa Ch 1984), and then:

b1) 12 g5 and now:

b11) 12...bxc3!? is interesting: 13 gxf6 cxb2+ 14 ♔xb2 ♖b8 (14...gxf6!?

Akopian) 15 ♗c1 gxf6 16 ♔a1 with compensation, Parligras-Raceanu, Romania 1999.

b12) 12...♘d7 transposes to note 'e3' to White's 12th move in Line C31 of Chapter 8, which is fully satisfactory for Black.

b2) 12 ♘a4!? ♘xb3+ (12...♘xe4!?) 13 axb3 ♘xe4 (the less consistent move 13...♗b7 is answered by 14 f3 ∞) 14 ♗f4 (scarcely better is 14 f4 ♗b7 15 f5 e5!, Eames-Hennigan, British League (4NCL) 2000/1) with a complicated position in which Black's chances are no worse:

b21) 14...♘f6 15 ♖he1 e5 (15...g6!? 16 ♗g5 ♗e7 Polugaevsky) 16 g5 ♘d7 17 ♗d2 ♖b8 18 f4 g6 19 ♕c4 ♕xc4 20 bxc4 ♗b7 21 fxe5 dxe5 22 c5 ♖c8 23 ♗f4 and after 23...♗g7 24 ♘b6 ♘xb6 25 ♗xe5 (I.Zaitsev & Zlotnik – Polugaevsky & Gulko, Moscow 1968) 25...♗xe5 26 ♖xe5+ ♔f8 27 cxb6 h6 or 23...♗xc5!? Black holds on.

b22) 14...♘c5!? 15 ♘f5 (15 ♖he1 I.Zaitsev) 15...e5, Cherkasov-Lysenko, Krasnodar 1983.

b23) 14...♗b7!? 15 f3 and now 15...e5! was given by *Schach-Archiv*, while Zaitsev recommended 15...♘f6, not fearing 16 ♘c5!? or 16 ♘b6!?.

**10...b5!** *(D)*

10...♗e7 11 g4! (11 ♗g5 b5! – *10...b5! 11 ♗g5 ♗e7!*) and then:

a) 11...♘d7 can be met by 12 f4 b5 13 g5!? – *11...b5 12 g5 ♘d7 13 f4!?*.

b) 11...b5 12 g5 ♘d7 13 f4!? (13 ♘f5?! exf5 14 ♘d5 ♕d8 15 ♗d4 ♗b7!; 13 h4!?) 13...b4 14 ♘b1 ♘c5 15 ♘d2 ♘xd3+ 16 ♕xd3 ± Kupreichik-G.Kuzmin, Moscow 1972.

c) 11...0-0 12 g5 ♘d7 13 f4 ♖e8 14 h4 b5. Black is in danger following the immediate 15 e5, when instead of 15...♘c5 16 ♗xh7+! ♔xh7 17 ♘f5 exf5 18 ♘d5 ♕c6 (Brinck-Claussen – Sher, Copenhagen 1993) 19 ♗xc5! ±, it is better to play 15...dxe5 16 ♘xe6 fxe6, with the point 17 ♕h5 ♘f8.

This position is hard to assess and is interesting for both sides. With the bishop on d3, the strategic pattern looks, in many ways, like the Scheveningen Variation. Black may consider that he is playing a Scheveningen with the extra tempo ...♘a5, but in reality the knight being on a5 can prove either an advantage or a problem for Black.

**11 a3**

The main move. Others:

a) 11 ♘b3 b4 12 ♘b1 with approximate equality.

b) 11 f4 b4!? (or 11...♗b7: 12 a3 – *11 a3 ♗b7 12 f4*; 12 ♗f2 is scarcely stronger) 12 ♘b1 (12 ♘a4?! ♗d7 13 b3 ♗xa4 14 bxa4 ♗e7) 12...e5! with good counterplay, Ljubojević-Musil, Yugoslavia 1975.

c) 11 ♗g5 ♗e7! (11...b4 is risky in view of 12 ♘d5 exd5 13 exd5+; e.g., 13...♗e7 14 ♗xf6 gxf6 15 ♖he1 ♖a7 16 ♕h5 ♕c5, Milu-Nevednichy, Bucharest 1994, 17 ♗f5! ♖c7 18 ♖e2

Stoica) 12 a3 (12 f4?! b4 13 ♘b1 e5! ∓ Rantanen-Reshevsky, Nice OL 1974; 12 ♖he1 b4 13 ♘b1 e5! 14 ♘b3 ♘xb3+ 15 axb3, A.Sokolov-Popović, Novi Sad 1984, and now 15...♘xe4 16 ♗xe7 ♘c5! is enticing) and here:

c1) Possibly it is satisfactory for Black to continue with 12...♗d7 13 f4 ♘c4 (13...♖c8!?) 14 ♖hf1 (14 ♕e1 0-0 15 ♗xc4 ♕xc4 16 e5 dxe5 17 fxe5 ♘d5 18 ♗xe7 ♘xe7 Rublevsky) 14...♖c8 (14...♘xa3 15 e5!; 14...0-0!?) 15 ♗xc4 ♕xc4 16 ♕e1 0-0, Rublevsky-Salov, Oviedo rpd 1992.

c2) 12...♗b7, with the point 13 f4 0-0, also looks playable, as after 13 ♗xf6 Black can play 13...♗xf6 14 ♗xb5+ axb5 15 ♘dxb5 ♕c5!.

c3) 12...♖b8 13 f4 (13 ♕e1 h6! 14 ♗h4 g5 15 ♗g3 e5 16 ♘f5 ♗xf5 17 exf5 b4 18 axb4 ♖xb4 19 h4 g4 20 ♕e3 0-0!! gives Black an advantage, Dimitrov-Zviagintsev, Barbera 1996) 13...b4 14 axb4 ♖xb4 with adequate counterplay, Ehlvest-Lerner, Tallinn 1986.

d) 11 g4 is the most interesting alternative:

d1) 11...♗b7 can be met by 12 g5 ♘d7 13 f4 ± (*NCO*) or 12 a3 – *11 a3 ♗b7 12 g4!.*

d2) 11...♗e7 – *10...♗e7 11 g4! b5.*

d3) After 11...♘d7!? there is 12 ♘f5, Kauppila-Kononen, Oulu 2000.

d4) 11...b4 and then:

d41) 12 g5!? and now:

d411) 12...♘d7 13 ♘b1 ♘c5 14 ♘d2 ♗b7 15 f4 d5 16 e5 ♘xd3+ 17 ♕xd3 ♘c4 (17...g6!? Akopian) 18 f5! is much better for White, Ghizdavu-Ungureanu, Romania 1971.

d412) 12...bxc3! is critical.

d42) 12 ♘b1 and then:

d421) After 12...♗b7 13 ♘d2 d5 (or 13...♗e7 14 g5 ♘d7 15 f4!) 14 ♗g5!? ♘xe4 15 ♘xe4 dxe4 16 ♗xe4 ♗e7 (not 16...♕e5? 17 ♘xe6! +–) 17 ♗xe7 Black still has some problems, Bokan-Lysenko, Sverdlovsk 1989.

d422) 12...e5! 13 ♘f5, and Black stands no worse after 13...g6 14 ♗g5 ♘d7 (14...♘xg4!?) 15 ♘e3 ♗b7!, Girkyan-Madl, Moscow wom OL 1994, or after 13...♗e6 14 b3 g6 15 g5 ♘d7 16 ♘h6 ♗g7 17 h4 ♘c5, Nunn-Salov, Wijk aan Zee 1992.

d43) 12 ♘a4 might lead to serious complications:

d431) 12...♗d7 13 g5! ♗xa4 14 gxf6 gxf6, and White may choose between 15 ♔b1!? (Vasiesiu-Tomescu, Bucharest 1998), 15 ♗xa6 (± *NCO*) and 15 ♕f3 (Lerner).

d432) 12...♗b7 13 ♘xc6! (13 ♔b1 can be answered by either 13...♗xe4!? or 13...♘d7!) 13...fxe6 14 ♗b6 ♕d7 (14...♕c6!? 15 b3! ♘xb3+ 16 axb3 ♗e7) 15 b3 ♘c6 (15...♗c6!? 16 g5 ♘g8 17 ♗xa5 ♗xa4 18 bxa4 ♕xa4 19 ♗b6 ♕xa2 and now 20 ♕g4 h5!? or 20 ♗d4!? b3!) 16 g5 ♘g8 17 f4 ♘ge7 18 ♗c4 and White gets a dangerous attack for the piece, Zaichik-Kovaliov, Borzhomi 1984.

d433) A calm and satisfactory line for Black is 12...♘d7!? 13 ♘b3 (13 b3 ♗b7!?) 13...♘xb3+ 14 axb3 ♗b7, Stellwagen-Dgebuadze, Wijk aan Zee 2000.

We now return to 11 a3 *(D)*:

**11...♗b7**

Other moves:

a) The idea 11...♗d7 12 g4 ♘c4 13 g5 ♘g8 (as played once by Gaprindashvili) looks suspicious.

b) 11...♖b8!? and then:

b1) 12 ♗g5 ♗e7 – *11 ♗g5 ♗e7!* *12 a3 ♖b8*.

b2) 12 ♖he1 ♘c4!? 13 ♗g5 ♗e7 14 f4 0-0 15 e5 dxe5 16 fxe5 ♘d5 17 ♗xe7 ♘xe7 with an acceptable position, Kaidanov-Ubilava, Kuibyshev 1986.

b3) 12 g4 and here:

b31) 12...♗e7 – *11...♗e7 12 g4!* *♖b8*.

b32) 12...♘c4 13 ♗xc4 (13 g5 ♘d7 14 ♖he1!?) 13...bxc4 14 g5 ♘d7 15 f4, and now playable is 15...♗e7 or maybe 15...♕b7 16 ♕xc4 ♕xb2+ 17 ♔d2 d5!? 18 exd5 ♘b6.

b33) Quite interesting for Black is 12...♘d7!? 13 f4 ♘b6 14 f5 ♘bc4 15 g5 b4 16 axb4 ♖xb4, Forster-Madl, Portorož 1998.

b4) The almost untested 12 f4! is probably the best response for White.

c) 11...♗e7 12 g4! (12 f4 ♗b7 – *11...♗b7 12 f4 ♗e7*; 12 ♗g5 – *11 ♗g5 ♗e7 12 a3*) and then:

c1) 12...♖b8 13 ♖he1!? ♘c4 (if 13...♘d7 then 14 ♘f5! Nunn) 14 g5 ♘xe3 (14...♘d7 15 ♘f5 exf5 16 ♘d5 ♕d8 17 exf5 0-0 18 ♕h5 ± Nunn-Pritchett, Bundesliga 1985/6) 15 ♕xe3 ♘g4 16 ♕g3 ♗xg5+ 17 f4 e5 18 ♘d5! ± (Akopian).

c2) 12...♗b7 13 g5 ♘d7 14 f4 (also promising is 14 h4!? ♘e5 15 f4 {or 15 h5!? *NCO*} 15...♘ec4 16 ♗xc4 ♕xc4 17 ♖d3 b4 18 b3 ♘xb3+ 19 cxb3 ♕c7 20 axb4 ♗xe4 21 ♖e1, Nunn-Arakhamia, Hastings 1994/5) and now:

c21) 14...♘c4? 15 ♘dxb5.

c22) 14...♘c5 15 ♔b1! (15 f5!? e5 16 ♗xb5+ axb5 17 ♘dxb5 ♕b8 18 f6, Tachilin-Ronin, Riga 1988) 15...♘c6 16 f5 ± Cosulich-Ungureanu, Siegen OL 1970.

c23) 14...♘b6!? deserves investigation.

c24) 14...♖c8 15 ♕h5 (15 f5 e5 and ...♘c4 – Conquest) 15...g6 16 ♕h6 ♗f8!? (16...♘c4 17 ♗xc4 ♕xc4 18 ♕g7 ♖f8 19 ♖he1 ♘c5 20 ♘dxb5! ± Conquest-Serper, Dhaka 1995) 17 ♕h3 ♗g7, and, now, instead of 18 ♗xb5 0-0! (Conquest), White could try 18 ♖he1 0-0 19 f5 (with an attack – A.Fedorov) or maybe even 18 f5!?.

**12 g4!**

Or:

a) 12 ♗g5 is harmless: 12...♗e7!? – *11 ♗g5 ♗e7! 12 a3 ♗b7*.

b) 12 f4 ♗e7 (12...♖c8!?) 13 g4 d5! 14 exd5 (14 ♗d2 dxe4 15 ♘xe4 0-0-0! ∓ Nunn-Van der Wiel, Leiden 1982) 14...♘xd5 15 ♘xd5 ♗xd5 16 ♖he1 ♘c4 17 f5 e5! 18 ♘f3, and, besides 18...0-0, which gave Black good play in Markland-Lamford, corr. 1981, 18...♘xb2!? 19 ♔xb2 ♗xa3+ 20 ♔b1 ♕c3 21 ♗d4 ♕b4+ 22 ♔a1 0-0-0! (Akopian) is interesting.

After the text-move (12 g4!), Black still has some problems:

a) 12...♗e7 – *11...♗e7 12 g4! ♗b7*.

b) 12...d5 13 exd5 ♘xd5 14 ♘dxb5 is not wholly clear but very dangerous for Black:

b1) 14...♕e5? 15 ♘xd5 ♗xd5 16 ♗b6! ±.

b2) 14...♕b8 15 ♘xd5 ♗xd5 16 ♘c3 ♗xh1 17 ♖xh1 ♕c7?! (17...♕c8!? Akopian, or maybe 17...♕b7 18 ♗e4 ♘c6) 18 ♘d5!! ♕c6 19 ♗xa6 ♖xa6 (19...♕xd5 20 ♖d1) 20 ♕xa6 ♘b3+ 21 ♔b1 ♕xd5 (Hawelko-Gaprindashvili, Polanica Zdroj 1986) 22 ♕c8+ ♔e7 23 ♖e1 +–.

b3) 14...axb5 15 ♗xb5+ ♔d8 16 ♘xd5 exd5 (16...♗xd5 17 ♖xd5+ exd5 18 ♖d1 ♗d6 19 ♖xd5 ♘b7 20 ♗a6! ±) 17 ♖d3 gives White very serious compensation, Nunn-Sosonko, Thessaloniki OL 1984.

c) 12...♖c8!? 13 g5 ♘d7 and then:

c1) 14 ♖he1 ♗e7 15 ♕h5 g6 (not 15...0-0?! 16 ♘xe6!) 16 ♕h6 ♘e5 17 ♕g7 ♖f8 18 f4 ♘ec4 leads to an extremely unclear game, A.Fedorov-Kasimdzhanov, Moscow 1996.

c2) 14 f4 ♘c4!? (a speciality of Inkiov; 14...♗e7 transposes to note 'c24' to Black's 11th move; 14...♘c5 15 ♔b1! ±) 15 ♘dxb5 axb5 16 ♘xb5 ♕b8 17 ♗xc4 ♗xe4 18 ♖he1 d5 19 ♗d3 ♗xd3 20 ♕xd3, and the assessment by *NCO* (±) awaits verification.

d) 12...♘d7!? 13 f4 ♘b6 (13...♖c8!? 14 g5 – *12...♖c8!? 13 g5 ♘d7 14 f4*) 14 f5 e5 15 ♘b3 ♘a4 (15...♘ac4?! 16 ♗xc4! ♘xc4 17 ♘d5, Howell-Madl, Hastings 1994/5) 16 ♗d2. Probably White's chances are a bit better.

Thus, the early ...♘a5!? is met with ♗d3! and is no better for Black than the conventional variations. Now, we move on to lines with ...♗e7 for Black and an early ♖hg1 for White.

**C)**

    **8...♕c7 9 0-0-0 ♗e7** *(D)*

*W*

**10 ♖hg1**

Otherwise:

a) 10 ♗b3 transposes to Line B of Chapter 10. Other alternatives are less significant:

b) 10 g4 ♘e5! 11 ♗b3 ♘exg4 12 ♖hg1 ♘xe3 13 ♕xe3 g6 14 f4 ♗d7 15 f5 e5 16 ♘f3 ♖f8 17 fxg6 (17 ♘g5!?) 17...fxg6 18 ♔b1 0-0-0 ∓ Velimirović-Cebalo, Kavala 1985.

c) 10 f4 0-0 (10...♘a5!?) 11 f5 (11 ♗b3 transposes to note 'b' to White's 11th move in Line B2 of Chapter 10) 11...♘xd4 (11...♘a5!? =) 12 ♗xd4 exf5 13 ♖hf1 ♗e6 ∞ Kaidanov-Ermolinsky, Kuibyshev 1986.

**10...♘a5!**

White's main hope is that Black plays 10...0-0, transposing to Line D1 (where 11 g4! is attractive for White).

However, I am not quite sure that 10...b5!? is any weaker than the text-move: 11 ♘xc6 ♕xc6 12 ♘xb5, and, in addition to 12...♘xe4 13 ♘a7 ♕b7 14 ♘xc8 ♕xc8 (Alburt-Vaiser, Kiev 1970), 12...0-0 and 12...♗d7 are also interesting.

**11 ♗d3**

11 ♗b3?! b5 12 g4 ♘xb3+ 13 axb3 b4 14 ♘a4 ♘xe4.

**11...b5!**

As compared to Line C, here ...♗e7 and ♖hg1 are included, and this circumstance does not allow White to count on any real advantage. For instance:

**12 g4**

12 a3 ♖b8 (12...e5 13 ♘f5 ♗xf5 14 exf5 d5 15 ♗g5 0-0-0!?, Zvonitsky-Kulinsky, Kharkov 1984) 13 g4 ♘c4!? 14 ♗xc4 bxc4 15 g5 ♘d7 16 f4 ♕b7 17 ♕xc4 (Kholmov-Zurakhov, USSR Ch (Kharkov) 1967) 17...♕xb2+ 18 ♔d2 d5!.

**12...b4**

Well grounded are 12...♗b7 and, particularly, 12...♘d7!? as 13 ♘f5 exf5 14 ♘d5 ♕d8 15 gxf5 ♗f6 (Sveshnikov-Popović, Novi Sad 1979), looks suspicious, and otherwise White is not getting much use out of the g1-rook.

**13 ♘b1**

Or 13 ♘a4 ♘d7! (but not 13...♗d7? 14 ♘b6!, Sax-Bellin, Teesside 1972).

**13...♗b7**

Less consistent here is 13...♘d7 14 ♘d2 ♘c5 15 ♔b1.

**14 ♘d2 d5 15 f3 dxe4 16 fxe4 ♘d7**

Black stands no worse, Shvidenko-Kurass, Kiev 1970.

**D)**

**8...♗e7 9 0-0-0 0-0 10 ♖hg1**

10 f4 is no better here than in Line C.

10 g4 is possible, and then:

a) 10...♘xd4 11 ♗xd4 b5 12 ♗b3 transposes to note 'd1' to Black's 10th move in Line A of Chapter 10, which is satisfactory for Black.

b) 10...♘e5 is even more important. It has the point 11 g5 ♘fg4! ∓.

Now:

**D1: 10...♕c7**     198
**D2: 10...♘xd4!**     198

## D1)

**10...♕c7 11 g4!**

An attack that saves the tempo ♗b3 may readily become killing here.

**11...♘xe4!?**

Or:

a) 11...♘d7 12 g5 ♘c5 13 ♕h5 g6 14 ♕h6 ♖e8 15 ♖g3 ♗f8 16 ♕h4 b5?! 17 ♗d5! ♗b7 18 ♘xc6 ♗xc6 19 ♗d4 +− Krivov-Upart, Minsk 1977. This is how the early ♖hg1 works against stereotyped play by Black!

b) After 11...♘a5, 12 ♗b3 transposes to Line B221 of Chapter 10, which appears promising for White. 12 ♗d3!? is also of interest.

c) 11...b5 12 g5! (12 ♗b3 transposes to Line B222 of Chapter 10) and then:

c1) 12...♘d7? 13 ♘d5! ±.

c2) 12...bxc4 13 gxf6 ♗xf6 14 ♕xc4 (14 ♘xc6 ♕xc6 15 ♗d4 ♗xd4! 16 ♖xd4 ♖b8 is unclear) 14...♗b7 (14...♗d7 is equivalent) and now:

c21) 15 ♘f5 exf5 16 ♘d5 ♕d8 17 ♗b6 ♗xb2+! 18 ♔xb2 ♕h4 promises little for White, Mariasin-Zborovsky, corr. 1971-2.

c22) Black can probably hold on after 15 ♘xc6 ♗xc6! (e.g. 16 ♗d4 ♗e5 Veličković) as well.

c23) 15 ♘d5 is interesting; for example, 15...exd5 16 exd5 ♖ac8 17 dxc6 ♗xc6 18 ♘f5 d5 19 ♖xg7+!? ♗xg7 20 ♕g4 f6 21 ♖g1 ♔h8 22 ♕xg7+ ♕xg7 23 ♖xg7 d4?! 24 ♗h6 ±.

c3) 12...♘xd4 13 ♗xd4 ♘d7 and then:

c31) 14 ♘d5 exd5 (14...♕d8!? is another idea) 15 ♗xd5 ♗b7 16 g6 ♗f6 17 ♕h5 (Mir.Pavlov-Barbulescu, Romanian Ch 1985) 17...♖fc8 deserves detailed analysis.

c32) 14 g6 hxg6 15 ♖xg6 fxg6 16 ♗xe6+ (Shadrina-Prudnikova, Russian wom Ch (Elista) 1995) 16...♔h7! is also very interesting.

c33) 14 ♗b3 transposes to the note to Black's 12th move in Line B23 of Chapter 10, where White has a dangerous initiative.

d) 11...♘xd4 12 ♗xd4 b5 and now: 13 g5 – *11...b5 12 g5! ♘xd4 13 ♗xd4*; 13 ♗b3 ♘d7 again transposes to the note to Black's 12th move in Line B23 of Chapter 10; 13 ♗d3!? is possible.

**12 ♘xe4 d5**

Now Black can scarcely get full equality after 13 ♗d3 dxe4 14 ♗xe4 e5 15 ♘f5 ♗e6 16 ♕f3 (not 16 ♘xg7? ♔xg7 17 g5 ♖h8!, Sax-Ermenkov, Vraca Z 1975) 16...♖fd8 or after 13 ♗xd5!? exd5 14 ♘c3.

## D2)

**10...♘xd4!**

It is difficult to recommend either 10...♘d7 11 g4!, or 10...♕e8 11 g4! ♘d7 (or 11...b5 12 g5) 12 g5 ♘c5 13 ♕h5!, Aleksandrov-Hausner, Mlada Boleslav 1974.

Little studied is 10...♗d7!? with the point 11 g4 b5 12 ♗b3 b4!, I.Zaitsev-Bukić, USSR-Yugoslavia 1968.

**11 ♗xd4 b5!**

Now:

a) 12 ♗b3 transposes to the note to White's 10th move in Line A of Chapter 10, which is satisfactory for Black.

b) No better for White is 12 e5 dxe5 13 ♗xe5 ♕a5! 14 ♗b3 ♗b7, I.Zaitsev-Grishchuk, St Petersburg 1999.

**Conclusion:** by responding correctly to 10 ♖hg1, Black solves his problems. Nevertheless, when played against an unprepared opponent, this idea can have an impressive effect.

# 12  5...♘c6 6 ♗c4 e6 7 0-0 a6 without ♗b3

1 e4 c5 2 ♘f3 d6 3 d4 cxd4 4 ♘xd4
♘f6 5 ♘c3 ♘c6 6 ♗c4 e6 7 0-0 a6 *(D)*

| | |
|---|---|
| **A: 8 a3** | 200 |
| **B: 8 a4** | 202 |

*W*

We have already discussed the main
positions with **8 ♗b3** in Chapters 8
and 9. In practice, White slightly more
frequently plays first **8 ♗e3**, and only
then 9 ♗b3. The difference is very
small here, but one nuance should be
mentioned. White can also play 8 ♗e3
intending a3 or a4 – for example, in
order to avoid 8 a4 ♕b6!?. However,
after 8...♕c7 (with the idea of 9...♘xd4
10 ♕xd4 ♘g4!) he either has to put
the bishop on b3 or proceed with 9
♕e2, after which it appears that 9...b5!
equalizes immediately.

Actually, both plans connected with
the reluctance of White to station the
bishop on b3 form the subject of this
chapter (this is all that remains from
the huge number of lines with ...a6).

Although the difference in the character of the struggle after a3 or a4 is
quite evident, these atypical Sozin lines
still have much in common. In either
case White provides for a sustainable
future of the c4-bishop, thereby con-
siderably reducing his strategic risk.
Black's risk is also reduced as White
loses an important tempo for prepar-
ing his assault. Comparatively slow
plans with an early advance of the a-
pawn have not attracted wide attention
as yet, but one can hardly miss the
growing interest in, primarily, the concept with a4 that was first adopted by
Kuzmin and V.Gurevich, and then by
Emms.

It is worth noting that the lines described in this chapter may arise out of
various lines:

5...e6 6 ♗c4 ♗e7 7 a3!? ♘c6 and
...a6;

5...a6 6 ♗c4 e6 7 a3 (7 a4) 7...♘c6;

5...a6 6 ♗c4 e6 7 0-0 ♗e7 8 a3 (8
a4) 8...♘c6;

5...♘c6 6 ♗c4 e6 7 ♗e3 a6 8 a3 (8
a4);

5...♘c6 6 ♗c4 e6 7 ♗e3 a6 8 ♕e2
♕c7 9 a4 ♗e7 10 0-0;

5...♘c6 6 ♗c4 e6 7 ♗e3 ♗e7 8 0-0
0-0 9 ♔h1 (9 a3 a6) 9...a6 10 a4.

Moreover, it should be added that the position in the previous diagram may also arise from the Fischer Attack move-order: 5...a6 6 ♗c4 e6 7 0-0 ♘c6.

We might say that the position in the diagram makes a convenient starting point for us to discuss the entire range of positions with 0-0, a3 (a4) for White and ...a6, ...♘c6 for Black. Let us advance from that starting point onwards.

## A)

**8 a3 ♗e7 9 ♗a2 0-0** *(D)*

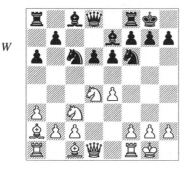

As a rule, White makes a choice between two options here:
**A1: 10 ♔h1**          200
**A2: 10 ♗e3**          201

10 f4 is also possible on the basis of 10...♕b6?! (10...d5!?) 11 ♗e3 ♕xb2 12 ♕d3 ±.

## A1)

**10 ♔h1 ♕c7**

This is a convenient but possibly not ideal method of development under the circumstances.

a) 10...♕b6?! 11 ♗e3!, Teschner-Smyslov, Dortmund 1961.

b) 10...♘xd4!? 11 ♕xd4 b5 12 f4 (12 ♗g5!? is another idea) 12...♗b7 13 f5 e5 14 ♕d3, and both the following lines are double-edged: 14...♖c8 15 ♗g5 ♖xc3, Stanec-Lerner, Vienna 1994, and 14...h6 15 ♗d2 a5 16 ♕xb5 ♗a6 17 ♕c6 ♗xf1 18 ♖xf1, Dvoirys-Cifuentes, Hoogeveen 2000.

c) 10...♗d7!? 11 f4. Now, besides 11...♕c8!? and 11...b5 12 f5 (12 ♗e3 ♖c8 – *10 ♗e3 ♗d7 11 f4 ♖c8 12 ♔h1 b5*), Black has 11...♖c8! with the point 12 f5?! ♘xd4 13 ♕xd4 exf5 14 exf5 ♖c5! ∓ Darga-Marthaler, Graz 1961. White should instead respond with 12 ♗e3 – *10 ♗e3 ♗d7 11 f4 ♖c8 12 ♔h1*.

A peculiar way to provoke ...♕c7 was introduced by Saltaev against Torre: 8 ♔h1!? ♕c7 9 a3 ♗e7 10 ♗a2.

**11 f4 ♗d7**

11...b5 12 f5 ♘xd4 13 ♕xd4 exf5 (13...e5?! 14 ♕d3 h6 15 ♘d5! ♘xd5 16 ♗xd5 ♗b7 17 ♗xb7 ♕xb7 18 f6! +− Saltaev; 13...♖b8!?) 14 exf5 ♗b7 15 ♗g5 h6! 16 ♗h4 ♕c6 with good chances for equalizing, Puc-Nedeljković, Yugoslav Ch (Sombor) 1957.

**12 f5**

12 ♘f3!? (in variations with the bishop on b3, this idea as a rule works badly, because of ...♘a5!) and now 12...♖ac8 13 ♕e1 ♕a5 14 ♗e3 ♕h5 15 ♖d1 ± Saltaev-Torre, Erevan OL 1996 or 12...b5 13 ♕e1 b4 14 axb4 ♘xb4 15 ♗b3 a5 16 ♘d4 ♕b7 17 e5 ± Saltaev-Yudasin, St Petersburg 1997.

**12...♘xd4 13 ♕xd4**

Now instead of 13...♘g4 14 ♗f4! ± or 13...e5 14 ♕d3 ♗c6? 15 ♗g5, Black should look for equality in variations of the type 13...♖ac8 14 ♗g5 h6 15 ♗h4 exf5 16 exf5 ♗c6 17 ♖ae1 ♖ce8!? and 13...♔h8 14 ♗g5 h6 15 ♗h4 exf5

16 exf5 ♗c6 17 ♖ae1 (17 ♖ad1!? Tolush) 17...♖ae8 18 ♖e2 ♗d8!, Kliavinsh-Tolush, Riga 1959. Therefore, it makes sense to play 13...exf5 at once, when 14 ♗g5!? is no stronger than 14 exf5 ♗c6.

## A2)
**10 ♗e3** *(D)*

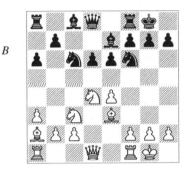

B

**10...♕c7**

Or:

a) 10...♘xd4 11 ♗xd4 b5 12 f4 (12 ♕e2 ♗b7 13 ♖ad1 ♕c7 14 f3 ♖ac8 is not too ambitious, Alexander-Unzicker, Munich OL 1958) 12...♗b7 makes it possible for White to take advantage of the bishop on a2, as compared to Fischer-Spassky, Reykjavik Wch (4) 1972, where the bishop stayed on b3: 13 ♕d3! (13 ♕e2 a5!) 13...♖c8 (not 13...a5? 14 e5 dxe5 15 fxe5 ♘d7 16 ♘xb5, and 16...♘c5 hits nothing) 14 ♖ad1 ♖xc3 15 ♕xc3 ♗xe4 16 ♗b1! ♕a8 17 ♕g3 and 18 c3, with an advantage, Petrushin-Pigusov, Rostov 1981.

b) 10...♗d7 and then:

b1) 11 ♕e2 ♖c8 12 ♖ad1 ♕c7 13 ♔h1 (13 f4!? ♘xd4 14 ♖xd4) 13...♘e5 14 ♗c1 ♘c4 15 ♖d3 ♕b6 16 ♗b3 ♕c5 17 ♖fd1 b5 with counterplay,

Bronstein-Najdorf, Argentina-USSR 1954.

b2) 11 f4 ♖c8 12 ♔h1 (scarcely stronger is 12 ♘xc6 bxc6 13 ♗c4 ♖b8, del Rio-Bruzon, Linares open 2001, but 12 ♕f3 seems logical) 12...b5 13 ♕f3 ♘xd4 14 ♗xd4 a5 15 ♗b3 ♗c6 16 ♖ae1 b4 17 axb4 axb4 18 ♘b1 with chances for both sides, Saltaev-Ermolinsky, Tashkent 1987.

**11 ♕e2**

If 11 f4, then instead of 11...♗d7 12 f5 (12 ♕f3!?) 12...♘xd4 13 ♗xd4 and 11...♘xd4 12 ♗xd4 e5 13 ♗e3 exf4 14 ♖xf4 ♗e6, which do not resolve all Black's problems, it seems better to play 11...b5!? 12 f5 (12 ♕f3 ♗b7 13 f5 ♘xd4! 14 ♗xd4 e5) 12...♘xd4 13 ♗xd4, and, after comparing the position with the similar line where the bishop is on b3, it is difficult to explain why altering the bishop's position by one square improves White's chances.

**11...b5**

11...♗d7 12 f4 b5 13 f5 ± Osnos-Udovčić, Leningrad 1967.

Now (after 11...b5) Saltaev has twice gained some advantage against the world chess grandees:

a) 12 ♔h1 ♗b7 13 f3 ♖fe8?! (this move is appropriate in the Sozin only when White threatens ♕h5 and ♖h3 with mate on h7) 14 ♖ad1 ♗f8 15 ♘xc6 ♕xc6 16 ♗d4 ♘d7 (Saltaev-Shirov, Erevan OL 1996) 17 f4! ♘c5 18 ♖de1 (Saltaev).

b) 12 ♖ad1 ♖b8 13 f3 ♘a5 14 ♗c1 b4 (weakening himself rather than his opponent) 15 axb4 ♖xb4 16 ♔h1, Saltaev-Topalov, Erevan OL 1996.

Playing against those rated 2750, one has nothing to lose, but the plan with f3 seems quite harmless.

## B)

**8 a4** *(D)*

*B*

White's strategic task is to create pressure against Black's position, proceeding step by step while preserving a territorial advantage. To achieve this, he has to be ready to meet ...d5.

**8...♗e7**

Or:

a) 8...♕c7 9 ♗a2 (9 ♗e3 ♘e5!?) 9...♗e7 10 ♗e3 – *8...♗e7 9 ♗e3 ♕c7 10 ♗a2*.

b) 8...♕b6 is akin to the Benko Variation (i.e. Line B of Chapter 14):

b1) 9 ♗e3 ♕xb2 is not correct for White here.

b2) 9 ♘b3! transposes to the note to Black's 8th move in Line B52 of Chapter 14, which is a little better for White.

**9 ♗e3**

Or:

a) 9 ♔h1 0-0 (9...♕b6!?), and if 10 f4?!, then 10...d5! with good play.

b) 9 ♗a2 0-0 10 ♔h1 and now:

b1) 10...♕c7 11 f4 ♘xd4 12 ♕xd4 ♘d7 (Saltaev-Savon, Alushta 1992) 13 f5!? ♗f6 14 ♕f2.

b2) 10...♘b4 11 ♗b3 d5 12 e5 ♘d7 13 f4 ♘c5 14 ♗e3 ♕c7 15 ♕d2

♗d7 (Savon-Poluliakhov, Volgograd 1994) 16 ♖ae1! is slightly better for White – Beliavsky and Mikhalchishin.

b3) 10...♕b6 11 ♘de2 ♖d8 (the alternative 11...♗d7 is less flexible) 12 ♗e3 ♕a5 13 ♗d2 ♕c7 is roughly equal, Saltaev-Dvoirys, Groningen 1992.

**9...0-0** *(D)*

Alternatively:

a) 9...♘b4 10 ♗b3 e5 and now 11 ♘de2 ♗e6 12 ♗g5 ♘d7! turned out to be satisfactory for Black in Emms-Rowson, Port Erin 1999, but 11 ♘f5!? is interesting; e.g., 11...♗xf5 12 exf5 ♕d7 13 ♗g5 ♕xf5 14 ♗xf6.

b) 9...♕c7 is not very logical because it weakens the idea of ...d5. However, it is difficult at this stage to say whether this factor brings actual benefits to White:

b1) 10 ♗a2 0-0 11 f4 ♗d7 12 f5 (12 ♕e2!?) 12...e5 13 ♘xc6?! ♗xc6 14 ♕d3 b5!, Lutikov-Suetin, Minsk 1952.

b2) 10 ♕e2 (this position arises from the move-order *7 ♗e3 a6 8 ♕e2 ♕c7 9 a4 ♗e7 10 0-0*) 10...0-0 and then:

b21) 11 ♔h1 – *9...0-0 10 ♔h1 ♕c7 11 ♕e2*.

b22) 11 f4 ♘xd4 (11...♗d7 12 f5 ♖ac8 13 ♗b3 ±; 11...e5!?; 11...♘xe4!?) 12 ♗xd4 e5 13 ♗e3 ♗e6! 14 ♗xe6 fxe6 and Black had extricated himself very cleverly in Conquest-Tukmakov, Iraklion 1992, as 15 f5? d5! 16 fxe6 d4 17 ♖xf6 ♗xf6 18 ♘d5 ♕c6 favours him.

b23) 11 ♖ad1 ♘e5!? (11...♗d7!? 12 f4 ♘xd4) 12 ♗b3 ♘eg4 13 ♗c1 d5, deserves attention, as in Rachela-Stefan, Slovakian Cht 1994/5.

**10 ♔h1**

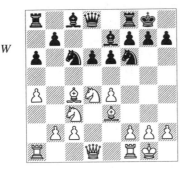

W

The main continuation. This preventive move is explained by the lines 10 f4?! d5! and 10 ♕e2 d5! (10...♕c7 – *9...♕c7 10 ♕e2 0-0*) 11 ♖fd1 (11 exd5 exd5 12 ♗b3 ♖e8 13 h3 ♗c5 with strong counterplay, Emms-Anastasian, Batumi Echt 1999) 11...♗d6 12 exd5 exd5 13 ♘xd5 ♘xd5 14 ♗xd5 ♗xh2+ and 15...♕xd5 = Ivanović-Kasparov, Bugojno 1982.

After 10 ♗b3, Black generates counterplay by way of 10...♗d7, and then ...♘a5!.

However, it makes sense to play 10 ♗a2!?; e.g., 10...♗d7 (10...♘b4 11 ♗b3) 11 f4 (11 ♕e2 ♖c8 12 f4 ♕a5 with the curious repetition 13 ♘b3 ♕c7 14 ♘d4 ♕a5 occurred in Donchev-Ribli, Thessaloniki OL 1988) 11...♘xd4 12 ♗xd4 ♗c6 13 ♕d3.

**10...♗d7**

Other moves:

a) 10...♘xd4 11 ♗xd4 e5 12 ♗e3 ♗e6 13 ♕d3 ♖c8 14 ♗b3 ± V.Gurevich-Sher, Berlin 1993.

b) 10...d5 11 exd5 exd5, and White can fight for an advantage with 12 ♗e2 as well as 12 ♗b3 ♖e8 13 h3 ♗e6 14 ♕f3 ♘e5 15 ♕e2 ♗b4 16 ♘xe6 fxe6 17 ♗d2, Emms-Krush, Hastings 2000.

c) 10...♖e8 and now:

c1) 11 ♗a2 ♘b4 (11...d5!?) 12 ♗b3 e5 13 ♘de2 ♗e6 14 ♘d5 ♘bxd5 15 exd5 ♗f5 16 a5 ± Kudrin-Browne, USA Ch (Greenville) 1983.

c2) 11 ♗b3 (the plan with ...♗d7, ...♖c8, ...♘a5, ...♘c4 is already a bit late here) 11...♗d7 12 f4 ♖c8 13 f5 (13 ♕f3 ♕a5 14 f5 ♘xd4 15 ♗xd4 ♕b4 16 ♖ad1 e5 17 ♘a2 ♕a5 18 ♗c3 ♕c7 19 ♘b4 ± V.Gurevich-Felsberger, Bratislava ECC 1996) 13...♘xd4 14 ♗xd4 e5 15 ♗e3 ♗c6? (not wholly clear is 15...♖xc3 16 bxc3 ♗c6!) 16 ♕d3 b5 17 axb5 axb5 18 ♗g5 ± Emms-Fressinet, Istanbul OL 2000.

d) 10...♕c7. This move is very often combined with a later ...♗d7 and a transposition to 10...♗d7, which we (very arbitrarily) have called the main line. Then:

d1) 11 f4?! d5! 12 exd5 ♘b4, Stefansson-Arnason, Oakham 1988.

d2) 11 ♗a2 ♗d7 (11...♘b4 12 ♗b3 b6 13 f4 ♗b7 14 ♕f3 ♖ad8 15 ♖ae1 ± G.Kuzmin-D.Gurevich, Moscow 1992; 11...b6 12 f4 ♗b7 13 ♕e1 ♘xd4 14 ♗xd4 e5 15 fxe5 dxe5 16 ♕g3 ♘d7 ± Galdunts-Nikolaev, St Petersburg 1992) 12 f4 – *10...♗d7 11 f4 ♕c7 12 ♗a2*.

d3) 11 ♕e2 and now Black has tried various moves:

d31) 11...♘xd4 12 ♗xd4 e5 13 ♗e3 ♗e6 14 ♗b3 h6 15 a5 ± Kudrin-King, Berne 1988.

d32) 11...♘e5 12 ♗b3 ♘eg4 13 f4! ♘xe3 14 ♕xe3 ♕c5 15 ♕d3!? ♗d7 16 ♖ad1 ♖ad8 17 ♕e2 ± G.Kuzmin-Ftáčnik, Dortmund 1981.

d33) 11...♘b4 12 ♗b3 (12 f4 d5! 13 exd5 ♘bxd5) 12...e5 13 ♘f3 h6 (13...♗g4 14 ♗g5 is slightly better for White) 14 a5 ♗g4 15 ♗b6 ♕c8 16

♖a4 with an advantage for White, V.Gurevich-Istratescu, Wattens 1993.

d34) 11...♖e8 12 ♗b3 ♗d7 13 f4 ♘a5 14 ♗a2 ♖ac8 15 ♖ae1 ♘c4 16 ♗c1 ♕b6 17 ♗xc4 ♕xd4 18 ♗b3 ♗c6 ± G.Kuzmin-Lerner, St Petersburg 1992.

d35) 11...♘a5 12 ♗a2 b6 13 ♖ad1 ♗b7 14 ♗c1 ♖ac8 15 f4 ♘c4 16 e5 (16 ♖f3!? *NCO*) 16...dxe5 17 fxe5 ♘d5 18 ♘xd5 ♗xd5 19 ♘f5 ♗xg2+ 20 ♕xg2 exf5 21 ♖xf5 ± Emms-Sutovsky, Harplinge 1998.

d36) 11...b6!? 12 f4 ♗b7 13 ♖ae1 (13 f5 d5 14 exd5 exd5 15 ♗b3 ♗c5 with sufficient counterplay, V.Gurevich-Ionov, Uzhgorod 1988; 13 ♖ad1 ♘xd4 14 ♗xd4 ♘xe4 15 ♘xe4 ♗xe4 16 ♗xe6 d5!) 13...♘b4 (13...♘xe4!?; 13...♘xd4!? 14 ♗xd4 ♘xe4) 14 ♗g1 ± Emms-de Firmian, Bundesliga 2000/1.

d37) 11...♖d8!? with the idea of ...d5 was played by GM Browne in the USA in 1994.

d38) 11...♗d7 12 f4 – *10...♗d7 11 f4 ♕c7!? 12 ♕e2.*

**11 f4**

11 ♗a2 ♖c8 12 f4 – *11 f4 ♖c8 12 ♗a2.*

11 ♕e2 ♖c8 (11...♕c7 can be met by 12 ♖ad1!? or 12 f4 – *11 f4 ♕c7!? 12 ♕e2*) and then:

a) 12 f4 – *11 f4 ♖c8 12 ♕e2.*

b) 12 ♗b3 ♘a5!?.

c) 12 ♗d3 ♘xd4 13 ♗xd4 e5 (another idea is 13...♕a5!?) 14 ♗e3 ♗e6 15 f4 exf4 16 ♗xf4 ♕a5 = Nijboer-Dorfman, Hilversum ECC 1993.

d) 12 ♖ad1 ♕c7 13 ♗b3 (13 ♗a2 ♘xd4!? 14 ♗xd4 ♕a5 15 ♗b3 e5 16 ♗e3 h6, Kudrin-de Firmian, USA Ch (Long Beach) 1989) 13...♕a5 (why not 13...♘a5 here?) 14 f4 ♘xd4 15

♖xd4 (15 ♗xd4!? e5 16 fxe5 dxe5 17 ♘d5) 15...♗c6 16 ♗d2 ♕h5 17 ♕xh5 ♘xh5 18 f5 with some advantage, Emms-Lutz, Istanbul OL 2000.

**11...♖c8** *(D)*

Or:

a) 11...♘xe4 12 ♘xe4 d5 and now:

a1) 13 f5 and here Black should avoid 13...exf5 14 ♗xd5 fxe4 15 ♕h5 ♗f6 16 ♘xc6 ♗xc6 17 ♗xc6 bxc6 18 ♖ad1 ♕e8 19 ♖xf6 gxf6 (G.Kuzmin-Ree, Bangalore 1981) 20 ♕g4+ ♔h8 21 ♗d4 +–. Instead, 13...dxc4!? 14 f6 gxf6 does not appear bad for Black.

a2) Better is 13 ♗xd5 exd5 14 ♘c3 ♘xd4 15 ♗xd4 ♗f5 16 ♕f3 ± Galdunts-Zilbershtein, Moscow 1991.

b) 11...♕c7!? is no worse than the text-move:

b1) 12 ♕e2 and then:

b11) 12...♘xe4 13 ♘xe4 d5 14 ♗d3 dxe4 15 ♗xe4 ♗f6 16 ♖ad1 ± V.Gurevich-Feher, Eger 1989.

b12) 12...♖fc8 13 ♗d3!? ± V.Gurevich-Palatnik, Kherson 1991.

b13) 12...♖fe8!? was tried in Panbukchian-Inkiov, Sofia 1989.

b14) 12...♖ac8 – *11...♖c8 12 ♕e2 ♕c7.*

b2) 12 ♗a2 and now:

b21) 12...♖ac8 – *11...♖c8 12 ♗a2 ♕c7.*

b22) 12...♘xd4 13 ♗xd4 ♗c6 14 ♕e2 is more pleasant for White.

b23) Very interesting is 12...♘a5 13 ♕e2 ♖fc8!? (13...♖ac8 – *11...♖c8 12 ♕e2 ♕c7 13 ♗a2 ♘a5*) 14 ♖ad1 b5 15 axb5 axb5 16 f5 e5 17 ♘dxb5 ♗xb5 18 ♕xb5 ♖ab8 19 ♕d3 ♖xb2 with chances for both sides, Kaminski-Filipenko, Pardubice 1996.

**12 ♕e2**

Or:

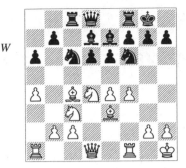

a) 12 ♗b3 ♘a5 is probably satisfactory for Black.

b) 12 ♗a2 and then:

b1) 12...♕a5!?

b2) 12...♕c7 13 ♕e2 (13 ♕f3 ♘xd4 14 ♗xd4 e5 15 ♗e3 exf4 16 ♗xf4 ♗e6 = Galdunts-K.Grigorian, Belgorod 1989) – *12 ♕e2 ♕c7 13 ♗a2*.

b3) 12...♘xd4 13 ♗xd4 (13 ♕xd4? ♘g4!, Ree-Wittmann, Holzoster 1981) 13...♗c6 14 ♕e2 b5 = Wittmann.

**12...♕c7**

12...♘a5 13 ♗d3! (13 ♗a2 ♖xc3) 13...♕c7 – *12...♕c7 13 ♗d3 ♘a5*.

**13 ♗a2**

White has two serious alternatives:

a) 13 ♘xc6 ♗xc6 14 ♗d3 ♘d7 and now rather than 15 ♗d4 ♗f6 = Chiburdanidze-Popović, Subotica (3) 1986. Chiburdanidze suggested 15 ♕h5 ± and Popović 15 b4!?.

b) 13 ♗d3 ♘xd4 (or: 13...♘b4 14 ♖f3, V.Gurevich-Ganin, Ukrainian Cht 1998; 13...♘a5 14 ♖ae1 ♘c4 15 ♗c1 is slightly better for White, V.Gurevich-V.Neverov, Kherson 1988) 14 ♗xd4 e5 15 ♗e3 exf4 (15...♖fe8 16 ♕f3!? exf4 17 ♕xf4! ♗e6 18 ♘d5!

with an advantage for White, V.Gurevich-Petitcunot, Le Touquet 2000) 16 ♗xf4 ♖fe8 17 ♗g5!? ♗e6 18 ♗xf6 ♗xf6 19 ♖xf6 gxf6 20 ♕h5 with compensation, Azarić-Djukanović, Budva 1996.

**13...♘xd4**

13...♘b4 14 ♗b3 d5 15 e5 ♘e4 was suggested by Greengard.

13...♘a5 14 ♖ad1 (also possible is 14 ♖ae1!?) 14...♘c4 15 ♗c1 and then:

a) 15...♘e8 16 ♘f5 ♗f6 17 ♘xd6 ♘exd6 18 e5 ♘e8 (if my source is correct, this happened in Mikhalchishin-Polajzer, Ptuj 1995) 19 ♗xc4 +–.

b) 15...♖fe8 16 ♖d3 ♗f8 17 ♗xc4 ♕xc4 18 e5 ♘d5 19 ♘e4! ± Kudrin-Chandler, Hastings 1986/7.

c) 15...♕c5 (recommended by Sadler in *BCM*) 16 e5 dxe5 17 fxe5 ♘e8 18 ♘f5 1-0 Emms-Joachim, Bundesliga 2000/1.

d) 15...h5!? is an unverified recommendation of Sadler.

e) 15...♖fd8 16 g4! (16 e5 ♘e8 17 exd6 ♗xd6! 18 f5 e5 ∞ G.Kuzmin-Savon, Moscow 1982), and now, instead of 16...♕c5? 17 g5 ♘e8 18 f5 e5 (18...♗f8 19 fxe6 fxe6 20 b3! and b4 +–) 19 ♘d5 ♗f8 20 b4 +– Emms-Shipov, Hastings 1998/9, 16...e5 enables Black to continue the struggle.

**14 ♗xd4 e5**

This idea of Dorfman's made it possible for Black to equalize in G.Kuzmin-Shneider, Enakievo 1997 (and later in Emms-Grishchuk, Esbjerg 2000) after 15 ♗e3 exf4 16 ♗xf4 ♗e6 17 a5 ♗xa2 18 ♖xa2 ♕c4 19 ♕f3 ♕e6 20 ♖a4 ♖c4 =.

# 13  5...♞c6 6 ♝c4 e6: Sozin and Velimirović without ...a6

**1 e4 c5 2 ♞f3 d6 3 d4 cxd4 4 ♞xd4 ♞f6 5 ♞c3 ♞c6 6 ♝c4 e6** *(D)*

This is the basic starting point for the Sozin & Velimirović complex.

We have already discussed all lines with 7...a6 and noticed that in them Black has the plan of ...♛c7, ...♞a5 and ...b5, which makes White seriously consider dropping the Velimirović scheme of ♛e2 and 0-0-0 in favour of Classical Sozin positions with f4. On the other hand, if Black plays 7...♝e7 and 8...0-0 (the main topic of this chapter), everything looks different: if White plays f4 and 0-0, Black can use his omission of ...a6 more effectively, and has more additional ideas than in the case where White plays ♝e3 and ♛e2.

Therefore, it is quite logical that the main introductory move, which

occurs much more often than any of the others, is **7 ♝e3** (planning to meet 7...♝e7 with 8 ♛e2).

Still, Fischer preferred the second most popular move **7 ♝b3** as he liked the idea discussed in Chapter 8: 7...a6 8 f4!? (however, it only occurred a few times in his games because his opponents usually answered 7 ♝b3 with 7...♝e7).

It is possible to begin with **7 0-0** (rejecting the Velimirović at once), but this does not make any particular sense – unless White intends to continue with a3 (e.g., 7...♝e7 8 a3 0-0 9 ♝a2, as played by GM Dvoirys several times recently).

Let us discuss all this in detail and in order:

After 7 a3!?, 7...♝e7 8 ♝a2 0-0 9 0-0 transposes to Line A.

## A)

**7 0-0 ♝e7**

For 7...a6, see Chapter 12.

**8 a3**

There is no sense in 8 ♚h1 0-0 9 f4 because of 9...d5!.

**8...0-0 9 ♝a2 ♞xd4!?**

Otherwise:

a) 9...a6 is also normal, and transposes to Line A of Chapter 12.

b) 9...♗d7 10 ♗e3 and then:

b1) 10...♘xd4 11 ♗xd4 ♗c6 (not 11...b5?! 12 ♗xf6!) 12 ♕d3 ±.

b2) 10...♘e5 is probably playable: 11 ♕e2 ♘eg4 (11...♖c8 12 ♖ad1, in preparation of ♗c1) 12 ♗d2 ♕b6 13 ♘b3 ♖fc8 (Medina Garcia-Polugaevsky, Las Palmas 1974) 14 h3! ♘e5 15 ♗e3 ♕a6! Polugaevsky.

**10 ♕xd4 b6!**

This is not an infrequent idea in positions with the pawn on a7.

**11 ♕d3**

Or:

a) 11 ♗g5 ♗a6!? 12 ♖fe1 ♕c7 13 ♖ad1 ♖fd8 = Sigurjonsson-Tukmakov, Reykjavik 1976.

b) 11 b4 ♗a6 12 ♖e1 ♕c7, Smirnov-Nikitin, Moscow 1966.

**11...♗b7 12 ♗f4 ♕c8!**

The queen is less useful on c7 under the circumstances.

**13 ♖fe1 ♖d8 14 ♖ad1 a6 15 a4 b5! 16 axb5 axb5 17 ♕xb5**

Now both 17...♘xe4 (Dvoirys-Zviagintsev, Samara 1998) and 17...♗xe4!? lead to an equal game.

**B)**

**7 ♗b3 ♗e7** *(D)*

Or:

a) 7...a6 is the subject of Chapters 8-10.

b) 7...♘a5 8 f4 ♘xb3 (8...a6 transposes to note 'c' after White's 8th move in Line A of Chapter 8) 9 axb3 b6 10 f5 ♕d7 11 ♗g5 ♗e7 12 ♕e2 0-0 13 0-0-0 ♘d5 14 ♕g4 ♘xc3 15 f6! ± Ivkov-Vasiukov, USSR-Yugoslavia 1962.

**8 0-0**

The main continuation here is 8 ♗e3, which transposes to Line C2.

8 f4 is less sensible here than after 7...a6. Black has the idea of 8...♘xd4!? 9 ♕xd4 0-0, when 10 0-0 transposes to the note to Black's 8th move, and maybe also 8...d5!?, and 8...♕a5 9 0-0 (better is 9 ♕d3 0-0 10 ♗d2, with unclear play) 9...d5! ∓ Ničevski-Korchnoi, Rovinj/Zagreb 1970.

**8...0-0**

It is possible to play 8...♘xd4!? 9 ♕xd4 0-0 10 f4 (10 ♔h1 – *8...0-0 9 ♔h1 ♘xd4 10 ♕xd4*) 10...b6 11 ♕d3 (11 ♔h1 transposes to note 'a' after Black's 10th move, and was the move-order used in Fischer-Geller) 11...♘d7 12 f5 ♘c5 13 ♕g3, and after 13...♔h8 14 ♗e3 ♗h4 15 ♕h3 ♘xb3 16 axb3 exf5 17 exf5 ♗f6 (Lanka) or 13...♗h4 14 ♕g4 ♗f6 (Kiik-Veingold, Finnish Cht 1999/00) Black's position appears satisfactory.

**9 ♔h1**

Again, the main move is 9 ♗e3, which transposes to Line C22.

9 f4 is unsuccessful in view of 9...d5! 10 e5 ♘xd4 11 ♕xd4 ♘g4 12 h3 (12 f5? ♕b6!, Estrin-Taimanov, Leningrad 1954) 12...b6 13 ♘a4 ♘h6 (13...♗d7?! 14 f5! Boleslavsky) 14 g4

f5 15 g5 ♘f7 16 ♗e3 ♗a6 with counterplay, L.Novikov-Boleslavsky, Minsk 1955.

**9...♘xd4!?**

Or:

a) 9...a6 transposes to note 'b' to White's 9th move in Line B3 of Chapter 8.

b) Another good alternative for Black is 9...♘a5!? 10 f4 (10 ♕d3 a6 11 ♗g5 b5 = Kruppa-R.Scherbakov, USSR Cht 1988) 10...b6; e.g., 11 e5 ♘e8 12 f5 (12 ♖f3 ♘xb3 13 ♘c6 ♕d7 14 ♘xe7+ ♕xe7 15 axb3 f6 ∓ Neikirkh-Botvinnik, Leipzig OL 1960), and now Geller recommended 12...dxe5 13 fxe6 exd4 14 exf7+ ♔h8 15 fxe8♕ ♕xe8, which looks sufficient, while Black should have other ideas as well.

**10 ♕xd4 b6**

White now has the following tries at his disposal:

a) 11 f4 ♗a6! 12 ♖f3 d5 13 exd5 ♗c5 14 ♕a4 ♗b7 15 ♗e3 exd5 16 ♗d4 (Fischer-Geller, Curaçao Ct 1962) and now 16...a6 gives Black excellent chances; e.g., 17 ♗xf6 gxf6 18 ♖d1 b5 19 ♘xb5 axb5 20 ♕xb5 ♕e7.

b) 11 f3 ♗b7 12 ♗e3 d5 (12...♕c7! Atalik) 13 exd5 ♘xd5 14 ♘xd5 ♗xd5 15 ♗xd5 ♗c5 16 ♕c3 with a small advantage for White, Mirumian-Atalik, Ankara Z 1995.

c) 11 ♗g5 ♗b7 12 f4 ♖c8 is assessed as promising for Black in view of 13 f5 ♖c5!, Ježek-Boleslavsky, Vienna Echt 1957.

Overall, the line with 9 ♔h1 should be placed in the category 'mostly harmless'.

**C)**

**7 ♗e3 ♗e7**

Or:

a) 7...a6 is the subject of Chapter 11.

b) 7...♘a5 8 ♗d3!? (after 8 ♗b3 Black may try something with ...b6) 8...a6. Now 9 ♕e2 transposes to Line A of Chapter 11. Not quite clear is 9 f4!? b5!? 10 e5 dxe5 11 fxe5 ♘d5 12 ♕f3 ♘xe3 13 ♕xa8 ♗e7, Yudasin-Rashkovsky, Kuibyshev 1986.

c) Incidentally, the early 7...♗d7!? has not been studied enough. Briefly:

c1) 8 ♕e2 ♖c8 (GM Enders played 8...♘a5 9 ♗d3 a6 several times; another possibility is 8...a6!?, transposing to note 'b' to Black's 8th move in Chapter 11) 9 ♗b3 (after 9 0-0-0, 9...♘a5! 10 ♗d3 e5!?, Brunner-Reeh, Gausdal 1991 is interesting) and now:

c11) 9...♘xd4 10 ♗xd4 b5 is unconvincing, Milu-Nisipeanu, Odorhieu Secuiesc 1993.

c12) 9...♘a5 10 f4!? (10 0-0 ♗e7 11 ♖ad1 0-0 =) 10...♖xc3 (10...e5! ∞ Akopian) 11 bxc3 ♘xe4 12 0-0 ♗e7?! 13 f5! ± (followed by ♘e6!), Palkovi-Tischbierek, Budapest 1986.

c13) 9...a6 is quite good, and transposes to note 'a' to White's 9th move in Line C1 of Chapter 8.

c2) 8 f4 ♘xe4!?.

c3) 8 0-0 makes sense in connection with a3 or a4, if Black replies 8...a6.

c4) 8 ♗b3! is my recommendation. White takes note of 8...a6 9 f4! b5 10 f5!, transposing to Line C1 of Chapter 8 (±).

We now return to 7...♗e7 *(D)*, after which White has these options:

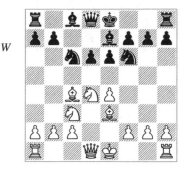

The last of these (Line C3) is by far the most important.

It is also necessary to mention 8 0-0 0-0:

a) 9 ♗b3 transposes to Line C22.

b) 9 f4?! is unsuccessful due to the typical answer 9...d5!.

c) 9 a3 gives Black a choice between 9...a6 10 ♗a2, transposing to Line A2 of Chapter 12, and Nunn's suggestion 9...♕c7!? 10 ♗a2 ♘e5.

d) 9 ♕e2 is inaccurate due to 9...a6 10 a4 d5! =.

e) At once 9 a4 is of some interest.

f) 9 ♔h1!? a6 (other possibilities are rarely tested) 10 a4 is a fairly interesting move-order, which transposes to Line B of Chapter 12.

## C1)

**8 f4 0-0**

8...d5?! is dubious owing to 9 ♗b5! ♗d7 10 e5.

After 8...a6, the simplest way for White to proceed is 9 ♗b3, transposing to Line C of Chapter 9. In the case of 9 ♕f3, he should be prepared for 9...♕c7!? 10 ♗b3 ♘xd4 11 ♗xd4 b5 as well as 9...♘xd4!? 10 ♗xd4 b5.

**9 ♕f3!?**

This gives independent value to the move 8 f4. The best response has not yet been defined. Certainly, Black has some ideas here...

**9...e5!?**

Other moves:

a) 9...a6 10 0-0-0! (avoiding 10 ♗b3 ♘xd4) 10...♕c7 (10...♘xd4 11 ♗xd4 b5? 12 e5) 11 ♗b3 transposes to Line C211 of Chapter 9.

b) 9...♕c7 10 ♗b3 a6 is probably no more precise than 9...a6.

c) 9...d5 needs substantiation – primarily after 10 exd5 exd5 11 ♘xd5.

d) 9...♕a5!? seems interesting:

d1) 10 0 0 0 ♘xd4 11 ♖xd4 (11 ♗xd4?! e5!) 11...♗d7 (with the idea of 12...b5!), Repkova-Galliamova, Erevan wom OL 1996.

d2) After 10 0-0, apart from the transpositional 10...♘xd4 11 ♗xd4 – 9...♘xd4 10 ♗xd4 ♕a5 11 0-0, Black may also try 10...♕b4.

e) 9...♘xd4 (this has occurred most frequently) 10 ♗xd4 and then:

e1) 10...e5 11 fxe5! (11 ♗e3 exf4 12 ♗xf4 ♕a5 13 ♗b3 ♗g4 and now rather than 14 ♕d3 d5!, Ankerst-Panchenko, Bled 1992, White could try 14 ♕g3!?) 11...dxe5 12 ♗xe5 ♘g4 13 ♗f4 ♕d4 14 ♗b3 ♗b4 15 ♖d1.

e2) 10...♕a5 11 0-0 (11 ♗b3 e5 12 ♗e3 ♗g4 13 ♕g3 ♗e6 = Howell-Krakops, Senden 1994) 11...e5 12 ♗e3 exf4 13 ♕xf4 ♗e6 14 ♗b3 ♕h5!? 15 h3 ♕g6 16 ♕f3. Instead of 16...a6 17 e5 ±, Onishchuk-Avrukh, Biel 1999, Avrukh recommended 16...♖fe8!? with good chances of equalizing.

**10 ♘xc6**

10 ♘f5 ♗xf5 11 exf5 exf4 12 ♗xf4 ♘e5 = Votava-Greenfeld, Rishon-le-Zion 1992.

**10...bxc6 11 f5 ♕a5 12 0-0-0**

Now:

a) 12...♖b8 and here 13 ♗b3 ♖xb3! followed by 14...d5 (as in Borkowski-Tupek, Slupsk 1992) appears to me a very promising sacrifice that White should avoid with 13 ♗d2!?.

b) 12...♗b7 13 ♗b3 d5 14 exd5 cxd5 15 ♘xd5 ♗xd5 16 ♗xd5 e4 17 ♗xe4 ♖ab8 18 ♗d5 ♖xb2 19 ♔xb2 ♘xd5 and now, instead of 20 ♕xd5 (where Black has at least a draw: 20...♗a3+ 21 ♔b1 ♕xd5 22 ♖xd5 ♖b8+ = de Firmian-Grishchuk, Esbjerg 2000), White should investigate 20 ♗d4.

## C2)

**8 ♗b3**

*7 ♗b3 ♗e7 8 ♗e3* is another way to reach this position.

**8...0-0** *(D)*

Or:

a) 8...a6 transposes to Chapters 9 and 10.

b) 8...♗d7 9 f4 (9 ♕e2 – *8 ♕e2 ♗d7!? 9 ♗b3*; in that line, 9 ♗b3 is hardly the best move; 9 g4!? ♘xd4 10 ♕xd4, De Vreugt-Bosboom, Wijk aan Zee 2001; 9 0-0 0-0 transposes to Line C221 of Chapter 13) 9...♘xd4 (9...0-0 – *8...0-0 9 f4 ♗d7*) 10 ♗xd4 ♗c6 11 ♕e2 b5 12 0-0-0 b4 13 ♗xf6!? favours White.

Now (after 8...0-0):

A good response to 9 ♖g1?! is 9...♕a5! 10 f3 e5 11 ♘de2 ♗e6 12 g4?! d5 ∓ Suetin-Galliamova, Naberezhnye Chelny 1993.

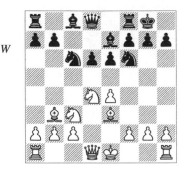

W

## C21)

**9 f4 ♘xd4**

The most critical. Other moves are no more than playable:

a) 9...e5 10 ♘f3 (10 ♘f5!? ♘xe4 11 ♘h6+ gxh6 12 ♘xe4; 10 fxe5!?) 10...♘g4 11 ♗d2 ♗e6 12 ♕e2 ♗xb3 13 cxb3 ♖c8 14 0-0 ♘f6 15 ♔h1 ♘d4! with counterplay for Black, Sigurjonsson-G.Kuzmin, Reykjavik 1978.

b) 9...♘a5 10 ♕f3!? (10 0-0 transposes to Line C222) 10...e5 (10...b6 11 0-0-0 ♗b7 12 g4 ♘xb3+ 13 axb3 ♖c8 14 g5 ♘d7 15 ♖hg1 ± Kundin-Chovnik, Israeli Cht 1998) 11 ♘f5 ♗xf5 12 exf5 ♘xb3 transposes to note 'c1' to Black's 10th move in Chapter 1.

c) 9...♗d7 10 ♕f3 (10 0-0 – *9 0-0 ♗d7 10 f4*; 10 ♕e2!? – *9 ♕e2 ♗d7 10 f4*) 10...♘xd4! 11 ♗xd4 ♗c6 (11...b5!? 12 e5 dxe5 13 fxe5 ♘e8 14 ♘e4 ♗c6 15 c3 b4, Stefansson-Dlugy, London Lloyds Bank 1987) 12 f5 (12 0-0-0 b5!; 12 g4 e5!; 12 a4!?, Plaskett-Ashley, Mermaid Beach 1998; 12 0-0 – *9 0-0 ♗d7 10 f4 ♘xd4 11 ♗xd4 ♗c6 12 ♕f3*) 12...e5 (12...exf5?! 13 ♕xf5 ♕c8 14 ♕f3 ±) 13 ♗e3 b5 14 0-0-0 ♕c7 15 g4 b4 probably gives Black adequate counterplay, Tatai-Huguet, Reggio Emilia 1967/8.

**10 ♗xd4**

As of now it is hard to say if 10 ♕xd4!? can revive this old variation. 10...♘g4 (10...b6 11 0-0-0 ♗b7 12 ♖he1 ♖c8 13 e5 ♘g4 14 exd6 ♗f6 15 ♕d3 ± Mikhalchishin-Kiss, Balatonbereny 1988; 10...♗d7 11 0-0-0 ♗c6 12 ♔b1 ♕a5 13 ♖hf1 b5 14 a3! ♖ab8 15 e5 dxe5 16 fxe5 ♘d7 17 ♖xf7! ± Istratescu-Hraček, Krynica Z 1998) 11 ♗d2 (11 ♗g1!?) 11...d5!? (calmer is 11...e5 12 ♕d3 exf4 13 ♗xf4 ♗e6!?, as GM Lanka has played twice) 12 exd5 (or 12 e5 b6 with strong counterplay) 12...♗f6 13 ♕g1 exd5 14 0-0-0 d4 and Black has hardly any problems, Gi.Hernandez-Vera, Cienfuegos 1996.

**10...b5!**

10...e5 was suggested by Euwe. Then:

a) 11 fxe5 dxe5 and now:

a1) 12 ♗e3 ♕xd1+ (less precise are 12...♘g4 13 ♕xd8! ♖xd8 14 ♗d2 and 12...♕a5 13 0-0 with the point 13...♘g4 14 ♕d5!) 13 ♖xd1 ♗b4 14 0-0 ♗xc3 15 bxc3 ♗g4 16 ♖de1 ♘xe4 17 ♗c1 ♘c5 = 18 ♗a3 ♘xb3 19 ♗xf8 ♘d2 and 20...♘c4 – Veličković.

a2) 12 ♗xe5 ♕a5 13 ♗xf6 ♗xf6 14 0-0, and Black can avoid the idea of 14...♗e6 15 ♘d5!? ♗xb2 16 ♖b1 with a certain initiative (Votava-Stocek, Czech Ch (Lazne Bohdanec) 1999) through 14...♗xc3!? 15 bxc3 ♗e6.

b) 11 ♗e3 ♘g4 12 ♗c1 (after 12 ♗d2 ♗h4+! 13 g3 ♘xh2 14 ♔f2 exf4 15 ♗xf4 ♘g4+ 16 ♔g2 ♗f6 17 ♘d5 ♗e6, Black has an extra pawn and enough defensive resources, Mitkov-R.Scherbakov, Belorechensk 1992) 12...exf4 13 ♗xf4 ♘e5 (13...♗f6 can be met by 14 ♕d2 ± or 14 ♕xd6!?) 14

0-0 ♗e6 15 ♔h1 with some advantage for White, Lastin-Scherbakov, Russian Ch (Elista) 1995.

**11 e5 dxe5 12 fxe5 ♘d7**

In this position White has failed for many years to demonstrate anything substantial:

a) After 13 ♕e2, it seems sufficient to play 13...♗c5!?.

b) 13 0-0 and then:

b1) 13...a6 transposes to Line C222 of Chapter 9.

b2) 13...b4!? 14 ♘e4 ♗b7 15 ♘d6 ♗xd6 16 exd6 ♕g5 17 ♕e2 and now not 17...♗d5?! 18 ♖ad1, as in Fischer-F.Olafsson, Stockholm IZ 1962, but 17...a5 = Stoica-Tischbierek, Calimanesti 1992.

b3) 13...♗c5 14 ♗xc5 ♘xc5 15 ♕xd8 ♖xd8 16 ♘xb5 ♗a6 17 ♗c4 ♖ab8 (alternatively, 17...♗xb5!? 18 ♗xb5 ♖ab8, Perez-Geller, Havana 1965) 18 a4 ♘xa4 = Fischer-Geller, Curaçao Ct 1962.

c) 13 ♕g4 ♗c5 (13...b4!? 14 ♘e4 ♗b7 15 ♘d6 ♗xd6 16 exd6 ♘f6, Stein-Gheorghiu, Reykjavik 1972, is an important alternative) 14 0-0-0 ♗xd4 (14...♕b6?! 15 ♘e4! ♗xd4 16 ♖xd4, Barle-Beliavsky, USSR-Yugoslavia 1971, 16...♔h8 17 ♘g5 ± Nunn) 15 ♕xd4 ♕g5+ 16 ♔b1 and now Razuvaev suggests 16...♖b8!? rather than 16...♕xe5 17 ♕xe5 ♘xe5 18 ♘xb5 ± Alexander-Hollis, Hastings 1962/3.

d) 13 ♕f3 ♖b8 14 0-0-0 (14 ♗xa7?! ♗h4+!, Ehlvest-Milos, Bali 2000; 14 ♘e4 ♗b7!) and now, instead of 14...♗b7 15 ♕g4 b4 16 ♗xa7 ♖a8 (Tatai-Zuckerman, Wijk aan Zee 1968) 17 ♘b5! with the point 17...♘xe5 18 ♕g3 ♕a5 19 ♕xe5 ♖xa7 20 ♖d7 ±, Black solves his problems by means of

14...♕c7!, as has been shown in practice in a number of games.

## C22)

**9 0-0** *(D)*

This is a more popular move-order than 9 f4 (in Fischer's games and in general).

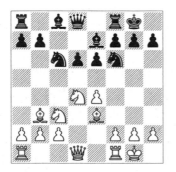

After 1972, 9...a6 and later 10 f4 ♘xd4 (see Chapter 9) came to the fore. The old continuations have now almost disappeared, although this may be rather undeserved.

**C221: 9...♗d7** 212
**C222: 9...♘a5** 214

Other moves:

a) 9...♕c7 10 f4 ♘a5 11 ♕f3 (or 11 f5!?) is promising for White.

b) 9...♕a5 10 f4 (10 ♔h1 ♘xd4 11 ♕xd4 b5 12 a3 ♗a6 ∞ Brunner-Korchnoi, Zurich (1) 1996) 10...♘xd4 (10...♘h5 11 ♕xh5 ♘xh5 12 f5 ±) 11 ♗xd4 e5 12 ♗f2 (12 ♗e3!? ♘g4 13 ♕e2) 12...exf4 13 ♗d4 ♗g4 14 ♕e1 is slightly better for White, Cirić-Korchnoi, Yugoslavia-USSR 1965.

c) 9...♘xd4 10 ♗xd4 b5 (10...b6 ±) 11 ♘xb5 ♗a6 (after 11...♘xe4, apart from 12 ♘xa7, also good is 12 c4!? a6

13 ♗c2 ♗b7 14 ♘c3 ± K.Müller-Cullip, Oakham jr 1992) 12 a4 (no advantage is gained by 12 c4 ♗xb5! 13 cxb5 ♘xe4 14 ♕g4 ♘f6 15 ♕e2, Fischer-Korchnoi, Rovinj/Zagreb 1970, 15...d5 Korchnoi) 12...♘xe4 13 c4! ± (Nunn).

## C221)

**9...♗d7 10 f4!**

If 10 ♕e2, then 10...♘xd4 11 ♗xd4 ♗c6 (or 11...b5 12 ♘xb5 ♗xb5 13 ♕xb5 ♘xe4 14 ♖ad1) 12 ♖ad1!? ♕a5 13 f4 e5 14 fxe5 dxe5 15 ♖f5 ♗c5 16 ♗f2 may give White some hope for an advantage, Gligorić-Pomar, Malaga 1961. It is simpler to proceed with 10...a6! 11 f4, transposing to note 'c1' to Black's 10th move in Line C22 of Chapter 9 (=).

**10...♘xd4!**

Or:

a) 10...♖c8 is poor in view of 11 ♘db5!.

b) 10...♕c8 is well met by 11 f5!, Fischer-Larsen, Denver Ct (5) 1971.

c) 10...a6 transposes to note 'c' to Black's 10th move in Line C22 of Chapter 9.

d) 10...♘a5 11 ♕f3 ♖c8 and now, rather than 12 g4 ♘c4 13 g5 ♘e8 14 ♗xc4 ♖xc4 15 h4 g6! 16 f5 gxf5 17 exf5 e5 ∞ Rittner-Simagin, corr. 1968, Nunn suggests 12 ♖ad1!? ♘c4 13 ♗c1 ±.

**11 ♗xd4** *(D)*
**11...♗c6**

Or 11...b5, and then:

a) After 12 e5 the game seems about equal.

b) 12 f5 b4 (12...e5 13 ♗e3 b4 14 ♘d5 ♘xe4!?) 13 fxe6 (Stoica-Atalik, Romanian Cht 1996) 13...fxe6 14 ♘e2 ♔h8! is also satisfactory for Black.

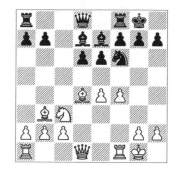

*B*

c) After 12 ♗xf6!?, I am unsure whether Black obtains full compensation for the two pawns in the variation 12...♗xf6 13 ♕xd6 b4 14 ♕xb4 a5 15 ♕d6 ♗xc3 16 bxc3 ♗b5 17 ♕xd8 ♖fxd8 18 ♖fb1 ♗c6.

**12 ♕e2**

Other continuations lead to chances for both sides:

a) 12 ♕f3 b5! 13 ♖ae1 b4 14 ♘d1 ♕c7 15 ♕g3 (Zso.Polgar-Ashley, New York 1989) 15...a5!?.

b) 12 ♕d3 b5 13 ♘xb5 (13 e5 dxe5 14 fxe5 ♘d7 and now 15 ♕e3 a5, Lutikov-Tukmakov, Odessa 1976, or 15 ♘e4 ♗xe4 16 ♕xe4 ♘c5, Christiansen-Yermolinsky, USA Ch (Seattle) 2000) 13...♗xe4!, Szabo-Benko, Hungarian Ch (Budapest) 1951.

c) 12 ♕e1 b5 13 ♖d1 ♕c7! = (rather than 13...b4 14 e5! ±) Benjamin-Kreiman, Connecticut 2000.

**12...b5**

Not 12...♕a5? 13 f5 e5 14 ♗f2 ± (Fischer-Pilnik, Santiago 1959) 14...b5 15 a3!.

12...♕c7 13 f5 (better is 13 ♖ad1 or 13 ♖ae1) 13...e5 14 ♗f2 b5! with counterplay, M.Kiselev-Bologan, St Petersburg 1996.

**13 ♘xb5**

There is no danger for Black in 13 ♖ad1 b4 14 e5 bxc3 15 exf6 ♗xf6 16 ♗xf6 ♕xf6 (16...gxf6 is risky) 17 ♖xd6 ♖ac8 (Nezhmetdinov-Geller, Gorky 1954) and if 18 f5, then 18...♕e7!.

**13...♗xb5**

13...♗xe4? 14 ♘xa7 ± Fischer-Saidy, New Jersey 1957.

13...e5? 14 fxe5 dxe5 15 ♗e3 a6 16 ♘c3 ♘xe4 17 ♖xf7 ± Fischer-Nievergelt, Zurich 1959.

**14 ♕xb5 ♘xe4**

In 1972 Fischer probably was ready to defend this position as White against Spassky, but we can only guess what he had in mind at the time...

**15 f5**

15 ♕d3 d5 16 c4 dxc4 17 ♗xc4 ♘d6 = Bannik-Boleslavsky, USSR Cht 1955.

**15...e5**

15...d5?! 16 fxe6 fxe6 is not sufficient in view of 17 ♕c6!.

15...♗f6 has occurred rather often:

a) 16 ♖ad1 ♗xd4+ 17 ♖xd4 d5 = Yudovich-Geller, Gorky 1954.

b) 16 ♕d3 and now:

b1) 16...d5 17 ♗xf6 (17 ♖ad1!?) 17...♘xf6 18 c4 (Fischer-R.Weinstein, USA Ch (New York) 1958/9) 18...♕b6+ 19 ♔h1 dxc4 20 ♕xc4 ± Nunn.

b2) Black can possibly equalize by playing 16...♗xd4+!? 17 ♕xd4 ♘c5, as in the game Winants-Gershon, Antwerp 1994.

c) 16 ♗xf6!? ♕xf6 17 ♖ad1 looks promising for White.

**16 ♗e3**

16 ♕d3!?.

**16...g5 17 ♕e2 ♗xe3+ 18 ♕xe3 ♘f6**

The game is equal, Chandler-Rachels, Manila IZ 1990.

**C222)**
**9...♘a5 10 f4 b6** *(D)*

10...♘xb3 11 axb3 e5 12 ♘f5 ♗xf5 13 exf5 exf4 14 ♖xf4 d5 15 ♕f3 with a slight advantage for White, Milos-Limp, São Paulo Z 1998.

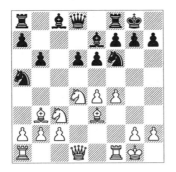

W

Lately, GM Ruslan Scherbakov has been trying to revive a rather forgotten plan with ...b6 and has achieved some success. Black wishes to maintain a strong defensive position and gradually to make use of the beneficial position of the bishop on b7.

**11 e5**
Or:
a) 11 ♕f3 ♗b7 12 g4 ♖c8 13 g5 ♖xc3! gave Black good play in Padevsky-Botvinnik, Moscow 1956. Nevertheless, Botvinnik was sceptical of the plan with ...b6.

b) 11 ♕d3 ♗b7 12 ♖fe1 ♕c8 13 f5 e5 14 ♘f3 ♘xb3 15 axb3 ♖d8 16 ♗f2 d5 17 exd5 ♘xd5 18 ♖xe5 with acceptable play for Black, Kotsur-R.Scherbakov, Tula 1999. Now 18...♘xc3!? 19 ♕xc3 ♗f6 = is sufficient.

c) 11 ♕e2 ♗b7 12 ♗f2 (Gochev-R.Scherbakov, Plovdiv 1990) 12...♖c8!? R.Scherbakov.

**11...dxe5**

In the 1950s and 1960s, 11...♘e8 12 f5! was studied in detail: 12...dxe5 (12...♘xb3 13 ♘c6! ♕c7 14 ♘xe7+ ♕xe7 15 f6 Geller; 12...exf5 can be met by 13 e6! or 13 ♗d5!?) 13 fxe6 and now:

a) 13...f6? 14 ♘f5 ♘xb3 15 ♘d5! +− Geller-Vatnikov, Kiev 1950.

b) 13...exd4?! 14 exf7+ ♔h8 15 fxe8♕ ♕xe8 16 ♗xd4, Romanovsky-Shamkovich, USSR 1956.

c) 13...fxe6!? should be met by 14 ♖xf8+! ± (but not 14 ♘xe6?! ♕d1 15 ♘xf8+ ♘xb3 16 ♖axd1 ♘d4).

d) 13...♘xb3 14 ♘c6! ♕d6! 15 ♕xd6 (15 ♘d5? ♗h4! is much better for Black, Bilek-T.Petrosian, Oberhausen Echt 1961) 15...♗xd6 16 axb3 ♗xe6 17 ♘xa7!? with a better ending for White, Fischer-Korchnoi, Curaçao Ct 1962.

**12 fxe5 ♘e8!**
The lines 12...♘d7 13 ♖xf7 ♘xe5 14 ♖xf8+ ♗xf8 15 ♗xe6+ and 12...♘d5 13 ♘xd5 exd5 14 ♕f3 clearly favour White.

After the text-move, the initial position of Scherbakov's variation arises. Up to now he has managed to obtain positions with chances for both sides where Black has cards up his sleeve.

**13 ♕h5!?**
Black's only weakness is the h7-pawn, so it is necessary to check whether it could withstand a direct assault. Other moves are less testing:

a) 13 ♕g4 ♕c7 14 ♘f3 ♘xb3 15 cxb3 ♗a6 16 ♖fd1 ♖d8 17 ♖xd8 ♕xd8 18 ♖d1 ♕c8 19 ♘d4 ½-½ Bezgodov-R.Scherbakov, Petropavlovsk 1999.

b) 13 ♕f3 ♗b7 14 ♕g3 (14 ♘xe6? ♕c8) 14...♘xb3 15 axb3 a6, with a long manoeuvring game ahead.

**13...g6**

Or:

a) 13...♗b7? 14 ♘xe6 +–.

b) After 13...♕c7, I propose 14 ♘d5!? exd5 15 ♗xd5 g6 16 ♕h6 ♘g7 17 ♗xa8 ♗a6 18 ♕f4.

c) 13...♘xb3 14 ♘c6 ♕c7 15 ♘xe7+ ♕xe7 16 axb3 is somewhat better for White, Sale-Dizdarević, Osijek 1993.

**14 ♕h6**

Alternatively:

a) 14 ♕g4 ♕c7 15 ♗h6 ♘g7 16 ♖ae1 ♘xb3 17 axb3 ♗b7 18 ♔h1 (or 18 ♗xg7 ♔xg7 19 ♕xe6 ♖ad8!? 20 ♘cb5 ♕c5 Cherny) 18...♖ad8 19 ♘f3 ♖d7 20 ♘g5 ♖d2 21 ♘ce4 ♖xc2 22 ♗xg7 h5! is at least no worse for Black, Kotsur-R.Scherbakov, Ekaterinburg 1999.

b) White's advantage is not felt either after 14 ♕e2 ♕c7 15 ♗h6 ♘g7 16 ♔h1 a6 17 ♖ad1 ♘xb3 18 axb3 ♗b7, Anisimov-R.Scherbakov, Cheliabinsk 1984.

**14...♕c7 15 ♘f3**

After 15...♗b7 16 ♘g5 ♗xg5 17 ♗xg5 ♕xe5 18 ♗e7, Black's compensation has to be proven.

**C23)**

**9 ♕e2** *(D)*

This position often arises after 7 ♗b3 ♗e7 8 ♗e3 0-0 9 ♕e2, and to make a general assessment of 7 ♗b3, it is important to know whether Black has important additional ideas (advantages) here as compared with 7 ♗e3 ♗e7 8 ♕e2 0-0 9 0-0-0 (Line C3).

We start with the variations where there is little or no difference:

a) More than half of the games simply transpose to the main lines of the Velimirović Attack via 9...a6 (Line A, Chapter 10) or via 9...♕c7 10 0-0-0 a6 (Line B2, Chapter 10).

b) 9...d5 10 0-0-0 – Line C32.

c) 9...♘xd4 10 ♗xd4 ♕a5 (10...e5 11 ♗e3 ±) 11 0-0-0 – Line C34.

d) 9...♕a5 10 0-0-0 (10 0-0-0!? ♘xd4 11 ♗xd4 b6 12 a4 ± de Firmian-Sosonko, Polanica Zdroj 1995) transposes to Line C34.

Then, two ideas for Black that have not been verified properly:

e) 9...♘d7!? 10 0-0-0 ♘c5.

f) 9...e5!?.

Finally, two rather well-known continuations that are claimed to reveal the drawbacks of an early ♗b3:

g) 9...♘a5!? and now:

g1) 10 0-0-0 – *7 ♗e3 ♗e7 8 ♕e2 0-0 9 0-0-0 ♘a5 10 ♗b3*.

g2) 10 g4 ♘xb3 11 axb3 d5! 12 e5 ♘e4 13 0-0 (13 ♘xe4 dxe4 14 ♘b5 {14 0-0? ♕a5 ∓} 14...a6 15 0-0 ♗d7 16 ♘c3 ♗c6 17 ♖fd1 ♕c7, Motylev-Panchenko, Kazan 1995, 18 ♗d4 ♗g5!? 19 ♘xe4 ♗f4 with compensation) 13...♘xc3 (13...♗d7!?) 14 bxc3 ♕c7 15 ♗d2 ♗d7 16 ♖ae1 a5!? 17 ♕d3 a4 18 ♖e3 a3!? 19 ♖h3 g6 (19...h6!?) 20 ♕e3 f6 21 ♖xh7 ♔xh7 22 ♕h6+ ♔g8 23 ♕xg6+ ♔h8 24 ♖e1 (Golubev-Weiler, Leuven 1994) 24...♕xe5! =.

g3) 10 f4 e5!? 11 ♘f3 ♘xb3 12 axb3 ♗g4 13 0-0-0 ♕a5 14 ♔b1 ♖ac8 with counterplay, A.Ivanov-Mochalov, Minsk 1985.

h) 9...♗d7!? and then:

h1) 10 0-0-0, transposing to Line C351, may be considered an achievement for Black (in the variation *7 ♗e3 ♗e7 8 ♕e2 0-0 9 0-0-0 ♗d7*, instead of *10 ♗b3, 10 f4!* is stronger).

h2) 10 0-0 transposes to the note to White's 10th move in Line C221 (=).

h3) 10 f4!? ♘xd4 11 ♗xd4 b5 (or 11...♕a5) has hardly been tried at all.

## C3)
8 ♕e2 *(D)*

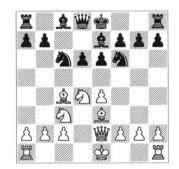

**8...0-0**

The other main line is 8...a6 (or, first, 8...♕c7 and then ...a6; e.g., 9 0-0-0 a6 transposes to Line C of Chapter 11) which transposes to Line D of Chapter 11.

Auxiliary possibilities are:

a) 8...d5 9 0-0-0 0-0 – *8...0-0 9 0-0-0 d5*.

b) 8...♕a5 9 0-0-0 0-0 – *8...0-0 9 0-0-0 ♕a5*.

c) 8...♘xd4 9 ♗xd4 ♗d7 (9...0-0 10 0-0-0 – *8...0-0 9 0-0-0 ♘xd4 10*

*♗xd4*) 10 0-0-0 (10 f4 ±) 10...♕a5? (10...♖c8 11 ♗xa7!?) 11 ♘b5! 0-0 (11...♗xb5 12 ♗xb5+ ♔f8 13 ♗c4 ♕g5+ 14 ♔b1 ♕xg2 15 ♖hg1 ♕h3 16 f4, Nunn, looks hopeless for Black) 12 ♘xd6 ± Nunn-Korchnoi, Brussels World Cup 1988.

d) 8...♘a5 9 ♗d3 (9 ♗b3 ♗d7!? – *8...♗d7 9 ♗b3 ♘a5*; interesting is 9 ♗b5+!? ♘d7 10 b4 ♕c7 11 ♗xd7+ ♗xd7 12 ♘db5) 9...0-0 (9...a6 transposes to note 'b' to Black's 9th move in Line A of Chapter 11, which is a little better for White; 9...e5 10 ♗b5+ ♔f8 11 ♘b3 a6 12 ♗d3, Ehlvest-I.Ivanov, New York 1990). Now after 10 f4 e5 11 ♘f3 exf4 12 ♗xf4 ♗e6 13 0-0-0 (13 ♘d4!?) 13...♖c8, Black obtains an acceptable position, Golubev-Lutsko, Kiev 1997, so it is worth considering 10 0-0, 10 g4, and in particular 10 0-0-0 – *8...0-0 9 0-0-0 ♘a5 10 ♗d3*.

e) 8...e5 should perhaps be met by 9 ♘f3 ± rather than 9 ♘f5 ♗xf5 10 exf5 ♘d4 11 ♗xd4 (11 ♕d3 d5! 12 ♗xd5 ♘xd5 13 ♗xd4 ♘b4! is much better for Black) 11...exd4 (Ernst-Kouatly, Manila OL 1992) 12 ♘b5!? d5 13 ♗b3 ♕a5+ 14 ♔f1.

f) 8...♗d7!? gained the support of several grandmasters in the 1990s, and for a while White had trouble getting to grips with it:

f1) 9 ♗b3 ♘a5!? (9...0-0 transposes to Line C23; 9...♖c8 10 f4 0-0 11 0-0 ♘a5 12 e5 ♘e8 13 ♕h5 ± Vouldis-Atalik, Karditsa 1996) 10 g4 (maybe something else?) 10...♘xb3 11 axb3 h5 with counterplay, A.Ivanov-Atalik, Chicago 1997.

f2) 9 0-0-0 ♖c8 (9...0-0 – *8...0-0 9 0-0-0 ♗d7*), and then:

f21) 10 ♘db5 ♘a5! 11 ♗b3 – *10 ♗b3 ♘a5 11 ♘db5*.

f22) 10 f4 ♘a5 (10...0-0 – *8...0-0 9 0-0-0 ♗d7 10 f4 ♖c8*) 11 ♗d3 ♖xc3 12 bxc3 ♕c7 deserves checking.

f23) 10 ♘xc6 bxc6! (10...♗xc6? 11 e5; 10...♖xc6 11 f3 a6 12 g4 b5 13 ♗b3 Lukacs) 11 g4 (11 f4 ♕a5 ∞ Avrukh) 11...0-0 (11...d5 12 g5! ♘xe4 13 ♘xe4 dxe4, D.Frolov-Ma.Tseitlin, St Petersburg 1997, 14 ♕g4! 0-0 15 h4 ± Avrukh) 12 g5 ♘e8, and now both 13 h4 d5 14 ♗b3 ♗b4! 15 h5 ♗xc3 16 bxc3 ♘d6 17 h6 g6 18 f3 c5, A.Sokolov-Zviagintsev, Russian Ch (St Petersburg) 1998, and 13 f4 d5 14 ♗d3 ♗b4 (Rechlis-Avrukh, Israeli Cht 2000) 15 ♘b1! (Avrukh) seem double-edged.

f24) 10 f3 0-0 (10...♘a5!? can be met by 11 ♗d3!? or 11 ♗b3 – *10 ♗b3 ♘a5 11 f3*) 11 g4 (11 ♘xc6 is recommended by Tsesarsky) 11...♘xd4 12 ♗xd4 ♕a5 13 ♗b3 b5 14 e5 is slightly better for White, Rogić-Greenfeld, Pardubice 1995.

f25) 10 ♗b3 ♘a5 (10...♘xd4 11 ♗xd4!? with the point 11...e5 12 ♗xa7 ♕a5 13 ♗e3 ♖xc3 14 ♗d2; 10...0-0 transposes to Line C351) 11 f3 (11 g4? ♖xc3!; White gains nothing through 11 ♘db5 ♘xb3+ 12 axb3 ♕a5!) 11...♘xb3+ (11...0-0 12 g4 ♘xb3+ will most likely come to the same thing) 12 axb3 (12 ♘xb3 a5!? 13 ♕f2 ♖xc3 14 bxc3 a4 gives Black compensation, Mortensen-Greenfeld, Moscow OL 1994; 12 cxb3!? Mortensen) 12...0-0 13 g4 ♕a5!? 14 ♔b1 ♘e8 15 ♕d2 ♔h8! (avoiding ♘d5) 16 h4 ♘c7 with the ideas of ...d5 or ...♘a6 and ...♘b4, Menoni-Greenfeld, Montecatini Terme 1997.

f3) Given that f4 is, as a rule, a good response to ...♗d7, it is strange that almost nobody has yet played 9 f4.

**9 0-0-0** *(D)*
9 ♗b3 transposes to Line C23.

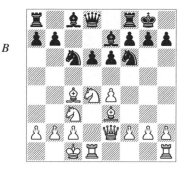

*B*

Should Black not wish to play the main variations of the Velimirović (9...a6 or 9...♕c7 10 ♗b3 a6 – in the latter case, however, 10 ♖hg1!? is interesting), then he has the following at his disposal:

**C31)**
**9...♘a5**
Now:

a) 10 ♗b3 and then:

a1) 10...♘xb3+ 11 axb3 ♕a5 12 ♔b1 ♗d7 13 g4 transposes to note 'd3' to Black's 10th move in Line C351.

a2) 10...♗d7 – *9...♗d7 10 ♗b3 ♘a5*.

b) 10 ♗d3 is probably more accurate. Now 10...a6 transposes to *7...a6 8*

♕e2 ♘a5 9 ♗d3! ♗e7 10 0-0-0 0-0 (note 'b1' to Black's 9th move in Line A of Chapter 11).

## C32)
### 9...d5 (D)

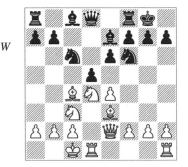

W

This move (suggested by Konstantinopolsky in 1966) does not quite equalize.

### 10 ♗b3
The other ideas are:

a) 10 ♘xe6!? (the only way to foist a tactical struggle on Black) 10...fxe6 11 exd5 ♘a5 12 dxe6, and now both 12...♕e8 13 ♗b5 ♘c6 (13...♕g6!?) 14 ♖he1 a6 15 ♗c4 b5, I.Zaitsev-Bitman, Moscow 1967, and 12...♕c7 13 ♗d5 (I.Zaitsev-Gik, Moscow 1967) 13...♘c6 14 ♕c4!? lead to a chaotic game.

b) 10 exd5 exd5 is hardly dangerous for Black. Approximate variations: 11 ♘f3 ♗e6; 11 ♘db5 ♗e6; 11 ♗b3 ♖e8 (11...♗b4!? 12 ♘db5 {12 ♕b5!?} 12...♗e6 13 ♗g5 ♖e8; Konstantinopolsky suggested 11...♘a5) 12 ♕b5 (12 ♘f3 ♗e6 13 h3 ♕a5 14 ♔b1 a6 Nunn) 12...♘b4 (12...♘a5? 13 ♘xd5) 13 a3 a6 14 ♕e2 ♘c6 15 ♖he1 ♗c5 Akopian.

c) 10 ♘f3 ♘xe4!? (10...♘b4 11 exd5 ♘bxd5 12 ♗d4 ± Ostojić-Hartston, Hastings 1967/8) 11 ♘xe4, and Black can proceed either by playing 11...♕a5 12 ♗d2 ♕a4 (12...♗b4 13 ♗xb4 ±; 12...♕b6!?) 13 ♗d3 ♕xa2!? (13...dxe4 14 ♕xe4 ♕xe4 15 ♗xe4 ± Boleslavsky) 14 ♘c3 ♕a1+ 15 ♘b1 e5! with compensation, or by 11...♕c7 12 ♗d3 (12 ♘eg5 dxc4 =) 12...dxe4 13 ♗xe4 e5! (= Nunn).

d) After 10 ♘b3, 10...♘xe4 11 ♘xe4 ♕c7 is probably again the most accurate and sufficient to equalize.

### 10...♘a5
After 10...♗b4 11 ♘db5!, 10...♖e8 11 ♘f3 or 10...♕a5 11 exd5 exd5 12 ♕b5!, Garibian-Yudovich, USSR 1968, White's chances are better.

### 11 e5
11 ♖he1 e5 12 ♘f3 ♘xb3+ 13 axb3 ♕a5 14 exd5 ♗b4 15 ♔b1 (15 ♘xe5? ♗xc3 16 bxc3 ♘e4!! –+; 15 ♗d2!?) 15...♗xc3 16 bxc3 ♘xd5 17 ♗d2 ♘xc3+?! (17...f6 18 ♘xe5 fxe5 19 ♕xe5 ♖f5 =; 17...♕xc3!?) 18 ♗xc3 ♕xc3 19 ♕xe5! gives White a slight advantage, Wedberg-Sosonko, Amsterdam 1984.

### 11...♘d7 12 f4
White has a small advantage. Now the following continuations have been seen:

a) 12...♘b6 13 ♔b1 (13 g4!? NCO) 13...♘xb3 14 cxb3 f6 15 exf6 (15 h4!?) 15...♗xf6 16 ♖he1 (16 ♘f3!?) 16...♕e8! = Hübner-Sosonko, Wijk aan Zee 1984.

b) 12...a6 13 ♖hf1 ♘xb3+ (13...b5 is met by 14 ♗xd5!) 14 axb3, Ahlander-L.Schneider, Stockholm 1986.

c) 12...♗b4 13 ♗d2 ♘c5 14 ♖hf1 ♘axb3+ 15 axb3 a5 16 ♔b1 ♗xc3 17

♗xc3 ♘e4 18 ♖f3, de Firmian-Sosonko, Lucerne Wcht 1989.

## C33)

**9...♘xd4**

This is similar to the line 9...♕a5 10 ♗b3 ♘xd4, but White has some additional ideas.

**10 ♗xd4**

10 ♖xd4!?.

**10...♕a5**

Now:

a) 11 ♗b3 – *9...♕a5 10 ♗b3 ♘xd4 11 ♗xd4* (Line C34).

b) 11 f4?! e5! = Yurtaev-Zhidkov, USSR 1978.

c) 11 e5!? dxe5 12 ♗xe5 b6 (12...♘d7!?) 13 ♖d4 (13 ♘b5 ♗a6 14 ♗c3 ♕a4 15 ♔b1 Nunn) 13...♗b7 and now Geller recommended 14 ♖hd1! (instead of 14 ♗b5 a6, Velimirović-Geller, Budapest 1973, 15 ♖a4 axb5 16 ♖xa5 ♖xa5).

d) 11 ♖hg1!? ♗d7 12 g4!? ♖fc8 (12...b5? 13 g5 ♘xe4 14 ♗d3!! Wolff) 13 g5 (13 ♗b3 transposes to note 'b' to Black's 12th move in Line C34) 13...♘e8 and now 14 ♔b1! is Christiansen's improvement over 14 f4 ♖xc4!! 15 ♕xc4 b5 with an unclear position, Brunner-Christiansen, Novi Sad OL 1990.

## C34)

**9...♕a5** *(D)*

**10 ♗b3**

Otherwise:

a) 10 g4?! is dubious because of 10...♘e5!, Šahović-Geller, Belgrade 1969, while 10...d5!? and 10...♘xd4!? are also interesting.

b) 10 ♘b3 ♕c7 11 f4 a6 12 g4 b5 13 ♗d3 is a double-edged form of the

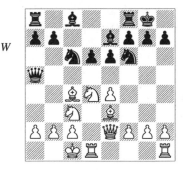

Anti-Sozin (see the note to White's 8th move in Line B5 of Chapter 14).

c) 10 f4!? ♘xd4 (10...♗d7 can be met by 11 ♘b3!? or 11 g4!? ♘xd4 12 ♖xd4 e5 13 ♖d5) 11 ♖xd4 a6 (11...e5 12 ♘d5!? ±) 12 ♗b3 (12 a3?! d5! 13 exd5 ♗xa3, A.Ivanov-Dlugy, USA Ch (Jacksonville) 1990).

d) 10 ♖hg1!? is of particular interest: 10...♘xd4 11 ♗xd4 ♗d7 transposes to Line C33, and if 10...♗d7, then 11 ♘b3!?.

**10...♘xd4**

10...♗d7!? is possibly better than its reputation: 11 ♘db5 (11 g4!? ♘xd4 12 ♖xd4 e5 13 ♘d5 Yudasin; 11 ♖hg1!?; 11 ♔b1!?) 11...d5 (11...♘e8 12 ♗f4 clearly favours White) is very interesting. For instance, 12 exd5 (unsuccessful is 12 ♗g5?! a6; 12 ♗d2 ♗b4 {12...dxe4!?} 13 e5 ♘xe5 14 ♕xe5 ♗xb5 15 a3 ♗xc3 {15...♗c4!?} 16 ♗xc3 ∞) 12...exd5, and as yet White has not shown anything:

a) 13 ♘xd5 ♘xd5 14 ♗xd5 ♘b4 15 ♘c3 ♗f5 16 ♗b3 ♖ac8 with the initiative for the pawn, Turlej-Gertz, corr. 1999.

b) 13 ♗d2 ♗b4! 14 a3 (or 14 ♘xd5 ♘xd5 15 ♗xd5 ♖ae8!) 14...♖fe8 15 ♕f1 a6! – Sek.

c) 13 ♘xa7 ♖xa7 14 ♘xd5 ♖aa8 15 ♗b6 (15 ♘xf6+ ♗xf6 16 ♖xd7 ♘b4!) 15...♕a6 16 ♗c4 ♕a4 17 ♗b3 ♕a6 with a repetition, Hunter-Dünhaupt, corr. 1970-1.

**11 ♗xd4**

11 ♖xd4!? ♗d7 and then: 12 ♖d3 ♗c6 13 ♗d2 ♕c7 14 g4 b5 15 g5 ♘d7 16 ♖h3 ♖fc8 is OK for Black, Dauga-Prieditis, corr. 1974; 12 g4!? e5 13 ♘d5 Geller; 12 ♖hd1!? ♗c6 13 f4, London-Dlugy, USA (4) 1986.

**11...♗d7**

11...♕g5+? 12 ♔b1 e5 (12...♕xg2 13 ♖hg1 ♕xh2 14 ♖h1 ♕f4 15 ♖dg1!) 13 h4 ♕xg2 14 ♖dg1 ♗g4 15 ♖xg2 ♗xe2 16 ♘xe2 exd4 17 ♘xd4 is much better for White – Fischer.

**12 ♖hg1**

There are some rare alternatives: 12 ♗xf6?! ♗xf6 13 ♖xd6 ♗c6; 12 f4?! e5!; little studied are 12 f3 and 12 ♖d3!? ♗c6 13 f4, Sveshnikov-Kogan, Lvov 1973.

The known alternative is 12 ♔b1, with the following continuations:

a) 12...b5?! 13 ♗xf6 ±.

b) 12...♖ad8?! 13 ♕e3! b6? (13...b5 14 a3 ± Fischer; 13...♗c6 14 ♗xa7 ♘d7 15 ♗d4! e5 16 ♘d5 ♗xd5 17 ♗c3 +–) 14 ♗xf6 gxf6 15 ♘d5! and White is winning, Fischer-Sofrevski, Skopje/Kruševo/Ohrid 1967.

c) 12...♗c6 13 f4 and now:

c1) 13...e5 14 ♗e3! favours White.

c2) 13...b5 14 e5! dxe5 15 ♕xe5 ± Fischer.

c3) 13...♖fe8 14 ♖hf1 (14 g4!? Sosonko) 14...♖ad8 – *13...♖ad8 14 ♖hf1! ♖fe8.*

c4) 13...♖ad8 14 ♖hf1! (14 f5 exf5 15 exf5 ♖d7 16 ♖hf1 ♗d8! Shamkovich; 14 g4 d5) and now:

c41) 14...♖fe8 can be met by 15 g4!? (Sosonko), or 15 e5 dxe5 16 fxe5 ♘d5 17 ♘e4 with a perceptible advantage for White, Rogić-Sosonko, Bükfürdo 1995.

c42) 14...b5 15 f5! (15 e5!? is also good) 15...b4 16 fxe6 bxc3 17 exf7+ (Murey and Boleslavsky suggested 17 ♖xf6!? with the point 17...gxf6 18 exf7+ ♔h8 19 ♕g4 ♖b8 20 ♕e6 ♕d8 21 ♖f1 ♖b4 22 ♗xc3 ♖xe4 23 ♖xf6 ♖e1+ 24 ♗xe1 ♗xf6 25 ♗a5!! +–) 17...♔h8 18 ♖f5 ♕b4 19 ♕f1! ♘xe4, and Fischer proved a win for White after 20 ♕f4!! (20 a3? ♕b7 21 ♕f4 ♗a4!! wins for Black, Fischer-Geller, Skopje/Kruševo/Ohrid 1967).

d) 12...♖fd8 Geller.

e) 12...♖fc8 13 f4 e5 14 ♘d5 ♘xd5 15 exd5 ♗b5 16 ♕e3 exd4 17 ♕xe7 d3! 18 cxd3 ♕b6 = Franzen-Stern, corr. 1994.

f) 12...♖ac8 13 f4 (13 ♕e1!?, Morozevich-Dlugy, ICC blitz 1999) 13...e5 14 ♘d5 ♘xd5 15 exd5 ♗f6 16 fxe5 ♗xe5 17 ♗xe5 ♖fe8 = de Firmian-Dlugy, USA Ch (Estes Park) 1987.

**12...♗c6**

Or:

a) 12...b5? 13 e5 dxe5 14 ♕xe5 ♖fc8 (14...♗c6 15 ♗xe6 +–) 15 g4 ♕c7 (15...♗c6 16 g5 ♘e8 17 g6 +–) 16 g5 ♘e8 17 ♘d5! ± Yudasin-Fedorowicz, Novi Sad OL 1990.

b) 12...♖fc8 13 g4 e5 (13...b5 14 e5! ♘e8 15 exd6 favours White, Romanishin-Zakharov, USSR 1974) 14 g5! (14 ♗e3 ♖xc3 15 ♗d2 is less convincing) 14...exd4 15 gxf6 ♗xf6 16 ♘d5 with an attack (Yudasin).

c) 12...♖ac8 13 g4 e5 14 ♗e3 (14 g5 is a serious alternative here) 14...♖xc3 15 ♗d2 ♗b5 16 ♕e1 ♖xc2+ 17 ♔xc2

♕a6 (17...♕c7+ 18 ♔b1!) 18 ♗g5
♘d5 ± A.Ivanov-Dlugy, Philadelphia
1989 (18...♗e2!?).

**13 g4 ♘d7**

13...e5 can be answered by 14 ♗e3!
♘xe4? 15 ♘xe4 ♗xe4 16 ♗d2 +−
(Geller) or 14 g5!?.

**14 ♔b1**

14 g5 ♗xg5+! 15 ♔b1 ♗f6 = Plan-
inc-Bertok, Novi Sad 1965; 14 f4!?.

**14...♖fe8**

Or: 14...b5 15 ♘d5! (or 15 g5 b4 16
♘d5) Bosch; 14...♘c5 15 g5 b5 16
♗f6! ± Bednarski-Kramer, Wijk aan
Zee 1969.

**15 g5**

Black now finds himself in danger.
We have to mention:

a) 15...b5 and then:

a1) 16 f4!? b4 (16...♘c5 17 f5 ♗f8
18 g6 ±) 17 f5 bxc3 18 fxe6 fxe6 19
♗xe6+ ♔h8 20 ♗xc3 Bosch.

a2) 16 g6 hxg6 17 ♖xg6 fxg6 (not
17...♗f6?, Bosch-Sosonko, Dutch Ch
(Amsterdam) 1996, 18 ♖xf6 gxf6 19
♕d2 +−) 18 ♗xe6+ ♔f8 19 ♕g4 ♗f6
20 ♗xd7 ♗xd7 21 ♕xd7 ♖ad8 and
Black just about remains in the game.

b) 15...♘c5 16 ♖g3 ♗f8 17 ♖h3
♘xb3 18 axb3 ♕xg5 (18...g6!?) 19 f4!
with an attack, Van der Wiel-Sosonko,
Dutch Ch (Rotterdam) 1998.

## C35)

**9...♗d7** *(D)*

Together with its improved version,
*8...♗d7!?*, the ...♗d7 theme is rather
topical nowadays. We shall discuss:
**C351: 10 ♗b3** 221
**C352: 10 f4!** 223

Otherwise:
a) 10 g4?! ♘xd4.

W

b) 10 ♖hg1 is not recommended either: 10...♖c8! 11 g4 (11 ♗b3 ♘a5 12
f3 is the least of all the evils) 11...♘e5
(11...♘xd4!?) 12 ♗d3 d5! ∓ Olesen-
Dlugy, Philadelphia 1994.

c) 10 f3 ♖c8 (10...♘a5!?; 10...a6)
transposes to note 'f24' to Black's 8th
move in Line C3.

## C351)

**10 ♗b3 ♖c8**

Or:

a) 10...♘xd4 11 ♗xd4 (11 ♖xd4!?
♕a5) and here:

a1) 11...♗c6 12 f4!? ♕a5 13 ♖hf1
b5 14 e5!, Tukmakov-Minkov, USSR
1967.

a2) 11...b5 12 e5! dxe5 13 ♗xe5
♕e8 14 ♘e4.

a3) 11...♕a5 transposes to Line
C34.

b) 10...a6 transposes to note 'b' to
Black's 10th move in Line A of Chapter 10.

c) 10...♕b8!? seems playable as of
now:

c1) 11 f4 ♘xd4! 12 ♗xd4 (scarcely
better is 12 ♖xd4 b5 13 f5 b4 14 fxe6
fxe6, Kholmov-Lein, USSR Ch (Kiev)
1964/5) 12...e5 = Balashov-Bykov,
USSR 1965.

c2) 11 ♔b1 (or 11 ♖he1) 11...♘xd4 12 ♗xd4 b5 13 e5 dxe5 14 ♗xe5 ♕b7 hardly promises anything for White.

c3) 11 g4 ♘xd4 12 ♗xd4 b5 (12...e5!? might be OK: 13 g5 exd4 14 gxf6 dxc3 or 13 ♗xe5 ♗xg4) 13 g5 (13 e5!? ♘e8) 13...♘e8 14 ♕h5 (14 ♖hg1!? b4 – *11 ♖hg1!? ♘xd4 12 ♗xd4 b5 13 g4 b4 14 g5 ♘e8*; 14 ♖dg1!?) 14...b4 15 ♖d3 bxc3! and now both 16 ♖h3 ♗xg5+ 17 ♕xg5 e5, Espig-Kirov, Timisoara 1972, and 16 f4 ♗c6!? 17 ♖e1 ♕b7 are likely to be in Black's favour.

c4) 11 ♖hg1!? ♘xd4 12 ♗xd4 b5 13 g4 (13 e5 dxe5 14 ♗xe5 ♕b7 15 g4 ♗c6 16 g5 ♘d7) 13...b4 14 g5 ♘e8, and instead of 15 ♘d5?! exd5 16 ♗xd5 g6! (T.Petrosian), White should test 15 ♘b1 or 15 ♘a4.

d) 10...♘a5!? (there is insufficient material to assess this plan) 11 g4 ♘xb3+ 12 axb3 and then:

d1) 12...d5!?.

d2) 12...a5!? 13 g5 ♘e8 and now, rather than 14 ♖hg1 a4 15 bxa4 ♗xa4 16 f4 ♗d7 ∞ Golubev-I.Sokolov, Moscow rpd 1994, 14 f4!? is interesting.

d3) 12...♕a5 13 ♔b1 (Nunn proposes 13 g5!?) and now:

d31) 13...♖fc8 14 g5 ♘e8 15 f4 ♘c7!? (15...b5 16 ♕g4 b4 17 ♘d5 ♗d8 18 h4 with an attack, Soltis-I.Ivanov, Boston 1988) 16 f5 exf5 17 exf5 ♗xf5 18 ♘xf5 ♕xf5 19 ♖hf1 with some compensation, Ribeiro-Khuzman, Benasque 1993.

d32) 13...♖fb8 14 g5 (14 f4 b5 15 e5 ♘e8, Velimirović-Van der Wiel, Reggio Emilia 1986/7) 14...♘e8 15 f4 b5 16 ♕g4 b4 17 ♘d5, Nelson-Frederic, corr. 1997.

We now return to 10...♖c8 (D):

W

**11 f4**

11 f3 ♘a5 (11...♘xd4!? 12 ♖xd4) – *8...♗d7 9 0-0-0 ♖c8 10 ♗b3 ♘a5 11 f3 0-0*.

11 ♘db5 ♘e8 and then:

a) It appears that 12 ♘xa7 ♘xa7 13 ♗xa7 b6 14 ♕a6 ♖c6 15 ♗a4 ♖xc3! 16 bxc3 (16 ♗xd7 ♖c7 17 ♗xe8 ♕xe8 18 ♗xb6 ♕c6 –+) 16...♘c7 17 ♕b7 ♗xa4 18 ♗xb6 ♗g5+! favours Black.

b) 12 g4 a6 13 ♘d4 b5 14 h4 ♘a5 15 g5 ♘xb3+ 16 axb3 b4 with strong counterplay, Franzen-Kochiev, Stary Smokovec 1982.

c) 12 f4 a6 13 ♘d4 ♘a5 14 g4 (Zapata-Limp, São Paulo 1997) 14...b5, and Black stands no worse.

**11...♘a5**

11...♕a5!? and then:

a) 12 f5 ♘xd4 13 ♖xd4 (13 ♗xd4?! is met by 13...e5!) 13...exf5 (13...e5 14 ♘d5!; 13...♖xc3 14 ♗d2 ♖xc2+ 15 ♔xc2 ♖c8+ 16 ♔b1 ♕e5 17 ♗c3 ±) 14 ♘d5 ♕d8 15 exf5 (15 ♘xe7+!? ♕xe7 16 exf5) 15...♗xf5 (15...♘xd5 16 ♖xd5 ± Khachian-Mirumian, Armenia 1993) 16 ♘xe7+ ♕xe7 17 ♕f3 with compensation, Khachian.

b) 12 ♘db5 d5 (12...♘e8!? 13 e5 d5 Anand) 13 f5 dxe4 (13...a6 14 exd5!?) 14 ♘xe4 (as an improvement, Nunn

proposed 14 ♖xd7!? ♘xd7 15 fxe6)
14...♘xe4 15 ♖xd7 exf5 16 ♘xa7 ♖c7
and Black has sufficient resources,
Nunn-Dlugy, Wijk aan Zee 1990.

**12 e5 ♘xb3+**

12...♘e8!? deserves some attention.

Now (after 12...♘xb3+):

a) 13 ♘xb3 dxe5 14 fxe5 ♘d5! 15
♘xd5 exd5 16 ♖xd5 ♕c7 (Boleslavsky), and Black should equalize step by
step.

b) 13 axb3 ♘e8 (13...dxe5 14 fxe5
and now 14...♘d5 15 ♘xd5 exd5 ± or
14...♘e8 15 ♘db5 a6 16 ♖xd7! ♕xd7
17 ♖d1 – Boleslavsky) 14 ♔b1 ♕a5 15
♗c1 dxe5 16 fxe5 ♘c7 17 ♖d3 ♖fd8
18 ♖h3 ♗e8 19 ♕e4 f5! 20 exf6 ♗g6
with sufficient counterplay, Szuk-Feher,
Budapest 1994.

### C352)

**10 f4! ♖c8** *(D)*

Or:

a) 10...♕h8?! 11 f5 ♘xd4 12 ♗xd4
(12 ♖xd4 ± Nunn) 12...b5 13 fxe6 ±.

b) 10...♕c8 11 ♘f3!? ♕c7 (11...a6
12 e5 ♘e8 13 h4!, Peters-Dlugy, Los
Angeles 1988) 12 ♔b1 a6 13 ♗d3 e5
(13...b5 14 e5!) 14 f5 ♘b4 (Wolff-
Dlugy, Toronto 1989) 15 ♗c4!? is
slightly better for White.

c) 10...♕c7 11 f5!? (11 ♗b3!?
♘xd4 12 ♖xd4; 11 ♘db5!? ♕b8 12
♕d2; 11 ♖hf1) 11...♘xd4 12 ♗xd4
exf5 13 exf5 ♗xf5 14 ♖de1 with compensation, Severodvinsk-Prokopievsk,
telegraph game between towns, 1967.

d) 10...a6 11 e5 dxe5 12 ♘xc6 bxc6
13 fxe5 ♘d5 14 ♘e4 ± Timman-Lju-
bojević, Novi Sad OL 1990.

e) 10...♘xd4 11 ♗xd4 ♗c6 (not
11...e5? 12 fxe5 ♗g4 13 exf6!) 12 f5

exf5 13 exf5 d5!? (13...♖e8) 14 ♗xf6
♗xf6 15 ♘xd5 ♗xd5 16 ♖xd5 ♕c7 ±
Yudasin.

**11 e5**

Or:

a) 11 ♗b3 – *10 ♗b3 ♖c8 11 f4.*

b) 11 ♘b3!? is curious, Borocz-
Feher, Hungarian Cht 1989.

c) 11 f5 ♘a5 (11...♘xd4!? 12 ♖xd4
exf5 13 exf5 ♗xf5 14 g4) 12 ♗d3 (12
fxe6!? ♘xc4 13 exd7 ♕xd7 14 ♗g5
Kholmov) 12...e5 13 ♘b3 b5! with a
good game for Black, Kholmov-Tal,
Riga (1) 1968.

d) 11 ♘xc6!? bxc6 (11...♗xc6 12
♗xa7!?) 12 e5 (12 g4!?) 12...♘d5 13
exd6 ♗xd6 14 ♕d3 with some advantage for White, Ashley-Avrukh, Wijk
aan Zee 2000.

**11...♘e8**

11...dxe5 12 ♘xc6 bxc6 13 fxe5
♘d5 14 ♘e4 ±.

**12 ♘xc6 ♗xc6 13 f5 exf5 14 e6
♔h8 15 exf7 ♘f6 16 ♗e6 ♗d7 17
♗b3! f4 18 ♗xf4 ♗g4 19 ♕e3 ♗xd1
20 ♖xd1**

White has more than adequate compensation, Topalov-Leko, Dortmund
1996.

# 14  Anti-Sozin: 5...♘c6 6 ♗c4 ♕b6 and 6...♗d7

**1 e4 c5 2 ♘f3 d6 3 d4 cxd4 4 ♘xd4 ♘f6 5 ♘c3 ♘c6 6 ♗c4** *(D)*

In the previous chapters (1-13) we described a whole range of positions with an early ...e6 (5...e6 6 ♗c4; 5...a6 6 ♗c4 e6; 5...♘c6 6 ♗c4 e6) and digressed from this topic just once in Chapter 2 when we considered some rare ideas for Black after 5...a6 6 ♗c4. Now it is time to talk about the avoidance of 6...e6 in the position shown in the diagram.

Two lines are of particular interest:

**A:  6...♗d7**　　225
**B:  6...♕b6**　　229

The other moves are:

a) 6...a6 – *5...a6 6 ♗c4 ♘c6* (note 'c' to Black's 6th move in Chapter 2).

b) 6...g6?! 7 ♘xc6! bxc6 8 e5 ♘g4. Now 9 e6?! f5 (Schlechter-Em.Lasker,

Berlin Wch (7) 1910) is not clear, but 9 exd6 provides White with better chances, and 9 ♗f4, with the point 9...d5 10 ♘xd5! ±, is even more critical.

c) 6...♘xd4?! 7 ♕xd4 e5 (7...e6 8 ♗g5! is a Richter-Rauzer with an extra tempo for White due to the difference between ♕d1xd4 and ♕d1-d2xd4) 8 ♕d3 with an obvious advantage for White.

d) 6...e5 is not entirely logical either:

d1) 7 ♘f5 is interesting but not too convincing. For instance: 7...♗xf5 (7...♗e6 8 ♘e3!?) 8 exf5 ♗e7 9 ♗g5 0-0 10 ♗xf6 ♗xf6 11 0-0 ♘d4 12 g4 ♖c8 13 ♗b3, Morović-Mohamed, Cap d'Agde rpd 1998.

d2) White gains some advantage through 7 ♘de2 ♗e6 8 ♗b3 ♗e7 9 0-0 0-0 10 f4 (or 10 ♔h1).

d3) 7 ♘f3 h6 8 0-0 ♗e7 9 ♖e1 0-0 10 ♘d5 ♗e6 11 ♗b3 ±.

e) 6...♘a5!? (this is at least better than 6...♘e5?, after which the black knight will inevitably be attacked later by f4) 7 ♗b5+!? (7 ♗d3 g6! =; 7 ♗e2!? e6 8 0-0 yields a little-studied position; 7 ♗b3 e6 transposes to note 'b' to Black's 7th move in Line B of Chapter 13) 7...♗d7 8 ♕e2 e6 9 ♗g5 ♗e7 10 0-0-0 a6 11 ♗xd7+ ♘xd7 12 ♗xe7 ♕xe7 13 ♘b3!? ♘xb3+ 14 axb3 ♖c8

15 ♛d2 ♖c6 16 ♖he1 0-0 17 ♖e3 ±
Hraček-Chernyshov, Czech Cht 2000.

## A)

**6...♝d7** *(D)*

This continuation has not received
much attention for a long time though
it still occurs occasionally in grandmaster play. By playing 6...♝d7, Black
preserves the possibility of ...e6 (with a
transposition to some lines with 6...e6
and ...♝d7) or ...g6 (if he wishes to obtain Dragon positions). Black used to
link 6...♝d7 mainly with the latter
plan, but it gradually became clear that
he encounters some problems there.

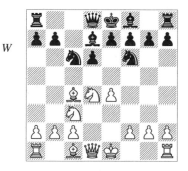

W

Now:

**A1: 7 ♝b3**    226
**A2: 7 0-0**    227

The other continuations are rare although at least two of them (7 ♝e3
and 7 ♞xc6) are of some interest:

a) 7 f4 g6! = Lipnitsky-Boleslav-
sky, Moscow 1950.

b) After 7 f3, Black can happily
choose between 7...♛b6! or any standard set-up with ...e6.

c) If 7 h3, the simplest is 7...e6!.

d) 7 ♝g5 should not worry Black:

d1) 7...♞xe4? 8 ♞xe4 ♛a5+ 9 c3
♛e5 10 ♝d3 d5 11 f4 +−.

d2) 7...♛b6 8 ♞b3 e6 transposes
to Line B531.

d3) 7...e6!? 8 ♞db5 (8 ♝xf6? ♛xf6
9 ♞d5 0-0-0! Koblenc), and Black
can continue with 8...♛b8 (which appears most reliable) or maybe 8...♛b6.

d4) 7...♛a5 8 ♝xf6 gxf6 leads to
positions with chances for both sides:

d41) 9 ♝d5 (Bronstein) 9...♞xd4!
10 ♛xd4 ♝g7.

d42) 9 ♞b3 ♛g5, and now 10 0-0
♖g8 11 g3 h5 12 ♞d5 ♖c8 (12...0-0-0!?
Nunn) 13 f4, Geller-Averbakh, Zurich
Ct 1953, or 10 g3 h5!? (10...f5 11 e5!?,
Kruppa-Sorokin, Kherson 1991) 11 f4
♛g4 12 ♝e2 ♛g6 13 ♛d2 f5 14 ♝f3
fxe4 15 ♝xe4 ♝f5, Brodsky-Naved-
nichy, Bucharest 1994.

e) 7 ♝e3!? ♞g4 (it is not consistent to play 7...e6 or 7...g6 8 f3!;
7...♖c8 8 ♝b3 ♞g4 9 0-0!? ♞xe3 10
fxe3 e6 deserves attention) 8 ♞xc6 (8
0-0?! ♞ce5! 9 ♝b3 ♞xe3 10 fxe3 e6
is clearly harmless for Black) 8...bxc6
(8...♞xe3? 9 ♝xf7+! +−) with a little-
studied position; e.g., 9 ♝f4 (9 ♝g5?!
♛b6; 9 ♝c1!?) 9...e5 10 ♝g3 (10
♝d2!? Gofshtein) 10...♝e7 11 h3!?
(avoiding ideas like 11 ♛e2 0-0 12 0-0
h5!, Gdanski-Nevednichy, Krynica Z
1998) 11...♞f6 12 0-0 with the idea of
♔h1 and f4.

f) 7 ♞xc6!? and then:

f1) 7...♝xc6 8 ♛e2, and White can
struggle for the initiative after 8...g6 9
♝g5 ♝g7 10 0-0-0 ♛a5 11 h4!? (11
♞d5) 11...0-0 12 ♔b1, Gi.Hernandez-
J.Armas, Cuba 1992, or 8...e6 9 ♝f4!,
Lein-Averbakh, USSR Ch (Baku) 1961,
but 8...♞xe4!? (Gofshtein) deserves attention.

f2) After 7...bxc6!? 8 0-0 e6 9 ♕e2 ♗e7 10 b3 d5 11 ♗d3 (Gi.Hernandez-Korchnoi, Moscow OL 1994) I would prefer to be White.

## A1)

**7 ♗b3** *(D)*

**7...g6**

This is the standard response, although Black enjoys a wide choice:

a) 7...♘xd4 8 ♕xd4 g6 is unpleasantly met by 9 ♕c4!, Madl-Gaprindashvili, Kishinev 1998.

b) 7...♕a5 8 0-0 is slightly better for White (e.g. 8...g6 9 h3 ♗g7 10 ♗e3 transposing to a Dragon).

c) 7...♖c8 and now:

c1) 8 ♗g5 ♕a5 9 ♗xf6 gxf6 10 0-0 is unclear; then 10...♕c5! was recommended by Bednarski.

c2) 8 f3!? a6 (8...g6 9 ♗e3!; 8...e6?! 9 ♘db5!) 9 ♗e3 e6 10 g4 ∞.

c3) 8 0-0! is simplest – *7 0-0 ♖c8 8 ♗b3*.

d) 7...a6 8 ♗e3 (8 f3 e6!; after 8 ♗g5!?, Taimanov's 8...♕a5 is not entirely convincing; 8 0-0!? – *7 0-0 a6 8 ♗b3 ±*) 8...♘g4 (8...♕a5!? 9 f4 ♘xb3 10 axb3 e5 may be playable, Bogdanović-Taimanov, Budva 1967) and now:

d1) 9 0-0!? ♘xe3 10 fxe3 e6 11 ♘xc6 bxc6 12 e5 d5 (Berzinsh-Antoniewski, Czech Cht 1998) 13 ♕g4! Berzinsh.

d2) 9 ♘xc6 bxc6 10 ♕f3 ♘f6 11 e5 (Kasparov/Nikitin) looks dangerous for Black.

e) 7...♘a5, with the point 8 f4 ♘xb3 9 axb3 e5, is of some interest.

f) 7...e6!? is likely to transpose to lines discussed in Chapter 13, but the moves ...♗d7 and ♗b3 restrict the possibilities of both Black and White. 8 ♗e3 ♗e7 transposes to note 'b' to Black's 8th move in Line C2 of Chapter 13.

**8 f3** *(D)*

With the idea of transposing to the Yugoslav Attack through 9 ♗e3.

Using the same idea, it is possible to play 8 ♗e3!? (Fischer) 8...♘g4 9 ♘xc6 bxc6 10 ♕f3 (10 ♗d4 e5! is satisfactory for Black, Velimirović-Ivanisević, Yugoslav Ch (Subotica) 2000; 10 ♕d4!? e5 11 ♕c4 ♕e7 12 ♗d2 ♗g7 13 f3 ♘f6 14 0-0-0 0-0 15 ♗g5, Smejkal-Hora, Pardubice 1965), and now:

a) 10...♘e5 11 ♕e2 ♗g7 12 f4 (12 h3 c5!) 12...♘g4 13 ♗d2 0-0 14 0-0 ♖b8 15 ♔h1, Ehlvest-de la Riva, Dos Hermanas open 1998, appears more promising for White.

b) Black can obtain a good game by 10...♘f6!? 11 ♗g5 ♗g7 12 e5 dxe5 13 0-0-0 0-0 14 ♗xf6 exf6!.

Other continuations (i.e. anything except 8 f3 and 8 ♗e3) allow Black to transpose to Dragon lines that are at least satisfactory for him; e.g., 8 h3 ♗g7 (8...♘xd4!?) 9 ♗e3 0-0 10 0-0 ♖c8.

**8...♘xd4**

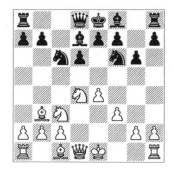

*B*

8...♘a5 9 ♗g5!? ♗g7 10 ♕d2 h6 11 ♗e3 ♖c8 12 0-0-0 with an advantage for White, Fischer-Gligorić, Yugoslavia Ct 1959.

8...♗g7!? 9 ♗e3 0-0 leads to a position that results both from the Dragon and the Accelerated Dragon. Due to the early ♗b3, Black has the resource 10 ♕d2 ♘xd4!? 11 ♗xd4 b5, and the attempt 10 h4!? has its disadvantages (as in the case of 10 ♕d2 ♖c8 11 0-0-0 ♘e5, the main move for White nowadays is not 12 h4 but 12 ♔b1!).

**9 ♕xd4 ♗g7 10 ♗g5**

10 ♗e3 0-0 11 ♕d2 b5! gives Black good counterplay.

**10...0-0**

An unclear alternative is 10...♕a5!? 11 ♕d2 ♖c8, and then:

a) 12 h4 ♗e6 13 ♘d5 ♕xd2+ 14 ♔xd2 ♗xd5 15 exd5 h6 is not dangerous for Black, Kudriashov-Averbakh, USSR Cht 1968.

b) 12 0-0 ♗e6 (12...♘h5 Makarychev) 13 ♗h6 with some initiative for White, Renet-Korchnoi, Swiss Cht 1995.

c) 12 0-0-0 ♖xc3 13 bxc3 0-0 (the alternatives are 13...h6 14 ♗e3! ♘xe4 15 fxe4 ♗xc3 16 ♕xc3 ♕xc3 17 ♗d4 +− and 13...♘xe4 14 fxe4 ♗xc3 15

♗xf7+ ♔xf7 16 ♕d5+ ± Makarychev) 14 ♔b1 (14 e5!?) 14...♖e8 (14...♗e6!? 15 ♗h6 Makarychev) 15 ♗h6 ♗xh6 16 ♕xh6 ♕xc3 17 ♕d2 ± de Firmian-Makarychev, Oslo 1984.

**11 0-0-0!**

Black again has adequate counterchances after 11 ♕d2 b5!.

Or 11 ♕e3 b5! 12 h4 b4 (12...a5 13 a4 bxa4 14 ♘xa4 ♖b8 15 h5 ♘xh5 16 g4 ♘f6 17 ♗h6 ♗xa4 18 ♗xg7 ♔xg7 19 ♖xa4 ♖b5 Ciocaltea-Stein, Caracas 1970, is probably also satisfactory) 13 ♘e2 a5 14 ♗h6 ♖c8 (14...♗xh6!? and 14...a4!? are other ideas for Black) 15 h5 ♗xh6 16 ♕xh6 (Saren-Robatsch, Forssa/Helsinki Z 1972), and Black holds on due to 16...a4! with the point 17 hxg6 axb3 18 g7 ♖e8 19 g4 ♕b6! 20 g5 ♕e3 (Florian).

**11...h6**

Or: 11...b5 12 e5!; 11...♕a5 12 ♕d2!; 11...♗e6 12 ♕d2 ± ♕a5 13 ♔b1 ♖fc8 14 h4 b5 15 h5 ♗xb3 16 cxb3 b4 17 ♘d5 ♘xd5 18 exd5 and White possesses the initiative, Parma-Averbakh, Titovo Užice 1965.

**12 ♗h4 ♗c6 13 ♕e3 ♘d7?!**

13...♕a5 ± T.Petrosian.

**14 ♖xd6! g5 15 ♗g6! e6 16 ♖xg7+ ♔xg7 17 ♗f2**

The position favours White, Tal-Stein, USSR Ch (Moscow) 1969.

**A2)**

**7 0-0** *(D)*

**7...g6**

This is more dubious here than after 7 ♗b3 (Line A1). Other ideas:

a) 7...a6 8 ♗b3! (8 ♗g5!? e6; 8 ♘xc6!? ♗xc6 9 ♖e1 e6 10 ♘d5, Jokšić-Shirazi, New York 1982) 8...e6 (8...g6 9 ♘xc6!) transposes to note 'b'

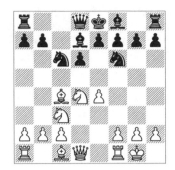

*B*

to Black's 8th move in Line B of Chapter 8 (±).

b) 7...♖c8 8 ♗b3 (8 ♗g5!?) and then 8...a6 9 ♗e3! ± (less convincing is 9 ♘xc6!? ♗xc6 10 ♖e1 e6, Soltis-Shirazi, New York 1987) or 8...g6 9 ♘xc6! ♗xc6 (9...bxc6 10 f4!) 10 ♖e1 (or 10 ♗g5 ♗g7 11 ♘d5) 10...♗g7 11 ♘d5 0-0 12 ♗g5 ♗xd5 13 exd5 – *7...g6 8 ♘xc6! ♗xc6 9 ♗g5 ♗g7 10 ♘d5 ♗xd5 11 exd5 0-0 12 ♖e1 ♖c8 13 ♗b3 ±.*

c) 7...e6 is more reliable. For instance, 8 ♗b3 ♗e7 9 ♗e3 0-0 transposes to Line C221 of Chapter 13.

**8 ♘xc6! ♗xc6**

After 8...bxc6 9 f4! Black has some difficulties with his development:

a) 9...♕c7? 10 e5! dxe5 11 fxe5 ♕xe5 12 ♗xf7+! ♔xf7 13 ♕xd7 (Boleslavsky).

b) 9...♘g4 10 ♕e2!? is better for White, Koopman-Makarychev, Groningen jr Ech 1973/4.

c) 9...♕a5 10 ♔h1 ♗g7 (Black should consider 10...♕h5!?) 11 e5! ±.

d) 9...♗g4 10 ♕d3 (10 ♕e1!? d5 11 ♗d3 dxe4 12 ♘xe4 ♗g7 13 ♘xf6+ ♗xf6 14 f5 gives White a slight advantage, A.Sokolov-Sax, Brussels 1988) 10...♗g7 11 h3 (not wholly clear is 11

e5 ♘d7 12 exd6 ♘b6 13 ♗a6 0-0, Nunn-Balashov, Toluca IZ 1982) 11...♗c8 12 e5 ♘d7 13 exd6 ♘b6 14 dxe7 ♕xe7 (14...♕d4+? 15 ♗e3 ♕xc4 16 ♕d8#) 15 ♗b3 0-0 16 ♗e3 ♖d8 17 ♕e2 (Chandler-Kupreichik, Minsk 1982) and now 17...♗xc3 18 bxc3 ♗a6 (Chandler) does not promise Black equality.

**9 ♗g5**

9 ♘d5 ♗g7 10 ♗g5 comes to the same thing.

A less consistent line is 9 ♕e2 ♗g7 10 ♗g5 (10 ♖d1 0-0!? 11 e5 ♘e8) 10...0-0 11 ♖ad1 ♕a5 12 ♘d5 ♗xd5 13 exd5 e5!, A.Sokolov-Korchnoi, Reykjavik World Cup 1988.

**9...♗g7 10 ♘d5 ♗xd5**

10...e6? 11 ♘xf6+ ♗xf6 12 ♗xf6 ♕xf6 13 ♕xd6 ♖d8 (13...♕xb2 14 ♖ab1 +−) 14 ♕a3 ±.

10...0-0!? 11 ♗xf6 gives White some advantage after any recapture on f6 (weaker is 11 ♖e1 e6!, when White has nothing better than 12 ♘xf6+ ♗xf6 13 ♗xf6 =).

**11 exd5 0-0**

11...♘e4!? 12 ♗b5+ ♔f8 13 ♗c1 h5, Lendwai-Robatsch, Austrian Cht 1995.

**12 ♖e1**

Practice has shown that White enjoys a small advantage here. After 12...♖c8 13 ♗b3 ♕d7 or 12...♕d7 followed by ...♖fc8, Black preserves great defensive resources but it is hardly possible to talk about equality.

Summing up: the rare ideas for White on move 7 require more testing. The main continuations, 7 ♗b3 and 7 0-0, make Black choose between 7...e6 and 7...g6. 7...e6 is satisfactory, but it is hard to say whether it is worthwhile to begin with 6...♗d7. As regards 7...g6, this move probably works better after 7 ♗b3 than it does after 7 0-0.

**B)**

**6...♕b6** *(D)*

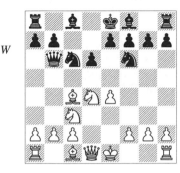

This currently popular line was introduced by Pal Benko at the end of the 1950s. It is clear that the queen will not stay on b6 for long but Black is ready to lose a tempo in order to disrupt White's attacking scheme.

White has to determine the character of further play by choosing between the main move 7 ♘b3, three topical alternatives (7 ♘xc6, 7 ♘de2 and 7 ♘db5) and the speculative gambit idea of 7 ♗e3.

**B1: 7 ♗e3?!**    229
**B2: 7 ♘db5!?**    230
**B3: 7 ♘de2!?**    235
**B4: 7 ♘xc6!?**    241
**B5: 7 ♘b3**    247

**B1)**

**7 ♗e3?! ♕xb2 8 ♘db5 ♕b4! 9 ♕e2** *(D)*

After 9 ♗d3 ♕a5 10 ♗d2 ♕d8 11 ♘d5 ♘xd5 12 exd5 ♘e5 13 ♗e2 a6 14 ♘d4 ♕c7 White obtained no genuine

compensation in the game Velimirović-Valvo, Krakow 1964.

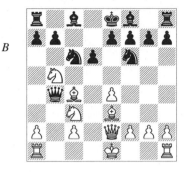

Black now has a number of promising possibilities:

a) 9...♗e6 10 ♗xe6 fxe6 11 0-0 is unclear, Polzin-Martinović, Austrian Cht 2000/1.

b) 9...♘e5 10 ♗b3 (10 ♖b1!? ♕xc4 11 ♕xc4 ♘xc4 12 ♘c7+ ♔d8 13 ♘xa8 ♘xe3 14 fxe3 b6 15 0-0 ♗b7 16 ♘xb6 axb6 17 ♖xb6 ∞ I.Zaitsev-Makarov, St Petersburg 1997) 10...a6 11 ♘c7+ (11 ♗d2 axb5 12 ♘xb5 ♕c5 13 ♗e3 and now 13...♕b4+ offers equality, while 13...♕c6!? 14 ♗d5 ♕d7 15 ♗b6 e6 is also possible) 11...♔d8 12 ♗d2 ♘xc7 13 ♘d5+ ♘xd5 14 ♗xb4 ♘xb4 (Pinski) – Black's chances are hardly worse.

c) 9...♘g4!? 10 f3 ♘xe4 (Miserendino-Zarnicki, Villa Martelli 1998) 11 ♗d4! (Olthof), with uncertain consequences.

d) 9...♘xe4 and then:

d1) 10 ♗d4 gives Black a good choice:

d11) 10...♗f5 11 a3 ♘xd4 (11...♕a5 12 0-0-0! ♘xd4 13 ♖xd4 ♘c3 14 ♘xd6+ ♔d8 15 ♘xb7++ ♔c7 16 ♘xa5 ♘xe2+ 17 ♗xe2 ± Dubinski) 12 axb4 ♘xe2 13 ♘xe4 ♖c8 with a good game (Lepeshkin).

d12) 10...♘xd4 11 ♕xe4 ♘xc2+! (11...♘c6 is risky in view of 12 ♖b1, Maslennikov-Kremenetsky, Moscow 1996, as is 11...e5 due to 12 0-0-0 ♕xc4 13 ♖xd4 ♕c6 14 ♘d5, Dubinsky-Grachev, Moscow 1996) 12 ♔d1 ♗f5! (12...f5 13 ♘c7+ ♔d8 14 ♕xc2! ♕xc4 15 ♘xa8 ♗d7 is possibly over-optimistic) 13 ♗xf7+ ♔d8! 14 ♕xf5 (14 ♕xb7!? ♖c8 15 ♕xa7) 14...♘xa1 15 ♗e8 ♔xe8 16 ♘c7+ ♔d8 17 ♘e6+ = Pinski.

d2) 10 ♗xf7+!? ♔xf7 11 ♖b1 ♕a5 12 ♕c4+ e6 (12...♗e6 13 ♕xe4 g6 14 0-0 ♗g7? 15 ♘xd6+ exd6 16 ♖xb7+ ± Lepeshkin) 13 ♕xe4 and now:

d21) 13...♕d8 can be met by 14 0-0 d5 15 ♕f3+ ♔g8 16 ♗f4.

d22) 13...d5 14 ♕f3+ ♔g8 15 0-0 ♕d8 16 ♗f4 (Dubinski-S.Kiselev, Moscow 1998) 16...a6 17 ♘c7 ♖a7 18 ♖fe1 ♕f6 19 ♘a4! (Dubinski) is unclear.

d23) Balinov recommended the line 13...♔g8 14 ♗d2 a6 with an advantage.

e) 9...♕a5 (the most solid reply) 10 ♗d2 ♕d8 11 ♘d5 ♘xd5 12 exd5 ♘e5 13 ♗b3 (13 f4 ♗g4 14 ♘xd6+ exd6 15 ♗b5+ ♗d7 16 fxe5 dxe5 17 ♕xe5+ ♕e7 = Pinski-P.Varga, Budapest 1997; 13 ♘a3!? I.Zaitsev) 13...a6 14 f4 (14 ♘a3!? g6 15 f4 ♘d7 16 ♘c4 Lepeshkin; 14 ♘d4 g6 15 f4 ♘d7 ∓ Ardeleanu-Nevednichy, Romanian Cht 1997) 14...♘g4! 15 ♘a3 (15 ♘d4 g6 16 ♗a4+ ♗d7 17 ♘e6 fxe6 18 ♗xd7+ ♕xd7 19 dxe6 ∓) and now:

e1) 15...b5 16 c4! ♗d7 17 cxb5 axb5 18 ♘xb5 ♕b6 19 ♗c4 is difficult for Black.

e2) 15...♕c7 16 ♘c4 b5 17 ♗a5 ♕c5 18 ♘b6 ♖b8 19 ♘xc8 ♕xc8 20 c4! also gives Black problems, Pinski-Galliamova, Koszalin 1997.

e3) 15...g6 16 ♗c3 ♖g8 17 ♘c4 b5 18 h3! bxc4 19 ♗a4+ ♗d7 20 ♗xd7+ ♕xd7 21 hxg4 (Pinski-Shishkin, Nadole 1997) 21...♗g7 leads to double-edged play.

e4) 15...♘f6 may be even stronger, Rosabal-B.Martinez, Placetas 2000.

On the whole, after 7 ♗e3 it is Black rather than White who is fighting for the advantage.

**B2)**
**7 ♘db5!? (D)**

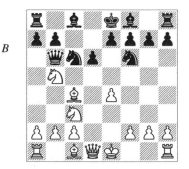

Though it is not a critical response to 6...♕b6, this move gives White good chances of obtaining a position in the usual spirit of the Sozin, and does not give Black relief from some objective opening problems.

Black faces a curious choice:

a) To transpose to a starting position of our Chapter 11 via 7...a6 8 ♗e3 ♕d8 9 ♘d4 e6 with a possible 10 ♕e2 and the Velimirović Attack.

b) To transpose to the Classical Sozin with an early ...♕c7: 7...a6 8

♗e3 ♕a5 9 ♘d4 e6 10 0-0 ♕c7!? 11 ♗b3. This is probably the best decision, although not very popular among the advocates of 6...♕b6.

c) To leave the queen on a5, thus reaching the Classical Sozin with an extra tempo of doubtful value: 7...a6 8 ♗e3 ♕a5 9 ♘d4 e6 10 0-0 ♗e7 11 ♗b3 0-0 – here, this will be our main line.

d) Not to agree to the Sozin structure (7...a6 8 ♗e3 ♕a5 9 ♘d4 e6) and to seek his fortune by deviating with 9...♘g4, 9...♘e5, 8...♕d8 9 ♘d4 ♘g4 or 7...♗g4.

**7...a6**

Or 7...♗g4, and then:

a) 8 f3 ♗d7 9 ♕e2 a6 10 ♗e3 ♕a5 11 ♘d4 b5 12 ♗b3 e6 with a double-edged game; e.g., 13 0-0-0 (13 a3; 13 ♕f2) 13...b4! (Velimirović) 14 ♘b1 (14 ♘d5!? exd5 15 exd5 ♘xd4 16 ♗xd4+ ♔d8 Kramnik) 14...♗e7 15 g4 (15 ♘d2? ♕c7 ∓ Kramnik) 15...♘xd4 (15...0-0!? 16 g5 ♘xd4 17 ♖xd4 ♗b5 18 ♕d2 ♘d7 Kramnik) 16 ♖xd4 e5 17 ♖dd1 (Topalov-Kramnik, Dos Hermanas 1996) 17...♕c7 18 ♘d2 a5 Kramnik.

b) 8 ♘d5! ♘xd5 9 ♕xg4 ♘f6 (a better idea than 9...♘db4?! 10 ♕e2 ♘e5 11 ♗b3 ♘bd3+ 12 cxd3 ♕xb5 13 d4! ± Macieja-Krush, Presov 2000) 10 ♕e2 ± Velimirović-Goldin, Yugoslav Cht 1996.

**8 ♗e3 ♕a5**

Or 8...♕d8 9 ♘d4 ♘g4!? (9...e6 transposes to Chapter 11) 10 ♘xc6 (10 0-0 ♘ce5 11 ♗b3 ♘xe3 12 fxe3 e6!, M.Schlosser-Goldin, Sochi 1989) 10...bxc6, and now:

a) 11 ♗d2 g6! (11...♘f6 12 0-0 e6 13 ♗d3 ± Velimirović-Barlov, Cetinje 1992) 12 h3 ♘f6 (12...♘e5!? 13 ♗b3 ♗g7) 13 ♗g5 ♗g7 14 ♕d2 0-0 15 0-0-0 (de Firmian-Zso.Polgar, Bermuda 1995) 15...♗e6!? (Cu.Hansen) with good chances for Black.

b) 11 ♗f4 e5 12 ♗g3 ♗e7 13 h3 ♘f6 14 0-0 0-0 15 ♔h1 g6 16 ♗h2 ♘h5 = Blasek-Khalifman, Bad Mergentheim 1989.

c) 11 ♗g5!? ♕b6 (or 11...h6 12 ♗d2!?) 12 ♕d2 h6 13 ♗h4 ♕xb2 (13...g5!? 14 ♗g3 ♗g7) 14 ♖b1 ♕a3 15 ♘d5 cxd5 16 ♗xd5 ♖a7 17 ♖b3 ♕a4 18 ♕c3 ♔d8 19 ♗c6 ♕xa2 20 f3 ♖c7 21 fxg4 ♗b7 22 ♖xb7 with a dangerous initiative, Tompa-Csom, Hungarian Ch (Budapest) 1976.

d) 11 ♕f3 ♘e5 12 ♕e2 e6 (12...g6 13 f4 ♘xc4 14 ♕xc4 ♗g7 15 ♗d4 ± G.Todorović-Z.Vuković, Yugoslav Ch (Kladovo) 1990) 13 0-0-0 (13 ♗b3 ♗e7 14 f4 ♘d7 15 g4?! ♗h4+!, Onishchuk-Sulypa, Donetsk Z 1998) 13...♗e7 (13...♘xc4 14 ♕xc4 ♕c7!? Ivanchuk) 14 ♗d4 (14 ♗b3 a5!? 15 f4 ♗a6 16 ♕d2 ♘d7 Gofshtein) 14...♕c7 (14...♘xc4 15 ♕xc4 ♕c7 16 ♗xg7 ♖g8 17 ♗h6 ♖xg2 18 ♖hg1 ♖g6 ∞ Ivanchuk) 15 ♗xe5 dxe5 16 ♘a4 0-0 17 ♖d3! (17 b3?! ♗d7!, Macieja-Ivanchuk, Polanica Zdroj 1998) 17...♕a5 18 b3 ♖b8 19 ♕d2 ♕xd2+ 20 ♔xd2 ± Ivanchuk-Kramnik, Linares 1998. As the game against Macieja was played later, we may assume that Ivanchuk had something in reserve.

**9 ♘d4** *(D)*

Black has won a tempo, but as a rule ...a6 and ...♕a5 combine poorly in the Sicilian, and the value of this tempo is therefore rather unclear.

**9...e6**

The alternative tries are:

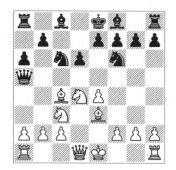

*B*

a) 9...♘xe4?! 10 ♕f3! and then:

a1) 10...♘xc3? 11 ♘xc6 ♕f5 12 ♕xf5 ♗xf5 13 ♘d4 +–.

a2) 10...♘e5 can be answered by 11 ♗xf7+ or 11 ♕xe4! ♘xc4 12 ♘b3 ♕c7 13 ♘d5 ♕c6 14 ♘d4 ♕d7 15 0-0-0 Boleslavsky.

a3) 10...♘f6 11 ♘xc6 ♕c7 12 ♘xe7!? gives White a clear advantage.

a4) 10...f5 11 ♘xc6 bxc6 12 0-0-0 d5 13 ♘xe4 (less convincing is 13 ♘xd5!?) 13...fxe4 (13...dxe4 14 ♕g3 e5 15 ♗g5 +–) 14 ♕h5+ g6 15 ♕e5 ♖g8 16 ♖xd5 cxd5 17 ♗xd5 ♕b5 18 ♕xe4 ♗f5 19 ♗c6+ +– Kindermann-Züger, Mendoza tt 1985.

b) 9...g6 10 0-0 (10 f3!? is possible; e.g., 10...♗g7 11 ♗b3 0-0 12 ♕d2 ♗d7 13 0-0-0 ♖fc8 14 h4 ♘e5 15 ♔b1 b5 16 ♗h6) 10...♗g7 11 ♘d5! ♘xd5 12 exd5 ♘e5 13 ♗b3 0-0 14 h3 ± Vladimirov-Zaichik, USSR 1979.

c) 9...♘xd4 and then:

c1) 10 ♗xd4!? e5 (10...♘xe4 11 0-0 ♘xc3 12 ♗xc3 ♕c7 13 ♕d3 gives White compensation – Onishchuk) 11 ♗e3 ♗e6 12 ♕d3 ± Onishchuk-Yermolinsky, Wijk aan Zee 1997.

c2) 10 ♕xd4 e6 11 ♗b3 ♗e7 12 0-0 (12 0-0-0 0-0 13 f4 ♘d7 14 g4 ♘c5 ∞ Gi.Hernandez-Damljanović,

Lyons 1990) 12...0-0 13 f4 ♘g4 14 ♗d2 ♕c7 (14...♗f6?! 15 e5!) 15 ♔h1 b5 (de Firmian-Damljanović, Erevan OL 1996) 16 a4 (Damljanović) with the point 16...♗f6 17 e5!.

d) 9...♘g4!? and now:

d1) 10 0-0!? ♘ce5! (10...♘xe3 11 fxe3 ♘e5 12 ♕h5! ±) 11 ♗b3 ♘xe3 12 fxe3 e6 13 ♕h5 g6 14 ♕h3 and now Black should play 14...♕d8!? rather than 14...♕c7?! 15 ♗a4+! ± Balzar-Dinstuhl, Bundesliga 2000/1.

d2) 10 ♘xc6 bxc6 11 ♗d2 (11 0-0 ♘xe3 12 fxe3 e6 13 ♕f3 ♖a7 14 ♖ad1 ♕e5 15 ♘a4!? with a sharp game, Ginsburg-Shmuter, Nikolaev Z 1993) 11...g6 (11...♘xf2?! can be met by Bilek's 12 ♕f3! or Sax's 12 ♗xf7+ ♔xf7 13 0-0!; 11...♕b6 deserves attention: 12 0-0 ♕d4!?, Ehlvest-Tella, Jyväskylä 1998, or 12 ♕e2 ♘e5 13 ♘a4 ♕c7 14 ♗b3 c5, de Firmian-Tella, Stockholm 1998) and now:

d21) 12 0-0? ♕e5! ∓ Sax.

d22) 12 ♗e2 ♘e5 13 f4 (13 ♘d5 ♕d8 14 ♘e3 ♗g7 15 ♗c3 0-0 16 f4 ♕b6! 17 ♕d2 ♘d7 18 ♘c4, Atalik-Kotronias, Greece 1998, 18...♕c5 Atalik) 13...♘d7 14 ♘d5 ♕d8 15 ♗c3 e5 16 ♘e3 ♘c5!? 17 ♗f3 ♘a4! 18 ♕d2 ♕b6 (Atalik) appears satisfactory for Black.

d23) 12 ♕e2 ♗g7 (12...♘e5?! 13 ♗b3 ♗g7 14 f4 ♘d7 15 ♕c4!) and here:

d231) 13 h3 ♘e5 14 ♗b3 ♕c7 15 f4 ♘d7 16 ♗e3 0-0 17 0-0 a5 ∞ de Firmian-Smirin, New York rpd 1995.

d232) 13 f4 0-0 14 0-0-0 ♕b6 15 h3 ♘f6 16 ♗b3 ♗e6 (16...a5 17 e5!, de Firmian-D.Gurevich, USA Ch (Estes Park) 1986) 17 e5 ♘d5 = de Firmian-Rachels, USA Ch (Long Beach) 1989.

d233) 13 ♗b3 0-0 14 0-0 ♘e5 15 f4 ♘d7 16 e5!? dxe5 17 f5 ♘f6 18 fxg6 hxg6 19 ♘e4 is awkward for Black, Sax-Radulov, Vrnjačka Banja 1974.

d234) 13 0-0-0 0-0 14 ♗b3 ♕c7 15 h4 h5!? 16 f3 ♘e5 17 g4 ♘xg4 18 fxg4 ♗xg4 and again Black's prospects are vague, M.Pavlović-Zaichik, Protvino 1988.

e) 9...♘e5!? and now:

e1) 10 ♗b3? ♘xe4.

e2) 10 ♘b3 ♕c7 11 ♗d3 (11 ♗e2 e6 transposes to Line B542) 11...e6 (11...g6 12 ♗g5!) and then:

e21) 12 0-0 b5!? =.

e22) 12 a4 ♗d7! 13 ♘d2 (13 ♕e2 ♖c8!) 13...♗c6 14 f4 ♘xd3+ 15 cxd3 d5 16 e5 d4! 17 ♗xd4 ♖d8, Macieja-Damljanović, Belgrade 1999.

e23) 12 f4 ♘c4 13 ♗c1!? (13 ♗xc4 again transposes to Line B542) 13...b5 14 ♕e2 ♗b7 15 a4 b4 followed by 16...d5 17 e5 ♘e4 gives Black sufficient counterchances.

e3) 10 ♗d3 ♘eg4!? (10...e6 11 f4!? ♘xd3+ 12 cxd3 ± Kramnik; 10...g6!?; 10...♘fg4!?) 11 ♗c1 (11 ♗d2? ♕b6! ∓) 11...g6 (11...♕b6 12 0-0! ♕xd4? 13 ♗b5+) 12 ♘b3! (12 f4 e5! 13 ♘b3 ♕b6 14 ♕e2 exf4 Kramnik) 12...♕b6 13 ♕e2!? (13 0-0 ♗g7 14 h3 ♘e5) 13...♗g7 14 f4 ♘h5! ("There is nothing else" – Kramnik) 15 ♘d5 (15 ♕f3? ♘xh2!; 15 ♗d2!? ♗xc3 16 bxc3 0-0 17 c4 Kramnik) 15...♕d8 16 ♗d2 (16 0-0 0-0 17 h3 ♘gf6 18 ♘xf6+ ♘xf6 = Kramnik) 16...e6! 17 ♗a5 (17 ♕xg4 exd5 18 ♕f3 0-0! Bönsch) 17...♕h4+ 18 g3 ♘xg3 19 ♘c7+ (19 hxg3 ♕xg3+ 20 ♔d2 exd5 and now 21 exd5+ ♔d7! or 21 ♖af1! ♘f6 22 exd5+ ♔f8 23 ♗b4 ♗g4! – Kramnik) 19...♔e7 20 hxg3 ♕xg3+ 21 ♔d1

♘f2+ = Topalov-Kramnik, Belgrade 1995.

**10 0-0 ♗e7**

Or:

a) 10...♕c7!? 11 ♗b3 – *6...e6 7 ♗b3 a6 8 ♗e3 ♕c7 9 0-0* (note 'a' to White's 9th move in Line C3 of Chapter 8).

b) 10...♘e5 11 ♗e2 ±.

c) 10...♗d7!? 11 ♗b3 ♖c8 (alternatively, 11...b5!?) 12 f4 ♕h5 13 ♕xh5 ♘xh5 14 f5 ♘xd4 15 ♗xd4 e5, Kontić-Simonović, Yugoslav Cht 1996.

**11 ♗b3**

11 f4 0-0 12 ♔h1 (12 f5? ♕c5) 12...♕c7! (12...♘xd4 13 ♗xd4 e5 14 ♗e3 ± Varavin-Kharlov, Russian Ch (Elista) 1996) and now:

a) 13 a4 – *6...e6 7 0-0 a6 8 a4 ♗e7 9 ♗e3 0-0 10 ♔h1 ♕c7 11 f4?!* (note 'd1' to Black's 10th move in Line B of Chapter 12).

b) 13 ♗b3 – *6...e6 7 ♗b3 a6 8 ♗e3 ♗e7 9 f4 0-0 10 0-0 ♕c7 11 ♔h1* (note 'a' to White's 11th move in Line C221 of Chapter 9).

**11...0-0**

Ricardi's 11...♗d7 12 f4 ♖c8!?, with the point 13 f5 ♘xd4 14 ♗xd4 e5 and 15...♖xc3, deserves attention.

**12 f4** *(D)*

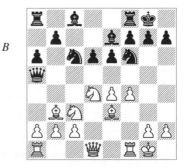

Black still has an extra tempo but the question remains whether the queen stands better on a5 than on d8.

**12...♗d7**

12...♘xd4 13 ♗xd4 (13 ♕xd4! transposes to note 'c2' to Black's 9th move) 13...e5! (13...b5? does not work with the queen on a5: 14 e5 dxe5 15 fxe5 ♘d7 16 ♘e4 ♗b7? 17 ♘f6+ +– Smirin) and then:

a) 14 fxe5 dxe5 15 ♗e3 ♘g4? (15...♗e6 =) 16 ♕d5! ± Gobet-Hort, Biel 1982.

b) 14 ♗f2 exf4 15 ♗d4 ♕g5!? = Soltis-Whitehead, USA Ch (Greenville) 1983.

c) 14 ♗e3 ♘g4 (14...exf4 15 ♖xf4 ♗e6 16 ♗d4! ± Velimirović-M.Mihaljčišin, Banja Luka 1981) 15 ♕e1 (15 ♘d5 can be met by 15...♘xe3, with the point 16 ♘xe7+ ♔h8 17 ♕xd6 ♖d8 18 ♕xe5?! ♕d2! –+) 15...♘xe3 16 ♕xe3 exf4 17 ♕xf4 ♗e6 ½-½ Sax-Dueball, Reggio Emilia 1973.

**13 f5**

Otherwise:

a) 13 ♕e1 is met by 13...♘g4!?.

b) 13 ♕f3 and now:

b1) 13...♕h5 14 ♕xh5 ♘xh5 15 f5 ♘xd4 16 ♗xd4 ♘f6 17 ♖ad1 ± Kožul.

b2) 13...♖ae8 14 ♘de2!? and now rather than 14...♔h8 15 g4 g5 16 e5! ± Velimirović-Kožul, Yugoslav Ch (Banja Vrucica) 1991, Black should try 14...h6!?, as in Korneev-Dokhoian, Berlin 1992.

b3) 13...♘xd4 14 ♗xd4 ♗c6 15 ♖ae1 (alternatively, 15 f5 exf5 = 16 ♕g3 ♘h5 17 ♕h3 ♗f6!, Golubev-Tukmakov, Odessa blitz 2000) 15...♖ae8 with the idea of ...♗d8 – Kožul.

c) 13 ♔h1 ♖ae8 (13...♕c7 14 f5; 13...♘xd4 14 ♗xd4 ♗c6 15 ♕d3 ±

Velimirović-Draško, Vrnjačka Banja 1985; 13...b5!? 14 a3 ♕c7 15 f5 ♘xd4, Ivanović-Čabrilo, Cetinje 1992) 14 ♕f3! (14 f5 ♘xd4 15 ♗xd4 exf5 16 exf5 ♗c6 17 ♕d3 transposes to note 'c' to White's 17th move) 14...♕c7 15 f5, Ivanović-Levin, Podebrady 1993.

**13...♘xd4**

13...e5 14 ♘f3! ♘g4 15 ♗d2 ♕c5+ 16 ♔h1 ♘f2+ 17 ♖xf2 ♕xf2 18 ♘d5 ± (Smirin).

**14 ♗xd4 exf5**

Otherwise:

a) 14...b5? 15 ♗xf6! ± Kengis-Lukin, USSR Cht 1990.

b) 14...e5?! 15 ♗f2!? ♗c6 16 ♗h4, Felsberger-Videki, Vienna 1990.

c) 14...♔h8 15 g4!.

d) 14...♖ad8 15 ♕f3 b5?! 16 fxe6! fxe6 17 ♕h3 d5 18 exd5 e5! (Korneev-Verat, Paris 1991) 19 d6+ ♔h8 20 dxe7 ♗xh3 21 ♗c5! ±.

e) 14...♖ac8 and now:

e1) 15 fxe6!? ♗xe6 (Bilek-Hort, Gothenburg 1971) 16 ♕d3 ± Bilek.

e2) 15 ♕e1 ♕c7 (15...♖fe8!?) 16 ♔h1 (16 fxe6!?) 16...b5 (Kindermann-Hjartarson, Thessaloniki OL 1984) 17 fxe6 ± Kindermann.

e3) 15 ♕f3 ♔h8 (15...e5?! 16 ♗f2 ♗c6 17 ♖ad1!; 15...exf5!?) 16 ♖ad1 (16 g4! Smirin) 16...b5! 17 ♗xf6 ♗xf6 18 ♖xd6 ♗c6 19 fxe6 b4 20 ♖xc6 ♖xc6 21 e5 ♕c5+ 22 ♔h1 bxc3 23 exf6 fxe6 24 fxg7+ ♔xg7 25 ♕g3+ = de Firmian-Smirin, Antwerp 1994.

**15 exf5**

15 ♘d5 ♘xd5 16 ♗xd5 ♖ab8 17 ♗c3 ♕c5+ 18 ♗d4 = Gulko.

**15...♗c6 16 ♕d3**

Or:

a) 16 ♕e1 ♖ae8 (16...♗d8 17 ♔h1!) 17 ♕g3 – *16 ♕d3 ♖ae8 17 ♕g3*.

b) 16 ♕d2 ♖ae8 17 ♖ad1 ♗d8 18 ♔h1 (18 ♕f4?! ♗b6!) 18...♘d7 19 ♕f4 ♗f6 20 ♗xf6 ♘xf6 21 ♖xd6 ♖e7 with compensation, Kengis-Kalinin, Würzburg 1994.

**16...♖ae8**

Alternatively:

a) 16...♖ac8?! 17 ♖ae1 ♕d8? 18 ♕e3 ♖e8 19 ♗b6 ♕d7 20 ♗e6! +−.

b) 16...♘d7!? 17 ♕g3 (17 ♖ad1 can be met by 17...♗f6!? or 17...♖ae8 − *16...♖ae8 17 ♖ad1 ♘d7*) 17...♗f6 18 ♕xd6 (18 ♖ad1!?) 18...♗xd4+ 19 ♕xd4 ♘f6, and now one possibility is 20 ♖ad1 ♖ae8 − *16...♖ae8 17 ♖ad1 ♘d7 18 ♕g3 ♗f6 19 ♕xd6 ♗xd4+ 20 ♕xd4 ♘f6.*

**17 ♖ad1**

Instead:

a) 17 ♖ae1?! ♗d8 =.

b) 17 ♕g3 ♗d8!? (other ideas are 17...♘h5!? and 17...d5!?) 18 ♔h1 (18 ♕xd6 ♗b6!) 18...d5 (with the idea of 19...♗c7) gives Black an acceptable position, Gi.Hernandez-Ivanović, Novi Sad OL 1990.

c) 17 ♔h1 b5 (17...♗d8 18 ♖ad1! − *17 ♖ad1 ♗d8 18 ♔h1*; 17...d5 ±; 17...♘d7!) 18 a3! (better than 18 ♕g3 b4!) 18...♕c7 (Kobaliya-Gonzalez Garcia, Linares 1998) 19 ♕g3! ♕b7 20 ♖ad1 ♗d8 21 ♘d5 ♔h8 22 ♘b4! ♗e4 23 ♗d5 with an advantage for White − Gonzalez Garcia.

**17...♘d7**

Or:

a) 17...b5? 18 ♕g3! ♘h5 (18...b4 19 ♘d5!) 19 ♕f2 ♗d8 20 ♗d5 ± Ehlvest-Ye Jiangchuan, Beijing 1998.

b) 17...d5!? 18 ♔h1 ±.

c) 17...♗d8 18 ♔h1 (18 ♕g3 ♗b6! ∓ Gulko) 18...♘d7 (18...♔h8 19 ♕g3!) 19 ♕g3 ♗f6 20 ♗d5! (stronger than

the alternative 20 ♕xd6 ♗xd4 21 ♕xd4 ♘f6, Kindermann-Gulko, Munich 1990) 20...♕b4 (20...♗xd5 21 ♘xd5 ♗xd4 22 ♖xd4 ♕b5 23 c4 ♕xb2 24 f6 g6 25 ♕xd6 +−; 20...♕c7 21 ♗xc6 ♕xc6 22 ♘d5 ± de Firmian) 21 ♗xf6 ♘xf6 22 ♗xc6 bxc6 23 ♖xd6 ± de Firmian-Kramnik, Erevan OL 1996.

**18 ♕g3**

18 ♘e4!? ♗xe4 (18...♘e5 19 ♕c3 ♕xc3 20 ♘xc3 ± Renet-Wang Zili, Geneva 1997) 19 ♕xe4 ♕c7, and Black organizes a defence through ...♘e5 and ...♗f6, Grigoriants-S.Kiselev, Moscow 1999.

**18...♗f6 19 ♕xd6 ♗xd4+ 20 ♕xd4 ♘f6 21 h3**

21 ♘d5 ♗xd5 22 ♗xd5 ♖d8 23 c4 = ½-½ Short-Kramnik, Novgorod 1996.

**21...♖e5 22 ♕f2 ♖fe8 23 ♖de1**

In the game Onishchuk-Svidler, Groningen FIDE 1997 there followed 23...h5 24 ♖xe5 ♖xe5 25 a3 ♗d7 (it is possibly better not to hurry winning back the pawn) 26 ♕d4 ♖xf5 27 ♖xf5 ±.

## B3)

**7 ♘de2!?**

In many ways this is quite a sensible continuation. White preserves the bishop on the a2-g8 diagonal and his e2-knight is placed somewhat passively but not badly − it may be activated later via ♘g3.

**7...e6** (D)

Development in the spirit of the Dragon (7...g6 8 ♗b3 ♗g7 9 ♗e3 ♕a5 10 f3 0-0 11 ♕d2 b5) seems to be less logical here.

**8 0-0**

8 a3 ♗e7 9 ♗a2 0-0 10 0-0 − *8 0-0 ♗e7 9 a3 0-0 10 ♗a2.*

Or 8 ♗b3 ♗e7 (more precise than 8...a6 9 ♗g5! ♗e7 10 ♗xf6, Velimir-ović-Radulov, Vršac 1973), and then:

a) Usually White proceeds with 9 0-0, which is equivalent to *8 0-0 ♗e7 9 ♗b3*.

b) 9 ♗g5? ♘g4, Velimirović-Popović, Zenica 1989.

c) 9 ♗e3 (taken together with ♘de2, this is a bit out of place) 9...♕c7 10 f4 (10 ♘f4 a6 11 g4 h6 12 ♕e2 b5 13 0-0-0 ♘e5 14 f3 g5 with counterplay, Ilinčić-Damljanović, Yugoslav Cht 1990) 10...a6 (10...0-0!?) 11 ♘g3 b5, and Black has no problems.

d) 9 ♕d3 a6 (9...0-0 10 f4 ♗d7 11 ♕f3!? ♘a5 12 e5?! ♗c6, Velimiro-vić-Komljenović, Umag 1972) 10 ♕g3 ♕c7 11 0-0 – *8 0-0 ♗e7 9 ♗b3 a6 10 ♕d3 ♕c7 11 ♕g3*.

e) 9 ♘g3!? (a fresh idea) 9...h5 (9...a6!?; 9...0-0) 10 ♗e3 ♕a5 11 f3 ♗d7 (11...g5!? Gulko) 12 ♕d2 ♘e5 13 0-0 ♖c8 14 ♕f2 ± De Vreugt-Gulko, Wijk aan Zee 2001.

**8...♗e7** *(D)*

There is not much sense in keeping the bishop on f8 any longer. However, Black frequently commences with 8...a6, which is less flexible under the circumstances:

a) 9 ♗b3 ♗e7 – 8...♗e7 9 ♗b3 a6.

b) 9 a3!? ♗e7 – 8...♗e7 9 a3 a6.

c) 9 ♗g5?! ♕c5! 10 ♗xf6 ♕xc4 11 ♗h4 ♘e5, Ljubojević-Ribli, Las Palmas 1974.

d) 9 ♗f4 ♘e5 10 ♗b3 ♗e7 (Van Riemsdijk-Hort, Bonn 1979; another possibility is 10...♕c7!?), and now the risky 11 ♘a4!? (Cvetković) or 11 ♔h1 with unclear play.

e) 9 ♔h1 ♗e7 10 ♘g3!? (10 f4!? 0-0 11 ♕e1 ♕c7 12 a4, Ljubisavljević-Radulov, Smederevska Palanka 1979) 10...0-0 11 f4 ♕c7 12 a4 ♗d7 13 f5 ♘e5 14 ♗b3 ♘c4 15 ♗xc4 ♕xc4 16 ♗g5 exf5? (16...h6!) 17 e5! +− Dvoi-rys-Andrianov, Ordzhonikidze 1978.

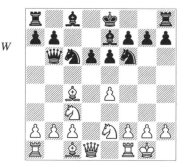

**9 ♗b3**

Here there is a choice. First, we mention several rare moves before moving on to better-established ideas:

a) 9 ♗d3!?.

b) 9 a4!?.

c) 9 ♕d3!? ♘e5 10 ♗b5+ (Tuk-makov).

d) 9 ♗g5 ♕c5 10 ♗xf6 ♗xf6 11 ♗b3 0-0 12 ♔h1 b5 13 f4 ∞ Velim-irović-Al.Khasin, Belgrade 1988.

e) No advantage is gained through 9 ♗e3 ♕c7!. For instance: 10 ♘g3 (10

♔h1 ♘g4!?) 10...a6 11 f4 (11 ♗b3 – 9 *♗b3 a6!? 10 ♗e3 ♕c7 11 ♘g3*; 11 a4 0-0 12 ♕e2 ♗d7 13 f4 ♖ac8 14 ♗d3 ♘a5, Zhang Pengxiang-Gershon, Erevan jr Wch 1999) 11...b5 (11...h5 12 ♗e2! g6 13 ♗f3) 12 ♗b3 ♘a5 13 f5 and now:

e1) 13...♘xb3 is imprecise: 14 cxb3 0-0 15 ♖c1 ♕b7 16 b4 a5 17 a3, Ivanović-Fedorowicz, Lone Pine 1981.

e2) 13...0-0! – *9 ♗b3 0-0 10 ♗e3 ♕c7 11 ♘g3 a6 12 f4 b5 13 f5 ♘a5 =.*

f) Of some interest is 9 ♔h1 0-0 10 ♗e3 (10 a3 – *9 a3 0-0 10 ♔h1*) 10...♕c7 (10...♕xb2? 11 a3 ♘g4 12 ♗b3) 11 f4 ♖d8 (11...a6!?) 12 ♗d3 a6 13 ♕e1 b5 14 ♕g3, Saltaev-Belikov, Moscow 1998.

g) 9 ♘g3 is quite possible; e.g., 9...0-0 10 a3!? – *9 a3 0-0 10 ♘g3.*

h) 9 a3 (the main alternative) 9...0-0 (9...a6 10 ♗a2 0-0 – *9...0-0 10 ♗a2 a6*) and now:

h1) 10 ♘g3 a6 11 ♔h1 ♘e5 12 ♗e2 ♕c6 13 f4 ♘g6 14 ♗d3 b5 15 ♘h5 (15 ♕e2!? ♗b7 16 ♗d2 is a little better for White – Dvoirys) 15...♗b7 16 f5 (Dvoirys-Lugovoi, Russian Ch (Elista) 1995) and now 16...exf5!? 17 ♖xf5 ♘xh5 18 ♕xh5 ♘e5 19 ♘d5 ♗d8 (Dvoirys) looks sufficient to reach equality.

h2) 10 ♔h1 ♘xe4!? (10...a6 11 ♗a2 – *10 ♗a2 a6 11 ♔h1*) 11 ♘xe4 d5 12 ♗xd5 exd5 13 ♕xd5 ♗e6 14 ♕h5 ♗c4 15 b3 g6 16 ♕f3 ♘d4 17 ♘xd4 ♗xf1 18 ♗e3 with compensation (Christiansen).

h3) 10 ♗a2 and here:

h31) 10...a6 11 ♔h1 (11 ♘g3 ♖d8 12 ♔h1 – *11 ♔h1 ♖d8 12 ♘g3*; 11 ♕d3!?, A.Sokolov-Petrov, Ohrid Ech 2001) 11...♕c7 (11...♖d8 12 ♘g3 ±

Kasparov-Teplitsky, Israel simul 1994; 11...♗d7 doesn't quite equalize either) 12 ♘g3 (12 f4 b5 13 f5! is possibly stronger, Kreiman-Waitzkin, USA jr Ch (New York) 1993) 12...b5 13 f4 ♘a5 14 f5 ♘c4 15 ♗xc4 ♕xc4 16 ♗g5 (Christiansen-Gulko, USA Ch (Salt Lake City) 1999) 16...h6! 17 ♗xf6 ♗xf6 18 ♕xd6 exf5 (18...♖d8!?) 19 exf5 ♗b7 with compensation – Christiansen.

h32) 10...♗d7 and now:

h321) 11 ♔h1 can be answered by either 11...♘g4!? (Lalić) or 11...♘e5 – *10...♘e5 11 ♔h1 ♗d7.*

h322) 11 ♕d3 ♘e5! 12 ♕g3 ♖ac8 13 ♔h1 (Saltaev-Riemersma, Agios Nikolaos 1995) 13...♗b5 gives Black strong counterplay.

h323) 11 ♘g3 ♖ac8 12 ♔h1 ♘e5 13 f4 (13 ♕e2 ♕a6! Lalić) 13...♘c4 14 ♕e2 ♕a6 (14...♕c6!? Timman) 15 e5 ♘e8 16 a4 ♗h4 17 ♘ge4 d5 18 ♖d1! with somewhat the better chances for White, Lalić-Timman, Kilkenny 1999.

h33) 10...♘e5 11 ♔h1 (11 h3 ♗d7 12 ♗e3 ♕c7 13 f4 ♘c4 14 ♗xc4 ♕xc4 15 e5 ♘e4!, Honfi-Drimer, Wijk aan Zee 1970) 11...♗d7 (11...♘ed7 12 ♘g3 ♕c6 13 f4 ± A.Sokolov-Ruban, St Petersburg Z 1993) 12 f4 ♘eg4 13 ♕e1!? (13 ♕d4 ♕xd4 14 ♘xd4 ♗d8!! ∓ Gullaksen-Yakovich, Gothenburg 2001) 13...♘e3 14 ♗xe3 ♕xe3 15 ♖d1 ♕b6 16 e5 ♘g4 17 exd6 ♗f6 ∞ Gofshtein.

**9...0-0**

9...♗d7 10 ♗g5 ♕c5 11 ♗e3 (11 ♕d2!) 11...♕a5 12 ♘d4!? (Hector-Damljanović, Palma de Mallorca 1989) 12...0-0! =.

Recently, 9...a6!? (preserving the possibility of ...h5) has received attention:

a) 10 ♘g3 h5!? 11 h3 h4 12 ♘ge2 ♘a5 13 ♔h1 ♕c7 14 a4 b6 15 ♗e3 ♗b7 16 ♕d4 d5 17 exd5 ♗c5 gives Black sufficient resources, Ki.Georgiev-Topalov, Las Palmas 1993.

b) 10 ♗e3 ♕c7 11 ♘g3 h5!? (11...0-0 – *9...0-0 10 ♗e3 ♕c7 11 ♘g3 a6*) 12 h3 h4 13 ♘ge2 b5 14 a3 ♗b7 with double-edged play, R.Gonzalez-Vera, Cienfuegos 1997.

c) 10 ♔h1 ♕c7 (10...0-0 – *9...0-0 10 ♔h1 a6*) 11 f4 (11 ♗g5 b5!; 11 ♘g3 h5!?) 11...♘a5 12 f5 0-0 13 ♘f4 ♘xb3 14 axb3 with a roughly equal game, Scholl-Csom, Amsterdam 1969.

d) 10 ♕d3 and then:

d1) 10...♗d7 11 ♔h1 (11 ♕g3 0-0 12 ♗h6 ♘e8 13 ♖ad1 ♘e5 = Kelleher-Lazetić, New York 1993) 11...♕c7 12 ♕g3 b5 13 a3 0-0 14 ♗h6 ♘e8 15 f4 ♘a5 16 f5 ♘xb3 17 cxb3 ♕d8 with an acceptable position, Reinderman-Svidler, Wijk aan Zee 1999.

d2) 10...♕c7 11 ♕g3. This position occurred in two Ljubojević-Kramnik blindfold games: 11...b5 12 a3 ♗b7 13 ♕xg7 ♖g8 14 ♕h6 0-0-0 15 f3 (Monaco 1996) seems unclear while 11...g6 12 ♗h6 b5 13 a3 ♗b7 14 ♕h3 ♘a5! 15 ♗g7 ♘xb3 (Monaco 1998) gave Black a good game.

e) 10 ♗g5 ♕c7 (10...♗d7 11 ♘g3 0-0-0?! 12 ♗e3 and 13 ♘a4 ± Plachetka-Kolesar, Pardubice 2000) 11 ♘g3 (11 ♕d2 0-0 – *9...0-0 10 ♗g5 ♕c7 11 ♕d2 a6*) 11...b5 12 ♘h5 (12 ♔h1? h5! 13 ♗xf6 gxf6 14 ♘xh5 ♗b7 ∓ Kasparov-Timman, Manila OL 1992; 12 f4 and 12 ♕d2 h5!? are unclear) 12...♘xh5 13 ♗xe7 ♕xe7 14 ♕xh5 0-0 15 ♖ad1 ♗b7 16 f4 ♘a5 17 f5 ♘xb3 18 f6 gxf6 19 ♖d3 f5 20 exf5 ± Arencibia-Becerra Rivero, Havana

1993; e.g., 20...exf5 21 axb3, when 21...♖e4 22 ♘d5 ♕a7+ 23 ♖f2! f6 24 ♖g3+ ♔h8 25 ♘f4 is a possible continuation.

We now return to the position after 9...0-0 *(D)*:

The key position emerges. Here, both sides may play flexibly and, so far, the accumulated material proves only that there is room for further improvements.

**10 ♗g5**

The other continuations are:

a) 10 ♗e3 ♕c7 11 ♘g3 (11 f4 may be met by 11...♘g4!) with roughly equal chances; for example:

a1) 11...♘a5 12 ♕e2 (12 f4!? is possible) 12...a6 13 f4 b5 14 f5 (14 ♖ad1 ♗b7 15 ♗d4 ♘xb3 16 axb3 ♖ac8 17 ♖f2, Espig-Pietzsch, Zinnowitz 1967, 17...b4!) 14...♘xb3, Filipowicz-Vasiukov, Moscow 1964.

a2) 11...a6 12 f4 b5 (12...♘a5 13 f5 ♘xb3 14 axb3 ♗d7) 13 f5 ♘a5 14 fxe6 fxe6 15 ♘f5 ♘xb3 is equal, Oral-Gabriel, Halle jr Wch 1995.

b) 10 ♕d3!? and then:

b1) 10...♖d8 11 ♕g3 ♕a5 (11...♗d7 12 ♗h6 ♗f8 13 ♖ad1 ± Vasiukov-S.Kiselev, Moscow 1987) 12 ♗e3 b5

13 a3 ♘e5 14 ♗d4 ♘c4 15 a4 ♘d2!
16 axb5 ♘xf1 17 ♖xa5 ♘xg3 18 hxg3
∞ Soltis-Arnason, New York 1989.

b2) 10...a6 11 ♕g3 ♔h8 12 ♗g5
♕c5 13 ♗e3 ♕a5 14 f4 b5 15 a3 ♕c7
16 ♘d4 with chances for both sides,
Bronstein-Gulko, Kishinev 1976 (this
position can arise from Chapter 6 via
the move-order *5...a6 6 ♗c4 e6 7 ♗b3
b5 8 0-0 ♗e7 9 ♕f3! ♕c7 10 ♕g3 0-0
11 a3 ♔h8!? 12 ♗e3 ♘c6 13 f4*).

b3) 10...♘a5 11 ♗e3 (11 ♕g3!?
♔h8 12 ♗e3) 11...♕c7 12 ♘b5 ♕b8
(12...♕c6!? 13 ♖fd1 a6) 13 ♗f4 ♖d8
14 ♖ad1 ♘e8 15 e5 ± Ljubojević-
Benko, New York 1985.

b4) 10...♗d7 11 ♕g3 and here:

b41) 11...♔h8 12 ♔h1 (12 ♗e3
♕a6! 13 ♖fd1 ♖ac4 14 ♗g5 ♘e5, Sol-
tis-Kožul, Palma de Mallorca 1989)
12...♕a6! 13 ♗g5 ♖ad8 ∞ Kožul.

b42) 11...♘e5!? 12 ♗e3 ♕a6! 13
♗d4 (13 ♖ae1!? b5 is an alternative)
13...b5!? (13...♘xe4 14 ♘xe4 ♕xe2
15 ♖fe1 ♕a6 16 ♘xd6 ±) 14 a3 ♕b7
(Ljubičić-Tukmakov, Pula 1994) 15 f4
♘c6 16 ♗e3 ♘a5 17 e5 ♘h5 18 ♕h3
g6 ∞ Tukmakov.

c) 10 ♔h1 and then:

c1) 10...a6 11 ♗g5 (11 ♕d3 ♕c7
12 ♕g3 ♔h8 = Soltis-Waitzkin, New
York 1992; 11 ♕e1!?) 11...♕c7 12 f4
b5 13 ♘g3 ♘a5 – *10 ♘g3 a6 11 ♔h1
♘a5 12 ♗g5 ♕c7 13 f4 b5*.

c2) 10...♘a5 and then: 11 ♘g3 –
*10 ♘g3 ♘a5 11 ♔h1*; 11 ♗g5 – *10
♗g5 ♘a5 11 ♔h1*.

c3) 10...♖d8 11 f4 d5 12 e5 ♘g4
13 ♕e1 with chances for both sides,
Zinn-Malich, East German Ch (Mag-
deburg) 1964.

d) 10 ♘g3 is another attractive option:

d1) 10...a6 and then:

d11) 11 ♗e3 ♕c7 – *10 ♗e3 ♕c7
11 ♘g3 a6*.

d12) 11 ♗g5 ♖d8 (11...♕c5 12
♕d2 ♕d4 13 ♕e2 ♕c5 14 ♗e3 ± Sem-
eniuk-Levin, USSR 1989; 11...♕c7 –
*10 ♗g5 ♕c7 11 ♘g3 a6*) 12 ♔h1 ♕c7
13 f4 b5 (13...h6 14 ♗xf6 ♗xf6 15
♘h5) 14 ♗xf6!? (14 f5 b4 leads to an
unclear position, Lamoureux-M.Sorin,
French Cht 1998) 14...♗xf6 15 ♘h5,
with attacking chances.

d13) 11 ♔h1 ♘a5 12 ♗g5 (12 f4
♕c7 13 f5 ♘xb3 14 axb3 ♗d7 is equal,
Ma.Ankerst-Minić, Novi Sad 1965)
and here:

d131) 12...♕c7 13 f4 b5 14 ♕e2
gives White some advantage, since after 14...b4, 15 e5! is strong, Donchev-
Züger, Lucerne OL 1982.

d132) 12...h6!? 13 ♗e3 (13 ♗xf6!?)
13...♕c6 14 f4 b5 15 e5 ♗b7 16 ♖f2
♘e8 favours Black, D.Schneider-Gol-
din, Connecticut 2000.

d2) 10...♖d8 11 ♔h1 (11 ♗g5 – *10
♗g5 ♖d8 11 ♘g3*) 11...♘a5 12 f4
♕a6!? (also playable is 12...♘xb3 13
axb3 ♕c6 14 ♕e2 a6 15 e5 ♘e8, Gdan-
ski-Kotronias, Moscow OL 1994) 13
♗e3 b5 14 f5 ♘xb3 15 axb3 ♕c6 16
♗g5 (Ki.Georgiev-Arnason, Palma de
Mallorca 1989) 16...b4 17 ♘ce2 e5 =
Arnason.

d3) 10...♗d7 11 ♔h1 ♘a5 –
*10...♘a5 11 ♔h1 ♗d7*.

d4) 10...♘a5 11 ♔h1 (11 ♗e3 ♕c6
12 f4 ♘c4 = Nunn; 11 ♘h5!? ♘xh5
12 ♕xh5 ♕c5 13 ♕g4 ♘c4 14 ♕e2
♘a5 15 ♗e3 ± K.Müller-Wahls, Hamburg 1991) 11...♘xb3 (11...a6 – *10...a6
11 ♔h1 ♘a5*; 11...♕c7 12 f4 ♗d7 13
♕e2 ♗c6 14 e5 with some initiative,
Gdanski-Kalinin, Bundesliga 1994/5;

following 11...♗d7, it is possible to play 12 f4 or 12 ♗g5 h6 13 ♗e3 ♕c7 14 f4 b5 15 e5!?, when White definitely has the initiative, Neukirkh-Pietrusiak, Rostock 1981) 12 axb3 ♕c6!? 13 ♗g5 h6 14 ♗xf6 ♗xf6 15 ♘h5 ♗e7!? 16 ♖xa7 ♖xa7 17 ♕d4 e5 18 ♕xa7 ♗e6 with compensation, Hector-Plachetka, Copenhagen 1990.

We now return to 10 ♗g5 *(D)*:

**10...♘a5**

The other possibilities are:

a) 10...a6?! 11 ♗xf6!, Chandler-Rivas, Minsk 1982.

b) 10...♕c5 11 ♗e3 (Saidy) ±.

c) 10...♘e5 11 ♘g3 h6 12 ♗xf6 ♗xf6 13 ♘h5 ♘d7 14 ♘xf6+ ♘xf6 15 ♕d3 ± M.Ankerst-Kožul, Bled 1993.

d) 10...♕c7 and here:

d1) 11 ♕d2 a6 (11...♘a5!? 12 ♖ad1 ♘xb3 13 axb3 ♖d8, Wedberg-Fedorowicz, New York 1990) 12 ♖ad1 ♖d8 13 ♘g3 b5 (13...♘a5 – *10...♘a5 11 ♘g3 ♕c7 12 ♕d2 a6 13 ♖ad1 ♖d8*) 14 ♖fe1 (14 f4 b4!?) and then:

d11) After 14...♗b7 15 ♗xf6!? ♗xf6 16 ♘h5 ♗e7 17 ♖e3 ♔h8, Quinteros-Radulov, Wijk aan Zee 1974, 18 ♘xg7!? looks dangerous for Black.

d12) 14...b4!?.

d13) 14...♘a5 – *10...♘a5 11 ♘g3 ♕c7 12 ♕d2 a6 13 ♖ad1 ♖d8 14 ♖fe1 b5!*.

d2) 11 ♘g3 a6 (11...♘a5 – *10...♘a5 11 ♘g3 a6*) 12 ♘h5 with a slight advantage (or maybe 12 f4!?).

e) 10...♖d8 and then:

e1) 11 ♔h1 ♘e5?! (11...♘a5 ± Anand) 12 f4 ♘eg4 13 ♕e1 ♕c5 14 ♘c1! ± Wahls-Mirallès, Lucerne Wcht 1989.

e2) 11 ♘g3 and here:

e21) 11...♕a5 12 f4! h6 (12...b5 13 a3!?, G.Kuzmin-Furman, Minsk 1976) 13 ♗xf6 ♗xf6 14 ♘h5 ♗xc3 15 bxc3 ♕xc3 16 ♕g4 with the initiative – Dokhoian.

e22) 11...d5 12 exd5 ♘xd5 13 ♘xd5 exd5 14 ♖e1! ± Ribli.

e23) 11...h6 12 ♗e3 (after 12 ♗xf6 ♗xf6 13 ♘h5, Dokhoian gives the lines 13...♗xc3 14 bxc3 ♕c5 15 ♔h1 d5!? 16 exd5 exd5 17 f4 ♕xc3 18 f5 with compensation and 13...♗e7 14 ♕g4 ♗f8 with unclear play) 12...♕a5 (12...♕c7 can be met by Dokhoian's 13 f4 or 13 ♘h5 ♗d7 14 f4 ♘a5 15 ♗d4! ± De Vreugt-Gulko, Esbjerg 2000) and now 13 h3!? gives White slightly the better chances, Levin-Dokhoian, Berlin 1992, and is better than 13 f4 d5! 14 e5 ♘e8 15 ♘ce2 d4! ∓ or 13 ♕e2 d5! (Dokhoian).

**11 ♘g3**

Or:

a) 11 ♕d3 ♕c5 =.

b) 11 ♕d2 ♕a6!? (11...♘xb3 12 axb3 a6 13 ♖fd1 ♖d8 14 ♗e3 ♕c7 15 ♗f4 is slightly better for White – Mirallès) 12 ♖ad1 ♘c4?! (12...♔h8 13 ♗xf6 gxf6 14 ♕h6 ♘xb3 15 axb3 ♖g8 16 ♘f4 ♗d7 ∞ Mirallès) 13 ♗xc4 ♕xc4 14 ♗xf6 gxf6 15 ♕h6 ♔h8 16

♘f4 ♖g8 17 ♖xd6 e5 (Wedberg-Mirallès, Haifa Echt 1989) 18 ♘cd5! ± (Mirallès).

c) 11 ♔h1 ♕c5 (11...a6 12 f4 ♕c7 13 ♘g3 – *10 ♘g3 a6 11 ♔h1 ♘a5 12 ♗g5 ♕c7 13 f4*) 12 f4 (12 ♗e3 ♕c7 =; 12 ♗f4 b5 ½-½ Wahls-Franco, Lucerne Wcht 1989) 12...b5 13 ♘g3, and here instead of 13...b4?, which is met by 14 e5! dxe5 15 ♗xf6! with an extremely dangerous attack for White, Fischer-Benko, Bled/Zagreb/Belgrade Ct 1959, Black must play 13...♘xb3 14 axb3 ♗b7 (14...b4!?) 15 ♘h5 ♔h8 = (Fischer), or, at once, 13...♗b7 14 ♘h5 (14 f5!?) 14...♔h8 (Kasparov and Nikitin's suggestion 14...b4!? is less convincing) with chances for both sides, Scholl-Langeweg, Amsterdam 1970.

**11...♕c5**

The following have been tested as well:

a) 11 b6 12 ♗e3 (unclear is 12 ♗xf6 ♗xf6 13 ♘h5 Dorfman) 12...♕c6 13 ♕e2 (13 f4 ♘c4 = Nunn; probably stronger is 13 ♘h5!?) 13...♘xb3 14 axb3 a6 15 f4 b5 16 e5 ♘e8! with a good game for Black, Thipsay-Dorfman, New Delhi 1982.

b) 11...♕c7 12 ♕d2 a6 13 ♖ad1 ♖d8 14 ♖fe1 b5! 15 ♘f5 (15 f3 ♗b7 ∓ Ribli) 15...exf5 16 ♗xf6 ♘xb3 17 axb3 ♗xf6 18 ♘d5 ♕d7! 19 ♘xf6+ (19 ♘b6? ♕c6 20 ♘xa8 ♗b7) 19...gxf6 20 ♕h6 ♗b7!? 21 ♖d3 f4 22 ♕xf4 ♔f8 23 ♕xf6 ♕e6 24 ♕h8+ ♔e7 25 ♕xh7 = Ljubojević-Ribli, Skopje OL 1972.

**12 ♕d2 b5 13 ♖ad1**

Now, instead of 13...♘xb3?! 14 cxb3 ♗b7 15 ♖c1 ♕b6 16 ♘h5 ± Ljubojević-Ree, Amsterdam 1975, or 13...♗b7

14 ♗e3 (14 ♘h5!? is also possible) 14...♕c6 (14...♘xb3!?) 15 ♘d5! with the advantage, Minić recommended 13...b4 14 ♘a4 ♕b5 with a complicated game.

We may conclude that 7 ♘de2 is a good choice for the player who is not well enough prepared for more forcing lines.

**B4)**

**7 ♘xc6!? bxc6 8 0-0** *(D)*

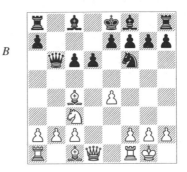

Like the other responses to 6...♕b6, 7 ♘xc6 has its own pros and cons. Having improved his opponent's pawn-structure, White is ahead in development. Black urgently needs to develop the f8-bishop by choosing one of three options:

**B41: 8...e5**     241
**B42: 8...e6**     242
**B43: 8...g6**     244

**B41)**

**8...e5**

Quite unpopular due to White's next move:

**9 ♗g5!**

Quiet development does not bring great advantage to White. For instance:

a) 9 ♕d3 ♗e7 10 ♗g5 0-0 11 b3 (11 ♗xf6 ♗xf6 12 ♕xd6 ♕xb2 = Sion Castro-Gi.Hernandez, Cordoba 1995) 11...♖d8 12 ♖ad1 ♗g4 13 ♗e3 ♕c7 14 ♖d2?! ♗h5!, Neelakantan-Annageldiev, Calcutta 1996.

b) 9 ♔h1 ♗e7 10 f4 0-0 11 ♕d3 (S.B.Hansen-Mortensen, Danish Ch (Esbjerg) 1997) 11...exf4 12 ♗xf4 ♘g4 13 ♕g3 ♕c5 14 ♗b3 ♘e5 followed by ...♗e6 (Mortensen).

c) 9 ♗e3 ♕xb2 10 ♕d3 deserves a certain amount of attention.

**9...♕xb2**

9...♗e7 10 ♗xf6 gxf6 11 b3 ♗a6 12 ♘a4 ♕a5 13 ♗xa6 ♕xa6 14 c4 ± Bangiev. Probably the least of all evils here is 9...♕c5!? ± with the idea of 10...♗e7, as in Tompa-Cserna, Hungarian Ch (Budapest) 1975.

**10 ♕d3 ♕b6**

10...♗e7 11 ♗xf6 gxf6 (11...♗xf6? 12 ♕xd6) 12 ♗b3 ♗e6 (12...a5? 13 ♖ab1 ♕a3 14 ♘b5 +− Vasiukov-Pietrusiak, Polanica Zdroj 1965) 13 ♗xe6 fxe6 14 ♖ab1 ♕a3 15 ♖b3 is much better for White.

**11 ♗xf6 gxf6 12 ♘d5 ♕d8**

12...cxd5 13 ♕xd5 ♕b7 14 ♖fb1! +−.

**13 ♖ab1!**

13 ♘e3 ♗h6 (13...♖g8!? Bologan) 14 ♖ad1 ♔e7 15 ♗b3 (15 ♕e2!? Bologan) and now, instead of 15...♗e6?! 16 ♘c4 d5? 17 ♗a4! +− Topalov-Gavrikov, Geneva rpd 1996, 15...♗xe3 ∞ is correct.

**13...♗e7**

Or: 13...cxd5? 14 ♕xd5 ♗e6 15 ♗b5+; 13...♗e6? 14 ♖b7!; 13...♗h6 14 ♘b4! ± K.Müller-Gabriel, Bundesliga 1997/8.

**14 ♘xe7**

The retreat of the knight to e3 or b4 also preserves the initiative.

**14...♔xe7**

Now:

a) White performed ineffectively in Ashley-Waitzkin, Bermuda 1997: 15 f4 ♕a5 16 ♔h1 ♖g8 17 ♗xf7? (17 f5!? Rechlis) 17...♔xf7 18 ♕xd6 ♕d8 19 ♕xc6 ♕d2!, etc.

b) Instead, I recommend 15 ♕a3 ± so as not to let the queen go to a5.

## B42)

**8...e6** (D)

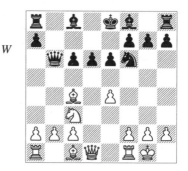

The game Topalov-Kramnik, Novgorod 1996 spoiled the reputation of this continuation.

**9 ♕e2**

Otherwise:

a) 9 ♗g5?! is well met by 9...♕c5!, Stanciu-Mititelu, Romania 1966.

b) 9 ♗b3?! ♗e7 10 ♗e3 ♕c7 11 f4 0-0 followed by ...d5!.

c) 9 ♗d3!? ♗e7 10 ♘a4 ♕c7 11 c4 is worth considering.

d) 9 b3 involves the same plan as the text-move, but it may be less accurate: 9...♗e7 (9...d5 10 exd5 cxd5 11 ♗b5+ ♗d7 12 ♗xd7+ ♘xd7 13 ♘xd5 exd5 14 ♖e1+ with an attack – *New in*

*Chess*) 10 ♗b2 0-0 11 ♕e2 with several possibilities for Black:

d1) 11...d5? 12 exd5 cxd5 13 ♗xd5 ±.

d2) 11...♘d7 – *9 ♕e2 ♘d7 10 b3 ♗e7 11 ♗b2 0-0.*

d3) 11...♗b7 12 e5!?.

d4) 11...♗c7 12 f4! d5 13 ♗d3.

d5) 11...♕a5 12 ♘a4 d5 13 e5 ♘d7 14 ♗d3 ♘b6 15 ♗c3 ♗b4 16 ♗xb4 ♕xb4 17 c3! ± De Vreugt-Van der Wiel, Amsterdam 1996.

d6) 11...e5!? 12 ♔h1 (12 ♘a4!? ♕c7 13 f4 exf4 14 e5 ♗g4 15 ♕e1, Tell-Trygstad, Stockholm 1998) 12...♕c7 13 ♖ae1 (13 f4? exf4 14 ♖xf4 d5) 13...♘d7 (13...g6!? *New in Chess*) 14 ♘a4 and here, instead of 14...♗b7 15 ♗d3 ♖fe8 16 c4 ♗g5 17 ♕c2 ± Karpov-Stein, USSR Ch (Leningrad) 1971, Karpov recommended 14...♗f6!.

e) 9 ♗f4!? is interesting:

e1) 9...d5? 10 exd5 exd5 11 ♘xd5! ±.

e2) 9...♕c5 10 ♕e2 ±.

e3) 9...♕xb2 10 ♕d3 ♕b4 (10...e5 11 ♗g5 transposes to Line B41) 11 ♖ab1 ♕c5 12 ♖fd1 with compensation, Fischer-Byrne, New York blitz 1971.

e4) 9...♕c7 10 ♕d3 (10 ♕e2 e5 11 ♗g5 ♗e7 = Minev) 10...♘h5!? (not all problems are solved by 10...♗e7 11 ♖ad1 e5 12 ♗g5, Britton-Speelman, London 1978, or 10...♘d7 11 ♕g3, Winants-Levin, Bundesliga 1996/7) 11 ♗e3 ♗e7 12 f4 ♘f6 13 ♖ae1 0-0 gives Black an acceptable position, Honfi-Čabrilo, Belgrade 1977.

**9...♘d7**

9...♗e7 10 e5 (10 b3 0-0 11 ♗b2 – *9 b3 ♗e7 10 ♗b2 0-0 11 ♕e2*) 10...dxe5 11 ♕xe5 0-0 (11...♗a6!? 12 ♗e3 ♕b7

13 ♗xa6 ♕xa6 14 ♗c5? ♘d7 15 ♕xg7 ♗f6 16 ♕h6 ♗xc3) 12 ♘a4 (12 ♕e2 ♗b7 13 b3 ♖ad8 14 ♗b2 c5 = B.Knežević-Damljanović, Belgrade 1998; 12 ♗b3?! ♗a6!) 12...♕b4 13 b3 with somewhat better chances for White, Nedev-Dorić, Plovdiv 1991.

**10 b3**

10 ♘a4 ♕a5 (10...♕c7) 11 b3 ♘e5 12 ♗d2 ♕c7 13 ♗a6 ± Gi.Hernandez-Yermolinsky, Chicago 1997.

**10...♗e7 11 ♗b2**

Or 11 ♘a4 ♕c7 12 ♗b2 0-0.

**11...0-0 12 ♘a4 ♕c7 13 f4 ♗b7**

Or:

a) 13...♘b6 14 ♘xb6 axb6 15 a4 (15 ♖f3! Krnić) 15...♖e8 and White only succeeded in drawing in Krnić-Radulov, Vršac 1973 after 16 ♖f3 b5 17 ♖g3 g6 18 ♕h5 (18 f5 bxc4 19 ♕h5 e5!, Krnić, also looks like a draw) 18...♗f8 19 f5 ♗g7 20 ♗xg7 gxh5.

b) 13...d5 14 ♗d3 (14 exd5 cxd5 15 ♗xd5? ♗c5+) 14...g6 15 c4 ♗f6 (Prié-Mirallès, French Cht 1989) 16 ♖ac1 with an advantage for White – Mirallès.

c) 13...e5!?.

**14 ♖ad1**

This is possibly stronger than the previously played 14 ♖f3 and 14 ♖ae1.

**14...♖ae8**

Unsuccessful are 14...c5 15 f5 ± (Khuzman) and 14...d5 15 ♗d3 ♗f6 (15...c5 16 exd5 ♗xd5 17 f5 ±) 16 e5 with an attack. Comparatively better continuations have been proposed: 14...♖fe8 ± (Kramnik) with the point 15 f5 e5, or 14...♖ad8 15 ♖d3 d5 (Topalov).

**15 ♖d3! c5**

Insufficient is 15...♗f6 16 ♗xf6 (16 e5! dxe5 17 fxe5 ♘xe5 18 ♖xf6 gxf6

19 ♖h3 ± Har-Zvi) 16...♘xf6 17 e5 dxe5 18 ♕xe5 (Kramnik) or 15...d5 16 ♖h3! ♘f6 17 e5!? (17 ♗d3 dxe4 18 ♗xe4 g6 is much better for White – Topalov) 17...♘e4 18 ♗d3 c5 19 ♘c3 f5 20 ♕h5! h6 21 ♕g6.

15...g6 16 ♖h3! ± (16 ♕h5 ♗f6! ∞; 16 f5 exf5! ∞ Golubev-Kuznetsov, Ukrainian Ch (Ordzhonikidze) 2001).

**16 ♗b5! ♗c6**

16...♖d8 17 ♗xd7! ♖xd7 18 ♕g4! g6 19 f5.

**17 ♗xc6 ♕xc6 18 c4**

White is much better, Topalov-Kramnik, Novgorod 1996.

## B43)

**8...g6** *(D)*

The topical continuation.

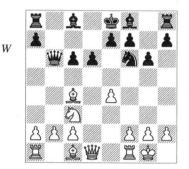

W

**9 e5!?**

Less radical attempts are:

a) 9 b3 ♗g7 10 ♗b2 0-0 with an equal position.

b) 9 ♗d3 ♗g7 10 ♘a4!? ♕c7 11 f4 (11 c4 e5!? {11...0-0 12 f4} 12 f4 exf4 Jokšić) 11...0-0 12 c4 gives both sides chances; for example, 12...e5 (12...♖b8 13 ♕e2 ♘d7, Gara-Jovanović, Budapest 1996; 12...♘g4!?, Velimirović-Damljanović, Ulcinj 1998) 13 f5 (13

fxe5?! ♘g4!) 13...d5, A.Kovačević-B.Knežević, Yugoslav Ch (Belgrade) 1998.

c) 9 ♗b3 ♗g7 10 ♗f4 (after 10 ♗e3, 10...♕a5!? 11 f4 0-0 is good enough) 10...♘d7 (10...0-0 11 e5 dxe5 12 ♗xe5 ± Prié-Mirallès, Chanac 1989; 10...♕c7 11 ♖e1 ♘g4 12 ♕d2 h6 13 ♖ad1 with the better chances for White, del Rio-Kožul, Ubeda 1996; 10...♕a5!?; 10...♗a6) 11 ♗g5 (11 ♕f3 0-0 12 ♗g5 ♕c7! = Kindermann-Pelletier, Portorož 1998) 11...♘c5!? (or 11...a5 12 ♕f3 ♘e5 13 ♕g3 ♗a6 14 ♖fe1 ♕c7 15 ♖ad1 and now, rather than 15...♘d7? 16 e5! ± Prié-Tukmakov, Aix-les-Bains 1991, Black should play 15...0-0 or 15...♘c4!?) 12 ♖e1 ♕c7 = del Rio-Pelletier, Medellin jr Wch 1996.

d) 9 ♗e3 and then:

d1) 9...♕xb2?! 10 ♗d4 e5 (and not 10...♕b4? 11 ♗xf6 exf6 12 ♕d4! ± Bosch-Kharlov, Leeuwarden 1993; 10...♕b7 11 e5 gives White compensation) 11 ♖b1 (11 ♘b5!? should probably be met by 11...exd4!? rather than 11...♕b4 12 ♘c7+ ♔e7 13 ♘xa8 ♕xc4 14 ♗xa7 ♕a6 15 ♗b8! ♘xe4 16 ♘c7) 11...♕a3 12 ♖b3 ♕a5 13 ♗e3 ♕c7 (13...♗e7 14 ♗g5 ♕c5 15 ♗xf6 ♗xf6 16 ♕f3 ♕xc4 17 ♕xf6 0-0 18 ♕xd6 ± M.Berkovich-Petrienko, USSR 1980) 14 ♗g5 ♗g7 15 ♗xf6 ♗xf6 16 ♕f3 (Arizmendi-Waitzkin, Bermuda 1999) 16...♗g7! 17 ♘d5! cxd5 18 ♗xd5 ♗e6 19 ♗xa8 ♗xb3 20 cxb3 0-0 21 ♗d5 ± Gofshtein.

d2) 9...♕c7 10 f4 ♗g7 11 ♗d4 (11 e5 ♘g4 12 ♗d4 0-0 – *11 ♗d4 0-0 12 e5 ♘g4*) 11...0-0 12 ♔h1 (12 e5 ♘g4 13 exd6 ♕xd6! 14 ♗xg7 ♔xg7 15 ♕xd6 exd6 16 ♖ae1 ♘f6 17 ♖e7 ♗d7

= del Rio-Gonzalez Garcia, Linares 1998; 12 h3 ♘d7 = Emms-Garcia Ilundain, Escaldes Z 1998) 12...♖b8 (12...e5 13 fxe5 dxe5 14 ♗c5 gives White a slight advantage, G.Todorović-Damljanović, Yugoslav Cht 1999) 13 ♗b3 ♗a6 with an equal game.

d3) 9...♕a5!? also seems to be satisfactory: 10 f4 ♗g7 11 e5 (11 h3 0-0 12 ♗b3 ♘d7 = Vlasov-Akhmadeev, St Petersburg 1999) 11...♘g4 12 ♗d4 c5!, Berndt-Popović, Austrian Cht 2000/1, with the point 13 ♗b5+ ♔f8.

e) 9 ♕e2 ♘g4 (9...♗g7?! 10 e5 dxe5 11 ♕xe5 gives White an advantage; e.g., 11...0-0 12 ♕xe7 ♗f5 13 ♗b3 ♖ae8 14 ♕d6 ♘g4 15 ♗f4 ♗xc3 16 bxc3 ♖e2 17 ♖ab1! +– Morović-Becerra Rivero, Cienfuegos 1996; 9...♘d7!? 10 ♗e3 ♕xb2 11 ♗d4 e5 12 ♖ab1 ♕a3 13 ♖b3 ♕a5 14 ♗e3 with compensation, Al Awadhi-Spraggett, Dubai OL 1986; 9...♗g4 10 ♕e1!, Madl P.Varga, Budapest 1997). Now:

e1) 10 b3 ♗g7 11 ♗b2 ♕a5 with a good game, Giaccio-Zarnicki, Villa Gesell 1998.

e2) 10 h3 ♘e5 11 ♗e3 (11 ♗b3 is better) 11...♕xb2 12 ♗d4 ♕b4! (Gofshtein) favours Black.

e3) 10 ♔h1 ♗g7 11 f4 0-0 12 ♗d3 (12 h3? ♘f6 13 e5 dxe5 14 fxe5 ♘h5 15 ♖f3 ♕d4! 16 g4 ♗xg4 17 hxg4 ♕xg4 18 ♘e4 ♗xe5 is much better for Black – Gershon) 12...a5 (12...♖b8 Gershon) 13 ♘a4 ♕d8!? with chances for both sides, De Vreugt-Gershon, Tel-Aviv 2000. Black intends ...e5 and ...♕h4.

e4) 10 ♗e3!? ♕c7 (10...♘xe3!? 11 fxe3 f6 Tyomkin) 11 ♗d4 e5 12 ♗e3 ♗g7 13 ♖ad1 0-0 14 ♕d3 d5 15 exd5 e4 16 d6 exd3 17 dxc7 dxc2 and it

looks like Black is equal, De Vreugt-Blehm, Erevan jr Wch 1999.

e5) 10 ♗b3 ♗g7 and then:

e51) 11 h3 ♘e5 12 ♗e3 ♕a6!? (12...♕a5 13 f4 ♗a6 14 ♕d2 ♘c4, Vasiukov-Mititelu, Budapest 1967, and 12...♗a6!? are also good) 13 f4 (13 ♕d2 ♘c4 14 ♗xc4 ♕xc4 ∓ Tyomkin) 13...♕xe2 14 ♘xe2 ♘d7 = Dervishi-Tyomkin, Verona 2000.

e52) 11 ♘a4 ♕a6 (11...♕b5!? is critical, with the point 12 c4 ♕e5! – Tyomkin) 12 c4 ♖b8 13 ♗d2 with some pressure, T.Thorhallsson-Tyomkin, Paget Parish 2001.

f) 9 ♕e1!? ♘g4 10 h3 ♘e5 11 ♘a4 ♕c7 (11...♕d4 12 ♗b3 with the point 12...♕a6? 13 ♗d2! ♗xf1 14 ♗c3 and White wins) 12 ♕c3!, Scheipl-Freise, Menden 1974.

**9...dxe5 10 ♕e2** *(D)*

**10...♕d4**

Or:

a) 10...♗g7?! – *9 ♕e2 ♗g7?! 10 e5 dxe5.*

b) 10...♘d7?! 11 ♘e4 ♗g7 12 ♗e3 ± (Morović).

c) 10...♕a5?! 11 f4 ± (Kantsler).

d) 10...♕c5!? 11 ♗e3 and now 11...♕a5 is a playable alternative to

11...♕d6, which transposes to the main line.

e) 10...♕c7 11 f4 (11 ♖e1!?) 11...e4 (11...exf4? 12 ♗xf4 ♕b6+ 13 ♗e3 ♗g4 14 ♕e1 with a decisive advantage) 12 ♘xe4 ♘xe4 13 ♕xe4 ♗g7 14 c3 0-0 15 ♗e3. This position has been tested in a number of games. White probably has a small advantage; for example, 15...♖b8 16 ♖f2 ♗f5 17 ♕f3 K.Müller-Csom, Lippstadt 1999.

**11 ♗e3**

Not 11 ♖d1? ♗g4!, Stocek-Goloshchapov, Mlada Boleslav 1995.

**11...♕d6!**

11...♕h4 12 f4! e4 (Nedev-Kotronias, Korinthos 1997; 12...♘g4 13 g3; 12...♗g4 13 ♕e1 ♕xe1 14 ♖axe1 exf4 15 ♗d4 ± Tsesarsky) 13 ♗f2!? ♕h5 14 ♘xe4 ♕xe2 15 ♘xf6+ exf6 16 ♗xe2 and White has an advantage.

**12 ♖ad1**

12 ♕f3?! is unsuccessful in view of 12...♗g4! 13 ♕g3 ♗g7, Jackova-Cmilyte, Erevan girls Wch 1999.

12 f4 contains a trap:

a) 12...e4? 13 ♖fd1! (better than 13 ♖ad1?! ♗g4 14 ♘xe4 ♕xd1!) 13...♗g4 (13...♕c7 14 ♘xe4 ♘xe4 15 ♗d4 ±) 14 ♖xd6 ♗xe2 15 ♖xc6 (or 15 ♖xf6) 15...♗xc4 16 ♖xc4 ± Tsesarsky.

b) However, 12...♗g7! is good (this was also pointed out by Tsesarsky): 13 fxe5 (13 ♖ad1? ♗g4; 13 ♖fd1 ♕c7!? 14 fxe5 ♘g4) 13...♕xe5 14 ♕f2 0-0, etc.

**12...♕c7 13 f4**

Or:

a) 13 ♖fe1 ♗g7 14 ♗g5 (14 ♗c5 – *13 ♗c5 ♗g7 14 ♖fe1*) 14...h6 15 ♗h4 ♘h5 16 ♘b5 cxb5 17 ♗xb5+ ♔f8 18 ♕c4 ♕b6 19 ♗xe7+ ♔g8 20 ♖d6 ♗e6 21 ♕e4 ♕xb5 22 ♕xa8+ ♔h7 −+

Florescu-Nevednichy, Miercirea Ciuc 1999.

b) 13 ♗c5!? ♗g7 (13...♗f5!?) and now:

b1) After 14 ♖fe1, both 14...0-0 15 ♕xe5 ♕xe5 16 ♖xe5 ♘d7 17 ♖xd7 (Kramnik) and 14...♘h5!? should suit Black.

b2) 14 f4 ♘d7 (14...♗g4?! 15 ♕xe5 ± Hamdouchi-M.Sorin, Montpellier 1999; 14...e4?! is also dubious in view of 15 ♘xe4) and now 15 ♗a3 ♘b6 is good for Black, Kornev-Akhmadeev, Russia 1998, so White should try 15 ♗xe7 ♔xe7 16 fxe5 ♖f8 17 ♕g4.

**13...♗g4**

13...♗g7? 14 fxe5 ♕xe5 15 ♗b6 ♕xe2 16 ♖d8#.

13...e4 14 ♘xe4 ♗g7 (14...♘xe4 15 ♗d4 ±) 15 ♗d4 0-0 16 ♘xf6+ ± Lakos-Pelletier, Portorož 1998.

**14 ♕f2**

14 ♘b5 ♕b7! ∓ Gofshtein.

**14...e4**

After 14...♗xd1?! 15 fxe5 ♕xe5 (15...♗xc2 16 exf6 ♗f5 17 g4!) 16 ♗d4 Black lacks a satisfactory defence:

a) 16...♕d6 17 ♗xf6 ♕xf6 (alternatively, 17...exf6 18 ♘e4 ♕e5 19 ♘xf6+ ♔d8 20 ♖xd1+ ♗d6 21 ♘e4! +−) 18 ♕c5 e5 19 ♗xf7+ +− Tsesarsky.

b) 16...♕c7 17 ♗xf6 exf6 18 ♖e1+ ♗e7 19 ♕xf6 0-0-0 20 ♖xe7 ♕b6+ 21 ♔h1 ± Mitenkov.

c) 16...♕f5 17 ♕e3.

d) 16...♕g5 17 ♗xf6 exf6 18 ♘e4 ♗c5 19 ♘xc5 0-0-0 20 ♘d3 ♔b8 21 ♖xd1 ♕g4 22 ♕g3+ ±.

**15 ♖de1 ♗f5!**

15...♗g7 16 h3! ♗f5 17 g4 ♗c8 18 ♗c5 ± Kramnik.

**16 h3 h5 17 ♗d4 ♗g7 18 b3 0-0**

18...h4 19 ♗xf6 ♗xf6 20 ♘xe4 ♗xe4 21 ♖xe4 ♖h5 (Schumi-Atalik, Bled 2001) 22 ♗d3!? is less convincing.

**19 ♗xf6 ♗xf6 20 ♘xe4 ♗xe4 21 ♖xe4 ♕b6**

½-½ Topalov-Kramnik, Novgorod 1997.

## B5)

**7 ♘b3**

This move is played more frequently than all the other moves put together. Whether it is good or bad, the b2-pawn is completely safe now and White is guaranteed a wide choice of continuations as the c1-bishop is free.

**7...e6** *(D)*

Or:

a) 7...g6 gives White at least a possibility to transpose to the position that usually arises out of the Accelerated Dragon through 8 ♗e3 ♕c7 9 ♗e2 ♗g7 10 0-0-0 ±.

b) 7...a6!? (avoiding 7...e6 8 ♗f4) 8 0-0 e6 transposes to the note to Black's 8th move in Line B52.

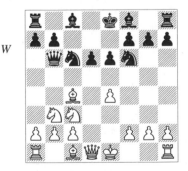

W

When the c4-bishop and the black queen have moved to more convenient squares, a huge range of Scheveningen positions may arise on the board. We shall quite briefly consider the continuations 8 ♗e3 and 8 0-0, which often lead to Scheveningen lines, and, in greater detail, more concrete variations with 8 ♗g5 and 8 ♗f4.

So:

**B51: 8 ♗e3** 247
**B52: 8 0-0** 248
**B53: 8 ♗g5** 253
**B54: 8 ♗f4** 261

Out of the other options it is necessary to mention 8 ♕e2. Usually, this move is linked with the idea of castling long: after, for example, 8...a6 9 f4 ♕c7 10 ♗e3 b5 11 ♗d3 followed by 0-0-0, or first g4, an intricate game commences that gives chances for both sides.

## B51)

**8 ♗e3**

8 0-0, followed by ♗e3, ♗d3 and f4, is the other possible introduction to the same arrangement (see Line B52).

As compared to 8 0-0 ♗e7 9 ♗e3, with the present move-order 8 ♗e3 the sides have certain additional possibilities. White has ideas with 0-0-0 or an early g4, and Black could try to do without ...♗e7; we shall see these ideas in the notes below.

**8...♕c7 9 ♗d3**

9 f4 a6 10 ♗d3 comes to the same thing.

**9...a6 10 f4** *(D)*

According to the widely adopted classification, this position and all its 'derivatives' are referred to as the Scheveningen. However, in practice they most often arise, as in our case, from the Sozin or from the Taimanov

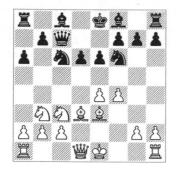

Variation. Also, it is curious to note that one may find a couple of hundred games that began 1 e4 c5 2 ♘f3 ♘c6 3 d4 cxd4 4 ♘xd4 ♕b6, where the position in the diagram arose with White to move. In many such instances Black, whose statistics are far from being catastrophic, was a famous grandmaster.

The most popular continuation is:
**10...b5 11 ♕f3**

White can play 11 g4!? or 11 ♕e2, which should be compared with 8 ♕e2.
**11...♗b7 12 0-0**

12 g4!? is an alternative.

Now (after 12 0-0):

a) 12...g6!? with a possible ...♗g7.

b) Black could also try 12...d5 13 exd5 ♘b4.

c) 12...♗e7 brings us to an important theoretical position, which we discuss in Line B52.

## B52)
**8 0-0** (D)

The flexible move. White holds in reserve the plans ♗g5 and ♗e3, ♗d3, f4 (allowing ...b5) in addition to the opportunity to make an early a4 advance.
**8...♗e7**

Very infrequently does Black play 8...a6, because in this instance 9 a4! gives White somewhat better chances: 9...♕c7 (9...♘a5 10 ♗e3 ♕c7 11 ♘xa5 ♕xa5 12 ♕d2 ♗e7 13 ♖fd1 with pressure, Mikhalchishin-Kožul, Slovenian Cht 1999; 9...♘e5 10 ♗e2 ±; 9...♗e7 10 a5 ♕c7 – 9...♕c7 10 a5! ♗e7) 10 a5! (10 ♗e3 b6), and now:

a) It is very risky for Black to play 10...♘xa5 11 ♘xa5 b6 12 e5 bxa5 (12...dxe5?! 13 ♕f3!) 13 exf6 (13 ♗xe6 dxe5!) 13...♕xc4 14 fxg7 (14 ♕f3!? is quite unclear, Vasiesiu-Solak, Bucharest 1997) 14...♗xg7 15 ♕xd6 ♗b7 (15...♖a7 16 ♖xa5 ± Nunn-Van der Wiel, Baden 1980), and now:

a1) 16 ♖xa5 ♗f6!?.

a2) 16 ♖d1 ♕c6! 17 ♕xc6+ ♗xc6 18 ♖d6 ♖c8!? 19 ♖xa5 ♗xc3 and now 20 ♖c5 (Franco-Marcussi, Los Polvorines 1980) 20...♗b4! 21 ♖cxc6! 0-0! 22 ♖xc8 ♖xc8 23 ♖d4 ♖xc2 24 ♗h6 ♗e7 = Nisipeanu/Stoica, or 20 bxc3 ♖g8 with the point 21 ♖c5 ♖xg2+ 22 ♔f1 ♖xh2 =.

a3) 16 ♗g5!? (± Nunn) 16...♕b4 17 ♕g3 ♖c8 (17...♕xb2? 18 ♗d2; 17...0-0? 18 ♗f6; 17...♖g8 18 ♖a4 ♕xb2 19 ♕c7 ♗f6 20 ♖b1 ♕xc3 21 ♕xb7 ♖d8 22 ♖c4! ♕e5 23 ♕c6+ ±)

18 ♖fd1 with the initiative, Pan-chenko-Zhidkov, Daugavpils 1974.

b) 10...♗e7 11 ♗e3 and then:

b1) 11...♘xa5?! 12 ♘xa5 b6 13 e5! dxe5 14 ♕f3 bxa5 15 ♕xa8 ♕xc4 16 ♖xa5 ± Pinter-Cserna, Hungarian Ch (Budapest) 1975.

b2) 11...♘e5?! 12 ♗e2 ♘c4 13 ♗xc4 ♕xc4 14 ♗c5! ♘xe4 15 ♕g4 (15 ♘xe4 ♕xe4 16 ♗xd6 seems not bad) 15...f5 (15...dxc5!?) 16 ♕xg7 ♗f6 17 ♘xe4 ♕xf1+ 18 ♔xf1 ♗xg7 19 ♘xd6+ ♔d7 20 ♖d1 ± Sofieva-Saunina, USSR wom Ch (Erevan) 1985.

b3) 11...♘d7 12 ♗d3 0-0 13 ♘a4 ± Nisipeanu/Stoica.

b4) 11...♘b4 12 ♗e2 ♗d7 13 f4 0-0 14 ♗f3 e5 (14...♖ac8 transposes to line 'c') 15 ♖f2 exf4 16 ♗xf4 ♖ad8 17 ♖d2 ± Nunn-Csom, Moscow Echt 1977.

c) 10...♗d7 11 ♗e2 ♖c8 12 f4 ♘b4 13 ♗f3 ♗e7 14 ♗e3 0-0 15 ♖f2 is slightly better for White, Kuczynski-Kožul, Ohrid Ech 2001.

**9 ♗e3**

9 ♗g5!? transposes to Line B532.

9 a4 is less sensible here than in the case of 8...a6. After 9...0-0 10 a5 ♕c7, Black plans 11...♗d7 and does not have, as a rule, any real difficulties.

**9...♕c7 10 f4**

An important but not adequately studied position arises after 10 ♗d3 a6 11 a4!? b6 12 f4. After 12...0-0 13 ♕f3 (13 g4 d5!? 14 e5 ♘d7 with counterplay, Marusenko-Zontakh, Kiev 1994) 13...♗b7 we have:

a) 14 ♕g3 ♖fe8 15 ♖ae1 (15 f5 ♘e5 16 fxe6 fxe6 17 ♘d4 ♗d8 18 ♕h3 ♕d7 Smirin) 15...♘d7 16 e5? ♘b4! with better chances for Black, Nijboer-Smirin, Tilburg 1993.

b) The more typical 14 ♕h3!? deserves attention; e.g., 14...♖fe8 15 ♖f3 ♘b4 16 ♖g3 ♘xd3 17 cxd3 ♔h8, and a draw was rather charitably accepted by White in V.Gurevich-Sakaev, Cappelle la Grande 1997.

**10...a6 11 ♗d3**

Again, 11 a4!? is a serious alternative here:

a) After 11...b6, 12 ♗d3 transposes to *10 ♗d3 a6 11 a4!? b6 12 f4*. Instead, the other version of Scheveningen, 12 ♗e2 ♗b7 13 ♗f3 0-0 = (as in Ilyin-Zhenevsky – Rokhlin, Leningrad 1926) appears to be less promising for White.

b) Black may deviate by playing 11...d5!? 12 exd5 ♘b4 13 ♗d3 (after 13 d6, 13...♗xd6 14 ♗b5+ ♗d7 15 ♗xd7+ ♕xd7 is sufficient for Black) 13...♘bxd5 (also possible is 13...exd5!? 14 ♗d4 0-0, de Firmian-Csom, Niš 1981) 14 ♘xd5 ♘xd5 15 ♗d4 (curious is 15 ♗d2 ♗f6 16 c4 ♕b6+? 17 ♔h1 ♘e3? 18 ♗xe3 ♕xe3 19 c5!! 1-0 Elseth-Grønn, Oslo 1991) 15...♗f6 (after 15...0-0!?, the double sacrifice 16 ♗xh7+ ♔xh7 17 ♕h5+ ♔g8 18 ♗xg7 ♔xg7 19 ♕g4+ yields merely a draw) 16 ♗e4!? ♗xd4+ (16...♘xf4 is critical) 17 ♕xd4 ± Nijboer-Mirallès, Lucerne Wcht 1989.

**11...b5 12 ♕f3 ♗b7** *(D)*

Black preserves possibilities of active struggle all over the board, including the kingside. 12...0-0 is considered to be a less flexible continuation here.

This is a standard position that has occurred in hundreds of games. Now:

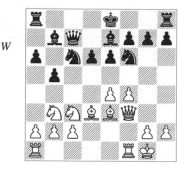

If 13 ♔h1, it is not bad to reply with 13...♖c8!?, and 13 g4 allows Black to start counterplay by means of 13...h6 or 13...g5!?.

## B521)
### 13 a3 ♖c8
13...0-0 14 ♕h3 and now:

a) The known line 14...b4 15 axb4 (or 15 ♘a4 bxa3 16 ♖xa3 ♘b4!?) 15...♘xb4 16 e5 dxe5 17 fxe5 ♕xe5 18 ♖a5 ♗d5 (18...♘xd3 19 ♖xe5 ♘xe5 20 ♘a5 ± Dückstein-Mikenda, Austria 1981), is, to my mind, dubious in view of 19 ♖xd5 (19 ♘xd5 exd5 20 ♗d4 ♕h5 21 ♕xh5 ♘xh5 = Minev-Polugaevsky, Moscow 1960) 19...exd5 20 ♖xf6 ♘xd3 21 ♖f5 ♕b8 22 ♘xd5 ♖e8 23 ♗d4 ♘b4 24 ♖h5 ♕c8 25 ♕g3 f6 26 ♗xf6 ♗c5+ 27 ♘d4 ♖a7 28 ♖g5.

b) 14...g6 15 f5! ± Hector-Hjartarson, Malmö 1995.

c) Black should probably proceed with the typical Scheveningen move 14...♖fe8, as in Zso.Polgar-Damljanović, Wijk aan Zee 1990.

### 14 ♖ae1
Or 14 ♕h3 h5!?, Georgadze-Cvetković, Sukhumi 1966.

### 14...0-0

14...b4!?.
### 15 ♕h3 b4
Black has sufficient counterplay, Kupreichik-Tal, USSR 1970.

## B522)
### 13 a4 (D)

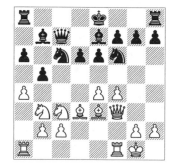

### 13...b4 14 ♘e2
14 ♘b1 e5!? 15 ♘1d2 exf4 16 ♕xf4 ♘e5 17 ♘d4 g6 with chances for both sides, Morozevich-Ruban, St Petersburg Z 1993.

### 14...♘a5
White has slightly the better prospects in the variations 14...a5 15 c4! (Gutman), 14...d5 15 e5, 14...e5 15 ♘g3 (Spassky-Marshalek, Leningrad 1960), 14...h5 15 a5! (Ghizdavu-Badilles, Skopje OL 1972) and 14...0-0 15 a5 (as in Ghizdavu-Carp, Romania 1972).

### 15 ♘xa5 ♕xa5 16 g4
Not dangerous for Black is 16 ♗d4 e5 (16...0-0 17 g4 e5!, A.Sokolov-Ionov, Russian Ch (Elista) 1995) 17 fxe5 dxe5 18 ♕f5 0-0!, Bogdanović-Szabo, Sarajevo 1972.

### 16...0-0
Otherwise:

a) 16...h6? 17 ♘g3 ± Tregubov.

b) 16...d5?! 17 e5 ♘e4 18 f5 was given by Bönsch.

c) 16...♘d7!? 17 g5 ♘c5, Ghizdavu-Szabo, Romania 1972.

d) 16...♕c7!? 17 g5 ♘d7 18 ♗d4?! (18 ♘d4 g6 ∞ Gutman) 18...0-0 19 ♕h5 e5! 20 f5 exd4 21 f6 ♘e5 22 ♖f4 ♖fe8 23 ♖h4 h6 24 ♘g3 ♕d8 25 ♖f1 ♗f8 26 ♘f5 ♖e6 27 ♖f2 d5 28 ♖g2 (J.Polgar-Damljanović, Wijk aan Zee 1990) 28...dxe4! with a winning position for Black.

e) 16...♖c8!? 17 g5 ♘d7 18 ♘g3 0-0 (18...g6!? Tregubov) 19 f5 ♘e5 20 ♕f4 exf5 21 ♘xf5 ♖fe8 22 ♗d4 ♗f8 with chances for both sides, Morozevich-Tregubov, Alushta 1994.

**17 g5 ♘d7 18 ♘d4**

18 ♕h3!? Ruban.

**18...g6**

18...♖fe8 is more reliable. For instance, 19 f5 ♘e5 20 ♕h3 exf5 21 ♘xf5 (Garbett-Jansa, Nice OL 1974) 21...♗f8!.

**19 ♕h3 ♘c5 20 f5**

Now, after 20...exf5 (20...♘xd3!? has the point 21 f6 ♖fe8 22 ♘xe6 ♘c5) 21 ♘xf5 gxf5 22 ♖xf5 ♕c7 (or 22...♗c8 23 ♕h6!) 23 ♕h6, Black may play 23...♕d7!? (instead of 23...d5 24 ♗d4 ♘e6 25 e5 ♗c5, Mortensen-Tukmakov, Reykjavik 1990, 26 ♖f6! +− or 23...♘xd3 24 cxd3 ± Zakhartsov-Ruban, Smolensk 1991), when I do not see anything better for White than 24 ♗d4 ♘e6 25 ♗e3.

**B523)**

**13 ♖ae1** *(D)*

**13...♘b4**

Or:

a) 13...h5 14 h3 h4 15 ♕f2 ♘h5 16 ♖d1 ♘g3 17 ♗b6 ♕c8 18 ♖fe1 ♗f6

19 e5! dxe5 20 ♘e4 ♘xe4 21 ♗xe4 ± Ghizdavu-Buza, Bucharest 1970.

b) 13...♖c8 14 ♕h3 ♘b4 15 ♘d4! (15 a3 ♘xd3 16 cxd3 e5!? 17 ♕g3 0-0 = Gheorghiu-Stein, Moscow 1971) 15...♘xd3 (15...0-0 16 g4 A.Frolov; 15...g6 16 ♔h1! h5 17 ♗g1 ♘xd3 18 cxd3 ♘g4 19 f5 gxf5 20 exf5 e5 21 f6!; 15...♕d7 16 a3 ♘xd3 17 cxd3 g6 18 ♘f3! d5 19 f5! – Gutman) 16 cxd3 b4 (16...0-0!? 17 g4) 17 ♘ce2 ♕a5 18 g4! h5 19 g5 ♘g4 20 g6 with an advantage for White, A.Frolov-Finegold, Groningen open 1993.

c) The popular alternative here is 13...0-0 14 ♕h3 (after 14 g4 ♘b4 15 g5 ♘d7 16 ♕h5, apart from Gutman's idea 16...♖fe8 17 ♖f3 ♘f8 18 ♖h3 d5, 16...f5! is good, Berndt-Klebel, Bundesliga 1997/8), and then:

c1) 14...g6 – *13 ♕h3 g6 14 ♖ae1 0-0*.

c2) 14...b4 15 ♘e2! ± Gutman.

c3) 14...♖fd8?! 15 g4 b4 16 g5! bxc3 17 gxf6 gxf6 (Ciocaltea-Tal, Havana OL 1966) 18 ♔f2! cxb2 19 ♖g1+ ♔h8 20 ♖g3 – Gutman.

c4) 14...♖ad8?! 15 g4 ♘b4 (15...b4 16 g5 ♘d7 17 ♘d5!) 16 g5 ♘d7 17 ♘d4! (17 f5 ♘xd3 18 cxd3 exf5 19 exf5 ♖fe8!) 17...♖fe8 18 ♖f3! – Gutman.

c5) 14...♖fe8!? 15 g4 ♘b4 16 g5 ♘d7 with a complicated game, Ulybin-Popović, Moscow 1989.

c6) 14...♘b4 and then:

c61) 15 g4 can be met by 15...d5!? 16 e5 ♘e4, Parr-Torre, Australia 1975, or 15...♖fe8 – *14...♖fe8 15 g4 ♘b4*.

c62) 15 ♘d4 ♖ae8!? 16 g4 ♘d7 17 g5?! ♘xd3 18 cxd3 ♘c5 19 ♖d1 b4 20 ♘ce2 f5!, Malakhov-Svidler, Russian Ch (Elista) 1997.

c63) 15 a3 ♘xd3 16 cxd3 and then:

c631) 16...♖ac8 17 ♘d4! ± Bünermann-Szymczak, Hamburg 1993.

c632) 16...♖fe8 17 f5! e5 18 g4 d5 19 ♖c1 ♕d8 20 g5 – Gutman.

c633) 16...e5!? transposes to note 'b' to White's 14th move.

**14 a3**

Or:

a) 14 ♕g3 g6 (14...0-0 15 f5 ± Espig-Cobo, Timisoara 1972) 15 a3 (15 ♗d4 ∞ Apicella-Mirallès, French Ch (Angers) 1990) 15...♘xd3 16 cxd3 ♖c8 17 ♖c1 ♕d7 18 ♘d4 ♘h5! 19 ♕h3 f5 = Tringov-Gheorghiu, Teesside 1972.

b) 14 ♕h3 e5!? (14...d5 15 e5 ♘e4 16 f5! ± Baklan-Kveinys, Bundesliga 1999/00; 14...♘d7 15 a3 ♘xd3 16 cxd3 ♘c5 17 ♘xc5 dxc5 18 f5 e5 19 ♕g3 ♗f6 20 ♖c1 ♖d8 21 d4! cxd4 22 ♘d5 ♕d6 23 ♘xf6+ gxf6 24 ♗d2 ± Ciocaltea-Darga, Germany 1971) 15 a3 ♘xd3 16 cxd3 0-0 17 ♖c1 ♕d8 with an acceptable position for Black, Minić-Csom, Siegen OL 1970.

c) 14 ♘d4!? ♖c8 (14...g6 15 a3 ♘xd3 16 cxd3 ♖c8 17 ♕h3 and now 17...♕d7 18 ♘f3!, Ulybin-Petrienko, Voronezh 1987, or 17...h5 18 ♔h1 ♕d7 19 ♘f3 ±) 15 a3 ♘xd3 16 cxd3 ♕d7 (16...g6 – *14...g6 15 a3 ♘xd3 16 cxd3 ♖c8*) 17 ♖e2!? (17 ♕g3 g6 18 h3 ♘h5!

19 ♕f2 f5, Brenjo-Damljanović, Yugoslav Cht 2001) 17...h5 18 h3 with some advantage for White, Ivanović-Gulko, Novi Sad OL 1990.

**14...♘xd3 15 cxd3 d5!?**

Or:

a) 15...♖c8 16 f5! e5 17 g4! – Gutman.

b) 15...0-0 16 ♖c1 (16 ♘d4 ♖fe8! Gutman; 16 ♕h3 – *13...0-0 14 ♕h3 ♘b4 15 a3 ♘xd3 16 cxd3*) 16...♕d8 17 ♘d4 ♘d7 18 b4 ♖c8 19 ♘ce2 with some advantage, Ciocaltea-Bobotsov, Bucharest 1973.

**16 ♖c1**

16 ♗d4 dxe4 17 ♘xe4 ♗d5! = Kasparov/Nikitin.

**16...dxe4 17 ♘xe4 ♗xe4 18 dxe4 ♕b7**

= Gutman.

## B524)

**13 ♕h3** *(D)*

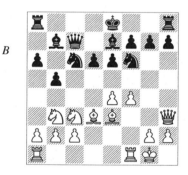

**13...♘b4**

Other possibilities:

a) 13...e5!?.

b) 13...b4 14 ♘e2 ±.

c) 13...♖b8 14 ♔h1 b4 15 ♘e2 e5 16 ♖ae1! ± Yudasin-Garcia Ilundain, Leon 1992.

d) 13...h5 14 a4 (14 ♔h1 ♘g4 15 ♗g1 g5!?, Mrdja-Zsu.Polgar, Rome 1989) 14...b4 15 ♘d1 ♘a5 (15...d5!? 16 exd5 ♘xd5 17 f5! ± Sax) 16 ♘xa5 ♕xa5 17 ♘f2 ± A.Sokolov-Makarychev, Sochi 1983.

e) 13...♖c8 14 a4 (14 ♖ae1! – *13 ♖ae1 ♖c8 14 ♕h3*) 14...b4 15 ♘b1 ♘a5! = 16 ♘xa5 ♕xa5 17 ♘d2 ♕h5 18 ♕xh5 ♘xh5 19 e5 g5 Gutman.

f) 13...g6 14 ♖ae1 0-0 15 f5!? exf5 16 exf5 ♘e5 17 ♗g5 ♖ae8 18 ♕h4 (A.Sokolov-Utasi, Moscow 1983) 18...♕d8 19 ♘d4 with an unclear position – Sokolov.

g) 13...0-0 and then:

g1) 14 a3!? – *13 a3 0-0 14 ♕h3*.

g2) A fresh idea is 14 ♖f3!? b4 15 ♘a4 a5 16 ♖g3 ♔h8 17 ♖f1 ♗a6 18 ♘d2, Ye Jiangchuan-Gulko, US-China (3) 2001.

g3) 14 g4 ♘d7 (14...b4 15 g5 ♘d7 16 ♘d5! exd5 17 exd5 g6 18 dxc6 ♕xc6 19 ♘a5! + Sax-Movsesian, Bundesliga 1997/8) 15 g5 ♘b4 16 ♘d4 ♖fe8 17 ♖f3 (17 f5 exf5!) 17...e5 18 ♘f5 exf4 19 ♖xf4 ♗xg5 20 ♕g3 with a dangerous initiative, Kozakov-Atalik, Lviv 2000.

**14 a3**

Or:

a) 14 ♖ae1 – *13 ♖ae1 ♘b4 14 ♕h3*.

b) 14 ♘d4 0-0 (14...♘xd3 15 cxd3 g6 16 a3 ♕d7 17 ♘f3 ± Belikov-S.Kiselev, Moscow 1995) 15 a3 ♘xd3 16 cxd3 transposes to the main line.

c) After 14 ♖ac1, instead of either 14...♘d7 15 a3 (15 f5!? e5 16 a3 Baklan) 15...♘xd3 16 cxd3 ♕d8 17 f5 e5?! 18 ♘d5! ± Baklan-Delchev, Istanbul OL 2000, or 14...e5 15 a3 ♘xd3 16 cxd3, which transposes to

the note to Black's 15th move, 14...0-0 is more reliable.

**14...♘xd3 15 cxd3 0-0**

15...e5 16 ♖ac1 ♕d8 17 ♘d2!? (17 fxe5 dxe5 18 ♕g3 0-0 19 ♘c5 ± Tal; 17 d4!? A.Frolov) 17...0-0 18 d4 ± A.Frolov-Shmuter, Nikolaev Z 1993.

**16 ♘d4**

This position occurred in Hartston-R.Byrne, Hastings 1971/2 and Belikov-Goldin, Russian Ch (Elista) 1995. White, who has active plans with g4 or ♖f3, ♖g3 and ♖f1, enjoys somewhat the better chances.

## B53)

**8 ♗g5** *(D)*

This popular idea has been moderately successful. Note also the move-order *8 0-0 ♗e7 9 ♗g5*.

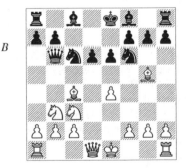

Let us discuss:

If 8...♘e5, then instead of 9 ♗b5+ ♗d7 10 ♗xf6 ♗xb5! 11 ♗xe5 dxe5 12 ♘xb5 ♕xb5 13 ♕e2 ♕a4 14 0-0 ♗e7 with an acceptable position for Black (Lukin-Oll, St Petersburg 1993),

9 ♗e2! is probably stronger. Then, in the case of 9...♗e7, 10 ♗e3! transposes to Line B541, which is advantageous for White.

### B531)
**8...♗d7!? 9 0-0**
Others:

a) 9 a4 ♘e5 10 ♗e2 ♗e7 11 f4 ♘g6 12 f5 ♘e5 13 a5 ♕c7 14 0-0 0-0 15 ♕e1 with chances for both sides, Velimirović-Sedlak, Subotica 2000.

b) 9 ♕e2 ♗e7 (9...♖c8!? 10 f4?! ♘d4! 11 ♘xd4 ♕xb2! 12 ♔d2 ♕b4, Savon-Stein, USSR Ch (Leningrad) 1971) 10 0-0-0 ♘e5 11 ♗b5 a6 12 ♗xd7+ ♘exd7 13 f4 ♕c7 14 ♖he1 0-0 = Armas-Kotronias, Wijk aan Zee 1995.

c) 9 ♗xf6 gxf6 10 ♕h5 ♖g8! (or 10...a6 – *8...a6 9 ♗xf6 gxf6 10 ♕h5 ♗d7*; 10...♖c8 11 0-0 – *9 0-0 ♖c8 10 ♗xf6! gxf6 11 ♕h5*) 11 0-0 ♖g6 (11...♘e5 12 ♗e2 ♖g6 13 ♕h4 ♗e7!? 14 ♔h1 f5 15 ♕xh7 f4 16 ♗h5 ♖g5 17 h4 ♖xh5 18 ♕xh5, Feigelson-Makarov, USSR 1988, 18...0-0-0 gives Black compensation – Makarov) 12 ♕h4 0-0-0 13 ♔h1 ♗e7 with good chances for Black, Hmadi-Dlugy, Tunis IZ 1985.

**9...♘e5**
Or:

a) 9...♗e7 – *8...♗e7 9 0-0 ♗d7*.

b) 9...a6 – *8...a6 9 0-0 ♗d7*.

c) 9...♖c8 (Agopov-Gavrikov, Finnish Cht 1998) 10 ♗xf6! gxf6 11 ♕h5 ♘d4 12 ♗d3 ♘xb3 13 axb3 ♖c5!? (13...a6 14 ♔h1 transposes to note 'b23' to White's 9th move in Line B533) 14 ♕f3!? ♖g5 15 ♖fe1 ♖hg8 16 ♗f1! ♗e7 17 b4!? f5 18 b5 fxe4 19 ♘xe4 ♖e5 and now V.Fedorov gives

20 ♘f6+ ♗xf6 21 ♕xf6 ♖xe1 22 ♖xe1 ♗xb5 23 ♖xe6+ = and 20 c4!?.

**10 ♗e2**
Now:

a) 10...♖c8!? 11 ♗xf6 gxf6 12 ♔h1 h5 13 f4 ♘c4 14 ♗xc4 ♖xc4 15 ♕d3 (Wolff-Shamkovich, New York 1992) 15...♖c8 (Wolff).

b) 10...♗e7 – *8...♗e7 9 0-0 ♘e5 10 ♗e2 ♗d7*.

### B532)
**8...♗e7 9 0-0**
This move is of particular interest because of the move-order *8 0-0 ♗e7 9 ♗g5*.

However, in this specific position it is more relevant to play 9 ♗xf6! gxf6:

a) 10 0-0 and now:

a1) 10...a6 – *8...a6 9 0-0 ♗e7 10 ♗xf6 gxf6*.

a2) 10...0-0 11 ♔h1 (11 ♕h5 – *10 ♕h5 0-0 11 0-0*) 11...♘e5 (11...♔h8 12 f4 ♖g8 13 a4 a6 14 ♕h5 ♖g7 15 a5 ♕d8 16 ♘a4 ± Brunner-Benjamin, Buenos Aires 1992) 12 ♗e2 ♔h8 13 f4 ♘g6 14 a4 ♖g8?! (14...♗d7 Dlugy) 15 a5 ♕c7 16 ♕d2 ♗d7 17 g3 ± de Firmian-Rachels, USA Ch (Jacksonville) 1990.

a3) 10...♗d7 11 ♔h1 (11 ♕h5 – *10 ♕h5 ♗d7 11 0-0*) 11...0-0-0 (11...0-0?! 12 f4 ♔h8 13 ♕h5 ± Fedorowicz) 12 a4 a6 13 ♕h5 ♘e5 14 ♗e2 transposes to note 'c22' to Black's 9th move in Line B533 (±).

b) 10 ♕h5 and then:

b1) 10...a6 11 0-0 – *8...a6 9 0-0 ♗e7 10 ♗xf6 gxf6 11 ♕h5*.

b2) 10...♗d7 11 0-0 ♘e5 (alternatively, 11...0-0-0, Antić-Timoshchenko, Belgrade GMA 1988, 12 a4!?) 12 ♗e2 0-0-0 13 ♔h1 ♖hg8 14 f4

♘g6 15 g3 ± Emms-Beckhuis, Münster 1995.

b3) 10...0-0 11 0-0 ♔h8 (11...♘e5 12 ♗e2 ♔h8 13 ♔h1 transposes to line 'b32') 12 ♔h1 and now:

b31) 12...♗d7 13 f4 ♖g8 (13...♗e8 14 ♕h3! Lukin) 14 ♕xf7 ♖g6 15 f5 ♖h6 16 ♗xe6 ♖f8 17 ♕xf8+ ♗xf8 18 ♗xd7 (½-½ Howell-Arlandi, Groningen jr Ech 1985) with good prospects for White; e.g., 18...♘e5 19 ♘d5 ♕a6 20 ♗e6 ♘g4 21 h3 ♕e2 22 ♖f3.

b32) 12...♘e5 13 ♗e2 (13 ♗d3 ♖g8 14 f4 ♘g6 15 ♘e2 ± Fedorowicz) 13...♖g8 (13...♗d7 14 a4 a6 transposes to note 'c24' to Black's 9th move in Line B533) 14 f4 ♘g6 15 ♕a5!? (a fresh idea; 15 ♖ad1 ♗d7 16 ♖d3 ♖ac8 17 f5 ♘e5 18 ♖h3 ♖g7 is unclear, Van Riemsdijk-Rachels, Manila IZ 1990) 15...♕xa5 16 ♘xa5 b6 17 ♘c6 ♗b7 (17...♖f8 18 ♘d8! ♖g7 19 ♖ad1 a6 20 ♗h5 Gofshtein) 18 ♘xe7 ♘xe7 19 ♖ad1 ♖ad8 20 ♗h5 ♔g7 ± Kaidanov-Fedorowicz, USA Ch (Seattle) 2000.

We now return to 9 0-0 *(D)*:

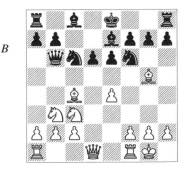

**9...♘e5**

The other continuations are:

a) 9...a6 transposes to note 'c' to Black's 9th move in Line B533.

b) 9...♗d7 10 ♔h1 (10 ♗xf6 gxf6 *– 9 ♗xf6 gxf6 10 0-0 ♗d7*) 10...♖c8!? (10...h6 11 ♗xf6 gxf6, Ma.Tseitlin-Stein, USSR Ch (Leningrad) 1971, 12 ♕h5 ± Nunn) 11 f4 (11 ♗xf6 ♗xf6!? 12 ♕xd6 ♘b4) 11...0-0 12 ♕e1 (12 e5? dxe5 13 ♗xf6 ♗xf6 14 ♕xd7 ♖cd8; 12 ♗xf6!?) 12...h6! 13 ♗h4 ♘b4 14 ♗d3 ♘xd3 15 cxd3 ♖fe8 16 e5?! ♘d5 17 ♘e4 dxe5 18 fxe5 ♕e3 ∓ Minasian-Khachian, Armenian Ch 1993.

c) 9...0-0 is another worthy try:

c1) 10 a4 ♘e5!? 11 ♗e2 a6 12 ♔h1 transposes to note 'a' to White's 12th move in Line B533.

c2) 10 ♔h1 ♖d8 (after 10...♕c7 or 10...a6, White can play 11 f4 at once) 11 ♕e2 (11 f4 d5!, Wang Pin-Wang Zili, Beijing 1993; 11 ♕e1 h6 12 ♗h4 ♘e5 13 ♗d3 ♘g6 14 ♗g3 e5 = Kindermann-Lobron, Dortmund 1990; 11 ♗d3 d5 12 exd5 ♘xd5 13 ♘xd5 ♖xd5 14 ♗xe7 ♘xe7 = Rublevsky-S.Kiselev, St Petersburg Z 1993) 11...♕c7 (11...♗d7!?; 11...a6!?; 11...♘xe4?! 12 ♗xe7 ♘xe7 13 ♕xe4 d5 14 ♗xd5 ♘xd5 15 ♘xd5 ♖xd5 16 ♖fd1 ± Kiselev/Gagarin) 12 f4 h6 13 ♗h4 a6 14 ♗d3 b5 15 ♖ae1 ♗b7 16 e5 ♘e8 17 ♗g3 ± Ivanović-Damljanović, Vršac 1989.

c3) The critical line is 10 ♗xf6!? ♗xf6 (10...gxf6 *– 9 ♗xf6 gxf6 10 0-0 0-0*) 11 ♕xd6 ♖d8. The pawn sacrifice should be correct, but some questions still remain here: 12 ♕g3 (12 ♕c5?! ♕xc5 13 ♘xc5 b6 favours Black), and now:

c31) 12...a5 13 a4 ♗e5 14 ♕h3 ♘b4 15 ♕h5! ♕c7 16 ♘b5 ♕xc4 (another idea is 16...♗xh2+!?) 17 ♕xe5 ♘xc2 (17...♕xc2!?) 18 ♖ad1 ♗d7 19

♘xa5! ± Sax-Ničevski, Porto San Giorgio 1992.

c32) 12...♛b4 13 ♗e2 (13 ♗d3!? ♗xc3 14 bxc3 ♛xc3 15 f4 Gorelov) 13...♗xc3 14 ♛xc3 ♛xe4 15 ♖fe1 and then:

c311) 15...♖b8 16 ♗f3 ♛b4 17 ♛xb4 ♘xb4 18 ♖ad1 ♖e8 19 ♖e4 ± A.Kuzmin-S.Kiselev, Moscow 1988.

c312) 15...♛e5 16 ♛xe5 ♘xe5 17 ♖ad1 ♗d7 18 f4 ♘g6 19 ♘a5 ♗c6 20 ♘xc6 bxc6 21 ♗f3 ♘e7 ± Nunn-Sax, Wijk aan Zee 1992.

c313) 15...♗d7 16 ♖ad1 (16 ♘c5 ♛b4!) 16...♛e5 (16...♛b4 17 ♛xb4 ♘xb4 18 c3 ♘d5 19 ♗f3 ± A.Kuzmin-Baikov, Moscow 1988) 17 ♛xe5 ♘xe5 transposes to line 'c312'.

c33) 12...♗e5 13 ♛h3 ♗d7 (13...a5 14 a4 – 12...a5 13 a4 ♗e5 14 ♛h3; 13...♘b4!?) and now:

c331) 14 ♖ad1 a5! (14...♘b4 15 ♘d2!? ♘xc2 16 ♗b3 ♘d4 17 ♘c4 ♛c7 18 ♛h5 is not so clear) 15 a4 ♘b4 with excellent compensation, Rublevsky-Goldin, St Petersburg Z 1993.

c332) 14 ♔h1 ♛b4 (14...♘b4 15 f4 ± Kindermann-Gomez Esteban, Palma de Mallorca 1989) 15 ♗d3 (15 ♗e2! ♗xc3 16 bxc3 ♛e7 17 f4 {± Bönsch} is not verified) 15...♗xc3 16 a3 (alternatively, 16 bxc3 ♛xc3 17 e5 g6 18 f4 ♘b4, Soltis-Lombardy, New York 1987) 16...♛e7 17 bxc3 e5 18 ♛e3 ♗e6 = Brunner-Khalifman, Lucerne Wcht 1993.

## 10 ♗e2 (D)

A game with chances for both sides can be obtained through 10 ♗d3 0-0 11 ♛e2 ♗d7 12 ♗e3 ♛c7 13 f4 ♘xd3 14 cxd3 b5, Kovaliov-Ruban, Budapest 1989, or 10 ♗b5+!? ♗d7 11 ♗xd7+ (11 a4 a6 12 a5 ♛c7 13 ♗d3

0-0 = Kontić-Levin, Podgorica 1993) 11...♘exd7 and then, for instance, 12 ♗e3 ♛c7 13 f4 a6 (13...0-0 14 ♛e2 ♘b6, Golubev-Serper, Leningrad 1989, 15 ♗d4!?) 14 ♛f3 0-0 15 g4 g6, Van der Wiel-Van Delft, Vlissingen 1998.

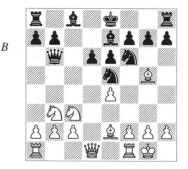

## 10...0-0

Or:

a) 10...a6 transposes to Line B533.

b) 10...♗d7!? and here:

b1) 11 ♗e3!? transposes to note 'b2' to White's 10th move in Line B543.

b2) 11 a4 0-0 12 a5 ♛c7 13 ♛d4 ♖fd8 14 h3 ♗e8 15 ♗f4 ♗c6 16 ♗g3 ♘g6 = A.Ivanov-Gi.Hernandez, Linares (Mexico) 1992.

b3) 11 ♛d2 0-0 12 ♖ad1 ♖ac8 13 ♗e3 ♛c7 14 f4 ♘eg4 15 ♗xg4 ♘xg4 16 ♗d4 ♗c6 17 ♛e2 ♘f6 18 e5 and here, rather than 18...dxe5 (Velimirović-Popović, Vršac 1989), 18...♘e8! = was recommended.

b4) 11 ♔h1 ♘g6 (11...0-0 – 10...0-0 11 ♔h1 ♗d7; 11...♖c8!? 12 ♗e3 ♛c7 13 ♘d2 0-0 14 f4 ♘g6 = Dimitrov-Kotronias, Athens 1989) 12 ♗e3 (12 f4? h6 Nunn) 12...♛c7 13 f4 0-0 14 ♛e1 (14 a4 ♗c6 15 ♗d3 ♘d7 16 ♘d4 ♗f6 = Arnason-Stefansson, Kopavogur

1994; 14 ♘d4!?) 14...♖fe8 (possibly stronger is 14...d5!?, as in Delacroix-Lucchini, corr. 1989) 15 ♖d1 ♗c6?! 16 ♗f3 d5 17 e5 ♘e4 18 ♘d4! with an advantage for White, Nunn-Tukmakov, Lugano 1986.

**11 ♔h1 ♗d7**

Otherwise:

a) 11...a6 again transposes to Line B533.

b) 11...♘g6!? 12 ♗e3 (12 a4 ♗d7 13 ♗e3 ♕c7 14 f4 – *10...♗d7 11 ♔h1 ♘g6 12 ♗e3 ♕c7 13 f4 0-0 14 a4 =*) 12...♕c7 13 f4 b6!? (or 13...♗d7 – *10...♗d7 11 ♔h1 ♘g6 12 ♗e3 ♕c7 13 f4 0-0*) 14 g3 ♗b7 15 ♗f3 ♖fd8 16 ♕e2 ♖ac8 and Black will obtain a good game by the manoeuvre ...♕b8-a8, de Firmian-Waitzkin, Las Vegas 1995.

**12 f4**

12 ♗e3 ♕c7 13 f4 ♘c4!? = Dimitrov-Atalik, Mangalia 1992.

**12...♘g6**

White now has a wide choice, but he has not demonstrated an advantage as yet:

a) 13 ♗xf6 ♗xf6 14 e5 ♗e7 15 exd6 ♗xd6! 16 ♘e4 ♗c6 17 ♘xd6 ♖fd8 = Yudasin-Al.Khasin, Kostroma 1985.

b) 13 e5 ♘e8 (13...dxe5? 14 ♗xf6) 14 ♗xe7 ♘xe7 15 ♗d3 (15 ♕d2!?) 15...♗c6 16 ♕h5?! (16 ♕e2 = *NCO*) 16...g6 followed by 17...♘f5! ∓, Minasian-Ruban, USSR Ch (Moscow) 1991.

c) 13 ♗h5 ♘xh5 (13...♖ad8!? 14 ♗xg6 fxg6! 15 ♕e2 ♖fe8! 16 e5 ♘d5 17 ♗xe7 ♖xe7 = Lukin-Lugovoi, St Petersburg 1994) 14 ♗xe7 and then:

c1) 14...♘g3+ 15 hxg3 ♘xe7 16 g4!? and now 16...f5 17 exf5 exf5 18 g5 ♗c6 19 ♕d4 ♘d5 20 ♘xd5 ♕xd4 21 ♘e7+ ♔f7 22 ♘xd4 ♔xe7 gives White a slight advantage, Rublevsky-Ruban, Smolensk 1991, or 16...♖ad8 17 ♕d2 ± Rublevsky-Lukin, St Petersburg 1994.

c2) 14...♘xe7! 15 ♕xh5 f5 with a good game for Black, Panbukchian-Ruban, Anapa 1992.

d) 13 ♕d2 ♗c6 = Kindermann-Brenke, Lippstadt 1993.

e) 13 ♗d3 ♖ad8! 14 ♕e2 (not 14 e5? dxe5 15 ♗xg6 fxg6 16 fxe5 ♗b5) 14...h6 15 f5?! hxg5 16 fxg6 fxg6 17 e5 ♘h5! with better chances, Pruess-Atalik, Los Angeles 2000.

f) 13 ♕d3 ♗c6! (13...h6? 14 ♗xf6 ♗xf6 15 e5; 13...♖ad8?! 14 f5 ♘e5 15 ♕g3 ♔h8 16 ♖f4!, Wahls-Wirthensohn, Hamburg 1991) 14 f5 (14 ♖ae1 d5!?, Lapshin-Lagoisky, corr. 1989-90) 14...exf5!? 15 exf5 (15 ♖xf5 ♖ae8 = Serper) 15...♘e5 16 ♕g3 ♖fe8 17 ♖ad1 ∞ Paronian-Serper, Tashkent 1992.

g) 13 f5!? ♘e5 14 ♕d2 (Serper) 14...♖ad8 and Black has quite a solid position.

## B533)

**8...a6** *(D)*

The most frequent answer to 8 ♗g5 – in playing this, Black assumes that now 9 ♗xf6 will be less effective than in the case of 8...♗e7.

**9 0-0**

Alternatively:

a) 9 ♕e2 ♗e7 10 0-0 0-0 11 ♔h1 ♕c7 12 f4 h6 (12...b5 =) 13 ♗h4 ♘xe4! is slightly better for Black, Parma-Saidy, Tel-Aviv OL 1964.

b) 9 ♗xf6!? gxf6 has not been developed adequately. Some lines:

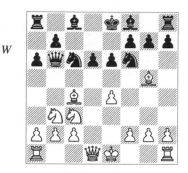

W

b1) 10 &e2!? &d7 (10...彎c7 might
be better) 11 0-0 &e7 12 含h1 (12
&h5 ②e5 ∞ Gulko) 12...h5 13 f4 and
now 13...0-0-0 14 a4 含b8 15 a5 彎c7
16 彎d2, Soltis-Čabrilo, New York
1988, or 13...h4 14 彎d2 ②a5 15 ②xa5
彎xa5 16 罝ab1! ± Fedorowicz-Gulko,
USA Ch (Salt Lake City) 1999.

b2) 10 彎h5 &d7 11 0-0 (here 11
罝f1!? deserves attention; e.g., 11...②e5
12 &e2 0-0-0 13 0-0-0 &e7 14 f4 ②g6
15 含b1 含b8 16 g3 ± Anka-Gonzalez
Garcia, Budapest 1993 or 11...罝c8!?
12 &d3 彎a7 13 0-0-0 b5, Killti-Kiik,
Hyvinkää 1996) and now:

b21) 11...彎c7 ± Kupreichik.

b22) 11...②d4 12 罝ad1 ②xc2?! 13
a3 罝c8 14 彎e2 a5 15 ②d5 ± Sutov-
sky-Shrentzel, Tel-Aviv 1993.

b23) 11...罝c8 12 含h1 ②d4 13 &d3
②xb3 14 axb3 彎c5 15 彎h3! h5 16 f4
h4 (16...&e7 17 f5 含d8 18 ②e2! 彎e5
19 ②f4, V.Fedorov-Ermolinsky, Leningrad 1980) 17 f5 &e7 (17...含e7 18
fxe6 fxe6 19 e5! ± or 17...彎e5!? 18
②d1! – V.Fedorov) 18 罝f4 ± V.Fedo-
rov-Kozlov, Erevan 1983.

b24) 11...②e5 12 &e2 and then:

b241) 12...②g6 13 g3 and here, instead of 13...0-0-0?! (V.Fedorov-Lukin,
Leningrad 1983) 14 a4! ± (Lukin),

Black should play 13...&g7!? with the
idea of ...0-0, as in V.Fedorov-Kuli-
kov, Leningrad 1980.

b242) 12...罝g8 13 含h1 罝g6 14
彎h4 (14 &d3?! ②g4! 15 含g1 罝g5 16
彎xh7 含e7!, Ehlvest-Salov, Leningrad
1984) with the point 14...罝h6 15 彎f4
罝g6 16 彎d2 (Nepomnishay).

**9...②e5**

Or:

a) 9...&d7 10 含h1 (10 &xf6 gxf6
11 彎h5 – *9 &xf6 gxf6 10 彎h5 &d7 11
0-0*) 10...&e7 (10...彎c7 11 &xf6 gxf6
12 彎h5 罝g8 {12...②e5 13 &e2 ±} 13
f4 罝g7 14 f5 ± A.Ivanov-Gulko, Moscow rpd 1992) 11 &xf6! (11 f4 彎c7
= Hermansen-Yermolinsky, Chicago
1994) 11...gxf6 12 彎h5 – *9...&e7 10
&xf6 gxf6 11 彎h5 &d7 12 含h1*.

b) 9...彎c7 10 &xf6 (10 a4 &e7 has
occurred, with roughly equal play)
10...gxf6 11 彎h5 罝g8!? (11...&d7!?;
after 11...b5 12 &d3 &b7 Black has
experienced difficulties; e.g., 13 f4
0-0-0 14 f5 彎e7 15 彎e2 d5 16 a4!,
Wahls-Lobron, Baden-Baden 1992) 12
f4 罝g6 13 含h1 (Emms-Atalik, Hastings 1995) 13...&d7 14 a4 ∞ *NCO*.

c) 9...&e7 and now:

c1) 10 含h1 彎c7 (10...②e5 11 &e2
– *9...②e5 10 &e2 &e7 11 含h1*) with
roughly equal play:

c11) 11 &d3 and then:

c111) 11...0-0 12 f4 (12 彎e2 =)
12...h6 (Ostojić-Polugaevsky, Skopje
1971) 13 &h4 ②xe4 14 &xe7 ②xc3
15 &xd6 ②xd1 16 &xc7 ②xb2 17 &e4
with compensation – Polugaevsky.

c112) 11...b5 12 f4 gives Black a
choice between 12...&b7 = Drimer-
Csom, Lugano OL 1968 and 12...h6!?
13 &xf6 &xf6 14 &xb5 &xc3 (Polugaevsky).

c12) 11 ♕e2 b5 12 ♗d3 ♗b7 13 f4
(13 a3 0-0 14 f4 b4 15 axb4 ♘xb4 16
e5 dxe5 17 fxe5 ♘fd5 18 ♘xd5 ♗xd5
19 ♗xe7 ♕xe7 = Ivanović-Čabrilo,
Yugoslav Ch (Kladovo) 1990) 13...b4!?,
but not 13...h6 14 ♗h4 ♘xe4?! 15
♕xe4! ♗xh4 16 f5! (Čabrilo).

c2) 10 ♗xf6 gxf6 11 ♕h5 (11 a4!?
♘a5 12 ♘xa5 ♕xa5 13 ♔h1 h5 14 f4
♗d7 15 ♕d3 h4 16 ♖f3 ♖c8 17 ♗b3
♖c5! 18 f5 ♖e5 with counterplay, de
Firmian-Smirin, New York rpd 1995)
with the following possibilities:

c21) 11...♘d4 12 ♔h1! (12 ♘xd4?!
♕xd4 13 ♗b3 b5, Kindermann-Lobron, Munich 1987; 12 ♖fd1 ♘xb3 13
axb3 ♖b8! 14 ♕h6 ♕c5 15 ♕g7 ♖f8
16 ♕xh7 b5 17 ♗d3 ♗b7 with compensation, Nunn-Martinović, Amsterdam 1985) 12...♘xb3 (12...♘xc2 13
♖ac1 ♘b4 14 f4) 13 axb3 ♕c5 (or
13...♖b8 14 f4 ♕c5 15 f5) 14 ♗b5+
♗d7 15 ♗xd7+ ♔xd7 (Arkhangel-
sky-S.Kiselev, USSR 1987) 16 ♕h3!
± Arkhangelsky.

c22) 11...♗d7 12 ♔h1 (another line
is 12 a4 ♘d4!?) 12...♘e5 (12...♖f8!?
13 f4 0-0-0 Kupreichik; 12...0-0-0 13
f4 ♖df8 14 a4 ♕c7 15 a5 ♘b4 16 ♕e2
± Sveshnikov-Vaiser, Volgodonsk 1983)
13 ♗e2 0-0-0 14 a4 (14 f4 is the alternative for White) 14...♔b8 15 a5 (15
f4 ♘g6 16 ♖ad1, Kupreichik-Kovacs,
Stary Smokovec 1975, 16...♕c7 –
Banas) 15...♕c7 16 f4 ♘g6 17 g3 ±
Fedorowicz-Rachels, USA Ch (Long
Beach) 1989.

c23) 11...0-0 12 ♔h1 ♘e5 13 ♗e2
– *11...♘e5 12 ♗e2 0-0 13 ♔h1.*

c24) 11...♘e5 12 ♗e2 (12 ♗d3!?)
12...0-0 13 ♔h1 ♔h8 14 a4 (14 f4
♘g6 15 ♖f3 was given as '±' by Mar-
tinović, but 15...♖g8 16 f5 ♘e5 17

♖h3 ♖g7 18 ♖f1 ♕d8 turned out to
be unclear in Topolowski-A.I.Frolov,
corr. 1990) 14...♗d7 15 a5 ♕c7 16
♘d2 ♘g6 (16...b5 17 axb6 ♕xb6 18
♖a2 ± Kupreichik; 16...♖g8!?) 17 ♘c4
♖ad8 18 f4 (Kupreichik-Radulov,
Plovdiv 1980) 18...♖g8! with the point
19 f5 ♘e5 20 ♘xe5 dxe5 21 ♕xf7
♖g7 22 ♕h5 exf5 – Kupreichik.

**10 ♗e2**
10 ♗d3!? ♗e7 (10...♗d7!?) 11 ♔h1
h6?! 12 ♗e3 ♕c7 13 f4 is slightly
better for White, S.Gross-Csom, Budapest 1993.

**10...♗e7 11 ♔h1** *(D)*
Alternatively:

a) 11 ♗e3!? transposes to note 'a'
to White's 11th move in Line B542.

b) 11 a4 0-0 12 a5 (12 ♔h1 – *11
♔h1 0-0 12 a4)* 12...♕c7 13 f4 (13
♘d2 ♗d7 14 f4 ♘g6 15 ♘c4 ♗c6 16
f5 ♘xe4 17 ♘xe4 ♗xe4 18 ♗xe7
♘xe7 19 fxe6 = M.Schlosser-Goldin,
Trnava 1989) 13...♘g6 (13...♘ed7 14
♔h1 h6 15 ♗h4 ♘c5 16 ♘xc5 ♕xc5
17 ♗f3 ± Tolnai-Gostiša, Maribor
1993) 14 ♗d3 h6 15 f5 ∞ Van Riems-
dijk-Franco, Havana 1991.

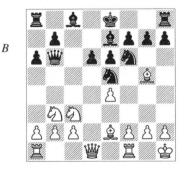

**11...0-0**
Or:

a) 11...h6?! 12 ♗e3 ♕c7 13 f4 with the initiative, Rublevsky-Baikov, USSR Cht 1991.

b) 11...h5 (Brunner-Lobron, Berne Z 1990) 12 ♗e3!? ♕c7 13 f4 is also promising for White.

c) 11...♕c7 12 f4 ♘ed7 (12...♘g6?! 13 f5 ♘e5 14 fxe6 ± Soylu-Radulov, Athens 1981; 12...♘c4?! 13 ♗xc4 ♕xc4 14 e5 ±; 12...♘c6!? is playable, as in Pablo Marin-Spraggett, Roses 1992) 13 a4 (in Pablo Marin-Garcia Ilundain, Manresa 1995, White did not manage to make progress after 13 f5 0-0 14 ♕e1 b5 15 a3 e5 16 ♕g3 ♔h8 17 ♕h4 ♗b7 18 ♖f3 ♖ac8 19 ♖h3 ♕d8 20 ♗f3 ♖g8 21 g4 ♘f8) 13...b6 14 ♗d3 ♗b7 15 ♕e2 h6 16 ♗h4 ± Minasian-Serper, Kherson 1991.

d) 11...♘g6!? 12 a4 (12 f4 h6!, Illescas-Franco, Leon 1989; 12 ♗e3!?) 12...♕c7 13 ♗e3 0-0 14 f4 ♗d7 15 ♕e1 b5! deserves attention, Burden-Stefansson, Reykjavik 1996.

**12 f4**

Or:

a) 12 a4 ♕c7 and then:

a1) 13 ♘d2 b6 = 14 ♗e3 ♗b7 15 f4 ♘ed7 16 ♗f3 ♖ac8 17 ♕e2 ♖fe8 18 g4? d5!, Kovaliov-Lerner, Simferopol 1988.

a2) 13 f4 ♘ed7!? 14 a5 b5 15 axb6 ♘xb6 16 ♕d3 h6 17 ♗h4 ♖b8 with good counterplay, D.Rodriguez-Serper, Tunja jr Wch 1989.

a3) 13 a5 h6 14 ♗e3 ♗d7 (better than 14...♘c4?! 15 ♗xc4 ♕xc4 16 ♘c5 ♕b4 17 ♖a4!?) 15 ♗b6 ♕c8 16 ♗d4 ♗c6 = Stefansson-Serper, Arnhem jr Ech 1989.

b) 12 ♕e1!? ♕c7 (12...♘g6!?) 13 f4 ♘g6 14 ♕g3 ♔h8 15 ♖ad1 b5 (15...h6 16 ♕h3 ♔g8 seems risky in view of 17

♗xh6) 16 a3 ♗b7 17 f5 exf5 18 exf5 ♘e5 19 ♖f4 ♖fe8 20 ♖h4 ♘ed7 21 ♘d4 ♗f8 22 ♗f3 with a slight advantage for White, Ehlvest-Popović, Belgrade 1989.

**12...♘g6 13 f5**

Otherwise:

a) 13 ♗d3 h6 14 f5 ♘e5 15 ♗h4 ♗d7 16 fxe6 (16 ♕e2!? was suggested in *Chess in the USSR*) 16...fxe6 17 ♕e2 ♖f7 18 ♗f2 ♕c7 19 ♗g1 ♖af8 20 ♘d4 ½-½ A.Sokolov-Tukmakov, USSR Ch (Odessa) 1989.

b) Probably 13 ♕e1 h6!? 14 f5 hxg5 15 fxg6 fxg6 should suit Black.

c) 13 ♗h5 (Sveshnikov) 13...♕c7 (13...♘xh5 14 ♗xe7 ± Brunner-Gulko, Munich 1990; 13...h6?! 14 ♗xg6 hxg5 15 ♗xf7+! ♖xf7 16 fxg5 ♗d7 17 e5! dxe5 18 gxf6 ♗xf6 19 ♘e4 ♗c6 20 ♕g4 ± Lukin/Sakaev) 14 ♗xg6 hxg6 (14...fxg6!? is more reliable, Tonning-Tukmakov, Copenhagen 1996) 15 ♕e1 (15 ♕e2 b5 16 e5 ♘e8 {16...b4!} 17 ♗xe7 ♕xe7 18 ♖ad1 ♗b7 19 ♘a5 ± A.Ivanov-Yermolinsky, USA Ch (Los Angeles) 1993) 15...b5 16 e5 (Lukin-Lerner, Kiev 1984; 16 ♕h4?! is met by 16...b4 with the point 17 ♖f3 bxc3 18 ♖xc3 ♕d7 19 ♖h3 ♘h5 20 ♗xe7 ♖e8 21 g4 e5 ∓ Lukin/Sakaev) 16...b4! 17 exf6 gxf6 (A.Neverov-Lukin, Blagoveshensk 1988) 18 ♘d5!? exd5 19 ♗h6 ♖e8 20 f5! ♗xf5 21 ♖xf5 ♗f8 22 ♗e3 gxf5 23 ♕g3+ ♔h7 24 ♘d4!? (24 ♕h3+ =) leads to unclear play – Lukin/Sakaev.

**13...♘e5 14 ♕d2**

The other possible development is 14 ♕e1!? ♗d7 15 ♕g3 ♔h8 16 ♖ad1 (16 ♖ae1!? Spraggett; 16 ♖f4!? leads to a tense game) 16...♖ae8 (16...♖ac8!?) 17 ♕h3 exf5 18 exf5 ♗c6!? 19 ♖d4

♘ed7 20 ♖h4 d5!? (20...♗d8!? Spraggett) 21 ♗e3 ♕c7 22 ♗d4 ♗d6, Pablo Marin-Spraggett, Barcelona 1993.

**14...♕c7**

14...♗d7 15 ♖ad1 (15 fxe6!? fxe6 16 ♖ad1) 15...exf5 16 ♘d4 ♖ac8 17 ♗xf6 ♗xf6 18 ♘d5 ♕d8 with equality, Emms-H.Jonsson, London Lloyds Bank 1994.

**15 ♖ad1**

Now:

a) 15...♘c4?! 16 ♗xc4 ♕xc4 17 ♗xf6 ♗xf6 18 ♕xd6 with a dangerous initiative.

b) 15...♔h8 16 ♗xf6 gxf6 17 ♘d4 ♖g8 (17...♗d7 18 ♗h5! with the idea of 19 ♗xf7!, Galdunts-Serper, Kherson 1991) 18 ♗h5 with better chances for White.

c) 15...♖d8 16 ♘d4!? ± Grabics-K.Grosar, Bled wom 1994.

d) 15...b5!? is worth investigating: 16 ♗xf6 ♗xf6 (16...gxf6 17 ♗h5 ♔h8 18 ♘d4 ± Gicev-Kožul, Skopje open 1991) 17 ♕xd6 ♕xd6 18 ♖xd6 ♗e7 (18...♖a7!?) 19 ♖dd1 ♖a7 with compensation (Galdunts).

**B54)**

**8 ♗f4** *(D)*

The hit of the 1990s.

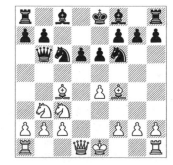

**8...♘e5 9 ♗e2**

9 ♗b5+!? has attracted some attention due to the efforts of GM Milos: 9...♗d7 (9...♘fd7!? is possibly playable) 10 ♗xd7+ (Black gets a good game after 10 ♗xe5?! dxe5 11 ♗xd7+ ♘xd7 12 ♕d3 a6 13 0-0-0 ♕c7, Istratescu-Arsović, Belgrade 1994, or 10 a4 a6 11 ♗xd7+ ♘fxd7 12 ♕e2 ♗e7 13 0-0 0-0 14 a5 ♕c7 15 ♗c1 ♘c4, Bischoff-Lau, Bundesliga 1992/3) 10...♘fxd7 (10...♘exd7!? 11 0-0 a6 12 ♗e3 ♕c7 13 f4 ♗e7 = An.Rodriguez-Ricardi, Cordoba Z 1998) 11 ♕e2 a6 (11...♖c8 12 ♖d1 ♗e7 13 0-0 0-0 14 ♔h1 ♕a6 {14...a6 is met by 15 ♗c1 with the idea of f4 and ♖d3 – Milos} 15 ♕xa6 bxa6 16 ♗c1 ± Milos-J.Polgar, São Paulo (2) 1996) and now:

a) 12 0-0-0 ♗e7 13 h4 ♕c7?! 14 ♗g5 ♘f6 15 f4 ♘c6 16 h5 h6 17 ♗h4 b5 18 ♔b1 b4 19 ♘a4 0-0 20 g4 ± Milos-Zarnicki, San Luis 1995.

b) 12 ♖d1 ♕c7 (12...♗e7 13 ♗c1 g5!? Yrjölä) 13 ♗c1 b5 14 f4 ♘c4 15 ♖d3 ♗e7 16 0-0 (Milos-Filgueira, Buenos Aires 1998) 16...♗f6!? Yrjölä (16...0-0!? 17 ♔h1 transposes to line 'c1').

c) 12 0-0 and then:

c1) 12...♗e7 13 ♖ad1 0-0 (13...♕c7 14 ♗c1 ♘f6 15 f4 ♘ed7 16 ♔h1 ♖c8 17 ♖d3 b5 18 a3 ± Milos-Fiorito, Mar del Plata 1996) 14 ♔h1 ♕c7 15 ♗c1 b5 16 f4 ♘c4 17 ♖d3 (Milos-Wang Zili, Groningen 1996) ± (Milos).

c2) 12...♕c7 13 ♖ae1 (13 ♖ad1 b5 has the point 14 ♗c1 b4! =) 13...♗e7 (13...b5 14 ♗c1 b4 15 ♘d1!) 14 ♗c1 g5!? (Milos-Yermolinsky, Groningen 1996) 15 f4! (Yermolinsky) is critical.

We now return to the position after 9 ♗e2 *(D)*:

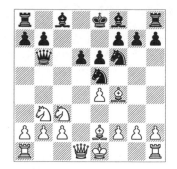

At first, White plans to attack the knight through ♗e3 and f4.

We shall consider:

**B541: 9...♗e7** 262
**B542: 9...a6** 263
**B543: 9...♗d7** 265

## B541)

**9...♗e7**

Anand selected this move against Kasparov in 1994. Recently 9...♗e7 has not been played in any top-level games.

**10 ♗e3!**

10 ♕d2 0-0! 11 0-0-0 a6 (the alternative 11...♕xf2!? 12 ♗e3 ♕h4 13 ♗g5 leads to a draw by repetition) 12 ♖hg1 ♕c7 13 g4 b5 with a good game, Zhao-Gabrielsen, Istanbul OL 2000.

10 g4 h6 (10...a6!) 11 h4!? (11 ♗e3 ♕c7 12 f4 ♘c4 13 ♗xc4 ♕xc4 14 ♕f3 e5 15 ♖g1 d5 ∞ Bach-Nevednichy, Romania 1995) 11...♗d7 12 ♖g1 ♗c6 13 ♗e3 ♕c7 14 ♕d4 ♘fd7 15 0-0-0! ♗xh4 16 f4 ♘g6 17 ♘b5 with the initiative, Kupreichik-Drollinger, Bundesliga 1998/9.

**10...♕c7 11 f4**

Unclear is 11 ♘b5; e.g., 11...♕b8 (11...♕c6!? Dolmatov) 12 f4 ♘c6 (12...♘g6 13 ♘c3 0-0 14 0-0 ♗d7) 13 ♘c3 0-0 14 g4 d5! 15 exd5 ♖d8 Nikitin.

**11...♘c4**

Or:

a) 11...♘c6 (this is a Scheveningen a tempo down for Black – the aim of 8 ♗f4 is completely achieved!) 12 ♗f3 a6 13 0-0 0-0 14 a4 b6 15 g4 with an advantage for White, Kasparov-Anand, Linares 1994.

b) 11...♘g6!? ±.

**12 ♗xa7!**

White has mostly tested two other lines, though without particular success:

a) 12 ♗xc4 ♕xc4 13 ♕f3 e5!? (13...0-0 14 0-0-0 ♗d7 15 e5 ♗c6 16 exf6 ♗xf3 17 fxe7 ♗xd1 18 exf8♕+ ♔xf8 19 ♖xd1 ♕c6 is given by Dolmatov; 13...a5!?) 14 f5 b5 15 ♘d2 (15 ♗g5?! b4!) 15...♕c6 16 ♗g5!? b4 (16...♗b7 17 ♗xf6 ♗xf6 18 ♕d3!) 17 ♘d5 ♘xd5 18 exd5 ♕xc2 19 ♗xe7 ♔xe7 20 0-0 f6 (Rublevsky-Svidler, Yugoslav Cht 1995; 20...♕xd2? 21 f6+) 21 ♘e4!? with compensation.

b) 12 ♘b5 ♕c6 13 ♗xc4 ♕xc4 14 ♕d3 ♕c6 and here:

b1) 15 ♘a5?! ♕d7 and then 16 e5 ♘d5 17 exd6?! ♗d8 18 ♗d2 a6 ∓ (Kasparov) or 16 ♘c4 ♘xe4!? 17 ♘xa7 b5!, Klimov-Lukin, St Petersburg 1995.

b2) 15 0-0-0 0-0 and now 16 ♘xd6 ♗xd6 17 ♕xd6 ♕xd6 18 ♖xd6 ♘xe4 = Lukin-Dranov, St Petersburg 1993, or 16 ♘c3 a6!?.

b3) 15 ♘3d4 ♕d7 16 0-0-0 0-0 (16...a6 also proved satisfactory for Black in the game Lastin-Lukin, Russian Ch (Elista) 1995) 17 e5 dxe5 18 fxe5 ♘g4 19 ♕e2 ♘xe3 (19...♘xe5? 20 ♘f3) 20 ♕xe3 = Rublevsky-Nevednichy, Yugoslav Cht 1995.

After the text-move (12 ♗xa7!) Black has problems: 12...♘xb2 13 ♘b5 ♛c6 14 ♛d4! or 12...e5 13 ♘b5 ♛c6 14 ♗xc4 ♛xc4 15 ♛d3! ± Vorobiov-Bakre, Moscow 1999.

### B542)
**9...a6** *(D)*

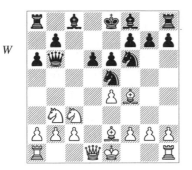

Kramnik successfully played this move in 1993 (against Ivanchuk) but later preferred 9...♗d7.

**10 ♗e3**
Others:

a) 10 g4 ♛c7 11 g5 ♘fd7 12 ♛d4 b5 13 0-0-0 ♖b8 14 ♗g3 b4 ∓ Cela-Kotronias, Athens 1996.

b) 10 a4 ♗d7!? (10...♛c7 11 a5 ♗e7 12 0-0 ♗d7 – *10...♗d7 11 a5 ♛c7 12 0-0 ♗e7*; 10...♗e7 11 a5 ♛c6!?, Milavsky-Vovsha, Petach Tikva 1996) 11 a5 (11 0-0 – *9...♗d7 10 0-0 a6 11 a4* =; 11 ♗e3 ♛c7 12 f4 ♘c4 13 ♗xc4 ♛xc4 14 ♛d3 ♖c8! ∓ Dervishi-Kotronias, Istanbul OL 2000) 11...♛c7 12 0-0 ♗e7 with chances for both sides, Verduga-Martin del Campo, Merida 1997.

c) 10 ♗g3!? and then:

c1) 10...♛c7 11 f4 ♘c4 12 e5! and now 12...♘xb2 13 ♛d4 ± or 12...dxe5 13 fxe5 ♘xe5 14 ♛d4 ♘fd7 15 0-0-0 ± Kramnik.

c2) 10...♘g6 11 f4 ♗d7 12 ♛d2 ♗c6 13 ♗f3 ♖d8 14 0-0-0 ♗e7 15 ♘d4 0-0 16 ♗f2 ♛c7 17 f5 with a slight advantage for White, Howell-Kožul, Bled 1995.

c3) 10...♗e7 11 f4 ♘c6 12 ♛d2 ♛c7 13 0-0-0 b5 14 e5! (Gdanski-Blehm, Warsaw 2001) 14...dxe5!? 15 fxe5 ♘d7.

c4) 10...h5 11 h3 (11 f4? ♘eg4; 11 f3 ♛c7 12 ♛d4 h4 13 ♗f2 b5 Kramnik) 11...♛c7 12 f4 (12 a4 ♗d7 13 ♛d4 ♖c8 = or 12 ♛d4 b5 13 a4 ♘c6 14 ♛e3 ♘b4! 15 ♗d3 bxa4 16 ♖xa4 ♖b8 = Kramnik) 12...♘c4 13 ♗xc4 (13 ♛d4 b5 and now 14 a4 e5! or 14 e5 dxe5 15 fxe5 ♗b7! Kramnik) 13...♛xc4 14 ♛f3 h4 15 ♗h2 (15 ♗f2 b5! 16 e5 ♘d5 =) 15...♗d7 16 0-0-0 ♖c8 with adequate counterplay, Ivanchuk-Kramnik, Linares 1993.

d) 10 0-0 and then:

d1) 10...♗e7 can be met by 11 a4 0-0 = Hamdouchi-Annageldiev, Moscow OL 1994 or 11 ♗e3 ♛c7 – *10 ♗e3 ♛c7 11 0-0 ♗e7.*

d2) 10...♛c7 11 a4 (11 ♗e3 – *10 ♗e3 ♛c7 11 0-0*) 11...♗d7 (11...b6 12 ♘d2 ♗b7 13 ♗e3 ♗e7 14 f4 ♘ed7 has also been played here) 12 ♘d2 ♗e7 13 a5 ♗c6 (13...♖c8 14 ♗e3 ♗c6 15 f4 ♘ed7 16 ♗f3 0-0 17 g4 d5 18 e5 ♘e8 19 ♘b3 g6 20 ♗d4 f6 is not bad either, Sion Castro-Gulko, Leon 1992) 14 ♗e3 ♘ed7 15 f4 ♘c5 16 ♗f3 0-0 17 b4 ♘cd7 18 g4 d5! Nikitin.

**10...♛c7** *(D)*
**11 f4**
This position may also arise from Line B2.

11 0-0 is the alternative:

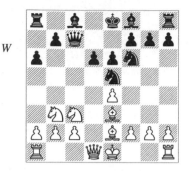

W

a) 11...♗e7 12 f4 ♘c4 13 ♗xc4 (again, this position can arise by transposition from Line B2) 13...♕xc4 14 ♕f3 (14 e5!? ♘e4 15 ♗d4 ♘xc3 16 bxc3, Brunner-Verat, Clichy 1991) 14...0-0 15 ♖ad1 e5?! (15...♕c7!?) 16 f5 b5 17 ♗g5 ± de Firmian-Sherzer, USA Ch (Jacksonville) 1990.

b) 11...b5!? 12 f4 (Pinski-Banas, Bojnice 1994) 12...♘c4!?, and now the continuation 13 ♗xc4 bxc4 14 e5 dxe5 15 fxe5 ♕xe5 16 ♕f3 cxb3 17 ♕xa8 ♕xe3+ 18 ♔h1 ♕c5 19 ♘a4 ♕c7 20 ♘b6 (Pinski/Umansky) seems dubious because of 20...♗c5!.

**11...♘c4**

11...♘c6?! (as happened in Christiansen-Yermolinsky, USA Ch (Chandler) 1997) leads to a position that usually occurs with Black to move (for example, Tate-Yermolinsky, Chicago 1994).

**12 ♗xc4 ♕xc4 13 ♕f3**

Or 13 ♕d3!?, and then:

a) 13...d5? 14 e5 ♘d7 15 ♕xc4 dxc4 16 ♘a5, Galdunts-Wiemer, St Ingbert 1994.

b) 13...b5 14 a4 (14 0-0!? ♗b7 15 a4 Rechlis) 14...♕xd3 15 cxd3 b4 16 ♘e2 with a slight advantage for White, Valerga-Braga, Villa Gesell 1997.

c) 13...♕xd3 14 cxd3 ♗d7 ±.

d) Possibly critical is 13...♕c7!? (this can arise from Line B2) 14 0-0-0 (14 ♗d4 b5! 15 e5 dxe5 16 ♗xe5 ♕d7) 14...b5 (14...♗e7 15 ♗d4!, Mikhaletz-Privalov, Galychyna 1997) 15 ♗d4 ♗b7 – Kotronias/Papatryfonos.

**13...♕c7**

There is definitely a choice here:

a) 13...d5?! 14 e5 ♘e4 15 ♘xe4 ♕xe4 16 ♕xe4 dxe4 17 0-0-0 with an advantage, I.Zaitsev-Serper, Moscow 1991.

b) 13...e5 14 ♖f1! (Mortensen; 14 fxe5!? dxe5 15 ♕g3; 14 f5?! b5 ∞ Solozhenkin-Lugovoi, St Petersburg 1995) 14...♗e6 (14...♗e7 15 fxe5 dxe5 16 ♘d5; 14...exf4 15 ♕xf4 ♗e6 16 ♗d4) 15 f5!.

c) 13...♗d7 14 0-0-0 and then:

c1) 14...b5? 15 e5! ♗c6 16 ♕h3 ±.

c2) 14...♕c7 15 g4 ♗c6 16 g5 and now, rather than 16...♘d7 17 ♖he1 (17 ♖hf1!? Istratescu) 17...♗e7 18 ♕h3! 0-0 19 f5 ± Istratescu-Pelletier, Erevan OL 1996, Black could try instead 16...♘xe4!? 17 ♘xe4 d5.

c3) 14...♖c8 and here:

c31) 15 ♗d4 can be met by 15...b5 16 a3 (Ivanchuk-Kramnik, Paris rpd 1995) 16...e5!? or the immediate 15...e5!?.

c32) 15 ♖d2 should be answered by 15...♕c7, with a rather unclear position, Losev-Belikov, Moscow 1998, rather than 15...b5 16 ♗b6! ♕c6 17 ♗a5 ♕a8 18 ♖e1 ♗e7 19 ♗b4 ± Sax-Tratar, Feldbach 1997.

d) A double-edged continuation is 13...♗e7 14 0-0-0 0-0 (14...♕c7!? 15 g4 b5) 15 g4 ♘d7 (15...a5?! 16 g5 ♘d7 17 a4! was played in Mortensen-Zavoronkov, Erevan OL 1996) 16 g5, when 16...b5!? 17 e5 d5 could be considered.

**14 0-0-0**

Or:

a) 14 g4?! b5 15 a3 (15 g5 b4!) and now 15...d5! is Rublevsky's recommendation, while 15...Hₐb7 is also not bad.

b) 14 ∰g3 b5 15 e5 dxe5 16 fxe5 b4!, J.R.Koch-Gi.Hernandez, Tunja jr Wch 1989.

c) 14 f5!? Hₑb8!? (14...b5 15 fxe6 fxe6 16 e5 Hₐb7 17 ∰h3 dxe5 18 ∰xe6+ ∰e7 19 ∰h3) 15 Hₐa7 Hₑa8 16 Hₐd4 e5 17 Hₐe3 b5 18 a3 Hₐb7 19 Hₐg5 ᠗d7 20 0-0 h6 21 Hₐh4 Hₐe7 22 Hₐxe7 ∲xe7 ∞ Nijboer-Van der Wiel, Wijk aan Zee 1996.

**14...b5 15 a3 Hₐb7 16 f5**

Both sides have chances in this complicated position. Instead of 16...exf5 17 ∰xf5 Hₐe7 18 Hₐd4 0-0 19 Hₑd3 ±, as in Rublevsky-Levin, Novgorod open 1995, it is better to proceed with 16...e5!? 17 Hₐg5 Hₑc8 18 ∰d3 ᠗d7 (Velimirović-Damljanović, Yugoslav Cht 1998) or to choose the sharp 16...Hₑc8 17 fxe6 fxe6 18 ᠗d4 (18 ∰h3 e5), when Black can continue 18...∰d7 (Cela-Kotronias, Ano Liosia 1997), 18...e5!? or maybe even 18...∰c4 19 Hₐg5 Hₐe7 20 ∰h3 ᠗xe4.

**B543)**

**9...Hₐd7 (D)**

This move is somewhat passive but quite reliable and (thanks to Kramnik) the most popular up to now. Note that plans with g4-g5 now make sense as an alternative to f4, since the d7-bishop blocks the retreat of the f6-knight.

**10 Hₐe3**

Otherwise:

a) 10 Hₐg3 Hₑc8! 11 f4 ᠗c4.

b) 10 0-0 Hₐe7 (10...∰c7!?; 10...a6 should be answered not by 11 a4 Hₑc8 {11...∰c7} 12 a5 ∰c7 13 Hₐg3 ᠗c4 14 Hₐxc4 ∰xc4 15 Hₐxd6 ᠗xe4 16 ᠗xe4 ∰xe4 17 Hₐxf8 Hₑxf8 18 ᠗d4 Hₐc6 = Jazbinsek-Kožul, Pula open 1997, but 11 Hₐe3! ∰c7 12 f4 ±) is interesting:

b1) 11 a4 0-0 (11...a6 12 a5 ∰c7 13 ᠗d2 0-0 14 Hₐe3 Hₐc6 15 f4 ᠗ed7 16 Hₐf3 e5 17 f5 b5 18 axb6 ᠗xb6 = Svidler-Ruban, Novosibirsk 1995) 12 a5 ∰c7 13 a6 Hₑfb8 (½-½ Kasparov-Kramnik, Horgen 1995; 13...Hₐc6 14 ∰d4 b6 15 ∰e3! ᠗g6 16 Hₐg3 e5 17 Hₑad1 Hₑad8 18 f4 exf4 19 Hₐxf4 ᠗xf4 20 ∰xf4 b5! = Rublevsky-Svidler, Novosibirsk 1995) 14 axb7 Hₑxb7 15 Hₐe3 Hₑb4 16 f3 a5 with a good game for Black, J.Polgar-Timman, Wijk aan Zee 2000.

b2) 11 Hₐe3 ∰c7 and then:

b21) 12 ᠗b5!? ∰b8 13 f4 ᠗c6!? 14 ᠗c3 0-0 15 g4 d5 16 exd5 ᠗b4! with compensation for Black, Novgorodsky-Kupreichik, Nizhny Novgorod 1998.

b22) 12 ᠗d2 and now Black has two satisfactory options:

b221) 12...Hₐc6 13 a4 ᠗ed7 14 f4 0-0 15 Hₐf3 Hₑfd8 and now 16 ∰e2, as played in Smirin-Ruban, Tilburg 1994, can be met by 16...♘e8! followed by ...♗f6 (Ruban). Alternatively, 16 ♘b5 ♗xb5 17 axb5 d5 18 e5 ♗c5 19 ♕e2 ♘e8 20 c3 ♕b6 is possible, Smirin-Yermolinsky, Philadelphia 1996.

b222) 12...0-0 13 f4 ♘g6 (another idea is 13...♘c6!?) 14 a4 (14 ♔h1 ♗c6 15 ♕e1 d5 16 e5 ♘e4 17 ♘cxe4 dxe4 18 ♘b3 ♘h4 = Smirin-Khalifman, Ischia 1996; 14 ♗d3 Ruban) 14...b6 (14...♗c6 15 ♘b5!?, Hamdouchi-Apicella, Tunis 1997) 15 ♗d3 ♗c6 16 ♕e2 ♖fe8 17 ♘b3 a6 18 ♖ae1 ♗b7 19 ♕f2 ♘d7 20 ♕f3 ♗f6 21 ♗d2 ♘c5 22 ♕h3 ½-½ Rublevsky-Makarov, Novosibirsk 1995.

b23) 12 f4 ♘c4 and now:

b231) 13 ♗d4!? and now Black should avoid 13...e5? 14 ♗xc4, Golubev-Mukhametov, Alushta 1997, and 13...♘xb2?! 14 ♘b5 ♗xb5 15 ♗xb5+ ♔f8 16 ♗xb2 ♕b6+ 17 ♘d4 a6 18 e5. Not so clear is 13...b5 14 ♕e1!? b4 (14...0-0 15 e5 dxe5 16 fxe5 ♘xe5 17 ♕g3 ♗d6 18 ♖xf6 ♘g6 19 ♖xg6) 15 e5 dxe5 16 fxe5 ♘xe5 17 ♕g3 bxc3 18 ♗xe5 ♕b6+ 19 ♗d4 ♕d6 20 ♕xc3 ♖c8. However, after 13...0-0 White has nothing better than 14 ♗xc4 ♕xc4 – 13 ♗xc4 ♕xc4 14 ♗d4 0-0.

b232) 13 ♗xc4 ♕xc4 and then:

b2321) 14 e5 ♘e4! 15 exd6 ♘xd6 16 ♗c5 ♘f5 17 ♗xe7 ♔xe7!? (Damljanović; 17...♘xe7 18 ♕d6 ♘f5 19 ♕a3 b5 20 ♕c5 ♕xc5+ 21 ♘xc5 ♗c6 22 b4 = Velimirović-Damljanović, Vršac 1989) 18 ♖e1 ♖hd8 19 ♕h5 g6 = Yermolinsky.

b2322) 14 ♗d4 0-0 (14...♖c8!?; the fact that Black has the untested 14...♗c6!? may justify, to some extent, the move-order with 13 ♗d4) 15

e5 (15 ♗xf6?! ♗xf6! 16 e5 ♗e7 17 exd6 ♗f6) 15...♘e8 (difficult to assess are 15...♘d5!? and 15...dxe5 16 fxe5 ♘d5 17 ♘e4!?, after which 17...♘e3?! is unsuccessful in view of 18 ♘f6+! gxf6 19 ♗xe3 ±) 16 exd6 (hardly advantageous are 16 ♖f3 f6 17 ♖h3 fxe5 18 fxe5 ♖f5, Velimirović-Popović, Novi Sad 2000, and 16 ♗c5!? ♗c6! 17 exd6 ♗xd6 18 ♗xd6 ♖d8 Lerner) 16...♗xd6 (16...♘xd6? 17 ♗c5 ♕a6 18 ♗xd6! ±) 17 ♘e4 and, instead of 17...♗c6? 18 ♘xd6 ♘xd6 19 ♗c5 ± Golubev-Lerner, Senden 1996, the most precise is probably 17...♗c7! 18 ♗c5 ♕xe4 19 ♕xd7 ♗b6 =.

c) 10 g4 (see comment to Black's 9th move):

c1) 10...h6 11 ♖g1 (11 f3!? ♖c8 12 ♕d2 a6 13 0-0-0 ♕c7 14 h4 b5 15 g5 ♘h5 16 ♗h2 hxg5 17 hxg5 g6, An.Rodriguez-Ricardi, Villa Gesell 1997, 18 a3 Rechlis) 11...g5 (Atalik gives 11...a6 12 ♗e3 ♕c7 13 f4 ♘c4 14 ♗xc4 ♕xc4 15 ♕f3 ♕c7 16 0-0-0 ♖c8 17 g5 with an attack and 11...♕c7 12 h4 ♗c6 13 f3 ♘g6 14 ♗g3 ♕b6 15 ♗f2 ♕c7 =) 12 ♗e3 ♕c7 13 h4! (Cela-Atalik, Ikaria 1996) 13...♗c6! with counterplay – Atalik.

c2) 10...♗c6! and then:

c21) 11 ♗e3 ♕c7 12 f3 h6 (better than 12...d5?! 13 g5 dxe4 14 f4! Atalik) 13 ♘d4 and now Black should play 13...a6! with chances for both sides, Ninov-Chernyshov, Djuni 1996 (rather than 13...d5?! 14 exd5 ♘xd5 15 ♘xd5 ♗xd5 16 ♗b5+ ± Kostakiev/Ninov).

c22) 11 f3 ♘g6 12 ♗g3 d5 13 exd5 (13 g5 ♘h5 14 exd5 ♘xg3 15 hxg3 ♖d8) 13...♘xd5 14 ♘xd5 ♗xd5 15 ♕d4 ♕xd4?! (15...♗b4+! 16 c3 ♕xd4

Short) 16 ♗b5+! ± J.Polgar-Short, Novgorod 1996.

d) 10 ♕d2 is more topical:

d1) 10...a6!? 11 ♗g5 (critical is 11 0-0-0 ♕c7) 11...♕c7 12 0-0 b5 13 a3 ♗e7 14 ♖ad1 ♘c4 = Ivanović-Damljanović, Vrnjačka Banja 1999.

d2) 10...♖c8 and now:

d21) 11 ♗e3 ♕c7 12 ♘b5 (consistent, but it does not give White an advantage) 12...♗xb5 13 ♗xb5+ ♘ed7! = Onishchuk-Tukmakov, Biel 1996.

d22) 11 f3!?.

d23) 11 0-0-0!? ♗e7 (11...♖xc3? 12 ♕xc3 ♘xe4 13 ♕d4 ♕xd4 14 ♖xd4 ♘xf2 15 ♖f1 ♘fg4 16 ♗xg4 ♘xg4 17 ♗xd6 Tukmakov) 12 f3 (or 12 ♗e3!?) deserves attention.

d3) 10...♗e7 11 0-0-0 (11 f3!? looks promising: 11...0-0 12 g4 ♗c6 13 ♗e3 ♕c7 14 g5 ♘fd7 15 f4 ♘g6 16 h4 ± Balashov-Lopushnoy, Russian Cht 1998, or 11...♕c7 12 ♘b5 ♗xb5 13 ♗xb5+ ♘c6 14 ♖d1 ♖d8 15 ♕a5 ♕d7 ± Gofshtein) and here:

d31) 11...♕xf2 12 ♖hf1 ♕xg2 13 ♖g1 (13 ♗xe5? dxe5 14 ♖xf6 0-0-0!! -+ Balashov) 13...♕f2 14 ♖xg7 with compensation – Kupreichik.

d32) Gofshtein recommended the continuation 11...♕c7!? 12 ♘b5 ♗xb5 13 ♗xb5+ ♔f8 but I am not sure whether he would play something like that in a tournament.

d33) 11...0-0 12 g4 (12 ♗e3 ♕c7 13 f4 ♘c4 14 ♗xc4 ♕xc4 15 e5 dxe5 16 fxe5 ♘d5 17 ♘xd5 exd5 18 ♕xd5 ± Kupreichik) 12...♗c6 (12...♘exg4 13 ♗xg4 ♘xg4 14 ♖hg1 favours White; e.g., 14...♘f6 15 e5!, Kupreichik-Lopushnoy, Russia Cup (Perm) 1998, or 14...e5 15 ♘d5 ♕d8 16 ♘xe7+ ♕xe7 17 ♗g3! – Kupreichik) 13 f3 and here:

d331) 13...♖fd8 14 h4 ♕c7 15 g5 ♘fd7 (15...♘h5? 16 ♗h2) 16 ♘d4! a6 17 h5 b5 18 ♖dg1, A.Fedorov-Lopushnoy, St Petersburg 1997.

d332) 13...a5 14 a4 ♕b4 15 ♕e1! Gofshtein.

d333) 13...♕c7 14 ♘d4 (14 h4!?) 14...a6 15 g5 ♘fd7 16 h4 b5 17 a3 (17 ♖dg1!? b4 18 ♘d1 ♗b5 A.Fedorov) 17...♘c5 18 h5 ♖fc8, and, as A.Fedorov asserts, both 19 ♗e3!? ♖ab8 20 g6 and 19 g6 (A.Fedorov-Gershon, St Vincent Ech 2000) 19...♗d7 20 gxf7+ ♔xf7 are unclear.

d34) 11...a6 12 g4 ♗c6 (Black should avoid 12...♘fxg4?! 13 ♖hg1!) 13 f3 ♕c7 (13...h6?! 14 h4) 14 g5 (14 ♘d4 b5 ∞ Ivanović-Damljanović, Yugoslav Cht 1999) 14...♘fd7 15 ♗e3 b5 16 f4 ∞ ♘g6!? (Konguvel-Bakre, Calcutta 1999) 17 h4!.

d35) 11...♗c6 12 ♗e3!? (12 f3 a6 13 g4 – *11...a6 12 g4 ♗c6 13 f3*) 12...♕c7 13 ♘b5 is interesting

**10...♕c7** *(D)*

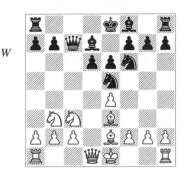

**11 f4**

Or:

a) 11 g4 d5! 12 exd5 ♗b4 with compensation, Movsesian-Lagunov, Bundesliga 1996/7.

b) 11 ♕d4 ♗e7 12 f4 ♘g6 (the alternative 12...♘c6 is also playable, as in the game Klimov-Makarov, St Petersburg 1999) 13 0-0-0 0-0 14 g4 e5 15 ♕d2 exf4 16 ♗xf4 ♖fc8 17 ♘d4 ♕a5 18 ♘b3 ♕c7 = J.Polgar-Kramnik, Novgorod 1996.

c) 11 ♘b5 and now:

c1) 11...♕b8 12 f4 enables White to keep an edge:

c11) 12...♘g6 13 f5!? exf5 (13...♘e5 14 0-0 ♗e7 15 ♗g5 0-0 16 ♗xf6 gxf6 17 ♕d2 ± Vereshagin-Makarov, Russian Cht 1997) 14 exf5 ♘e5 15 ♕d4 a6 16 ♘c3 ♗xf5 17 0-0 ♗e6 18 ♖xf6! gxf6 19 ♘d5 with compensation for White, A.Sokolov-Nevednichy, Yugoslav Cht 1995.

c12) 12...♘eg4 13 ♗xg4 (not 13 ♘xd6+? ♗xd6 14 ♗xg4 in view of 14...♗xf4) 13...♗xb5 (13...♘xg4? 14 ♘xd6+ ♗xd6 15 ♕xg4) 14 ♗f3 e5 (14...♗e7 15 ♘d4 ♗d7 16 ♕d3 ♕c7 17 0-0 a6 18 c4 ± A.Sokolov-Al.Khasin, Russian Ch (Elista) 1994) 15 a4 (15 f5?! ♕c7 16 ♖c1 d5 17 exd5 ♗c4, Ermekov-Al.Khasin, Omsk 1996; 15 ♕d2 ♗e7 16 g4!? Rechlis) 15...♗c6 16 ♕d3 ♗e7 17 c4 0-0 (17...exf4!?) 18 f5 ± Lastin-Dragomaretsky, Moscow 1995.

c2) 11...♗xb5! 12 ♗xb5+ ♘c6 equalizes:

c21) 13 ♘d2 can be answered by 13...d5 = A.Sokolov-Belikov, Russian Ch (Elista) 1995, or 13...a6 14 ♗d3 d5.

c22) 13 ♕f3 a6 14 ♗d3 d5 = J.Polgar-Kramnik, Dortmund 1996.

c23) 13 ♗d3 d5 14 exd5 ♘xd5 15 ♗d2 ♗e7 = Velimirović-Damljanović, Vrnjačka Banja 1999.

**11...♘c4 12 ♗xc4 ♕xc4** (D)

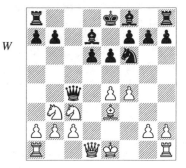

W

**13 ♕d3**

Nothing is gained by 13 ♕d4 ♕xd4 14 ♗xd4 ♗c6 15 ♘a5 ♗e7, Losev-Iskusnykh, Moscow 2001.

Or 13 ♕f3, and now:

a) 13...e5?! can be countered in three ways: 14 ♖f1!? Mortensen; 14 f5!? Pupo; or 14 fxe5!? dxe5 15 ♕g3, Blees-Pupo, Cienfuegos 1997.

b) 13...♗c6 14 ♗d4 (14 ♘d4 ♗e7 15 0-0-0? d5 16 e5 ♘e4 17 ♘xe4 dxe4 18 ♕g3 ♕xa2 19 ♕xg7 ♖f8 20 ♘xc6 bxc6 21 ♕xh7 ♗b4! –+ Saulin-Dragomaretsky, Moscow 1995) 14...♗e7 (14...♘xe4? 15 ♘xe4 f5 16 ♕h5+! wins for White) 15 0-0-0 0-0 16 ♖he1 a5 (16...♖fc8 Cu.Hansen) 17 ♖d3! with the better chances for White, Mortensen-Cu.Hansen, Esbjerg 1997.

c) 13...b5!?.

d) 13...♕c7! 14 0-0-0 ♖c8 with the initiative – Atalik.

**13...♕xd3**

Or 13...♕c7?! 14 0-0-0 ♖c8 15 ♗d4! ± Istratescu; 13...b5 14 ♕xc4 bxc4 15 ♘d2 d5 16 ♗d4 (±) Atalik.

**14 cxd3**

In the resulting ending White has a certain, though hardly significant, advantage.

**14...♗e7**

14...h5!? 15 a4 h4 16 h3 a6 (or
16...♖h5 17 0-0 ♗e7 18 ♖fc1 ♗d8 19
♘d2! b6 20 ♘f3 ♖c8 21 ♘d4 a6 22
b4 ± Istratescu-Atalik, Kastoria 1996)
17 0-0 ♗e7 18 ♘a5 ♖h5 19 ♘c4 and
White has some advantage, Stoica-
Gabriel, Romanian Cht 1998.

**15 a4**

15 ♖c1 0-0 16 h3 ♖fc8 (16...h5!?)
17 g4! ♗c6 18 ♖h2 (18 ♔e2 d5 19 e5
♘d7 20 ♘d4 g5 Atalik) 18...e5! 19
♖hc2 exf4 20 ♗xf4 ♖e8 21 ♘d4 d5
with an equal position, Istratescu-Atalik, Aegina 1996.

**15...0-0 16 h3**

Now:

a) 16...e5?! is well met by 17 0-0
♗e6 18 ♘a5!, Istratescu-S.Kiselev,
Bucharest 1998.

b) After 16...♖fc8 17 0-0 Black can
choose between 17...♗h6, as in Der-
vishi-Efimov, St Vincent Ech 2000,
and Stoica's 17...♗d8!?.

c) 16 h5 17 ♘d2 h4 18 0-0 (Bru-
zon-Pupo, Havana 1998) 18...d5 19 e5
♘h5 Pupo.

Summing up: Black does not en-
counter great problems in the variation 6...♕b6, but he has plenty of
small ones and it is high time White
learned how to turn them to good account. I believe that the quite favourable statistics for Black in the Benko
Variation are due to the fact that
'White' Sozin players pay, as a rule,
much more (if not all!) of their attention to more fascinating variations
with ...e6, and in practical 6...♕b6
games Black is often better prepared.

To conclude the theme of the queen
advance and the book as a whole, I offer a statistical sample of the best performances in Sozin games (source:
games from the period 1990-2000 taken
from the *ChessBase Mega Database
2001*; the performances achieved by
Topalov and Gelfand, who played a
small number of games, are shown as
an exception).

**White**

Topalov (10 games) 2796; Short
(15) 2781; Rublevsky (22) 2627; de
Firmian (39) 2617; Gi.Hernandez (30)
2595; Zapata (35) 2587; Galdunts (15)
2577; Golubev (27) 2575; Rogić (17)
2573; Milos (16) 2553; K.Müller (44)
2545; Saltaev (36) 2544; Mitkov (20)
2544; Emms (41) 2500; Istratescu (43)
2498 ... Velimirović (30) 2463

**Black**

Kramnik (15) 2765; Kasparov (16)
2675; Gelfand (9) 2629; Damljanović
(19) 2612; Dvoirys (16) 2584; Lerner
(14) 2552; Makarov (17) 2542; Atalik
(15) 2530; Nevednichy (16) 2499; Kožul (25) 2487; Scherbakov (15) 2487;
S.Kiselev (15) 2480; Yermolinsky (15)
2463; Vaulin (19) 2454; D.Gurevich
(20) 2450; Cebalo (15) 2448

Though this study is somewhat ar-
bitrary, it is hard to miss the fact that
the list of the best performers as Black
contains the names of at least eight
adepts of 6...♕b6. Well... I don't think
that the originator of the attack,
Veniamin Sozin, would have been dis-
appointed by such a circumstance.

# Index of Variations

## Chapter Guide

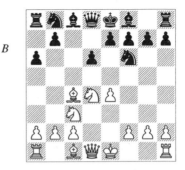

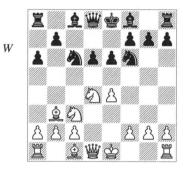